THE
GARDEN PRIMER

THE
GARDEN
PRIMER

BARBARA DAMROSCH

Illustrations by
Ray Maher
and Carol Bolt

A REGINA RYAN BOOK

WORKMAN PUBLISHING, NEW YORK

Library of Congress Cataloging-in-Publication Data
Damrosch, Barbara. The garden primer.
Bibliography: p. Includes index.
1. Gardening. I. Title. SB453.D318 1988 635 86-40545
ISBN 0-89480-317-4 ISBN 0-89480-316-6 (pbk.)

Cover and book design: Susan Aronson Stirling
Cover photograph: Gary Gunderson

Grateful acknowledgment is made for permission to reprint: page 298,
copyright © 1978 by Marge Piercy, reprinted from *The Twelve-Spoked
Wheel Flashing* by Marge Piercy, by permission of Alfred A. Knopf,
Inc.; page 309, from *Herbs of a Rhyming Gardener* by Elisabeth
Morss, reprinted by courtesy of Branden Publishing Company; page
327, from "Beautiful Old Age," *The Complete Poems of D.H.
Lawrence,* ed. Vivian de Sola Pinto and F. Warren Roberts, copyright
© 1964, 1971 by Angelo Ravagli and C. M. Weekley, Executors of
the Estate of Frieda Lawrence Ravagli, all rights reserved, reprinted by
permission of Viking Penguin Inc. and Curtis Brown Limited; page
372, William Carlos Williams, *Collected Poems, Volume I
(1909–1939),* copyright © 1938 by New Directions Publishing
Corporation.

Illustrations for chapter openings, tools (and tool shed), vegetables,
fruits and those appearing on pages 50, 56, 188, 193, 196 and 205
were drawn by Ray Maher. All other illustrations, including those on
pages 192–3, 332 and 379, were drawn by Carol Bolt. The landscape
and garden plans were rendered by Ludvik Tomazic.

Workman Publishing Company, Inc.
708 Broadway
New York, NY 10003
Printed in the United States of America

First printing October 1988
10 9 8 7 6 5 4 3 2 1

Acknowledgments

A number of people made the writing of this book an easier, more pleasant task than it would otherwise have been. Regina Ryan helped to launch the project and I am grateful to her for her meticulous editing and many insightful suggestions. Paul Frese gave every word his careful eye and allowed me to draw on his voluminous knowledge of plants and gardening. I thank Peter Workman for all his energy and encouragement, and for the fine staff that kept this project on track: Susan Aronson Stirling, Barbara Scott-Goodman, Mary Wilkinson, Bob Gilbert, Ludvik Tomazic, Wayne Kirn, Mark Freiman, Lynn Strong, Gabrielle Maubric, Catherine Mayer, David Schiller, Carol McKeown, Bert Snyder, Andrea Bass, Carolan Workman and, above all, my editor Sally Kovalchick, who always makes hard work fun.

I have been extremely fortunate to draw on the talents of Ray Maher and Carol Bolt, who both worked heroically to put my thoughts into pictures. I thank Castle Freeman for his meticulous copy-editing, Catherine Dorsey for her thorough index and Maggie Higgins for much help along the way. Jacqueline Miller, Sandra Pandora and William Fairbairn of Cramer and Anderson spared some busy hours and Jean Crawford at Time-Life Books also lent assistance. The Hickory Stick Book Shop in Washington Depot, Connecticut, the Oliver Wolcott Library in Litchfield, Connecticut, and the Fairfield County Cooperative Extension Service in Bethel, Connecticut, were always there when I needed them.

Jan Ohms of Van Engelen Bulbs was extremely helpful. Other gardening friends who gave advice throughout this project, as always, include Mary Ann and Frederick McGourty of Hillside Gardens in Norfolk, Connecticut, Glenn Waruch and John Owen of Claire's Garden Center in Patterson, New York, David Johnson, Jr. of Branching Out in Litchfield, Connecticut, David Smith of White Flower Farm in Litchfield, Connecticut, Melvin Lee Bristol of Lee Bristol Nursery in Sherman, Connecticut, Robert Towne, Jr. and Robert Kourik. Hans Bauer kept me at peace with my computer and John and Mary Fahey lent me their office. My friends Sarah Warner and Lauren Lieberman kept me sane.

I am especially grateful to Christopher Kerrigan and Evan Alter for their willing help and constant good cheer, to my parents Eleanor and Douglas Damrosch, to my sisters Eloise MacMurray and Anne Williams, and most of all to Burton Alter, who encouraged me at every step and made it all possible.

CONTENTS

Green Side Up

I firmly believe that in order to learn anything you have to be willing to ask dumb questions. A lot of people say to me, "I don't know *anything* about gardening," and some of them just let it go at that. Intimidated by the sheer volume of gardening lore they find around them, much of it very scientific and arcane, they leave gardening to those who presumably have lots of time to read and better yet, have a "green thumb." But others, unable to resist a pastime they suspect may be a lot of fun, wade right in. I love people who ask things like "Why do you prune plants?" and "What is mulch?" and "What part of the plant do you stick in the ground?"

The aim of this book is to answer as many elementary questions about gardening as possible. I may not be able to anticipate everything you want to ask, but I will explain to you how pruning can make your plants bushier, more compact or more fruitful. I will tell you that mulch is a layer of material such as shredded bark that you lay down on the ground chiefly to keep weeds from growing and to keep the soil moist. And I will try to come to your aid when you are standing there alone in the garden, holding a plant that looks like an amorphous tangle, and you have no idea what to do with it. If I could go out into the garden with you I would tell you what my friends Mary Ann and Frederick McGourty, professional growers, tell their fledgling workers: "Plant it with the green side up." Everyone has to start somewhere.

I am the first to admit I have my own idiosyncratic approach when it comes to gardening and gardening knowledge. Someone once called me an "old-fashioned dirt gardener," and I guess the description fits. I use relatively few commercial fertilizers and almost no pesticides. I prefer hand tools to power ones. I like to take cues from the way nature gardens, and also from the gardens of the past. I read as much as I can about scientific advances in horticulture and I'm usually willing to try something new; but I must say that most of what I do when I garden has come from just plain experience. There is no substitute for spending time in your garden and using all your senses to judge what is going on there. Are your plants' leaves a healthy green? Does your soil feel porous and fluffy when you stick your fingers into it? Does your sick plant have bugs on it or is there evidence of disease? Far more gardens fail because the gardener is absent or not paying attention than because he or she lacks erudition. Yes, you need to know your ABCs, but the more you garden, the more you will know what works and what doesn't and what problems to look for.

One of the hazards of writing a gardening book is that the author is addressing gardeners in many different localities with many different climates, soil types and selections of plants to choose from. The more exact the information I give you, the less accurately it may pertain to the specific conditions of your very own yard. I have to tell you what to add to your soil, for example, without knowing what is already in it. I have tried, therefore, to steer away from formulas, though there are times when saying "Add some fertilizer" is not enough. ("Should I add a spoonful or a bucketful?" I hear you asking.) So use my recommendations as a starting point, and try to learn as much as you can about your own garden's needs. Local resources such as nurseries, universities and the Cooperative Extension Service can be very helpful.

You will find most of the general information about gardening in the first four chapters of this book; the rest deals with specific kinds of plants and how to grow them. Use the book by going back to the early chapters if you need to have one of those basic questions answered. The index will help you if a cross-reference does not steer you to the answer at just the point when you need it.

Gardening, for all its down-to-earthness, has always had some mystery about it, a mystery that each culture had its own ways of expressing. In ancient times you might have a village maiden dance around the fire to impress the corn god, or you might make a burnt offering of the harvest to thank the deity that made it all possible. Now we do soil tests, take clones and even try to become gods ourselves in our quest to create new genetic plant material. But try as we may, I don't think we will ever shed so much light on gardening that we dampen the awe a gardener feels when the first vegetable seedlings start to come up in spring. We may never explain things like why we are attracted to flowers just as butterflies and bees are, even though normally we have no role in their pollination. Perhaps their form and fragrance are somehow luring us to some fateful role in their survival. I don't think we'll ever know all there is to know about gardening, and I'm just as glad there will always be some magic about it.

So just go out there and start doing it. It is often said that a green thumb is a dirty thumb. Choose good spots for your gardens, prepare the soil well, keep a close eye on things. And remember: the green side is always up.

Barbara Damrosch

PLANNING YOUR PROPERTY

The gardening bug can bite at any moment. Sometimes it's on a warm day in March when the earth is just starting to smell like earth. Itching to get out there and dig, an eager gardener rushes out and buys some seeds, digs up some soil, and scans the instructions on the packets to see which seeds can be planted "as soon as the ground can be worked." The peas can, so in they go.

Sometimes the bug bites on a Saturday in late June. A couple out for a drive passes a nursery where everything is 25 percent off. They pick out two dozen shrubs, forty perennials and a magnificent copper beech tree. When the plants are delivered the next day they triumphantly "find a place for everything."

There is no doubt that these gardeners are having a good time. But acting on impulse does not always produce satisfying results. The pea planter later decides that the front yard was not the best spot for the vegetable garden—once the tomato stakes have reared their 6-foot heads and the squash vines have taken off across the lawn and into the street. And the bargain hunters find that in five years their weekend purchases (and the many that have followed) are an unrelated collection of this and that, and their landscaping has a spotty look with no unifying theme. In fifteen years the precious copper beech has to be moved at great expense because it is right where the new addition to the house has to go. So much for bargains.

You Need a Plan

Such mishaps can be avoided by some advance planning, however, and without taking any of the fun out of gardening. In fact for some people the planning is the best part. I like to do it in the lull after the winter holidays when the first color-filled plant catalogs start to arrive, and gardening is a grand fantasy—weedless, bugless and crowned with success. It is a time when I am not being rushed into planting jobs that must be done on time and can stand back and take an honest look at the property as a whole.

Other chapters in this book will give you help in planning the individual segments of your landscape. Chapter 15 will help you to choose and place trees for shade, ornament and other purposes. Chapter 14 will show you ways to use various shrubs in the landscape—shrub borders and plantings near the house, for example. The chapters on lawns and ground covers, perennials, annuals, herbs, bulbs, roses, vines, vegetables, fruits and wildflowers will help you to design gardens with these particular plants and place them in the landscape. As you read, however, it's important that you keep thinking about how all these plantings will look together.

It is especially important to consider the overall look of the house and grounds when you build a new home, because you are starting from scratch; but it is also useful when you move into a home that previous owners have landscaped in a way that may or may not suit your taste and lifestyle. And even if you have lived there awhile it is good to rethink the plan from time to time and make sure the whole thing works. A new structure or addition to existing buildings might need to be incorporated into your scheme. A shift in your way of life—new children coming along, or older ones moving away, for example—might prompt some changes. Or you might just decide the place needs a fresh look.

One purpose of landscape planning is to reconcile the needs of different members of the household. Sometimes when I am called in to help people with their property I feel like a family counselor. The husband is thinking "lawn" for a spot where the wife is thinking "flowers" (or vice versa). The couple's concept of their yard as an elegant setting for their jewel of a home conflicts with their children's use of it as a ballfield. Often one member of the household (a man as often as a woman) is a gardener and the other is not. The gardener may anticipate the other's help in the form of interest, ideas and hard labor, but rarely will he or she get it. One may love to spend money on plants, tools, power equipment, while the other balks. And who asks the family dog? No one, because it wouldn't do any good. Chances are that the dog will run where it wants, dig where it wants and take its own chosen path from point A to point B whether you make the path flagstone or brick.

While it may not always be possible to reconcile everyone's needs, you can arrange your property in such a way that everyone will coexist, enjoy themselves and take pride in their surroundings. My suggestion is that you actually map out your property on graph paper, sketch in your ideas and create a simple master plan that you can follow in years to come. Here is how you do it.

Getting to Know Your Property

The first thing to do, before you ever put pencil to paper, is to take a long, careful look at your property. If the place is newly acquired, or if you have never gardened seriously before, there are probably a lot of basic things you don't yet know. Some of these you can find out right away; others you will learn only after you have lived there for a while. I sometimes advise people not to take any major steps until they have been in their house for a full year.

CHECK YOUR PROPERTY LINES AND UTILITIES

First of all make sure you have a surveyor's map of the property, and walk the boundaries. Don't rely on someone else's vague indication of them—find all the little markers. Anything you build or plant on your neighbor's land you might have to unbuild or unplant in the future. Next find out where all your underground service lines are: buried electrical cables, water pipes, sewer lines or septic tanks and leach fields, underground oil tanks, etc. You want to know what you will encounter if someone digs in any given spot, either by hand or with machinery. Driving over a septic field with a heavy truck can cause it to cave in; driving over water lines can damage them, too. Also look above you and be aware of any power lines or telephone wires that may interfere with trees or shrubs when they reach their full height.

CHECK THE ORIENTATION

Get a clear idea of where north, south, east and west are, either from the surveyor's plan, a compass or by watching the sun. Many plants prefer a specific exposure. And remember that the position of the sun changes at different times of the year. A spot that is shady in summer may be sunny in winter and vice versa. Make a note of how much sun each part of the property gets and at what times of the day. Whether a site is shaded, and in particular what kind of shade it gets, will strongly affect what you choose to plant there (page 37). You may need to cut down trees, or plant trees, to alter the degree of light.

UNDERSTAND THE CLIMATE

You should be aware of your climate's vital statistics: what is the coldest winter temperature you are likely to experience? This will affect what plants you choose to grow and how you grow them (page 42). If you live in a climate where temperatures fall below freezing, what are the dates of the average first frost in fall and the average last frost in spring? These dates will affect how you plan your vegetable garden as well as the way you grow any tender plants that can't take frost. If the weather is very dry or very wet where you live, you probably know it already, but it might be useful to get some statistics on annual rainfall, too. All these facts can be obtained from your local Cooperative Extension Service.

The direction of the prevailing winds at various times of the year is also something to be aware of. Winds, especially strong ones, can dry your plants in summer, chill them in winter, slow their growth, knock down tall vegetables and flowers and even ruin the shapes of shrubs and some trees. They may also affect your own comfort. If you have strong winds you'll have to plant in sheltered areas, or erect a windbreak of some sort such as a tall wood fence, or plant a living windbreak in the form of a hedge.

TOPOGRAPHICAL FEATURES

Look closely at the way the land is formed, and think about how this will affect the way you use it. Any major changes that require grading of the site (moving soil to change the level or degree of slope) should be done first, so you don't have to disrupt areas after they have been planted. Very often they are changes for which you will need both expert advice and heavy equipment. For instance, if the land is so hilly that you cannot walk around it comfortably, chances are you will not be able to garden comfortably there either. Your planting areas will be easier to tend, more attractive to look at, and less prone to water run-off if you terrace them, using retaining walls of stone or timbers, and building steps of stone or wood to lead you comfortably and attractively from one level to another. It is important that all these features be installed correctly, allowing for water drainage, so that they will be permanent. Unless you are particularly good at this kind of engineering, hire a contractor to do it.

Grading may also have to be done if the property is very rocky. You may want to have a bulldozer remove rocks and add topsoil. Or, if the rocks are very large, use them as assets in your plantings by creating a rock garden. Determine which rocks are the visible outcroppings of ledge under the soil, and don't plan to put deep-rooted trees and shrubs in these areas. If it is important to you to have a flat play area, or a flat site for a formal garden, do the grading now, even if you won't be planting for a few years.

WATER

How does water behave on the property? Does it gush down slopes, eroding soil as it goes? Does it collect in puddles that don't drain, making the soil soggy? You may need to have a drainage system installed, plant slopes with vegetation to slow erosion, or even, if water collects and doesn't drain, make a virtue of your problem by having a pond dug. If the ground is too dry, consider having an irrigation or sprinkling system put in.

SOIL

What is the soil like? Refer to the discussion of soil beginning on page 21, and see if there are any changes that need to be made in yours that might require heavy equipment. This is particularly important if there has been recent construction on the property. Rocks, rubble and building debris may have been buried in certain areas; either avoid planting deep-rooted plants in those places or have the obstacles dug out. The soil may have been compacted by trucks and bulldozers driving over it and may need to be power tilled. And the topsoil layer may have been stripped off and not adequately replaced, or not replaced at all. If so, you will have to have topsoil brought in and spread over the area.

At this point you may be shouting, "Stop! We just wanted to put in some early peas and a few shrubs, and now you have us calling in the Army Corps of Engineers." No, my point is that if major, earth-moving changes are going to be needed, I would rather do them first, if possible, so I'll only mess up the place once; or at least I'd plan around them so that I won't end up spending more time and money to rearrange things later. It's easy to move a pea patch, but not a large vegetable garden or a 30-foot tree.

EXISTING PLANTS

What is already growing on your land? It may take you a while to find and identify all the trees, shrubs and herbaceous plants growing on your property, and to decide which ones to keep and which ones to take out. Some people get rid of too little because they are afraid they will kill something valuable and not easily replaced. Others get rid of too much in their eagerness to let in light and air, open up a view or make room for new plantings. Identify and evaluate the plants already on your property before you take drastic measures; or get in a landscaper or tree surgeon to advise you.

VIEWS

Look at your house in relation to everything that is around it. Are there eyesores you'd prefer not to see? Some can be removed, such as your tumble-down shed and rusted '55 pickup. Others must be screened from view, such as your neighbor's rusted pickup. There may, on the other hand, be attractive vistas that should be highlighted, either by cutting trees to open the view or by planting some that will frame it. Think of all the "lines of sight" there are on your property: the view of the house from the street, the view as you walk up the path, the views from all the windows. A view across a lawn might be enhanced by an attractive planting at the far side, or a view into a woodland area might be more dramatic if a path were cut into the woods to let you see still farther.

PRIVACY

Think about how much privacy you need. Should there be tall fences for instant screening, or have you the patience to wait for a hedge to grow? (The sooner you plant it, the better.) What creatures are likely to roam across the yard: dogs? children? cows? "Good fences make good neighbors," Robert Frost once wrote.

Mapping the Property

After you've taken a good hard look around you and answered these basic questions, make a map of what is on your place. You don't have to be an experienced draftsman to do this—it's very easy. And you will learn even more about your property while you are doing it. All you need is some graph paper, a piece of wood or a bulletin board to thumbtack it to, and a 100-foot measuring tape. A scale ruler is useful for translating feet into inches—I use a scale of ¼ inch = 1 foot for large areas, and ½ inch = 1 foot for small areas and detailed plantings such as flower gardens. But you can also just let each side of a square on the graph paper represent a foot, or half a foot, and count squares as you draw your lines.

I figure out how large a sheet of paper I will need to measure the whole area; sometimes I have to use several sheets and map various areas separately. Then I start with the buildings. I position the house, garage and other structures in such a way that I'll have room to map the areas around them that need landscaping. If there are architect's drawings of the buildings I can save some time by tracing those outlines onto my plan, as long as I am using the same scale. Otherwise I simply measure with my long tape. I rarely have a partner to hold one end, so I just stick a screwdriver through the metal loop at the end and then into the ground to anchor the tape.

After the buildings, I measure the size and position of all the other important features such as trees, shrubs, boundaries, stone walls, paths and large rocks. I draw them on the plan and label them "existing maple," "existing stone wall" and so forth. For trees and shrubs, I indicate both the location of the trunk and the spread of its branches by a circle with a dot in the middle (with young plants I draw in the spread they will have when full grown). I note details such as the position of the well cover or the pipe where the oil tank is filled, and the height from the ground of windows I will be planting things under—anything I think might be relevant to my planning.

When I have mapped everything my plan is ready to be filled in with all the new features I want to add—new trees, gardens, paths, decks or whatever. That's the fun part. But if you've never done it before you might ask, "How do I begin?" I suggest you stop for a while and do some hard thinking first.

When you landscape your home you are really doing two things: creating an environment that will be a pleasure to look at and also creating one that will be used. After you have a good sense of what is there on your property, you need to think very carefully about what will happen on it. I always feel that the best way to understand this is to compare the inside of the house with what is around it. Homes are divided into rooms for reasons—chiefly to give the people who use them private space and to separate different activities from one another. This is just as true outdoors. The grounds surrounding the great English estates were often divided into distinct "garden rooms" separated by walls or hedges. This is rarely done today, but it is helpful to think of outdoor spaces as "rooms" that must serve different purposes and must have different looks to them. Some features will be purely ornamental, such as a shrub planting that frames an important entrance; some, such as lawns or swimming pools, will be used for recreation; others, such as storage or work areas, will be strictly utilitarian.

These areas must all be tied together in a way that looks attractive and is also easy to live with. You must plan the best way to get from one outdoor space to another, just as you plan the traffic between indoor rooms. Even an informal landscape plan should define the different areas within it and lead you subtly but deliberately from one to the next. A visitor should not be confused about which door to enter. And even the most fun-loving households function best if different spaces are well defined, both those that specific people use and those that are used in common.

Getting Ideas

I think it is very helpful to drive around your community, and other communities, and see what people have done to enhance their homes. You don't want to merely copy someone else's landscaping, but you may get some ideas you hadn't thought of. And when looking at places in your area you will get a sense of what plants do best there.

You should also take note of the style of your home and consider what style of landscaping will best complement it. For example, a large Victorian house would be set off by a sweeping lawn, stately trees, large-specimen shrubs set at a distance from the house and perhaps some plots of bedding annuals. A colonial house could well be enhanced by a cottage garden of herbs and flowers inside a picket fence. A contemporary wooden house stained in a natural color might look good with a Japanese-style planting, or with the abstract masses provided by interesting foliage plants such as cacti, ornamental grasses or dwarf evergreens. Can you mix styles? Yes, if you do it with care. Suppose you love Japanese gardens but have a 1770 colonial. A Japanese garden won't look odd if you plant it at a distance from the house, reached by a mossy path, or if you simply apply the Japanese aesthetic to a naturalized planting of native shrubs and trees near the

house, avoiding everything that would look incongruous such as stone Buddhas or a pagoda. You might want to do some research on historic gardening styles and tasteful ways to use them.

Very often an older home in a formal style looks best with plantings and walkways that are geometrically laid out and rather symmetrical, like those in the plan in Figure 1. There is a strong central axis to this property, running from the front walk to the front door, through the central hall of the house, out the back door and into a series of sharply defined garden spaces: the terrace, the lawn and gardens, and the pool. A design like this need not be rigid, and its regularity can be softened with the placement and textures of the plantings. But there is a solidity and regularity about it that echoes the feeling of the architecture.

Compare this plan to the one for a contemporary home in Figure 2, in which neither the front yard, the backyard nor the house has any axis at all. The landscape contains many of the same features as the other plan; both are on 135-by-200-foot lots that slope gently down to the west, with the front of the house facing east. But there are more curved lines, odd angles, and changes of direction in the second plan, just as there are in the house itself.

Your house may not be at either extreme, but somewhere in the middle, and it may require a landscape plan that combines formal and informal features. Or it may be very rustic, or in a rural setting where there are wild areas to develop in attractive ways (see Chapter 16). Your property may be much smaller or much larger than that considered in these two plans, which are for typical suburban lots less than half an acre in size. But these will serve to illustrate how different landscaping needs might be reconciled within a limited space.

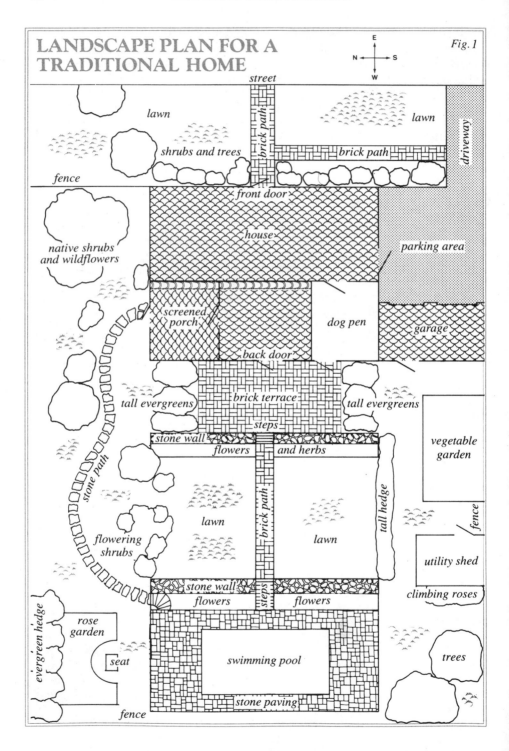

LANDSCAPE PLAN FOR A TRADITIONAL HOME — Fig. 1

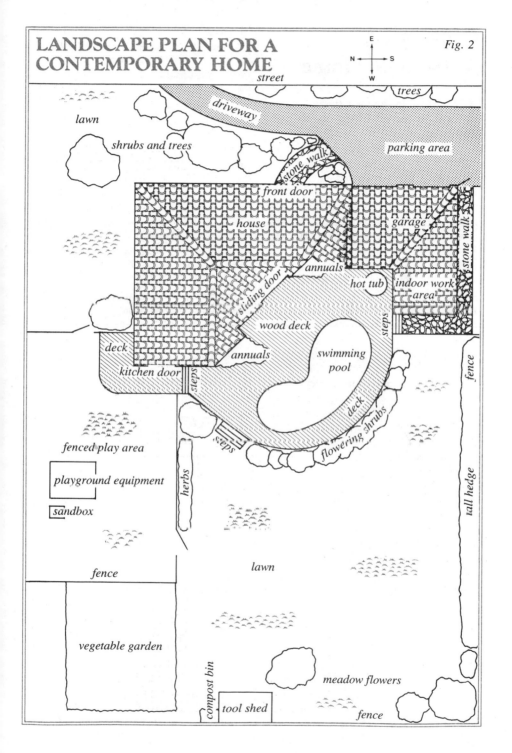

LANDSCAPE PLAN FOR A CONTEMPORARY HOME

Fig. 2

A Plan for a Traditional Home

The house in Figure 1 (page 10) can be approached by the brick path leading from the street or the one from the driveway. Either way, the first sight you have of the house is the front, framed by a fairly symmetrical planting of trees and shrubs and a well-maintained lawn. The plantings accentuate the lines of the house and contribute to a feeling of dignity and solidity. The areas behind the house are, for the most part, given an equally formal treatment. The aim has been to provide spaces for recreation in an enclosed, private setting. The back door opens onto a brick terrace flanked by tall, columnar evergreens. A brick path then leads you through the lawn area to the swimming pool. The changes in elevation have been dealt with by keeping all the areas flat and connecting them with a short flight of steps and stone retaining walls. At the base of each wall is a long, narrow flower border, which could contain annuals, perennials or both. The border closest to the house contains some herbs.

The use of brick for all the paths unifies the front and rear areas, as does the use of gray flagstones to pave both the terrace and the area around the pool; the gray stone of the walls ties in with these as well. In the northwest corner is a small formal rose garden, backed by an evergreen hedge. It is meant to be viewed from the pool, and is placed on an axis with it, at right angles to the central axis of the property. The side yard to the north is shaded partly by the house and partly by some trees that have been deliberately planted to give dappled shade. This tiny woodland is planted with native shrubs and wild-flowers, and an informal stone path winds through it, connecting the screen porch with the pool. A tall row of flowering shrubs has been planted between the lawn and the woodland to give shade to the latter and to separate the formal and informal areas.

The south side of the property is given over to utility areas: garage, dog pen, vegetable garden and utility shed. The shed contains tools for the garden and equipment for maintaining the pool, and is placed close to both. Nevertheless, all the utility features, even the tidy vegetable garden, are separated from the formal areas. Most of the property has been fenced to satisfy the legal requirement for enclosing a pool. The fence also prevents the dog from running out into the street, but he can also be confined to his pen when no one is home, to keep him out of mischief.

A Plan for a Contemporary Home

The plantings in front of the house in Figure 2 (page 11) are designed to hide the entrance to the house rather than accentuate it. You can see the roofline from the street, but the rest of the house unfolds gradually as you drive up to it and then turn onto the path that leads to the front door. The trees and shrubs planted on either side of the drive and the walk give a sense of mystery and expectation to the entrance.

The house has been designed and sited in a way that gives it a southwestern exposure, so as to keep the back of the house as private as possible but also let in a lot of light. A sliding door leading from the living room/family room in back opens directly onto a wooden deck surrounding a pool and a hot tub. The deck curves around the northwest corner of the house, where the kitchen is. Here the deck overlooks a small fenced play area for young children, where their mother can keep a close eye on them from the kitchen window when she is indoors.

It happens that this family is more interested in growing vegetables and herbs than flowers, so there are relatively large areas for food plants and only a few small annual beds near the pool for color. A hedge of flowering shrubs, many of them fragrant, follows the curved lower edge of the deck. These are not tall enough to block the sun, but they give a sense of enclosure to the pool. A much taller hedge to the south prevents anyone from looking into the yard on that side. In the southwest corner is a little "wild meadow" of grass and perennial wildflowers (see Chapter 16). The rest of the lawn is as large as space will permit so the children can run around.

Drawing Your Own Plan

When you are ready to do your own landscaping plan, you will be dealing with a whole set of unique requirements: yours and your family's, those of the spaces you have to work with and of the amount of landscaping you can afford. Very rarely are ready-made plans such as the ones shown here carried out in their entirety. They must be adapted to each household. Nor are plans usually executed all at once. They evolve in stages. I would start, for example, by planting the trees and shrubs in front of the house and taking care of some basic immediate needs such as the children's play area. I'd save such features as pools, terraces and rose gardens

until I had the time and money to tackle them. If you can foresee the need for these features now, you will have set aside a spot for them where they will work best.

It may take you quite a while to figure out how to put all the pieces of a landscaping plan together. I find it helps to lay sheets of tracing paper over the plan and sketch different layouts to see what might work. Keep going out and looking at the actual site as you work, seeing things from different angles to help you visualize them, and staking out lines where features like gardens or pools will go. If you have trouble seeing how your bird's-eye-view plan will look in real life, you can even take photographs of the house, enlarge them, trace the general outlines onto tracing paper and draw in your proposed plantings or construction projects to see how they will look.

Principles of Garden Design

Each part of your property will present a different kind of design challenge. There are specific tricks to designing with roses, shrubs or any plant group; they are discussed elsewhere in this book. But certain principles hold true for all phases of garden design. These are balance, contrast and unity—the basic elements of all art. And in fact what you are doing in landscaping is really just painting a picture using plants instead of brushstrokes. Try to imagine each glimpse of your property and the areas within it, framed as if they were pictures, and try to make that picture both interesting and harmonious.

BALANCE

If you have ever assembled the furniture

in a room, put together a still life, or created any kind of composition at all, you know that balance is necessary. Picture a room in which all the tall furniture is at one end and the low pieces are at the other; it doesn't work. Plants must also be balanced in a composition. In a formal garden design the balance has a lot of symmetry—as in Figure 1, where the tall evergreens flank the terrace. In a more informal plan the balance is more subtle: instead of duplicating a form on one side with a mirror image on the other, you provide masses of equal weight on each side, even though their contours are not the same. What kind of contours your plant picture will have will depend on the sizes and shapes of the individual plants and on how they are grouped. An example might be a doorway planting in which the groups of plants on each side of the door have equal weight visually, even though several different species with different forms—cone-shaped, columnar, low and spreading—are used.

Balance is not achieved with contours alone. You also need to think about a balance of color, of light and dark tones, and texture. You don't want a flower garden, for example, where all the blue flowers wind up at one end or all the bright-toned ones, or all the ones with a daisylike shape.

CONTRAST

One of the things that makes any garden design interesting is contrast. Just think how varied plants are—how many different ways flowers are colored; how many different textures evergreens can have—how trees can vary from the huge, dense head of a maple or beech to the open branches and small leaves of a birch or an aspen. As you get to know plants better, you will find contrasts you never thought of: leaves marked in several colors, bark in colors like red or green. You will find ways to combine similar plants that differ slightly—mixing five different ground covers to make a richly patterned carpet, for example, or planting three different ferns, like three different patterns of lace. Some contrasts will become your favorites—perhaps pink roses against a background of dark evergreens, or yellow goldenrod and blue chicory together in a wild meadow.

UNITY

Giving your plant pictures a feeling of unity is something that simply takes practice. One thing that will help you a lot is to use repetition at the same time that you are using contrast to arouse interest. A single element that you use throughout the composition may help tie it together. In a flower garden it might be clumps of white feverfew dotted throughout the bed. In a shrub planting it might be a ground cover that unifies the whole. It might even be a construction material, such as the stone and brick used in Figure 1, above.

Very often the trick of a unified design lies in not planting too many different things. I find that the more I learn about plants, the more different ones I want to try to grow and the more I risk letting the yard become a motley jumble of this and that. It is very hard to be a designer of plants and a collector of plants at the same time. Look at the living pictures in your gardens with this in mind. Are they designs or collections? And if you are an inveterate collector, perhaps there is something—like a ground cover or edging or background hedge—that you can plant to unify your design. Plants can become like stray cats that you can't turn away, but a yard that is a vast horticultural orphanage will not be a showplace. If you have too

What to Do Yourself

Whether you tackle a gardening task yourself will depend on many things: how much physical strength you have, how much knowledge you have, how much time you have and often simply how much interest you have in taking on the project. The following lists may help you to make the decision.

Good do-it-yourself tasks:
Minor grading and terracing
Correcting minor drainage problems
Erecting masonry walls up to 1 foot high
Drawing a landscape plan
Installing a small ornamental pool
Pruning and spraying small trees
Building raised beds
Transplanting bare-root shrubs and trees
Planting balled-and-burlapped trees if the ball is not too heavy
Sinking fence posts
Constructing simple fences and gates
Building good garden soil
Installing simple above-ground irrigation systems
Making compost
Planting a new lawn or restoring an old one
Training vines
Designing and planting a perennial garden
Making compost bins
Building a cold frame
Laying an informal fieldstone walk and establishing creeping plants between the stones

Learning to monitor insect populations so that you can recognize them at different stages of their life cycles and also know when they are most active

Usually best done by a pro:
Major grading and terracing
Making tree wells
Correcting major drainage problems
Erecting masonry walls higher than 1 foot
Felling trees
Pruning, spraying and cabling large trees
Removing large stumps and boulders
Diagnosing disease problems and often insect pests as well
Soil testing
Planting balled-and-burlapped shrubs and trees with heavy root balls
Digging and balling a shrub or tree
Sinking posts in very rocky or compacted soil
Building large arbors
Large-scale spraying, even with low-toxicity products
Planning and/or carrying out woodlot management
Installing underground irrigation systems
Building retaining walls to hold up earth on a steep slope. (Whether of wood or masonry, such walls must be properly anchored, and drainage systems must be built into them. Otherwise they will be pushed outward.)
Digging out large tree stumps

much of something, give it away or compost it. It is not a federal crime to kill a garden plant.

Another factor to keep in mind is the element of time. A garden may be a picture, but it is one that changes from day to day, or hour to hour. The flowers that bloom in your yard in May will not be blooming in August, so you'll need to plant others. The red autumn leaves on your Japanese maple will be handsome at 4:00 P.M. but spectacular at 6:00 P.M. when the sun is setting behind them—if you plant the tree to the west. The swimming pool will look attractive and inviting in summer, but less so in winter with the cover on it; if this bothers you, site the pool at a distance from the house. And always keep in mind the ultimate size and spread of everything you plant, whether it is a tall tree, a broad shrub or a flowering plant that may creep all over your garden.

How Much to Tackle Yourself

This and other aspects of landscape design may be a bit overwhelming to you if you are still unfamiliar with plants and the way they grow. You may decide you need to get help from someone skilled in landscape design either to start you off with an overall plan or help you with specific areas. But as you learn more you will enjoy trying your hand at these projects, which will give you the feeling of creating your own little world of color, fragrance, light and shade.

You need to make similar choices when it comes to the physical work of gardening. Don't take on more than you have the time, money, strength or expertise to handle, either in the initial preparation or the yearly maintenance. I truly hope that you are not one of those people who, like me, believe they can do anything and must learn the hard way which things they cannot do, cannot do well, or refuse to do regularly. The list of jobs I have learned to shun includes dry-wall construction, tree felling, terrace building and all forms of lawn care. You may shine at all these but have no patience with weeding or deep digging a bed. Most people who garden like to do at least some of the work themselves because they enjoy it; it is good for them physically and takes their mind off things that cause them stress. Others find that what they want most after a long, hard week is to take the time to smell the flowers—flowers planted by someone else. This is fine too.

So use common sense in scheduling your projects. And when you are sitting by the fire in winter, ordering plants and seeds, don't plan a monster. Plan gardens you will *enjoy* getting to when they need attention. After all, that's the whole point.

WHAT PLANTS NEED

Good gardening is very simple, really. You just have to learn to think like a plant. You can memorize sets of instructions if you want to, collect charts and tables, test and retest your soil and follow precise recipes for soil mixes and compost. But you will accomplish more simply by learning a bit about how plants are constructed, how they grow and what they want out of life. Once you understand what makes plants tick, you'll understand what you need to do to help them grow well (only a few rather uncomplicated things). You'll also learn how to read the sign language by which plants tell you what they need. Some plants may have fussy preferences—many of them dealt with in the other chapters in this book—but most have the same universal needs.

How Plants Function

Plants, like people, need food for survival, growth and reproduction. They manufacture their food by means of a process called "photosynthesis," from elements they find in the air, water and soil. Sunlight provides the energy for this activity—which is in reality a chain of chemical reactions.

To get what it needs from the air, a plant "breathes," inhaling carbon dioxide and exhaling oxygen—just the opposite of animal respiration. To get what it needs from the soil, it absorbs water, oxygen and certain nutrients, the most important of which are compounds of nitrogen, phosphorus and potassium, followed closely by sulfur, calcium and magnesium (certain other chemicals, known as "trace elements," must be in the soil in small quantities).

Plants also make their own vitamins and digestive enzymes, and the hor-mones that govern their longings and desires, called "tropisms." One of these (phototropism) makes a plant want to lean or grow toward a source of light and to face its flowers toward the sun. Another (hydrotropism) makes it turn its roots in the direction of water.

Working with plants gives you a great respect for them. Though silent and slow, they are resilient, relentless. We may feel quite powerful dispatching a row of garden weeds with a hoe in an instant. But turn our backs for a week or two, and there they all are again. I once went on a camping trip in the South American jungle and saw that the paths we had made with machetes on our way to the campsite had started to seal us in when we hacked our way out again a mere week later. To this day I always see a little bit of the jungle in plants, even the ones in my civilized northern garden.

PLANT STRUCTURE

To see how plants work, let's look more closely at the parts of a typical one, from the bottom up (Figure 3). A plant's roots are, in a sense, its feet, since they anchor it to the ground, but they also are responsible for absorbing all those vital elements from the soil. It is thus very important to keep in mind what a plant's roots are up to—all the more so because you can't see them. The roots' absorption of nutrients takes place through microscopic projections called "root hairs"; these hairs also take in oxygen from the soil, release carbon dioxide and absorb water. The roots store water and nutrients (sometimes for long periods, in enlarged portions such as bulbs or tubers), then send them up to the leaves via fine channels, like our veins, in the stems.

One of the plant stem's main functions is support. Unless a plant is a

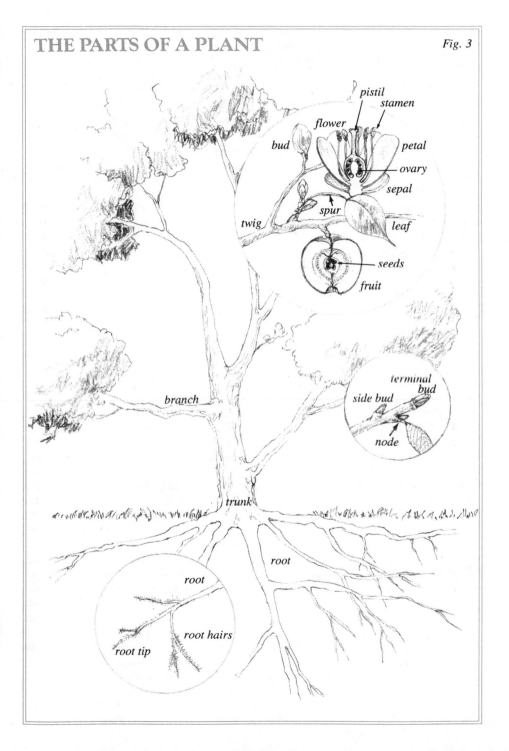

THE PARTS OF A PLANT

Fig. 3

pistil

stamen

flower

bud

petal

ovary

sepal

twig

spur

leaf

seeds

fruit

terminal bud

side bud

node

branch

trunk

root

root

root hairs

root tip

creeper by nature, it is always thinking "up"—trying to get its leaves up into a place where there is light and good circulation of air, and competing with other plants that are trying to do the same thing. Stems (trunks and branches in the case of woody plants) are also the plant's most important conductors of materials—its circulatory system, so to speak. They bring the leaves raw materials gathered by the roots and take away food that the leaves manufacture, using some of it for their own growth and returning the rest to the roots so that they too can grow.

Though stems make some food, it is primarily in the leaves that food production takes place, from the water and nutrients brought up by the stems from the roots. On the leaves' undersides are tiny pores called "stomata" through which carbon dioxide enters. This gas is combined with the water and nutrients by means of the green chlorophyll in the leaves. This process produces the carbohydrates that nourish the plant. The byproducts of these chemical reactions—water vapor and oxygen—pass out through the stomata into the air (this is called "transpiration"). The more leaves a plant has, the more food it can make, and the more it can grow.

PLANT GROWTH

A plant is always growing—all over. The most dramatic growth points are the tips of the roots and the buds at the tips of the stems (called "terminal buds"). But growth also occurs at side buds, where new stems form. Some plants, called "annual" plants, grow to maturity in one season, reproduce, and then die. Others, which are "perennial," produce new plants but continue to grow themselves, persisting from season to season. From the gardener's viewpoint it is important with both annuals and

perennials to keep a plant's growth vigorous during the full course of its normal life.

PLANT REPRODUCTION

Plants reproduce in different ways. One way is by means of seeds. Some of a plant's terminal buds turn into leaves, but others turn into flowers, which, as far as the plant is concerned, exist solely for the purpose of reproduction. A flower performs its show of color and fragrance for the benefit of bees, butterflies, hummingbirds and other creatures that pollinate it. While these various creatures are burrowing around in the blossom to get nectar, they transfer pollen from a male part of the flower, called a "stamen," onto a female part, called a "pistil" (a biology teacher once told me I could remember which is which by thinking "pistil-packing mama"), and the flower is thereby fertilized. (Occasionally the male and female parts are on separate plants.) After fertilization, the flower can produce fruits or seed heads containing the seeds. These are then transported by gravity, by the wind, by water, by traveling animals who carry the seeds on their fur, or by birds that eat the fruits. The seeds land or are dropped at another spot where the life of a new plant begins.

Plants can also reproduce by vegetative means, such as sending up new shoots from their roots or underground stems ("stolons") or by forming small bulblets at the sides of a food-storing bulb. Your plants may decide that they want to put most of their energy into one or another form of reproduction, but it is often desirable for you to change their minds. If you are trying to encourage a large harvest of fruits or a showy display of flowers, you may want to chop off "suckers," the new plants that come up from the roots. Or you may want to cut seed heads off plants that have flowered, so that they will concentrate on forming good, productive root systems instead. (Decisions such as these are discussed in more detail in the chapters on specific types of plants.)

Plants Need Good Soil

Since so much of what plants need if they are to do well comes from the soil, establishing a good soil is the most important thing you can do for plants. But gardeners often don't understand what a "good soil" is or how they can achieve it. They may think that it means simply improving soil fertility, and this in turn means going out and buying a bag of "evergreen food," "bulb food" or "rose food" (just as they would buy "dog food," "horse feed" or "rabbit chow") and sprinkling it on their gardens. But good soil is soil with good structure as well as good fertility, and structure is something that you must work to build. Improving soil structure isn't difficult to do, but it does require that you understand some basic things about your soil.

SOIL LAYERS

What is soil? Most soils are composed of inorganic mineral particles, air, water and organic matter—matter that was once living plant or animal tissue—in varying amounts. If you go out in the garden right now and dig a straight-sided hole to the depth of your spade, you will see something like the cross-section drawing of soil on page 17. Most likely, the upper layer—the topsoil—will be considerably darker in color, lighter in texture and easier to dig than the lower layer—the subsoil—

because the topsoil contains more organic matter. In the upper layer you will find more plant roots and more soil organisms than in the denser subsoil, though some deeper-rooted plants and some earthworms will probably have entered the subsoil as well. The subsoil is important: plant roots bring important minerals up from it, and it can be improved just as the topsoil can. When we speak of the soil structure in a garden, however, we are usually talking about the topsoil layer.

Soils vary enormously from one part of the country to another. Your topsoil may be dark brown, light brown or a brick red, depending on the kinds of minerals it contains and the amount of moisture and organic matter in it. It may be only a few inches deep, or it may be a foot deep. It may be full of rocks, or it may be fairly rock-free.

SOIL STRUCTURE

Soils are classified according to the size of the particles of which they are composed. At one extreme is coarse gravel, with particles larger than 5 millimeters in diameter; at the other is clay, with particles smaller than .005 millimeter. In between is a gradation of soils with particles of decreasing size: fine gravel, coarse sand, fine sand, sandy loam, loam, silt loam and silt. The soils with larger particles are generally characterized as "light" or "sandy" soils; those with small ones are "heavy" or "clay" soils. Loam, the happy medium, is usually considered the ideal type of soil.

Each type of soil texture has its virtues. In light soils, both water and air can move freely among the large particles, so that these soils tend to be well drained and rich in oxygen. Light soils warm up fast in spring, thus stimulating early plant growth. They are also easy for plant roots to penetrate as they grow.

On the negative side, water may drain out of light soils too quickly, taking nutrients with it and leaving the soil both dry and infertile.

In clay soils there is little space among the particles for air and water to circulate, so that these soils are often waterlogged and poorly drained. This can rob plant roots of oxygen and cause them to rot. Since clay soils are dense, they are harder for roots to penetrate. (Imagine poking your fingers through sand, then through clay, and you'll sense what the same process feels like for plant roots.) Clay soils also warm up more slowly in spring. On the other hand, because they hold water and nutrients well, they are often fertile (this is also because clay particles have negatively charged ions that attract positively charged particles of elements important for plants). And they retain moisture better than sandy soils do in hot, dry weather.

Different plants like different soils. Some plants that need particularly good drainage are most at home in sandy soils and have evolved with roots deep enough to withstand their dryness. Others that need the extra fertility and moisture of clay soil have strong roots that don't mind the extra push it takes to penetrate them. But the ideal soil for most plants is loam, and if we are trying to grow a wide range of plants, loam is what most of us would like to have.

What kind of soil do you have in your garden? Squeeze a handful of it. Does it form a tight ball that doesn't come apart when you tap it? Is it sticky when wet but hard and lumpy when dry? If so you have a clay soil. If it runs through your fingers and doesn't form a ball, it's sandy. If it holds together, but breaks when you tap it, it's loam.

The size of the particles in your soil is not the only important factor in soil structure. How the particles are orga-nized also matters. Ideally, soil particles are clustered together in groups and are not distinct as, for example, sand particles usually are. Nor are the particles so close together that they form a tight mass, as with clay. Rather, the particles of the best soils are like crumbs of homemade bread. In fact when we describe good structure we often say the soil has a "crumb," or "tilth." And usually a soil has crumb because it is rich in organic matter. What you want is a "friable" soil, one that feels light, almost fluffy, and is easy to stick your fingers into. It is inviting to plants, inviting to earthworms, which will always populate your garden if you have good soil, and inviting to you! You'll find it a joy to work in because it is easy to dig and because weeds pull out of it easily.

Now let's get back to your own soil. What if you have squeezed your handful, and found out that it is dry and sandy, or heavy and sticky, and on top of that has no "crumb." Don't despair. Only in the direst of situations would you need to replace your soil by bringing in good (and expensive) loam, or to adjust your soil by adding large amounts of soil of the opposite texture. Fortunately there is one easy way to improve your soil no matter what is wrong with its structure: add organic matter.

THE ROLE OF ORGANIC MATTER

Organic matter is simply dead plant or animal tissue. Unless all your topsoil has been removed, there is some of it in your soil. Above ground, animals have left their carcasses and excrement, plants have died and leaves have fallen. Below ground, organisms such as worms and moles have also left car-casses and excrement, and plant roots have died and rotted. The actions of burrowing creatures, of growing plant roots, and of the freezing and thawing of the soil have mixed all these into the soil, even bringing some of the surface matter to the layers below, especially to the topsoil layer.

This varied collection of organic materials does a number of things for the soil that are greatly appreciated by plants. In the soil, plant and animal matter decomposes into a substance called "humus." Humus contains sticky gums that bind soil particles together into those all-important clusters, or crumbs—not densely, as with tightly packed clay, but with spaces through which water and air can pass. Thus organic matter, in the form of humus, helps to aerate the soil. It also makes it more able to conduct water, retaining some for plants to use, but letting the excess drain away. This is how adding organic matter can improve both clay and sandy soils.

Organic matter also contains important nutritional elements that plants need. In the process of decay, living things return to the soil the substances from which they were built so that other living things can use them. This happens through the action of soil microorganisms, which break down organic matter into its basic elements, in forms that can be readily absorbed by plant roots. Thus organic matter in the soil gives it a good structure and makes it fertile at the same time.

SOIL FERTILITY

For the most part, plant life is more healthy and abundant in soils that are fertile—that is, rich in nutrients. But what, really, does this mean? Let's go back to the major elements that plants need from the soil to manufacture their food, and let's consider how nature—or the gardener—supplies them.

Nitrogen. Soil nitrogen is converted to nitrates by "nitrogen-fixing" bacteria that take the nitrogen and change it, or "fix" it into a form that plants can use. Nitrogen maintains plants' green color and is largely responsible for good leaf and stem growth. The effect of feeding nitrogen to plants is fast and dramatic—you can see the stems shoot up and new leaves unfurl, suffused with a healthy green color. To the plant, a dose of nitrogen probably feels something like the way a candy bar feels to us: like a shot of quick energy.

Important as nitrogen is to plants, they can sometimes suffer from an excess of it, especially if other important elements are lacking. You'll notice that rapid growth produced by nitrogen is often rather soft and vulnerable, easily succumbing to cold and disease and making the plant attractive to sucking insects. The stems may be weak and need staking. Nitrogen may also produce too much leaf and stem growth instead of a good root system, or instead of producing desirable fruits and flowers. So you have to learn when your plants need extra nitrogen—when you want to green up your lawn, for example, or make an ornamental foliage plant like a fern more showy, or produce a quick, abundant row of lettuce. And you learn when plants don't need nitrogen: before the onset of cold weather, which would kill soft new growth, and when you want your plants to bloom heavily or get their roots well established instead of growing tall or leafy.

Though I use nitrogen with some caution I am always on the lookout for a nitrogen deficiency. Nitrogen is an element that is used up by plants very quickly. It is also highly soluble in water and thus leaches out of the soil quickly. If your plants run out of it you'll see pale foliage and spindly growth.

Spring is the best time to feed nitrogen to outdoor plants, for several reasons: because that's when you want lots of new growth, because the nitrogen is more available to the plants in warm weather when nitrogen-fixing soil bacteria are most active, and finally because nitrogen added in fall may leach away by springtime.

Phosphorus. Phosphorus is especially important for the root development of a plant. It also helps the plant to produce fruit and seeds and resist disease. It is one of those pluses a gardener can give to plants to make sure they do better than average.

When I dig a permanent bed for perennials where good root growth must continue for years, or if I am transplanting a plant and want it to put out fresh new roots right away, I try to make sure there is plenty of phosphorus available in the soil. Root-vegetable crops and flower bulbs also need a lot of phosphorus. It is not highly soluble and thus can be applied in fall.

Potassium. Potassium is essential for plant growth and for resistance to disease. It is highly soluble and leaches out quickly, so that if your soil is deficient in potassium you have to keep adding more from time to time.

Most mineral deficiencies in the soil are hard for the average gardener to spot because their symptoms can be similar to those of many other problems, such as pollution or disease. If your plants are growing poorly despite your best efforts, it is a good idea to have your soil tested (page 25). In certain parts of the country, local soils are commonly deficient in a specific mineral—say, boron, magnesium or calcium. A soil test will pick this up.

SOIL PH

Another thing that determines whether you have "good soil" is the soil's level of acidity or alkalinity, as measured by the pH factor—expressed as a number on a scale of 1.0 to 14.0, with 7.0 representing a "neutral" pH. As the numbers decrease from 7.0 they indicate greater acidity; as they increase from 7.0 they indicate greater alkalinity. The pH of most soils is between 4.5 and 8.0.

The main reason to be concerned with soil pH is not the direct effect of excessively acid or alkaline soil substances on the plants themselves, but the effect the pH has on important soil minerals. These are much more available to plants in soil that is close to neutral than in soil that is either very acid ("sour") or very alkaline ("sweet"). The action of soil bacteria is also thought to be more vigorous when soil pH is between 6.0 and 7.0.

Most plants have specific preferences as to soil pH. There are some that like really acid soil: heathers, rhododendrons and blueberries are notorious examples. Others prefer alkaline soil: these include baby's breath, delphiniums and beets. But most garden plants will tolerate a large pH range. Furthermore, if you have a healthy soil that is well supplied with nutrients and organic matter, and that is also well aerated and full of earthworms and microorganisms, its pH doesn't matter much. The overall good condition of the soil will act as a buffer against any deviations from the ideal pH for any given plant.

It is only when your soil is extremely acid or alkaline that you have to do anything about it. A soil test is probably the easiest way for you to check the pH of your soil. (For ways to alter soil pH see page 33.)

Having your soil tested. If you are new to gardening or are simply unsure about the nature of the soil in your garden, a soil test is a good idea. You will learn a lot about your soil. Most tests will tell you how much of the important elements your soil has (excluding nitrogen, which is hard to measure), how acid or alkaline it is, and what you need to add, in what amounts, to bring your soil to optimum condition (depending on what you are planning to grow). Some test results will also include the clay and humus content of your soil and even the levels of lead or other toxic elements. (If you notice flecks of paint in your soil from nearby buildings or fences, be sure to have the soil tested for lead. Don't grow edible crops in places where the lead level is high.)

You can buy fairly inexpensive soil kits that will test for pH and many nutrients, but I think it is easier to have your soil tested professionally. You will also get more complete information that way. For a very small fee, the local Cooperative Extension Service will provide you with a mailer and full instructions for digging up and sending soil for testing, and they will send you back a computer printout with the results. Private labs cost more but will sometimes provide more information. The best time to test the soil is before you start your garden or add nutrients to it. If you want to test an established garden, do it in fall.

How to Improve Your Soil

Once you understand what your plants want from your soil—good structure, available nutrients and the proper pH—and have determined how well equipped that soil is to provide these things, you need to decide how to make up for any deficiencies the soil has. My own approach is always to seek out good sources of organic matter and to add that to the soil, thereby enriching it and giving it a good structure at the

same time. This is, after all, the way nature has been improving the soil for millions of years. As I'll explain, adding organic matter does not always give my plants everything they want, but it does give them so much that it is the point at which I always begin.

ADDING ORGANIC MATTER

If nature has already put organic matter in your soil, why add more? Because few soils have a perfect structure to begin with, and because, after all, when you garden you want to give your plants an even more luxurious environment than nature usually provides. Furthermore, organic matter is not an addition you make just once and then forget about. It is always decomposing and being used by the plants; it must therefore always be replenished. Even the most permanent plantings such as trees, shrubs and deep-rooted perennials benefit by a surface mulch of organic matter that can, as it decomposes, be worked into the soil.

Although there are many kinds of organic matter to choose from, here are some of the most commonly used:

Animal manures. The manures of farm animals are very popular soil amendments because they provide good tilth and are high in nutrients as well. But there are a few things about them you need to know in order to use them profitably. Most contain a high percentage of nitrogen, relative to the other major nutrients, and a low percentage of phosphorus. So you might avoid them when you want to encourage root formation but not abundant growth of stems and leaves.

Manures can also be harmful to plants if they have not sufficiently decomposed. If you look at a pile of fresh horse manure on a cold morning, you will see billows of steam rising from it because of the heat it is giving off during decomposition, and you'll be able to smell the ammonia in it as well. Both heat and caustic ammonia can burn plants' roots, just as they can burn your own hands. Some manures are more apt to hurt your plants than others: chicken and rabbit manure, for example, are very "hot" and should be added to the garden only when thoroughly rotted.

I use a great deal of animal manure in my garden, but I never use any that is fresh. Well-rotted manure is odorless, and looks like dark soil. Often people who raise animals have piles of it that have been sitting around for years, and they are glad to have it carted away. Or they will sell it to you for less than it would cost to buy it in bags. But I have often splurged on bagged composted cow manure when I did not have a handy farm source, because my plants seem to consider it such a treat.

There are other considerations in judging a particular manure source: one is the percentage of animal excrement versus animal bedding (such as straw, sawdust or shavings). The bedding is good organic matter too, but it is lower in nutrients, more acidic and slower to decompose than pure manure. Another drawback is that manure and bedding can contain viable seeds from hay or other animal feeds, and these can sprout in your garden, so you have to weigh the risk of introducing weeds against the benefits to your soil. Finally, never use manures from dogs, cats or humans, for all of these can transmit diseases to your soil and then to you.

Plant humus. The most common form of decomposed plant matter that is sold commercially is peat or peat moss. This is made up of plants—usually sphagnum or other mosses—that have decomposed very slowly in boggy places. (Sphagnum peat is not to be confused with the undecomposed sphag-

num moss that is used to keep plants moist when packed for shipping or to line hanging-plant baskets.)

Peat moss comes in compressed, plastic-wrapped bales of various sizes, usually 2, 4 or 6 cubic feet. It is very, very dry. If you add peat moss to your soil directly it will draw the moisture out of the soil just as a blotter would, so be sure to moisten it first. Before I use peat moss, I either split the bale in two by cutting the plastic with a knife and letting water from a hose run slowly into the peat for a few hours, or I spread it on top of the garden and turn a sprinkler on it until the whole layer is wet before I dig it into the soil.

You can also buy "peat humus." This is more decomposed than peat moss, and much more moist. It comes in smaller bags and is darker, heavier and more expensive.

I find that no commerical product can lighten the soil in a large area as efficiently as peat moss can, if properly moistened, because it is relatively inexpensive and light to handle. I often use it in combination with rotted manure, however, because peat moss is relatively low in nutrients; I add as much manure as I need to give fertility to the soil.

Grass clippings are a convenient source of plant humus, but don't dig them into a planted garden if they have just been cut, because they decompose rapidly and the heat will burn plant roots. I avoid them if they are full of weed seeds (such as dandelions), and I never use clippings from lawns treated with herbicides such as 2,4-D, which will harm garden plants.

Plant debris such as weeds that have not yet gone to seed, annual crops that have finished producing or thinnings from the vegetable garden are all good sources of humus. These can be tilled directly into the soil. And you can till under annual crops in fall after they have finished producing. But don't till under plants that have suffered from diseases or insect infestations during the growing season, because both can winter over in the soil.

Cover crops. Sometimes gardeners plant crops just to provide organic matter for their soil, especially in vegetable gardens. These are called "cover crops" or "green manures" and are tilled under after a while. They are especially good if you have a large garden because they spare you from having to bring in a lot of material from somewhere else.

Planting cover crops benefits your garden in a number of ways. The growing roots help to keep the soil loose, moist and aerated on land that is being left fallow. Deep-rooted cover crops bring valuable minerals up to the topsoil from the subsoil, something that shallower-rooted garden crops can't do. Cover crops also keep rainfall from eroding the soil, and in many cases help to keep perennial weeds from growing. After the cover crops are turned under, they not only add organic matter for good tilth, but often return more nutrients to the soil than they consumed. Since some of the nutrients already in the soil would leach away if the ground were fallow, this is a double bonus.

What you decide to grow as a cover crop depends partly on your climate and partly on what you are trying to achieve. You might want a cover crop that will grow for an entire year, from one spring to another, to take care of a plot you are not going to use or want to revitalize thoroughly as part of your garden-rotation scheme (page 197). If so, plant a deep-rooted perennial crop such as alfalfa, perennial rye or one of the clovers (see below for the benefits of each). On the other hand, use an annual cover crop if you want a quick-growing green manure to follow early vegetables, a spring cover crop to precede later-

planted ones, or a crop for the fallow summer period in a hot-climate garden. Some of these are annual rye (called "ryegrass"), buckwheat, hairy vetch, crimson clover and winter barley. I think annual cover crops are easier to deal with because you don't have to worry about perennial roots remaining in the soil and resprouting.

Cover crops that are especially good at holding down weeds are buckwheat and winter rye—the latter being a biennial that will survive the winter even in the north but will stop growing and die if you mow it in spring. Cover crops that are best at enriching the soil are those that are members of the pea family (legumes) such as the clovers, the vetches or, best of all, alfalfa. Legumes enrich the soil through the process of nitrogen fixation, described on page 215. They have bacteria called "rhizobia" living in nodules that grow on their roots. The legumes will use some of it up, but residual nitrogen will be available for other plants that grow in the same soil after the legumes have been removed or tilled under. You can help the process of nitrogen fixation along by dusting the seeds of the legume crop with a powder called an "inoculant." There are different inoculants for various legume crops, so check to make sure you've got the right one for your crop.

The most popular way to till under a cover crop is with a rear-mounted rotary tiller, but this machine cannot handle crops after they have gotten tall and thick-stalked. Either till your cover crop under when the plants are soft, green and about a foot tall or, if they've gotten tall and tough, mow them first, put the cuttings on the compost pile or use them as mulch, and then till the rest in. You can also dig a cover crop under by hand, especially if you are only dealing with a small area.

As a rule, it is not advisable to plant a new crop right after a green cover crop has been tilled under, because it will not have decomposed sufficiently to provide nutrients. Wait a month or so. A good plan is to plant an annual crop in late summer or fall. The plants will die over the winter and start decomposing, but their roots will still hold the soil. By spring, it will be time to till them in.

There are many different cover crops you can grow, and some will be better for your own climate than others. Your best bet is to talk to local farmers, farm-supply stores, nurseries or the Cooperative Extension Service to find out what works best in your area.

MAKING COMPOST

Another good way to add organic matter—and nutrients—to the soil is through compost. Compost is simply a big casserole of organic matter that you assemble yourself and then leave to "cook" awhile. The cooking—or decomposing—takes place fastest under these conditions: plenty of moisture, some heat and some air, all in the presence of microorganisms that speed decay.

I think the best reason to make compost is that it enables you to recycle the debris from your garden and many of the scraps from your kitchen and put them back into growing things, so that nothing is wasted. You may never become like the compost fanatics who feel they are letting down the whole planet if they send a potato peeling through the garbage disposal. But chances are that if you try composting you will find it a handy way to deal with garden refuse and obtain a great soil amendment at the same time—one that is not only free of charge, but right next to your garden where you need it.

Compost is made by piling layers of organic material, usually interspersed with layers of soil, in a heap, keeping it moistened with a hose and letting the pile decompose. This happens very quickly at the inside of the pile—the temperature there can get as high as 160 degrees—though the whole pile will eventually decay if it sits long enough. Patient (or lazy) composters do just that—let it sit. Those who want their compost faster turn their piles, bringing the material on the outside to the inside with a pitchfork or some such implement so that it too will have its chance at the "hot spot." (A handy way to do this is to turn the pile onto a spot next to it, then turn it back to the original spot, as shown in Figure 4.) Industrious composters turn their piles as often as once a week; doing it even once after a few months of warm weather will bring you more quickly to the finished product: a dark, moist substance that may not have the soillike consistency of finished humus but is broken down enough so that you can easily till it into the garden.

Every composter has his or her own recipe—usually, as with most good casseroles, a blend of whatever good things come to hand (see page 30 for some suggestions). But basically what you need are some materials like twigs, bark and thick roots that provide bulk but break down slowly; and other materials that break down faster and hasten the decomposition of the bulky ones—high-nitrogen substances such as manure, dried blood, fish emulsion or soft green-plant debris, and even soil, which introduces decay-causing microorganisms into the pile. Adding lime or wood ashes to your layers is also a good idea, especially if your materials are acidic ones such as leaves, manure or sawdust (wood ashes also contribute phosphorus).

Many gardeners are now using gasoline- or electric-powered shredders to break up compost materials and thereby speed decomposition, especially if they use a lot of autumn leaves, which tend to mat and sit in the pile wihout doing much. I would not buy anything this expensive just to make compost, but it might be a good tool to share with a few neighbors.

You can "cook" your compost in a number of different containers. It is easier to stack your pile if you enclose it, and it will also look tidier this way if your compost operation is in full view. The compost bins shown in Figure 4 have been built of wood frames with wire mesh stretched across them on three sides and one side left open for turning. The mesh lets air into the pile to help activate it. Bins can be constructed of wooden boards; logs stacked in a square, log-cabin style; or cement blocks stacked with air spaces between them. Or you might use a piece of snow fence, supported by metal stakes. There are many composting apparatuses on the market, but most of them seem to me too small, too expensive, or both, and I like the do-it-yourself approach better. You may come up with your own ingenious compost receptacle. Some gardeners even use old 55-gallon drums with holes punched or drilled in the sides.

Your compost is "done" when it has broken down into pieces small enough to use easily, depending on what job you are doing. For jobs like planting shrubs and trees, or for use as a mulch, it can be fairly coarse textured. For

USING COMPOST BINS

Fig. 4

A compost bin is left open at the top so that you can dump materials into it. The ones shown here are open in front as well, for easier turning. Remove compost from a bin with a manure fork, piling it on the ground in front of the bin; then return it to the bin in such a way that the material from the edges of the bin is put into the center. While the compost in the left bin is "cooking," the other is ready for fresh materials.

The Makings of Compost

Materials to use:
Farm animal manure
Autumn leaves and twigs
Grass clippings
Nonanimal kitchen scraps, such as
    fruit and vegetable peelings, corn
    husks and carrot tops
Animal remains from slaughter-
    houses, such as steamed bone
    meal, dried blood, and hoof and
    horn meal
Eggshells
Farm animal bedding, such as straw
    and shavings
Used mulch, such as chips and hay
Wood ashes
Seaweed, with the salt washed off
Alfalfa meal, or unused cat litter
    made from alfalfa meal
Sawdust and shavings from
    lumberyards
By-products from locally grown
    crops, such as spent hops or
    tobacco stems
Sod that has been removed in order
    to make new beds
Coffee grounds
Bulbs that have been discarded after
    forcing
The tops of perennials cut back in
    fall
Silt removed from the bottom of gar-
    den pools and ponds
Fallen fruit

Materials to use with caution:
Fish scraps, which are a good
    nitrogen source but may attract
    animals unless well buried in
    the pile

Annual weeds, which may contain
    weed seeds; compost them
    thoroughly
Perennial weeds, whose roots may
    regenerate; compost them
    thoroughly
Spent crops from the vegetable
    garden; don't use diseased crops
Corncobs, grapefruit rind, etc.;
    these decompose very slowly,
    and raccoons can scatter corncobs
    that are not well buried in the pile

Materials to avoid:
Animal kitchen scraps, which will
    attract rats and other vermin
Manure from dogs, cats or humans,
    which can transmit diseases
Colored newspapers, books and
    magazines, which may contain
    toxic inks
Plastic materials, which will not
    decompose
Grass clippings containing residual
    weed killers, which will kill
    garden plants
Any refuse from black walnut,
    eucalyptus and red cedar trees,
    which will inhibit the growth of
    garden plants
Coal and charcoal ashes, which
    contain toxic residues

enriching a seed bed or a potting mixture, you want compost that has broken down so much that it looks almost like soil and is so decomposed that you cannot easily see what materials went into it. When I worked at my friend Lee Bristol's nursery in Sherman, Connecticut, he kept several compost piles going at once. Most of them were huge mounds in varying stages of decay; even the oldest one was rather coarse textured, but it was perfect for outdoor planting. He also kept a four-sided wooden bin with a removable board at the bottom of one side, from which he extracted very fine compost that had been sitting for about five years. We used this for jobs like starting seeds. If you want very fine compost without the long wait, take some coarse compost and sift it through hardware cloth nailed taut to a frame (a small window frame would be just right).

Can you let a compost pile sit indefinitely? No. Eventually the organic matter will break down completely, your pile will dwindle, and the microorganisms in it will no longer be active. So get it while it's hot!

ADDING MORE NUTRIENTS TO THE SOIL

As I've explained above, much of the organic matter that you add to your soil to improve its structure also makes it more fertile. If you incorporate manure, plant residues, cover crops or compost into your soil, it may be that you won't have to add anything else.

On the other hand, maybe you will. Some kinds of organic matter—peat moss, for example—are less nutritious than others, or are lacking in some important elements that your plants need. So you need to find materials to add to your soil solely for the purpose of increasing its fertility.

You may also need to fertilize a specific plant by giving it an extra dose of nutrients at some point in its growth. You can dig some fertilizer into the bottom of a planting hole and mix some into the soil with which you fill the hole. You can dig fertilizer into the soil around certain plants as they grow, and "side dress" or "top dress" plants by spreading fertilizer on the surface of the soil around them. You can also apply fertilizer in liquid form, either by watering the plant with a fertilizer solution or by "foliar feeding"—spraying the solution directly on the plant's leaves.

The fertilizer you use might consist of some of the organic materials mentioned in the preceding sections, but here you would be applying them chiefly for their nutritional value, not to change the structure of the soil. Before feeding a plant, always ask yourself, "What kind of food does this plant really want?" Keep in mind the three basic elements that plants need to get from the soil (pages 23–24)—nitrogen, phosphorus and potassium—what kind of growth they produce in plants, and when that growth should occur.

Organic versus inorganic fertilizers. Nitrogen, phosphorus and potassium can be obtained from organic sources (animal and vegetable matter) or from inorganic fertilizers produced by the petrochemical industry. Some gardeners are passionately committed to one or the other approach, some don't care and use whatever they have around, and others use different fertilizers in different situations.

People who favor inorganic, or "chemical" fertilizers say that they are less expensive than organic preparations, act more quickly and are often easier to apply; further, they feel the plants don't know the difference between elements from organic and inorganic sources. All plant nutrients are "chemical" compounds, after all, and are absorbed and used in the same way.

"Organic" gardeners, on the other hand, refuse to use any petrochemical products, as well as any manmade pesticides and weed killers, because they are concerned about the toxic properties of all of these and their effect on the soil (and other parts of the environment as well). They say that overuse of chemical fertilizers kills beneficial soil organisms —with the result that soon nutrients are no longer made in the soil, and the only way plants can obtain readily available nourishment is from more chemical fertilizers. These products, they say, also lead to the build-up of chemical residues in the soil, which can be bad for plant growth.

I agree that there are dangers in the overuse of these fertilizers and that overusing them is very easy to do, especially if you just scatter handfuls of fertilizer grains about. I have tried them in the past from time to time, particularly on ornamental plants when I have wanted to get them off to a fast start. But now I find I tend to use chemical fertilizers less and less. I prefer to add organic materials that I am sure will have a safe, long-lasting effect on the soil. But it is good to know about both approaches and how to use them. •

When you buy fertilizers commercially, most are labeled with a formula that states the percentage of nitrogen, phosphorus and potassium that the preparations contain. The chemical symbols for these three elements are N, P and K, respectively, and the elements are referred to by their symbols in many discussions of them and on fertilizer bags, so it is worth memorizing them. (If, like most people, you forget which element is P and which is K, use a memory device such as "Phosphorus is P because the word has two P's in it.") If a bag of fertilizer says it is "5–10–5," for example, that means that it contains 5 percent N, 10 percent P and 5 percent K. You can then figure out, if you want to, how many pounds of each element you are adding to your soil. For example, a 100-pound bag of 5–10–5 would supply 5 pounds of nitrogen to your garden, 10 pounds of phosphorus and 5 pounds of potassium. The rest is inert filler. Both organic and inorganic commercial fertilizers are labeled using these initial letters.

Organic sources. If I want a good, steady nitrogen source that will break down over a period of time and simultaneously improve soil texture, I add well-rotted manure. Manure is also good to use if you have lightened the soil with a material that is relatively poor in nutrients, like vermiculite or peat moss; but since in this case the soil texture is already good, you might apply a less bulky nitrogen source such as cottonseed meal. For a fast-acting nitrogen supply, use a liquid source that will go straight to the plant roots, such as liquid fish emulsion diluted according to the directions on the bottle, or "manure tea," made by soaking manure in a bucket or tub of warm water for several hours or overnight. Although "dried activated" sewage sludge is a nitrogenous fertilizer, I don't use it. It is supposed to be free of disease-causing bacteria if it has been heat-treated, but I'm concerned that sludge might contain PCBs or other toxic wastes.

Sources of organic phosphorus include bone meal and hoof and horn meal (both are slaughterhouse by-products). Rock phosphate, which is not an organic product but a naturally occurring, ground-up mineral, is also a phosphorus source favored by organic gardeners. If you use manure as a fertilizer it is a good idea to add one of these, since manure is relatively low in phosphorus.

Organic potassium can be found in

the wood ashes from your stove or fireplace. It is also found in leaves and in compost made from them. If your garden site once had trees on it, chances are that there is a fair amount of potassium in your soil from all the leaves that have fallen. Mineral sources also favored by organic gardeners include crushed granite and greensand (glauconite), a mineral deposit found on the ocean floor.

You can also buy commercial organic preparations that are "complete" fertilizers—mixtures of the three essential nutrients—nitrogen, phosphorus and potassium—in pelleted form. Sometimes you will see organic and inorganic nitrogen combined together in one product, and the label will say something like "40 percent of the N is organic." The reason for combining the two is that the inorganic nitrogen will act quickly to start the plant's growth, and the slower-acting organic nitrogen will provide for future growth.

Inorganic fertilizers. Most inorganic fertilizers sold are complete ones, with all the essential nutrients. Their contents are explained by the N P K formula, and there are many different formulations available. You can also buy bags of these nutrients singly. Superphosphate—a highly activated form of rock phosphate—provides a rapidly available supply of phosphorus. Double and triple superphosphates supply two and three times as much. Using too much of any of them can cause mineral imbalances in your soil, so don't be careless with them. A quarter-pound of regular superphosphate per square yard of soil is a safe amount if you're digging the soil to a depth of one foot; add another quarter-pound to the subsoil if you're double digging (page 34). Muriate of potash is a synthetic product that raises the potassium level of the soil.

"Slow-release" fertilizers provide nutrients over a long period of time; these are often used for fertilizing shrubs and trees. Some are collections of little pellets that you dig in or sprinkle over the soil; others look like large white pills and are placed in the bottom of a planting hole. There are also commercial products designed to take care of mineral deficiencies (such as a boron deficiency), either singly or in combination. There is no need to add these unless a problem shows up on a soil test. If it does, consult a soil expert; your local Extension Service will most likely be able to help you here.

ADJUSTING YOUR SOIL'S PH

As explained on page 24, you may not need to do anything about your soil's pH. But if a soil test indicates you need to correct it, this can easily be done.

To raise the pH of soil that is too acidic, lime is usually added. "Lime" is the common name for calcium carbonate, a compound that also helps compensate for the calcium deficiencies to which acid soils are sometimes prone. Bone meal and wood ashes also raise soil pH.

A general rule of thumb for adding lime is that 5 to 10 pounds of it per 100 square feet of soil will raise the pH one scale interval. This amount depends on what your soil is like. For example, you will need more lime to raise the pH if your soil is clay. It's best to follow the recommendation that comes with your soil test results.

The best all-purpose liming product to use is dolomitic limestone, a fine white powder that comes in large or small bags and contains magnesium as well. "Quicklime" is a product that neutralizes acid soil much faster than other preparations, but it is too caustic for garden use. "Hydrated lime" is safer, but it too can harm plants and should be applied only to soil that you will not be planting for several months; it also will revert to ordinary lime if the bag sits around for a while.

Where I live, the soil is very acid, with a pH as low as 4.8—and even lower than that when mulches such as shredded bark are used. As a result, every fall I add at least 10 pounds of dolomitic limestone to every 100 square feet of my vegetable and flower gardens. But even in gardens where I haven't used any lime at all, I am amazed at how well everything seems to grow, even in such acid soil.

In many parts of the country, especially in the Great Plains and dry, western areas, the soil is often very alkaline. You also might have a portion of your property that is alkaline because of the lime present in some building materials—the area next to a mortared wall or concrete foundation, for example. To lower soil pH, ground sulfur can be added—but carefully, since too much can be harmful. (Again, follow the recommendations included with the soil test results.) Calcium sulfate, which adds calcium as well, can also be used, as can iron sulfate or aluminum sulfate. But the best solution is to dig in a lot of organic matter that is very acid, such as peat moss, sawdust, leaves, bark and manure. Fertilizers designed for "acid-loving plants" can benefit too-alkaline soil, but applying quantities of these products year after year can cause your soil to become much too acid, so use them conservatively.

TILLING YOUR SOIL

How you dig in organic matter, fertilizers, lime and other soil amendments is just as important as what you add. You want to work these materials into the soil as thoroughly as possible and as deeply as necessary for the plants you want to grow—only about 6 inches for lawn grasses, but as much as 2 feet for some deep-rooted perennials. This procedure—which also loosens the soil and breaks up large clumps—is called "tilling." For growing crops on a large scale, tilling is done with heavy power equipment, and it is still the custom in some areas to have a local farmer come in and plow up the family vegetable plot with his tractor. More often nowadays people have smaller gardens and usually till their own plots.

Tilling a new bed. If I am making a new garden, whether it is for vegetables, flowers or anything else, I almost always avoid power equipment and till by hand, arduous as this is, using a spade or a digging fork to turn over the soil and mix in soil amendments. Some people use a rototiller for this job, but I don't, for several reasons. One is that new garden ground usually contains perennial weeds, which mechanical tilling chops up into thousands of little pieces that grow into thousands of new weeds. It's possible to remove weeds as you go along when you dig by hand. (See page 54 for ways to remove weeds.) Another reason to till by hand is that a new bed needs to be tilled deeply—at least a foot deep—and even a deep-tined rototiller can't go down that far. Also, rototillers don't remove rocks, of which my soil has a great abundance. If you are planting a shallow-rooted crop like lawn grass or certain ground covers, a rototiller is very useful, but the weeds should still be removed by hand.

When I till a deep bed I try to improve on nature by loosening, lightening and enriching not only the topsoil layer but also some of the subsoil below that. There are two ways to do this—double digging, and a deluxe version of double digging, both illustrated in Figure 5. In the first method I remove the soil from a section of the bed to the depth of a spade and set it aside. Then I loosen the soil under it with a digging fork, working organic matter, lime and whatever else the soil needs into the subsoil. I replace the topsoil layer, but only after I have added soil amendments to it as well. Then I repeat the whole procedure with the next strip of garden, continuing until I have dug it all.

In deluxe double digging I remove both the topsoil and subsoil from a strip, keeping the two separate, and I move them to the opposite end of the bed. Then I remove both soils from the next strip and put them in the first hole, but with the topsoil and subsoil inverted. As in the first digging method, I add soil amendments to both soils. The process continues strip by strip, to the end of the bed, with the soil from the first trench going into the last. But please note: this method will only work if you lighten and enrich the subsoil to the point where it is like excellent topsoil—otherwise you will just have a bed of clumpy, infertile subsoil with an exquisite under-layer, which will reward only deep-rooted plants that choose to sample it. Also note that with either method, the strips you dig up must be of uniform width so that you can fill all the trenches evenly.

I only use the deluxe double dig-ging method for beds that will hold deep-rooted plants such as roses, aspar-agus and deep-rooted herbaceous peren-nials. But I might use the simpler method for a bed of annual flowers or for a vegetable garden, where many crops have fairly deep roots and surface tilling alone would be inadequate. Once, when making a very large bed by the deluxe method, I used a 23-horsepower tractor with a bucket attach-ment to help dig soil out of each 3-foot-wide trench and fill the next. The loader wasn't very precise in handling the sub-soil layer, and I had to do much of the work by hand, but a small backhoe attachment probably would have han-dled the subsoil layer too.

While I was digging that bed, peo-ple who wandered by thought I was crazy. There were many jokes about the series of graves I was digging and how their headstones should read. But the deep, fluffy, moisture-retentive soil that resulted was no joke. Roots were en-couraged by that wonderful texture to grow deep down where the moisture was more constant, and instead of finding subsoil down there, they found black gold!

When the bed was first finished it looked like a raised bed, because it was almost a foot higher than the surround-ing earth, but it gradually settled. If you double dig a bed, try to do it in fall so it can settle a bit before planting time and fill in air pockets that might dry out the plants' roots.

Tilling an established bed. Once a bed has been put in, the tilling should be done every year, preferably in fall when the soil is not wet and easily compacted. Annual tilling is much less of a chore than creating a new bed. It can easily be accomplished with hand tools or with a deep-tined rototiller. (But use the roto-tiller with care: overtilling can pulverize soil to the point that it loses its crumb.) Even just a light forking over of an established bed will help, exposing clumps of soil that winter freezing and thawing will break up further.

Plants Need Light

As everyone knows, mushrooms grow well in the dark, and seeds germinate in the darkness of the soil and will even send up pale shoots without light. In most cases, however, plants need light to carry on food production. While the requirement for light is virtu-ally universal, nonetheless different

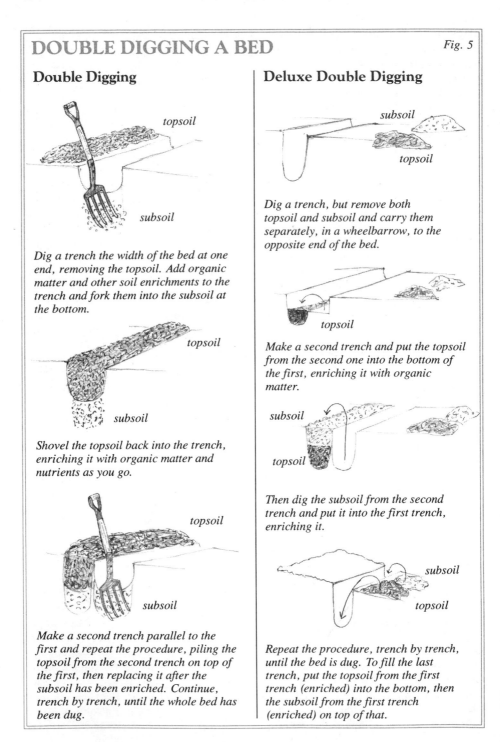

DOUBLE DIGGING A BED   *Fig. 5*

Double Digging

topsoil

subsoil

Dig a trench the width of the bed at one end, removing the topsoil. Add organic matter and other soil enrichments to the trench and fork them into the subsoil at the bottom.

topsoil

subsoil

Shovel the topsoil back into the trench, enriching it with organic matter and nutrients as you go.

topsoil

subsoil

Make a second trench parallel to the first and repeat the procedure, piling the topsoil from the second trench on top of the first, then replacing it after the subsoil has been enriched. Continue, trench by trench, until the whole bed has been dug.

Deluxe Double Digging

subsoil

topsoil

Dig a trench, but remove both topsoil and subsoil and carry them separately, in a wheelbarrow, to the opposite end of the bed.

topsoil

Make a second trench and put the topsoil from the second one into the bottom of the first, enriching it with organic matter.

subsoil

topsoil

Then dig the subsoil from the second trench and put it into the first trench, enriching it.

subsoil

topsoil

Repeat the procedure, trench by trench, until the bed is dug. To fill the last trench, put the topsoil from the first trench (enriched) into the bottom, then the subsoil from the first trench (enriched) on top of that.

plants need different degrees of light. Some must have bright sunlight to do well, others tolerate or prefer part shade, and some even prefer full shade. Plants small enough to be kept indoors will do well grown in artificial light.

Before I plant something outdoors, I try to have a good idea of what its light requirements are, so that I can choose an appropriate site for it. But even so, I also watch the plant as it grows, to make sure I've made the right choice. If the plant has too little light it will say so by putting out few leaves and remaining short; or conversely, it may send out long, leggy shoots or lean in an attempt to reach the light. If the sun is too strong for a plant it will wilt, and the leaves may look scorched.

Sometimes the decision to plant in light or shade is purely aesthetic. For example, day lilies and azaleas may grow well in shade but have few flowers, and burning bush grows well in shade but its fall foliage is less colorful there. Coleus may thrive in sun, but its leaf variegations will be less striking than they would be in shade. Lilies and roses will thrive in sun, but if it is too strong their flower colors may fade.

DEGREES OF LIGHT

To give a plant the amount of light it needs, it is important to understand all the different degrees of light and shade. Light requirements are often affected by other site factors and by the climate.

Full sun. Usually a plant that is said to prefer "full sun" needs at least 6 hours of sun a day, during the "prime time" for sun—10:00 A.M. to 6:00 P.M. Daylight Saving Time. This includes most fruits and vegetables and most flowers. When I grow plants that are particularly sun-loving, such as tomatoes and sunflowers, I try to give them even more sun than that. If you have a choice between a site with morning sun and a site with afternoon sun, keep in mind that afternoon sun is stronger, and that midday sun is the strongest of all.

If you live in a cool climate you'll find yourself trying to make the most of your sun, but if you live in a warm one, you'll probably find yourself trying to temper the sun, especially for plants like Oriental poppy and bellflower, which are basically sun-loving but can't take too much heat. For these, morning sun or part shade at midday may be preferable to full sun. In dry climates you may also have to guard some plants against full sun. Not only will soil moisture be lost through evaporation in a sunny site, but the air will be drier, and plants will lose moisture through their leaves.

Light shade or part shade. Plants that prefer neither full sun nor full shade should be given shade during the hours when the sun is strongest or else grown in a spot where the sunlight is broken in some way. This condition is variously described as "filtered light" and "dappled shade." The most common way to provide it is by planting in the shade of a tree such as a crab apple or mountain ash, which do not cast full shade but let spots of light come through their branches. A broad-leaved evergreen such as boxwood, which must be protected against winter sun, could get enough shade from leafless tree limbs in the same manner. You might also find sites that are more shaded at one time of the year than another, as the sun changes its course. These can be used advantageously to suit the needs of particular plants. A site with winter shade would suit boxwood, for example, and one with winter sun would be perfect for a February daphne, to encourage early bloom. Dappled shade can also be provided artificially by the use of lath structures—thin, narrow pieces of wood nailed in rows or crisscrossed so that some part of the plant is always shaded as the sun moves across the sky.

Bright shade. Even a spot that gets no sun at all can be filled with light. The area under a tree whose branches start at a considerable height on the trunk will often be filled with light from the areas around it. A sunless spot next to the white wall of a house might receive reflected light from the house, especially if sun shines on the wall. Often, plants described as liking part shade will do all right in bright shade.

Full shade and deep shade. A site in full shade that gets neither direct sun nor reflected light will only sustain truly shade-loving plants. In very deep shade almost nothing will grow. Full shade on the north side of a house may be bright enough to grow plants like hostas and rhododendrons, however, and full shade underneath a broad-leaved deciduous tree such as a beech or maple might be appropriate for ferns and shade-loving ground covers like sweet woodruff. But under the overhanging branches of large evergreen trees you may find that a mulch is your only alternative to bare soil. (In fact many evergreens, such as pines, provide a fine mulch of their own in the form of dropped needles.)

Naturally, in the case of deciduous trees, time of year makes a big difference in the shade they cast. There are some plants that don't mind being shaded in summer and fall as long as they get sun shining through leafless branches in spring, for example, spring-blooming woodland wildflowers. By the time the trees above them have leafed out, they have completed all or most of their growth cycles; some even become dormant and disappear from view until the following spring. Although I always try to include some summer-blooming shade plants, such as astilbes, in my "shade garden" it is always in its fullest glory in springtime.

Finding the perfect balance of sun and shade for the plants you grow may take some juggling—giving a plant just enough sun to bloom well, without burning its foliage, for example. You might have to try a plant in one spot, then move it if it doesn't perform as well as it should. If there is too little sun on your property you may have to cut down some trees, or "limb" some (cut off branches) to let in bright shade under them. On the other hand, if there is too little shade you might need to plant some trees, choosing those that will admit just the amount of light you need, or you might have to build a lath screen or arbor to shade certain plants. The portable frame shown on page 205 will provide temporary shade for smaller plants.

Plants Need Water

All the chemical reactions that take place in plants require the presence of water. All movement of nutrients through plants and through the soil requires water. And water is also needed to give plant parts "turgor," or firmness. You can see what happens to a plant when it dries out: the leaves shrivel, the stems flop, and the roots look like a handful of limp spaghetti. On the other hand, the changes wrought in a plant by too much water are just as dramatic as those wrought by too little. Below ground, roots growing in water-logged soil, robbed of the oxygen they need, soon die and turn into a rotting mess, as does the rest of the plant. Above ground, plant stems and crowns, sitting in puddles or soggy ground, can also rot. Leaves that stay too wet are more susceptible to diseases. And some plant diseases travel through the medium of water. A gardener working in a largely healthy plot on a wet day may later find he or she has left a trail of leaf-spot mildew and blight through the garden, spread from a few diseased plants.

ACHIEVING THE RIGHT BALANCE

Obviously you need to make sure that your plants have the right amount of water, neither too much nor too little. This means you have to get to know your plants and their individual needs. Just as with light, the moisture requirements of plants vary greatly from species to species. For example, plants native to dry climates, like cacti and succulents, have evolved in such a way that they can store water in their stems and leaves, while plants native to bogs and other wet places have roots that can "breathe" in water, like fish. Even with different species native to one climate, needs can vary according to plant structure. Shallow-rooted plants need water more often than deep-rooted ones. Young plants, and plants that have been root-pruned or transplanted, usually need extra water to help build new root systems. Many also need more water at the time they set their flowers—otherwise the flowers may drop—or when fruits or vegetables are maturing, especially juicy ones like tomatoes.

The amount of water available to a plant depends on more than just how much falls from the sky or from your hose. The amount and strength of the sun, and to a lesser extent of the wind and heat, influence how much water is retained by the soil and how much will evaporate before plants can use it. If your site has strong sun or a lot of wind, or if the weather is hot, you'll have to work harder at keeping the soil moist. Shady sites where air circulates poorly may stay too moist and lead to plant diseases. Another fact not always accounted for is the effect of frozen soil on a plant's water supply. If plants, especially evergreens, go into the winter with their roots in dry soil they may suffer, because rain and melting snow will not reach their roots through frozen soil. "Winter burn" of broad-leaved evergreens can be caused by the harsh, scorching effect of sun on snow, but more often than not it's from the roots' having had insufficient moisture before the ground has frozen.

The type of soil in which the plant is growing also makes a big difference, as explained on pages 21–22. Sandy soils hold water poorly. Clay soils hold it well and may in fact drain poorly. Soils of either type that are rich in organic matter hold moisture well, but also release the excess.

CORRECTING SITE PROBLEMS

Anything you can do to improve the site of your garden before you plant will save you work later on, and solving water problems is no exception. First consider whether you need to do any grading. Go out and look at the site sometime when it has been raining all day, and see what the water is doing.

Steep slopes. If the site is on a slope, chances are the water is running downhill at a great rate and not staying where it might be doing the plants some good. It may even be taking the soil with it, leaving gullies. In this case your best bet is to terrace the land by cutting into the hill to make flat beds and retaining the soil above them with low stone walls or timbers. If you can achieve your goal with retaining walls a foot high or less, terracing is a fairly simple matter, but if your slope is quite steep and requires higher walls, you will need to build masonry footings to support them and install drainage tiles in the bank to prevent excess water from pushing the wall outward. If you use timbers, you will have to anchor them into the bank. I would immediately hire, or at least consult, a professional who specializes in this type of work, and I suggest you do too. Another option, of course, is to look for a flatter area for your garden. And you can also consider plantings that will help to retain the soil on a steep bank, such as bearberry (*Arctostaphylos uva-ursi*) or shore juniper (*Juniperus conferta*)—both of them seaside plants that are used to keep sand dunes from eroding—or day lilies (*Hemerocallis*), whose fingerlike roots grip the soil. You can also make miniature retaining walls for each plant by making a flat, round planting area shored up by a saucer like the one pictured on page 52, with the saucer only on the downhill side.

Poor drainage. If you look at your rained-on site and it is a sea of puddles, you'll need to find a way to make them drain off. If the problem is not severe, you can probably devise your own common-sense solution. If you're like most people, you enjoyed fooling around with water as a child, making it stay, making it go—whether it was in the sandbox, a stream that you dammed up, or on the beach. Just do what you did then: make a berm of earth to channel water the way you want it to go, or dig a gulley to take it away, then fill the gulley with crushed stone (you can even cover the stone with a few inches of earth). Or you can lay lengths of perforated plastic pipe. Just make sure your gulley slopes downhill and has somewhere appropriate to go (not your lawn or driveway, or your neighbor's). Simply placing a layer of crushed stone under the soil in your bed may help drainage, but if the problem is severe or if the soil around the bed is very compacted, the layer will act as a sump into which water will flow and where it will stay, rotting your plants' roots. If your drainage problem is very severe, you

may need a curtain drain that goes below frost level. In this case I would reach for the Yellow Pages.

Drainage problems may not always be visible, even when it rains. There may be a layer of hardpan (compacted soil) below the surface soil where water collects. This situation will harm any deep-rooted plants you try to grow there. Usually you encounter the problem with your first attempt to plant a tree. You find you need to pickaxe to make the planting hole, and then, in due course, the tree dies. You can avoid such disappointments by first digging a test hole and filling it with water. If the soil is hard to dig and the water sits there for more than an hour without draining into the soil around it, you should choose a new site or get professional assistance.

In most cases, the best way for a beginning gardener to deal with poor drainage is to build a raised bed, especially if you are growing relatively small plants such as vegetables, flowers, herbs, bulbs, roses and small shrubs. Follow the directions for the simple wooden bed on page 190, or build one out of railroad ties, landscaping timbers or stones. More elaborate ones can be built with mortared stone or bricks.

In preparing your site, also remember that tilling the soil deeply (page 34) and adding plenty of organic matter will improve a site that drains either too slowly or too fast. If the problem is not too severe, you may find that adding organic matter is all you need to do.

WATERING

Watering is a basic part of planting, as discussed on page 51 and in other sections dealing with specific plants. And it is very important to keep the soil around new plants moist, whether they are tiny vegetable, flower or grass seedlings or a recently planted shrub or tree. (Bulbs, which are dormant when planted, are an exception.)

While garden plants are growing, the need to water them varies with the type of plant, the climate and the weather. Established trees and shrubs, in an average climate, don't need to be watered except during very dry summers or (especially if they are evergreens) during a dry fall. According to the usual rule of thumb, vegetable and flower gardens don't need to be watered unless the rainfall is less than 1 inch a week. But moisture-loving plants will need more water and drought-tolerant plants less. Mulched gardens, closely planted gardens and gardens with clay soil or soil rich in organic matter may get by with no watering even if less than an inch of rain falls. For raised-bed gardens, gardens in warm climates or gardens with sandy soil an inch may be too little. In my climate, where severe droughts are rare, I water plants only when they are newly planted, then mulch to keep watering at a minimum (page 63). I take extra care to water summer-seeded vegetable crops and to keep them moistened. I soak the soil around fruiting vegetables, such as tomatoes and peppers, when it is hot, and I water vegetables that need extra moisture, such as carrots and celery, during their growth. I also water plants like dahlias that bloom poorly when their roots are dry, and I check my flower gardens in dry weather to see if anything is drooping.

I always try to keep a close eye on both the plants and the soil to see whether either needs more water. Plants are tricky, especially young ones with small root systems. These may wilt during the hot part of the day but revive later on. (Some mature plants, such as *Ligularia* and *Pulmonaria*, will wilt and revive, too.) But no plant should be ignored if it stays wilted for more than a few hours; if it passes a certain point it will not recover.

Checking the soil for moisture is easy—just dig down and see if it is moist under the surface. It doesn't much matter whether the soil surface is moist because you just watered it, or dry because the sun is out; it's the soil underneath, where the roots are, that counts.

There are a number of ways to give your garden extra water, as discussed in the chapter on garden gear (page 95). But here are some points to remember:

Try to water deeply or not at all. Everyone runs out of patience standing there with a hose and is apt to skimp at the end, but it's better to water only part of the garden and really soak it, or use a soaker hose or drip-irrigation system. Barely wetting the ground may actually do harm, by causing roots to grow up to the surface, only to be burned by the hot sun. Another trick is to put containers such as coffee cans with holes punched in them at intervals among the plants and fill them with water that can then soak down into the ground. Planting in furrows (page 191) or with saucers (page 52) will also help more water to soak in.

Try not to wet the leaves. Misting houseplants indoors is often beneficial but wetting the leaves of outdoor plants can burn them if the sun is out, as the droplets act like lenses that concentrate the sun's rays. Wetting can also promote disease organisms if leaves are wet at night. If diseases are a particular risk in your garden, water in the morning, at ground level, and don't work around the plants when they are wet. Or use a soaker hose or drip-irrigation system and avoid hoses and sprinklers that wet the leaves.

Don't waste water. It's a valuable resource that is getting scarcer. Don't let your lawn sprinkler run forever, and

don't let water run down a slope use-
lessly; give the soil only what it can
absorb.

The Importance of Climate

S ometimes we choose to grow plants
that adapt very easily to our climate,
and sometimes we choose ones that are
not well adapted but that are so beautiful
or useful that they are worth some extra
trouble to make them grow or are worth
growing even if they cannot carry out
their whole growth cycle. Dahlias, for
example, do not survive the winter in
my flower garden as they would in
warm Mexico, but I am willing to dig
them up and store them over the winter
so that I can have their glorious late-
summer bloom. Tomato plants only live
one summer in my vegetable garden,
whereas they live much longer than that
in Peru—but so what? I simply sow new
seeds each year. On the other hand I try
to give dahlias and tomatoes the warmest, sunniest growing conditions I can,
to make them feel at home and produce
better.

If I lived in a hot climate my situation would be reversed. There would be
plants I'd want to grow, such as delphiniums, that would resent the hot summer,
and others, like daffodils, that would
mind the absence of a cold winter to
send them into a dormant, resting state.
I might be able to grow delphiniums as
early-summer annuals, buying new ones
each year. And I could give my daffodils an artificial winter by putting them
into cold storage before planting them in
late fall or early winter. But by and
large, if I lived in a warm region I would
choose among the many warm-climate
plants that northern gardeners wish they
could grow.

WINTER HARDINESS ZONES

It is not always possible to predict
whether a plant will flourish in your
garden. One general indicator that is
widely used is the United States Department of Agriculture table and accompanying map of winter hardiness zones,
shown on page 614. In this system the
United States and most of Canada are
divided into numbered zones based on
average minimum winter temperature.
Plants are assigned a hardiness zone
based on how low a temperature they are
able to survive. For example a plant that
is rated hardy to Zone 5, where I live, is
expected to survive temperatures as low
as −20 degrees Fahrenheit. But a plant
rated hardy to Zone 9 will probably not
survive temperatures lower than 20 degrees above zero. If you do not know
how low the temperatures go in your
area, get the figure for the annual average minimum from your local Extension
Service office.

I take hardiness ratings of plants
with a grain of salt, however. For one
thing, a good many of them are only
estimates that will continue to be reas-
sessed and refined as more data on each
plant becomes available. (A more defin-
itive zone map is currently being prepared by the U.S. National Arboretum.)
For another, hardiness zones are applied
with a broad brush: they may refer to
your geographical area but not to your
particular yard. Your windy hill might
be Zone 6, while your neighbor's protected valley next door might be Zone 7.
Or, on an even smaller scale, your lawn
might be Zone 7 but the garden next to
the south wall of your house, Zone 8.
Try to identify these "microclimates"
on your property so that you can choose
the right site for your plants. South- or
west-facing exposures are warmest,
northern ones are coldest. The area
around a swimming pool is often hotter

(and drier) than the rest of your yard because of the reflected glare off the water and the proximity of paving materials that hold and reflect heat. Often the plants themselves will tell you which spots are warm and which are cold: the same plant may bloom or leaf out earlier in one spot than another.

Also bear in mind that it doesn't get down to the lowest temperature every year. For example in my Zone 5, there may be many Zone-6 plants I can grow—most of the time. It's a gamble, to be sure, but I don't mind if the plants are, say, some asters I bought at $4 a pot. On the other hand, if they are $50 azaleas I would certainly think twice about growing one that wasn't rated Zone 5, and that might be killed by a rare −20-degree spell in winter.

Another problem is that hardiness ratings take into account only one climatic factor: minimum winter temperature. Some of the important factors they omit are the *maximum* temperature a plant can stand, degree of dryness or moisture, light requirements and the type of soil plants prefer. Therefore a plant that is hardy in your zone may still do poorly for any of these other reasons.

You should also be aware that there are several different zone maps, with different systems of zone numbering; the USDA one is simply the one most commonly used. So when you are told a plant's zone, check to see which map your source is using, and use the temperature chart to see which zone is yours on that particular map.

Whether you live in a windy area is also important in your choice of plants, as is whether there are particularly windy spots on your property. A windy site calls for relatively short or strong-stemmed plants that will not be pushed over by the wind; and since wind is drying, plants in windy locations should be able to withstand dryness well. Plants native to the seashore resist wind well; their leaves have tiny hairs on them that help to prevent evaporation of water.

Plants Need a Good Start

If you are a Freudian you believe that birth traumas and subsequent experiences in people's early lives can mark them for life. If you are a non-Freudian you consider this hogwash, holding that everyone is born with a certain personality, and beyond that your life is what you make of it.

I'm not entirely sure which theory is true where humans are concerned, but with plants I'm a Freudian all the way. Yes, a rhododendron is born a rhododendron and will always curl up its leaves self-protectively on cold winter days, only to become an extroverted mound of bright-flowered joy when it gets sufficiently warm in spring. But how large that mound is, and how glorious its display, depends on *you*, its parent, who can start it off by cramming its little roots into a stingy hole filled with meager soil, or give it a wonderful environment rich in love, care and compost. Whether you are planting a tiny seed, or transplanting a large tree, the same principle applies.

GROWING PLANTS FROM SEED

The seeds that gardeners most often sow are annual vegetables and herbs, such as lettuce and dill, or they are annual plants grown for their flowers and leaves, such as marigolds and coleus. But in fact many kinds of plants can be started from seed: perennials, bulbs, even shrubs and trees. The only reason we don't usually grow these plants from seed is that they take a long time to reach a mature size and may take up too much of our space and time while we are waiting for them to perform. So we buy them in a more mature state and then transplant them to our gardens. Nevertheless there is something very satisfying about growing a plant from a single seed, whether you start the seed indoors or out.

Starting seeds indoors The main reason we start seeds indoors is to get a jump on the growing season with plants that will not withstand frost, but it is also a way of starting a plant's life in a controlled environment and making the most of every seed sown. Whether you start seeds indoors, and how many, depends on how much space you have. There are a number of systems for starting seeds, and you'll probably develop one that best suits your household.

I start seeds in a commercially prepared soilless mix that is primarily composed of peat moss, but you can also make your own mix from various combinations of peat, perlite, vermiculite and even soil from outdoors. I don't use commercial potting soils, because I've found most to be of poor quality.

Soil you dig for seed starting should be sterilized in the oven for a few hours at 180 degrees before use. You sterilize it to kill disease organisms in soil, such as the fungus that causes "damping off," and also to kill weed seeds in the soil. In the garden you wouldn't want sterile soil—you'd want your soil crawling with beneficial microbes—but for the few weeks your seedlings spend in your starting medium, sterile soil is best. When I blend indoor soil mixes, I do it in a large plastic tub.

You can start seeds in just about any container that is at least 2 inches deep and has holes for drainage. I space small seeds about a half-inch apart, if possible, in small plastic flats (large-seeded plants like winter squash I sow directly into peat pots or cell packs—flats divided into individual compartments). It's very hard to space tiny seeds, but I try, because this gives each one a better chance to form a root system. It also means I don't have to waste a lot of seeds. Most seed packets give you many, many more seeds than you need, and since most seeds will be almost as good the next year, and often for several years, I usually don't plant the whole packet at once.

I moisten the planting mix thoroughly, place my seeds on the surface, cover them with a very fine layer of dry mix, then moisten the surface with a spray bottle. I identify the seeds in the flat by sticking a little wooden marker in the corner, marked in indelible ink, and I cover the flat with plastic wrap to keep the moisture in. The flat goes into a larger plastic tray that holds about six flats and is then set under a fluorescent light in the basement. I suspend the light from the ceiling with two chains so that it hangs just a few inches above the flat (Figure 6). Most seeds aren't aware of the light, although some seeds are light-sensitive. Those I don't cover with dirt; I just press them lightly onto the soil surface. The seed packets will tell you which are light-sensitive. Even in the case of seeds that are not light-sensitive, the slight heat emanating from the bulb helps them to germinate faster. I use two industrial-type lighting fixtures, each 4 feet long, with wide-spectrum fluorescent bulbs designed for starting plants (all bought at the local hardware store), and I set the flats on two old card tables.

I keep an eye on the flats of seeds, and as soon as the little green sprouts appear I take off the plastic wrap. I also take it off if I see any signs of mold from excessive moisture. As the seedlings grow I gradually raise the lights so that they are always several inches away from the plants. If something is growing

STARTING SEEDS INDOORS

Fig. 6

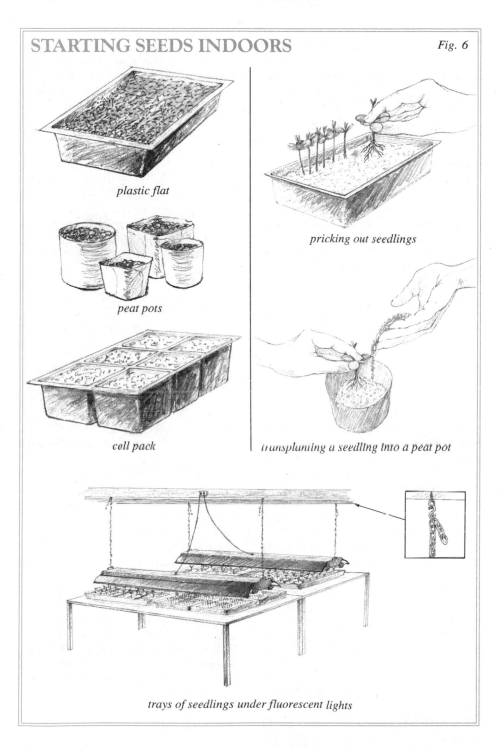

plastic flat

peat pots

cell pack

pricking out seedlings

transplanting a seedling into a peat pot

trays of seedlings under fluorescent lights

so fast that I expect it will be planting size before planting time, I take it away and put it on a sunny, but cooler, windowsill. If I'm trying to hurry up warm-season crops like eggplant and peppers, I give them good seats under the center of the bulb, where the light is the strongest, and I set an electric food-warming tray under them—one that has variable settings and can be turned to "low," since the single-setting type gets too hot.

Although all the advice I've ever read on this subject tells you that you must turn out the lights at night to simulate a normal growing day, I leave the lights over my seedlings on all the time, and it never affects the plants adversely. I check the flats at least once a day to make sure the planting mix is not drying out, and I pour water not on the delicate seedlings but into the trays, where it is absorbed through the holes in the flats. But I give them only what the soil can absorb and don't let them sit in water.

After the plants develop their second set of leaves, I transplant them into containers that will give their roots more room to develop. This operation is called "pricking out." Those plants that particularly resent transplanting now go into individual peat pots that can be set in the soil with a minimum of root disturbance. The rest go into larger flats, spaced a few inches apart, or into plastic cell packs. Some gardeners use expanding peat pellets or soil blocks made with a gadget called a "soil blocker." You can start seeds directly in any of these and skip the small flats, but starting in small flats saves space.

How you move tiny seedlings is important; they look too fragile to deal with, but they'll be fine if you grasp them by the leaves, not the spindly stems. You can use a kitchen fork or plant label to help dislodge them, but I find they will usually lift out easily by

the leaves if my planting mix is a light one. I select the strongest seedlings and discard any that have little or no root system attached.

To plant the seedlings you can either dangle the roots and sprinkle dry soil mix around them or else make a hole with your finger, insert the roots and then sprinkle. Plant them a bit deeper than they were in the first flat, to give the stems more support. The mix can be the same kind you sowed the seed in or it can be one with more soil. I fertilize the transplanted seedlings with a weak solution of a liquid fertilizer, but I try not to get any on the delicate leaves, which burn easily. I start to feed plants that were directly seeded into peat pots some weak fertilizer when they have their second set of leaves.

As the pricked-out seedlings accumulate I am always glad that I have labeled them meticulously. The label from the original small flat goes in the first pot or cell in a vertical row as I look at the flat, reading from bottom to top and left to right; this is the same order I will follow later on when I plant them in rows in the garden. Even with this great system, of course, there are sometimes mixups. I remember once I got the cosmos all mixed up with the Florence fennel, because they have very similar leaves. Going by the one pot of each that had the label actually in it, however, I was able to distinguish the very different branching patterns that the stems had, and separate them. (Even so, there were two purple cosmos plants blooming in the fennel row at midsummer!)

Luckily I don't plant all the different seeds at once, so that they're all at different stages, and in different places, at any given time. It's sort of like an elementary school. Some are started early either because they need a longer time to germinate or to reach transplanting size. After a while my two card tables start to get very crowded, and I move some of the more advanced classes up to the sunny windowsill, making room for the lower grades under the lights. As the weather starts to get warm, I even start moving some of them outdoors to "harden off" (that is, get used to cold, wind and strong sun to toughen up the leaves and stems) in a spot where I can keep a close eye on them. I bring the little plants in at night for the first few days—and even after that if the weather is cold or windy, day or night. Eventually some are able to graduate to the garden, and others can be promoted from the fluorescent lights to the window. This way the whole house isn't filled with seedlings—it just seems that way.

Planting seedlings outdoors. When it is the right time to set the plants in the ground (see the appropriate chapters for specific kinds of plants, especially annuals and vegetables), I make sure the ground in the garden is ready, then carry down a tray or two, filled with as many plants as I know I can plant that day. (They should not be left unplanted in the garden overnight to dry out or tip over.) I water these seedlings thoroughly so that they will come out of their containers with soil clinging to the roots.

If some plants are growing in peat pots, I tear off the top edge of the pot before planting it in the garden so that it won't draw moisture out of the soil like a wick, and I carefully slit the pot on two sides and remove the bottom. In other words I leave just enough of the pot so that the soil around the roots stays put when I set the plant in the ground. Peat pots are supposed to decompose fast and permit the roots to spread out, but I've found that they don't. When I pull up spent crops in fall, I've noticed that many have peat pots that are still quite intact, and some roots have clearly had a tough time penetrating them.

To plant each seedling I make a hole with a broad trowel, fill the hole with water from a watering can, let the water sink in, set the plant in the hole a little deeper than it was in the pot, and firm the soil around it. If the plant likes plenty of water I'll make a small saucer around it to catch rain. If it needs something extra such as rotted manure (for tomatoes) or extra lime (for larkspur) I'll dig that in before I plant, using a shovel, over an area about a foot wide. Then I'll stake it or label it or mulch it, depending on the type of garden and the needs of that particular plant. If I've bought seedlings of vegetables, herbs or annual flowers from a nursery, I set those into the garden just the way I do those I've grown myself.

Starting seeds outdoors. Fun as it is to start seeds indoors in early spring, I am grateful for those that can go straight into the garden, either because (like lettuce or alyssum) they can take some frost, or because (like zinnias and summer squash) they grow so fast that they make up the difference.

If the area I am planting is fairly large, I draw an iron rake through it, smoothing the surface and removing from the top inch or two of soil stones and debris that might impede small seedlings' growth. If I am planting in rows, I stretch out a string tied to a stake as a guide in making the row straight, then I make a furrow several inches deep with the blade of a hoe held at an angle. I soak the furrow very thoroughly with water several times, then place my seeds in the bottom, trying to space them sparsely, even though this is hard with very tiny seeds. Then I pick up some dry earth and rub it between my hands, letting a light, powdery covering fall over the seeds. For large seeds that I plant more deeply, I poke a hole for each one with my finger and drop it in. Some large seeds, such as corn and some beans, go in furrows. Some, like peas, usually go in wide rows. Others are planted in what are called "hills"— not mounds, but circles or groups of seeds—that I later thin to the strongest few or the strongest one. However I plant them, I always press the soil down with my hands to make sure the seeds are in contact with the soil.

I leave my seed furrows concave because this helps to keep the seeds and seedlings moist and also marks the rows so that I know where the seeds are. For wide vegetable rows or blocks or patches I am seeding in a flower garden, I just plant in broader, well-moistened areas covered with soil sifted through my hands. If it is dry I also sprinkle the top with a fine mist from the hose. For seeds that germinate slowly, especially in warm weather, it is helpful to spread moist burlap or hay over the seed bed until the seedlings emerge, or to sow them along with a "nurse crop" such as radishes that will shade the ground and help keep it moist.

When the seedlings are several inches high they can be thinned to the appropriate distance apart, either by pulling up some of them or by snipping them with scissors to avoid disturbing the roots of those left. You can also transplant the thinnings elsewhere.

If you have a "nursery-bed" section of your garden, you can raise seedlings there, then transplant them into the

USING A COLD FRAME

Fig. 7

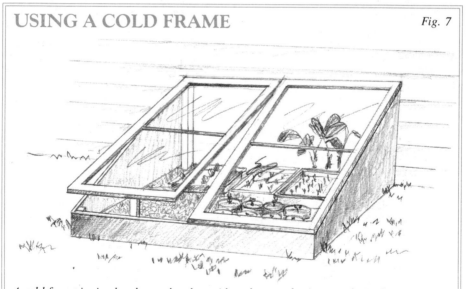

A cold frame is simply a bottomless box with a glass or plastic top to let in the sunlight. Old storm windows are perfect, attached to the box at the top with hinges so they can be propped open when it's too hot inside. Build the sides with pressure-treated lumber or plywood painted with linseed oil, bracing the corners with 2-by-2s. The windows should face the south and tilt at least 45 degrees for the best solar efficiency, so make the back of the box higher than the front. Enrich the soil inside so you can sow early and late lettuce crops or winter over tender perennials. Set flats of seedlings in the box to give them an early start or to harden them off before planting. For extra protection, bank the sides with hay bales and cover the frame with hay or old blankets on cold nights.

place where they will eventually grow. A part of the vegetable garden, for example, might provide a nursery for seedlings of annual flowers that will eventually be used as bedding plants elsewhere, or as fill-ins for the perennial border. A cold frame (Figure 7) also makes a good nursery bed.

PLANTING HERBACEOUS PERENNIALS

Herbaceous perennials are plants whose stems are generally soft and green (herbaceous), rather than hard and woody like those of shrubs. "Perennial" means that, unlike the annual vegetables and flowers discussed above, they last more than one year in your garden. Most of them go dormant during the winter, meaning that they have no green growth to be seen above the ground. How to design and prepare beds for perennials, and when to plant them, are discussed in detail in Chapter 6, and to some extent in Chapters 8 and 12 since some herbs and ground covers are perennials of this type.

Planting bare-root. Certain perennials can be grown successfully from seed, either sown directly in the garden or sown indoors and transplanted outdoors as seedlings, in the manner described above. But most perennials are planted when they are dormant or just starting to sprout, and often "bareroot," with no soil around the roots.

Planting perennials bare-root is easy, but you have to be well aware of one very important thing: those roots absolutely mustn't dry out. If they do they will never recover. This means you have to keep the roots moist, but also protect them from the sun and wind. If you order perennials by mail, they will usually come carefully wrapped in damp sphagnum moss or some such packing material (though some nurseries are be-

ginning to ship perennials in small peat or plastic containers). If you can't plant them right away, either pot them up (page 582) or heel them into the ground. Heeling in means digging a trench in a cool, shady spot and laying the plants in it, in a row with their crowns (the place where stem and roots join) at soil level, then watering them and covering the roots with soil. Plants can be held that way for quite a while, but if growth starts they will eventually resent being crowded together, so don't let a heeling-in trench become a permanent residence. When you get ready to plant your bare-root perennials, never leave them lying on the ground unprotected while you are digging their holes. Cover them with moist burlap or some mulch material such as hay or black plastic.

I make my planting holes with a broad trowel or a shovel, depending on the size of the plants. If I feel the soil needs improvement, I might mix in some compost or bone meal but I avoid chemical fertilizers, because they might burn the roots. I set the plant in the hole so that the crown is just at the soil surface, because burying it any deeper may cause the plant to rot; then I spread the roots out in the hole and fill it part way with soil and the rest of the way with water. When the water has sunk in I fill the hole up with soil and firm it well so that there are no air pockets. Some perennials have special planting requirements; for these see page 150.

Plants in containers. Perennials that you have bought potted up (or that you have potted yourself) are planted in much the same way. If you must keep them for a while before planting them, set them in a level, shaded or semi-shaded spot where they can be watered conveniently. Water the pot before removing the plant to soak the soil, then knock the plant out of the pot (page 50). If the plant has been growing in the pot for a long time it may be "potbound" or "rootbound"—the roots will be thick, matted, and growing round and round in the pot. To encourage roots to start growing outward, slit the mass of roots vertically every few inches with a knife or pruners, and break up the roots at the bottom as well. This may sound like a brutal thing to do when I've just told you to pamper a plant's roots, but it's the kind of "tough love" roots need. Left alone, they'll just keep growing round and round in their holes and either rot, or starve, or both. If the plants are in peat pots you can plant them in the pots, but tear off the rims and slit the sides vertically in several places to help the roots to escape. (For staking newly planted perennials, see page 155.)

KNOCKING A PLANT OUT OF A POT

Fig. 8

If you are transplanting perennials from one place to another or replanting ones that you have divided, it is best to do it when the weather is fairly cool and moist and when the plants are dormant. If you must do it during the heat of summer, keep them thoroughly watered till their roots are established, and cut the stems back to just a few inches, so the plants will not lose a lot of moisture through the leaves. (For dividing perennials, see page 151.)

PLANTING SHRUBS AND TREES

Woody plants are usually planted singly, in individually prepared holes, rather than together in prepared beds. (One exception is hedge plants, which may be planted in a long trench.) How you make that planting hole is important. Woody plants have two kinds of roots, each for a different purpose. One kind goes down very deep into the soil (more deeply with some species than with others) and is there primarily to support the plant; the other kind spreads out for a great distance through the topsoil and upper subsoil layers. These are called "feeder roots," because through them the plant absorbs nutrients. The feeder roots need particular encouragement, so it is more important to dig a wide hole for the plant than a deep one.

Planting bare-root. Many shrubs and trees that establish themselves easily are sold bare-root. Planting is almost always done when the plant is dormant, usually in early spring but sometimes in fall after the leaves have fallen, and it is usually done when the plant is quite young. When you buy bare-root trees in a nursery, or order them by mail, they won't look like much. Often they have been, quite properly, pruned back hard. Don't let that discourage you.

The plant's roots want to be good

and moist when you plant them. Soaking them for a few hours (but no longer than overnight) will help; so will "puddling in." This means mixing up soil and water in a tub or bucket so that it is the consistency of gravy and sloshing the roots around in it. This mud gravy will keep the root hairs moist and help them start to grow.

Dig a hole a few inches deeper than the roots and quite a bit wider. Set aside any subsoil and rocks you dig up, and put any sod clumps in a pile. It is also a good idea to break up the soil along the bottom and sides of the hole so that roots will be encouraged to venture out laterally. Recent studies show that making a luxurious hole for a plant, filled with loose, light, rich soil, can sometimes encourage plant roots to stay in the hole, circling round and round, especially if the soil around the hole is very heavy or compacted. Most times this will not happen, but the extra forking around the edges of the planting hole is good insurance. It is also a good idea to loosen the soil surface near the hole and dig in some organic matter to encourage feeder roots to spread out there.

Set the tree or shrub in the hole (Figure 9) so that the beginning of the trunk is just above the soil surface (you will see a line where the trunk bark changes color and the roots begin). It is important not to plant the trunk below ground, because the roots can be deprived of food, water and air if they are too far down. Better to err on the side of planting too high, in case the plant settles in the hole. If the plant is a grafted one such as a dwarf fruit tree (there will be a bump where the top part has been joined onto the rootstock), the graft union should usually be above ground.

Spread the roots out in the hole and start filling the hole with the topsoil you dug out, mixed with some organic matter such as compost or peat moss. It is

also wise to add a high-phosphorus fertilizer, such as bone meal, to aid in root development. As you work, make sure you don't leave air pockets, which can dry the roots. Firm the soil with your feet, but take care that the roots aren't damaged. When the hole is about two-thirds full, add water from a hose or bucket till it reaches the top, and let the water sink in. The water not only keeps the roots moist but also helps to settle the soil in the hole.

Then fill the hole the rest of the way with more topsoil and organic matter. Use the subsoil and rocks to build a small saucer, or circular dike, around the plant to hold water. (Sod clumps can also be used for the dike, or they can be placed in the bottom of the hole, grassy side down.) Your last steps are to pour water into the saucer, then apply several inches of mulch such as shredded bark to keep the soil around the trunk moist and free of weeds. Keep the mulch at least 6 inches away from the plant, however, to keep the trunk from getting too damp. Trees whose trunks are susceptible to sun scald, particularly young fruit trees, can be protected by painting them with a white tree paint designed for this purpose.

Balled-and-burlapped plants. Many trees and shrubs that you buy will be "B-and-B"—balled and burlapped—either because they resent being transplanted bare-root or so that you can plant them even when they are not dormant. A nursery will dig the plant in the field with a ball of soil around it and wrap up the root ball, usually with burlap and twine. The plant can be transported, held for a while, and planted in this state. I would not advise trying to dig a root ball yourself unless you are dealing with an easy-to-move plant or one whose life you don't mind putting at risk. Digging a ball without the soil falling apart is, as a friend of mine once

PLANTING SHRUBS AND TREES

Fig. 9

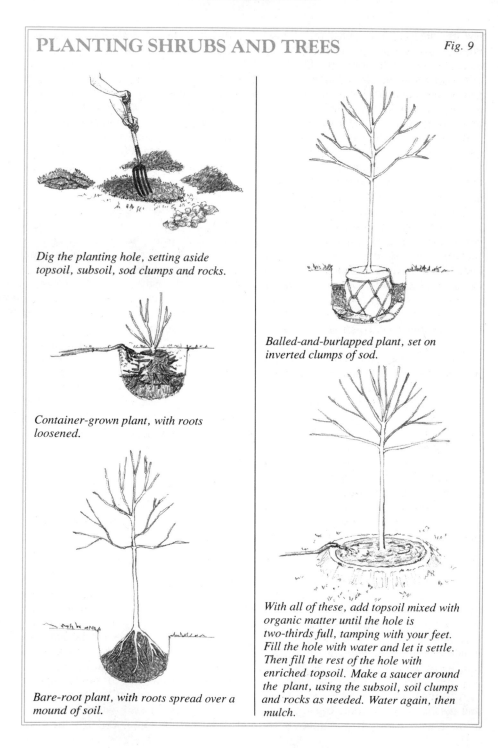

Dig the planting hole, setting aside topsoil, subsoil, sod clumps and rocks.

Container-grown plant, with roots loosened.

Balled-and-burlapped plant, set on inverted clumps of sod.

Bare-root plant, with roots spread over a mound of soil.

With all of these, add topsoil mixed with organic matter until the hole is two-thirds full, tamping with your feet. Fill the hole with water and let it settle. Then fill the rest of the hole with enriched topsoil. Make a saucer around the plant, using the subsoil, soil clumps and rocks as needed. Water again, then mulch.

put it, "like carving a ball of melting butter," and wrapping and tying it can be tricky, too, if the root ball is large.

Plants you buy B-and-B should be kept in the shade, covered with piles of mulch, and moistened with a hose until you can plant them. Treat the root ball very carefully, sliding it, not rolling it, and never dropping it on the ground. Lower it into the planting hole *gently.* If you are taking a heavy ball off a truck, slide it down a stout wooden plank. You might even want to borrow or rent a hand cart designed for moving plants. These look like the dollies you move furniture with, but the upright part is curved to hold the root ball in place.

B-and-B shrubs and trees are planted much the same way as bare-root stock, except that the size of the hole has to be calculated more carefully. It is very frustrating to dig a large hole, lower a large root ball into it, then find that the hole is too deep and the ball too heavy to lift out again. The best way to avoid this is to measure the height of the ball, then lay a tool handle flat across the top of the hole and measure from the handle to the center of the bottom of the hole, adjusting the depth accordingly. Another trick is to put upside-down sod clumps in the bottom of the hole, lower the ball, then add or remove sod clumps as needed until the bottom of the trunk is just above the soil surface.

Once the ball is in the hole you can remove the burlap, but only if the ball is a very firm one. It is safest not to remove it at all. Burlap is easily penetrated by most roots, and both the burlap and the twine will rot quickly. But if the burlap is left sticking out so that it is exposed to air, it can quickly draw moisture out of the soil, so it is a good idea to loosen the burlap near the trunk, roll it back and cut it away. If the wrapping and the twine are made of plastic you must remove them. I also remove the metal cages that sometimes encase root balls, cutting them away with wire cutters so that the metal doesn't harm the plant's roots when they grow larger. Fill the hole just as for a bare-rooted plant, firming the soil around the ball with your feet, watering, composting and mulching in the same way.

CONTAINER-GROWN PLANTS

Woody plants that have been grown in containers can be planted even when they are not dormant. They are planted like B-and-B plants, but first you must remove them from their containers, which are usually plastic or metal. Trees and shrubs in plastic pots can be knocked out by the method shown on page 50, but plants in metal cans are a different story. I have never once succeeded in extricating a plant from a metal can without cutting the can apart with wire cutters or tinsnips.

For advice on when to plant shrubs and trees and how to stake them, and for special procedures to use with specific plants, see Chapters 14 and 15.

Dealing with Weeds

"A weed," my mother used to say, "is just the right plant in the wrong place." To me this is much more accurate than defining weeds as "wild" plants as opposed to "garden" ones. Many wild plants are appropriate in gardens. In fact a large number of the plants we regard as wildflowers are actually plants imported from other countries as garden flowers, which have escaped into the wild, liked the environment and naturalized themselves. And many a garden plant, fine in one spot, can be an unwelcome guest in another. Even the right plant in the right spot can be weedy if there is too much of it; in that case you must "weed" it out along with the pigweed, man-underground and fall panic grass. (Why do weeds always have the best names?)

It sometimes seems that weeds will put up with anything, but this is not so. All plants have some preferences as to climate, soil type, degree of sun and moisture. In fact, if you are looking at a new piece of ground with an eye to gardening on it, you can tell a lot about the conditions on the spot by noting which weeds are there by choice. A field of goldenrod is apt to have rather dry, poor soil; one with burdock, on the other hand, will be moister and richer in organic matter.

Every now and then some particularly attractive weed, like Cinderella, will be lifted from the ranks of weedhood because of some particularly attractive trait. Nurseries will start selling it, hybridizers will start looking for ways to improve it. Butterfly weed, with its showy red-orange flowers and popularity with butterflies, is a fairly recent example. But your garden may have its own Cinderellas that are simply your own pet weeds. For instance, I once developed an affection for purslane when working in a nursery because I could snack on it as I weeded (its leaves have a pleasant, crunchy texture and a mild taste). And when something crops up in my flower garden that might have potential, I'll sometimes let it bloom and see if I like the way it looks there. You'd never know that the wild white yarrow next to my red hybrid yarrow wasn't planted there deliberately.

But let's face it: weeds are often just plain weeds, and you need a good way to keep them under control. It does no good to give your plants first-class soil if they must share it with weeds, which will compete with your plants for everything they need in life: nutrients, water, light, air and space—both above ground and below.

ANNUAL WEEDS

How you deal with weeds depends partly on whether they are annuals or perennials. You can never quite eradicate annual weeds, because they make so many seeds—seeds that are blown or carried into your garden or are simply lying there dormant in your soil, waiting for your hoe or trowel to bring them just close enough to the surface to allow them to sprout. Unfortunately, in the very act of weeding you make it possible for new weeds to grow. This is why mulching is so helpful. It won't keep every annual weed from germinating, but it will drastically cut down on their number. Some mulches, however, such as hay and other grass crops, may introduce many seeds of their own to the ground they're put on. Applied thickly they will keep the seeds from sprouting, but the seeds may sprout later with a vengeance whenever the mulch is removed. Fortunately there are mulches like salt hay and shredded bark that are relatively weed-free. (For more information about mulches, see page 63.) On soil that is not being gardened, cover crops (page 27) will also keep most weeds from growing.

If you are not using a mulch, the best way to deal with annual weeds is simply to get them while they are very tiny and keep after them. It is so easy to put off weeding when weeds are small, inconspicuous and not staring you in the face, but believe me, this is the time to attack them. Small weeds are thwarted just by slicing them with a narrow-bladed hoe such as a scuffle hoe, or with the side of a trowel, which either severs the plant from the roots or brings the roots to the soil surface, causing the plant to immediately wilt and die. With this technique you don't even need to cart piles of weeds away—just leave them where they fall.

Experienced gardeners all know they must strike when weeds are small, but even the best let the weeds get ahead of them from time to time. When this happens there is no alternative but to get out there and pull weeds. With some weeds the job is just that—pulling. The ones with soft, water-filled stems come out easily when you yank them, and in fact many weeds can be pulled if you grasp them just at soil level. But if you break them off and leave the root in the ground, you're just pruning the weed and encouraging it to branch and regrow more bushy and glorious than ever. When pulling mature weeds I always have a trowel handy for the ones that resist a tug. I stick the point of the trowel under the roots to loosen them from the soil, and *then* I yank the weed.

Sometimes, if I'm rushed, I'll just spread the weeds I've pulled between the rows of my vegetable garden as a temporary mulch, until I can get around to composting them. A blanket of dead weeds is not very attractive, but it keeps new ones from growing.

PERENNIAL WEEDS

Some perennial weeds go to seed the way annuals do, but their roots are their real weapons. Most perennials reproduce themselves from their root systems, and even from parts of roots that may remain in the ground after you pull or dig them up. Therefore it is important, when you go after perennial weeds, that you get the whole plant. Weeding them with a hoe when they're small will often work, just as it does for annual weeds, but once perennials get large you need to be more careful, especially if the weeds spread by runners, or "stolons"—underground stems that run

through the soil and send up new plants when they get close to the surface. A digging fork is the best tool for removing these, because it is less likely to break the roots than a spade is. Almost as pernicious as weeds that produce stolons are the weeds with long, skinny taproots, like dandelions and the various docks. Even if you leave just a tip of that root when you pull it, a new plant can sprout. Sometimes these pull out easily if they're growing in loose soil, but if you hit a stubborn one, the dandelion weeder shown on page 88 can help you get the whole weed out. Mulch will control perennial weeds to some degree, but it won't help much if a number of the weeds' roots are present in the soil before you put down the mulch; many will come right up through the mulch. Black plastic will smother them if left on long enough, but it could take a year. And if there are holes in the plastic to let water in or to let a cultivated plant come up, weeds with stolons will search around under the plastic till they find those holes, and come up there.

I can hear you saying, "How am I supposed to know whether a weed is annual or perennial? I can't even tell whether something is a weed!" Unfortunately the only way to learn these things is by experience, and this means spending time in the garden weeding and really looking at the plants that are there—weed and nonweed. If you recognize the foliage and growth habits of the plants that are supposed to be there, then you know the rest are weeds by process of elimination. It is also useful to have an illustrated guide to native plants so that you can identify weeds that appear. The list of common weeds (page 58) may help you pinpoint some, but there are many more that I hadn't the space to list. In general, perennial weeds have deeper, more vigorous, and more pronounced root systems than annuals and are harder to get out of the ground. Just be on the lookout for ones like these, and try to get all the roots.

PREPARING A NEW BED

Keeping an established garden free of weeds is challenge enough, but the big task is removing them from a spot that is not yet a garden. Obviously, removing all the weeds first, especially perennial ones, will save you much work and aggravation later on. There are several ways to go about this. One is to dig out any woody plants and then cut all the herbaceous ones close to the ground with a mower, brush cutter, string trimmer, or with a hand tool such as a sickle or scythe. Then spread sheets of heavy black plastic on the area for a year; afterward, till under the dead weeds. If

EDGING A BED WITH A SPADE *Fig. 10*

you can't wait a year to start the garden, you can dig all the weeds out by hand with a digging fork, or whatever it takes to get rid of them all.

If the site has lawn sod you must strip it off—hard work, but necessary. Just chopping sod up with a tiller will not help; the grass will soon regrow. First mark the shape of the bed with a string tied to a stake, using it just as you would a ruler or compass and marking the edge with small stakes or a sprinkling of lime. Curved or free-form edges can be laid out with a garden hose. Then edge the bed along these lines with a sharp spade. If you can't slice through the sod easily, lift the spade above your head with both hands as shown in Figure 10 and bring it down hard. (Don't worry: your aim will improve with practice.) Then either roll back the sod in strips or slice under it just below the surface, trying to remove as little of the topsoil along with the sod as possible. I sometimes cut stubborn sod into blocks and shake the excess soil out of the roots, block by block. I lift the sod with a digging fork and shake it. You can also rent a gasoline-powered sod stripper to make the job easier. Compost the sod, and remove any weed roots left behind in the soil.

Another alternative in preparing a new bed, whether the site has weeds or not, is to use a herbicide. I used to be categorically against chemical weed killers, but recently I've made an exception: I will occasionally use a glyphosate herbicide to prepare a new bed or help control perennial weeds in an established one. There are several brands available; the label will indicate glyphosate as the major active ingredient. These products have a low toxicity to animal life and no residual life in the soil. They should be kept out of ponds and streams, however, and as with any weed killer, you should rinse out any spraying equipment you use before reusing it to spray garden plants.

Glyphosates are "systemic" herbicides, meaning that no matter what part of the plant you spray, they will permeate the whole plant, including those awful underground roots. "Contact" herbicides, by contrast, kill only the part of the plant they touch. Glyphosates are also "nonselective," meaning that they will kill any plant they touch, whether it be broad leaved or grassy, friend or foe. So if you are using such a weed killer on, say, perennial grasses in the garden, you must either spray extremely carefully or brush it on each leaf with one of those disposable foam brushes sold in paint stores. I find this trick especially handy in plantings such as pachysandra or creeping junipers, where it would be impossible to disentangle grass stolons from the roots of the planting itself.

Glyphosate herbicides usually take about a week to do the job, longer in cool weather when plant growth has slowed down. You may have to use several applications for persistent weeds.

GARDEN EDGINGS

Another way to minimize weeds in the garden is to edge it with a barrier to deter weeds that come in from surrounding areas, including the lawn. Such invasions can be a real problem, and edgings do help. Edgings also give the garden a tidy, well-defined look. They can be as simple as a prefabricated metal or plastic strip or as elaborate as a row of flagstones set in sand or stone dust. They are all fairly easy to construct, even the flagstones. Some good edgings are shown in Figure 11.

GARDEN EDGINGS

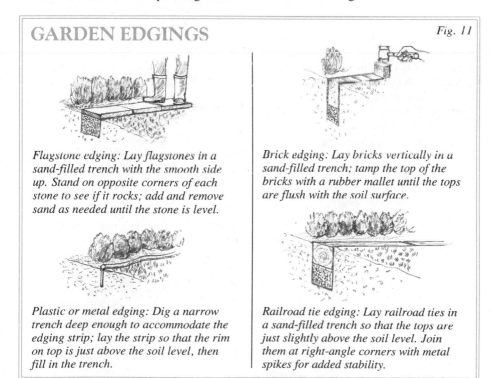

Fig. 11

Flagstone edging: Lay flagstones in a sand-filled trench with the smooth side up. Stand on opposite corners of each stone to see if it rocks; add and remove sand as needed until the stone is level.

Brick edging: Lay bricks vertically in a sand-filled trench; tamp the top of the bricks with a rubber mallet until the tops are flush with the soil surface.

Plastic or metal edging: Dig a narrow trench deep enough to accommodate the edging strip; lay the strip so that the rim on top is just above the soil level, then fill in the trench.

Railroad tie edging: Lay railroad ties in a sand-filled trench so that the tops are just slightly above the soil level. Join them at right-angle corners with metal spikes for added stability.

Some Common Weeds

If these plants were human they would probably have their pictures hanging in the post office. You no doubt have some of them where you live, but plant life varies so much from one locale to another that you'll need a guide to native plants to identify your own local criminal element. And please note that some of these weeds are the "right" plant if they are growing in the right place.

Bindweed. *Convolvulus arvensis.* A deep-rooted perennial with pink-white flowers shaped like those of the morning glory, to which it is related, this vine should be eradicated before it can twine around your garden plants and smother them. Nasty roots. Pulling encourages new growth.

Burdock. *Arctium lappa.* You can recognize burdock by its fuzzy purple-pink flowers and the round burrs that stick to you, your dog and anything else that moves. It is a biennial: the seeds that fall one year will grow the next. Don't let burdock go to seed. When you spot its large rosette of broad, hairy leaves, yank up its deep taproot. (Fortunately it chooses soils that are loose and humusy, and the root can be pulled rather easily.) If you are so inclined, you can eat these roots, which taste something like parsnips but are blander and less sweet.

Canada Thistle. *Cirsium arvense.* If you can look at this weed objectively, it's a handsome plant, with fuzzy purple flowers from mid-summer to fall. But the very prickly leaves are not something you want to step on in bare feet. An extremely hardy perennial, it spreads both by suckers from the roots and by seed. Put on leather gloves and try digging out the taproot, but some may remain. If thistle is a serious problem use a systemic herbicide.

Chickweed. *Stellaria media.* Chickweed loves the fertile soil of gardens but will make do with just about any soil if it has to. An annual

with delicate foliage and dainty, starlike white flowers, it looks harmless but makes seeds like crazy from spring to fall and also roots along the stem. Fortunately it is easy to pull out.

garden because they are perennials and their deep taproots are hard to dig out. The best way to keep them out of the lawn is to mow them before the seeds start to blow around. Some gardeners kill dandelions with broad-leaf weed killers, but I'd rather live with a few of them in the lawn.

Crabgrass. *Digitaria sanguinalis.* This annual grass spreads out from the center in a stiff, flat rosette. It tolerates even the inhospitable soil of a packed, gravelly driveway, but is equally happy filling any bare spot in your lawn, garden or shrub border. The best prevention is to have no bare spots—by keeping the lawn healthy and by mulching your gardens. If crabgrass appears, dig it out (it's hard to grasp with your fingers) before it can go to seed.

Dandelion. *Taraxacum officinale.* Dandelions need no introduction. I think their yellow flowers and fluffy round seed heads are pretty in the lawn, but they are a nuisance in the

Dodder. *Cuscuta gronovii* and other *Cuscuta* species. This slender annual vine is the ill-famed "tares" referred to in the Bible (as in "wheat and tares"). Like bindweed, it twines around plants and kills them, but unlike bindweed it is actually parasitic on the host plant, rooting in it to suck its juices while its own roots atrophy and die. It spreads by seed. Pull it off the host plant as soon as you spot it.

Goldenrod. *Solidago canadensis* and a number of other *Solidago* spe-

cies. A handsome plant, it has been hybridized and sold for gardens. This perennial spreads both by its roots and by seed.

Ground Ivy. *Glechoma hederacea.* Also called "gill-over-the-ground," this is a pretty weed with small round leaves and small blue flowers in spring. Usually it sneaks from the lawn into your gardens by means of thin, almost invisible runners. In the right spot it makes a nice deciduous perennial ground cover, but I try to keep it pulled out if it starts to approach any shrubs, particularly low-growing evergreens. If it gets into their branches the needles don't grow, and the plant's shape is distorted.

Jewelweed. *Impatiens capensis.* I'm happier to have this large, hardy annual growing in a moist field or

beside brooks than some of the less-attractive plants that might colonize those areas instead. It has pretty orange flowers followed by small green seed pods that explode when you touch them (hence its other name, "snapweed"). I used to love to make them do that when I was a child. But I don't want those pods exploding all over my garden to make more jewelweed. Fortunately, it is a soft, fleshy plant that is easy to pull out before it reaches the seed stage.

Johnson Grass. *Sorghum halepense.* This warm-climate pest is a tall perennial grass with wide blades and vigorous creeping rootstocks. You can make a lifelong career of pulling it out—or use a systemic herbicide.

Lamb's Quarters. *Chenopodium album.* How this weed got to be associated with so many animals, I'll never know, but it also goes by the names of "pigweed," "fat hen" and "white goosefoot." An annual that likes any garden soil, it has ragged-edged leaves and grows as tall as 6 feet. On the plus side it is easy to pull out and is delicious cooked like creamed spinach. But it grows very fast, and unless you consume an awful lot of creamed greens there is always too much of it.

Poison Ivy. *Rhus radicans.* I spent my whole childhood learning how to recognize this plant in all its guises: the three shiny yellow-green leaves as they first unfold; the three medium green leaves when half grown; the three large dark green leaves at maturity; the three red-orange leaves in fall; the ropelike vines; the underground roots with the fuzz on them. This vigorous perennial clinging vine gives most people a blistering rash if any part of the plant is touched, at any time of

the year. I once got a bad case from dead leaves in fall when doing a college biology project on soil organisms. Exterminate it with a systemic herbicide.

Purslane. *Portulaca oleracea.* Here's another one that looks innocent—but watch out. It resembles garden portulaca, but the water-storing leaves are rounder and fatter, and its small yellow flowers are not as showy. Like garden portulaca it spreads easily by seed, especially in tilled ground. It also has a habit of rooting into the ground wherever you throw it, so drought-proof are its roots. Therefore if you use dead weeds for mulch, exclude the purslane.

Quack Grass. *Agropyron repens.* This weed heads my own personal enemies list. Other names for it include "witch grass" and "couch grass." It spreads both by seed and by long, white stolons that are very hard to eradicate; I recommend glyphosate herbicide or black plastic.

Ragweed. *Ambrosia artemisiifolia.* I don't know which is worse—what ragweed does to my garden or what it does to my nose. It grows at least 3 feet tall and sometimes taller than I am. Its flower spikes make vast amounts of hay-fever-producing pollen in late summer and fall. Ragweed blooms at the same time as goldenrod, which is often unjustly blamed for people's sneezes and itchy eyes. A deep-rooted annual, ragweed chooses soil that has been tilled, whether it is your garden or a cornfield, and should be pulled out before it has a chance to flower and form all that pollen.

Stinging Nettle. *Urtica dioica.* Unlike the thistle, which *looks* dangerous, this plant resembles many other, more innocent weeds. I never recognize it until I've grabbed hold of it and gotten a handful of minute daggers. These are stinging hairs too small to see, and they must surely have evolved for the nettle's self-defense, in order to make the gardener drop rather than pull up the plant. A perennial, it grows to 4 feet and spreads by underground roots.

Shepherd's Purse. *Capsella bursa-pastoris.* This common annual or biennial weed grows to 3 feet, with arrow-shaped leaves on top and a rosette of leaves on the bottom. Flowers are small and white. Dig out the thin taproot.

Wild Strawberry. *Fragaria virginiana.* How can such a charming plant, with its white flowers and sweet red fruit, be deemed a pest? I've seen it charm its way into many a garden where the gardener doesn't have the heart to do it in. But it is a persistent perennial plant that creeps by small threadlike runners above the ground, and soon it is everywhere. If you like it, find a safe spot in which to naturalize it.

Mulch

I don't know who invented mulch, but I'm sure I know where the idea came from. If you go out into the woods and examine the ground you will see a perfectly mulched garden. On the surface of the ground are leaves that have fallen recently; below them are layers of leaves from seasons past in increasingly advanced stages of decomposition. The more decomposed leaves near the top make up a crumbly substance called "lead mold"; below that is a thin layer of "duff"—leaf mold that has crumbled almost to a powder; and below that is soil—beautiful, dark, rich, light, moist, humusy soil. Forest soil is so good because of the leaf covering, which is nature's mulch. And achieving that kind of soil is one of the reasons why people mulch their gardens.

THE BENEFITS OF MULCH

Mulch is simply a surface covering that we apply to our garden soil. There are many, many different materials we can mulch with, but before I advise you about which ones are best to use, let's look at some of the things mulch does.

Keeps weeds down. As explained above, mulch won't keep every weed from coming up, especially if the roots of perennial weeds are in the soil. It will, however, keep down enough of them so that your weeding labor will be reduced enormously, and, at the same time, the condition of mulched soil will also make weeds easier to pull. Get out as many weeds as you can before you mulch, and if some do come up, try to pull them without bringing soil up on top of the mulch where more weeds might grow. This may mean pushing aside the mulch to get at a weed, especially if a trowel is required to dig it up.

Conserves soil moisture. A mulch will keep moisture from evaporating from the soil surface. This is especially useful during hot, dry weather. Depending on your climate, you may have to do little or no watering if you mulch. By absorbing rainfall, a mulch can make the most of a good rain, holding water that would otherwise run off and letting it trickle down to the soil. And by holding moisture in the soil in fall, mulch helps prevent winter burn (page 490).

Keeps soil cooler in summer, warmer in winter. The temperature of mulched soil is more constant than that of unmulched soil. Mulch allows you to temper both extreme heat and extreme cold by several degrees. A mulch that keeps the soil cooler in summer not only prevents moisture from evaporating but also helps to protect plants that are intolerant of high temperatures. A number of plants such as lilies and clematis don't mind warmth on their stems and leaves but need to have their roots kept cool. In the winter a mulch may also prevent the death of certain plants that are not quite winter-hardy in your climate, just by keeping the soil a few degrees warmer than unmulched soil. More important, mulched soil experiences less of the alternate freezing and thawing that can damage the roots of plants and even heave them out of the ground.

Attracts earthworms. Earthworms work hard to cultivate your garden soil, but they don't like soil that is too hot and will stay in the subsoil to get cool. A soil cooled by mulch will bring them closer to the surface.

Prevents soil erosion. Rainfall will not wash soil away if the surface has been mulched, even on a steep slope.

Improves soil structure. Mulches consisting of organic matter decompose and gradually work their way into the soil, thereby improving its structure (page 21). This is what happens in the forest, and it can happen in your garden.

Improves soil fertility. These same organic mulches break down and provide the soil with nutrients that the plants need.

Keeps plants and their fruits clean. Plants growing in mulch are not spattered by rain or water from your hose. Crops such as tomatoes and melons, which may rest on the ground, will stay cleaner and be less prone to rot and freer from disease. Mulch also keeps flowers that flop over, such as peonies and daffodils, from getting spattered with soil.

Provides a place to walk. A mulched path in a garden, whether it is down the middle of a vegetable garden or winding its way through a wildflower garden in the woods, won't get muddy and won't need to be weeded.

Makes plantings more attractive. A mulched garden usually looks tidy and allows you to step on the soil without leaving footprints. Mulch can also be an important design feature: using the same mulch throughout a bed with a variety of different plants ties it all together. You can relate a number of different plantings to one another by using the same mulching material for all of them.

WHEN NOT TO MULCH

Mulch does have certain drawbacks, and there are times when even a confirmed mulcher may forgo it, use it with caution or use it only during a specific part of the season.

Mulch can keep the soil too cool or moist. In the cool climate where I live, early spring is called "mud season." It is the time when everything, including the soil, needs to make the most of the sun's warmth and drying power so that planting can begin. Mulch is often withheld or moved aside until the soil is warmer and drier.

Mulch can cause plants to rot.

Plants that are particularly sensitive to winter moisture (such as coral bells and blanketflower) may rot and die if water collects around their crowns (the place where the roots and stems join). Either don't grow these plants in mulched beds, or draw the mulch away in fall. Another solution is to apply the mulch thickly between the plants but leave the soil right around them bare.

Seeded areas and young seedlings can't be mulched. Don't mulch a newly planted area until the plants are tall enough so that the mulch won't smother them. An exception would be a very light mulch, such as strands of salt hay, which will partly shade the soil, keep it moist, prevent erosion and aid seed germination. This technique is especially useful for lawns that are seeded in hot weather. Or, a heavier mulch such as wet burlap might be placed on the seeded area to help germination, but it must be removed as soon as the seeds are up.

Mulch can impoverish the soil. Some woody mulches such as chips or sawdust are said to deplete the soil of nitrogen initially, while they are decomposing. This has never happened to me, as far as I can see, and I am sure that the eventual full decomposition of the mulch adds more nitrogen than it takes away. If plants growing in mulch lose their green color, however, this may be the cause. The problem can be corrected by pouring a liquid-nitrogen source such as fish emulsion through the mulch.

Mulches attract pests. Mice and other rodents often burrow in mulch, either to nest or to look for seeds, and they can nibble on garden plants while they are there. Mulch can also be a hiding place for slugs and snails, which can do serious damage. If you have problems with these or other pests, don't use mulch on susceptible crops.

How you use mulch is a combina-

Mulching Materials

Here are some of the mulches you can try. I have left out a few that are widely used, such as peat moss (it can form a crust that sheds rain) and newspaper (I think it looks ugly). In applying all these mulches, try not to bury the plants you are mulching, and smooth the surface of the mulch so that it doesn't look lumpy. Most of these will need to be replenished from time to time, for mulch, like compost, is not so much a product as a process. For one thing it is always decomposing, and for another it is often disturbed in the course of weeding and planting, during which mulch is worked into the soil. This is fine if you've chosen a mulch material that returns organic matter to the beds—you're mulching and composting at the same time.

Autumn Leaves. Raking leaves into shrub beds at the edge of the lawn is a good way to make use of them. They tend to mat heavily around herbaceous plants, however, especially flat ones such as maple leaves. Curly ones, such as oak leaves, make a more aerated mulch.

Black Plastic. For the use of black plastic in the vegetable garden see page 192; for killing weeds, see page 55. Many people use it to mulch beds or paths, covering it with a more attractive substance like bark or chips or gravel. Employed this way, plastic will keep weeds from coming up, but I find it always works its way up to the surface eventually. Use it if you can live with this problem, but if you use it in a bed, make a few holes in it so that rainwater can seep through, unless you're using one of the new plastic sheeting materials that are perforated with small holes to let moisture seep through to the soil.

Buckwheat Hulls. This tidy, elegant mulch looks especially good in flower gardens and rose beds, spread about 2 inches deep. The hulls are tiny, dark gray papery disks that are easy to sprinkle on the garden from large bags. Since it is very light, some weeds will push right up through it, but it does prevent many annual weed seeds from germinating and will help keep the soil moist. Its major drawback is that it blows around, wanders into the lawn, slides down hills, and is totally dispersed by any leaf-blowing machine that comes near it. I use it whenever I want to give a fairly flat bed a formal look, and simply replace it each year in early summer.

Cocoa Shells. These are sold in bags and make a good, light mulch. Don't worry if your garden smells of chocolate at first. The odor soon disappears.

Evergreen Branches. The branches of evergreen trees make an excellent winter mulch for gardens such as perennial beds, where you don't want moist materials matting around the plants. They hold the snow and keep it from blowing away or being melted by the sun. Apply them when the ground freezes. About this same time abandoned Christmas trees can provide a handy supply.

Grass Clippings. These are a convenient source, though perhaps they look a bit messy in an ornamental planting. They decompose very rapidly and can burn herbaceous plants, so don't pile them closely around vegetables or flowers. Never use clippings from a lawn that has been treated with broad-leaf weed killers.

Hay. Hay is the most traditional mulch because it is so handy. What else can you do with hay that has been spoiled by an untimely rain or by green weeds that have rotted in the bales? Sell it for mulch, often at a higher price than the good hay used for horses. Try to get a second or, better yet, a third cutting that will contain fewer seeds. A hay bale breaks apart in "flakes" or "books." Simply lay these side by side between the rows of your vegetable garden.

Locally Available By-Products. In your quest for the perfect mulch, check to see what local farms or plants have organic waste materials that might be suitable. Some that people use for mulches are spent hops from breweries, tobacco stems, ground corncobs, shredded cornstalks, sugar-cane residue, cottonseed hulls, peanut hulls and nut shells.

Manufactured Cloth Mulches. There are some fabrics on the market that are less obtrusive than plastic and might be worth investigating, though I haven't myself tried them. I have also heard that biodegradable, plasticlike films will be available in the near future; these, too, bear watching.

Pine Needles. Pine trees shed their old needles, and you can find them lying on the ground under the trees. If you have a source of pine needles, these make a beautiful mulch for ornamental gardens, especially shrub plantings. They are rather acidic.

Root Mulch. This marvelous mulch is almost impossible to find in bulk and is expensive to buy in bags. It is ground-up plant roots that have a dark color and are moist and easy to apply. This mulch stays put better than any I've ever used, even on a slope.

Salt Hay. This is a better, although a much more expensive, alternative to ordinary hay. It is a wild seaside grass that is harvested when it floats into shore on the water. Seeds in it will germinate only under salty conditions, not in your garden. I find that salt hay decays more slowly than regular hay; I can use it a second year.

Seaweed (Kelp). Seaweed is an excellent mulch if you live by the ocean. Wash off the salt first.

Shavings and Sawdust. These can be used as mulch too, but remember that the more finely pulverized a wood product is, the faster it will decompose and the sooner it will need to be replaced. These also look rather unnatural until they weather.

Shredded Bark. This is an excellent mulch, particularly for shrubs and trees, and one that is readily available. You can buy it in bags at a garden center, but try to get it in bulk if you want to mulch large areas. I buy it from sawmills that strip the bark off the logs they are cutting into lumber—a bucket loader simply dumps it into the back of my pickup truck. But often you can get truckloads delivered. I lay it down about 4 inches thick, less for herbaceous plantings. The bark weathers to a natural grayish color; I think it is a lot more attractive than the "bark nuggets" that are also sold in bags, because it doesn't look so artificial.

Stones. If you put down a mulch of small stones or pebbles several inches thick, you can suppress most weeds and provide a nice dry surface for plants whose foliage can rot if it lies on moist ground. I think organic materials are more attractive as mulches than stones are, but I can see where a stone mulch might look fine in a contemporary or Japanese-style setting. Round, black Mexican beach pebbles are beautiful as a

mulch, especially when they're wet, but alas, they are very costly. You might try them in a small, special plot.

Straw. Straw is the stubble that remains after a grain crop has been cut; it is harvested after it has dried and is relatively free of viable seeds. Use it like hay.

Wood Chips. The best wood chips are the ones whose branches, twigs and bark have all been put through a chipper, because they look much like the litter on the forest floor. A tree surgeon may be able to sell you some, or you may find a place where land is being cleared and there are piles of it that you can beg or buy. Chips are also available at sawmills and in bags, but these are very light colored and take a while to weather to a more attractive gray.

tion of trial and error and common sense. Some gardeners use mulches so religiously that they claim they never even have to till their gardens. They insist their mulch just sits there and solves all their problems. In many cases this may be true. My advice is to experiment with several mulching materials that are readily available, using the list on page 65 for suggestions.

What to Do About Bugs

Every garden has some insects that the gardener would just as soon do without. I must admit I don't pay a great deal of attention to bugs, because they

rarely do serious damage. I tolerate a few chewed leaves or flowers in my ornamental plantings, and with my food crops I follow the old wisdom that holds, "one for the bugs, one for me," planting enough so that my yields are good despite occasional nibblers. Admittedly my arugula, which I share with some local flea beetles, will never be photographed by *Gourmet* magazine.

More serious infestations do need a gardener's attention, however, especially since some insects can spread plant diseases. It is important to know some safe ways to deal with them. Fortunately gardeners are becoming more aware that using toxic sprays and dusts can be dangerous to themselves and their families, to their pets, to wildlife and even to their plants. So today there is considerable interest in safe means of insect control.

A large network of insect and plant life exists in every garden. This network fits together in such complex ways that I will never fully understand them. It changes from season to season, for insect (and plant) populations are always in flux. Certain "bad" insects eat some of my plants, but there are in turn "good" insects that attack the bad ones. If I destroyed all the insects in my garden, I'd not only be destroying the bug eaters but also insects that perform other useful functions, such as the bees that pollinate my plants and the butterflies and moths I enjoy watching. And even if I find a means of controlling only the "bad" plant eaters, I run the risk of depriving the bug eaters of their food supply, so that they leave my garden and cause the plant eaters to be all the more numerous. Sometimes I'll try to get rid of unwelcome visitors that are threatening something I've worked hard to grow, but I don't worry about rounding up the whole gang, just diminishing their numbers.

Each plant that gardeners grow has particular insects that consider it their favorite food, and each part of the country has its own notorious insects to deal with. Vegetables tend to be "buggier" in the south than they are in the northeast, where I live. But our fruit crops in the northeast are much buggier than those of growers I've talked to on the west coast. You will probably need more specific information than I can give you about all the creatures that might eat your plants and what you can do about them (it's a huge topic), and you'll need to consult local experts or some of the sources listed beginning on page 618. But the decision about what forms of pest control you are comfortable with is finally yours. I, for one, would no sooner use an "all-purpose"

spray that killed all the bugs in my garden than I would a spray that killed all the gray hairs on my head—and all the brown ones, too.

Insects vary in the way they damage plants. Some suck out the plant juices; some chew on the leaves or other plant parts; others bore into the stems, leaves or roots. Some carry specific diseases to plants or create wounds that leave them open to infection, or simply weaken plants so that they resist disease less easily than healthy plants would. Insects may do damage while they are in their growing stages (as larvae) or after they have changed into the adult form in which they reproduce—or both. If you are on the warpath against a specific insect you should check an insect field guide so that you can recognize it in its different stages. Sometimes gardeners unwittingly kill an insect that they would like to protect, such as a butterfly, because they only recognize its adult form, not the suspicious-looking caterpillar that takes a few bites of something they prize. Or they fail to control an insect because they go after it in the adult stage, after the larvae have done their damage. Often when there is insect damage you can't even see the culprit because it is too tiny, because it has hidden itself somewhere in the plant, or because it does its work in the soil. Sometimes an insect is not even at fault—a disease is, or a mineral deficiency in the soil or some other cause of physical stress. When in doubt on any of these counts, *don't spray.* Get a positive identification first. If you put the affected plant parts in a plastic bag and take or mail them to your Extension Service, they can usually identify the perpetrator for you.

INTEGRATED PEST MANAGEMENT

You may not need to spray at all. People have found, over the years, that insects often develop a resistance to the chemicals used to control them, so that not only is spraying risky, it is often futile. As a result, many commercial growers are now using a practice called IPM, or "Integrated Pest Management." It often involves a spray program but also employs deterrents such as crop rotation, hand picking, natural predators, sterilizing and releasing male insects that will mate but produce no young, using insect diseases, using traps—and most important of all, identifying the specific pests, pinpointing the time and place of the damage they cause and being selective about any toxic material that is applied. Poisons are starting to be viewed as a last resort, and the indiscriminate use of wide-spectrum ones has been somewhat reduced.

You can practice a home gardener's version of IPM. Try using some of the insect remedies that follow here, starting with the safest ones, which are listed first. If you grow food crops in a communal garden, where each person has a plot and many crops are being grown, it may seem as if every bug in the world has found its way there, and control of them may be a tricky matter. You are at the mercy not only of your neighbors' bugs, but also of any sprays they use that might drift over onto your plants. By meeting together and planning a safe, coordinated attack, you may be able to help one another identify problem insects before they spread, so you can tackle them at the proper stage and come up with the safest means of control.

FORMS OF INSECT CONTROL

Plant extra for bugs. If something cuts back on your harvest one year, figure how many more plants you'll need next year if the visitor comes back.

Time your plantings. If the planting date for a food crop is flexible, you can sometimes time it to avoid a pest—for example, you can grow radishes after root maggots are no longer active (in late summer and fall). You can also grow seedlings in large containers until they have enough foliage to withstand an insect attack, then transplant them into the garden.

Grow a trap crop. On the other hand you might plant a "sacrifice" radish crop so the maggots will eat that and not your broccoli.

Avoid high-risk plants. Sometimes a plant is not worth repeating if you grow it and find it is a magnet for a specific pest that is hard to control. Grow those that are less susceptible.

Wait for a pest to move on. Many insects migrate or come in cycles. You might get a severe infestation of gypsy moths or tent caterpillars for a few years, for instance; I've seen gypsy moths defoliate entire hillsides one year and not the next. Usually trees and shrubs thus attacked will recover in time as the plague moves elsewhere.

Rotate your crops. If you grow an annual food crop in the same place each year, the insects will often overwinter in the soil and come back stronger than ever. Foil them so that they hatch out without their favorite food handy; some may never find where you've moved it and will die out or leave.

Encourage beneficial predators. Many creatures that prey on insect pests will appear in your garden of their own accord, but there are things you can do to encourage them. Birds eat a lot of

SOME COMMON INSECT PREDATORS

Fig. 12

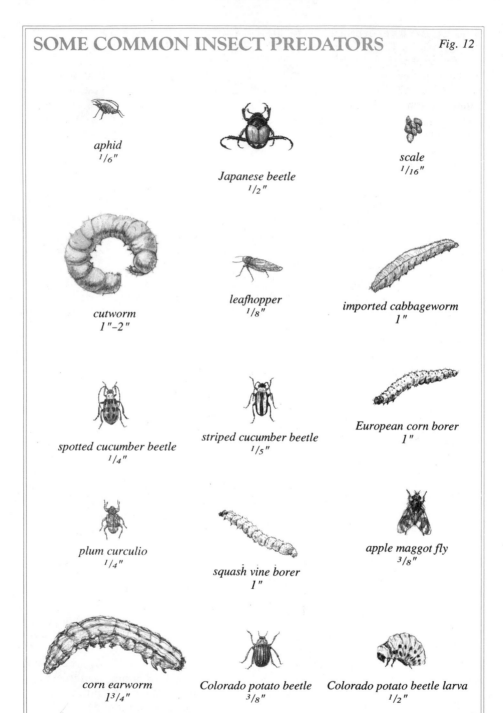

aphid
$^1/_6''$

Japanese beetle
$^1/_2''$

scale
$^1/_{16}''$

cutworm
$1''-2''$

leafhopper
$^1/_8''$

imported cabbageworm
$1''$

spotted cucumber beetle
$^1/_4''$

striped cucumber beetle
$^1/_5''$

European corn borer
$1''$

plum curculio
$^1/_4''$

squash vine borer
$1''$

apple maggot fly
$^3/_8''$

corn earworm
$1^3/_4''$

Colorado potato beetle
$^3/_8''$

Colorado potato beetle larva
$^1/_2''$

insects; give them trees and shrubs near the garden in which to nest. Toads do their part as well; give them flowerpots to hide in, propped open with a rock. Spiders, of course, trap and eat insects (they are not, strictly speaking, insects themselves.) Some of the insects that eat insect pests are ladybugs, lacewings, praying mantises, ant lions, damsel bugs, pirate bugs, syrphid flies, ichneumon flies, assassin bugs and fireflies (Figure 13). Many of these can be bought in bulk and released in your garden, but frankly it is usually a waste of money because chances are they'll eat a few bugs and then move on. Lace-

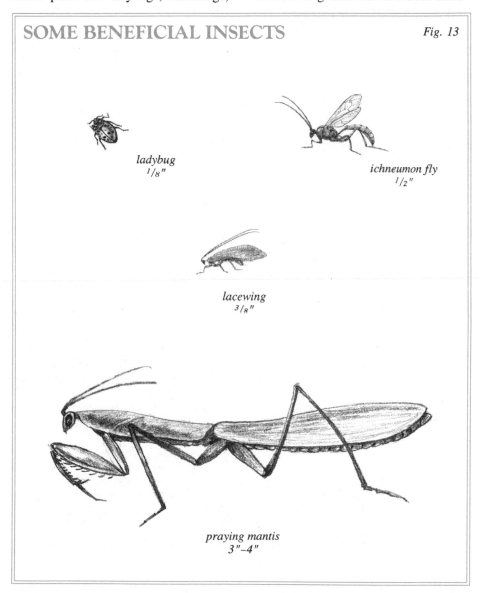

SOME BENEFICIAL INSECTS

Fig. 13

ladybug
¹/₈"

ichneumon fly
¹/₂"

lacewing
³/₈"

praying mantis
3"–4"

wings are a notable exception and will stick around to prey on mealybugs, aphids, mites, thrips, scale insects and whiteflies, so you might give these a try. But the best way to encourage all beneficial predators in your garden is to avoid using poisons.

Cover the plants. If insects attack your young plants while they are most vulnerable, try protecting them during this stage with the agricultural fabric described on page 206. You can even leave the fabric on all season. One commercial seed producer I talked to told me these fabrics had virtually solved his pest-control problems. They are particularly helpful for insects such as leafhoppers that don't sit still long enough for you to pick them off. You will have to remove the fabric in order to weed, however, and also when the plants are setting flowers and are being pollinated by insects.

Physical barriers. Cutworms, which sever the stems of young plants just beneath the soil surface, can be deterred by setting collars made of paper cups or some such thing around susceptible seedlings such as tomatoes and peppers. The collars should extend about an inch above the soil and an inch below it. Tarpaper mats spread on the ground are said to deter root maggots (lay the tarpaper on the ground and plant through holes you make in it). Aluminum foil spread on the ground may discourage striped cucumber beetles, Mexican bean beetles, spider mites, leafhoppers and squash bugs.

Control the weeds. A lot of weeds growing in the garden and just outside it can harbor insect pests. They can harbor beneficial insects too, but if your garden is particularly "buggy" try to keep the weeds down, and mow weedy areas around its perimeter.

Use repellents. Some insects that eat food crops or ornamental plants are said to be deterred by sprays made of garlic or ground-up hot peppers. It's always worth a try, but be sure to reapply if rain washes them off.

Use bug juice. Many gardeners claim that if you collect pest insects in a jar, purée the bugs in water in an old blender, strain the concoction, and spray it back on the plants, it will discourage others from returning.

Turn loose the chickens. They may eat good bugs as well as bad and they may nibble away at some plants, but if left there for short stretches chickens may help to cut down on some serious pests, such as potato beetles.

Pick off the bugs. This is probably the most useful insect control there is. Picking bugs off your plants and dropping them into jars filled with kerosene may not be your favorite way to spend time, nor will you get them all. But you don't need to: even getting half the offending bugs may solve your problem. If you have children you might give them a chance to earn spending money by paying them a per-bug or per-cupful fee. Not all insects can be picked easily, of course. Some are too small, some won't sit still and some are high above your head, eating your trees. But many are easy. Some, like Japanese beetles and potato beetles, drop to the ground when disturbed, so you can just knock them or shake them into a container, or onto a cloth spread on the ground. Prowl for slugs with a flashlight at night, and check their hiding places (under rocks and boards, for instance) by day.

Spray with a hose. Many pests such as aphids and spider mites can easily be knocked off with the force of a garden hose. Aphids are tiny sucking insects (usually green) that appear in throngs on plant leaves; the leaves are often crinkled or distorted. Spider mites are too small to really see, but they give the leaves a dotted, stippled look and you can sometimes spot the tiny webs they make on the undersides of the leaves. Be sure, when you are hosing off these pests, that you hit the undersides of the leaves, too.

Trap them. You can outfox many pests with clever traps. Slugs and earwigs can be lured into saucers of beer sunk in the ground up to the rims. Male Japanese beetles can be lured by traps containing pheromones (sex attractants) of the female beetles. Whiteflies can be lured while in flight to a piece of wood or metal painted bright yellow and smeared with a sticky substance like molasses that works like old-fashioned flypaper. Probably the most ingenious insect trap around is a sticky red ball on which apple maggots will lay their eggs, thinking it is a ripe apple! You can buy these from mail-order catalogs or make them out of croquet balls. (These sticky traps are also used to monitor insect infestations so that the right bugs can be attacked at the right time.)

Destroy their nests. Tent caterpillars, which build webs in the forks of trees in spring (particularly cherry trees), and fall webworms, which build webs at the ends of tree branches in fall, can be curbed if you break apart their nests and scrape the caterpillars into cans of kerosene or alcohol.

Use dormant oil sprays. These oil sprays are applied only when the temperature is between 45 and 85 degrees Fahrenheit, to deciduous woody plants while they are in a dormant state, usually just before their buds begin to swell. (There are similar formulations that can be applied later in the season and will not burn leaves the way dormant oils can.) These are important controls for scale insects, which look like small bumps (usually brown) on the twigs and branches of woody plants but which are actually sucking insects. Like many other sucking insects (including

whiteflies and aphids), scale insects secrete a sticky substance called "honeydew," which in turn attracts a black fungus disease called "sooty mold." Dormant oil sprays also help to control such pests as spider mites, psyllids (such as pear psylla) and leaf rollers.

Use soap sprays. Spraying infested plants with soapsuds is an old-fashioned remedy for such insects as aphids, earwigs, psyllids, sawflies, leaf miners (which make tunnels in leaves), spider mites, thrips and scale. Household soaps and detergents can burn plant leaves, however, and it is less risky to buy a commercially prepared insect soap spray and use the concentration recommended on the label.

Diatomaceous earth. This material consists of the fossilized remains of diatoms, tiny sea creatures. It damages the soft bodies of crawlers such as slugs and cabbage worms. It is harmful to breathe, however, and I would worry about hurting harmless caterpillars, too.

BT. BT stands for a bacterium called *Bacillus thuringiensis.* Sold under names such as Dipel and Thuricide, it is a disease you can give to your bagworms, gypsy moths, tent caterpillars, webworms, tomato hornworms, European corn borers and cabbage worms. Milky spore disease, another bacterium, will eliminate many of your Japanese beetles. These remedies are rather expensive to apply and, again, I worry about upsetting the balance of nature and wiping out bugs I want.

Natural organic poisons. Certain plant extracts can kill insects with less risk to humans and other warm-blooded animals than most chemical sprays present, but they all carry some risks. All can harm beneficial insects, and none should ever be applied to plants in bloom, especially at times when bees are active. Pyrethrum, made from ground-up flowers of the chrysanthemum family, kills a number of insects, and the residue it leaves on edible crops breaks down very quickly; but it can kill some beneficial insects and fish, too, if it drifts or drains into streams or ponds. Rotenone, made from ground-up derris root, is more powerful; its residue lasts up to a week. While it won't hurt humans or pets, it kills fish and beneficial insects. Ryania has a fairly low toxicity and helps cope with worms such as European corn borer; sabadilla dust kills many insects—including bees; nicotine is quite toxic, and I do not advise using it. In general, be wary of any product that claims to kill "pest" insects but spare the "beneficial" ones. This is very unlikely to be true.

As you can see, I've put even the "natural" poison sprays low on my list, because they are either something to use if all else fails, or not to use at all, depending on your philosophy. If you do use these or any other toxic materials in the garden, follow these safety rules:

Read the labels, use only as directed and heed all warnings.

Keep poisons in original containers, away from children and pets.

Don't breathe sprays and dusts.

Try not to spill poisons or splash them on humans or pets.

Don't smoke while using them.

Cover food or water in the area that might be consumed by people or pets.

Always deal with poisons in a well-ventilated area.

Don't mix them together.

Don't use them on windy days.

Be careful not to contaminate streams, ponds and other water sources.

Wash yourself with soap and water after handling them; wash and flush out any equipment used to apply them.

Keep empty poison containers out of harm's way, then take them to a toxic-materials recovery site; *don't* send them to the town dump.

Coping with Diseases

Plant diseases are not easy for the home gardener to diagnose or treat. There are so many different ones— ranging from those that make ornamental plants unsightly to those that kill or weaken food plants or make their fruits inedible or unappetizing—and it is hard to match the disease with the cure without being an expert. Even if you can get your disease identified, the cures available to you may be ineffective. Fortunately there is quite a bit you can do to prevent plant diseases or at least keep them under control.

DISEASE PREVENTION

Here are some steps you can take to keep your gardens healthy. As with pest control, there are commercial products that can be applied if prevention fails, but you may find that you can get by without using them.

Grow disease-resistant varieties. Commercial producers of plants and seeds are always coming up with new varieties that resist the most common diseases of plants. And in fact gardeners have been doing the same thing for centuries simply by selecting the healthiest, most vigorous specimens from which to save their seed or take their cuttings. If certain diseases haunt your garden, be on the lookout for varieties that are said to resist them. Certain species of plants may also be more prone to disease in your climate than others because your climate is too different from their native ones. You might simply choose to grow those that do well in your area instead. Sometimes diseases are aggravated by growing a susceptible plant in large numbers. For example the more lilies you grow, the more apt your flowers are to get lily virus, so being content with a few healthy specimens may make sense.

Buy disease-free seed. Sometimes a plant disease will permeate a given locality so that none of the seed or stock raised there commercially can be totally free of it. You might check with your local Extension Service, state university or nurseryman to find out if there are specific diseases associated with certain plants or seeds you wish to grow. They can also advise you about where disease-free material is grown and sold. Always try to buy seeds and plants from reputable sources, and examine plants you buy for signs of disease before you bring them home.

Practice crop rotation. This practice, described on page 197, applies mostly to food gardens, but if ornamental plants do succumb to disease it is wise to try them again in a new location as well, since disease organisms can persist in the soil.

Don't work in wet gardens, if possible. As you move among wet plants you can easily spread diseases.

Keep plants dry. Obviously your plants are going to get wet when it rains, but keeping foliage unnecessarily moist can promote disease. Water plants at ground level whenever you can.

Control disease-spreading insects. Cucumber wilt, for example, is spread by the striped cucumber beetle, so to thwart the disease you thwart the bug.

Keep your plants vigorous. You know that you get fewer colds if you exercise, eat right, get plenty of sleep and all those other things your mother taught you. It's the same with plants. If they have great soil, no weeds, and ample water, chances are they will have few diseases or only mild cases.

Don't crowd plants. Good air circu-lation among plants helps prevent many diseases.

Don't reuse potting soil. This is especially important if the previous tenant of that soil was sick. If throwing out soil seems wasteful, sterilize it in the oven for a few hours at 180 degrees.

Disinfect contaminated tools. If you're pruning out diseased portions of a plant, dip your pruners in a chlorine solution between cuts.

Destroy diseased plants. Tilling under diseased plants or putting them on the compost heap just perpetuates the problem. Burn them, or bury them at least 6 inches deep in a spot other than the garden.

Keep a tidy garden. Clean up plant debris after you harvest a food crop, and cut back herbaceous perennials after their foliage dies down in fall. Disease organisms will have less chance of wintering over.

Replace the soil. As a last resort, if a disease keeps recurring each year, you can remove the top 2 or 3 inches of soil, and with it, the disease organism. Replace with new, disease-free soil.

COMMON PLANT DISEASES

Here are some major categories of diseases that may befall your plants. They can be caused by fungi, bacteria or viruses.

Leaf-spot diseases. These are fungus diseases that afflict both woody and herbaceous plants. There are many different ones, but in general they appear as round spots that are often a series of concentric circles in shades of brown, yellow or black (if the circles are numerous they merge to form blotches). Sometimes they affect a plant's looks only, and can be ignored, but I have occasionally seen bad cases kill plants. The fungi overwinter in fallen leaves, so it is best to rake up the leaves of affected plants and destroy them, and to destroy the whole plant if it dies. Fungicides applied in spring as the leaves start to appear can help.

Fusarium wilt. This fungus lives in the soil and attacks plants' roots. Scar tissue forms, which blocks the circulation of fluids, and the plant wilts. There is no treatment the home gardener can apply, but you can fight the wilt by growing resistant varieties, rotating crops, pulling up and destroying afflicted plants and not letting the soil get too acid.

Mildews. Mildews afflict such diverse plants as phlox, beans, lilacs and roses. Downy mildew produces white patches on the leaves in wet weather; powdery mildew turns the leaves a powdery white and occurs when it is hot and humid. Benomyl is a common remedy for ornamental plants, but often it does not work. Sulfur dust can be effective on many ornamental and food plants. And many plants, such as roses, have mildew-resistant varieties. Usually I simply try not to look at the mildew on my phlox and lilacs.

Botrytis This fungus disease produces brown or gray areas on leaves and stems in humid weather. Prune out and destroy all affected parts. Benomyl is sometimes effective.

Rust. Yet another fungus, rust produces pustules on the undersides of leaves; these are sometimes rust colored but can also be red, yellow, brown or black. Rust is treated with fungicides, but try to find resistant varieties.

Anthracnose. A lot of things get anthracnose, from maple trees and dogwoods to cucumbers and beans. It is not always east to identify, but it produces spots on leaves, or on pods in the case of beans. Western seeds and plants are less likely to carry it.

Canker. Cankers can be either fungal or bacterial. They produce sunken areas on the twigs, stems and trunks of woody plants. Prune them out, and if too much of the plant is affected for this to help, destroy it.

Crown galls. This bacterial disease of woody plants produces knobby growths that block circulation of fluids. Usually the plant must be destroyed.

Other bacterial diseases. Plants afflicted with bacteria can show slime and rot, wilt, spots and any number of other symptoms. Bacteria tend to spread quickly so it is wise to get any plant in very bad shape out of your garden fast. Plants growing in moist, nitrogen-rich soil in hot, humid weather are the most susceptible.

Four-Legged Marauders

People from the city who move to my area often ask what they can plant to attract wildlife to their yards. "That's easy," I tell them. "Plant lettuce, corn, broccoli, beans, berries, day lilies, yews. . . ." The list is very long.

I don't mean to sound cynical. I can empathize with folk who are tired of looking at concrete and want to look at deer, rabbits and raccoons. I'm the same way. But unfortunately, many of us who start gardening in these parts wind up regarding these creatures much the way we once regarded muggers, burglars and welfare cheats. The trick is to find ways to enjoy the presence of wildlife and still have a garden.

I won't waste your time listing the dozens of repellents that gardeners claim work on this or that pest. No doubt some are effective. Yes, you can try dabbing your ornamentals with Tabasco sauce, cayenne pepper and every Cajun, Creole or Szechuan seasoning on the market; you can round up human hair from all the local beauticians and barbers to hang in bags around your property, and you can haunt zoos that are willing to part with their lion dung. But the best remedies are either to plant things that your local wildlife doesn't care for or to erect physical barriers. I do not recommend poisoning them, gassing them, shooting them or trapping them.

KNOW THE CREATURES' HABITS

You may not know what is eating your plants. Finding out about your local wildlife by consulting field guides may help you to identify the culprit. And talk to local gardeners and farmers. Each area has its own special varmints. Here are some of the most common ones.

Rabbits. Rabbits will eat a wide variety of plants. They love salad crops like lettuce but will also gnaw the bark of fruit trees, often girdling and killing them. Rabbits reproduce prolifically, as we all know, and the little ones are the hungriest of all. Protect young fruit trees as soon as they are planted by wrapping the trunks in cylinders of hardware cloth that are buried 1 to 2 inches in the ground, and extend at least 18 inches up the tree (for more information see page 530). The cylinder should not constrict the growth of the trunk or prevent the tree from forming feeder roots below the surface.

In the vegetable garden make sure the first 2 feet of your fence is rabbit fencing, 1-by-2-inch mesh, and bury it 6 inches deep or bend it outward to rest on 6 inches of soil to discourage burrowing. Baby bunnies can squeeze through anything less closely woven than that.

For unfenced flowers and other herbaceous plants use the portable frames shown on page 205 with rabbit fence or 1-inch chicken wire stretched over

them, until the plants are large enough to withstand a little nibbling.

Woodchucks. Some people call them "groundhogs." They are fat, lumbering and rather lovable except when they are eating your peas. Woodchucks are not supposed to climb fences, but I once saw a huge one hauling its heavy self over a 4-foot fence that I had built, and I've heard of them climbing much higher. They are not supposed to burrow under the fence if you bury the wire a foot down, but one did, and came up right in the middle of my beans, so you might want to go deeper than that.

Deer. It's funny, but as an area gets more built up and suburban it often has more deer. Though they are woodland creatures, deer prefer the outskirts of woodlands, or clearings in them, where they can find fresh new growth on shrubs and other understory plants. When they see former farmland growing up in scrub, or homeowners planting day lilies and phlox or rows of yews and arborvitae on one-acre lots—"Ah," say the deer, "progress!"

Deer will leap very high fences to get into a garden, and you need one about 8 feet tall to deter them effectively. Some people have had good luck with fencing that is lower but extends upwards at a 45-degree angle, and some put deer fence flat on the ground, on the theory that deer don't like to put their hooves through mesh. Commercial orchards and tree farms often use electrified strands of wire. Hardware and farm-supply stores supply apparatus for electric fencing, as do mail-order outfits, but I still feel a very tall fence is the best solution if deer are a problem.

Wrap ornamental shrubs that deer like in chicken wire supported with metal stakes in wintertime, removing it in spring when everything has leafed out and they have a wider choice of forage. Emerging tulips and other herbaceous plants can be protected by the movable frames shown on page 205 or some other cage of your own devising. By the time the plants are too tall for the frames the deer will have lost interest. There are also a number of deer repellents.

Raccoons. Raccoons will raid your garbage can if the lid isn't tight, but the only plant they seriously threaten is corn. See page 242 for some tactical suggestions.

Rodents. Mice, moles and voles can do the same thing to young fruit trees that rabbits can and are foiled by the same methods. But voles often gnaw on the roots as well. You can destroy them by putting mousetraps, baited with something tasty like apple or peanut butter, in their runways. Also avoid using mulch within a foot of tree trunks because it can be a haven for rodents. For problems with flower bulbs see page 398. Moles can make a lawn very lumpy, but they are blamed unjustly for a lot of damage actually done by mice, which use mole tunnels as runs. As far as I'm concerned, moles earn their keep in the lawn by eating Japanese beetle grubs that hatch there, so I leave them alone.

Birds. Protect newly planted seeds from birds with mulch or mesh-covered frames. Plastic netting is effective on fruit crops such as raspberries, blueberries and cherries. Or just grow enough for you *and* the birds and pick regularly.

The Larger Community

G ardening is essentially the creation, for certain plants, of a more luxurious, consistent and protected environment than those plants would find in the wild. By giving them this environment we control nature, just as plant growers have for thousands of years.

Sometimes, in our desire to achieve a predictable outcome from all our hard work, we lose sight of how much we and the other living things in nature all depend on one another. Plant and animal life is a chain of interdependence: plants feeding animals, animals feeding plants, plants feeding plants and animals feeding animals. Even the death and decay of organisms is a vital part of the process. When we destroy living things that are part of the chain, we always run some risk of disrupting it, and destroying their habitats can amount to the same thing. Good gardening is sometimes a matter of leaving nature alone— of not draining a swamp on your property that harbors wildlife, of not clearing your woods of all the underbrush and logs where creatures hide, of realizing that even your soil is alive—with insects, reptiles, mammals and microbes—and so is not the place for toxic substances. We garden in a world that is in constant motion, motion that our clumsy efforts to control the environment can bring to a halt.

My own philosophy is that most of the time I can't predict what the outcome of my manipulating the natural world will be, because that world is so complex. Therefore, although I sometimes regulate this or that aspect of it, I try to do the very minimum and avoid any measures I feel might be harmful. I don't try to be a perfect gardener; I don't judge my success by the number of flowers on a plant or the size of a fruit. I happen to think that safe gardening practices give equally good—or better—results than those that tamper thoughtlessly with the balance of nature. But even if they did not I'd probably use them anyway. If I've enjoyed growing my garden, and the countryside around it is still humming with life, that's a large part of the harvest.

GARDENING
GEAR

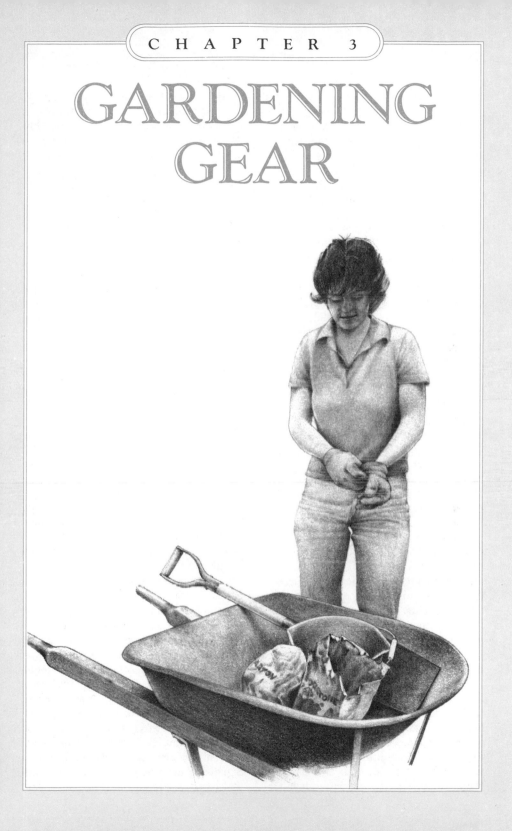

Most gardeners have a close relationship with their tools, even though that relationship can take different forms. Some have a whole wall of specialized tools and gadgets displayed on nails and pegboards, where they can reach like surgeons for the one that is perfect for the task at hand. Others have only a few simple implements to which they are nonetheless very attached. The handles fit their hands like a familiar glove, and woe betide the friend, spouse or child who borrows and loses them. There are also gardeners who long to form such attachments to their tools but dare not because they lose at least two shovels and three trowels each season.

I confess I am the few-simple-tools type. I like to have some well-made, versatile ones that I can count on and feel comfortable with. There is a wide range of prices of garden tools nowadays, from cheap to · exorbitant, but there are few real bargains—you get what you pay for. If you buy a cheap tool, chances are the handle will break or the working end will bend or fall off; and the tool may not even be well designed for efficient performance. Given an unlimited budget I might be the gardener with the great wall of tools, but I'd rather be extravagant about plants instead. So I try to choose tools that give me the most for my money. This means deciding on the few that will do the most for me, then buying top-of-the-line products (or close to it) and perhaps picking up some specialized ones here and there at tag sales.

But what if you are the inveterate tool loser who is afraid to buy good tools? Here's a suggestion: we all know tools can masquerade as sticks, or hide under piles of weeds to be composted, or wander over into someone else's yard. Why not paint all the handles bright blue? (Red-and-yellow handles work well up until fall, when they start pretending they are fallen leaves.) Tell everyone that your tools are the blue ones, then guard them with your life.

Deciding Which Tools to Buy

A beginning gardener can waste a lot of money buying the wrong tools. So it is worth finding out something about which ones are out there, what they do, and which will do the jobs you need to do. The list of basic tools that follows will acquaint you with most of the important ones and help you to choose among them. But first some generalizations about quality.

When you go to buy tools you will notice that even within a specific brand there is usually a range of prices for a single type of tool. There might be a cheap version and an expensive version, or there might be even three or four versions, each with a different price tag. When in doubt, buy the best or next-best tool. Paying a lot of money for something does not always guarantee that you'll get quality, but with tools, more often than not it does. And there are certain things to look for that will make your choice less blind. Every tool has certain construction features that make it function best, and as you get to know tools you will notice these, but here are some criteria that you can apply to most tools in general.

What metal is used? The best tools are of good steel that is labeled "tempered," or "heat-treated," and has been "forged" or "drop-forged," as opposed to stamped out of sheet metal. Stainless-steel tools are even better because they do not rust, but they are usually very expensive. The better tools have a solid feel to them because they are made out of heavier-gauge metal than cheap ones. Lighter-weight tools are easy to wield comfortably, but make sure that the tool is light because of its design (a smaller blade or shorter handle, for example), and not because it has been made of flimsy materials.

Look at the handles. Some tools, especially small ones, have metal or plastic handles, but for the most part tool handles are made out of wood. Wood is light and durable, and most people like the feel of wood-handled tools—I know I do. Look for handles made of straight-grained ash, not just an anonymous "hardwood," and check to see that they have no knots or other flaws. Avoid tools with handles that have been painted. That paint may be concealing faults in the wood. Better to add your own coat of paint if you like.

Check the sockets. The way in which the working end of the tool is joined to the handle is equally important. Generally what I look for here is called "solid-shank" construction. Most tools have a socket that the handle fits into; this socket and the working part should be all one piece, not two pieces of metal welded together. In some types of tools the wood is held in the socket simply by a tight fit. (See the mattock in Figure 14 for an example.) But the majority of tool heads have some piece of hardware, such as a rivet, that keeps them on. Look for solid, heavy-duty hardware. A wood screw is not adequate to hold a tool onto its handle and a rivet should go all the way through the handle to the other side.

Evaluate size and weight. If you are a beginning gardener I strongly recommend that you visit either a good, old-fashioned hardware store or an agricultural-supply store. You may end up buying some of your tools from a mail-order supplier since some carry specialized or particularly fine tools that are hard to find elsewhere, but I think it is important to actually hold in your hand some different kinds of tools, in different weights and sizes, and find one that matches your own size and strength. Keep in mind that a large, heavy tool can often do more work as long as you can wield it comfortably, but it will slow you down if you have to strain too hard. Similarly a small, light version of the same tool may force you to work very fast to compensate for the lesser amount of work it accomplishes. The handle length may also make a difference. Sometimes holding a tool in the store won't tell you what using it is like; if so, try to borrow one from a friend and use it for a while. Tools that last a lifetime are worth little if they're the wrong ones.

Basic Tools

M any garden tools are very simple but at the same time very versatile. You can perform a lot of different tasks with each one; this is why you really don't need to own very many of them. But for the purpose of discussion, tools can be grouped according to their chief function.

TOOLS FOR DIGGING AND PLANTING

Much of gardening is just making holes in the ground so that you can put plants in them. How you make those holes, and what you make them with, depends on what your ground is like, what is going to go into the hole and what size and shape hole you need to accommodate it. Since digging is the most tiring gardening task, it makes sense to dig with something that is sharp, efficient and just heavy enough to do the job. You don't need to be lifting a too-heavy tool

TOOLS FOR DIGGING AND PLANTING

Fig. 14

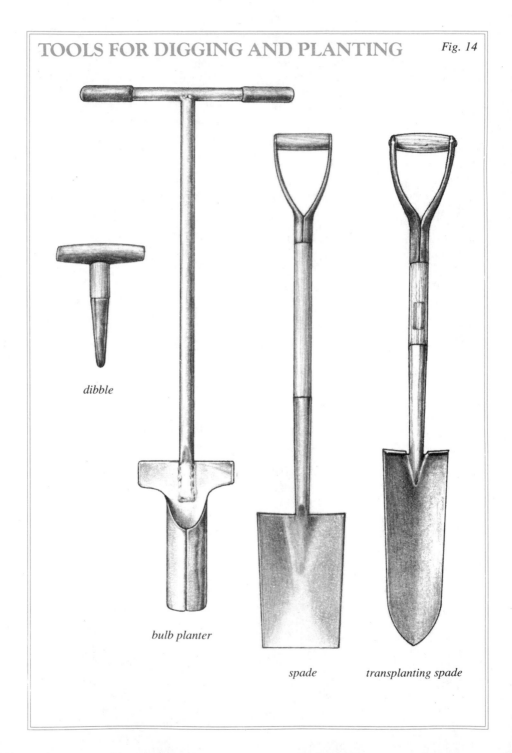

dibble

bulb planter

spade

transplanting spade

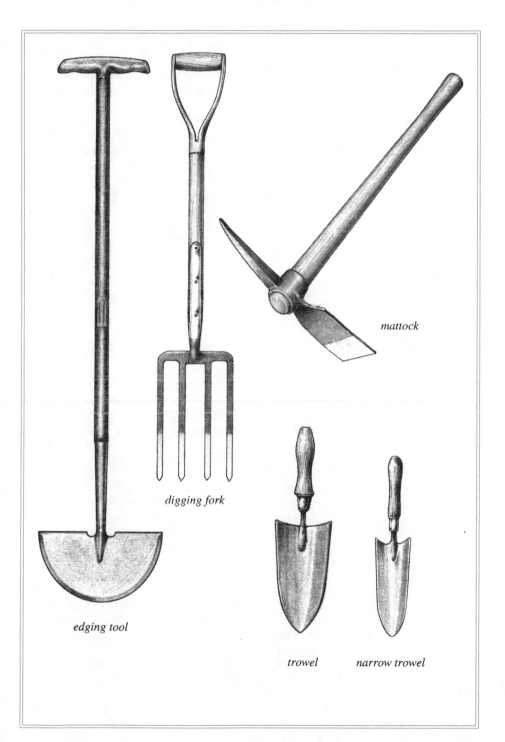

mattock

digging fork

edging tool

trowel   narrow trowel

along with all that dirt. Of the tools listed below, the ones I find really essential are the trowel, the spade and the digging fork.

Trowel. This indispensable little tool is used for digging small holes for planting and transplanting annuals, perennials, vegetables and other relatively small plants. You not only dig the hole with it, but also lift the plants and move them to their new locations. Trowels are also very handy for mixing small amounts of soil and for weeding and cultivating. The broader one in Figure 14 has the widest range of uses, but the narrow one is handy for making smaller holes, for digging out an individual weed, and for working among plants that are close together. I own both, and I usually take both with me when I go out to the garden, but you could begin with just the larger one. Look for trowels that have been forged or cast. Cheap trowels will bend at the tip or the handle as soon as they encounter a stubborn rock.

Bulb planter. I plant small bulbs with a trowel and large ones with a spade, but some gardeners I know feel that a bulb planter is a quick way to make a lot of holes for bulbs, all exactly the right size. Use the hand version in Figure 14 if you do not have to go too deep, but for larger bulbs like narcissus and tulips, use the long-handled model also shown there. It is used by pressing down with the foot to remove a plug of earth that you then replace over the bulb. The dibble shown in Figure 14 is for planting small bulbs or making holes to accommodate large seeds such as those of peas, corn and nasturtiums.

Spade. When I need a bigger hole than I can make with even my large trowel, I reach for either a spade or a shovel. They have slightly different uses, but first let's be clear about which is which. A spade has a relatively flat, usually rectangular blade; a shovel has a curved, scooped-out blade that can be a number of shapes, the most common being a round arc that comes to a point. For a typical spade see Figure 14; for a standard "round-point shovel" see Figure 15.

I use a spade to make holes with straight sides for planting trees, shrubs and big clumps of perennials, and to dig up those same plants in order to transplant them. I also use it to edge a bed cleanly and slice through sod, weeds and even tough shrub roots. It is the only tool that will dig up a shrub with a root ball around it, keeping the earth intact. A spade is more of a precision digger than a shovel is. It will not lift and carry soil as efficiently as a shovel will, but it can lift enough soil during planting jobs that you often do not have to change tools. If you are digging with your spade and encounter something you cannot drive the spade through with your foot, take the handle in both hands, lift the spade vertically till your hands are just above your head, and plunge the blade straight down so that it slices through the stubborn obstacle. It is amazing what you can cut through this way (see Figure 10).

In order to perform such feats a spade should have a D-shaped handle— the kind shown in Figure 14. It is also handy to have a foot rest on your spade—a narrow strip on top of the blade where you can place the sole of your boot while digging, for less wear and tear on your foot. I think a spade is important enough to warrant spending extra money for a good one and taking the time to keep it clean, oiled and sharpened.

Transplanting spade (Figure 14). This is a long, skinny version of the standard spade. It will dig a deep, steep-sided hole, and since it is narrow it will get in among tightly planted clumps where you want to disturb only the roots of the plant you are digging up.

Edging tool (Figure 14). This is handy for putting a tidy edge on a bed. It is not as heavy as a spade and will not cut as deeply, but if you have a lot of beds to edge and if neither the grass nor the earth is very hard to slice through, you might want a light tool like this on hand.

Digging fork (Figure 14). Also called a "spading fork," this tool has four heavy, flat tines and is used for loosening soil, for digging up large clumps of weeds, and for digging perennial clumps for dividing or transplanting. I reach for my fork instead of my spade when I am tilling up soil that is firmly packed. The fork tines will break up clumps more efficiently than the blade of a spade will, because the digging motion alone breaks them without any additional chopping up. I also reach for it when I want to lift a clump of plants and leave the soil behind—weeds I am getting rid of, or a plant like a day lily that I want to move bare-root. I lift the weed clump with the fork and shake it hard to make the soil fall off. (The day lily clump I lift and shake *gently*.) I keep two of these forks on hand to use back-to-back when I divide large, dense perennial clumps (page 151). It is not worth buying a cheap one, because the tines will soon get bent out of shape.

Mattock. This tool is useful for breaking up hard, stony soil that a digging fork cannot handle. It is also good for severing roots and for making planting holes, especially if you're standing on a slope, where a chopping motion is easier to make than a digging motion. There are several different kinds, but I prefer the one shown in Figure 14, which has a broad blade on one end and a pick (like that of a pickaxe) on the other. The pick will take care of extremely hard soil, and it is handy to have both tools on one handle so that you can switch back and forth if need be. (A single-bladed mattock is easier to use because it is lighter, but unfortunately they are hard to find.) The joint of head and handle is not a socket but an eye attachment (in fact the tool is very similar to one called an "eye hoe"). Make sure the handle is good and strong and fits into the eye with a good tight fit.

TOOLS FOR LIFTING

There are many lifting tools in gardening, each designed to lift materials of different textures and weights. The one essential one is a round-point shovel. Whether you need any others depends on what materials you are dealing with.

Round-point shovel (Figure 15). No manual tool moves earth quite as efficiently as this one. I use it for turning soil over, for making planting holes with rounded sides, for removing dirt that I've loosened with some other tool such as a fork or spade, and for filling in the dirt after I've put a tree or shrub into the hole. I load soil, compost, sand, gravel and other materials into a wheelbarrow with it. I use it when I am grading to move and distribute soil, which I then even out with a rake. I use it to mix together soil, fertilizer and other materials in a wheelbarrow or in a planting hole. I use it to mix concrete in a wheelbarrow and put the concrete mix where it is needed.

There are shovels with short D-handles, but I find a long-handled one the most versatile and the most comfortable to use. Once again, since this is an important tool I use all the time, I make sure that I buy a good one.

Scoop shovel. This shovel is much larger than the one described above and is squared-off rather than rounded (see Figure 15). I use it for picking up materials that are lighter and more loosely

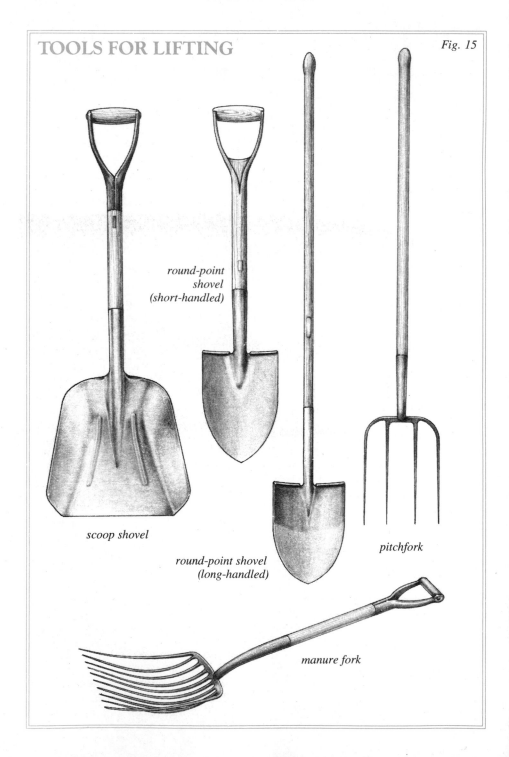

TOOLS FOR LIFTING

Fig. 15

round-point shovel (short-handled)

scoop shovel

round-point shovel (long-handled)

pitchfork

manure fork

packed than soil, such as sawdust or light, well-composted manure. It does not have a heavy, sharp blade that is angled for cutting into the ground, but it holds a lot of material, so you can move a large pile quickly with it.

Manure fork. I would not be without this tool because I like to mulch with shredded bark, and this tool is perfect for lifting it off a truck and into a wheelbarrow or onto a storage pile. I also use it to move manure that is not too fine textured and to turn the compost pile. It will not hold mulches that fall through the tines, however, such as small chips. This is why it is used to muck out horse stalls: large clumps of manure stay on the fork while you shake the finer bedding material back onto the stall floor. The more tines the fork has, the closer together they will be, and the more kinds of material you can move with it. A ten- or twelve-tine fork (Figure 15) is ideal, and can be bought at farm supply stores.

Pitchfork (Figure 15). A pitchfork with just three or four slender tines will only move something light and bulky like loose hay or straw, but it does this beautifully and lets you avoid having to wield a heavier fork. You may move loose hay for mulch only occasionally, but if you can pick up this common item for a few dollars at a yard sale it will save you some labor.

TOOLS FOR WEEDING AND CULTIVATING

You can weed your garden without having to buy any special weeding tools. In fact I will often head out to weed the garden with just a trowel for the weeds I can't pull up with my hands and a digging fork for really stubborn clumps. But there are some tools that can make the job much easier, and one of them—the hoe—I consider essential if I am growing my vegetables in rows.

Garden hoe. No garden tool comes in more shapes and sizes than the hoe, because so many specialized ones have been designed for various purposes. Often these pertain to specific crops, so that the list of available hoes almost sounds like a produce market: "onion hoe," "beet hoe," "grape hoe," "potato hoe" and so forth. Some gardeners like to own several hoes, each dedicated to a different task, but if you are going to invest in just one, the basic garden hoe is the most versatile. These vary in size and shape, but the 6-inch one shown in Figure 16 is the one I would choose. It is used for chopping annual weeds so that they can't regrow and for moving soil around in the garden. You can use it to push soil up around a plant or draw the soil away. By holding the blade at an angle you can make a furrow with the hoe in order to plant seeds. You can also cultivate the soil with it, breaking up the surface to let in air and moisture; in fact when you use a hoe you are weeding and cultivating at the same time. (If you mulch your garden you will not be able to hoe it, except when a crop is newly planted and mulch has not yet been applied.) Hoes come with short handles, but I like to work with the long ones to avoid bending over. Hoes don't get the rough treatment that some tools do, but I still buy good ones that won't bend, and I always keep them sharpened.

Scuffle hoe. Scuffle hoes come in many different shapes, but the principle on which they work is always the same. Instead of just pulling them toward you, as you do the garden hoe, you can both pull them and push them because they are sharp on two sides. To get rid of annual weeds you "scuffle" the hoe back and forth just below the soil surface, severing the weed stems. The first time I tried this hoe I knew I'd found a

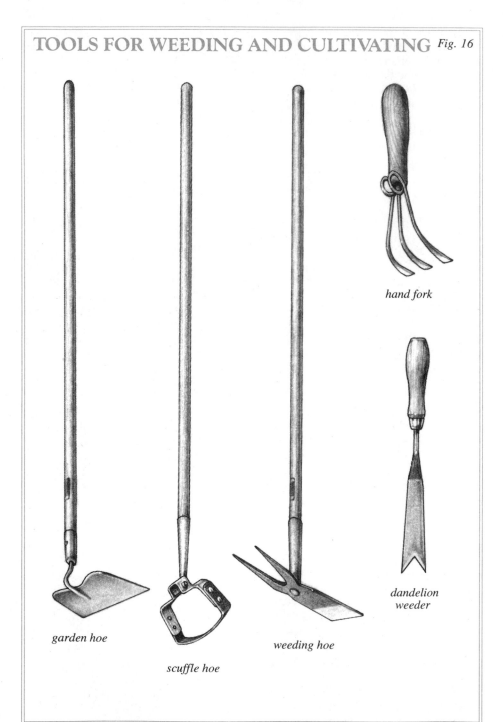

TOOLS FOR WEEDING AND CULTIVATING *Fig. 16*

hand fork

dandelion weeder

garden hoe

scuffle hoe

weeding hoe

really efficient tool. Since most scuffle hoes are not good at hilling or furrowing, you'll probably want to own a regular garden hoe as well. Most scuffle hoes look like the one in Figure 16, but others are triangular. Some are called "action hoes" and swing back and forth as you work them.

Weeding hoe (Figure 16). I grew up using this hoe, which has a hoeing blade on one end and a forked weed puller on the other. To some degree it will pull out stubborn perennial weeds by the roots (if you just chopped them they would resprout). It is an advantage to be able to do this as you encounter these weeds while hoeing and not to have to bend over and dig them out with a hand tool.

Hand fork. Also called a "hand cultivator," this tool looks like Captain Hook's right hand (Figure 16). It is for weeding and cultivating while you are kneeling or sitting on the ground. It works faster than a trowel does but less precisely; and I find it is easy to be careless with it and zap a valuable plant. Nonetheless I include it because so many people do like it, and it is always included, along with a trowel and a dandelion weeder, in sets of "essential small tools." A long-handled version with curved flat tines can be useful because it both cultivates the soil and lifts out the weeds.

Dandelion weeder. This long, skinny, notched tool (Figure 16) is also called a "dock digger," a "daisy grubber" and an "asparagus knife." It is for getting long, thin objects out of the ground in one piece, both those you don't want, such as taprooted dock and dandelion, and those you do, such as asparagus (if you want to cut the stalk below the surface). These are useful as taproot weeders only if you follow the line of the root precisely, because if you miss and cut it, it will break off and regenerate. I usually take a chance on

either pulling taprooted weeds out or digging them with a trowel, but your aim may be better than mine.

TOOLS FOR RAKING

Dragging the tines of a rake through the soil can do many things: take something out of the soil, work something into it and change the contours of it. Those tines will also remove plant debris, such as dead stems and leaves, from a bed. Rakes vary in their weight and construction according to how deep the tines need to go.

Level-head rake. The simplest kind of rake is made of steel, has a long handle and is flat on top, as shown in Figure 17. It is an important tool if you are creating new beds or lawns; use it for grading and smoothing the soil. Moving large amounts of earth is laborious with a rake, but for changing the contours by several inches the tool is highly efficient. Soil can be pulled toward you by using the rake with the tines down, or it can be pushed away from you if you keep the tines up. Bringing the tines down hard on the surface can break up compacted soil that will not yield by just drawing the rake across it. You can incorporate fertilizer or lime into the top layer of soil with a back-and-forth motion of the tines, or you can drag the rake through the soil to remove sticks, stones and even small weeds—use it to cultivate vegetable rows that are spaced far apart. Some gardeners even drag it through wide rows of seedlings to thin them.

Bow rake. This rake is just the same as the one above except that it has a bow across the top (Figure 17). I prefer the level-head rake because I can turn it upside down for finer smoothing, but some people like the springier action you get from a bow rake and say that it makes the work easier.

TOOLS FOR RAKING

Fig. 17

level-head rake

lawn rake

bow rake

Lawn rake (Figure 17). Also called a "leaf rake" or a "fan rake," this tool is usually used on grass to remove leaves, clippings or sticks that have fallen from nearby trees. But it is just as useful for clearing surface debris off the soil of a garden bed to make it look tidy after you've been working on it. It even erases handprints and footprints. It is also extremely valuable for cleaning out debris from perennial beds in fall. Lawn rakes are made of either bamboo, metal or plastic. Bamboo is the most attractive and has the most spring to it, but the strips do not last forever, even when gently used and stored under cover. The tines of metal lawn rakes get bent out of shape very easily. And both of these can come apart where the tines are joined together unless they are of very good construction, so if you buy these types, buy good ones. The plastic rakes are much more durable; the tines rarely break or bend even when used by over-zealous small boys, though the handle can get loose in the socket. I buy a plastic rake in an obnoxious shade like bright pink, so that it cannot get lost no matter where someone abandons it.

TOOLS FOR MOVING ROCKS

For me, rocks turn up most often when I am digging, so I am apt to tackle the rock first with whatever digging tool I am using, whether it's a trowel, a spade or whatever. If I can't pry it out with a spade or shovel, even after uncovering it, I'll see if I can wiggle it with a crowbar, and then I decide whether to bother getting it out. I know that if the rock wiggles it is not ledge, and I can get it out if I have to, but it is important to know when to abandon lighter tools and move on to heavier-duty ones. Digging tools can be dulled and damaged by using them as mining tools, and there are better things to use on rocks. (The mattock is an exception.)

Potato hook (Figure 18). Also called a "potato hoe," this tool is designed to lift potatoes out of the soil without scratching them. It has long, curved, hooklike tines that wrap around the potato. It is a good tool to have even if you don't grow potatoes, because it will scoop potato-sized rocks out of a garden or field.

Crowbar. A crowbar is used to pry rocks up out of the ground and roll them out of the way. It works as a lever and needs a fulcrum. If the rock is sitting at the bottom of a hole, the side of the hole can be a fulcrum, but often the best thing is to put another, smaller rock next to the one you want to move and get leverage from that. Crowbars come in different sizes; the heavier ones can lift more weight. Buy one with a chisel-shaped end (Figure 18) to help it slide underneath a rock. Unless you can't do, or prefer not to do, heavy work of this sort, a crowbar is a very handy tool to have around. It is also the perfect tool for making holes for bean poles, tomato stakes and posts for pillar roses; and holes for deep-feeding the roots of shrubs and trees. Use the smaller crowbar for this purpose, and the large, heavy kind to remove rocks.

Come-along (Figure 18). This little device will turn even the most petite gardener into Paul Bunyan. I have used it to remove huge boulders from gardens. By attaching one end of it to the rock and another to a tree or other stable object, you can winch the rock along with a lever. Rocks too large for the come-along will break its metal ropes; for them you must move up to a power winch. But ultimately, some rocks are just not worth removing! Plant around them or cover them with extra soil instead.

TOOLS FOR MOVING ROCKS   *Fig. 18*

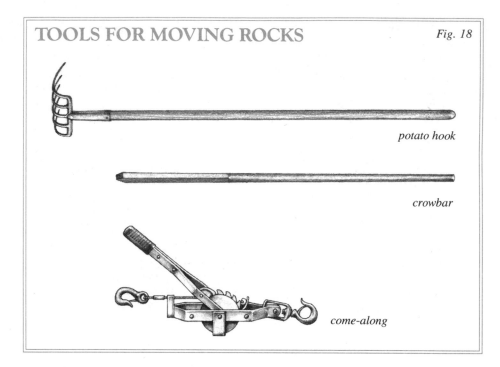

potato hook

crowbar

come-along

TOOLS FOR PRUNING AND CUTTING

This is one area where I especially like to have fine-quality tools. Cutting tools are often more complicated mechanically than the kind used for jobs like digging. Good ones can be quite expensive but if cared for properly will be your friends for life. I make sure I have a succession of implements that cut stems and branches of increasing sizes so that I don't damage any by asking them to do a job that will overtax them. Formulas that specify twig and branch diameters that these tools will cut do not take into account how an individual tool is made or the density of the stem that is being cut. Therefore pay attention to the way a tool is reacting. If it will not cut a stem without being forced, go get the tool that will cut it comfortably.

Pruning knife (Figure 19). This is a small, curved knife that folds up and can be carried easily in a gardener's pocket, taking up a lot less space than your hand pruners. It will always be there to cut off a dead twig, poke into a woody stem to look for borers, and perform a host of handy little tasks during the course of the day—if you keep it sharp. It's great for cutting dead stems off perennials and for trimming the tips of evergreens.

Hand pruners. These are among the most important tools a gardener can own. They are also called "secateurs." They cut herbaceous stems, woody twigs and small branches, and are used for such jobs as pruning roses and other shrubs, cutting back perennials, and harvesting herbs. If I were to be extravagant about only one tool, it would be this one—and good pruners *are* expensive. If you treat yourself to a good pair, get them with brightly colored handles so that you do not lose your prize.

Two kinds of pruners are generally available: the anvil type and the bypass

TOOLS FOR PRUNING AND CUTTING *Fig. 19*

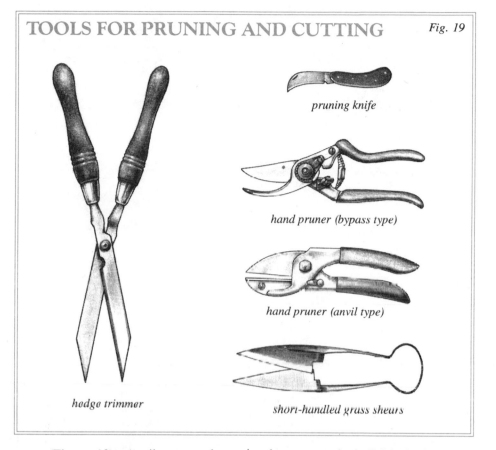

pruning knife

hand pruner (bypass type)

hand pruner (anvil type)

hedge trimmer

short-handled grass shears

type (Figure 19). Anvil pruners have one moving blade that closes against a fixed piece of softer material in the same plane. Bypass pruners have two moving blades that bypass each other just like those of scissors, except that the blades are curved. Both are good and do pretty much the same job, so you don't really need both. Gardeners usually have their preferences; I use a bypass pruner because I can get closer to the branch when I cut off a twig than I can with anvil pruners.

It is important to keep your pruners free of dirt when they're not in use and to keep them oiled. You might get into the habit of wiping them with an oily rag and hanging them up on a nail or hook whenever you have finished using them. Pruners also need to be sharpened periodically.

Loppers (Figure 20). If your hand pruner won't cut something, use long-handled pruners, also called "loppers." These are similar, but larger and heavier with two long handles. They will cut twigs and small branches of shrubs and trees. I have an ancient pair of wood-handled loppers that work fine, but I have seen new, metal-handled ones that seem sturdy and easy to use. Loppers come with both anvil and bypass blades, although I see the bypass type most often. Sometimes loppers are geared, to make them more powerful. They also come in various sizes. The smaller ones

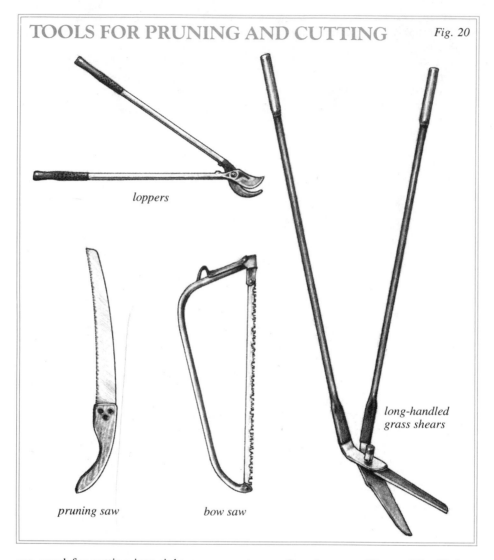

TOOLS FOR PRUNING AND CUTTING

Fig. 20

loppers

pruning saw

bow saw

long-handled grass shears

are good for getting into tight spaces—when you're pruning roses, for example. The larger ones will cut branches of greater diameter.

Bow saw (Figure 20). If my loppers can't cut a thick branch, and if there are not a lot of other branches in the way, I might reach for a bow saw—an efficient hand saw that holds the blade at two ends and will charge through quite a bit of wood quickly.

Pruning saw (Figure 20). If there are a lot of branches in my way I reach for a pruning saw, because its curved blade, held at one end by a small wooden handle, can fit in among the branches and cut effectively. I sometimes use it to cut big, tough roots that are too thick for my loppers or mattock when I am removing a stump from the ground. Pruning saws come in varying lengths from about 9 inches to well over

20. If you are a serious tree pruner you'll probably have several sizes, including one on a long pole for pruning up high.

Obviously there are branches—and trunks—beyond the capability of a pruning saw, and when you get to one, you reach for an axe or a chain saw. These two are more in the realm of woodsmanship than gardening; but a gardener should always have tools with which she or he can cut off a dead, diseased or superfluous limb from a valuable tree.

Grass shears (Figures 19 and 20). These are useful for trimming grass at the edges of lawns and flower beds, but keep them dry, rust-free, sharpened and well oiled. Both long- and short-handled shears are available. The short-handled kind shown in Figure 19 has a nice spring to it—but my advice is to try working several in the store, and see which you feel will do the job without tiring your hand. If you have a lot of trimming to do you might want to invest in battery-powered shears or even a string trimmer (page 100).

Hedge trimmers (Figure 19). These are similar to grass shears but have longer blades that can cut twigs of shrubs. They are useful if you have a hedge that must be kept within bounds, but I do not like to use them to prune shrubs. Most gardeners overuse them (page 495). They are handy for deadheading and cutting back perennials in fall, however, because you can cut more stems at a time with them than you can with hand pruners.

TOOLS FOR WATERING

Watering equipment has become so complicated that you almost need to be an engineer to understand it. I stick to the simplest devices, namely a watering can, a hose and a nozzle, but then I have the luxury of living in a climate where drought is only an occasional problem. Though I'm not an expert on waterers, I do feel I should make you aware of some of the options you have if water is a pressing need in your garden.

Watering can. I use my watering can a lot: for starting seeds indoors, for taking care of houseplants and container-grown plants on the terrace, and for planting perennial clumps or annual and vegetable seedlings in the garden. It is much easier to moisten my planting holes with the can than to uncoil several lengths of hose and drag them across the lawn. A long-spouted can will reach under plant foliage to avoid wetting it, but I find it is more apt to spill when you carry it than a short-spouted can, so I usually use that (Figure 21). I use my can most often without the rose attachment so the water will flow faster, but I put on the rose to give newly planted seeds or delicate seedlings a gentle spray.

Hose. A garden hose is like a lover that you can't live with and can't live without. No scientific advance, to my knowledge, has yet tamed its willful nature, and hoses will probably continue to knock over plants, get kinks in them and get run over by cars for as long as there are gardeners. I store mine tightly coiled on a reel that I like about as much as I like my hose. It always tips over when I unwind the hose. But there are occasions, such as spring planting and August drought fighting, when I use the hose a lot. Life with it is less of a living hell if I observe these rules: coil it up when not in use so it won't be damaged; drain it and store it indoors in winter; be especially careful not to run over or otherwise damage its couplings, since leaky couplings make the hose useless. Buy the very best rubber hose you can find. It is well worth the investment, not only because good rubber and couplings will last much longer than inferior products, but because a good hose handles better. Plastic hose is hard and won't roll up easily; it will also crack in cold weather.

Nozzles. These come in a wide variety of forms. Some are simple switches that allow you to turn the hose on or off at a distance from the faucet. Others have an adjustable spray. Others have a trigger device that gives you a very long stream. For my birthday my son gave me a nozzle that combines the spray and the trigger and locks in any position I want it to. I love it, especially when I am feeling lazy, because I can stand in one spot and give most of my vegetable garden just the right amount of water without moving an inch. Sometimes I like to use the on/off type, though, to just let water run down a row of plants. By not letting the water wet the foliage I am helping to ward off disease, and I am also delivering more water to the plants in a shorter time. There is also an excellent device called a "water wand," which emits streams of water at the end of a long pole so that you can water the soil underneath the plants' foliage without bending over. Buy good hose nozzles whenever possible.

Sprinklers. I think these are useful on lawns, but I don't advise using them in the garden because they get the foliage wet. There are many kinds, from the simple whirling device shown in Figure 21 to sprinklers that walk around your lawn by themselves. Some sprinklers rotate in a full circle, others oscillate. I like the rotating ones because I have trouble remembering which way the other kind is oscillating and invariably walk right into the spray. Some sprinklers are metal, some are plastic; either is fine as long as it is sturdy and well made.

Irrigation systems. The systems used to water large areas at a time are too varied and numerous to cover here,

but they are worth investigating if you have need of them. In some areas they mean the difference between having and not having a garden. Irrigators can be as simple as a 15-foot-long canvas soaker hose (Figure 21) that slowly leaks water into the area where you place it, or as complex as a large system of interconnecting pipes that emit little jets of water through holes or tiny nozzles. Some of these devices can be buried in the soil; others must lie on top of or under a layer of mulch. Some are very expensive; others come in kit form to cut costs and make them more adaptable to your needs. Often gardeners invent their own systems, using whatever ingenious combinations of hardware they can find. Try to find gardeners who have different irrigators and go watch them in action before you invest in an elaborate system. Not only will you learn what type of system will best fill your needs, but you will be alerted to brands that really work and those that are not worth their price.

Sprayers. Whether you believe in using chemical sprays in your garden or not, you will probably need to own some kind of sprayer. In choosing one, consider the volume of spray you need to use and the kind of stream you want the sprayer to deliver. The simplest type is just a pump bottle—for this you can use an empty window-cleaner bottle. The old-fashioned "flit-gun" type will also deliver an atomized spray efficiently. For larger jobs you can use either a trombone sprayer, which you operate by sticking one end in a bucket of solution you have mixed and then spray, or a compressed-air sprayer, which forces water out in a stream because you have compressed the air inside with a pump. Some of these can be carried on your back. There are even power sprayers, though these are far beyond the needs of the average gar-

TOOLS FOR WATERING

Fig. 21

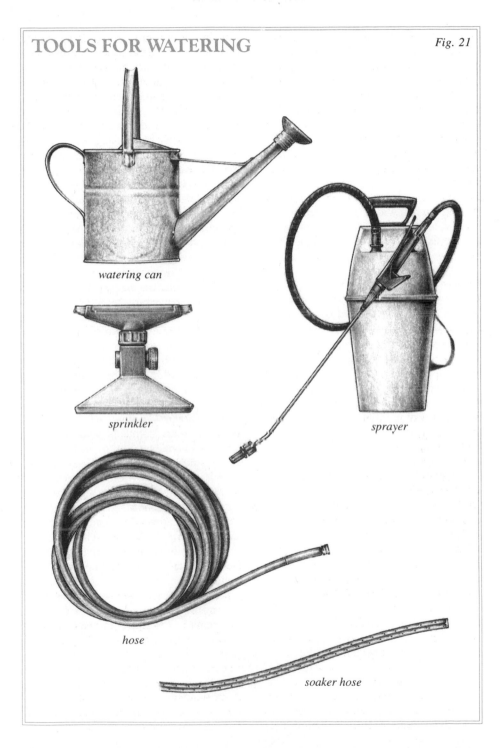

watering can

sprinkler

sprayer

hose

soaker hose

dener. I recommend either the window-cleaner bottle or a compressed-air sprayer like the one in Figure 21, with whatever capacity suits your needs—usually anywhere from 1½ to 5 gallons. Remember when you choose that even 1 gallon of water weighs 8 pounds and is heavy to carry around. If you want to spray something at a distance (up in a tree, for example) and hit it with deadly accuracy, get a trombone sprayer; but always be careful not to loosen the tip too much when you adjust the spray. As I know from experience, nothing is worse than shooting your sprayer tip right into a bed of poison ivy.

TOOLS FOR HAULING

Gardening always involves moving around a lot of bulky and/or heavy materials: soil, compost, heavy bags of lime, large bags of peat, rocks, gravel, big piles of weeds, tools. It is important to have something to carry them in that you will feel comfortable using. The two most common devices available are wheelbarrows and carts. Each has slightly different uses and virtues, as you will find if you are lucky enough to own both. But most of us must choose which one will do the most for us.

Wheelbarrow (Figure 22). A wheelbarrow's greatest virtue is its maneuverability. Because it has only a single wheel, you can guide it along a narrow path, around obstacles, even along a plank laid over a muddy spot or leading up into the bed of a truck. You can mix soil in it, even concrete for jobs like sinking gate posts. You can load all your tools, fertilizers and pots or flats of plants into the wheelbarrow and then head for the garden. I have always used a metal contractor's wheelbarrow with a 4½-cubic-foot capacity. I recently tried out a friend's plastic version of the same thing and found it lighter than mine,

though sturdy, so you might like to try that one. But I do recommend buying a professional-quality barrow rather than a "garden" model unless you have a small yard or cannot wheel heavy loads. Be on guard that equipment geared to the homeowner rather than the professional is often of less sturdy construction. A 5½-cubic-foot wheelbarrow may be the answer if you are stronger than I am, but I find that I cannot wheel it easily if it is full of anything heavy.

Two-wheeled cart (Figure 22). A large, box-shaped wooden cart will allow you to carry a much larger, heavier load than a wheelbarrow will, because the weight is distributed over the two wheels. There are many of these carts on the market now, and they are extremely popular. You can fit a great deal more of bulky matter, such as leaves or bales of mulch hay, in a cart than you can in a wheelbarrow. The disadvantages: most of them are harder to dump with, so you may have to shovel out your load when you arrive at your destination (though some models have fold-down or removable sides). And carts are far less maneuverable than wheelbarrows, since you have to get those big wheels and that big box around things. They are also inconvenient, if not downright hazardous, on steep ground. I once put a load of gravel in a garden cart and headed downhill with it. The load felt deceptively light on level ground, but on the incline the center of gravity shifted suddenly and the cart literally ran away from me. With a wheelbarrow, a load that would take it down the hill would also make it too tippy on level ground, so you would be less likely to make the mistake of overfilling it. You cannot mix concrete in a wooden cart, but you can get a lot of working gear in it to take to the garden, and you can use it as a nice flat work station when you get there. It even makes a good potting

TOOLS FOR HAULING

Fig. 22

wheelbarrow

two-wheeled cart

bench. There are also many smaller garden carts on the market, many of them plastic or metal. But beware of flimsy construction, and buy a small, light-weight cart only if you are doing very light hauling.

Baskets and buckets. Alas, they don't make as many peck baskets, bushel baskets and bean baskets as they used to. They are my favorite containers for picking up weeds and for other tasks where I want a light, not-too-large container. Modern life has its plusses though, such as plastic containers, 2-gallon size and up, to keep fertilizers and other supplies in. Sooner or later all paper sacks rip, or get wet and disintegrate, especially if your storage area has

a damp floor. I try to remember to put the sacks into a suitable plastic container *before* this happens. Plastic tubs and buckets are also good for making potting-soil mixes or mixing up batches of liquid fertilizer. I also use them for carrying just the amount of dry fertilizer I need out to the garden, so I don't have to put the whole bag in the wheel-barrow.

Power Equipment

I am the kind of gardener who prefers hand tools to power tools. They don't make a loud noise and vibrate; they are simple to use and take care of; they are less expensive to buy and repair. If properly chosen, hand tools make work lighter—but not so light that I don't get the good physical exercise that is one of my reasons for gardening. I've built up some strong muscles from years as a gardener, all from using hand tools.

But there are times when a power tool can save so much tedious work that even I break down and use them. I used to mow the lawn with a hand-pushed reel mower, cut down trees with an axe, and saw up the logs with a bow saw. But those jobs were taking too great a percentage of my time, so I switched to a power lawn mower and chainsaw, even though I can't say I really enjoy using either. For some reason the only pull-start device I can operate with ease is a lettuce spinner.

Selecting power equipment for the garden is a tricky matter that is beyond the scope of this book. If there is something you think you need, make a research project out of acquiring it: talk to fellow amateur gardeners and also to professionals who might be familiar with the equipment. Talk to a number of dealers, compare prices and gather as much technical information as you can in order to make an intelligent purchase. Here are a few brief comments about which machines are most useful to the gardener.

Lawn mower. If you want to mow your own lawn, invest in a *good* power mower. They are made in an enormous range of sizes and prices these days, from the simplest rotary mower to big ride-on lawn tractors that can perform other jobs as well, depending on what attachments you buy for them, such as tillers and brush hogs. Even small walk-behind mowers have extra features, such as baggers to collect clippings, and many are self-propelled. Some even float on a cushion of air like a hover-craft, and thereby avoid obstacles such as rocks and edgings. My advice is that if you have a choice between a good mower with few extras and an economy machine with many of them, choose the first. The self-propelling mechanism on a cheap machine will wear out quickly, and this applies to other features as well.

String trimmer. This handy tool is a pole with a small engine at your end (although sometimes the engine is at the bottom) and a string made out of tough plastic monofilament at the other. The string whips around at high speed, cutting grass and weeds. The machine works efficiently and weighs only about 10 pounds. It is great for edging lawns or just keeping weeds down for a tidy look. Don't use it close to tree trunks, especially young ones; it can nick and even girdle the trunks, thereby damaging or killing the trees. A larger version of this tool cuts brush, sometimes with a nylon string, sometimes with a circular-saw blade, but it is more dangerous and should be used with great caution.

Rotary tiller. These machines are becoming almost standard equipment for people with large vegetable gardens and even for those who do a lot of yard work. They have revolving tines that can cultivate the soil to varying depths— anywhere from a few inches to a foot, depending on the condition of the soil and the size of the tiller. With most you can adjust the depth of cultivation. Some have a hilling and furrowing attachment, which is handy at planting time. Their chief uses are for tilling a garden in preparation for planting and for incorporating lime, fertilizer and organic matter into the soil. They are also good for turning under cover crops (page 27) and can be useful in breaking up the soil for new lawns. The best rototillers have the tines in back and are operated by standing off to the side. This way neither the wheels nor your feet compact the soil after tilling.

I have used rototillers quite a bit and have liked them, but I have also discovered their limitations. Contrary to what most people believe, the tiller is not an effective machine for creating a new bed, especially if there are weeds and sod growing on the site. It does not cultivate deeply enough, and it breaks up the roots of perennial weeds and grasses, which only makes more of them come up. If tillers are overused they can pulverize the soil too finely, destroy its structure and cause organic matter to be used up too quickly—though I do not think this is enough of a danger to preclude using a tiller altogether. With all this in mind, you may decide that this is a machine to rent, borrow or share, rather than rush out and buy only to have it not earn its keep.

Shredder. Zealous composters love this machine. They can chop up materials such as leaves and thereby greatly speed up decomposition. There are both electric and gasoline-powered models. Ones big enough to really do the job are noisy, expensive, and take up enough storage space to make you wonder if they are worth the use they get—often just a week or two in autumn at leaf time. But since good compost is such a valuable thing to have, you might consider renting a shredder in fall or sharing the purchase cost with several other people.

Other Aids

There are a multitude of items to be found in gardeners' tool sheds in addition to tools, some of them essential, some of them necessary only for specific gardening situations you may or may not encounter—netting to keep birds off fruit, for example. Others, such as devices for starting seeds, are dealt with in other chapters of this book.

Some are items that, while essential to the gardener, are really part of the carpenter's or household-tool department, such as a 100-foot tape (Figure 23) for measuring beds, scissors to take out to the garden to snip twine for tying tomatoes—and to snip off a few ripe tomatoes while you're at it—or a broom to sweep off the flagstones after you've messed them up by weeding. A "garden line" or "planting line" (a pointed piece of metal with a long cord attached) is also helpful for laying out nice straight rows.

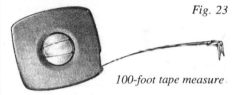

Fig. 23

100-foot tape measure

You will no doubt accumulate your own collection of miscellaneous paraphernalia. I find that I do try to keep my own collection rather sparse. Catalogs arrive with hundreds of suggestions about "gardening aids you cannot do without," most of them expensive, brightly colored and made of plastic. I usually flip through the catalog and decide I can do without all of them. My advice is: keep gardening simple. Buy a few good implements and treat them well.

Maintaining and Storing Garden Gear

Taking care of tools means not leaving them out in the rain, cleaning the dirt off them when you have finished using them and oiling them all over to keep metal parts from rusting, mechanisms moving smoothly and wooden handles from deteriorating. Gardeners use various kinds of oil; motor oil is as good as anything. Either keep an oil-soaked rag handy for wiping tools, or fill a plastic bucket with sand mixed with a quart of oil. Dip metal tools in it after use to clean and oil them at the same time.

Tools, from hand pruners to spades and hoes, will also do a faster, cleaner job if they are sharpened from time to time. Use a hand file for most tools, drawing it repeatedly across the side of the tool that is making the cut. (In the case of a hoe, this would be the side facing you as you work.) Look at the blade first to see which side was sharpened originally (sometimes both sides

ORGANIZING YOUR STORAGE AREA

are sharpened) and at what angle. For cutting tools such as pruners, a whetstone is best. I use a hand file and stone, but a friend of mine has told me that his electric grindstone was well worth the investment for keeping his tools in working order.

Power equipment should always be stored out of the weather and kept clean and dry. At the end of the season, machines like lawn mowers and rotary tillers should be run until they are out of gas, their spark plugs should be disconnected, and they should be thoroughly cleaned. It is also a good time to make minor repairs, sharpen blades, change the oil and replace air filters.

Wheelbarrows and carts should go under cover. If you ever have to keep them outdoors in rain or snow, upend them so that water does not sit in them and rust the metal or rot the wood.

It is much easier to take care of tools when you have a good place to store them. If you have a large tool shed or a spacious area in your garage where you can put them, all the better; but even a tiny shed or corner of the garage can work if you organize it well. You can get by with just a pegboard or row of nails from which to hang small hand tools, and a barrel to stick long-handled tools into—handle down and working end up, for quick identification. Figure 24 shows how a modest-sized storage area might be organized by putting long tools in a barrel, and hanging tools with a D-grip on the wall and small tools on a pegboard. The workbench provides a surface for jobs like marking plant labels, sorting packages of seeds, even starting seeds in flats without having to bring the mess indoors. Shelves underneath it provide space for pots, fertilizers and other supplies. And there is space on the floor where bagged supplies can sit upright in their plastic containers. If the area is large enough to accommodate big items like lawn mowers, all the better.

Fig. 24

What to Wear

Only a woman would bring this up, right? Wrong. In my experience male gardeners are forever discussing the best boot, the best pants. The best gardening clothing for you is just as much a matter of personal taste as the best tools, and you'll end up wearing what feels comfortable.

Boots. Good, sturdy work boots with leather soles are long lasting and are the best to wear if you are out spading all day; the spading will be easier on the soles of your feet. But boots with rubber feet and high leather tops feel better if it's wet or cold. And sneakers feel right if it's hot and you're not spading a lot.

Pants. Heavy-duty cotton trousers sold as "work pants" are probably sensible—they are sturdy and long wearing. Overalls have nice big pockets to put things like pruners or fence staples in, but I've given up on overalls mainly because you have to undo the straps to shed an extra sweater or shirt, and if you wear those on top you have to shed them to get to the straps. I admit I'm the most comfortable in my worn-out Calvins, or in old corduroys that are soft and supple from many washings.

Shirts. In my New England climate gardeners wear layers of clothing because the temperature can change so drastically during the course of the day. I might start out wearing a tee shirt, a flannel shirt, a sweatshirt or sweater and maybe even an old parka on top of that, then shed all but the tee shirt as the sun, and my work, heat me up. (Though even in heat you might choose to leave on a long-sleeved shirt as protection against thorns, poison ivy, sunburn and stinging insects.)

Hats. Many gardeners like to wear a big-brimmed hat for shade. A wide hat also discourages gnats, because they don't like to come under the brim. A bandana helps to keep hair off your face, and you can soak it in water to keep your head cool when it is very hot.

Gloves. Gardening gloves (Figure

Fig. 25

gardening gloves

25) are essential. They keep your hands from getting rubbed raw from very long, hard jobs, and are crucial if you are dealing with thorny plants like roses and scratchy ones like junipers. Leather gloves give you the most protection, but lightweight cotton ones that fit your hands neatly are best for weeding. If you prune a lot of prickly shrubs, buy a pair of heavy fabric gloves long enough to cover your wrists, with leather palms and fingertips.

Frankly I hate to wear gloves, because they're hot and because I garden so much by feel: how the soil texture feels, how moist the soil is, what a plant's root system feels like. But there are times when I want to keep my hands and nails clean or avoid poison ivy, and then I force myself to work in gloves.

(An important note about poison ivy: all parts of the plant are poisonous, even the roots, and at any time of the year. Even dead leaves will give you the rash. Poison ivy's irritating oil will stay on your gloves, shoes, pants, shirt and tools, so handle all these with as much caution as the plant itself if you have been working in a spot where it is growing. Many people think their rash is spreading when they are just reinfecting themselves every day by putting on contaminated gloves or sneakers.)

Whatever clothes you wear for gardening, be aware that they will be permanently grubby, and that you really need a separate wardrobe for gardening and other outside chores. Getting dirty just goes with the territory.

CHAPTER 4

HOW TO BUY PLANTS

You've decided what kinds of gardens you want and where you want to put them. You've gained some understanding of how plants grow, where they need help, and what kind of equipment you need to give them that help. You've prepared your soil, and now you're actually ready to go out and buy those plants and seeds and see them through life.

This is where you can get a case of cold feet. All along I've been saying, "Choose the right plant" for your climate; "Choose the right plant" for your soil type; "Choose the right plant" for the setting. You have some idea of what to buy. But now it's real life, and you're standing in a crowded nursery surrounded by green leaves, and they all look alike, except that they have different labels on them, mostly in Latin.

Plant Names

Threading your way through the nursery circus needn't be a nightmare, and I'll give you a brief Survivor's Guide to plant nurseries in a minute; but first a few words about those Latin names, because there they are, and ignoring them won't make them go away. In fact they are very useful and can save you a lot of trouble. If you only grow basic vegetables and fruits you will come across Latin names much less often than you will if you grow ornamental plants; nevertheless, plant nomenclature is worth understanding. All the plant descriptions in this book give Latin names as well as common names and can be used as a reference when you are planning your garden. (In many cases the Latin name has become the most common way to identify the plant.) Knowing both will help you know exactly what you're getting.

A plant's botanical name usually consists of two Latin words written in italics. The first designates the "genus" (plural, "genera") to which the plant belongs—a group of plants with similar characteristics. The second designates the plant's "species"—a smaller group within the genus. The species name usually describes one outstanding characteristic of the plants in that group.

For example, let's take a familiar plant, the Johnny-jump-up. Its common name suits it well, because after going to seed it jumps up all over your garden. Its Latin name, *Viola tricolor,* tells you that it belongs to the genus *Viola* and that its species name is *tricolor,* describing its petals, which are marked with three colors: blue, white and yellow.

Since few of us speak Latin, why not stick with a perfectly good name like Johnny-jump-up? While that might work fine for Johnny-jump-up, it gets confusing when a plant has several names. For example, *Monarda didyma* is commonly known as bee balm, or bergamot or Oswego tea. *Stachys lanata* is variously called lamb's ears, woolly betony and Saviour's flannel. And for an even more complicated example, consider the common purple lilac. Its botanical name is *Syringa vulgaris.* But there is another plant, a shrub with fragrant white flowers, whose common name is sometimes "syringa" (I don't know why) and sometimes "mock orange" (because the flowers look and smell like orange blossoms). It is neither a lilac nor an orange, and its Latin genus name is *Philadelphus.* If you went shopping for what you called "syringa" (meaning *Philadelphus*), you might end up buying a lilac by mistake, since the plant could well be labeled with its Latin name, *Syringa.*

The best way to avoid muddles like these when you go to buy a plant is to call it by the name that does not vary—the Latin one—or at least have it handy should any confusion arise. (Sometimes, indeed, Latin names change too, because botanists do not always agree on them either, but this does not happen often.) You may feel awkward or downright pretentious using Latin names, but they will save you from getting the wrong plant. A rose by any other name may smell as sweet, but if you are not careful it may turn out to be a hellebore (if it's a "Christmas rose") or a hibiscus (if it's a "rose of Sharon").

And what is *Syringa vulgaris*? A "vulgar lilac"? Actually, *vulgaris* just means "common" or "ordinary." A friend of mine is still kidding me about the "vulgar plant" I put in his garden—*Calluna vulgaris,* or common heather. For some other species names and their English translations, see page 108.

Sometimes the genus and species names are followed by a third denoting a "variety" within the species. A variety is a subdivision of a species composed of plants that differ from other members of the species in minor ways. For example, *Syringa vulgaris alba* is a white variety of common lilac. There can even be a fourth name, denoting a "subvariety," as in *Chamaecyparis pisifera* 'Filifera Aurea': gold-thread false cypress, or, more fully, "plant looking like (*Chaemae-*) cypress (*-cyparis*) that is pea bearing (*pisifera*), threadlike (filifera) and gold (aurea)."

Hybrids and Cultivars

If the variety name of a plant is in Latin, it has appeared naturally without human intervention from plants cross-pollinating in the wild or from the appearance of a mutation. But if the variety is a non-Latin name, capitalized and in single quotes, as in *Syringa vulgaris* 'President Lincoln,' it was produced by human intervention and is thus a cultivated variety, or cultivar. Sometimes cultivars are created by cross-pollinating (hybridizing) two or more unlike species or cultivars possessing different traits to produce another, and other times by finding a mutant specimen with unusual characteristics and propagating it by dividing plants or by taking cuttings and rooting them.

The propagation of plants to obtain new varieties is a complex topic, but there are some simple things in this regard that it is useful for the shopper to know. The human hand has produced thousands of new plants that not only grow better in our gardens but also make gardening more fun. Some, such as rust-proof asparagus, have been developed to resist specific diseases. Others better withstand climatic problems—for example, spinach that thrives even when it's hot, and tomatoes that set fruit even when it's cold. We have created giant fruits and flowers and miniature fruits and flowers. We search for colors never found in nature, as in the elusive blue rose, and even for the absence of color, as in the quest for the white marigold or white day lily—surely a search as long and obsessive as Captain Ahab's. I'll discuss some of the new varieties I consider outstanding in the chapters dealing with individual plants.

CULTIVARS VS. SPECIES

A wild plant from which garden cultivars have been derived is often referred to as "the species." The common lilac I mentioned is a good example of a species that is still as familiar as the named varieties it has produced. Usually this is not the case. Hybrid roses, for example, are more familiar to us than most species of wild rose.

Species plants vary greatly in their suitability to the garden. In vegetables hybrids are almost always considered an

Guide to Botanical Names

The following list contains some of the common Latin (and occasionally Greek) descriptive words found in plant names, with their translations. The endings may vary; for example, words ending in *-a* can also end in *-us,* those ending in *-is* can also end in *-e.* But you'll always be able to recognize the root word, which stays the same.

aestivalis—of summer
alba—white
alpinus—alpine
alta—tall
amara—bitter
amethystina—violet
angustifolia—narrow-leaved
annua—annual
aquifolia—sharp-leaved
arborea—treelike
arenaria—of sandy places
argentea—silver
armata—armed
arvensis—of the fields
atropurpurea—dark purple-red
aurantica—orange
aurea—gold
auriculata—with ears
australis—southern
autumnalis—of autumn
azurea—sky blue
baccata—berrylike
barbata—barbed or bearded
biennis—biennial
blanda—mild, pleasant
borealis—northern
caerulea—blue
caesia—blue-gray
caespitosa—tufted
campanulata—bell-shaped
campestris—of the fields
canadensis—of the New World
candida—white
capitata—headlike
cardinalis—red

centifolia—many-leaved
cerea—waxy
chinensis—of China
chrysos—gold
cilians—fringed
cinerea—light gray
citrina—yellow
citriodorus—lemon-scented
coccinea—scarlet red
coelestina—sky blue
compacta—compact
concolor—of one color
conferta—crowded
conica—cone-shaped
contorta—twisted
cordata—heart-shaped
cordifolia—with heart-shaped leaves
cornuta—horned
coronata—crowned
crassa—thick, fleshy
cristata—crested
crocea—yellow
cruenta—bloody
cyanea—blue
damosa—bushy
decumbens—lying down
decussata—at right angles
disticha—with two rows
divaricata—spreading
diversa—varying
edulis—edible
elata—tall
elegans—slender, elegant
excelsa—tall
eximia—distinguished
fastigiata—compactly erect
filifera—slender, thread-like

flabellata—fan-shaped
flava—yellow
flore pleno—with double flowers
floribunda—flowering freely
foetida—strong- or ill-smelling
fragrans—fragrant
glauca—grayish white
glomerata—clustered
gracilis—slender
granda—large, showy
grandiflora—large-flowered
helix—twisting
herbacea—herbaceous, not woody
heterophylla—with leaves of different shapes
hortensis—of gardens
hyemalis—of winter
incana—gray
insularis—of islands
intermedia—intermediate in color, shape, habit
lacianata—fringed or jagged
lactiflora—white-flowered
laevigata—smooth
lanata—woolly
lanceolata—lance-shaped
lancifolia—spear-shaped
latifolia—broad-leaved
liana—climbing
lignea—woody
littoralis—of the shore
lobata—lobed
lutea—yellow-orange
maculata—spotted

marginalis—margined
maritima—of the sea
meleagris—spotted
microphylla—small-leaved
minor—small
mollis—soft, hairy
montana—of the mountains
moschata—musk-scented
mucronata—pointed
multiflora—many-flowered
mutabile—changeable
nana—dwarf
nigra—black
nivalis—white, or growing near snow
nivea—white
nodulosa—with nodules
nummularia—round, coin-shaped
nutans—nodding
obtusa—blunt, flattened
occidentalis—western
odorata—fragrant
officinalis—medicinal, of the apothecaries
orientalis—eastern
palustris—of swamps
paniculata—with loosely branched flowers
parvifolia—small-leaved
patens—open-formed, spreading
patula—spreading
pendula—weeping, hanging
perennis—perennial
pilosa—shaggy
pinnata—feather-shaped
pisifera—pea-bearing

platyphylla—broad-leaved
plena—full, double
plicata—with pleated petals
plumaria—plumed
plumosa—feathery
praecox—early
praestans—excellent
pratensis—of meadows
procumbens—trailing
procurrens—extending
prostrata—prostrate
pulchra—beautiful
pulsatilla—shaking in the wind
pumila—dwarf, small
punctata—dotted
pungens—sharp, pointed
pura—pure, clean
purpurea—purple
pusila—small and insignificant
pyramidalis—conical
quinquefolia—with five leaflets
radicans—rooting as it creeps
regalis—stately, regal
repens—creeping
reptans—creeping
reticulata—veined, netted
riparia—of river banks
rivala, rivalara—of brooks
rosea—rose-colored
rotundifolia—round-leaved
rubra—red
rufus—ruddy
rugosa—wrinkled
rupestris—growing on rocks

saccharata—sweet
sacramentosa—having long runners
sagittalis—arrow-shaped
salicifolia—with willow-like leaves
sanguinea—red
saxatilis—living among rocks
scaber—rough
scariosa—thin, shriveled
sempervirens—everliving or evergreen
serpyllum—mat-forming
simplex—undivided
speciosa—showy
spectabilis—spectacular
spicata—spiked
spinulosa—spiny
spuria—false
stelleriana—starlike
stolonifera—with rooted runners
suffruticosa—shrubby
superba—magnificent
tectorum—of roofs
tenua—thin
tormentosa—woolly, hairy
uliginosa—of marshy places
variegata—irregularly colored
vegetus—of vigorous growth
verna—of spring
vernalis—of summer
verticallata—arranged in a whorl
violetta—violet-colored
viscaria—with sticky stems

improvement over the species. Most have undergone extensive hybridization for productivity, hardiness, and good flavor. Even "heirloom" vegetable varieties are hybrids that were bred long ago, not original species.

Among ornamental plants original species are more commonly grown than they are among vegetables, but they are still far less available than cultivars. Only occasionally does the flower gardener have a choice, though some cultivars are closer to the original species than others. Often the choice is simply a matter of taste. For instance, I prefer the red-and-yellow columbine (*Aquilegia canadensis*) that is native to the eastern United States, to the showy hybrids that never survive even a year in my garden. I like single hollyhocks (*Alcea rosea*), which are old-fashioned cultivars, better than the modern "powder puff" doubles that collapse of their own weight when it rains, then lie on the ground like soggy Kleenex.

Species plants are often more fragrant than hybrids as well, an example being the tall white *Nicotiana alata*. The fragrance has almost been bred out of many modern rose and sweet pea varieties in favor of size and color variation. Some heliotropes, plants once prized for their sweet scent, now have no fragrance at all. On the other hand I am always delighted to find a hybrid aster that doesn't flop or is especially hardy in my zone. I suppose what I like best is the chance to explore both species and hybrids, to see what is new and better each year but at the same time to keep an eye out for original species or great-but-forgotten hybrids that have become newly available.

As indicated above, original species are not easy to come by. Often you can only obtain them by mail order, and often only as seeds. But another advantage of original species is that you can save their seeds and grow plants that will "breed true," or be similar to their parents. (Seeds from most hybrids revert to something unpredictable.) Species seeds are a fine gift to pass from gardener to gardener.

Where to Buy Plants

N ow for the actual shopping. The best way to buy plants is almost always to go to a well-established nursery that guarantees its plants and actually grows much of its own stock. It can be a large nursery or a tiny one; the important thing is the quality of its plants. Ask the proprietors if they grow their own. Most places "buy in" at least some of their material either because of crop failures or because it is hard to grow everything for which there is a demand unless you sell a very specialized range of plants. But if you do find a place where the owner is a grower, the chances are good that she or he can give you more dependable, disease-free plants and will be more knowledgeable about them. Most nursery owners, to one degree or another, do know Latin names and can discuss the relative merits of different varieties. Even if the person who waits on you is there for brawn and not expertise, the owner or manager of a nursery is usually on hand to shed light on any mysteries.

Today plants seem to be sold everywhere—supermarkets, discount houses, roadside stands—as well as nurseries and garden centers. They often cost less at places like supermarkets than they do in nurseries, and like most people I sometimes toss a box of petunias or an African violet into my grocery cart along with the chicken parts and yogurt. Often as not supermarket plants work out fine, but you have to know what to look for (see below). Even if they have been well grown, plants in the supermarket are at the mercy of the produce staff who may not water them regularly. The azaleas and roses standing outside next to the shopping carts may or may not be hardy in your region, and no one is likely to know whether they are or aren't. Nevertheless, it is sometimes worth giving them a try—if they are labeled as a variety that you know, and if they look like healthy, bushy plants.

One kind of place where I tend to trust the plants is a church fair or benefit plant sale. Plants at such affairs are usually grown by local people—good gardeners who either are standing right there or can be found if you have a question. Garden clubs and plant societies are also good places to swap plants and knowledge with other gardeners.

What to Look for

You might have to poke around nurseries for a while before you feel confident about judging the quality of the plants you see, but if you look closely you can easily tell what to avoid:

Plants with yellowed leaves. A number of things can cause yellowing, all of them bad.

Plants with wilted leaves. A good watering might perk them up. *Might.* But you don't know if they've been neglected often, thus permanently weakening the plant.

Tall, spindly plants. Whether you are buying annuals, perennials or shrubs, you generally want compact, bushy plants with many stems. Taller is usually not better and often indicates that the plant suffered from lack of light during growth, was not pinched or pruned enough, or has been growing in a pot for too long.

Plants in bloom. Many nurseries display these most prominently, because blooming plants lure the most buyers. But if you have a choice between a plant in flower and one that hasn't bloomed or even budded yet, choose the latter. Dormant shrubs and trees, perennials a few inches high or barely showing, and annuals no more than 6 inches high are all preferable. Let them do their growing in your garden, not in nursery pots.

Signs of bugs or diseases. Look for insect bodies, stickiness, oddly distorted leaves or crowns, blackened areas, mushy or rotten places, spots, blotches, streaks, holes or jagged bites taken out of the leaves. Not only will the plants have been weakened by the problem, but the insect or disease may spread to other plants in your garden.

Weeds in the pots. These are robbing the plant of water and food and show general neglect by the nursery.

Potbound plants with roots crawling out of the bottom of the pots. These are often starved, and may contain girdling roots that have wound their way around the pot as they grew and can strangle the main root years later.

Plants with little, undeveloped roots. These plants will come out of the pot if you pull only slightly. If you can choose between a plant that has been in the pot awhile and a plant that was potted yesterday, choose the former.

Nicks, scars and cracks in woody trunks and stems. These may have weakened the plant, can let in disease, and show general neglect.

Balled plants where the ball is dry or damaged. Balled-and-burlapped trees and shrubs must be kept watered and handled very carefully. If the ball of earth is broken up so that it feels like a bag of loose soil when you tip it, never buy the plant. The roots will surely have suffered and are a poor risk for transplanting.

Taking Your Plants Home

Make sure you have a good level place on the floor or in the trunk of your car where the plants can sit upright without their tops bending over. Wear something you can get dirty (plant shopping is just an extension of gardening), and bring newspaper to put under the plants. If you are carrying them in the bed of a truck, put the plants near the cab, out of the wind, or better yet put a tarp over them to protect them from drying and breaking, especially if it is a long ride home. If you must tilt the tall plants, lean them toward the rear of the truck. Leaning with, not against the wind, they will be less battered.

Try to have sites chosen and planting areas ready for the new plants before you go shopping, so that they do not sit around for a long time unplanted. People often buy too much at one time, just because good plants are so hard to resist. If you must hold plants over, set them in shade or semishade. Put them close to the hose so that you can keep pots and root balls well moistened. Piling mulch around balled plants helps to keep them from drying out.

Mail-Order Plants

Shopping by mail is an acceptable alternative once you know a little more about what you want. The best reason to order by mail is that a greater variety of plants is available to you, especially after you have amassed a good collection of catalogs. (See the list of Mail-Order Sources beginning on page 618.) You can also buy very young plants in quantity and save money.

Read the plant descriptions in the catalogs very carefully. It is important to know not only the Latin names of the plants you are ordering, but something about their age and size as well. The more reputable the supplier, the more it will tell you about its plants. If perennials are described as "seedlings" or "cuttings," expect something much smaller than plants that are called "large divisions." Among woody plants, "one-year grafts" will be smaller than "two-year-old plants." Specific plants sometimes have their own terminologies. A peony division might be described as having "three eyes" or "five eyes." New shoots will emerge for each eye, and the five-eyed division will be a larger, more expensive plant than the three-eyed. Sometimes the size of the pot it comes in will be the key piece of information in determining the size of a mail-order plant: "2¼-inch," "4-inch," and so on.

The plants that arrive in the mail will usually be dormant, because that is the best way to ship most of them. That's fine, since it is best to plant them at this stage, anyway; there will be less transplanting shock than there would be if plants had grown stems or leafed out. But be prepared for something that may look rather insignificant at first. I once ordered a hundred young rugosa rose plants for a client's hedge, knowing they would make a fine show eventually. I could wrap one hand around the whole bundle. Planted, the roses looked like a row of little sticks—*if* you got up close. If you moved back a few steps they were completely invisible. "They grow really fast," I reassured neighbors passing by. At the end of the day I had fears that my client would feel a little shortchanged, and I decided I had better give her some older plants. The next day I dug up the sticks, planted them at my own house, and at my client's I put in a row of 2½-foot potted roses that were bushy and leafed out. Some were even starting to bloom. That night I got phone calls asking me where I had gotten the Amazing Fast-Growing Rose, and although I told everyone the whole tale, I fear I still bask in some undeserved glory on that street. The "sticks" at home did well and caught up to the others, but it took a few years.

Try to place your mail order well before planting time, to be sure of getting the varieties you want. Usually the nursery will ship at the best time to plant what you have ordered; sometimes they will ask you to specify a date when you will be there to receive the plants.

Some mail-order companies do a great job of packing, some don't, and you may not be able to predict this in advance. Usually plants are shipped bare-root—i.e., without soil. When you get your order it is important to open the package right away, water the plants and either plant them or store them in the proper way. For bare-root woody plants, heel them into the ground (page 49) and keep them watered until you can plant them. For herbaceous plants it is usually best to pot them up in compost or in rich, light soil and set them outdoors in semishade to harden them off (get them used to outdoor conditions) for a week or two before you plant them. Protect any tender, new growth from the burning sun. Then plant them along with their new compost or soil after they have made some growth. They appreciate the easy transition.

The biggest drawback to mail ordering is the exaggerated claims made by many of the catalogs, both in their pictures and their text. The giant blossoms in heightened colors, the hedges spilling over with thousands of blooms, could only have been photographed on a distant planet discovered by the Starship *Enterprise*. Sometimes catalog plants have made-up names, presumably more evocative than the real ones, common *or* botanical, that leave you guessing. (Just what is "Golden Twinkles," anyway?) This is more of a problem in the big, soup-to-nuts catalogs than in those of the smaller, more specialized nurseries; but I look through all of them and sometimes turn up a real find even among those gaudy pages.

Much of plant shopping is trial and error, but it does help you to learn about plants, and it can also be fun. In addition to nurseries, there are many places to learn about new plants by actually seeing them: friends' gardens; botanical gardens and arboreta; public parks and private gardens that are at times open to the public; flower shows and other exhibitions. Also try to notice plants when you travel. Often things that are common or even weeds in a distant place are exotic specimens at home, yet may do well there given the proper care. You can learn a lot about plants by seeing how they grow in their native setting. Then if you want to try them, track them down when you get home. Usually there's a catalog somewhere that lists them, even if it takes some detective work to find it. You may have to get a plant importer's license for that plant if you can only obtain it abroad, but this is not especially difficult to do. Your Cooperative Extension Service may be able to put you in touch with plant societies that can help you locate hard-to-find plants.

CHAPTER 5

ANNUALS

Have you ever noticed how specific personality types are drawn to specific types of gardening? Take the vegetable grower: a fine, upstanding soul if there ever was one, the sort who not only recycles his soda bottles but always rinses them first. Perennial gardeners are notorious overachievers who are as apt to run a marathon as they are to double-dig their grand herbaceous borders. If you are very close friends with a rose gardener you know that she is a romantic who wears lace in places that will never show. You'll forgive your neighborhood alpine-plant collector her touch of snobbery and the dwarf-conifer enthusiast his touch of arrogance, because both are so erudite, and they can always help you finish your crossword puzzle. Lawn fetishists wash the dishes between courses and pick white lint off their white suits, but you can count on them for anything.

You may feel that I have pinned some rather unfair generalizations on your fellow gardeners, and perhaps I have. But I am sure that you will accept without argument the fact that all gardeners who grow annuals are complete hedonists. Not only do they seek sensory delights with abandon and without guilt, but they manage to escape any form of drudgery that might take time away from those enjoyments. They will only ski if there is a chair lift, and they tend to eat their ice cream before dinner.

The reason annuals are perfect for them is that annuals give such spectacular results with such little labor. Nothing else blooms with such profusion and for such a long stretch of time, so if you want a riot of color, annuals are your answer. Not only do they bloom abundantly, they do it quickly. Gratification is, if not instant, then certainly not long delayed; you can have mature plantings in a matter of weeks. Nor will your senses ever become jaded with annuals; you can plant a totally different color scheme or totally different plants each season. And best of all, annuals are just about the easiest plants to grow. If you have insecurities about how you will pan out as a gardener, try growing some annuals. Your success will fill you with the courage to go on to some of the trickier plants—unless of course you are such a pleasure-lover that you simply stick with annuals for good.

Since there is a bit of the hedonist in all of us, most gardeners always grow some annuals, even though their main focus may be elsewhere. There are so many ways you can use them! Annuals mixed in a bed are glorious, but they are also a fine addition to a perennial border, and they add a touch of a summer color in front of evergreen shrubs. Since so many annuals are ideal as cut flowers, many people have an annual garden just for cutting. Annuals also make ideal container plants, set on a patio, next to a pool, in window boxes or on windowsills indoors. Some even make good houseplants.

What Is an Annual?

A true annual is a plant that completes its entire life cycle in one season. Typically it grows from a seed in spring, quickly becoming a mature-sized plant and quickly producing a great abundance of flowers. It does this because its only, or primary, means of reproducing itself is from seed. So an annual makes as many seed-producing flowers as it can. That's why, if you pick the flowers, even more will come—one reason why annuals are ideal flowers to grow for cutting. After producing and dropping the seeds, the plant dies, though often, in cold climates, it is frost that arbitrarily ends the growth period. If the annual has been in a climate and soil that suit it, the seeds that have fallen by the season's end will winter over on the ground and sprout in spring, starting the cycle over again.

There are also a number of plants that are technically perennials but are often spoken of as annuals simply because they are grown the way annuals are. These are plants that are perennial only in warm climates and will not withstand winter temperatures in cold regions. So a new crop is started each year. Not surprisingly, these "tender perennials" are chosen for this role because, unlike most perennials, they grow to flowering size the first season and then bloom for a particularly long time, so that you don't mind having to replant them each year. Some perennials, such as coleus, geraniums (*Pelargonium* species), impatiens, nicotiana and wax begonias, are grown as tender annuals. Others, such as alyssum, pansies, snapdragons and lantana, are grown as hardy annuals. But don't count on any of them to winter over in regions where there is frost.

A few common plants we often treat as annuals are actually biennials— plants that take two years to complete their growth cycle and normally produce flowers and seeds in their second year. Forget-me-not and larkspur are examples; they can be sown in fall for spring germination or in late summer to produce seedlings that will winter over. (For more information about biennials see page 140.)

There are also several different kinds of true annuals. The terms can be a little confusing, but you'll find it is worth learning to understand them, because if you know what kind of annual you are growing it helps you to remember how to grow it properly.

Tender annuals. These are plants that cannot take frost, either as young seedlings or as mature plants. Many common annuals belong in this category, such as ageratum, nasturtium, portulaca, red salvia, zinnia and verbena. These plants cannot be sown in the ground or set out as transplanted seedlings until after danger of frost has passed. Hence they are usually started indoors, so that by the time it is safe to plant the seedlings they are at least several inches tall. A few tender annuals, such as zinnias and marigolds, grow so quickly that they are often sown directly in the ground after danger of frost has passed.

Hardy annuals. These can take some frost, the amount varying from one plant to another. This means that you can sow them directly in the garden in early spring as soon as the ground can be worked, or even the previous fall, especially in milder climates. It also means that they will not be cut down by the first frost in fall but will bloom a while longer. This is a great advantage, for you will often have one early frost followed by several weeks of frost-free nights, and the blooming period of your garden will thus be substantially lengthened. Some hardy annuals are bachelor's button and calendula.

Gardeners sometimes start hardy annuals indoors, just to give them warmer, more controlled growing conditions in which they can grow to relatively large size before transplanting. But these must be hardened off (page 47) if they are to be set out while it is still cold.

Half-hardy annuals. These are plants that will take a few degrees of frost, but not as much as hardy annuals will. They cannot be fall-planted in cold areas. Some examples are cleome, *Cosmos bipinnatus* and petunia.

Warm-weather annuals. These are annuals that grow and bloom best during warm weather. More often than not they are tender annuals such as zinnias, but this is not always the case. Lobelia, for example, is a hardy annual but likes warm weather. And many of the perennials grown as annuals prefer warm weather, such as nicotiana, geraniums and blue salvia.

Cool-weather annuals. These are usually hardy annuals such as bachelor's button, or else perennials treated as annuals such as larkspur. But some tender annuals, such as nasturtiums and African daisies (*Arctotis*), are also cool-weather plants—in other words they can't take either frost or extreme heat. They may stop blooming or even die in the heat of the summer, especially in warm climates. Gardeners in these regions either choose warm-weather annuals instead, grow the cool-weather ones in partial shade, or plant a second crop of them for fall or winter bloom.

With some cool-weather annuals day length is as much a factor as heat. They succeed better in northern regions where summer days are long than they do in the south where summer days are shorter.

Growing Annuals

Annuals do not have complicated growing requirements, but paying attention to a few simple needs will ensure a better show. Probably some do better in your climate or soil type than others; you can learn which ones by trial and error—experience is easy to get, since you are starting with new plants each year—or you can ask the advice of local nurserymen and fellow gardeners.

PLANTING SCHEDULE

As explained above, when you plant and what you plant are very important. When you are growing perennials your important statistics are the minimum winter temperature in your area and the coldest temperature zone a given plant will tolerate. With annuals the important information is the first and last average frost dates for your area and whether a given plant will tolerate frost. Individual species' requirements are given in the List of Annuals in this chapter, but you can easily see that your planting will fall into several distinct tasks. First you will start some plants from seeds indoors in early spring and start others in early spring directly in the garden. Then, after the last likely frost, you will set out the seedlings you have raised indoors and perhaps sow a few other types directly in the garden.

Another alternative is to buy started seedlings in a nursery. Many gardeners do this, since the plants are fairly inexpensive, and if this is your first garden you may want to try this approach. (For advice about buying annual seedlings see page 111.) The cost of started plants can mount up if you are growing a lot of plants, however; and if you have the time and space to do it, there is much satisfaction in starting your own annuals from seed. I find that, for one thing, there is much more variety in the annuals available from seed catalogs than there is at most nurseries. I am lucky enough to have a local grower, Glenn Waruch, of Claire's Garden Center in Patterson, New York, who experiments with new plants and entices me to do likewise. I always buy a few started plants from Glenn. "Try some Dahlberg daisies, Barbara, you'll love them," he says, holding out a flat of tiny, yellow, starlike flowers. "Or some nierembergia—the flowers are little blue or white bells and bloom like crazy." So try them I do. Not all garden centers have the vision to see beyond petunias, but I predict that in the near future more and more will, and you will be able to grow many interesting annuals from purchased transplants.

Because of space limitations, most of the annuals included in the list in this chapter are the familiar ones, but don't let that stop you from investigating new ones. The advice that follows will help you to grow most annuals. For new ones consult the directions on the seed packet or in the catalog. You'll usually find them very explicit.

SOIL REQUIREMENTS

In a bed of annuals the soil does not have to be dug as deeply as it does for perennials, because most annuals are fairly shallow rooted. But keep in mind that the deeper you loosen the soil and lighten it with organic matter, the more it will retain moisture, and the more the roots will reach down into the soil. And make sure you have removed rocks and perennial weeds. For the most part annuals like a fertile soil a little richer than what you would use for perennials. Some like the soil to be quite rich— zinnias, pansies and marigolds, for example. Others, such as nasturtiums, cosmos and portulaca prefer a slightly poor soil. My advice is to try to please the majority that fall in between when you prepare your bed.

In general, too much nitrogen can cause some annuals to produce a great deal of leaf and stem growth and few flowers, or leaves that hide the flowers through sheer abundance. Work about a tablespoon of balanced fertilizer into the hole for transplants, and feed the ones that need extra fertility a few weeks later with a liquid fertilizer. In areas with sandy soil where nutrients can leach away, time-release fertilizers can be helpful. You must also consider soil acidity. Most annuals are comfortable with a pH between 5.5 and 7.0. (See page 33 for information about pH and how to correct it.)

PLANTING ANNUALS

Be sure to give sun-loving annuals a site that gets at least six hours of sun a day. And don't plant any annuals in a spot where tree roots take up space and rob the soil of moisture. If drainage is poor, plant in raised beds. For information about planting techniques in general, see page 47; for specifics about individual plants see the second half of this chapter.

How closely you space your annuals is partly up to you. They don't like to be crammed together, but plants spaced too far apart will take a long time to produce much of a show and will leave more bare ground to weed. As you get to know your plants you will be able to visualize how wide each one will become when mature, and you will give the bushy ones more space than the skinny ones.

GROWING REQUIREMENTS

All you need to do while your annuals are growing is keep them well weeded, or mulched with a few inches of a light mulch such as buckwheat hulls. Keep in mind that some annuals, particularly petunias, will rot if the mulch is right up next to the stems. Make sure the plants don't dry out. Most annuals need to be watered more than perennials do. Some of the tall ones may need staking.

Some annuals can be made bushier and more free-flowering if they are pinched to make them branch (page 156). Ageratum, coleus, snapdragons and petunias all respond to pinching. If you are starting them indoors, pinch them when they are a few inches high. You can also pinch plants you have sown directly in the garden when they are 4–6 inches tall.

Another big favor you can do your annuals is to pick them. This is really just pinching, with a plus—bouquets of flowers. You can also deadhead the plants (remove spent blooms). This will not only make them bloom more, but your border will look tidier. Don't, however, deadhead the blooms on plants that you want to self-sow. Some annuals such as alyssum, cleome, snapdragons, portulaca and petunias will drop seed in your garden and come up next year as volunteers. If they come up in the wrong place you can transplant the seedlings. But you will find that some hybrid annuals do not breed true to seed and will not be as attractive as the parent plants.

PESTS AND DISEASES

In my climate annuals are rarely damaged very badly by insects or by disease, but this is not true in all parts of the country. Most insects that plague annuals (such as aphids) can be controlled with insecticidal soaps, but the best way to combat disease is to choose resistant varieties and to practice the safeguards described on pages 74–76.

Designing with Annuals

For many gardeners annuals are their most creative outlet, because they can achieve so many different effects quickly. You might start by imitating something you have seen in someone else's garden or patio, or follow some of the suggestions here. But in future seasons you will probably come up with your own unique flower combinations.

ANNUAL BORDERS

Whether an annual border actually *borders* something (like a path, a house wall, or the edge of a lawn) or is a free-standing "island border," such a collection of annuals massed together can add spectacular color to your surroundings. A garden like this is not difficult to plant because you do not have to worry about blooming periods; all the flowers will bloom at pretty much the same time—usually from early or midsummer up until frost. The only factors you have to keep in mind, then, are color combinations, heights, and plant forms—that is, upright plants versus bushy ones, broad leaves versus fernlike ones, and different flower shapes: flat umbels, spikes, big round clusters, daisy shapes, misty bunches of tiny flowers, and so forth. The more you combine different forms, and the more careful you are not to hide a short plant with a tall one, the more effective the picture will be.

Color choice is a very personal thing. Some people want annual beds to be full of very strong, hot, bright colors; other people like a more muted look. The garden plan shown in Figure 26 is one combination I have used many times, with a number of variations, that gives a lot of brightness but with some blues and whites to soften the impact a little.

This garden was conceived simply by making a list of annual flowers I particularly like and dividing them into three groups based on height (Figure 26). First I thought of some favorite tall flowers: white cleome and a cosmos variety I particularly love called 'Diablo,' which is a very bright red-orange, has smaller flowers than the tall purple-pink-white cosmos, and grows on a bushy, many-branched plant. Then I wrote down some medium-height plants: blue salvia and 'Cut and Come Again' zinnias. For shorter plants I thought of blue-violet ageratum, white alyssum and a favorite red French marigold called 'Red Wheels.'

Looking at the list, I realized that I

had a lot of red, white and blue—a good, crisp combination, I thought. But I didn't want the garden to look like an American flag, so I added my favorite calendula to the "short" list—the single type in a rich shade of yellow. The 'Cut and Come Again' zinnias would be in mixed shades that included yellow, pink and salmon, for still more variety. The plan shows how I arranged these plants in a border 5 feet wide and 12 feet long. Tall plants are in the back, medium-height plants in the middle, and low plants in the front.

If I had wanted this border to have more warm colors I would perhaps have put in some large yellow marigolds and eliminated some of the blue flowers. If I had wanted to tone it down, on the other hand, and give it a misty "English-garden" look, I would have taken out the bright red and orange flowers and added larkspur, stock and love-in-a-mist (*Nigella*). For the cleome and cosmos I would have chosen varieties that bloom in the pink-purple range. I might also have added some white-leaved annuals such as *Cineraria maritima*. A dark red foliage accent could be attractive, too, such as 'Dark Opal' basil and purple perilla.

If the garden were in shade I would have selected a different group of plants, beginning with early-blooming pansies and forget-me-nots; after danger of frost is past I would plant impatiens, wax begonias and perhaps monkey-flower (*Mimulus*), with a dark red coleus as a foliage accent.

BEDDING PLANTS

One traditional way to use annuals is as "bedding plants": a large number of a single species are planted, usually in a single color, and usually in a formal arrangement. Sometimes several contrasting plants are used this way, in concentric rings, for example. The shape of the bed tends to be very regular and geometric, and the bed is often outlined with a material such as brick or with a very low clipped hedge plant such as box or germander. In Victorian times this style of gardening was very popular, and bedding plants would be nurtured in greenhouses so that they would all be exactly the right height, and in full bloom, at the time they were needed for the display.

While many modern gardeners now consider formal garden beds to be more appropriate to public or institutional plantings than to the home garden, they can still be effective if you have a Victorian home, or even just a rather formal house and yard. Tastefully done, this kind of bed can be charming. If you are choosing plants for such a design, look for annuals of low or medium height that will be tidy and uniform in shape, such as most begonias, small marigolds such as 'Lemon Drop,' ageratum, alyssum, verbena, and foliage plants such as annual dusty miller (*Cineraria maritima*).

ANNUALS IN CONTAINERS

Annuals make perfect container plants for outdoor use in cool climates because you don't have to worry about what to do with them at summer's end. Many annuals can be brought inside and grown as houseplants (see Bringing Annuals Indoors, page 124), but if you have no interest in doing this, you can throw out the plants after frost and start over again next year when you are starting to spend more time outdoors.

Finding ways to use annuals in containers can really get people's imaginations going, though not always in the right direction. No empty receptacle is safe from a gardener on the prowl for a place to plant petunias, whether it's a

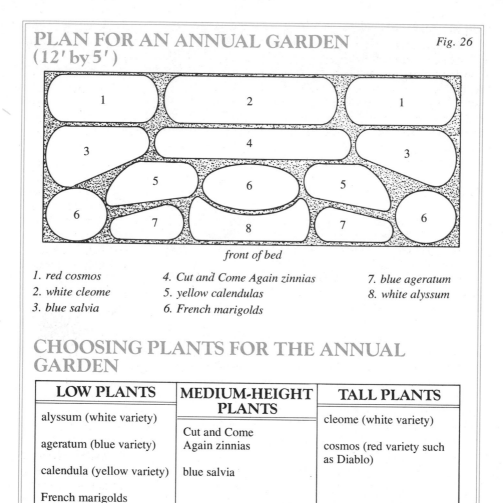

PLAN FOR AN ANNUAL GARDEN (12' by 5')

Fig. 26

front of bed

1. red cosmos
2. white cleome
3. blue salvia

4. Cut and Come Again zinnias
5. yellow calendulas
6. French marigolds

7. blue ageratum
8. white alyssum

CHOOSING PLANTS FOR THE ANNUAL GARDEN

LOW PLANTS	MEDIUM-HEIGHT PLANTS	TALL PLANTS
alyssum (white variety)	Cut and Come Again zinnias	cleome (white variety)
ageratum (blue variety)		cosmos (red variety such as Diablo)
calendula (yellow variety)	blue salvia	
French marigolds (red variety such as Red Wheels)		

wheelbarrow, an old sled or a chamber pot. I personally can do without most forms of front-lawn cuteness, including unexpected plant containers. But I do like to find attractive containers for annuals—a retangular terra-cotta pot with particularly nice carvings on it, a wooden box that has weathered to a gray color, a shiny, dark brown ceramic jar.

What makes this kind of gardening fun is not only choosing the containers and plants and finding artful ways to place them, either alone or in attractive groupings, but also finding combinations to use within a container. Let's take the classic wooden whiskey barrel, cut in half, available at many garden centers. You might put two or three pink Martha Washington geraniums in the center, then plant some dusty miller around them, and then add four or five variegated trailing vinca plants that will hang over the edge. Or you might start with the geraniums, then surround them with white annual baby's-breath and add a trailing flower such as verbena. It will take some trial and error before you know just how much of each plant you need for a given container. Give container-grown annuals a nice light soil, water regularly and feed about once a month with a time-release fertilizer.

CUTTING GARDENS

Annuals are ideal plants for cutting gardens because they produce so many flowers, and cutting only makes them more productive. If my main flower garden consists of annuals or has annuals in it, I find I can usually rob enough flowers from it for bouquets without spoiling the display, especially if I use flowers from the fields and roadsides in my bouquets too—something I really like to do. But if you need so many cut flowers that you would spoil your ornamental garden by cutting them there, a separate cutting garden is the answer.

Such a garden is not always grown to look good, though it is never an unattractive sight. Often the flowers in it are raised like a vegetable crop—in straight single rows that can be mulched, in blocks, or in wide rows. One of the most popular ways to grow cut flowers is in the vegetable garden itself. I always do this, just as added insurance that I will always have some flowers to cut. I choose ones that have fairly long stems and last a long time in water, like zinnias, bachelor's button and snapdragons. I don't plant dwarf or compact varieties for this purpose, because these are usually short stemmed.

OTHER USES FOR ANNUALS

There are also many special situations where annuals can provide a quick—and pretty—fix. Let's say you have an ugly, slightly sandy patch of soil where weeds are going to grow unless you get there first. Let some trailing nasturtiums ramble over it. Perhaps you have been forced by law to put an ugly wire fence around your swimming pool. Plant morning glories all over it; even if they don't totally hide the fence, your eye will be drawn not to the fence but to the flowers. When you are planting near the pool, choose annuals that will tolerate what is, in effect, a hot microclimate within your yard. Heat and sun reflected from decking, stone coping and the pool water itself can really bake plants. Choose species such as portulaca, marigolds, nasturtiums, and any white-leaved annuals that are relatively comfortable in these conditions.

Is your vegetable garden in the front yard because that is the only sunny part of your property? Make it an ornamental garden by alternating vegetables with tidy rows or blocks of zinnias and marigolds, and plant tall sunflowers along the north side of the fence where they won't cast shade on your crops. Annuals look lovely in herb gardens, too.

And finally, never underestimate the power of annuals tucked into a perennial border. The perennial purist (the overachiever, remember?) would probably consider this cheating, but I find annuals very helpful in filling gaps here and there and providing dependable continuous color in an all-summer garden. You might also plant a garden in which annuals take over after spring-blooming bulbs and perennials, and are in turn followed by fall-blooming perennials such as asters, sedum and chrysanthemums. The easiest annuals to use with perennials are those that are tall and showy but not broad and bushy (such as snapdragons)—these will help you save space.

Bringing Annuals Indoors

Many of the flowers we grow as annuals make fine houseplants. Some you can simply dig up and bring indoors before frost; others you would do better to start from cuttings taken from your plants while they are growing in the garden. To bring whole plants indoors, take younger, smaller plants, pot them up in a good soil mix (page 584), then condition them for indoor life by keeping them outdoors in their pots for a few weeks before frost. But be sure to bring them in if frost is imminent.

What better consolation on the morning you find that the first hard frost of fall has blackened your annual garden than to know that healthy plants are coming along on a sunny windowsill indoors. Not all will be long lived like your other houseplants, but they will provide a cheerful show in winter, and you can even take cuttings of them to extend the bloom even longer. If your plants are still thriving by spring you can replant them in the garden, or else take cuttings for spring planting. (Among annuals that should last all winter are geraniums, impatiens and coleus.) Here are some of the plants that respond well to indoor culture:

Alyssum. Dig up a clump, pot it, and bring it inside. Or divide a large clump into several; each will become larger.

Coleus. Whole plants may be dug up, cut back to a few inches tall, and regrown in a pot. Or take stem cuttings and root them.

Geranium. Dig the plant up and cut it back at least by half, then fertilize with a balanced liquid fertilizer. Or take stem cuttings and root them.

Impatiens. Taking stem cuttings is the best method and works well for all types of impatiens. Pinch them to make them bushy. New Guinea impatiens is especially popular as a houseplant.

Lantana. The whole plant may be dug up and brought indoors. Usually it is best to cut it back hard and let it put out fresh growth. You can also take stem cuttings and root them.

Nasturtium. Take stem cuttings and root them.

Pansy. Try pansies only if you keep your house cool. Dig up, pot, and bring inside. Cut back to encourage fresh new growth and fertilize with a balanced liquid fertilizer.

Petunia. Dig up, pot, cut back and bring inside. You might have luck taking stem cuttings and rooting them.

Portulaca. Dig up and pot, or take stem cuttings. Easy to transplant.

Verbena. Dig up, pot, and bring inside.

Wax Begonia. Transplant to pots or take stem cuttings.

LIST OF ANNUALS

This list of twenty-five annuals no doubt contains many that are familiar to you. All are popular plants that are commonly seen in gardens because they make a colorful display and because they are easy to grow. In some cases I mention specific varieties or series of varieties that you might try, but it is hard to keep up with all the new varieties that come out each year—in many cases each seed company has its own series of varieties. Besides, nurseries and other places that sell annuals locally do not always label flats of annuals with the variety. If you order annual seeds by mail, you will have a better chance to experiment with varieties and to decide which you like best. You can also explore some of the many annuals I haven't the space to list here. So start with these old favorites, then select some new ones to experiment with from the catalogs listed on page 618.

AGERATUM
Ageratum houstonianum

DESCRIPTION: I like this plant, sometimes called "flossflower," because its masses of intense violet-blue, fuzzy flowers show up even from afar and do not recede into the background as blue flowers often will. A tender annual, it sometimes grows as tall as 2 feet, but most commercial varieties are compact mounds that are less than a foot high. Sometimes the flowers are white or pink.

HOW TO GROW: Plants are usually started indoors six to eight weeks before the last frost, then set out into the garden after all danger of frost has passed. They are slow to get started and are therefore most effective planted closely—about 8 inches apart. They prefer full sun but do fairly well in light shade, especially in hot climates. Pinching them back once will make the plants more bushy, but it is not necessary.

ALYSSUM (SWEET ALYSSUM)
Lobularia maritima

DESCRIPTION: A perennial usually grown as a hardy annual, alyssum may grow as tall as a foot, but is usually no more than 6 inches tall, spreading in wide clumps. The tiny, profuse flowers form a carpet, usually white but often purple and sometimes pink. It is a good edging plant, but the best thing about it is that you can easily grab little clumps of it whenever you need them and stick them into whatever odd corner needs a carpetlike plant—even the soil between flagstones. The flowers are fragrant and have a long period of bloom, from spring till after the first hard frosts.

HOW TO GROW: Sow alyssum directly in the garden as early in spring as you can work the soil, or start indoors, pressing the seeds lightly into the surface of your planting medium since they need light to germinate. Transplant them into the garden in clumps without thinning. They prefer cool weather and will often self-sow.

BACHELOR'S BUTTON (CORNFLOWER)
Centaurea cyanus

DESCRIPTION: I find a spot for this hardy annual every year because it keeps right on blooming long after most annuals have turned into frost-killed heaps and adds a touch of real blue to my chrysanthemum bouquets. The plants grow up to 3 feet tall but are usually about 2 feet, with long grayish leaves. Flowers are 1–1½ inches wide, rather raggedy and usually a bright medium blue, but sometimes white, pink or purple. Plants of different colors may be sold separately or in mixtures. They often continue to bloom very late in the season, even past frost. (Another *Cen-*

taurea species, *C. cineraria,* is an annual grown for its white foliage, and is one of the plants called "dusty miller.")

HOW TO GROW: These are cool-weather plants that can be sown directly in the garden in early spring. You can also try sowing in fall for spring bloom, especially in warm climates. Plants may also be started indoors. Plant in full sun, 8–12 inches apart.

CALENDULA
Calendula officinalis

DESCRIPTION: In colonial times this hardy annual was called "pot marigold" because of its use as a cooked vegetable. I grow it for its intense shades of orange and yellow, and because it is long blooming after frost. The daisylike flowers can also be cream colored; some are single, some double, though I much prefer the simplicity of the single ones. All are long-lasting as cut flowers.

HOW TO GROW: Calendulas are easy to grow from seed. Sow very early in spring indoors, or sow directly in the soil in early spring, ¼ inch deep. Gardeners in warm climates can sow seeds in late summer for bloom all fall and winter. The plants may mildew in muggy weather. They like cool days, full sun and fertile soil. They do best planted about a foot apart.

CLEOME (SPIDER FLOWER)
Cleome spinosa

DESCRIPTION: This half-hardy annual is prized for its huge, dainty heads of pink, white or lavender blossoms, with long wavy stamens. They usually grow 3–4 feet tall, sometimes 5, and seem both monumental and dainty at the same time. They are strongly fragrant, bordering on smelly, and as such are a poor choice as a cut flower, but they are truly elegant in the rear of the flower garden.

HOW TO GROW: Sow indoors six to eight weeks before the last average frost, or outdoors in the garden after all danger of frost has passed. Thin to at least a foot apart. Cleome is a warm-weather plant, moderately drought-tolerant. It will often self-sow.

COLEUS
Coleus hybridus

DESCRIPTION: A tender perennial grown as a tender annual, coleus is loved for its dramatically variegated leaves in shades of red, green, yellow and white. Both the shapes of the markings and the shapes of the leaves vary from variety to variety and can be effective in mixtures or in plantings of one color. They are often used in planters, pots and window boxes as well as in beds. Tall varieties grow as tall as 3 feet, shorter ones as low as 6 inches.

HOW TO GROW: It is best to buy started plants in the colors and leaf forms you desire. Growing coleus from seed is slow. If you want to try it, sow indoors as early as ten weeks before the last expected frost. Sprinkle the tiny seeds on top of the soil and gently press them into it rather than covering them, and keep the soil moist and warm during germination. Transplant seedlings into the permanent location after danger of frost has passed. Coleus plants should be spaced at least a foot apart; they can grow quite broad. Young plants can be pinched (page 156) to make them compact and bushy. A warm-weather plant, coleus can grow in full sun in some climates, but part shade will prevent wilting in hot weather and produce stronger colors. A light mulch will help keep the soil moist, but don't mound the mulch around the plant stems.

COSMOS
Cosmos

*Cosmos
sulphureus*   *Cosmos bipinnatus*

DESCRIPTION: The most common varieties are hybrids of *Cosmos bipinnatus,* a half-hardy annual with daisylike flowers sometimes as large as 4 inches across, in shades of pink and red or white. Plants have airy, threadlike foliage and usually grow about 4 feet tall, sometimes taller (the 'sensation' hybrids are shorter). They are ideal for the back of the annual garden. I also use them to fill in between clumps of tall perennials such as asters and phlox. Hybrids of *C. sulphureus* are shorter, usually about 3 feet, and have red, yellow or orange flowers that are usually about 2 inches across and sometimes double. They are tender annuals. This is the preferred species for very hot climates. If you have never tried this type of cosmos you are missing a great flower. Plants have airy but bushy foliage and bloom very profusely.

HOW TO GROW: Sow seeds outdoors after the last expected frost, or indoors about six weeks before. For optimum bloom, plant in full sun or part shade in soil that is not too rich or too moist. Plant at least 12 inches apart. Tall varieties often need staking, but can be pinched (page 156) if you want shorter plants and more bloom.

FORGET-ME-NOT
Myosotis sylvatica (*M. alpestris*)

DESCRIPTION: Hardy biennials often grown as hardy annuals, forget-me-nots are typically bright blue but sometimes pink or white. Usually no more than a foot tall, they are often grown among spring bulbs or are naturalized in woodland and water gardens. They also make good edging plants.

HOW TO GROW: There are several ways to grow forget-me-nots. Easily grown from seed, they may be sown in fall when spring bulbs are planted, to germinate in spring for spring and early-summer bloom. They may be sown in late summer in a cold frame to produce seedlings that will winter over in a protected setting. Or they may be sown indoors in March and transplanted outside later in the spring. Plants do not need thinning, and often self-sow under their favorite conditions: moist, humusy soil in light shade. These cool-weather plants will not bloom during the heat of August, but a self-sown crop may appear in fall in warm climates.

GERANIUM
Pelargonium

DESCRIPTION: Tender perennials grown as tender annuals north of Zone 8, these are the much-loved bright geraniums seen on windowsills, on terraces and in gardens everywhere. Most are

ivy geranium

zonal geranium

varieties of *Pelargonium* × *hortorum* (zonal geranium), which forms a large, shrubby plant in frost-free climates but grows about 2 feet tall in colder ones. The large flower clusters can be red, pink, salmon, orange or white. Martha Washington geraniums (*P. domesticum*) are shorter, with pink, red or white flowers. The flowers in each cluster are large, rather like those of azaleas, often with a blotch of a darker shade. Ivy geranium (*P. peltatum*) is a trailing plant often used in window boxes. There are also a number of species grown less for their flowers than for their leaves; these have various scents such as apple and lemon and are popular in herb gardens.

HOW TO GROW: Seeds can be sown indoors in late winter or early spring in soil kept warm for better germination. Growing from seed can be slow, and therefore many gardeners prefer to buy a few plants the first year, then take cutting each year for next year's crop or for a supply of bright houseplants in winter. On the other hand, growing from seed is apt to produce plants that are free from the diseases that cause leaves to yellow. These diseases may be carried over if geraniums are propagated from cuttings. Seeds of a number of hybrids are now available.

Geraniums are warm-weather plants and relatively drought-tolerant, but intense heat can be fatal to them, and cool nights are best. Martha Washington geraniums need a period of cool weather to bloom and thus are not satisfactory for hot climates. All like full sun but can take a bit of shade, especially in hot areas. Plant in not overly fertile, well-drained soil, 12–15 inches apart in the garden. Cut them back to half their height in late winter or early spring in climates where they are perennial. Give pot-grown geraniums plenty of light so they will not be leggy. Often a large pot with several plants looks best.

IMPATIENS
Impatiens

single

double

New Guinea impatiens

DESCRIPTION: These tender perennials grown as tender annuals will always come to the rescue of the gardener who wants plenty of color but whose house is surrounded by shade (though they will do well in full sun too). The most familiar species is *Impatiens wallerana,* which is also, paradoxically, called "patience plant" or "patient Lucy." Plants are sometimes upright, reaching to 15 inches or so, but they are also often low and sprawling, and each plant may cover a wide area before summer's end. Colors are vibrant reds, pinks, salmons, purples and oranges as well as white and bicolors. Some have double flowers like tiny camellias. The 'Super Elfin' series are large flowered and especially compact. All are good container plants, even indoors. 'New Guinea' impatiens is a tender annual with red, pink or purple flowers, often larger than those of the usual impatiens. It also has strikingly variegated leaves and has recently become popular as a container plant or houseplant. It requires full sun to fully bring out the colors in its foliage.

HOW TO GROW: Sow seeds indoors six to eight weeks before the last frost. Sowing outdoors after the danger of frost has passed would give you very late-flowering plants. Press seeds lightly into the soil surface and keep soil moist and warm for faster germination. These are warm-weather plants that will not take any frost, but they do like the soil to be somewhat cool and moist; make sure it has plenty of organic matter worked in. Impatiens stems are very soft and fleshy and will be obliterated by any foot traffic, so they should not be planted in a spot well traveled by dogs or people. Plants can be pinched (page 156) to make them more compact and bushy. They are also extremely easy to grow from cuttings.

LANTANA
Lantana

DESCRIPTION: Lantanas are perennials grown as half-hardy annuals in most climates, or wintered over indoors. *Lantana camara* can grow as tall as 10 feet in very warm climates but is usually no more than 3 feet tall, and dwarf varieties no taller than 18 inches are very popular. Little round flower heads are clusters of tiny flowers in shades of red, pink, yellow and orange, sometimes all in one cluster. 'Alba' is a white variety. Trailing lantana (*L. sellowiana*) is less hardy, with trailing stems and flowers that are usually combinations of lavender and yellow. Both are excellent container plants but are also grown in gardens, the trailing kind as a ground cover.

HOW TO GROW: Lantanas are warm-weather plants. Sow seeds indoors in late winter because they take a long time to germinate. In warm climates sow outdoors in the garden. Many gardeners buy plants and then take stem cuttings when they need new ones to bring indoors for winter display and for a source of new cuttings for the following season. Plants can also be dug up, cut back to 5 or 6 inches, and kept dormant in a frost-free basement until early spring with just enough water to keep them alive but not enough to produce new growth.

LARKSPUR
Consolida ambigua (Delphinium ajacis)

DESCRIPTION: If you love delphiniums but don't have the patience it takes to grow them, these hardy annuals may cheer you up. Their flower spikes look like those of delphiniums, but are shorter and more delicate. Heights vary, but 2 feet is common. Colors are shades of blue, lavender, pink, purple, salmon and also white. Some are branched and some are upright. Twelve-inch dwarfs are also available. Plants have attractive, fernlike foliage. The bloom period is not as long as it is for some annuals, as flowers peter out before summer's end; but larkspur makes an excellent, long-lasting cut flower.

HOW TO GROW: Seeds can be sown directly in the garden as early in spring as you can work the soil or, in warm climates, in late summer to produce some growth on plants, which will bloom in early spring. In cold regions you can sow about the time of the first frost and let the seeds lie dormant in winter for early bloom. Seeds started indoors should be sown in peat pots and thinned to one plant for each pot to minimize the difficulty of transplanting. Larkspur likes full sun but will take part shade, and prefers part shade in hot zones. Plants in the garden should be at least a foot apart, in fertile, well-drained soil. Keep roots cool with a light mulch, especially in hot climates. Tall plants may need staking.

LOBELIA (EDGING LOBELIA)
Lobelia erinus

DESCRIPTION: A hardy annual, rarely taller than 8 inches, whose flowers are almost always blue. Some shades are

among the most intense blues of any garden plant. In some varieties, such as 'Crystal Palace,' the foliage is tinged with red. Some have trailing stems and make good container plants. Lobelia is also used as an edging plant in flower gardens.

HOW TO GROW: Sow seeds indoors in late winter or early spring, ten to twelve weeks before the last expected frost. Sprinkle them on top of the soil and press lightly. After danger of frost is past, transplant in unthinned clumps a few inches wide, and set clumps about 6 inches apart. The plants grow best in cool areas and appreciate full sun except in hot climates, where they do best with some afternoon shade. Soil should be fertile and moist, but well drained.

MARIGOLD
Tagetes

DESCRIPTION: Even if you have never grown anything in your life, it is very hard not to succeed with marigolds, and it is hard not to enjoy their sunny profusion. Hybrids of these pungent-smelling, half-hardy annuals are derived from several species. *Tagetes erecta* is called African marigold but is actually from Mexico. Flowers are often large, anywhere from 2 to 6 inches across, and tall—as high as 3 feet. Colors range from off-white to yellow, orange and red. The 'Climax' series, with big, ball-like flowers, is typical of the tall types. Burpee's 'Lady' series is a good selection of intermediate marigolds, about 1½ feet tall. *T. patula*, French marigold (also from Mexico), grows anywhere from 6 to 18 inches high; flowers are yellow, orange and red, often bicolored, and either single or double. I think the singles are more striking. *T. tenuifolia* 'Pumila' is a dwarf marigold, 12 inches tall or less, with yellow or orange flowers.

African marigold

French marigold

HOW TO GROW: Sow seeds outdoors on or just before the last average frost date in fertile soil, and in full sun except in very hot climates. Seeds can also be started indoors six weeks or so before the last frost. Marigolds are warm-weather plants that make bushy growth quickly and are quite tolerant of drought. Tall varieties can go at least 12–18 inches apart, dwarf ones 6–8 inches.

NASTURTIUM
Tropaeolum majus

DESCRIPTION: Nasturtiums are tender annuals and a garden favorite because they are so easy to grow. The flowers are about 2 inches across, with ruffled, spurred petals in shades of red, orange, yellow, gold, salmon, dark pink and dark red. Stems are long and curving but rather breakable, and leaves are light green and round. Both flowers and leaves are edible in salads or as garnishes. Some varieties, such as the 'Tom Thumb' series, are dwarfs that grow only to a foot; others are vines that can attain great lengths in warm climates. These look good in hanging baskets, spilling onto paths or terraces, or as a covering for banks or stone walls. I like the semitrailing 'Gleam' hybrids with their large double flowers. Bloom lasts until frost.

HOW TO GROW: The large seeds can be sown a few weeks before the last frost, directly in the ground, at about the distance apart that you want them to grow (6 inches for dwarfs, and up to 12 inches for larger types). If you start them indoors, sow earlier in individual peat pots, and set the pots in the ground after danger of frost is past. They like full sun, and rather dry, sandy, infertile soil. Watering or fertilizing them too much will result in big leafy plants that hide the flowers.

NICOTIANA (FLOWERING TOBACCO)
Nicotiana alata

DESCRIPTION: A perennial grown as a tender annual, this is a smaller relative of the plant grown for cigarette tobacco. It has trumpet-shaped flowers 2–4 inches long and smells sweet at night, especially the tall, old-fashioned, white kind. (You might have to sift through a few seed catalogs to find the latter, but the quest will be worth it.) Hybrids are available in red, pink, lavender, purple and white. The 'Nicki' hybrids are dwarfs that grow 12–18 inches tall.

They are popular because, unlike some nicotianas, their flowers stay open all day. Other varieties may reach 3 feet or more.

HOW TO GROW: Start seeds indoors four to six weeks before the last average frost, then transplant to the garden after frost danger, spacing 9–12 inches apart depending on height. They like an alkaline soil and plenty of moisture in dry weather. Warm-weather plants, they prefer full sun but will tolerate part shade.

PANSY
Viola tricolor hortensis

DESCRIPTION: Pansies are perennials but are short lived in many areas and so are often grown as hardy annuals or biennials. Hybrids come in just about every color imaginable, many bicolored or tricolored, with the familiar "faces" that most people remember from their childhoods. Most plants are about 8 inches tall. They are used in window boxes and planters as well as in gardens. Like most gardeners, I find the spring pansy show a welcome sight, but boy, can they sulk in hot weather! Fortunately most of them revive when it gets cool at the summer's end, and there are all those little faces again. In mild climates they will bloom all winter.

HOW TO GROW: Pansies can be sown indoors ten to twelve weeks before the last average frost, but be sure to sow them shallowly, keeping the seed tray dark, moist and cool. Transplant them into the garden in the spring in fertile, humusy, moist soil; you should move them early enough so that they can establish good root systems before the weather gets too warm. A more reliable method is to sow seeds in summer or fall for bloom the following spring. In cold climates this is best done in a cold frame, though some gardeners have good results by mulching the seedlings heavily. Left to their own devices, a few pansies will often overwinter or self-sow, even in cold zones. Frequent picking or deadheading will give you more compact plants and profuse bloom.

PETUNIA
Petunia × hybrida

DESCRIPTION: Petunias are half-hardy annuals and are related to the potato and other members of the nightshade family (page 184). Their familiar trumpet-shaped flowers come in many shapes, sizes and colors, from the old-fashioned single flowers to modern hybrids that are striped, double, ruffled and sometimes very large—at least 4 inches across for the "grandifloras." The new "multiflora" petunias are small and single and bloom very profusely; they are also disease-resistant. Since petunias make compact plants with masses of color, they are excellent in flower bor-

ruffled *single*

double *petunias* *double-ruffled*

ders. I find that the more modest, simpler petunias are less decimated by heavy rainstorms than the more flamboyant ones; the latter, however, are fine as container plants in sheltered locations. The trailing petunias, such as the grandifloras, are especially effective in pots, planters and boxes. Petunia colors are virtually unlimited; there are even striped, bicolored ones. Height ranges from 6-inch dwarfs to 18-inch full-sized plants.

HOW TO GROW: Sow seeds indoors eight to ten weeks before the last frost, dropping the tiny seeds onto the soil surface and pressing lightly with the fingers. Keep the seedlings cool, and transplant them carefully to individual peat pots when each seedling has four leaves. They can be set out in the garden 12–18 inches apart after danger of frost in fairly fertile soil. Some petunias, especially the doubles, are slow to grow from seed, and you may be better off with nursery-grown seedlings.

Petunias are warm-weather plants but they sometimes do poorly during hot weather. If they look straggly and aren't blooming well, cut them back to a few inches tall and feed them liquid fertilizer that you water in well. Petunias will self-sow readily, but the seedlings will rarely look anything like the parents.

PORTULACA
Portulaca grandiflora

DESCRIPTION: Portulacas are often thought of as rock-garden plants because they do so well in that setting. They are tender annuals with succulent, needle-shaped leaves and trailing stems 6–8 inches long. The flowers are bright and papery-textured in shades of pink, red, yellow, salmon, orange, purple and white. They are usually sold in mixtures, not as single colors. They open in sun but close at night and on cloudy days. Since they are gloriously drought-tolerant, I put them in pots, window boxes, or any container that I might forget to water from time to time.

HOW TO GROW: Transplanting being difficult, it is best to start seed directly in the garden when the soil is warm. A warm, sunny exposure is essential, as is a site with well-drained soil. Thinning is not necessary. They will tolerate poor soil as well as hot, dry conditions. On top of all that, they will self-sow!

SALVIA (SAGE)
Salvia

DESCRIPTION: Of a number of salvias grown in the garden, my favorite is *Salvia farinacea* (blue salvia, or mealy-cup sage). A tender perennial grown as a half-hardy annual in most climates, it has blue flower spikes 2–3 feet long that are as attractive and long lasting in the garden as they are in bouquets. Others include *Salvia splendens,* or scarlet sage, which is a perennial grown as a tender annual and has brilliant red flowers and handsome dark green foliage. Varieties come in a number of heights from about 9 inches to 2 feet. Choose the one that best suits your garden. This is such a controversial plant that I have even heard of an Anti-Red-Salvia League. It is often grown in masses and as such *can* be too much of a good thing. I am not such a salvia snob as to pass it over altogether, but I do like it best in small groups with other plants that tone it down a little.

SNAPDRAGON
Antirrhinum majus

DESCRIPTION: Snapdragons are perennials grown as half-hardy annuals. Flowers grow on spikes of varying heights, from 6 inches to 4 feet. 'Rocket' varieties are tall; 'Sentinel' are somewhat shorter; 'Floral Carpet' is very low but spreads widely. Colors can be pink, red, yellow, orange, purple, rust and white. There is always a place for their strong, vertical accents in the flower garden, and I find they bloom long after frost has cut down many other plants. As a bonus they are a long-lasting cut flower, so plant extras.

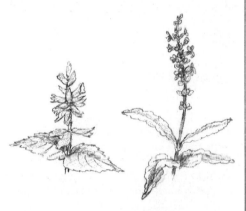

HOW TO GROW: Though it is usually best to buy started plants, salvias can be started indoors six to eight weeks before the last average frost. Seed must be kept warm to germinate. Transplant after danger of frost is past. Plant in full sun (light shade in hot climates), spacing about a foot apart. Salvias can also be sown directly in the ground after the weather has warmed up, but unfortunately they take a long time to flower when grown this way. They like warm but not excessively dry weather and need to be watered in drought unless they're well mulched.

HOW TO GROW: Sow seeds indoors at least six weeks before the last frost, and transplant to the garden 6–8 inches apart, as soon as you have some vigorous seedlings about 4 inches tall. They like full sun and will thrive in light shade but will have fewer blooms. They are cool-weather plants that can be sown in August in warm climates for fall blooms, or in winter for early-spring bloom. They like fertile, slightly alkaline soil. Pinch at 4 inches for bushier plants and more flower spikes. Cutting the flowers helps them to keep blooming. They will often self-sow.

STOCK
Matthiola

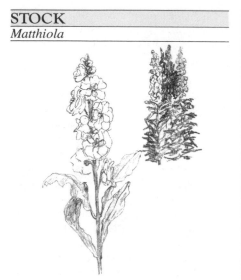

DESCRIPTION: Stock is an old-fashioned plant that is grown less than it used to be. It deserves a comeback. The common garden stock is *Matthiola incana* 'Annua,' a biennial often grown as a hardy annual. It grows 1–3 feet tall, with spikes of small, fragrant flowers in shades of blue, purple, pink, yellow and white. 'Ten Weeks' and 'Column' are popular strains; 'Trysomic' varieties are best for hot climates. *M. longipetala* (*M. bicornis*), "evening" or "night-scented" stock, is a hardy annual that grows up to 1½ feet tall and is very fragrant at night. The flowers, which are purple, lavender or white, are single and not very showy. In fact there is not much reason to look at evening stock. Plant it mixed in with something bushy and showy, near a patio or open window, and enjoy the scent in the evening.

HOW TO GROW: Sow seeds indoors very early or outdoors as soon as you can work the soil. Stock is a cool-weather plant that can also be sown in late summer in hot climates for winter and spring bloom. It likes fairly rich soil with plenty of moisture, and full sun (evening stock will tolerate part shade).

VERBENA
Verbena × *hybrida*

hanging

low-growing

DESCRIPTION: Verbenas are tender annuals grown for their clusters of tiny, fragrant flowers in shades of red, pink, purple, lavender and white. Never more than 12 inches high, many are shorter. Some verbenas have trailing stems.

HOW TO GROW: Sow seeds indoors very early in light, warm soil. Gemination can take a long time, so many gardeners buy started plants. Transplant into the garden 8–12 inches apart in fairly fertile soil after danger of frost is past. They will form wide clumps. They are warm-weather plants that prefer sun, but light shade is a blessing in hot, dry areas.

WAX BEGONIA
Begonia semperflorens cultorum

DESCRIPTION: A tender perennial treated as a tender annual, the wax begonia is grown partly for its pink, red and white flowers and partly for its fleshy leaves, which can be green, red or bronze. It grows 8–12 inches tall and is a good source of summer color for either shaded or sunny gardens. It is a subtle plant; combining several different varieties can be particularly effective. You can depend on wax begonias to be covered with flowers all summer, and in

conditions they like, each plant will make a large clump.

HOW TO GROW. These are slow to grow from seed, so I purchase mine as seedlings. You can, however, sow seed indoors four to six weeks before the last average frost, in a light, warm place. Transplant to the garden, 8–12 inches apart, after danger of frost has passed. Light shade is ideal for healthy leaves and abundant bloom.

ZINNIA
Zinnia

DESCRIPTION: Zinnias are tender annuals that all gardeners love because they make a great show and are easy to grow. Flowers are flat or rounded heads of petals, like overlapping scales, in every color except blue. Height and flower sizes also vary. Modern hybrids are derived from *Zinnia elegans, Z. angustifolia* and *Z. haageana,* and range in height from 12 inches to 3 feet. Large, tall zinnias such as the 'Zenith' strain or the 'California Giants' are good for the back of the garden. 'Cut and Come Again' zinnias are bushy plants of moderate height that are full of buttonlike flowers and bloom all the more if cut.

'Thumbelina' zinnias grow about 6 inches high. All bloom until frost, and none need staking.

HOW TO GROW: You can sow zinnia seeds indoors about 4 weeks before the last frost and set out in moist, fairly rich soil, 8–18 inches apart depending on the size of the variety. Large zinnias will not branch properly if planted too closely. Too-close planting may also lead to mildew. Use peat pots since they do not like to be transplanted. Since zinnias germinate and grow so quickly, it is also possible to sow them directly in the garden after danger of frost. Leaves may mildew, but this will not affect bloom. If the mildew bothers you, use a fungicide. Water in drought, but try to keep water off the leaves, since this can make the mildew worse. Zinnias are warm-weather plants, and make excellent long-lasting cut flowers.

tall-growing doubles

single tall-growing

short-growing

CHAPTER 6

PERENNIALS

The last ten years have seen a strong, renewed interest in perennials. Will it last? Gardening, like anything else, has its fads and changing currents. Remember terrarium fever in the fifties? (Perhaps you still have a few moldy fish tanks in your cellar as a reminder.) Or the houseplant jungles of the seventies? (Hardware and grocery stores that could hardly restock spider plants fast enough have now gone back to selling hardware and groceries.) Now it's perennials; but I predict that they are here to stay.

To me, growing perennials is the most satisfying form of ornamental gardening. A bed of them in full bloom, with its glowing patterns of color, is a real showstopper. But it's more than that. The garden's performance changes every day, every month, every year, and I find myself totally absorbed in the ongoing production. The garden is not a set piece but a process.

A perennial is a plant that does not die after a season's growth but renews itself each year. (People sometimes speak of a certain perennial being an "annual" in their gardens; but this only means that the plant does not survive the cold winters or hot summers of their climate.) Technically this category includes trees, shrubs, hardy bulbs, your lawn, several vegetables, some houseplants and a number of other growing things. But usually when we talk about "perennials" we mean a large group of garden plants grown solely for ornament, often for their flowers. Most are "herbaceous" perennials, which means that their stems are green and soft, not brown and woody like those of a shrub. The soft growth usually dies in fall, but the roots are alive and well underground. In early spring you can see signs of life all over your perennial bed—little bumps or points of new growth that turn into little green sprouts,

a different shape for each plant. As you learn about perennials you come to recognize them even at the "bump" stage, and it is wonderful to watch them all come to life.

Biennials and perennials are often grouped together. A biennial is a plant that takes two seasons to complete its growth cycle. If started from seed one year, it will generally not flower until the next; and after flowering once, the plant may persist, but it is not likely ever to produce another showy flowering. A biennial's growth cycle is, then, something like that of a hardy annual rather than like that of a perennial, since hardy annuals are often sown in fall for bloom the following season. But the plants we call biennials can generally be sown earlier in the season than hardy annuals, and they can winter over as fair-sized plants. It is thus easier to grow them in a permanent perennial bed than in an annual bed that is tilled up after frost. Some common garden biennials are Canterbury bells (*Campanula medium*), hollyhocks (*Alcea rosea*), foxgloves (*Digitalis* species) and sweet William (*Dianthus barbatus*).

Some common perennials that most people recognize are chrysanthemums, day lilies, peonies and iris. But these fine old standards are only the beginning. There are hundreds and hundreds of garden perennials for you to discover and combine in color pictures that are yours alone. This is why gardening with perennials can become—let me warn you—addicting. By the time my perennial bed is starting to show signs of life in early April, I always have a list of new things I want to try in it and ideas about rearranging it to make this year's show even better than last year's.

"Now wait," you may say. "I thought the whole point about perennials was that they are permanent—that you can plant them once and then never have to touch them again." Not true, and if a maintenance-free flower garden is your chief goal, you had best forgo perennials. Perennials not only need some yearly care, such as feeding, staking and cutting back after blooming, but many of them must be divided every few years to keep the clumps healthy and vigorous. You also need to experiment a bit to see which flowers do best in your own climate and even in your own yard, discarding some and trying new ones.

Another common misconception about perennials is that they bloom all season long, the way annuals do. Not so. Most of them bloom for a few weeks, some even less. A few, which you will come to cherish, might bloom from a month to six weeks or longer. Many will come up with a second flowering or a scattered continuous one through the rest of the season if you cut back flower stalks after bloom. By combining plants that flower at different times, you can ensure that there is always something blooming, but doing so takes skillful planning, and you will always have many spots where nothing is colorful at the moment. Planning such a garden is like conducting an orchestra that won't sit still. By the time the violins show up, the flutes are breaking for lunch; when you finally get the trumpet's attention, the oboes have wandered off.

But what a show if you manage to make such a garden work! If you doubt it, find some photographs of the great herbaceous borders in full bloom on the estates of England. They have a monumental quality that you cannot achieve with annuals. And in a cool climate like mine there is an added advantage to a perennial garden: most annuals do not bloom profusely until at least early summer and are cut down by the first frost, whereas many perennials bloom in

spring or fall months during which night frosts are common. As I write this a heavy April snow is falling on my perennial bed full of spring flowers, with no ill effects at all.

What Kind of Garden?

There are many different ways of using perennials, some of them very simple. An effective planting can be designed with just one species. Take day lilies, for example. If you have ever seen the wild orange ones growing along the road in early summer, you know that their bloom lasts only a few weeks. But if you were to plant the old-fashioned lemon lily, which still blooms earliest of all, and then plant a succession of hybrid varieties that bloom at different times, you could have a day lily bed in bloom from spring to early fall. (Catalogs that list day lilies usually specify blooming times.) A day lily planting like this might edge a lawn, or a driveway, or even work as a naturalized planting on a steep bank, where the plants' vigorous roots will help keep the soil from eroding.

You might find a spot for an all-iris bed in late spring, or an all-chrysanthemum bed in fall. Or plant an all-hosta bed in a shady spot; this stalwart perennial is grown not so much for its flowers, nice as they are, but for the varied shapes and colors of its leaves— large and blue-green, small and wavy with white markings, green edged in yellow, yellow edged in green, and many others. When different species and varieties of hostas are combined the effect is lovely.

In fact you might take any one of the plants in the List of Perennials and plant it in a mass to lend color to a spot even briefly. Globeflowers (*Trollius*), for example, have blossoms that look like giant yellow or orange buttercups with lights glowing inside them. A bed of these in part shade, blooming in late spring or early summer, will be so beautiful that you won't mind having to look elsewhere for your color later in the season. For summer you might also try a bed of feathery astilbes or, like my neighbor Jean Orr, grow a profusion of tall rose and purple foxgloves against a barn. For fall you could plant a bed composed of tall and short asters or a bed of tall, late-blooming sedums in mixed shades.

Combining two species together can also be very effective. Try a bed of yellow yarrow and blue veronica together. Or plant tall blue-flowering autumn monkshood with a silvery foliage plant such as 'Silver King' artemisia. Or mass columbines and lupines together; both are spring-flowering self-sowers that will naturalize together in harmony. You might even mingle a few particularly fast- and low-growing perennials like foamflower, lamium and ajuga to make a flowery carpet.

If you are anything like me, though, you will want to try your hand at an old-fashioned perennial border. It need not be large, grand and formal like those English borders I mentioned above, and you will not need a squadron of hired gardeners to keep it beautiful. But you will need two things: careful planning and excellent preparation for your bed. Both will pay off in less work and a better effect later on.

Planning

The first thing you need to decide is in what season you want your garden to be effective. There are a number of choices. Here are some of them:

A GARDEN FOR SPRING AND EARLY SUMMER

The mainstay of this garden might be iris, columbines, lupines, Oriental poppies, pinks, bellflowers, gas plant, coral bells and perhaps some of the early veronicas. If the bed were in partial shade, you would eliminate the iris, poppies, pinks and gas plant and add some more shade-tolerant perennials such as bleeding heart, foxgloves, wild blue phlox, globeflowers, primrose and perennial geraniums. To extend the blooming season, you might precede these with spring bulbs such as crocus, grape hyacinth and miniature narcissus whose foliage would later be hidden by the perennials. Then in the gaps between the perennials you would plant tall or bushy annuals such as zinnias and orange cosmos, which would take over after the perennials have finished blooming. You might also plan to have your summer bloom elsewhere on the property. If you go away for the summer, and only care about spring bloom, you might forget the annuals altogether.

A SUMMER GARDEN

By planning carefully you can keep a border in bloom for several months in the summer. In my New England climate, prime time would be July and August; in a warmer part of the country, you would focus on June and July or even May and June, before the intense summer heat gets the best of your plants.

The beginning of the show is the easiest—early to midsummer is the favorite blooming time for most perennials, such as yarrow, bee balm, sundrops, butterfly weed, coreopsis, most veronicas, gaillardias, day lilies, scabiosa, balloon flower, Shasta daisies, loosestrife, phlox and sea lavender. But many of these also bloom into late summer—such as day lilies, bee balm, phlox, loosestrife and Shasta daisies—especially if you look for late-blooming varieties. Many, such as pinks, coreopsis, Shasta daisies and delphiniums, will rebloom if flower stalks are cut. And still others are late-summer plants, such as coneflowers, gayfeather and false sunflower. The last is particularly useful because it fills that void between the last major summer flowers such as phlox and the first fall ones such as chrysanthemums and asters. (Similar bridge plants for this time of year are *Helenium, Helianthus* and *Rudbeckia.*)

There is no reason why you cannot extend your summer garden's season by planting spring- and fall-blooming perennials or by putting annuals in gaps between perennial clumps. But remember that any space occupied by these will diminish the space available for the summer-blooming perennials. One solution might be to plant a mixed collection of tulips that will bloom over a period of several weeks in late spring (see Chapter 10), but treat them as annuals. Tulip foliage is rather ugly after the plants have bloomed, and the flowers are often only at their best the first year. They are also relatively inexpensive to replace. I would simply dig them up after bloom and plant chrysanthemums in their place. These will grow into bushy clumps and then bloom in fall. Or I might grow the chrysanthemums in a nursery bed during the summer and transplant them into the border, full grown, in fall. I could even buy full-grown chrysanthemum clumps each fall and treat them as annuals.

A FALL GARDEN

A garden planted for fall display might start with some of the bridge plants, planted along with the real fall bloomers such as autumn monkshood, late sedums such as 'Autumn Joy,' asters and chrysanthemums. A fall garden can be quite beautiful, with many of the flowers having the same hues as autumn leaves but with the contrast of pink chrysanthemums, the blues of monkshoods, the wonderful rose and deep purple of asters and the crisp accents of white asters and mums.

You may decide that having different gardens for different parts of the season works best for your property. For example you might want a spring garden that is close to the house and easily seen from indoors, a summer garden near a pool or patio where you spend your summer hours, and a fall garden at the far edge of the lawn where its blazing colors can be best appreciated. You might want a summer garden at a summer house, or a spring and fall garden if you travel during the summer.

If you have limited time and space and can only have one garden, try planting one with spring bulbs and perennials followed by summer annuals, followed by tall perennials that bloom even after frost. This solution is particularly useful in cold climates where annuals have a short season.

Site

M ost perennials are sun loving, and need at least six hours of sun per day to grow and bloom well. So the first question asked in planning a border is usually, "Where is a good sunny spot?" Keep in mind that afternoon sun is stronger than morning sun. Thus in cool climates a garden that faced south or west would be ideal, and an eastern exposure would be preferred in hot climates where afternoon sun is too strong. But an ideal exposure will not do you much good if the spot is one you will never see. Another factor: some flowers, such as the sunflower types, daisies and daffodils, will actually turn to face the sun. With in-the-round flower shapes this is not a consideration: astilbes look the same from any direction. And with some sites it may not matter. My daffodils are far across the lawn, and I can't tell that they are facing the other way, only that the sun is backlighting them beautifully and making them glow. With the pansies near the kitchen window it makes more of a difference. A pansy with its back to you is not very interesting.

If you do not have a sunny site, do not despair. There are some perennials that actually prefer shade during part of the day, or better yet, filtered light such as that provided by a tree that lets some sun in. More often than not these are spring-flowering perennials that would be woodland plants if they lived in the wild, blooming before the trees are heavy with leaves. If you try some of these out of necessity, you will probably decide you are fortunate to have a spot for a shady garden. Flower colors sometimes look more vibrant in dappled shade than they do in strong sunlight, which can wash them out.

You do need a site with good drainage. Most perennials will rot if water collects around them and sits there, especially in winter. If your choice site is wet, the easiest way to correct the problem is to grow the plants in a raised bed.

Your site will also need to be free of encroaching roots from trees and shrubs. Most perennials will not tolerate competition from those roots, which not only take up space but also rob the soil of moisture and fertility. Here again a raised bed is the best solution. Bring in at least 8 inches of new soil to spread over the root-ridden area, enrich it, and enclose it with a stone, brick or wooden edging.

Size of the Garden

If you have only a small amount of time to spend in your perennial garden, stick to one of moderate size, say between 10 and 20 feet long. Figure that you may need to spend several days on the initial preparation and then a few hours each week maintaining it. In subsequent years you will not only have to do the regular maintenance but will have to spend at least a full day in spring and fall dividing plants and putting things in order.

Deciding how wide to make the bed is tricky: if you make it as narrow as 3 feet, it will be easy to tend, and you will not have to worry as much about plants' hiding one another as you would with a wide border. On the other hand, the wider the border, the more you will be able to give the effect of continuous bloom, since you can have many overlapping drifts of plants with at least one drift in bloom at any given time. You might start with a narrow border, then try a wide one after you become experienced with more plants and know their relative heights and periods of bloom.

Expense is less a consideration than you might think. True, to fill a 50- by 8-foot bed with big clumps of nursery-grown perennials can cost well over a thousand dollars. But you can also buy only a third of the full number of plants and then wait for them to form larger clumps, filling in the gaps with annuals in the meantime. In a few years you will be dividing some and even giving extras away. You may also fill your garden up with friends' donations, though keep in mind that these gifts are usually of plants that love to take over your garden. Spreaders such as *Oenothera pilosella* (sundrops, often called evening primrose) or bee balm are worth growing as long as you weed out the excess from time to time. But if someone offers you *Lathyrus latifolius* (perennial sweet pea) say "Thanks but no thanks"; it does not just crowd other plants—it obliterates them. Once perennial sweet pea is established, you will never get all of its ropelike roots out of your garden. (See page 158 for some other notorious overachievers.)

Shape of the Garden

A "perennial border" usually means simply a "perennial bed," though often the plot does border something: a lawn, a path, a fence, a wall, a building. It can also be a free-standing, or "island" bed, surrounded by lawn, ground cover, or paving. Beds can have formal geometrical shapes or they can be free-form, with sweeping S-curves. The important thing to remember in planning them is that an island bed will be seen from all sides; thus the tall plants will go in the middle, the medium-height plants on either side of them, and the low plants along the entire edge. In a bed that backs up to a building, hedge or other such feature, the tall plants will go in back, and the others will descend in height toward the viewer. Which shape you make your bed is partly a matter of style—is the property formal or informal in feeling?—and partly a matter of how the bed will best be viewed.

Backdrops and Edgings

I like a perennial garden to have a "frame" around it like a picture. If you are lucky enough to have a tall stone or brick wall in the right location, this will be an excellent backdrop as long as it does not cast too much shade on the garden, and as long as the rear plants start at least 3 feet out from the wall for good air circulation. A tall hedge is also very effective—evergreens such as yew, holly, hemlock, boxwood and arborvitae are some attractive choices, but a deciduous hedge can also be effective. I have a lilac hedge behind my flower garden. The house, barn or garage can also be a backdrop, as can a tall wooden fence.

An edging provides visual definition in front of the bed. It also can be a helpful physical barrier between the lawn and the garden. Your lawn grass and your pinks or creeping veronica will not, by themselves, stay on the correct side of an imaginary line you call "the edge of the garden." But they will respect an edging of flagstones, or bricks sunk vertically on end. A metal or plastic edging strip will also keep them in check but without the pleasing visual effect. I like to have an edging a foot wide. One wheel of the lawn mower can rest on it, and foreground perennials can spill out attractively onto the edging and still not be cropped by the mower.

Choosing the Plants

The List of Perennials describes forty common, easy-to-grow perennials and a few good species or varieties of each. As you come to realize how many different kinds there are, you will understand how difficult it was to narrow the list down to just forty. I did this so that I could describe each, give some advice about growing it, and include an identifying illustration. The perennials in this list, all of which can be grown in most parts of the country, should give you a good start, but I urge you to poke around nurseries and try some new ones each year. Seek out knowledgeable growers, salespeople and gardening friends, and get the benefit of their experience. There are also plant societies (listed in the back of the book) devoted to the culture of individual perennials such as iris and chrysanthemums. Their newsletters often list members whose gardens are sometimes open to the public. Visiting these wonderful gardens will alert you to new varieties to try, even within a plant group that is familiar to you. Finally, use plants such as perennial herbs, small shrubs and bulbs from the lists in other chapters in this book. Spring bulbs will often complement spring perennial gardens, and I often use summer bulbs such as lilies and dahlias for summer gardens.

In some instances your choices will be influenced by the nature of the site. If your garden is partially shaded, look for shade-tolerant plants in the descriptions. If it is very dry, look for those that tolerate dryness. If your property is very windy, you might want to avoid tall plants such as delphiniums, which blow over easily, though of course any plant can be staked. If your soil is either very acid or very alkaline, this might influence your choices, but since soil pH is easily brought within the ideal range for most perennials, 5.5–6.5, acidity need not be a determining criterion. Winter hardiness zones (page 613) should always be taken into account, but remember that they are not hard-and-fast rules; a protected site, or winter protection, may allow you to grow plants that are said to be too tender for your zone. Chrysanthemums are a good example. Few are winter-hardy where I live, but they will often survive if mulched with a thick, loose material such as straw, held down with evergreen boughs or black plastic.

In order to make your final selection of flowers for a specific garden you will have to keep several things in mind at once: color, height and blooming period. There are several ways to make

this simpler. I start by making a chart like the one shown in Figure 27. Let's say I am choosing plants for a sunny border 20 feet long and 5 feet wide. I want it to bloom for as much of the summer as possible, but with a bed this small, in my area, my best bet is to aim for July and August bloom, with some starting in June and some still left in early September.

As I go through the list of plants available I mark down the ones that appeal to me and place them on the chart according to their blooming period (indicated at the top) and their approximate height (indicated at the left side). For those with long bloom periods, and for foliage plants with long periods of effectiveness, I draw an arrow to the point where I think the plants' show will end. I always put down more than I can fit into the bed, then eliminate some. Usually I find I have too many plants in the middle height range. Or perhaps I've picked too many white flowers, or too many pink ones. In fact I often make the final choice on the basis of color. For example the column for the last week in June gives me yellow coreopsis, red-orange 'Enchantment' lilies and blanketflowers, blue delphiniums, veronicas and bluebells, white Shasta daisies and 'Miss Lingard' phlox—a strong, fresh combination I like in the garden at that time of year. Sometimes I'll select a specific variety of a plant at this point to complete the total picture. For example if my "July" column needs a strong red shade I might choose a red bee balm like 'Cambridge Scarlet' rather than a pink or lavender one.

Drawing the Plan

The next step is to translate the chart into the bird's-eye-view plan shown in Figure 31, drawing in the

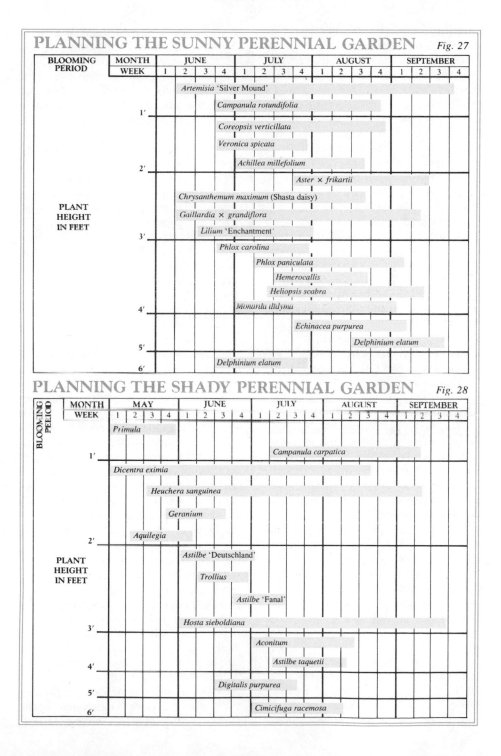

PLANNING THE SUNNY PERENNIAL GARDEN   *Fig. 27*

BLOOMING PERIOD	MONTH	JUNE				JULY				AUGUST				SEPTEMBER			
	WEEK	1	2	3	4	1	2	3	4	1	2	3	4	1	2	3	4

PLANT HEIGHT IN FEET

- Artemisia 'Silver Mound'
- Campanula rotundifolia
- Coreopsis verticillata
- Veronica spicata
- Achillea millefolium
- Aster × frikartii
- Chrysanthemum maximum (Shasta daisy)
- Gaillardia × grandiflora
- Lilium 'Enchantment'
- Phlox carolina
- Phlox paniculata
- Hemerocallis
- Heliopsis scabra
- Monarda didyma
- Echinacea purpurea
- Delphinium elatum
- Delphinium elatum

1' 2' 3' 4' 5' 6'

PLANNING THE SHADY PERENNIAL GARDEN   *Fig. 28*

BLOOMING PERIOD	MONTH	MAY				JUNE				JULY				AUGUST				SEPTEMBER			
	WEEK	1	2	3	4	1	2	3	4	1	2	3	4	1	2	3	4	1	2	3	4

PLANT HEIGHT IN FEET

- Primula
- Campanula carpatica
- Dicentra eximia
- Heuchera sanguinea
- Geranium
- Aquilegia
- Astilbe 'Deutschland'
- Trollius
- Astilbe 'Fanal'
- Hosta sieboldiana
- Aconitum
- Astilbe taquetii
- Digitalis purpurea
- Cimicifuga racemosa

1' 2' 3' 4' 5' 6'

areas that each plant will occupy in the garden. Keeping in mind the size the plant will become, I draw a shape that indicates the number of plants that will make up each clump. Thus the phlox are in clumps of three, for a good show even the first year; the delphiniums are planted with a bit more space in between them than the phlox; the blanketflowers are planted singly because each one will eventually form a large clump.

I start the plan with the tall plants at the back of the border, then work forward to the front. As I place each one I think about how it will look in relation to the plants on all sides of it. Consider heights carefully. For instance the delphiniums will be tall when they bloom in early summer, but when they rebloom later they will be shorter than they were the first time. The yarrow, coreopsis and bluebells in front of them will not, however, be tall enough to hide the delphiniums. The phlox in front of the 'Enchantment' lilies may be tall enough to hide them, but only after the lilies have finished blooming. The 'Frikartii' asters, though medium height, were put in the front of the border because they tend to flop forward—and to my mind look pretty this way.

Also consider color juxtapositions: The blue veronica will look nice with the yellow coreopsis next to it. The salmon color of phlox 'Sir John Falstaff' will go better next to the yellow heliopsis than one of the pink or purple phlox varieties would, but the pink phlox in the center will go well with the purple coneflower on either side of it. The Shasta daisies and phlox 'Miss Lingard' will provide a running theme of white through the middle of the border, to set off the bright colors of the other plants. The 'Silver Mound' artemisias at each corner will lend a silvery foliage accent for the whole season.

As you build your border always imagine that you are looking at it head-on, or from whichever position you will actually be in when you view it. You should try to space out your plants for each blooming period so that you can see color dotted throughout the whole border at any given time, not just a big lump of it in one spot. The bed does not have to be symmetrical, like the one shown here, but it should have balance to it. (I sometimes like to start with symmetry, then as years go by let the border take on a less ordered scheme as I add and subtract plants.) Sometimes it is helpful to make several different border plans, one for each part of the blooming season, just to check for large gaps in the flow of color. You can do this by placing several pieces of tracing paper over the original plan one at a time and by drawing on them only the plants that will be in bloom at roughly the same time. Another thing to keep in mind is what the foliage of each plant will look like after it has finished blooming. Will it be attractive like the grassy foliage of Siberian iris? Or will it look messy and dried out like that of Oriental poppy? In the latter case you would try to arrange for a bushy mid- or late-season plant such as phlox to grow up and hide the unsightly early-blooming one.

You do not *have* to do all this on paper. If I am starting a garden from scratch I will sometimes just set out all the pots where I think they should go, then stare at them, think about them, rearrange them, and plant them only after I am sure of the right position for each. But if you are new to laying out perennials, a plan is very helpful, especially since you need to know what heights, colors and bloom periods you will need before you go shopping. Even if yours is an "accumulation" garden, with many plants scavenged from friends, it is nice to have a master scheme to refer to, even though you may constantly make substitutions in it.

The second plan shown here (Figure 32) is for a semishaded garden in the the ell of a house, or perhaps bounded on the short side by a fence. It spans a long season, beginning in spring with primroses, wild columbines, coral bells, and a low-growing form of bleeding heart. Next are violet-blue perennial geraniums, rosy foxgloves, orange-gold trollius and a succession of astilbes: an early white, a July-blooming red and a tall, late pink. Blue Carpathian harebells start in July at the front of the bed, blue monkshood at the rear, along with the tall, fuzzy white spikes of snakeroot. The hostas bloom too but are chiefly there as foliage accents—one with large blue-green leaves, another with large green ones edged in yellow. It is not a showy garden with a riot of color, but there is always something blooming in it. There are many foliage contrasts such as the broad-leaved hostas next to the ferny-leaved astilbes and bleeding hearts, or the bluish leaves of the columbines next to the apple-green leaves of the primroses. For more color you could tuck in small spring bulbs such as glory-of-the-snow or miniature narcissus, then add some pansies or impatiens here and there wherever you find small gaps.

Preparing the Bed

I deally a perennial bed should be prepared in fall, then allowed to settle. I admit that I have planted many beds in spring immediately after preparation, out of necessity or sheer impatience. But if you can muster the foresight fall preparation is better, especially if you are giving the bed first-class treatment and digging it very deeply.

When you get a perennial bed ready you are providing space for long-term residents, not short-term tenants. Thus while you might prepare your vegetable or annual garden hastily one year, vowing to better it the following season, with perennials you have only one chance to make good. You will be dividing or moving some of them in years to come (phlox, yarrow, day lilies, for example) but others form deep root systems and resent being transplanted. Oriental poppies, balloon flower, peonies, butterfly weed, gas plant and sea lavender are best left alone; others such as loosestrife (*Lythrum*) and Siberian iris can be divided, but there is usually no need to. Picture what your perennials will want: a weed-free soil that has been loosened to a good depth, with organic matter added to it for perfect tilth, and sufficient nutrients for proper growth (see Chapter 2). Even though you will be fertilizing and cultivating the top layer every year, the lower layers must be improved at the start.

I am fanatical about perennial beds and dig mine to a depth of almost 2 feet (although you do not have to go this far—one foot might suffice). I use either the basic or deluxe methods of double digging described on page 35, depending on how much energy I have and what kind of plants will occupy the beds. If there will be small shrubs such as roses in the bed, or if it will contain large, deep-rooted perennial clumps, I go the full 2 feet, adding generous amounts of rotted manure and peat to the subsoil layer, together with a handful or so each of wood ashes and superphosphate (0-20-0) for each 3–4 cubic feet of soil. When I am done the subsoil looks like topsoil, and the soil surface is almost a foot higher than it was before I started (though it will later settle to almost its original level). And it is the kind of loose, fluffy soil that you can dig with your fingers, without so much as a trowel.

If I have done my job right, I do not really need to add any more fertilizer to the soil when I set in the plants. The manure supplies plenty of nitrogen, the superphosphate supplies phosphorus and the ashes supply potassium. If you do not have a source of manure or rich plant humus, use plenty of peat moss to lighten the soil and add a commercial fertilizer to the soil in the amounts suggested on the package. Refer to the discussion of fertilizers on page 31, and be sure that the peat you add has been moistened (page 26).

Planting and Dividing

P erennials reproduce vegetatively—that is, by sending up new stems from the roots, rhizomes or tubers. Those same plants also reproduce by seeds, but most are cultivars that will not breed true. Since most perennials take longer to attain flowering size than annuals, most gardeners grow them from clump divisions they buy in a nursery or obtain from friends rather than from seed. But there are a few perennials that you might try growing from seed. Some, such as feverfew, blanket-flower and coreopsis, can grow to flowering size in one season and will usually breed true to the original seed-producing plant. I also like to grow a number of self-sowers—plants that will seed themselves in my garden—such as feverfew, foxgloves, lupines and columbines. They may not always breed true, or come up where I want them (in front of, not behind, a taller plant for example)

PLANTING PERENNIALS

Fig. 29

Plant fibrous-rooted perennials with the roots spread out and the crown at soil level.

Plant bearded iris with the rhizome right at soil level; mound slightly if drainage is less than perfect.

Plant Oriental poppies in a hole deep enough for the taproot, with the crown an inch or two below the soil surface.

Plant peonies in a deep hole with compost, firmed well, in the bottom. The pink "eyes" (buds) should be 1–2 inches below the soil surface.

Plant day lilies in groups by spreading the roots against a cone-shaped mound of compost in the center of the hole; keep crowns at soil level.

but the seedlings are easily moved. Working with them gives the garden a natural but controlled look, as if things were allowed to happen accidentally. As permanent as a perennial garden is, I like to have, say, 25 percent of it in flux. There should always be a few places where I can try out new kinds, add some bright annuals and put in a striking foliage plant or a useful and attractive herb.

The best time to plant perennials is when they are just starting to show signs of life. If you order them by mail, they will be shipped in this near-dormant state and, with any luck, they'll arrive at the proper time for planting: when the ground has thawed but is no longer too damp for digging—April to May in my climate. If you place your order in February you stand a better chance of getting your delivery on time, as well as a better shot at finding the varieties you want. Often the plants arrive with some fresh new growth on them. These young shoots are very soft and tender because they have emerged under greenhouse conditions or even in transit. I pot up my mail-order arrivals in a rich potting medium (say, one-third compost, one-third soilless mix and one-third soil) and then harden them off in a spot protected from hot sun, wind and freezing temperatures. After a few weeks I plant them with their potful of loose, rich soil.

If you buy your plants at a nursery, you should also look for ones that are just starting to show healthy new growth, not ones that are tall and flowering in their pots. If you are not planting them right away, place them in a partly shaded area and keep them well watered.

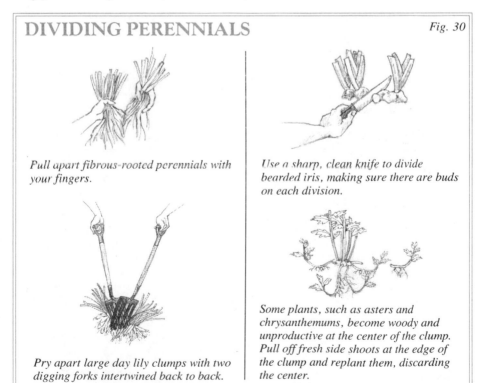

DIVIDING PERENNIALS

Fig. 30

Pull apart fibrous-rooted perennials with your fingers.

Use a sharp, clean knife to divide bearded iris, making sure there are buds on each division.

Pry apart large day lily clumps with two digging forks intertwined back to back.

Some plants, such as asters and chrysanthemums, become woody and unproductive at the center of the clump. Pull off fresh side shoots at the edge of the clump and replant them, discarding the center.

PLAN FOR A SUNNY PERENNIAL GARDEN (20' by 5')

Fig. 31

1. *Artemisia* 'Silver Mound'

2. *Aster* × *frikartii*

3. *Campanula rotundifolia* (bluebell)

4. *Veronica spicata* 'Blue Spires'

5. *Coreopsis verticillata* 'Zagreb' (threadleaf coreopsis)

6. *Lilium* 'Enchantment'

7. *Chrysanthemum maximum* 'Polaris' (Shasta daisy)

8. *Gaillardia* × *grandiflora* 'Monarch Strain'

9. *Achillea* 'Red Beauty' (yarrow)

10. *Phlox carolina* 'Miss Lingard'

11. *Monarda didyma* 'Cambridge Scarlet' (bee balm)

12. *Phlox paniculata* 'Sir John Falstaff'

13. *Phlox paniculata* 'Dodo Hanbury Forbes'

14. *Heliopsis scabra* 'Incomparabilis'

15. *Delphinium elatum* 'Blue Skies'

16. *Delphinium elatum* 'King Arthur'

17. *Hemerocallis* 'Hyperion' (day lily)

18. *Hemerocallis* 'Evergold' (day lily)

19. *Echinacea purpurea* 'Bright Star' (purple coneflower)

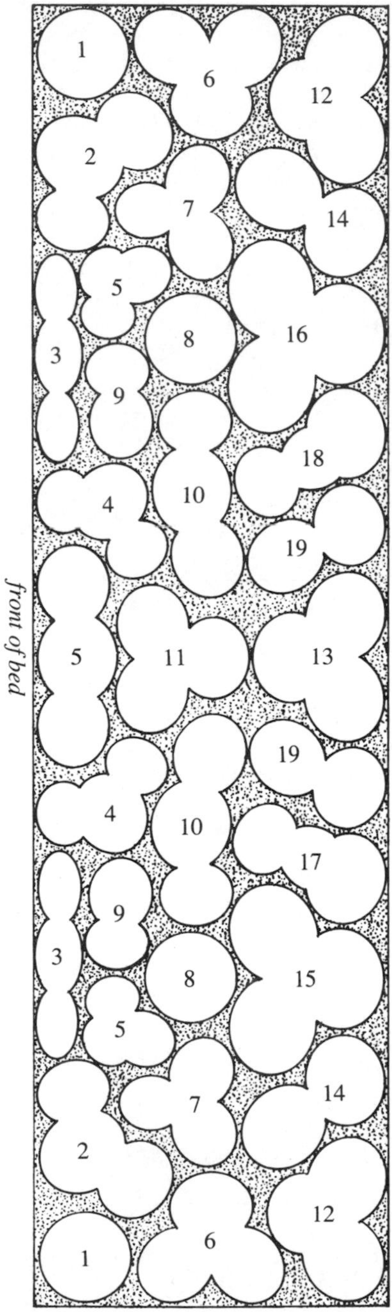

PLAN FOR A SHADY PERENNIAL GARDEN (15½' by 8')

Fig. 32

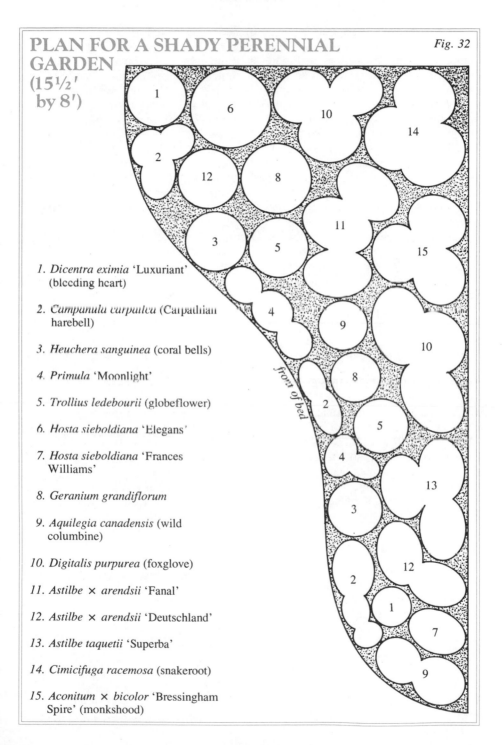

1. *Dicentra eximia* 'Luxuriant' (bleeding heart)

2. *Campanula carpatica* (Carpathian harebell)

3. *Heuchera sanguinea* (coral bells)

4. *Primula* 'Moonlight'

5. *Trollius ledebourii* (globeflower)

6. *Hosta sieboldiana* 'Elegans'

7. *Hosta sieboldiana* 'Frances Williams'

8. *Geranium grandiflorum*

9. *Aquilegia canadensis* (wild columbine)

10. *Digitalis purpurea* (foxglove)

11. *Astilbe* × *arendsii* 'Fanal'

12. *Astilbe* × *arendsii* 'Deutschland'

13. *Astilbe taquetii* 'Superba'

14. *Cimicifuga racemosa* (snakeroot)

15. *Aconitum* × *bicolor* 'Bressingham Spire' (monkshood)

Wherever you obtain your perennials you should plant them carefully, according to the instructions in Figure 29. Keep them watered for a week or two to get them established.

After your garden has been growing for a year or two, some plants will need dividing. Follow the instructions in Figure 30. Usually division is done in early spring. Make your new divisions and plant them at the same time you would plant purchased ones, when the perennials' new growth is just starting to emerge.

Some perennials can be divided and/or planted in late summer or fall. Poppies and peonies prefer fall planting, for example. Other early bloomers such as coral bells and bleeding heart can also be done then. Late-blooming perennials such as asters, chrysanthemums, rudbeckia and phlox, however, should be divided and/or planted in spring.

Division not only keeps plants that require it healthy, but it provides you with lots of new plants and is the easiest way to obtain them. You can also propagate new plants from your garden by taking stem or root cuttings and by saving seeds after your plants have bloomed. But remember that most of the plants in your garden were probably hybrids and will not breed true from seed.

Maintenance

Keeping a perennial bed pretty is not arduous; it consists of a series of small tasks performed regularly.

WEEDING

I find that a mulch cuts out most of the worst job—weeding. If you have removed most traces of perennial weeds from the soil during preparation, you need only inhibit the annual weeds with a 2-inch layer of mulch. I like something light such as buckwheat hulls, root mulch (chopped-up roots, sold in bags) or leaf mold. I try not to mound it around the plants themselves, because the crowns of many perennials are subject to rot or disease and are best kept relatively dry, even though the surrounding soil must be kept moist. A mulch will also lessen the need for watering. A light mulch will have to be replaced or added to each year, since it will decompose and since you will disturb it by dividing plants and by pulling out those perennial weeds that find their way into the garden from the edges, from bits of root still in the soil, or from seeds that drift into the garden.

WINTER PROTECTION

Mulching for winter protection is another matter entirely. It is helpful to protect plants that are not quite winter-hardy in your area or to keep fall-planted perennials from being heaved out of the soil by alternate freezing and thawing. But it is best done with salt hay, straw or evergreen boughs, which will catch and hold the snow, not with flat leaves such as maple, which can mat around the plants and promote disease. Oak leaves, which don't mat, are all right. If you have a cold frame (page 48) you can dig up perennials that may not survive your winter, keep them in the frame until early spring, then replant them where they were before.

STAKING

Whether to stake perennials or not is a fairly subjective matter. Some tall ones such as delphiniums or hollyhocks must almost always be staked. Even the healthiest, strongest-stemmed plants can be decimated within minutes by a sudden thunderstorm or strong wind. With others, such as Shasta daisies, which flop over without the stems actually breaking, it is a matter of appearance; if you prefer the natural look of some floppy plants to the neat, staked look, let them flop. When I do stake I try to do it as unobtrusively as possible, using green, inconspicuous stakes and twine, and never anything plastic. (Some methods of staking various perennials are shown in Figure 33.) I also try to stake them before it is too late. Even if the stem does not break when the plant flops you have problems: the stem will start to grow straight up, so that when you finally get around to righting it again, its top will be heading in a sideways direction. If the plant is at the front of the border it is sometimes better to just leave the flopped stem alone. In fact some gardeners deliberately flop the front stems of certain plants forward at the front of the clumps and "peg" them into the earth; they will grow straight up from the pegs to give a low, bushy display of color.

WATERING

I almost never water my perennials—only those I have just planted or those that look wilted during dry weather. If you live in a dry climate, however, you may need to be more vigilant. It is best to water plants at soil level, either by standing there with a hose or water wand and letting the water flow onto the soil at the base of the plant, or by laying down a soaker hose (page 97). Sprinklers are handy but get the foliage wet and can thereby make your plants more prone to disease.

STAKING PERENNIALS

Fig. 33

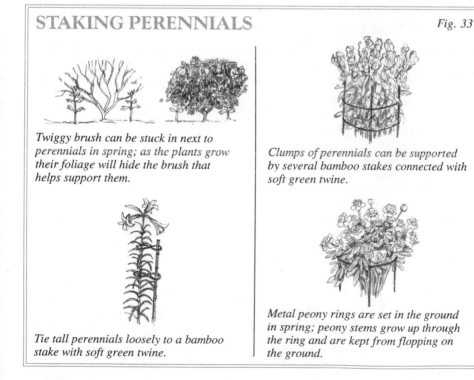

Twiggy brush can be stuck in next to perennials in spring; as the plants grow their foliage will hide the brush that helps support them.

Clumps of perennials can be supported by several bamboo stakes connected with soft green twine.

Tie tall perennials loosely to a bamboo stake with soft green twine.

Metal peony rings are set in the ground in spring; peony stems grow up through the ring and are kept from flopping on the ground.

CONTROLLING PESTS AND DISEASES

I rarely have any serious problems with insects on my perennials. The occasional aphid or leaf miner seldom does much damage, and I am always reluctant to use even the relatively nontoxic sprays on them, for fear I will harm the insects I want in my flower garden such as butterflies, bees and ladybugs. If there is severly distorted growth from root nematodes, it is best to destroy the plants before others are infested.

Diseases are occasionally a problem in muggy summer weather when I sometimes see fungus diseases such as powdery mildew or septoria. Fungicides are sometimes effective, as is destroying plant debris, especially that of diseased plants. I also try to give the plants plenty of air circulation by not crowding them or growing them in too enclosed a spot. Keeping the supply of moisture fairly constant through mulch and good drainage is also a deterrent to disease.

OTHER CHORES

There are also a few little tasks that are not necessary for the plants' survival or health but that will make them showier. ''Deadheading'' means cutting off flowers that have finished blooming. This will not only make the garden look tidier, but it will also cause the plant to put energy into growth and not into seed formation. And it will keep plants that do not breed true to seed from producing unwanted seedlings. (Obviously you should not deadhead all the blossoms if you are eager to have a particular plant self-sow.)

''Pinching'' (Figure 34) will encourage plants such as chrysanthemums and asters to become bushier by making them branch, but it should be stopped soon enough in the season to allow the plant to bloom at its proper time. Cutting back the flowering stems of some plants, especially delphiniums, painted daisies and yarrow, will cause them to rebloom either continuously or later on in the season.

And that's about it. Each spring I scatter a handful of fertilizer for every square yard or so, using a high-phosphorus one such as those designed for bulbs. This is because I am always trying to encourage root development, not lush foliage. And I constantly watch the garden picture as it unfolds from week to week, day to day. I get to know the plants so that I can recognize them by their foliage and growth habit, even when they are not in flower.

PINCHING TO PRODUCE BUSHY GROWTH   *Fig. 34*

Making Changes in the Garden

After your bed has been in place for a long time, the soil may become depleted in the lower layer, and the organic matter you originally tilled into the soil may break down. This may also be true of an old bed you inherited when you moved to a new home. The best thing to do is remove all the plants in early spring and temporarily heel them into a nursery bed (page 49). Then double dig the soil in the bed just as if you were starting from scratch. Many of the clumps will need dividing anyway, and double digging is also a good chance to remove any perennial weeds and grasses that have worked their way into established clumps. Either sacrifice taprooted plants that can't be moved successfully, or work around them.

Even without taking such drastic measures, there is always something I want to change in my garden. Sometimes it can be done as soon as I spot it: one of the phlox I bought was mislabeled by the nursery and is the wrong color, so I dig it up with as much soil around it as possible, move it, and water it well. A veronica I expected to be 2 feet tall is 3, and is hiding a dwarf phlox, so I might move one or the other in similar fashion. On the other hand it might be a hot week in August when I would rather wait till a cooler, moister time of year, so I make a note of this and other things to do at a future time. In spring my list might read: "Move the tall veronica. Regal lilies are hiding Siberian iris 'Cambridge.' Bed needs move lavender shades. 'Miss Lingard' phlox is spindly; move it to a sunnier spot. Painted daisy is being engulfed by bee balm. Shasta daisy looks lonesome at left end of bed; buy two more. Try some *Sanguisorba canadensis* next year."

Taking frequent photographs is also a good way to keep accurate records, using a wide-angle lens if possible to get the border all in and maintain good detail in a broad depth of field. And this way when you tell friends, as every perennial gardener does, that they "should have seen the border two weeks ago when it was *really* gorgeous," you can actually prove it!

Perennials That Spread

Many plants start out fine in your garden, then are too much of a good thing. Some are wild species; some are "civilized" cultivars. Often there is a legend about whatever villain introduced them to the regions where they grow. A spready plant may have been brought here by foreigners; in other cases an infamous past member of the Garden Club did the deed.

Many of these plants are beautiful if used in the right way. Some can go in the perennial bed if you weed out the extras; some are fine if you give them a spot to themselves where they can't cause trouble—naturalized in a meadow, or used as a ground cover; some are so invasive that you shouldn't get involved with them at all. This list does not cover all the trespassers on your precious soil, but here are sixteen to watch out for.

Aster. *Aster*, dwarf hybrids. Most tall hybrid asters merely form large clumps, though some original species such as *Aster novi-belgii* can self-sow. It is the sly little hybrids such as the 6-inch 'Romany' that are grown with caution. Unless you want a spreader, buy dwarf asters only when the catalog says "compact," or "forms a tidy cushion."

Bee Balm. *Monarda didyma*, *M. fistulosa*. Bees, butterflies, hummingbirds and most gardeners agree that this plant has its place in the garden despite its spreading roots. The more rich and moist your soil, the more you will have to remove each year; if your garden is very small, make another choice.

Bouncing Bet. *Saponaria officinalis*. Considered a wildflower, bouncing Bet was brought to North America in colonial times, and has naturalized. It has pretty pink flowers that are especially profuse at night, but may bounce all over your garden; it's best in a wild setting.

Chinese Lantern. *Physalis alkekengi*. I love this plant—and its little papery orange "lanterns" are beautiful in dried arrangements. But grow it by itself in a moist spot.

Coneflower. *Rudbeckia*. This species includes the wild brown-eyed Susan, which some garden cultivars resemble. Others have ball-shaped yellow flowers, like the tall, old-fashioned 'Golden Glow.' They are good plants if you divide them frequently, but in warm climates and moist soils they can be a nuisance.

Creeping Bellflower (Rampion). *Campanula rapunculoides*. Rampant it is, creep it does. Three feet tall, with handsome long-blooming blue flowers, it looks like a useful plant until the roots spread all over your garden. Many of the low-growing bellflowers are also creepers but are so attractive that most gardeners make peace with them.

Goutweed (Bishops' Weed). *Aegopodium podagraria*. This plant has attractive, often variegated foliage like that of astilbe. The flowers look like Queen Anne's lace, bloom for a very long time, and are great to have nearby for flower arrangements. Resist the temptation. It makes a good ground cover for a spot more distant (about 2 miles).

Loosestrife. *Lysimachia* species. Yellow loosestrife (*Lysimachia punctata*) is an attractive plant for early summer but too invasive for small gardens. Another plant called loosestrife, *Lythrum salicaria* is the tall, spiky purple plant you see in wet meadows. The species is such a bad spreader that it is illegal to sell it in some areas. It can crop up surreptitiously in wildflower mixes. The roots colonize a meadow so tenaciously that usually you can never eradicate them. Loosestrife's cultivars, however, are well behaved.

Obedient Plant (False Dragonhead). *Physostegia virginiana.* This hardy plant is valuable for its tall snapdragonlike flowers in late summer. Would that it *were* obedient. I say grow it anyway, but dig it up every year or so and replant only what you need. It spreads most vigorously in moist, light soils.

Perennial Pea. *Lathyrus latifolius.* The flowers are handsome and long-blooming clusters in shades of pink, lavender and white. Its evils are described on page 145.

Plume Poppy. *Macleaya* species (*Bocconia*). Some forms are worse than others, but in all cases use this plant with caution. Some gardeners like the tall, pinkish, plumelike flowers in the back of the border; others put it elsewhere. It doesn't matter: unless you confine the roots it will soon be everywhere.

Ribbon Grass (Gardener's Garters). *Phalaris arundinacea picta.* This attractive grass has white stripes. Ornamental grasses can be a fine addition to the perennial border, but this is not one to try. Except in very poor, dry soil it is invasive.

Sundrop. *Oenothera pilosella.* This plant's common name is usually erroneously given as "evening primrose" (unlike some *Oenothera* species, it is day-blooming). But there is no mistaking the plant. It has straight, 2-foot stems with clusters of bright yellow flowers at the top and little rosettes of leaves at the bottom. I like it for its color and just pull out the extras; they spread close to the soil surface and are easy to remove.

Tansy. *Tanacetum vulgare.* This herb is another escapee that was brought over by the early settlers and now makes mischief all over the country. The clusters of buttonlike flowers atop 3-foot stems are pretty along a split-rail fence. It is pungent-smelling, bitter-tasting, even poisonous. And it spreads wildly.

Valerian. *Valeriana officinalis.* This tall, vigorous plant bears pinkish flowers in midsummer that are almost too fragrant. It, too, was imported by the colonists and will gladly colonize your garden. Another plant called "valerian," *Centranthus ruber*, is a little better behaved but not much. Both have their place in the scheme of things, but perhaps not in your garden.

Violets. *Viola odorata.* People love the common "sweet violet," but it self-sows everywhere. Confederate violet (*Viola papilionifera*) is a lovely white violet streaked with blue. It will march through your garden faster than Robert E. Lee.

LIST OF PERENNIALS

This list of forty perennials will give you a start in planning your garden. Most of them are familiar favorites; some may be new to you. With only a few exceptions, they are among the easiest perennials to grow. Many, many fine plants were omitted for lack of space, and in most cases the entries describe only some of the species and cultivars available. (For the distinction between species, varieties and cultivars, see page 107.)

In the How to Grow sections below, I have assumed that you are giving the plants the kind of "lowest common denominator" soil that you provide when you are growing a number of different plants with slightly different needs. In some cases you may alter the soil in your garden to grow plants with specific requirements—for example you might create a bed with woodsy soil, very rich in organic matter, for a partly shaded garden of woodland species. Usually, however, the plants must make some sort of accommodation to your soil. If you have a soil condition that is common to your area—dry and sandy, for example—look for plants I describe as preferring those conditions.

ARTEMISIA
Artemisia

DESCRIPTION: Artemisias are treasured by the gardener for their white or silvery foliage. Their flowers are relatively uninteresting, but the leaves are effective as a lightening or softening accent all season long. They vary greatly in leaf shape and growing habit. *Artemisia schmidtiana* 'Silver Mound' makes a low, silvery mound. When you stroke it, it feels like a soft, fluffy cat; when the wind blows, it undulates as if it were alive. Zone 4. Southernwood (*A. abrotanum*) makes a large mound that can be rather sprawly if not clipped. Zone 5. *A. ludoviciana albula* 'Silver King' has tall plumes, 2–3½ feet. Zone 5. Beach wormwood (*A. stellerana*) is the whitest of the group; its foliage is chalk white, toothed and woolly. Its stems grow to 2 feet but tend to flop along the ground. Zone 4.

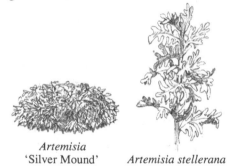

Artemisia 'Silver Mound'   *Artemisia stellerana*

HOW TO GROW: Provide all varieties with good drainage, especially in winter. They prefer dryish, not-too-fertile soil. All are easily divided. 'Silver King' can be invasive and should be weeded out from time to time. If Artemisias become leggy, cut them back in summer; fresh new growth will start to appear right away.

ASTER
Aster

DESCRIPTION: The glory of the fall garden, asters range in height from 6 feet tall to just above the ground. Colors are shades of purple, lavender, pink, red, blue and white. In zones where they are hardy, the plants tend to be very vigorous; some are even invasive. Most garden hybrids are derived from one of two native species. From *Aster novae-angliae* (New England aster) come 'Harrington's Pink,' pale to medium pink and up to 6 feet tall, and 'Alma Potschke,' which is 3 feet tall and a strong pink. Zone 5. From *A. novi-belgii* (New York aster) come many varieties including 'Marie Ballard,' light blue, 3–4 feet; 'Crimson Brocade,' reddish pink, 3 feet; and 'Eventide,' purple, 3–4 feet. Zone 5. Dwarf varieties include 'Snow Flurry,' which is white, and 'Audrey,' which is blue-violet. Zone 5. *A. × frikartii* is a very long blooming aster that begins flowering in summer and grows 2–3 feet tall. Zone 6.

HOW TO GROW: Asters like moist but well-drained soil and plenty of sun. Most form big clumps that are best divided every few years by replanting shoots from the outside of the clumps. Tall varieties must often be staked, but the stems can be pinched early in the season to make the plants more erect as well as more compact and free-flowering. (This may, however, delay bloom.) With some of the dwarf varieties you must remove some plants each year to prevent them from taking over. Mulch varieties that are not winter-hardy in your zone with evergreen boughs. Remove self-sown seedlings, for they will not come up the same color

Aster × frikartii   *Aster* 'Harrington's Pink'

as the parent plant if they are hybrids and not an original species.

ASTILBE
Astilbe × arendsii

DESCRIPTION: What would I do for summer bloom in my shade garden without astilbes? The plants have plumelike flowers and fernlike leaves and bloom from early to late summer depending on the variety. Colors are shades of pink, red and white; heights range from 8 inches to 4 feet. 'Europa,' pale pink, and the white 'Deutschland' grow 2 feet tall, with early-summer bloom. Good midsummer varieties include 'Fanal,' dark red and 2–2½ feet tall, 'Ostrich Plume,' deep coral and 3–3½ feet, and 'Avalanche,' white and 3–3½ feet. The pink *Astilbe taquetii* 'Superba' grows up to 4 feet tall and blooms late in the summer. The dwarf *A. chinensis* 'Pumila' is lavender-pink, 8–12 inches tall and blooms in late summer. All are Zone 5.

HOW TO GROW: These vigorous, trouble-free plants prefer fertile, fairly acid, and moist but well-drained soil. They need partial shade. They spread readily and if space is limited may need to be divided frequently. This can be done in spring or fall.

BALLOON FLOWER
Platycodon grandiflorus

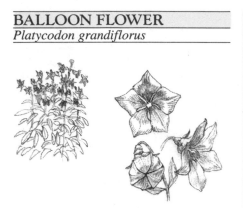

DESCRIPTION: This is a fine, old-fashioned plant with flowers the shape of open bells, some single and some double, in colors that are never garish: blue, pink or white. It is perfect for the "English garden" look. It blooms in midsummer on stems that are usually 2–3 feet tall. 'Mariesii' is a short blue variety with single flowers, 1½ feet tall. 'Shell Pink' is a popular pink variety; 'Album' is white. All are Zone 4.

HOW TO GROW: Sun is preferable, but platycodon will tolerate some shade. Provide light, slightly acid, moist but well-drained soil. Sandy soils are more suitable than clay. The plant forms long-lived clumps that do not require division, though it may be done in spring if you dig out the long taproot very carefully. Watch out for the shoots, which are slow to emerge in spring. Don't trample them when you are working the soil in their general vicinity. You can mark the spot in fall as a safeguard.

BEE BALM (BERGAMOT)
Monarda

DESCRIPTION: Bee balm is a bit over-zealous, but still a good, dependable perennial for the middle of the border. Strong upright stems bear bright flowers 2–3 inches across that are clusters of tiny tubes. They are beloved by hum-mingbirds and butterflies and worth growing for this feature alone. Flowers, which appear in midsummer, are shades of red, lavender, pink, mahogany and white. Hybrids of *Monarda didyma* include the red 'Cambridge Scarlet' and 'Croftway Pink,' both about 3 feet tall. *M. fistulosa* (wild bergamot) has lavender flowers and may get as tall as 5 feet in the garden; it tends to grow rampant.

HOW TO GROW: Bee balm spreads underground by runners. Unless you are allowing it to naturalize in a spot with plenty of space, you will need to weed out the excess every year or two. But the plant is widely grown because it is easy and trouble-free, especially in cool climates. It prefers sun or partial shade, and a rich moist soil. Of the two species, *M. fistulosa* tolerates heat and dry soil better.

BELLFLOWER
Campanula

DESCRIPTION: Whatever kind of flower garden you have, there is a bellflower for you. The flowers vary considerably in shape and size; though most are blue, some are violet or purple, and some are white. They are beautiful in pastel gardens, with roses, or just anywhere you want a blue accent. Some grow on plants of mid-border height, others on low cushions, others on long, trailing stems. Most bloom in early summer, but

Campanula   *Campanula*
persicifolia   *carpatica*

some, especially the low-growing varieties, will continue to flower, though less heavily, throughout the season. *Campanula persicifolia* 'Grandiflora,' the popular peach-leaved bellflower, is available in blue varieties such as 'Telham Beauty' and a white one, 'Alba.' It grows 2–3 feet tall. Zone 4. *C. glomerata* also grows up to 2 feet; its variety 'Superba' is a wonderful rich purple, 'Crown of Snow' is white. Zone 3–4. Low-growing bellflowers include *C. carpatica*, blue or white, 6–10 inches tall, Zone 4; *C. garganica,* blue, 6 inches, Zone 5; *C. poscharskyana*, lavender, 12 inches tall but sprawling, Zone 4; *C. rotundifolia* is blue and 1–2 feet, but the variety 'Olympica' is more compact. Hardy to Zone 2, this last species can be weedy in some gardens.

HOW TO GROW: Bellflowers like sun but will do well in light shade, especially in hot climates. Provide moist, moderately fertile, well-drained soil. Sometimes slug control may be necessary (pages 72–73). Weed out the invasive types as needed; cut back tall varieties after flowering to encourage them to bloom again.

BLANKETFLOWER
Gaillardia × grandiflora

DESCRIPTION: Gaillardias look like large daisies, with bold, bright markings like those of an American Indian blanket, in patterns of red, yellows and golds. Most grow about 2½ feet tall, but there are also dwarf varieties. They bloom in summer over a long period and are a good choice if your climate is hot and dry. Varieties include the mixed-colored 'Monarch Strain,' and solids such as dark red 'Burgundy' and 'Yellow Queen.' Multicolored 'Goblin' grows a foot tall. All are Zone 4.

HOW TO GROW: In moist, humid areas the plants may develop fungus diseases in summer or succumb to rot from winter moisture. Avoid mulching them, and give them light, well-drained soil, preferably on the sandy side. Gaillardias can be grown fairly quickly from seed, and will flower the first year. In spring, watch for new shoots that may appear quite a distance from the original clump. If the center of the clump dies, discard it and replant the side shoots.

BLEEDING HEART
Dicentra

DESCRIPTION: When most people think of bleeding heart they picture an old-fashioned spring perennial with long, arching stems from which dangle small, pink, heart-shaped flowers. This is *Dicentra spectabilis*, well named because it really is spectacular. After the plant blooms, its long, rather gawky foliage courteously disappears. It grows about 3 feet tall and requires a space about that wide. Zone 3. Several long-blooming

*Dicentra
eximia*

Dicentra spectabilis

short species have recently become popular; these have attractive, fringed, grayish green foliage and deep pink flowers. (White forms of both tall and short are available, though these are somewhat less vigorous than the pink ones.) *Dicentra eximia* grows 12–18 inches and blooms from spring to fall. 'Bountiful' and 'Luxuriant' are the available varieties. Zone 4.

HOW TO GROW: All bleeding hearts prefer partial shade. The short ones may thrive in full sun, but the flowers will appear sunburned and untidy. You may cut the foliage of the tall ones back immediately after bloom if you like. Give both types fertile soil with plenty of organic matter and good drainage.

BUTTERFLY WEED
Asclepias tuberosa

DESCRIPTION: One of several species of native milkweeds, this showy plant attracts not only the "milkweed butterfly" (monarch) but many other butterflies as well. It only blooms for a few weeks in summer but earns its keep with its bright orange flower clusters, the ease with which you can grow it, and of course the butterfly show. As with other

milkweeds, its large seed pods spill forth handfuls of white fluff in fall. Stems can be 1½–2 feet tall, even 3 feet as the clumps become well established. Most plants sold are the native species, although hybrids will probably be available soon with different color gradations, including pink. Zone 4.

HOW TO GROW: Butterfly weed prefers a light, sandy soil. It will grow fine in average soil as long as it has good drainage. Because of its deep taproot the plant withstands drought well. If you must move young plants, do it carefully, lifting all of the taproot; established clumps are best left alone and will often self-sow. The plants may be grown easily from seed sown in sandy soil or propagated with cuttings in deep pots to accommodate the taproots. Cuttings can even be rooted in frozen-juice cans. The shoots are late to appear in spring.

CHRYSANTHEMUM
Chrysanthemum

DESCRIPTION: The familiar garden "mum" comes in many shapes, from little pompons the size of a dime, to huge "spiders." Some are shaped like daisies; some, called "spoons," are nests of little spoon-shaped petals. The most familiar are the large, round ones with many petals, which are classified as "decorative" mums, and the easy-to-grow "cushion mums," which grow up

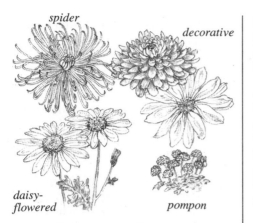

spider

decorative

daisy-flowered

pompon

to 15 inches tall. Colors include everything but blue, and heights range from less than a foot tall to 4 feet. Several other *Chrysanthemum* species are also popular garden plants. Most start blooming in late summer and continue through fall. Try cold-hardy types such as the Cheyenne series in cold climates. Zones 5–6.

Hybrids of several other *Chrysanthemum* species are popular garden flowers. Painted daisy (called *Pyrethrum roseum*, *C. coccineum* or *C. roseum*) has daisylike flowers in shades of red, pink, lavender and white, grows 1–3 feet tall and blooms in early summer. Zone 4. Feverfew (*C. parthenium*) has white-and-yellow buttonlike blooms, is 2–3 feet tall and blooms from early summer to fall, making it a splendid garden plant. Though the plant is short-lived in some climates, it will self-sow. Zone 5. *C.* × *rubellum* 'Clara Curtis' has pink flowers on 1–2 foot stems in mid- and late summer. Zone 4. See also Shasta Daisy.

HOW TO GROW: In cold climates mums are often treated as annuals. However if you want to try wintering them over, dig them up in fall and put them in a protected place such as a cold frame. Or try mulching them with evergreen boughs. Divide them in spring (or fall, in warm

climates) discarding the centers of the clumps and replanting the side shoots. Pinch until early summer to get bushy plants and abundant fall flowers.

Give painted daisies fertile soil and cut back spent flowers to encourage rebloom. Feverfew will tolerate light shade; the other species are sun loving. Give all *Chrysanthemum* species moderately fertile, moist but well-drained soil.

COLUMBINE
Aquilegia

DESCRIPTION: Both the flowers and leaves of columbines have a dainty, airy quality. Many of the flowers have long spurs, and they come in every color, including bicolors in which the inner row of petals is one color, the outer petals (sepals) and the spurs another. Heights also vary. Most bloom in mid- to late spring. *Aquilegia canadensis* (common columbine) is yellow and red and grows 1–2 feet. *A. caerulea* (Colorado or Rocky Mountain columbine) is blue and white and grows up to 3 feet tall. Both are native American wildflowers. *A. chrysantha* is yellow, 2–3 feet. *A. vulgaris* is shades of blue and rose and grows up to 3 feet. *A. flabellata* (Japanese fan columbine) is as short as 6 inches (though sometimes as tall as 1½ feet), with bluish leaves; available varieties are usually white or blue and white. In addition there are many hy-

brids: 'McKana' and 'Dragon Fly' hybrids in mixed shades are medium
height; 'Biedermeier' strain are mixed
and shorter. 'Snow Queen' is white;
'Crimson Star' is red; 'Maxi Star' is
yellow. In general, the species are Zone
4. The hybrids Zone 5.

HOW TO GROW: Columbines do well in
either full sun or part shade. They only
transplant well when small, and are
sometimes short-lived, but have a strong
tendency to self-sow, and volunteer
seedlings can be moved to the desired
location. All need well-drained soil.
Leaf miners, which make white tunnels
in the leaves, do considerable harm in
some gardens, but when the tunnels are
merely unsightly they are best ignored.

CONEFLOWER
Rudbeckia

DESCRIPTION: These are cheerful,
bright flowers and among the easiest
perennials to grow. The common black-
eyed Susan is the most familiar one, and
many garden hybrids resemble it. Others have double, ponpon-shaped
flowers. Purple coneflower, an excellent garden plant, is often called a rudbeckia, though it is more precisely *Echi-*

nacea purpurea. Most coneflowers
bloom from mid- to late summer until
frost, a time when it is hard to find good
choices for the garden, so many gardeners are willing to overlook their tendency to spread. Often the solution is to
naturalize them in a place where they
can't get into trouble.

    Rudbeckia fulgida 'Goldsturm' has
single yellow flowers and grows about 2
feet. Zone 4. *R. laciniata* 'Gold Drop'
is a double that grows 2–3 feet. *R. nitida*
'Goldquelle' is a 4-foot double. Zone 3.
Purple coneflower grows as tall as 4 feet
and is usually purple with a raised, iri-
descent, rust-colored center. Zone 3.

HOW TO GROW: These vigorous plants
form clumps that are best divided every
few years. They are not fussy about
soil. Most need full sun, but purple
coneflower will take part shade.

CORAL BELLS
Heuchera sanguinea

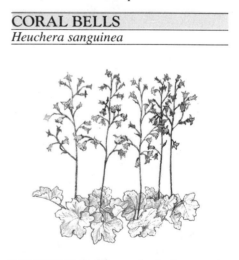

DESCRIPTION: These plants form mats
of leaves close to the ground and send
up wiry stems with tiny bells dangling
from them, usually in shades of pink
and red. Though not large and showy,
those little dancing bells are a welcome
addition to the garden in early summer,
and will often produce scattered blooms
later on. The foliage is evergreen in

most climates. Hybrids are usually red, sometimes pink or white. 'Pluie de Feu' is red and 18 inches tall; 'Bressingham' hybrids are mixed colors and heights. 'Santa Ana Cardinal,' a tall red, is a good variety for warm climates. All are Zone 4. *Heucherella*, a cross between coral bells and a white forest wildflower called *Tiarella cordifolia* (foamflower) is a spreading, pink-flowering perennial, 12–18 inches tall. Zone 3.

HOW TO GROW: Coral bells need moist, fertile soil enriched with organic matter. They like moisture but require good drainage, especially in winter. Either full sun or part shade is suitable. Easy to grow, they are best used at or near the front of the border. Divide after several years, and cut back flower stems after blooming to encourage rebloom.

COREOPSIS
Coreopsis

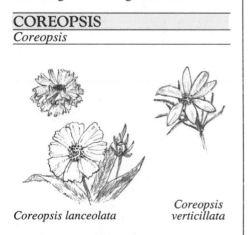

Coreopsis lanceolata *Coreopsis verticillata*

DESCRIPTION: These summer-blooming plants usually look like slightly ragged yellow daisies. I like them because they are easy to grow and have a fairly long flowering period. *Coreopsis lanceolata* is generally 2–3 feet tall. The variety 'Sunray' has double flowers. 'Goldfink' is 12 inches tall or less. 'Baby Sun' is 12–20 inches. Zone 4. *C. verticillata* (threadleaf coreopsis), though less familiar to gardeners, is a

real find. It has a rather spidery foliage and a very long bloom period. The variety 'Moonbeam' is 2 feet tall and has pale yellow flowers that fit wonderfully in gardens where a strong yellow would be too much. 'Zagreb' is 18 inches or less. 'Golden Shower' is 3 feet and bright yellow. All are Zone 3.

HOW TO GROW: These plants tolerate relatively infertile soil, self-sow, and are very easy to divide. They are sun loving, but *C. verticillata* and its hybrids will take part shade well.

DAY LILY
Hemerocallis

DESCRIPTION: Day lilies are one of the most satisfying plants you can grow because they are very easy and very colorful. They grow from rhizomes and are not the same plant as the true lily (*Lilium*), which grows from a bulb. Most people are familiar with the orange day lily that blooms along roadsides for a few weeks early in summer; but not everyone knows about the modern hybrids, derived from several different species, which bloom at different times from late June well into September, and in colors ranging from dark red, bright red, pink and peach to orange, gold and yellow. There are also bicolors. Heights range from 2 to 4 feet for the flower stems, but the foliage remains a fairly low mound. 'Hyperion' is a fragrant, summer-blooming yellow hybrid. 'Evergold' is a standard gold one. 'Prairie Sunset' is a good peach shade. But there are thousands of hybrids to choose from, with scores of new ones appearing each year. These include dwarf varieties, and varieties with very small flowers, double flowers and very large flowers. The fragrant, old-fashioned lemon lily (*Hemerocallis flava* or *H. lilioasphodelus*) is still popular. Most day lilies are Zones 3–4.

HOW TO GROW: Day lilies like soil of average fertility with plenty of organic matter. They will thrive in part shade, especially in hot regions, but bloom best in sun. Clumps become large and will bloom well without division, but can be more easily divided for propagation before the clumps become huge.

DELPHINIUM
Delphinium

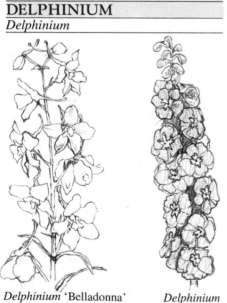

Delphinium 'Belladonna'   *Delphinium elatum*

DESCRIPTION: My idea of luxury is to always have plenty of delphiniums. They are not reliable in my climate, so I must replace many of them each year.

But I do it gladly, not only for their magnificent flower spikes in the garden, but also for summer bouquets. They require extra attention, but they earn it. The most spectacular ones are hybrids of *Delphinium elatum*, which are tall and grand—often upwards of 5 feet. Among these are the 'Giant Pacific' series, which come in many shades and are often bicolored—each flower along the spike having the center, or "bee," in a contrasting color. The vivid blue varieties such as 'Blue Skies' are my favorites, but I always grow a purple, too, such as 'King Arthur,' and a mauve, such as 'Astolat.' The dwarf 'Blue Fountains' hybrids are similar but only 2 feet tall. Zone 3.

Several delphiniums are a bit more reliable and very beautiful in their own way. 'Belladonna' (light blue) and 'Bellamosum' (dark blue) are 3–5 feet with an open-form spike. Zone 4. 'Connecticut Yankee' is a bushy 2½ feet in a number of shades. Zone 4. Chinese delphiniums (*D. chinense*) are less than 2 feet and a very intense blue.

HOW TO GROW: Delphiniums prefer climates with cool summers, where their stems grow tall and strong, and where they are free from diseases that attack them—diseases aggravated by hot, muggy weather. Choose a sunny location, if possible one protected from the wind. Even there they will probably need to be staked. The stake should reach to the point where the flower spike starts. Give them a very rich, alkaline soil. I dig a cupful of lime into the hole before planting, and top dress established clumps with a cup of lime each spring. I also top dress with a balanced granular or liquid fertilizer in spring and after the plants bloom. Avoid mulching around the crowns (the place where the stems join the roots), as this can cause rot. Remove all but five of the strongest stems in each clump in the spring, and cut off spent flowers after they bloom in early summer. Then cut back the stems when you see new growth start to appear. Most will bloom a second time in late summer, but with tall varieties the blooms from the second flowering will be shorter. Delphiniums will bloom the first year from seed.

FALSE SUNFLOWER
Heliopsis helianthoides scabra

semidouble

single   *double*

DESCRIPTION: This tall plant with daisylike yellow flowers is wonderful for bridging the gap between summer flowers such as phlox and fall flowers such as asters. Some are double; some are single. Most grow 3 or 4 feet tall and have a long flowering period. Hybrids include 'Karat,' a single, and 'Golden Plume,' a double. Zone 4.

HOW TO GROW: The plants will tolerate some shade but are more upright and free flowering in sun. Soil need not be very rich. Division is not a necessity but is easily done for propagation.

FOXGLOVE
Digitalis

DESCRIPTION: Gardeners who love romantic, old-fashioned flowers can rarely

resist growing foxgloves, even though some of the species are not reliably perennial in all climates. Many are biennials, forming rosettes of foliage the first year, blooming the second and becoming unproductive after that. They are happy to self-sow, however, if conditions suit them. Flowers occur on tall spikes in shades of rose, purple, yellow or white, depending on variety. The spikes rise in early summer from a low mound of broad leaves. I like to place them so the spikes emerge from clumps of ferns in partly shaded corners.

Digitalis ambigua (*D. grandiflora*) is the longest-lived species; it has pale yellow or cream-colored flowers, and grows 3 feet tall. Zone 4. *D.* × *mertonensis* has 3-foot spikes of pink flowers, which sometimes grow much taller. Zone 5. *D. purpurea* is rose colored, and the tall Excelsior hybrids are mixed shades.

HOW TO GROW: Give foxgloves fairly fertile, well-drained soil containing plenty of organic matter. Plant in partial shade. Cut stems of spent flowers to promote rebloom, but leave some of them if you want them to self-sow. Dividing established clumps will prolong vigor.

GAS PLANT
Dictamnus albus (D. fraxinella)

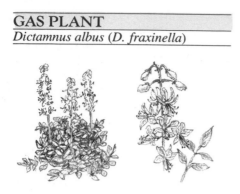

DESCRIPTION: Gas plant is a good thing to establish in your garden. It takes a few years to make a good show, but after that it will stalwartly produce airy pink or white flower spikes on tall stems in late spring or early summer. The name derives from a gas produced by the plants on humid summer nights that can, some claim, be ignited with a match. Touching the plant produces an allergic reaction in some people. The species is white, but *Dictamnus albus* 'Purpureus' is pinkish purple, and 'Rubrus' is red. All are usually 3 feet tall. Zones 3–4.

HOW TO GROW: Gas plant will eventually form thick, permanent clumps that live a long time and will not require division (in fact they may not survive dividing). The plants are taprooted and like a moist, well-drained, fertile, humusy soil. Either sun or part shade suits them. They are grown most successfully by sowing seeds in fall; these will germinate the following spring.

GAYFEATHER (BLAZING STAR)
Liatris

DESCRIPTION: These flowers, usually pinkish purple but sometimes white, look like little bunches of wavy string along a tall spike. They grow anywhere from 2 to 6 feet tall and bloom in late summer and early fall. They are native American wildflowers suited to a variety of habitats, depending on the species. But all are vigorous growers that do well in gardens and can even be naturalized as meadow flowers. *Liatris scariosa* has pink-purple flowers and grows from 3 to 4 feet tall. 'White Spires' is a white cultivar. *L. spicata* 'Kobold' is a 2-foot variety with purplish flowers. Both Zone 4.

HOW TO GROW: Gayfeather grows from little round corms or tuberous roots. The soil can be rather infertile, but it should be deep and light if at all possible. Choose a sunny location. Plants may be propagated from seed sown in spring or from division in spring. One plant is sufficient to form a sizable clump in the garden.

GERANIUM
Geranium

DESCRIPTION: These are the hardy geraniums as distinguished from the plants commonly called geraniums, which are tender perennials of the genus *Pelargonium*. Hardy geraniums grow in a mound anywhere from a few inches to a few feet tall, with five-petaled blossoms in shades of pink, crimson, purple, lavender and blue, usually about an inch wide but sometimes larger. Depending on variety they bloom from late spring to well into the summer, and some are long blooming. Most are vigorous and very easy to grow. Once you discover this fine family of plants you will want to grow them all.

Here are a few of the many attractive species and varieties that you can grow: The pink *Geranium dalmaticum* 'A. T. Johnson' and 'Wargrave Pink' are low-growing varieties. Zone 5. 'Johnson's Blue' grows to 12 inches. Zone 5. *G. sanguineum* forms a big mound a foot high but much wider, with magenta blooms that often repeat. The variety 'Lancastriense' is lower growing, its flowers pale pink streaked with red; it is a longer, later bloomer. Both Zone 4. *G. endressii* is a pink variety that grows 12–18 inches. Zone 3. *G. grandiflorum* 'Plenum,' one of my favorites, bears large, intensely violet-blue flowers on 2-foot stems in early summer. Zone 4.

HOW TO GROW: Most of the hardy geraniums prefer light shade, especially in climates with hot summers, but *G. sanguineum* is especially sun tolerant. They like moist, well-drained soils. Most form large clumps that need not be divided but that can be increased by carefully pulling a small clump away from the parent plant.

GLOBEFLOWER
Trollius

DESCRIPTION: These lovely flowers look like large, round versions of the

Trollius ledebourii   *Trollius europaeus*

buttercups to which they are related. Colors range from light yellow to deep orange. Bloom is in late spring or early summer but will sometimes repeat throughout the summer. *Trollius europaeus* is a bright yellow species that grows up to 2 feet tall. *T. ledebourii* is taller and more likely to be orange. Zones 5–6.

HOW TO GROW: Globeflower can do well in full sun but does best in partial shade. Give it fertile, moist soil. It is slow to make big clumps. Established plants rarely need to be divided, though for propagation this can be done in fall.

HOSTA
Hosta

DESCRIPTION: These plants are grown for their unusual leaves, which vary greatly in size, shape and markings. Colors range from pale green to deep blue-green, and many have attractive markings in white, yellow or a paler shade of green. Some leaves are very large, some are wavy. The flowers are less showy than the leaves but are a welcome addition to the shade garden in late summer when few other shade-loving plants are blooming. They are lavender or white bells dangling from tall stems. Many of the white-flowered species are fragrant. Hostas make good edging plants, and those with pale coloring are good for lighting up shady corners of the garden.

Though the hostas are far too numerous to list, here are a few good ones to try. *Hosta sieboldiana* forms big clumps of huge bluish leaves. The variety 'Frances Williams' is edged in lighter green. *H. fortunei* 'Albo-picta' has yellow-green leaves edged in dark green. The common *H. undulata* has a small, wavy leaf with cream-colored markings. All Zone 4.

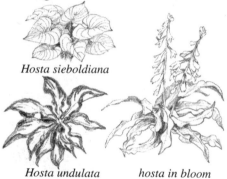

Hosta sieboldiana

Hosta undulata   *hosta in bloom*

HOW TO GROW: Hostas are easy, vigorous plants that will thrive in light or even deep shade. They like rich, moist soil but need good drainage in winter. Slugs may need to be controlled. Division is easy and may be done in spring and fall.

IRIS
Iris

DESCRIPTION: The most familiar member of this group is the "bearded" iris (*Iris* × *germanica*) that blooms in late spring. The large, handsome flowers are composed of three ruffled petals called "standards," which stand upright, and three petals called "falls," which hang down. The range of color is extraordinary—every color except bright red; sometimes the falls and standards are

bearded iris   Japanese iris   Siberian iris

colored differently. The gray-green, swordlike leaves are easy to hide with other plants after the flowers have bloomed so they will not take up visual space. For this reason I like to use iris in the border, although other gardeners prefer to mass them by themselves, which creates a lovely effect. Heights range from 2 to 4 feet. Zone 4.

The two other types well worth exploring are Siberian iris (*I. sibirica*) and Japanese iris (*I. ensata*, also called *I. kaempferi*). Siberian iris quickly forms large clumps of slender upright leaves. The flowers are more dainty than those of bearded iris; shades include blues, purples, rose and white, some with exquisitely veined markings. Zone 4. Japanese iris is similar, but the flowers are much larger and bloom a bit later. Zone 5. (For iris that grow from bulbs, see Chapter 10.)

HOW TO GROW: The roots of bearded iris are fat rhizomes that are prone to rot and to infestation by root maggots. I fight both problems by dipping the roots in a ten-to-one chlorine solution whenever I dig them up to divide them, but the best prevention for rot and maggots is to plant the roots so that the tops are visible. You can plant them on a soil mound if drainage is less than perfect.

They like fairly rich, alkaline soil and are generally planted in late summer.

The roots of Japanese and Siberian iris are long and stringy. The plants like moist, slightly acid soil that is rich in humus. Divide Japanese iris every few years. Siberian clumps can be left undisturbed, but for purposes of propagation, divide with a sharp spade or digging fork. The roots of old clumps become densely matted together but can be pried apart with two digging forks worked back to back (Figure 30).

LOOSESTRIFE
Lythrum salicaria

DESCRIPTION: Loosestrife is a good plant for the back of the border, with its tall upright spikes of pink or purple flowers that do not need staking. The hybrids, unlike some of the wild species, will not take over. Plant each one singly—it will form a woody, shrublike clump that is long-lived and will not need division. They bloom for many weeks in mid- to late summer. 'Morden's Pink' is a popular tall variety. 'Rose Queen' is a shorter plant, 2½ feet tall and 'Happy' is shorter still—only 18 inches. All Zone 4.

HOW TO GROW: Give loosestrife fairly fertile soil. Some wild species grow in very wet sites, but the hybrids seem to be moderately drought resistant and can be grown either in a wet place such as next to a pond, or in the garden. They prefer full sun but will tolerate part shade. Division is not necessary, but it can be done in spring for propagation.

LUPINE
Lupinus

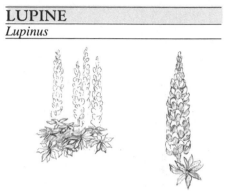

DESCRIPTION: These tall, spikelike flower clusters can be truly spectacular in a garden that suits them. With most species this means in a cool climate where the stems grow thick and sturdy. There are, however, some species suited to warmer parts of the country. Bluebonnet, the State Flower of Texas, is an annual lupine. Many native lupines have blue flowers or flowers in shades of rose, lavender or white. Those most commonly sold, the 'Russell' hybrids, cover a full range of blue, purple, red, pink, yellow, rust, cream and white, with many bicolored combinations. These grow 2–4 feet and may need staking. Zone 5.

HOW TO GROW: Lupines prefer deep, moist, rich acid soil and will grow in sun or light shade. Fertilize well when they are planted, then top dress each year. Mulching will help to keep the roots cool and the plants vigorous. They are not very long-lived in most gardens but will often self-sow. To grow new ones from seed, nick the seeds with a file to hasten germination, then plant them in peat pots or flats filled with sandy soil.

MONKSHOOD
Aconitum

DESCRIPTION: These plants produce tall spikes of flowers, usually blue, which do look like a throng of hooded monks—hence the name. They are a fine plant for the middle or back of the border in late summer or fall. The clumps can be left undisturbed. Beware: all parts of the plant are poisonous. Monkshoods for the garden come from a number of different species. Some good varieties include 'Bressingham Spire,' a 3-foot lavender-blue flower; 'Bicolor,' a taller plant with blue-and-white flowers; and 'Spark's Variety,' which is tall, late blooming, and dark blue.

HOW TO GROW: Monkshood prefers part shade but will grow in full sun if the soil is kept moist. Soil should also be moderately fertile, light, well-drained, and deeply cultivated to accommodate the extensive root system. It does best in cool climates where the stems grow strong and are less likely to need staking. Division is tricky and not necessary, so clumps are best left alone.

PEONY
Paeonia

DESCRIPTION: Peony flowers are classified as "doubles" (huge round balls with many petals), "semidoubles" (with fewer petals), "singles"(with one sparser row of overlapping petals surrounding a handsome cluster of gold stamens in the center) and "Japanese" (single, with a nest of showy, petallike stamens in the center). Colors range from dark maroon, to bright red, to pink, to white and occasionally yellow. Many, especially the pale ones, are fragrant. They grow on long, arching stems in a mound of dark green foliage about 3 feet high and 3 feet wide. The plants do not bloom for long, although you can choose varieties that bloom for several overlapping periods, and the foliage is attractive all summer and into fall, when it turns a pleasing gold color. *Paeonia tenuifolia* (fern-leaved peony) is low growing and admired for both its handsome foliage and its dark red flowers. "Tree peonies" are really shrubs that grow into a mound about 5 feet high and 5 feet wide; there is a wider range of flower colors among the tree peonies than with the herbaceous kind, including yellows, golds and some with spectaculary streaked markings.

By choosing a selection of early, midseason and late varieties you can keep a peony bed in bloom for as long as 6 weeks; this is a good idea because they make a good cut flower as well as a grand show in the garden. Some of the many hybrid peony varieties are 'Kansas,' a bright red double; 'Festiva Maxima,' a beautiful variety over 100 years old, which is a white-flecked double with traces of red; and 'Mrs. Franklin D. Roosevelt,' a pale pink double.

HOW TO GROW: Peonies are planted in fall in deep, well-drained soil enriched with organic matter. Plant as shown in Figure 29, making sure the "eyes" are no more than 2 inches below the soil surface, because planting too deep may result in failure to bloom. Peonies usu-

double   *single*   *Japanese*

peonies

ally do very well when planted right, even though they may take a few years to get established and bloom well. They are not suitable for climates with very warm winters. Staking with peony rings (Figure 33) will keep the blooms more attractive, especially when it rains. If you have planted your peonies correctly and they still do not bloom after several years, other conditions may be at fault, such as excessive moisture or drought, too much heat or too much shade, as well as various pests and diseases. To keep plants healthy, always clean up dead foliage at the season's end. Heavy feeding may also encourage the plants to bloom. Dig a trowelful of a balanced fertilizer into the soil around each one in early spring and again after flowering.

PHLOX
Phlox

DESCRIPTION: Most people are familiar with the tall garden phlox that is the glory of the summer garden, with its big clusters of red, pink, salmon, lavender, purple or white blossoms. However, there are also a number of earlier and shorter varieties, some less than a foot tall, that are well worth exploring. *Phlox paniculata*, the standard garden phlox, usually grows 2½–4 feet tall and looks best massed in large clumps of one color each. Good varieties include the bright red 'Starfire,' pink 'Dodo Hanbury Forbes' and salmon 'Sir John Falstaff.' Zone 4. Carolina phlox (*P. carolina* or *P. suffruticosa*) is slightly shorter, with looser flower clusters, and starts blooming earlier, usually the end of June. 'Miss Lingard' is the common white variety; 'Rosalinde' is pink. Zone 5. Low-growing phlox include the spring-blooming wild blue phlox (*P. divaricata*), which prefers light shade; and moss pink (*P. subulata*) with pink, purple, red or white blooms. Both are excellent as edging plants and in rock gardens. Both Zone 4.

Phlox paniculata   *Phlox subulata*

HOW TO GROW: All phlox like light, fertile soil with ample organic matter to retain moisture and good drainage. Provide adequate air circulation around the plants by not crowding them. This will help to forestall the white mildew that often disfigures the leaves of the tall garden phlox; fungicides may also help. Divide clumps of tall varieties every few years, replanting the side shoots. Clumps also flower best when thinned to about five stems. Remove spent blooms to prevent plants from going to seed (seedlings will all be magenta).

PINKS
Dianthus

*Dianthus ×
allwoodii* 'Alpinus'

*Dianthus ×
allwoodii* 'Doris'   *Dianthus deltoides*

DESCRIPTION: These flowers are often pink, but are sometimes shades of red or white, and sometimes marked with several colors. Some are shaped like small carnations (to which pinks are related); others have fewer petals, sometimes with ragged edges. Some have a pleasant, clovelike scent. The foliage is often very pretty, usually in shades of grayish or bluish green. Pinks are generally short—many grow close to the ground in matlike carpets. The tallest are rarely more than 1½ feet high. They usually flower in spring or early summer, but some continue to produce blooms all summer, especially if cut back.

Maiden pink (*Dianthus deltoides*) produces tiny, single dark pink or white flowers on short stems in late spring, and self-sows. Grass pink (*D. plumarius*) is usually about a foot tall, with bluish foliage and multicolored flowers. Both are Zone 4. Cheddar pink (*D. gratianopolitanus*, also called *D. caesius*), is a low-growing, spreading pink flower with grayish leaves; the variety 'Tiny Rubies' is very low and abundant with bright pink flowers. Zone 5. *D.* × *allwoodii* hybrids such as 'Doris' and 'Ian' have larger flowers and are hardy only to Zone 6, but the low-growing variety 'Alpinus' is hardy

to Zone 4. In warm climates you can grow carnations, also called clove pinks (*D. caryophyllus*). Zone 8. Sweet William (*D. barbatus*) is a tender perennial best treated as a biennial or self-sowing annual.

HOW TO GROW: All pinks need excellent drainage and prefer slightly alkaline soil. Do not mulch the crowns. Remove spent flowers to encourage rebloom, and cut back long-stemmed varieties if they get dry and scraggly in midsummer. Mat-forming varieties can be left alone unless they take up too much space, but clump-forming ones such as carnations and the *Dianthus* × *allwoodii* hybrids may need to be divided every few years to keep them attractive and vigorous. They can also be increased by layering or taking cuttings.

POPPY
Papaver orientale

DESCRIPTION: The Oriental poppy's showy flowers appear for—at most—a week or two in late spring or early summer in gorgeous shades of red, pink, orange and salmon, as well as white. They are borne on stems 2½–3 feet high above foliage that looks, alas, quite messy as summer wears on, then disappears. They can be grown in a bed by themselves, or tucked in among later-blooming plants whose foliage will fill in and hide that of the poppies.

There are many varieties to choose from, including the pink 'Helen Elizabeth,' 'Barr's White' and 'Carmine,' which is red with black markings. The 'Minicap' series will do better than most in hot climates.

HOW TO GROW: Poppies are planted in late summer or early fall. They rarely need division, and propagation is best done by taking root cuttings several inches long. They prefer sun, except in hot climates where some light shade is best during the hot part of the day. They are not fussy about soil, but poor drainage will cause them to rot, especially during the winter. Mulching should be avoided for the same reason.

PRIMROSE
Primula

Primula × polyantha   Primula japonica

DESCRIPTION: I am not sure why Shakespeare had his "primrose path" lead to "dalliance," but a primrose path is certainly a colorful way to lead a visitor to your door. The most characteristic primrose color is yellow, but there are many other colors available. All the species have cheerful, spring-blooming flowers, and most are easy to grow. Some have evergreen leaves, and some will rebloom a little in fall.

The most commonly sold primroses are hybrids of *Primula × polyantha*; these come in just about any color you can name, many of them bicolored. The "candelabra" types, which include Japanese primrose (*P. japonica*), have clusters of pink, purple or white flowers atop stems as tall as 2 feet, and they bloom in late spring. Zone 6. Japanese star primrose (*P. sieboldii*) is shorter, in rosy shades. It is hardy to Zone 5. The Barnhaven strain is particularly vigorous.

HOW TO GROW: Primroses prefer part shade and humusy, moisture-retentive soil. The candelabra types like the soil to be wet. None of them do well in very hot climates. The species can be grown from seed; hybrids are propagated easily by division. Division also renews vigor. Do it right after they have finished blooming, at least every other year.

SCABIOSA (PINCUSHION FLOWER)
Scabiosa caucasica

DESCRIPTION: These lacy blue or white flowers do look something like a pincushion. You need a good mass of them to create a showy effect in the border, but they are easy to grow, long-blooming and a good cut flower. Most grow 1½–2½ feet tall and bloom from early to late summer. Some good varieties are 'House Hybrids,' which are mixed shades of blue, 'Clive Greaves,' a lavender-blue and 'Miss Wilmott,' which is white.

HOW TO GROW: Scabiosa prefers sun except in hot climates. It needs moist, light, slightly alkaline soil with good drainage. It rarely need division, but if you like you can divide it in early spring. It is also a good perennial to grow from seed.

SEA LAVENDER
Limonium latifolium

DESCRIPTION: This plant is not grown as often as it should be. It is a good front-of-the-border plant with a flat rosette of dark green leaves and airy, lavender-colored flowers on long, thin stems. It gives much the same effect as baby's breath both in the garden and in flower arrangements, and it blooms for a long period in summer. Grow either the original species or the variety 'Violetta,' which has darker flowers.

HOW TO GROW: The plant needs sun and a deep, sandy loam that is well drained but not too fertile, or the stems will be floppy. It is slow to establish, but once it gets going, you can take divisions from the sides of the clump for propagation.

SEDUM (STONECROP)
Sedum

DESCRIPTION: Sedums are succulents—they have thick, fleshy leaves filled with water. There are an enormous number of them, most of which are good rock-

garden plants, especially the low-growing ones. Some of these are also good ground covers. I find the larger species very effective in borders. Most species have attractive flowers; some are also grown for their leaves, which are colorful and/or variegated.

Sedum acre (gold moss) is a yellow-flowering prostrate creeper that is ideal as an edging, in rock gardens, and even in cracks between paving stones. *S. spurium* forms a 6-inch mat and blooms in a variety of colors. *S. kamtschaticum* forms clumps a foot high or less and bears yellow flowers in the latter half of the summer. Good border types include *S. spectabile*, whose varieties 'Meteor' and 'Brilliant' bear reddish pink flowers in late summer, and 'Autumn Joy,' with pink flowers in fall that turn a deep mahogany and leave seed heads that are pretty all winter. All Zone 4.

HOW TO GROW: Sedums need good drainage, especially in winter, but are otherwise not fussy about soil requirements. They are very easy to propagate by stem or leaf cuttings or from seed. Division is easy but not often necessary.

SHASTA DAISY
Chrysanthemum × *superbum*
(*C. maximum*)

DESCRIPTION: These are always white but can be either single or double, tall or

single

double

short. They generally bloom for a long time in summer, especially if the flower stems are cut, and are a good white accent. 'Alaska' and 'Polaris' are among the hardiest tall varieties; both single, both Zone 4. 'Marconi' is a double variety. Zone 5. 'Little Miss Muffet' is a single that grows about a foot tall.

HOW TO GROW: Provide rich, moist, well-drained soil. In hot climates provide light shade. Pinching the stems in early summer will make the tall varieties bushier. Clumps are sometimes short-lived; established ones respond well to division.

SNAKEROOT (BUGBANE)
Cimicifuga

DESCRIPTION: This woodland plant, native to the eastern United States, is not well known but truly a delight to grow. Its flowers are tall, fuzzy white spikes. The leaves are attractive and fernlike, rather like that of astilbe. *Cimicifuga racemosa* grows 5–6 feet tall, sometimes even taller, and flowers in mid- to late summer (sometimes earlier). *C. simplex* grows about 3 feet tall and blooms in fall. Both Zone 4.

HOW TO GROW: Both species like part shade and moist, woodsy soil, but *C. simplex* will do well in full sun. Division is not necessary, but the stems often need to be staked up to where the flower begins.

SUNDROP
Oenothera

DESCRIPTION: The sundrops commonly found in gardens are mistakenly called "evening primrose"; some *Oenothera* do bloom at night, but not these. They resemble large, spread-open buttercups and bloom in early summer, with some repeat bloom as summer goes on. *O. pilosella* (sometimes labeled *O. fruticosa*) is the weedy variety gardeners tend to complain about. But it is a great perennial to plant if you want a lot of sunny yellow in your garden and you want it quickly. *O. missourensis* has larger flowers, grows low to the ground, and is not a spreader. 'Fyrverkeri' is long blooming. All Zone 5.

HOW TO GROW: All are sun loving and tolerant of dry, infertile soil. Those that enjoy your garden too much can easily be weeded out, for they are shallow rooted. Try them in a spot where you want a lot of color quickly.

VERONICA (SPEEDWELL)
Veronica

DESCRIPTION: Veronicas are usually blue but sometimes lavender, pink or white. The flowers are spiky and range in height from 4 feet to a few inches. Bloom period varies from early to late summer. *Veronica spicata* 'Blue Peter' grows up to 2 feet and blooms in mid-summer. 'Icicle' is white and a long bloomer. 'Red Fox' is medium height and fairly early. *V. prostrata* 'Heavenly Blue' is low and mat forming and early blooming. *V. incana* is similar but has striking white leaves as well as blue flowers.

HOW TO GROW: These plants like sun but will take some shade. They need adequate moisture but good drainage as well. The soil should be moderately fertile. They are easily divided in spring or fall. Cutting back spent blooms may encourage rebloom.

YARROW (MILFOIL)
Achillea

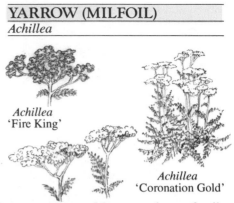

Achillea 'Fire King'

Achillea 'Coronation Gold'

DESCRIPTION: Many people are familiar with the wild white yarrow with its flat clusters of flowers, but most garden specimens are yellow, and some are pink or red. All have ferny leaves, sometimes with a grayish cast. They are easy to grow and bloom for a long time in summer. Most hybrids are varieties of *Achillea millefolium* or *A. filipendulina*. 'Moonshine' is a pale yellow with gray leaves and grows up to 2 feet. 'Coronation Gold' is bright yellow with greener leaves, and grows to 3 feet. 'Fire King' is 2 feet and pinkish red. 'Gold Plate' is among the tallest. *A. tomentosa* is a very pleasing low variety that forms a mat of whitish leaves and has flowers less than a foot tall. It is nice in the rock garden or at the front of the border.

HOW TO GROW: Yarrows are sun loving and drought resistant. Some are rather spready and need to be divided frequently. All, in fact, benefit by division every few years in fall or early spring.

CHAPTER 7

VEGETABLES

Why Grow Your Own Vegetables?

V egetable gardening is so popular that to many people it *is* gardening. When they parcel out the limited time, space and resources they have for gardening, the vegetable garden gets a mighty share; only lawns, on the average, get more. In fact about half of the families in the United States have some sort of vegetable garden.

Why, with ample fresh produce available year-round in the supermarkets, is this tradition still alive and well? Sometimes the initial goal is to save money. If gardeners are efficient and diligent they often do so, but not, I would guess, very often. Usually I hear them joke in fall about the squash that cost them a dollar apiece to grow, or the peas that were fifty cents a pod after figuring the cost of the fence, tools, fertilizer and other aids, and the cost of their time. The following spring, undaunted by these economics, they are back in their gardens again.

I grow my own vegetables for two reasons: the quality of the crops I can produce myself, and the quality of the time I spend doing it. There is no question that food picked fresh from my garden tastes better than food that is picked six states away, rides in a truck, sits in storage areas, waits in display bins in the store, rides home in my car, then idles in the refrigerator until it is the right item for the menu. Vegetables ripened in the garden and eaten right away have many more vitamins, too. I also appreciate the fact that I can control what chemical fertilizers, if any, are used to grow my vegetables and whether they are sprayed with pesticides and other possibly harmful substances. And as I investigate the selection of vegeta-

bles available to me as a home gardener, I realize more and more how much better it is than that in the produce department. Supermarket vegetables are usually bred for ease of transportation and storage, uniform size and color, and the ability of the crop to bear all at once for most efficient harvest. In choosing what to grow in my garden, on the other hand, I look for better flavors and nutrition, new and unusual varieties to try out and, quite often, a crop that does *not* mature all at once, so that I can pick it over a long period of time.

All these are benefits I have discovered during the course of growing vegetables, but they are not what motivated me in the first place. Initially it was simply the itch to get out there in the spring, to smell the warm earth, and to grub around in the garden all spring, summer and fall in the sunshine, feeling fit and contented, watching my bounty ripen. The harvest was extra. I think there is a basic satisfaction in growing food for the table, and that most of us who do it enjoy the activity of gardening itself just as much as the result.

What Is a Vegetable?

B otanically, the term "vegetable" means nothing. When we speak of vegetables we mean an odd assortment of plants, mostly annual and soft stemmed, that we grow for food. Generally we exclude those that taste sweet and most of the grain crops such as rice and wheat. A few vegetables are perennial, such as asparagus, rhubarb, horseradish, Jerusalem artichoke and (in tropical climates only) peppers.

The distinction between a "fruit" and a "vegetable" is a wholly unscientific one. "Fruit" is the botanical term for the part of a plant that contains the seeds. Thus the tomato plant is grown for its fruit, as are the eggplant and the pepper. But vegetables vary widely in terms of which part of the plant is eaten. Often it is the leaves, as with lettuce, spinach, cabbage, Swiss chard and all the crops we call "greens," cooked or otherwise. Onions are also, strictly speaking, a leaf crop, even though the bulbs (actually leaf bases) grow underground. Other vegetables, such as rhubarb, celery and, oddly enough, turnips and potatoes, are not "root vegetables," but are actually enlarged stems. True root crops include carrots, parsnips and beets. Those usually grown for the seeds inside the fruits include peas and corn. Those grown for the edible flowers are cauliflower and broccoli.

Sometimes vegetables are grouped together according to their botanical families. You can grow prize vegetables without ever knowing their Latin names, but it does help to know something about vegetable families for quite practical reasons. Many of the plants within the main groups of vegetables have similar characteristics, have the same problems, and are grown in similar ways. And organizing your garden by plant groups will help you to rotate crops from year to year and thereby avoid some of the diseases that plants within the same groups have in common. Also, the family names crop up quite frequently in garden literature. Use the following list as a reference, so when someone mentions, say, the brassicas, you will know what they are talking about.

Which Vegetables Should You Grow?

The first criterion should be your appetite and that of the people you live with. A friend of mine used to grow a bumper crop of pumpkins every year, no small feat in the north country. Stacked in crates from floor to ceiling each fall, they provided his large family with months of the nutritious pumpkin pudding he took pride in making. Unfortunately no one in his household could stand pumpkin pudding except him, so he finally admitted defeat and settled for a few pumpkin plants for jack-o'-lanterns. If your tribe loves beets, plant beets. If they like lettuce, plant lettuce. You might even get them involved in helping you take care of the garden that way (not likely, I realize, but worth a try).

But although I have advised planting vegetables you know and like, I still think that a vegetable garden is a golden opportunity to try the new and unfamiliar. Often having a garden is the only way you can eat certain things: French string beans, Italian salad greens, Oriental vegetables or the new "baby vegetables" ("small-fruited" varieties as opposed to varieties where the plant itself is dwarf or compact). Some may be novelties that you try only once; others may become a regular feature of your garden. Mail-Order Sources, beginning on page 618, include some suppliers of seeds for unusual crops. Some of the catalogs give you more detailed descriptions and directions for growing than I have space for here.

WORKING WITH YOUR CLIMATE

In deciding what to grow, it is wise to take your climate into account. Each region has a set of vegetables that are easier to grow than others. Southerners have no trouble with okra, sweet potatoes, eggplant and peanuts. Northerners have an easy time with cool-weather crops such as broccoli, peas, lettuce and

Vegetable Families

Solanaceae. Called the "tobacco" or "nightshade" family, it includes not only these but also tomatoes, peppers, potatoes and eggplants. (I call them "ratatouille vegetables" because so many of them go into that dish.) Some are toxic, have toxic parts (like potato sprouts) or are toxic for certain people. But as a group they are rich in vitamin C. All are warm-weather plants that like rich, moist soil. Solanaceae are disease-prone, so it is important to rotate them.

Cruciferae. Most are in the genus *Brassica,* often called "cabbage" or "mustard" vegetables, or "cole crops." Besides cabbage and mustard greens, the brassicas includes broccoli, Brussels sprouts, cauliflower, kale, collards, turnip, rutabaga and kohlrabi. Other garden Cruciferae are watercress, garden cress and radishes. All are cool-weather crops that like a moderately rich soil, with plenty of organic matter to maintain a steady supply of moisture. Root maggots, cutworms and cabbage worms can be a problem. They share a number of diseases such as blackleg.

Leguminosae. Called "legumes" or the "pea family," these are all the peas and beans, including soybeans and peanuts. Clover is also a legume. Rich in protein, they are good for you and good for your soil; nodules growing on their roots fix the nitrogen in the soil for plants to use. Cold tolerance varies, but all legumes have large, fast-germinating seeds that are usually sown directly in the garden. They share certain diseases that can spread if you move among their leaves when wet.

Cucurbitaceae. Called "cucurbits" or the "cucumber family," the group includes squash, pumpkins, melons and gourds as well as cucumbers. All are warm-weather plants and most produce vigorous, fast-growing vines that need fertile soil amply supplied with organic matter. The cucumber beetle afflicts them all, as do many diseases.

Umbelliferae. Carrots, parsnips and celery belong to this family, as well as many edibles grouped under "herbs," such as parsley and dill. They all have an "umbel" flower shape (that of a Queen Anne's lace). All are cold-weather crops with few diseases or pests. They like a deep, loose soil. Their major problem is poor germination, and all need a pulverized, moistened soil to sprout.

Compositae. In this family are some salad plants, notably lettuce, endive and chickory, and the root crops salsify and scorzonera. These easy crops like cool weather.

Liliaceae. The lily family contains all the onion-type vegetables and also asparagus. Members of the onion group like to be started in cool weather; they need a rich soil, plentiful moisture and good drainage.

Chenopodiaceae. These are spinach, Swiss chard and beets. Apart from spinach, which bolts in heat, all are problem-free plants.

cabbage. Gardeners in wet climates can grow celery; those in dry ones can grow sweet potatoes.

If you are a beginning gardener my advice is to start with the crops that thrive near you. Ask your neighbors what grows well for them, or ask local nurserymen or your Extension Service. It is also helpful to start with some crops that are notoriously easy to grow anywhere because they are not fussy plants: lettuce, radishes, tomatoes, beets, summer squash, cucumbers and Swiss chard. Then, with a few gardening seasons behind you, try anything, even vegetables less well suited to your climate. The gardening magazines are full of stories about people who have grown the "wrong" vegetable against improbable odds with a few tricks and attention to details. Often it is just a matter of choosing the right variety, such as a heat-resistant spinach or a cold-resistant tomato.

Individual vegetables, how to grow them, and what varieties to grow are discussed on pages 210–305 of this chapter. But it is important to get an overview of how vegetable gardens are planned in relation to climate—how the growing schedules vary from one region to the next. In the north, where I live, my gardening fortunes rise and fall on my observation of two important dates: the last frost in spring, and the first frost in fall. Unfortunately I never know what these dates are going to be. All I know is that the average last frost in spring for my locality is June 1, and the average first frost in fall is September 17. By keeping my mind on these dates, my eye on the weather, and my ear tuned to the forecast on the radio, I can at least set up a gardening schedule. In my case it will mean starting the seeds of some plants indoors in March or April and transplanting the young plants to the garden after danger of frost has passed. Other crops will be sown directly into the garden as the weather becomes right for each one. Some spring crops will be harvested early; in their place I will plant successions of summer crops; some crops planted in spring and harvested in summer will be followed by fall crops. When that fateful first frost threatens, a lot of vegetables will leave my garden and go into the freezer, into canning jars, and into the cellar, or they will be hung on strings in the kitchen. But a lot of rugged ones will keep right on producing despite the frost. A few will even stay in the ground over the winter, to be harvested in early spring.

If I lived in the Deep South, I might preserve some of my food, but I would not be in such a frenzy about it as my northern locale obliges me to be. Down there it is possible to eat vegetables fresh from the garden all year long. Instead of one or two successions of most crops, I could have three successions of many of them. I would still keep an eye out for frost, since some vegetables cannot tolerate even a touch of it, but my main worry would be the summer heat, which would bring much of my vegetable production to a standstill. While some of my crops would thrive during the hot stretch, for many it would be the fallow season. In the south, I would make the most of the temperate days of spring and fall.

Temperature and moisture are not the only factors that vary from one part of the country to another. With certain vegetables you must also take day length into account. In the north, days start to shorten dramatically at summer's end, an effect that is much less pronounced in the south. This makes cauliflower, for example, a better crop in the north, because the heads start to develop when the days become noticeably shorter. The ability of onions to form bulbs is also affected by decreasing day length.

There are actually "short-day" onions more appropriate to southern gardens than the "long-day" onions that thrive up north. Questions of how day length influences growth are considered in more detail under specific vegetables.

The number of sunny days is another factor. Some parts of the country, the Pacific Northwest for example, have so many rainy, cloudy or foggy days during the growing season that gardeners there have to choose vegetables that will tolerate the relative lack of sun. In general most vegetables are sun loving, especially tomatoes, peppers and eggplant. And none will do well in true shade. But some will tolerate more cloudy days than others, or a yard that is semishaded beyond remedy. These include beets, cabbage, carrots, kale, leeks, lettuce and other greens, onions, turnips, peas, and Brussels sprouts.

How Big a Garden Do You Need?

This is a very important decision. I think the most common mistake made by new gardeners (and often old ones) is that they plant too much—too many crops, too many seeds, too many plants. Either the upkeep overwhelms them and much of the garden succumbs to weeds, bugs or drought, or the harvest is too bountiful, and they cannot keep up with the picking, let alone the eating and preserving. If you are really sure that you want a large garden and will spend the time needed to bring it to harvest, by all means plant one. But I would hate to see you discouraged forever by a garden that failed because it was too ambitious. You will probably find it more fun and rewarding to start small.

In fact you may want to stay small. I have had a number of different kinds and sizes of vegetable gardens, depending on where I was living, how long I expected to stay there, how many people I was feeding, and how overcommitted I was in other areas of my life at the time. One garden, in a hayfield next to a rented apartment, was about 6 feet by 6 feet and contained two cherry tomato plants, two rows of lettuce and some basil. It served its purpose perfectly. By alternating the two lettuce rows I had good salads all summer, and when frost threatened I picked all the cherry tomatoes and marinated them in jars of vinaigrette in the refrigerator (even with two plants I had a surplus of tomatoes).

Another year, living in a more permanent residence, I planted an enormous garden—about 45 by 60 feet—considering the fact that I was only feeding two people. It was elaborately fenced against intruders (with moderate success) and had thirty-five or forty crops, from snow peas to corn to about five kinds of dried beans. I canned a number of crops and stored root crops in the basement in winter. It took three months to clear land for that garden, to dig it, condition its soil, fence it and plant it, and during that time I did nothing else, enjoying it all. It required considerable upkeep all summer, even with mulches, and when canning time came I again did nothing else. The following year I was working for a nursery and had far less time for the garden. So I planted only a quarter of the area. Even without the big initial task of preparation, I knew that was all I would be able to manage in a few daylight hours after work each week.

Another year, in a hayfield next to a rented house, I dug and planted a 15- by 30-foot plot that was just right for salad crops, a variety of cooking greens, tomatoes, peppers and herbs. I also mixed in a lot of red and orange nasturtiums, yellow calendulas, and blue morning glories on the modest chicken-wire fence. The garden produced food for three people, with some extras for friends, and took an average of half a day's work per week.

The next garden was about 20 by 40 feet, with a picket fence around it and a colonial-style gate. The entire plot was divided into raised beds with 2-foot paths between them. I dug out all the topsoil in the paths and put it into the raised beds, then filled the paths with builder's sand. All this construction took several months, with me working every weekend. Knowing I would have limited time to garden or preserve food, I sowed only crops I would eat during the growing season, together with perennial herbs and a lot of annual and perennial flowers. I mixed all these together, the way the early settlers would have done. A small row of roses outside the fence at one end was my sole concession to formality, and all the gardening I did went on in that one little garden, which I mulched for easier maintenance. In subsequent years the garden was even easier, because it was all ready for me in the spring and so easy to care for thereafter. Mind you, if I neglected it for a few weeks it suffered, but two to four hours of care each week was about all it needed.

Now I am living somewhere else, feeding more people, and cultivating another large garden that includes canning and storing crops—and this time some freezing crops as well. The garden is some distance from the house, so I am growing most of my cooking herbs in pots nearer the kitchen for easy snipping. Herbs are easier to grow this way anyway, since many of the perennial ones grow rampant in the garden.

I have gone through this lengthy history to indicate that there are a number of ways to have a vegetable garden, and to show you what kind of questions you need to ask yourself in order to plan yours. How many will you be feeding? (Account for company, too, if you do a lot of entertaining.) Will you be canning, freezing or drying part of your harvest, and if so how much? Do you have a place for winter storage where the vegetables will stay cool but not freeze? How much space do you have for a garden—and that means sunny, well-drained space close enough to the house to be tended and watered. Realistically, how much time will you have to care for it? Will it be a food garden only, or one that combines food and flowers?

Allotting the right amount of space for each crop can be a little tricky. I tend to be mistrustful of formulas for specific crops that predict your yield "per 100 feet of row" or some such figure. With so much variation in soil, climate and care from one garden to the next (or one year to the next), yields will vary. Planting styles these days are less uniform than they used to be, as well. We do not always plant in rows, and plant spacing also varies a great deal. I have tried to give a few guidelines in the individual vegetable sections, but you will have to work out your own spacing by seeing what works best for you. When in doubt, plant less, not more.

One encouraging trend in food gardening these days is that more people seem aware of different possibilities for laying out vegetable gardens. Fifteen years ago garden geography was pretty standard: a large rectangular plot tilled up each spring and planted in parallel rows. Gardeners are becoming more resourceful about using small spaces for vegetable growing or perhaps having several different gardens: a salad-and-herb garden near the house, and a large garden for big crops at some distance. Or a vegetable garden with flowers in it, either tucked in as ornaments or planted in rows to be cut for bouquets. Or even a vegetable garden grown entirely in containers, either for ease of cultivation or for lack of tillable ground.

Choosing the Site

Deciding where to put the garden is a matter of juggling several different needs, some of them yours and some the garden's. A committee composed of your vegetables would unanimously select the sunniest spot on your property, a place where water never collects in puddles after a rain but always drains away nicely, where the ground slopes slightly toward the south. The soil there would be neither porous sand nor heavy clay, neither full of stones nor tightly compacted—and of course it would be fertile. I have a perfect spot exactly like that. It is also large enough for the most ambitious garden, and it's right near both the house and the hose spigot. Unfortunately it is the lawn, and no one in the house is ready to consign it to vegetables, not even me. So the garden is a long way from the house, and I

ROW STYLES

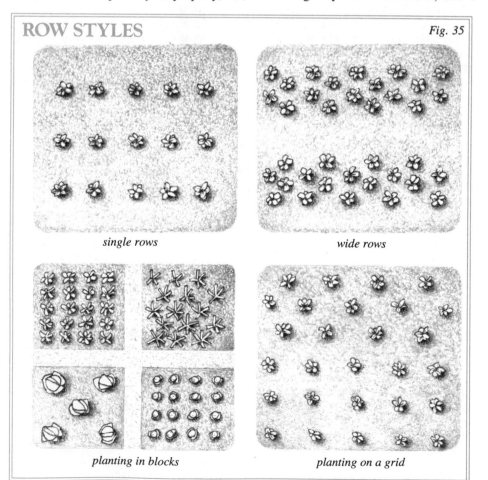

Fig. 35

single rows

wide rows

planting in blocks

planting on a grid

water it with a hose I share with the horses—although after mulching I do not have to water often.

Almost every site problem can be corrected. Trees can often be cut down to let in more light. Tree roots below the surface are a big problem, but growing vegetables in high raised beds can make even a root-ridden site a possibility, as long as sun shines in under the branches. Poor drainage can be corrected by raised beds (Figure 36) or drainage systems. Poor soil can always be improved (page 25), and slopes can be terraced (page 6). A garden near the house that detracts from its formal look can be hidden by a hedge or fence if the house does not cast a shadow on the garden. Or you can work hard at making the garden beautiful by planting it in tidy rows or blocks with ornamental paths of brick or flagstone and by edging blocks of vegetables with flowering annuals. Even vegetables themselves can look beautiful combined together if they are staked as needed and weeded regularly.

Styles of Vegetable Gardening

After you decide where to put the garden, figure out what kind of layout it will have. Traditional single rows, wide rows or blocks? Raised beds or level ones? Paths in the garden or just wide spacing between rows? Mulch or no mulch? These questions are all interrelated: the answers depend partly on your own climate, soil conditions and other site considerations, but they are also very subjective. Gardeners tend to be dogmatic about which systems are best because for one reason or another one system is exactly right for them. My advice is to try gardening in different ways from year to year or even in one part of the garden or another in the same year, and find the style that suits you.

Here are the results of my own experience:

Rows. I sometimes like to plant vegetables close together in blocks or wide rows. I find that I get larger yields in a smaller space, and can therefore afford to use more space for paths in the garden. This method, as opposed to traditional single rows, is called "intensive" gardening and has become increasingly popular. But I do not always use it. I find that tomatoes, for example, no matter how clever and industrious you are about your staking or trellising, don't like to be crowded together. They need sun all around them. Their vines are also very rampant and are never far from total chaos; crowding them creates a jungle.

I also find that it's easier to mulch a garden that is planted in rows. The theory behind intensive planting holds that the lush growth of the plants will form a "natural mulch" that will shade the ground, force out weeds and conserve moisture, but this does not always happen, especially with skinny plants like onions, and plants whose foliage is never very lush like carrots and parsnips. With a single row you can lay mulch between the rows and really keep weeds down and the soil moist.

Raised beds. I like to use raised beds in most of the garden. They take a lot of work to build, but they save me time in subsequent years because these tidy beds are easy to tend. I can sit in the paths between them and don't have to lean over very far to weed. I make them small enough (usually not more than 4 feet wide) so that I can reach into the middle from either side and never have to step on the soil inside them—helpful in keeping that ideal loose and fluffy texture. The soil also warms up faster in these beds, giving my spring crops an earlier start.

Simply because I have *made* these garden spaces with the sweat of my brow, I find I am always trying to make the most efficient use of them and so I plant them rather intensively. But I have learned the hard way not to let raised beds get out of hand. Crops thrive in these little plots of warm, luxurious soil, and unless I am careful about how many plants I put into them, my tidy arrangement can become a jungle. I make them as simply as possible (Figure 36), digging out the topsoil between them, putting it into the beds, and then filling these corridors with the most inert substance I can find. I tried builder's sand and gravel, but found that these are exhausting to move and that weeds will eventually grow in them, especially after several years of my spilling the soil out of the beds and into the paths while I work them. Some weeds, such as horsetails, will grow in anything; my own self-sowing chives are another notorious culprit. A thick bark mulch is a better material for paths. It can be easily removed and tossed on the compost pile if it becomes full of soil, or more bark can be added on top of it.

For a large garden with a number of space-consuming crops such as corn, squash, potatoes and beans, a raised-bed system is usually just too ambitious. In this case a good solution is to make half the garden raised beds and half of it flat.

You may find that if you live in a very warm climate, raised beds will not work for you at all. Even where I live I

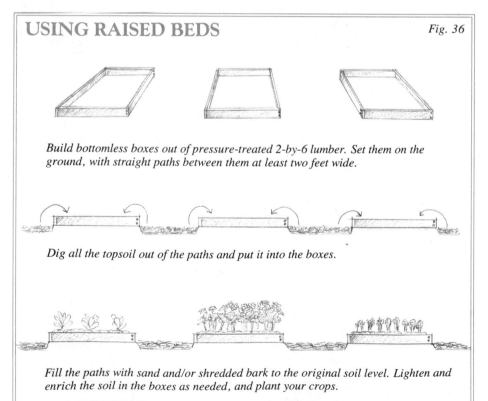

USING RAISED BEDS   *Fig. 36*

Build bottomless boxes out of pressure-treated 2-by-6 lumber. Set them on the ground, with straight paths between them at least two feet wide.

Dig all the topsoil out of the paths and put it into the boxes.

Fill the paths with sand and/or shredded bark to the original soil level. Lighten and enrich the soil in the boxes as needed, and plant your crops.

have found that they dry out much faster than flat ones, and with some crops I have to be extra careful about keeping the beds moist. Since they are relatively small plots, this is not difficult, but if you find yourself engaged in a constant struggle to keep your garden soil moist and cool, raised beds may not be for you. You might even consider planting in rows that are actually shallow trenches, which will collect more rainwater and partly shade the plants' roots (Figure 37).

Paths. I consider garden paths very important. I like to have a lot of them, and I make most of them at least 2 feet wide so I can wheel a wheelbarrow through them, set a bushel basket down anywhere on them, and sit in them while I work. In my ideal garden they would be permanently installed in brick, beautifully laid in perfect geometry throughout the garden in a basket-weave or herringbone pattern. Alas, my vegetable garden is not funded for that sort of thing, and chances are yours is not either. Instead of the bark paths described

above, you might choose to make grass strips that can be mowed like a lawn; those planted in annual grasses can even be tilled under in fall with the rest of the garden if you are not using raised beds.

Mulch. I am a great believer in mulch in the vegetable garden. It does not totally deter weeds, but depending on what kind of mulch you use, it can cut weeding time down by as much as 75 percent. You will need to do much less watering, too. Although some people have more problems with garden pests such as slugs when they use mulch, others find that they have less.

My favorite mulch material is salt hay, a type of hay that grows by the seashore. Whatever weed seeds it contains apparently germinate only in salty conditions, not in your garden, and so unlike regular barn hay, it will not produce weeds. It is rather stiff, and handfuls of it are awkward to arrange around plants, but this same quality makes it easy to remove so that you can pull up dead plants in fall or expose the soil in spring to let it warm up or to plant. I

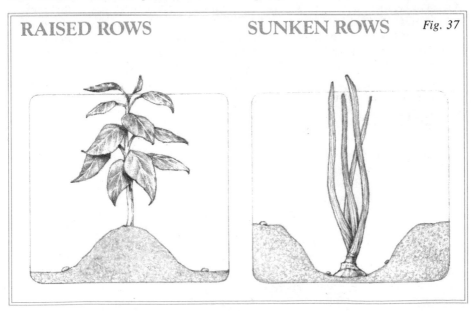

RAISED ROWS   SUNKEN ROWS   *Fig. 37*

have corners of the garden here and there where I keep piles of hay handy until they're needed. I reuse mulch if it does not look moldy but always buy a new bale or two each spring to add to what I have.

Remember that mulch keeps garden soil cool. You want it there in hot weather, but not in early spring when you are eager to have the soil warm up. I apply mulch around transplants if the soil is sufficiently warm, and around growing plants started from seed when they are about 6 inches tall. I also spread salt hay very thinly over seeds I have sown that need very steady moisture for germination, such as carrots, but I'm careful not to mulch so thickly that the seedlings cannot come up through the mulch.

Other mulches work well for other gardeners. Black plastic has multitudes of devotees. Gardeners carpet their vegetable plots with it, then cut slits in the sheets for the transplanted seedlings. They claim it keeps the ground warm, moist and weed-free. All this is true. My only objection to plastic is the way it looks. I prefer a more natural style in the garden. But I confess I have used black plastic from time to time.

Planning the Vegetable Garden

I think it is a good idea to draw a sketch of your garden, even before you order your seeds. You may end up deviating from that neat plan for one reason or another, but the garden will be a more successful one if it has been well coordinated at the beginning. I really enjoy drawing my garden plan, especially if it is 10 degrees outside with a foot of snow on the ground; the plan makes spring seem more real. And I

find I buy seeds more judiciously. Instead of buying everything I like in the catalogs, I consider more realistically how many crops I will have space to grow.

There are a lot of factors to consider in planning a vegetable garden, even after you have decided how large a garden you want, what you want to grow in it, and how much of each crop you want to grow. When you draw your plan you will need to know how to space the plants, where to place crops so that they can be grown conveniently and with the proper degree of light, how to interplant one crop with another, how to plant crops in succession to ensure the maximum harvest, and how to rotate groups of vegetables year by year to ward off disease. I will explain, one by one, how these decisions are made. The list may seem a little daunting at first, but none of these principles will be difficult to follow if you plant only as much garden as you have the time, space and experience to handle. After a while much of the planning will start to seem automatic. The garden may sometimes resemble a jigsaw puzzle that will never quite fall into place, and sometimes it will just not be possible to reconcile all the requirements with one another—to plan for a succession of crops, but still practice crop rotation, for example. Usually your plan will represent a series of compromises.

There are an infinite number of vegetable-garden schemes that could be devised according to your own preferences and climate, and it seems very arbitrary to present only two suggested plans. But since this is the easiest way to illustrate the principles involved, try to see these two plans as examples of what one might do, not as strict models to follow.

The small garden in Figure 39 is the kind you might plan if you have a small yard or little time for gardening, and not many people to feed (though it will produce more than you might expect). It is also a good garden to begin with if you are not very experienced. It is surrounded by a fence and divided into small beds, two of which run the length of the fence and contain some crops that the fence will support. The beds can be raised or flat, according to your preference, and are all separated by 2-foot-wide paths.

The second garden (Figure 40) is laid out the same way, but some of the beds are larger. Again, the beds might be raised, flat, or a combination of the two. The area at the eastern end of the garden is for perennial crops. Both gardens are designed to have rows running north–south, where there are rows, to reduce the possibility of taller crops shading shorter ones. The larger garden produces many more vegetables and more varieties; consequently, it requires much more care.

What if you would like to start small but graduate to larger gardens as you gain experience? Does this mean

BUILDING A GARDEN FENCE AND GATE   *Fig. 38*

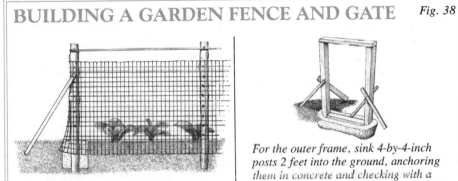

For the fence, use cedar, locust, redwood or wood treated with a preservative. Posts should be 8 feet long (or 10 feet to keep out deer) and sunk at least 2 feet into the ground. Sink corner posts in concrete and/or brace as shown. Use heavy-gauge wire mesh and bury the bottom at least 6 inches deep to deter animals from digging under.

To build the gate, make an inner frame of 2-by-4s nailed together. Nail boards across it diagonally to keep it square.

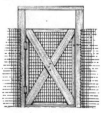

For the outer frame, sink 4-by-4-inch posts 2 feet into the ground, anchoring them in concrete and checking with a level to make sure they are upright. Nail on temporary braces as shown. At the same time, sink a pressure-treated 2-by-4 in concrete for the doorsill, making it flush with the surface of the ground and using a level to make sure it is perfectly horizontal.

When the concrete is thoroughly dry, remove the bracing lumber and attach the inner frame to the outer frame with hinges. Use a heavy metal hook and eye as a latch, and stretch a section of mesh across the gate, stapling it in place.

that you have to fence and refence each year? Not necessarily. You might fence a big area but leave it untilled, or till it and plant a cover crop (page 27) or plant it with annual flowers until you are ready to fill it with more vegetables. Or you might use a simple, inexpensive fence on metal posts that you can re-arrange the following year.

For both of these gardens you would probably want to make a number of changes based on your own needs. For example the two blocks of early peas in the large garden will be fine for a few tasty early-summer meals, but if you want a freezer full of them you would have to devote a larger area to them, perhaps eliminating the limas. You might have no interest in growing witloof chicory but want to include something I have not, such as cauli-flower. You might have a particular in-terest, such as ethnic vegetables. You might want additional space for flowers

(though with this plan you can still tuck them in the corners of the beds or fill in a vacant row with them here and there). You might want to change the layout as well, allowing for more large blocks of space with traditional rows in them, especially if you are growing more large-space crops such as shell beans, winter squash, sweet potatoes or corn.

In the section on individual vegeta-bles I suggest the proper spacing for each one; sometimes I give one figure for traditional-row planting and one for wide-row or block-style planting. But there are no hard-and-fast rules for planting distance. Close planting may produce smaller plants but more of them, so that in many cases the yield will be greater per square foot. I simply find these small, closely planted beds easier to tend and would rather have the luxury of all those paths to work in than extra space between plants that must be mulched or weeded.

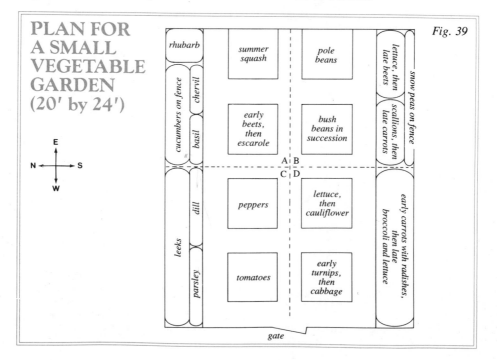

PLAN FOR A SMALL VEGETABLE GARDEN (20′ by 24′)

Fig. 39

PLAN FOR A LARGE VEGETABLE GARDEN (40' by 60')

Fig. 40

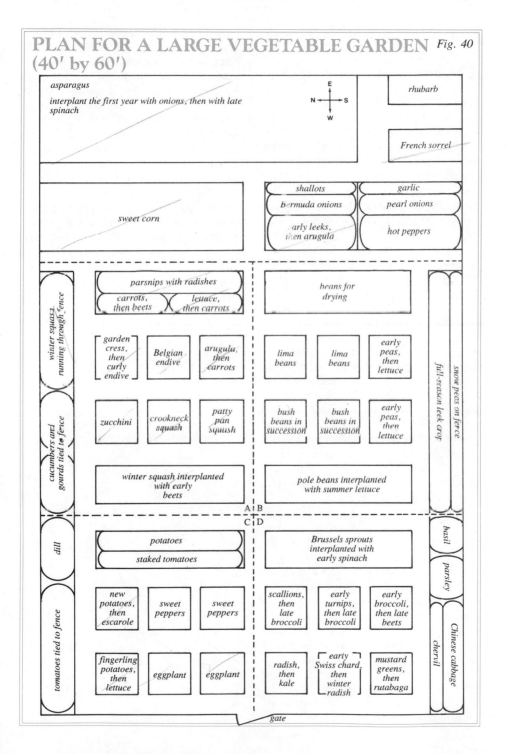

asparagus

interplant the first year with onions, then with late spinach

rhubarb

French sorrel

N E S W

sweet corn

shallots

Bermuda onions

early leeks, then arugula

garlic

pearl onions

hot peppers

winter squash running through fence

parsnips with radishes

carrots, then beets

lettuce, then carrots

beans for drying

garden cress, then curly endive

Belgian endive

arugula, then carrots

lima beans

lima beans

early peas, then lettuce

cucumbers and gourds tied to fence

zucchini

crookneck squash

patty pan squash

bush beans in succession

bush beans in succession

early peas, then lettuce

full-season leek crop

snow peas on fence

winter squash interplanted with early beets

pole beans interplanted with summer lettuce

A B
C D

dill

potatoes

staked tomatoes

Brussels sprouts interplanted with early spinach

basil

parsley

tomatoes tied to fence

new potatoes, then escarole

sweet peppers

sweet peppers

scallions, then late broccoli

early turnips, then late broccoli

early broccoli, then late beets

Chinese cabbage

chervil

fingerling potatoes, then lettuce

eggplant

eggplant

radish, then kale

early Swiss chard, then winter radish

mustard greens, then rutabaga

gate

Succession Planting

Planting crops in succession is a good way to make the most of your precious garden space. Sometimes it means planting several successions of the same crop. In the small plan there is a spring carrot crop (planted together with radishes to shade the carrot seedlings), then a summer carrot crop planted in another spot to mature in fall. There are also early and late beet and lettuce crops in different locations. The early crop of bush beans is harvested, and then a second crop planted in the same spot. The longer the growing season in your area, the more successions of the same crop you can have.

The other way to plan successions is to have a late crop of one vegetable follow an early crop of another. Cool-weather spring crops such as peas, lettuce or turnips can then be followed by crops that do well late in the season such as escarole, cabbage or broccoli. Many gardeners do not realize that there is a whole group of vegetables that can be planted in late summer to mature in time for a fall harvest: Brussels sprouts, broccoli, Chinese cabbage, parsnips, carrots, peas, radishes, turnips, spinach, Swiss chard, bush beans and kale to name some. Sometimes you can find started plants in garden centers in summer, but for good variety you usually have to grow them from seed starting in June or July. Some gardeners even have luck sowing seeds of certain crops just before frost so that they will be ready to sprout when the ground thaws, even if it is too wet to be worked. Lettuce, radishes, beets, onions and spinach are some you might try this way.

In the large garden plan there are many, many such successions, and you will no doubt find good combinations of your own. You will notice that some crops do not succeed each other but stay in the same place all season, such as eggplant and peppers. But even these crops that take a long time to mature can be part of successions in a climate with a more extended growing season. Pay attention to the needs of each vegetable as outlined in the section on each, and allow plenty of time for the crop to mature before frost if it is not frost-hardy, or before hot weather if it is not heat-tolerant. For example, if you live in a very warm climate, you will grow your cool-weather crops such as lettuce, peas, radishes, spinach, Brussels sprouts, cabbage, cauliflower, kale and Swiss chard right through the winter, then follow them with warm-weather crops like okra, sweet potatoes, eggplant and tomatoes.

INTER-PLANTING

Fig. 41

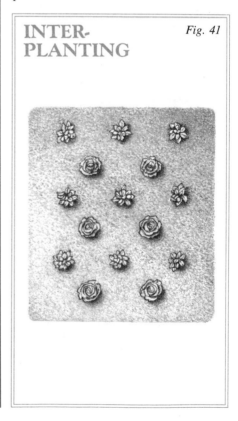

Interplanting

Interplanting means growing two crops in the same spot. You can do this with alternating rows, or in a grid pattern (Figure 41). Usually a relatively small, fast-maturing plant is inter-planted with a large, slow-growing plant that will take a while to use up the space allotted for it in the garden. So, for example, the large winter squash patch in the big garden has early beets in it that are pulled long before the squash vines are long and the leaves large. The Brussels sprouts are interplanted with early spinach that must be harvested before the heat of summer. The broccoli in the small garden has a few heads of lettuce growing among it. You will find that there are several crops—lettuce, scallions, radishes, the cresses and other small greens, for example—that can be stuck in odd corners of the garden so conveniently that you will always have some somewhere, ready for picking. You may not even need to include them in your plan. (But keep records of where they grew, for the purpose of crop rota-tion.) Another trick is to interplant something that dislikes the hot summer sun, like lettuce or spinach, with a tall vegetable like pole beans. The greens will tolerate the partial shade cast by the beans, and their tendency to bolt will be lessened.

Crop Rotation

Crop rotation is the practice of changing the location of the crops from one year to the next. There are two reasons to do this. The first is so that the diseases and insect larvae that plague a particular crop during the summer and then lie in wait for it in the soil over the winter will be disappointed the next year and peter out. This practice will not, by itself, totally prevent diseases or pests in your garden, but it will help, and the longer you can wait before repeating a crop, the better. The other reason is that crops vary in their nutritional needs, and therefore deplete the soil in different ways. If you grow one crop in the same place each year, the soil will become deficient in certain elements. While these nutritional deficiencies could be corrected by fertilizing, rotating is just that much easier on your soil, and you will find that you need to fertilize less. The legume crops even improve the soil, and rotating them through the garden spreads this benefit around.

Crop rotation is practiced a great deal in commercial agriculture, but frankly, home gardeners tend to be care-less about it, because it can be confus-ing. Following a whole field of beets with a whole field of corn is not hard to keep track of. But what if you are grow-ing 30 tiny little crops in one garden? It requires pretty careful record-keeping as well as skillful jigsaw puzzle-making. Unfortunately the problems that afflict one vegetable often afflict all the mem-bers of that vegetable's family, as men-tioned above. They share some diseases and pests with other families, but not as many as they share with each other. So to properly rotate your tomatoes, you have to avoid not only a spot where tomatoes have grown recently but also peppers, eggplant and potatoes. This also makes the possibilities for succes-sion planting more limited. For exam-ple, you might be tempted to follow an early bean crop with broccoli, only to find from your records that broccoli grew on that spot the past year. This is the point at which most people give up.

I think it is still worth doing, though, and there are ways to make it work. I have worked out a "four-quad-rant" method by which I can rotate my garden by plant groups. In the two plans shown on pages 194 and 195 I have divided each garden into four quadrants: A, B, C and D. In each one I have segregated the vegetables from the four large vegetable families that benefit the most from rotation. Thus the A section contains the cucurbits (cucumbers, squash, gourds), B contains the legumes (peas, beans), C contains the cabbage family (Brussels sprouts, broccoli, ruta-baga, etc.) and D contains tomatoes and their relatives. Each family is rotated clockwise as a group each year, so that four years will elapse before any family returns to the same spot.

There are other vegetable crops that can benefit from crop rotation but do not belong to these families—lettuce, carrots and onions, for example. To make the scheme perfect you would have to create more sections, or attach each of these to one of the other quadrants. But I find it easier to just insert these crops where they fit in well, trying not to repeat them in the same spot two years in a row. Lettuce, for example, is so handy to stick in here and there, and onions have such purported insect-repelling qualities, that I hate to restrict either to just one quadrant. Radishes, though members of the cabbage family, are also too useful to confine to one block since they can be used as a "nurse crop" (page 280). You also may find that you want to grow much more from one family than another, and that four more-or-less-equal quadrants will not work unless you leave extra space in each one, as I have done. This space can be either filled up with the family, used for the free-floating vegetables, or planted in flowers. The space at the upper right is also useful for the over-flow, as well as for segregating two varieties of the same vegetable that can cross-pollinate if grown together, such as sweet and hot peppers (page 274).

Companion Planting

M uch has been said about the powers of one plant to repel the pests that attack another, and I often see long lists of "companion plants" that if planted side by side will help each other out. Radishes are said to repel the squash-vine borer. Marigolds are sup-posed to keep rabbits and nematodes away from everything. I do not know how many of these assertions have actu-ally been proven successful, though if you have found some combinations that work for you, by all means use them. I find that with so many other consider-ations to think about in planning the garden, this one usually comes last—though I do scatter plenty of onions and marigolds throughout the garden just in case.

Vegetable Varieties

C hoosing vegetable varieties from catalogs can be bewildering. There are so many of them, and it is hard to know how much to believe from the descriptions, which naturally tell you only the good things and none of the bad. Exaggeration runs even more rampant with the accompanying photos, in which each plant is impossibly laden with vegetables of impossible size, in impossible colors. Until you know your way around the seed company circus it is best to buy from the most reputable, well-established sources you can find.

I like to have a number of different catalogs on hand so as to get a good composite picture of what is available. In any category there are always some tried-and-true favorites that everybody sells. If you stick to those instead of experimenting with the latest rage you can't go too far wrong. But some new varieties are genuine improvements over the old ones; perhaps they bear more abundantly or quickly, withstand cold or heat better, grow on a more compact plant, or resist certain diseases. Bear in mind that these traits are often geared to specific gardening needs—cold climates, for example, or lack of space.

Sometimes you will see a vegetable variety labeled AAS. This means that it is an All-America Selection, having been selected by a large group of experts who have grown it in many trial plots across the country, and that it has beaten out all the rest in its field. But it still may not be the one for you, since those bred for limited parts of the country rarely win the award. I have found the best approach is to find a seed company that specializes in growing seeds for my own particular region. These seeds have given me the most trouble-free plants and abundant harvests. But of course the final test is how they taste to you when they finally make it to the table. You might not like super-super-sweet corn; or you might find that the extra-extra-early pea (like many other extra-early crops) is not as flavorful as the one you have to wait another two weeks for. Or that the bush winter squash are not as tasty as the less convenient vine ones, but that perhaps the convenience is worth it.

You can of course buy seeds in a nursery, or even in the hardware store. But you will never have as many varieties to choose from as you would by mail. And if most of your vegetables come from flats of plants started in the garden center, you may never even know which varieties you are growing. Most gardeners end up buying started plants at some point; they haven't had time to start seeds indoors early, or there was no bright, warm spot to do it in.

This has certainly happened to me. But if you cannot experiment with varieties, you do miss some of the fun of gardening. Most of the information about specific varieties can be found in the individual vegetable sections of this chapter. Refer also to the list of old-fashioned, or "heirloom," varieties on page 200 and the list of varieties for small spaces on page 203.

Getting the Garden Ready

If I am starting a new garden, I like to prepare the soil in fall. There is just not enough time in the spring to remove whatever is growing in the plot, till it, get the soil the way I want it, and then plant. If I find myself in this predicament, I know I will have to forgo some early crops the first year.

Even with an established garden there is a lot to do, because first you must wait until the ground can be worked in spring. This phrase sometimes puzzles new gardeners. When *can* the soil be worked? In most regions workable soil comes when the ground is not only free of frost but also sufficiently dried out. Some seeds will rot if the ground is too wet, but even more important, the soil's texture can be damaged by working it while it is still mucky from spring rains and melting snows. Digging it up only compacts it further.

You can tell that soil is too wet if it forms a firm ball when you squeeze it, but frankly the best way to learn what good soil is, is by working some wet soil and seeing what happens to it. Always keep good soil texture in your mind and try to achieve it whenever you can. Good soil is light and fluffy. Thrust your fingers into the soil, pretend they

Heirloom Vegetable Varieties You Can Grow

Many of the vegetables our ancestors grew have been abandoned in favor of modern hybrids, which tend to be earlier producing and more resistant to disease. But many of the old favorites are worth growing because of their good flavor and because of the fact that they often produce over a longer period rather than having been bred for commercial harvest at one specific time. Most are open-pollinated, non-hybrid varieties that can be grown from seed saved from last year's crop or passed on from friend to friend. By participating in such exchanges you might even help to save some of the rarer varieties from extinction. Here are some you can try. Dates, when given, are approximate. (For companies that sell old varieties, see page 625.)

Beans. *Pole Beans:* 'Kentucky Wonder' ('Old Homestead'), great flavor. 'Scarlet Runner,' a colonial variety with beautiful red flowers. 'Lazy Wife,' a stringless bean. *Limas:* 'White Dutch Runner' ('Oregon Lima'), for the pacific northwest. 'Hopi' ('Bandy') lima, a native-American strain for southern areas. 'Henderson's Bush Lima,' an old bush lima. 'King of the Garden,' an old pole lima. *Shell Beans:* 'Jacob's Cattle,' white with maroon blotches, native to the American southwest. 'Speckled Cranberry' ('Wren's Egg'), red-speckled pods. 'Black Turtle,' an old-fashioned soup bean. 'Swedish Brown,' good bean for baking, early 1800s.

Beets. 'Detroit Dark Red,' the old standby, dates from 1892. 'Winter Keeper,' long keeping and vigorous.

Broccoli. 'Calabrese' ('Italian Sprouting'), forms sideshoots. 'Romanesco,' an old Italian variety with spectacular yellow conical heads, flowers in a spiral pattern.

Brussels Sprouts. 'Catskill' ('Long Island Improved'), an old semidwarf. 'Early Dwarf Danish, early, with short plants.

Cabbage. 'Early Jersey Wakefield,' matures early (1840). 'Late Flat Dutch,' dependable, with good flavor (1860). 'Danish Ballhead,' good for storage (1887). 'All Seasons' ('Wisconsin'), yellows resistant.

Carrot. 'Danvers Half-Long' (1871). 'Early Scarlet Horn,' an old "baby" carrot. 'Nantes' (1870). 'Oxheart,' short and fat (1884).

Cauliflower. 'Early Snowball,' early producer (1888). 'Autumn Giant,' very large (1885).

Celery. 'Giant Pascal,' the old favorite. 'Golden Self-Blanching,' does not need to be blanched.

Corn. *Sweet Corn:* 'Country Gentleman' ('Shoe Peg'), small, sweet white kernels (1890). 'Golden Bantam,' small ears (1853). 'Black Mexican,' a blue-black corn (1863). 'Stowell's Evergreen,' a fine old late corn with a long harvest (1840).

Corn for Meal: 'Taos Pueblo White Flour,' a pre-Columbian corn that makes very fine white flour. 'Mandan Bride' and other Mandan strains are multicolored Indian corn; also attractive as an ornamental corn.

Cucumber. 'Long Green Improved,' a slicing cucumber (1870). 'Straight Eight' and 'Marketmore 76,' both old slicing favorites. 'Boston Pickling,' an old pickling cucumber (late 1800s).

Eggplant. 'Black beauty,' the old favorite for warm climates. 'Early Long Purple,' better for cooler areas (1880s)

Kale. 'Green Scotch Curled,' very hardy (1865).

Leek. 'Giant Musselburgh,' grows very large (1850–1870).

Lettuce. 'Black Seeded Simpson,' a fast crop (late 1880s). 'Parris Island White,' an old favorite cos. 'Mescher,' a fine old butterhead. 'Prizehead,' leaves tipped with red (1880). 'Four Seasons,' heat- and cold-tolerant (1880). 'Iceberg,' the standard crisp-head (1894).

Onion. 'Red Wethersfield.' 'Yellow Globe Danvers' (1850). 'Southport Red Globe' (1836). 'Ailsa Craig.'

Parsnip. 'Hollow Crown' (1850). 'Guernsey.'

Pea. 'Alaska,' cold-tolerant. 'Thomas Laxton.' 3-foot vines (1897). 'Alderman' ('Tall Telephone'), large peas, tall vines (1861). 'Little Marvel,' early and a heavy bearer (1908).

Pepper. 'Bullnose,' the oldest green bell pepper (1759). 'Long Red Cayenne' (1828).

Potato. 'Green Mountain.' 'Irish Cobbler.' Finger-shaped 'Fingerling,' with yellow flesh.

Pumpkin. 'New England Pie' ('Small Sugar') (1863). 'Connecticut Field' (1700s).

Radish. 'Round Black Spanish' (1824). 'China Rose.' 'French Breakfast' (1885).

Squash. *Summer:* 'Yellow Crookneck.' 'White Bush Scallop' ('Patty Pan'). 'Cocozelle,' the original zucchini (1856). *Winter:* 'Delicata,' small and striped. 'True Hubbard,' large and green (1857). 'Turk's Turban,' edible ornamental (1800).

Tomato. 'Ponderosa,' old, large-fruited variety. 'Yellow Pear,' small, yellow, sweet and pear-shaped (1852). 'Marglobe,' red and juicy (1900). 'Earliana,' early variety (1900). 'Red Cherry,' an old red cherry tomato (1865).

Turnip. 'Purple White Glove,' the old standard, still grown (1890s). 'Golden Ball' (1859).

are roots that have to grow through it, and try to make that job as easy for them as possible.

What your soil needs in general and how to provide it is discussed in Chapter 2. You may want to begin by having a soil test done for your future vegetable plot (page 25). The test results will come with recommendations about what to add to give your soil the right pH and amount of nutrients for basic vegetable gardening.

One thing that may confuse you is the fact that various vegetables have different requirements with respect to soil texture, soil fertility and soil pH. How, if you are continually changing the location of the crops in the garden, can you provide precisely what each one needs? You can't always do this. The best you can do is to establish soil with a good texture by adding plenty of organic matter; have the soil moderately fertile and well balanced chemically, without an overabundance of any one element; and keep the pH somewhere beween 6.0 and 7.0.

It is still helpful to know what each crop prefers, however. This way if your soil has a particular condition—very acid, very sandy, very low in an essential nutritional element, you will know which crops will need special attention. You can make careful seasonal applications of lime, sulfur, fertilizer or whatever a particular crop needs for its growth period, but don't add excessive amounts that the next crop growing in that spot will not appreciate. For instance digging some wood ashes and bone meal into the soil will benefit your root crops; and adding some fish emulsion or blood meal will provide nitrogen for the leafy crops such as lettuce. Sometimes you will be told to "top dress" or "side dress" a crop if it is a heavy feeder, or if you need to hasten it along in order to bring it to maturity

before frost or before hot weather. One method is to lay manure or a balanced fertilizer on top of the soil next to the plant and allow it to slowly leach down into the soil. A faster-acting method is to top dress with a liquid fertilizer. Some gardeners make a "manure tea" for this purpose by steeping manure in buckets of water. The same can be done with compost, dried blood, fish emulsion and other soluble materials. Some crops that feed heavily and profit by this kind of attention are asparagus, cabbage, celery, corn, eggplant, rhubarb, squash and tomatoes. But keep in mind that the next crop might not want the soil full of manure (such as carrots) or full of lime (such as potatoes).

In discussing specific vegetables, I have in some instances been specific about amounts of a given fertilizer to add for a crop at a particular stage in its life. But please keep in mind that the usefulness of such advice is limited by the fact that I do not know what your soil is like: what nutrients are already there; whether the soil is heavy and will retain nutrients you add or whether it is sandy and will allow them to leach out of it; whether you live in a warm climate where organic matter decomposes quickly. I would rather you familiarize yourself with the few simple basics of plant nutrition, then *watch* how your plants grow, looking for signs of excess or insufficiency until you know what you can safely add, and when.

Planting Your Crops

The basic techniques of planting, transplanting and thinning are discussed in detail in Chapter 2. Specific information about planting individual vegetables is covered later in this chapter. Here I want to give you some advice

Baby Vegetables and Vegetables for Small Spaces

Many vegetable varieties are dwarf or compact-shaped plants, which makes them good choices for small-space or even container gardens. In some cases they are bush varieties of vegetables that more commonly grow on long vines. Many, though not all, produce small or "baby" fruits; in other cases the fruits are average size.

Beets. Beets are a good small-space crop in general. Try 'Little Ball' or 'Gladiator.'

Broccoli. Broccoli 'Raab' ('Rabb,' 'Di Rapa') grows on small plants and so takes up less space than the heading types.

Cabbage. 'Modern Dwarf,' 'Hybrid Salarite' (Savoy type), 'Minicole,' 'Red Acre' (red).

Carrots. Carrots are a small-space crop in general. For tiny ones try 'Little Finger,' 'Lady Finger,' 'Gold Nugget.'

Cauliflower. 'Snowball.'

Corn. For a space-saving corn grow 'Honey Cream,' with 7-inch ears and stalks 5–6 feet tall. For even tinier corn grow 'Golden Midget,' with 4-inch ears on stalks less than 3½ feet tall. For popcorn in a container try 'Mini Hybrid.'

Cucumber. 'Pot Luck,' 'Bush Champion,' 'Spacemaster,' 'Patio Pik.'

Eggplant. 'White Egg,' 'Modern Midget,' 'New York Improved,' 'Early Black Egg.'

Lettuce. Any lettuce is a space saver, but especially 'Little Gem' and 'Tom Thumb.' Also grow small greens such as garden cress.

Onions. Most onions are good small-space crops, especially scallions. Also try garlic and shallots. 'White Portugal' is a tiny white round onion that can be grown from seed.

Parsnip. In general a crop that takes up little space as long as the soil is deep.

Peas. 'Mighty Midget,' 'Tiny Tim,' 'Little Marvel.'

Peppers. Most peppers take up little space and do well in containers; any of the hot ones are particularly ornamental in containers. For small sweet peppers try 'Park's Pot.'

Pumpkin. 'Small Sugar,' 'Spirit,' 'Cheyenne.'

Radish. All are good for small spaces.

Squash. *Summer:* 'Creamy,' 'Hybrid Daytona' (crookneck), 'Benning's Green Tint' (patty pan type). *Winter:* 'Gold Nugget,' 'Table King Bush Acorn,' 'Butterbush,' 'Sweet Dumpling.'

Tomato. 'Patio,' 'Pixie,' 'Tiny Tim,' 'Small Fry,' 'Goldie.'

about planting vegetable gardens in general.

Vegetable crops vary in how and when they are planted. This is fortunate, because it means that not all the work of planting has to be done at one time. You can plan your labors more easily if you keep the following chronology in mind.

Some vegetable seeds can be sown directly in the ground as early as you can work the soil; these include peas, beets, lettuce, onions, radishes, spinach and turnips. Others, such as corn, beans and squash, are sown directly in the garden, but not until danger of frost has passed. In cool climates with shorter growing seasons, some seeds, such as tomatoes, Brussels sprouts, cauliflower, celery, eggplant and cabbage, are generally sown indoors and then set out in the garden when there is little or no danger of frost. (In warm climates with a long growing season it is often unnecessary to do this.)

With quick-growing crops that are planted in succession you have a considerable choice of planting times and will probably evolve your own schedule for each one. For example, if you want to harvest a crop towards the end of the season, just find out how long the plant will take to mature and count backwards from the ideal harvest time to find the ideal planting time. This may take a little practice at first. Seed companies tell you how many days each variety takes to mature, but unfortunately these estimates can vary dramatically from one seed seller to another. They can also vary dramatically in your garden depending on where you live and what kind of weather you are having. And to top it off, it is not always clear whether the calculation of days to maturity has been made from the time of sowing the seed or the time of setting out a transplant. The numbers are not entirely useless, since they do give you a means of comparing one variety with another, as long as you realize that they are not very exact.

Even after danger of frost has long since passed, you may want to start your late crops in a separate place, either indoors in a sunny spot, in a greenhouse, in a cold frame, or even in a separate "nursery-bed" corner of your garden. This way they only take up a tiny bit of space while they are small, freeing up the garden for early crops that need it more. Later, when they are ready to be transplanted in a permanent place, there will be gaps waiting where the early crops have been harvested.

Moving seedlings from indoors to the garden can be very hard on them, because plants grown indoors tend to have soft, tender stems and leaves that are easily injured by either extreme cold or hot sun. Therefore many gardeners "harden off" their plants before moving them permanently to the garden. They bring the seedlings, still in their flats or peat pots, outside and expose them gradually to cold, sun and wind. The best way is to start about two weeks before planting time, leaving them out for a few hours each day and increasing the time until they are out all the time. But always bring the tender plants back indoors if frost threatens. By planting time you will notice that the leaves and stems look tougher, thicker and better able to withstand the elements on their own.

Many gardeners use devices such as cloches, hot caps, grow tunnels or portable cold frames and mini-greenhouses to get a head start on early crops. There is an ever-growing number of these on the market in countless different designs. The general purpose of all of them is to trap the warmth from the sun during the day and hold some of it around the plant and the soil during the night, causing the plant to grow faster

A SYSTEM OF FRAMES TO PROTECT YOUR GARDEN

Fig. 42

You can build a series of simple wooden frames all the same size that can serve a variety of purposes in your garden. The ones shown are pieces of 2-by-4-inch pressure-treated lumber nailed together at the corners, all of them 4 feet by 4 feet. Various materials are then stapled or nailed over them.

Stacked frames can provide several kinds of protection at once; for example, you might cover your summer lettuce crop with chicken wire against the rabbits, and lath for shade. Spacers (empty frames) made of 2-by-4s or 2-by 6s can be stacked under the protecting frames to make them taller as plants grow, and any frames can be set over raised beds. For long beds, set a series of frames next to each other, keeping each frame small enough so that you can lift it easily.

Clear plastic is stretched over a frame as protection against frost. The frame is then set over young plants.

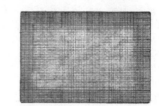

Agricultural fabric over the frame wards off insect pests and also provides some frost protection.

Black plastic keeps weeds from growing in a bed that is not being used.

Chicken wire over the frame protects against rabbits, deer and other predators. Use plastic netting or metal screening to keep birds from eating newly planted seeds. Screening will also keep out mice.

Lath (narrow strips of wood) protects plants from excessive sun in summer. Snow fence can be nailed to the frame to make assembly even easier.

by day and escape frost damage by night. Larger versions are used to cover mature plants in fall or winter to extend the harvest. Originally these devices were made of glass; modern versions are usually plastic or fiberglass. They vary in cost, ease of assembly and use, durability and stability against wind. Some of them work, but most make weeding and watering difficult. The biggest problem is ventilation. The air can get too hot inside the cloche or tunnel and bake the plants. Those with vents to let heat out and rainwater in give less protection from cold; those that are opened and shut manually take much time and vigilance. Usually the heat-holding devices that cover the largest area provide the greatest protection from frost.

All in all it is up to you whether the extra growth these gadgets afford is worth the bother. Many gardeners find them a great help. I do recommend that unless you live in a frost-free climate you keep some form of protection on hand in case an unexpectedly late spring frost is forecast. For individual plants the easiest thing to use is a plastic gallon jug with the bottom cut out. Either stick it into the soil around the plant, or cut the bottom on three sides for a flap, which you can anchor with a stone. If you leave the jug on during the day, be sure to unscrew the top if it is hot. You should also have some big sheets of clear plastic that you can throw over a large number of plants, weighted at the sides with stones. Use this for fall frosts as well. In addition buy some large pieces (say 20 by 20 feet) of the new agricultural fabrics such as Reemay or Agronet, which afford a few degrees of frost protection for plants of any size. These also keep out most insect predators during the growing season. They are so lightweight that most plants can grow to their full height under them,

pushing up the fabric, as long as you leave some slack when you anchor them. They let in water and light and can be removed for weeding. Note: you must remove the fabric at times when certain crops, such as cucumbers, are being pollinated by bees.

If you want to go in for more elaborate protection devices, I recommend building a series of wooden frames all the same size that you can use for a variety of purposes (Figure 42). Pick a specific size, say 4 by 4 feet or 4 by 6 feet, and plan your garden so that rows or blocks of plants will fit under the frames. Then just nail pressure-treated 2-by-4s or 2-by-6s together and nail or staple whatever material you need over the top: agricultural fabric or metal screening to keep out harmful insects, chicken wire to keep out rabbits and other nibblers, heavy clear plastic or storm windows for frost protection, plastic netting to keep out birds, lath or snow fence to provide shade for plants that bolt (see page 251) in summer heat, or black plastic to keep an unplanted area weed-free. These frames are easy to build, light enough to transport but heavy enough to stay put. They can be stacked on top of each other if more than one material is needed at once. Keep plenty of empty frames on hand to stack as spacers, adding more as needed for tall plants. This system works particularly well if you garden in raised beds. Just make the frames exactly the same size as your beds. Ones with plastic or glass should be slid open, or propped open with a stick on hot days, to let cooler air in.

Another season-extender for your vegetables is a permanent cold frame in which you can sow or harden off seedlings in spring and even sow crops in fall for overwintering. See page 48 for instructions on how to build one.

Taking Care of the Garden

M aintenance is the hard part—not because it requires a great amount of skill, but because it is so easy to neglect. I know I always have more time, energy and enthusiasm for gardening in spring, after being indoors for much of the winter, than I do in summer when there are so many other things to do, like playing tennis or cooling off in the lake. This is why it is so important to plant an area that you can realistically, not hypothetically, take care of. It also helps to know what your gardening priorities are.

WEEDING

In maintaining the garden, the most important activity by far is weeding. Weeds compete with garden plants for all the necessities: light, nutrients, water, air. They sometimes harbor insect pests and even diseases. It is virtually impossible to have your garden produce much of anything if you do not keep weeds out of it.

One way to minimize weeds greatly is to mulch, although even a mulch will let some weeds through. Some annual weed seeds already in the soil will poke up through the mulch or fall into it and sprout. Roots of perennial weeds that have not been eradicated from the soil will sprout and push up through it valiantly. But your labors will be greatly lessened if you mulch, especially since some weeds are easier to pull from mulched soil. It is also worth taking the trouble to weed a strip several feet wide around the outside of the garden, if it is weedy there, and mulch that because some weeds will send runners in.

Your biggest weed battles will be in early spring—I think of it as "weed season"—when so many of the annual weeds are sprouting. At this point mulch won't help because most of your seedlings are so small that mulch might smother them. Mulch may also prevent the ground from warming up and in so doing hinder both germination and growth. The best way to deal with these early weeds is by repeated, careful cultivating—that is, by disturbing the soil with a cultivator, a hoe, a hand rake or whatever works best for you—so that the tiny weed roots are dislodged, exposed to air and killed. You must be careful not to uproot the young seedlings sprouting among them, and you will often find yourself pulling weeds with your fingertips where they are close to the plants, which is picky work, but necessary.

But even after weed season, and even with a well-mulched garden, you must—I repeat, must—weed. You will benefit yourself and save yourself much labor if you catch weeds when they are *tiny*. Try to get yourself to weed an hour here, an hour there, instead of ignoring the garden for a week or two and then spending all day weeding it. Going in to weed often forces you to notice other problems as well and catch them before they get out of hand.

HARVESTING

The second most important maintenance task is picking. Most vegetables have an optimum time when they should be picked, and some, such as edible-pod peas, are at their best only on a specific day. Corn must also be picked promptly—or the raccoons will do it for you. With other crops, such as snap beans, cucumbers, broccoli, summer squash and okra, you must keep picking continuously or the plants will slow down and even stop production. With many vegetables such as salad greens, the harvest starts long before the plant is mature. You can eat even the smallest thinnings, then thin some more the week after and eat those.

PEST CONTROL

Looking out for bugs and diseases is important because they can ruin a whole harvest, often very quickly. This topic receives more discussion in Chapter 2. Some of the cautions offered there are particularly important when you are dealing with edible crops. I do not like to put any toxic substances in my vegetable garden. Even if I waited the required number of "days to harvest," which is always specified on the can of spray, I would worry about the stuff straying to plants nearby that I might be picking and eating at the time I spray. I also worry about the effect of these sprays on insects that are beneficial to the garden, such as bees, praying mantises and ladybugs.

My preference is, whenever possible, to use nonchemical means such as picking the bugs off, washing them off with a soap spray, and covering young plants with a mesh-covered frame. If all else fails I will use rotenone or another nontoxic substance; but bearing in mind that even these can harm bees, especially early in the day when they are feeding, I use them only as a last resort. A squash blossom, for example, blooms for only one day, and nothing should interfere with a bee's pollinating it. As far as diseases go I will occasionally apply a vegetable fungicide. But in general I fight diseases by cleaning up garden debris promptly, by rotating crops, by selecting disease-resistant varieties, and by giving the plants great soil and everything else their hearts desire to keep them as robust as possible. I have not had many problems with plant dis-

eases, and many other gardeners have had the same experience.

Above all, if you do see something odd on your plants that is obviously not doing them any good, find out exactly what the problem is, either by consulting this or other books or by taking a sample of the plant (and the bug, if you can) to the Extension Service for identification. There is nothing worse than a gardener who, at the first sign of any problem (or even before), says "Oh, I've got to *spray*," without knowing what the problem is—an insect, a disease, a soil deficiency or just rotten weather. "All-purpose" sprays may be profitable to the seller, but they will not do your garden's ecology, or your own body, any good.

WATERING

It amazes me how much gardeners disagree about the need for water in their vegetable gardens. The traditional wisdom holds that a garden needs an inch of water per week during the growing season. If it does not get that inch from rainfall, the moisture must be provided by watering. If the weather is very hot, however, either because of your climate or because of a heat wave, your garden may need more than an inch of water a week, but if you mulch the garden you may get by with less.

Some people maintain that this is far too little water if you want to have really spectacular yields. Many vegetables, such as tomatoes and cucumbers, are largely composed of water, and it is claimed that by using a drip-irrigation system, you can ensure a great yield of these vegetables—and of everything else. Having never tried these systems, I cannot judge, and so I would not try to dissuade you from using them. In fact they are probably a good idea if you live in a particularly dry climate. The systems on the market can be very expensive if your garden is large, though many gardeners find ingenious ways of rigging up homemade drip systems with lengths of leaky hose and various combinations of hardware.

Why can't you simply put your lawn sprinkler in the garden and let it gradually soak everything as you move it from place to place? You can, but if you do you'll wet the leaves of your plants, and there is always more risk of disease when the leaves of plants get wet. Notice how many more mildews and other fungus diseases appear when it is very rainy, or in August when there is a lot of humidity in the air.

What do I do? Preferring the simplest possible methods, I get by with a combination of mulch and deep soaking with a plain old hose whenever it is dry. I just let it run out of the hose without a nozzle, because I do not like the plants' leaves to get wet. I am also a firm believer in presoaking furrows at planting time, and I make little circular dams of earth around individual plants, especially tomatoes, so that the plant sits in a saucer that catches and holds water. Even with mulch, this is a good idea.

OTHER CHORES

There is not much else you need to do to keep your garden in good shape. Some crops do require special kinds of attention. The tall or sprawling ones need to be staked or trellised, as discussed in the individual sections that follow. And a number of vegetables can be partly covered to "blanch" (whiten) them, tenderize them, or make them less bitter. The most common vegetables that are blanched are celery, leeks, broccoli, asparagus and Belgian endive. Blanching is variously done by putting boards over the plants, tying the plants' own leaves over the edible portions, or mounding earth over the parts to be blanched. With some vegetables, such as cauliflower, this is almost always done; with others, such as asparagus, it is optional and more a matter of appearance than anything else. In recent years, however, research has shown that unblanched vegetables have more nutrients than blanched ones do, and thus blanching has started to go out of fashion. Just as with flour and rice, the trend has shifted away from whiteness toward natural color and greater nutritional value. If you do blanch vegetables, make sure you peek into their dark hideaways from time to time to make sure they are not rotting, mildewing or being eaten.

HOUSEKEEPING

One more task—cleaning up. This should begin as soon as you have a crop you are finished with, either because it has succumbed to a plague or because it has been harvested. Unless it is a perennial crop, or unless it did indeed have a plague, it should be pulled up and put on the compost pile. This will help keep the garden free of disease and insect pests, add to your store of composting material, and possibly provide space for a succession crop. By the time the ground has frozen, *everything* should be out of there except the perennial vegetables, any crops you are overwintering in the ground for spring harvest, seed you have sown for spring sprouting or any cover crops you may have planted. If your winters are mild your cleaning up and replanting will go on all year long. If your winters are severe it is time to hibernate along with your garden, waiting for the seed catalogs to come, reevaluating the year's garden and deciding what to try next year. The fantasy will be a much more enticing one if the garden is all tidied up and ready for those first seeds to go in.

Asparagus

I think that planting asparagus is one of the best investments a gardener can make. It is a crop that asks a great deal of you at first: a lot of space in your garden, a lot of work preparing the bed, and a three-year wait before you can harvest your first full crop. But provided you pay attention to a few rules of good maintenance, nothing you can grow will give you quite such a good return.

Asparagus is one of the few perennial vegetables—that is, one of the few that comes back each year without being replanted. A well-established bed can produce for decades, giving you crops that, if you had to buy them in the store, would be expensive and never as savory as those fresh-picked, home-grown spears in spring. It also freezes beautifully, retaining its fresh taste and bright green color. If I could freeze only one

vegetable I would freeze asparagus. I even like looking at the plants, with their tall, fernlike foliage—bright green in summer, then yellow-orange in fall—plus, on the female plants, the added visual bonus of red berries.

SITE

To grow enough asparagus for a family of four—about fifty plants—you need 250 square feet of land. The spot should be sunny, if possible. Even though asparagus will tolerate some shade, full sun will give you more vigorous plants that can better ward off disease. Asparagus is generally grown in a plot by itself, for it is so tall that it easily shades most plants growing next to it. The first year, before the ferns are tall enough to cast much shade, you can plant crops such as beans between the asparagus rows. In subsequent years, interplant with early crops such as radishes and lettuce, which are harvested before the ferns reach their full seasonal growth.

SOIL

Since asparagus is a perennial, the bed it grows in will be a permanent one. The only chance you will have to give your asparagus the luxurious soil preparation it needs is before you plant, so do it then. This means removing as many perennial weeds from the bed as possible, including pieces of their roots, which can resprout. When mature, the asparagus will form a dense mat of deep roots from which you cannot disentangle these invaders. Perennial grass, especially, can quickly destroy the bed if the bed is neglected. I never rototill a new bed unless I have removed all the weeds first with a digging fork.

Asparagus is a hungry plant, so I dig a lot of fertilizer into the whole bed—a 6-inch layer of rotted manure if I have it, plus a phosphorus source such as bone meal and a potassium source such as wood ashes. If you are using fertilizer in pellet form, make sure you also add plenty of organic matter, such as peat moss, too. A 6-inch layer, spread on the bed and dug in thoroughly, should be enough, but use more if the soil is heavy, since asparagus prefers a sandy loam. Double digging the bed (page 36) would make the soil texture even better. Add lime too, if the pH is more acid than the preferred 6.0–7.0.

PLANTING

Asparagus can be grown from seed, but gardeners rarely do that for the crop takes too long from seed. The best method is to buy one-year-old roots, or "crowns," from a local nursery or mail-order supplier. Some parts of the country have had problems with an airborne fusarium wilt of asparagus. Check with your Extension Service, and if fusarium wilt is a problem in your area, be sure you order disease-free roots from a reputable nursery in a part of the country that has not been affected, or else grow your plants from seed. Seeds are started indoors three months before planting and set out as 12-inch plants a month after the last frost. Plant them in trenches the same way you do the roots (Figure 43).

Asparagus roots are long, white, and hang like the tentacles of an octopus from the center of the crown, where you can see little white tips ready to sprout. When I first saw a bin of these crowns for sale I was surprised to find them lying exposed to the air. Up to a point asparagus roots will withstand exposure to air. Nonetheless make sure they look fresh and firm, not limp and wrinkled. The less stress the roots encounter, the more vigorous the plants will be. If they arrive by mail and you cannot plant

PLANTING ASPARAGUS

Fig. 43

them right away, keep them in their package, or wrap in sphagnum moss that is slightly damp (not wet). Try to plant them as soon as possible.

If you live in a warm climate, plant asparagus roots in fall. In a cooler one the proper time is early spring, about four weeks before the last average frost date. Try to prepare the bed the previous fall, to give it a chance to settle.

I plant asparagus in rows, leaving a good 4 feet between them, because I like to be able to walk between the rows without compacting the soil around the plants or stepping on the young shoots. For each planting row I dig a series of trenches a foot deep and 18 inches wide. I add a few more inches of compost or manure to the bottom of the trench, then make mounds of compost or light, rich soil, one for each plant, spacing them 18 inches apart. The top of each mound should be about 6 inches below the soil surface.

I drape the "tentacles" over the mounds that I have made (Figure 43), with the tips about 6 inches below the soil surface. Then I start to fill the trench with soil, firming it gently around the roots and covering the tips

with 2 or 3 inches of soil. As the spears grow, I gradually fill the trench up with soil. In subsequent years the crowns will work their way closer to the surface.

GROWING

Keep a new bed watered if it is a dry spring, and cultivate very lightly to keep it free of weeds, being careful not to damage the emerging shoots. When the plants are mature, it is usually not necessary to water the bed, because the roots go down so deep.

A few puny spears will come up the year that you plant. Don't pick them! If the whole plant is to mature, you must let the first spears grow into the foliage that makes food for the long roots to store. Do not cut the foliage down until late winter or until it dies down by itself. Even as it turns yellow, it will be helping the plant to grow. Besides, that bright color is a welcome sight in winter when everything else looks dead. At the end of winter it is a good precaution to cut the old foliage down and burn it or

haul it away, since it can harbor diseases or the eggs of the asparagus beetle.

The second spring there will be more spears than there were the year before. Don't pick them yet, except for the few that are as thick as your finger. Just keep waiting, watering and mulching; and top dress with compost, manure or a liquid fertilizer after harvest and again in fall. (You may top dress at these times in subsequent years also.)

PESTS AND DISEASES

The chief insect plague is the asparagus beetle. These can be controlled in all but the direst cases by picking them off when they appear and destroying the dead stalks at the end of the season.

Asparagus rust is a common disease, but most modern varieties are rust-resistant. Fusarium wilt can be fought by obtaining disease-free roots and burning plant debris. Also, do everything you can to raise a vigorous crop that will do its own part in resisting disease: prepare the soil well, feed, weed, mulch and keep an eye out for insect predators that may weaken the plants.

HARVEST

The third spring there will be many more spears. Okay, *now* pick them—but only the ones that are finger-sized, and only for two to four weeks.

How you pick asparagus is a burning issue with some people. There are the snappers, and there are the cutters. Nature has arranged for the asparagus spear to break off at a point where it starts to be tender and cook nicely, so snapping works fine. So does cutting, as long as you use a sharp knife and try not to injure the emerging shoots nearby, especially if you are cutting below the soil surface in order to get a longer spear. The spears should be cut when they are about 8 inches above the ground, before the scales on the tips have begun to open.

In subsequent years, pick all the finger-sized ones you want for six to eight weeks, or until the weather is hot and the spears are coming up thin and spindly. If you want a really early harvest you can pull the mulch away from one row to let the ground warm up faster. Some people also lengthen the picking season by planting some crowns very deep initially, so that they come up later and can be picked longer.

VARIETIES

The most commonly grown asparagus variety is 'Mary Washington.' This and the other Washington varieties have been bred for rust resistance, as have 'Early California 500,' 'Hybrid Waltham,' 'Jersey Centennial' and 'Jersey Giant.' The last is also resistant to fusarium wilt. 'Brock Imperial' is a high yielder, and 'Princeville' is a southern variety.

Beans

Y ou can grow beans in a small garden, but there are so many interesting kinds of beans that they may lure you into planting a larger one just so you can include them all. The most familiar ones are "string beans," so called because they used to have inedible strings running down the spines before this trait was bred out of them. These are also called "snap beans" because they snap in two when ready for picking. They are eaten pods and all. They can be green or yellow; if yellow, they are called "wax beans." There are varieties in either color that grow short and are called "bush beans,"

and varieties that grow long vines and are called "pole beans." Those that are raised for the beans inside the pod are called "shell beans." Of these some, such as limas, are eaten fresh; others, such as navy beans, kidney beans and soybeans, are dried.

Beans have a way of twining their way out of these categories, though. Many a snap bean that has grown past the tasty-pod stage can be picked for the bean inside it, and many shell beans can be eaten either fresh or dried. Green beans, wax beans and limas can all be either bush or pole. "Half-runners," popular in the south, are somewhere

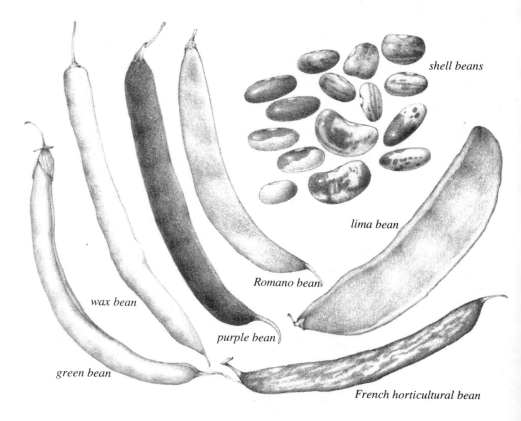

shell beans

lima bean

Romano bean

wax bean

purple bean

green bean

French horticultural bean

between a bush and a pole type. There are also a number of southern peas, such as black-eyed peas, that are often discussed with beans. ("Pea" and "bean" are rather loose terms that describe a number of different legumes, all closely related.) These are sometimes eaten fresh, and sometimes dried.

My advice is to try a lot of different beans—a few new ones each year. Most people wind up with some pretty strong favorites. I love to eat and freeze fresh beans in the summer, but I also love to have rows of dried ones in big glass jars on my shelves, all in contrasting shapes and colors. One of my favorites is a large, fat white bean with dark red speckles called 'Jacob's Cattle,' which not only tastes good but looks pretty, either in jars or on the plate.

All beans are rich in vitamins, and the shelled kind are rich in protein, too. Soybeans, especially, are terrifically good for you. I probably have had one soyburger too many at vegetarian tables to be a true fan, and I confess I thanked the critter that ate the one crop of soybeans I ever tried to grow. But their virtues are many; in addition to being nourishing, soybeans have value as a green manure (page 27).

Beans are a fast, easy, abundant summer crop that needs plenty of sun and will produce little but mildew in foggy climates. Too much intense heat in summer will cause the blossoms to drop, and cold, heavy, wet soil in spring will rot the seeds. But given a reasonable three-month summer, you should be able to grow most beans if you choose varieties geared to your region.

SITE

Plant beans in a spot where they will get full sun and good drainage. Early crops will benefit from soil that warms up quickly in spring. These factors make beans good candidates for raised-bed culture. I find this is not always practical if I am growing a number of different kinds of dried beans and want to give them a lot of space (I'd need to build a lot of beds). But for an early, quick crop of snap beans, raised beds are great. I also make sure I choose a spot where the beans will not cast shade on other crops, unless they are ones that appreciate some shading in midsummer, such as lettuce. And I avoid planting beans where other legumes have grown recently.

SOIL

The soil in which beans grow can have a neutral to slightly acid pH (6.0–7.0). They like any good loam with plenty of organic matter added, but they don't need a great deal of feeding. "Nitrogen-fixing" bacteria in nodules that form on beans' roots convert atmospheric, gaseous nitrogen into nitrogen compounds in the soil, making nitrogen available to plants, and thereby fertilizing and enriching the soil. Dusting the seeds with the proper bacterial inoculant, *Rhizobium phaseoli*, will speed up this process. A fertilizer like 5–10–5, not one that is very high in nitrogen, is best for planting.

PLANTING

If you want to start eating beans early—six to eight weeks after the last average frost—plant some bush beans, either green or wax. They will produce all at once, which is handy for both the commercial grower and the home gardener whose chief goal is to fill the freezer. You can also sow new plantings every ten days or so for succession crops.

Pole beans take longer to bear—ten or eleven weeks—but then keep bearing until frost, so they are the joy of the gardener who wants to pick and eat fresh beans over a long period of time. They are also great space savers because they will ultimately produce about three times the yield of the bush types in the same amount of garden space. Except in very warm climates, they are generally sown in one planting.

Lima beans take a long time, so choose ''early'' varieties up north. So do soybeans, but these can make fast progress in spring even if it is a bit chilly. Fava beans, which are big fat shell beans, also respond well to early sowing.

Bean seeds are almost always sown directly in the garden, but not until after danger of frost has passed. None of them is frost-hardy, and they will make a very slow start if the soil is colder than 65 degrees (though if you try an extra-early row you might get lucky with it). Plant these early beans 1 inch deep; later ones should go 1½–2 inches deep. Moisten the soil well when you plant, and make sure that the seeds will be coming up through fine soil, patted firm but not hard and crusty. If the soil in your garden tends to be lumpy, rub the lumps between your hands, letting the soil fall onto the seeds.

I like to plant bush beans in a wide row or block. Seeds spaced about 4 inches apart will not have to be thinned later. Planting pole beans is a bit more complicated, because you first have to decide what kind of support you are going to give the vines. I use either single unpeeled saplings, 8 feet long and about 2 inches in diameter, or else three thinner ones placed 3–4 feet apart in a triangle, and joined tepee-style on top with a stout string (Figure 44). Either way I make sure I sink the poles deep enough in the ground so that they will not blow over (at least a foot, 2 feet for the thicker ones). I sow about six seeds in a circle around each pole, about 6 inches from it, then later thin these to three seedlings per pole. The vines then twist their way up the poles as they grow.

Another good and popular way to support pole beans is on a trellis that runs the length of the row. Trellises work if they are sturdy enough to support what will be a pretty heavy crop, and if they provide vertical strings or wires for the vines to twist around; horizontal strings or meshes seem to confuse the beans, and you can wind up with a tangled mess. Install your trellis before you plant, then sow a row of seeds on either side of it, with the beans about 4 inches apart.

GROWING

Mulch is good for beans because they are shallow rooted and can easily be damaged by cultivating and weeding. They also are more prone to disease when wet, and mulch cuts down on the need for watering. I try not to mess with beans when they are wet because it is touching the wet plants that spreads disease from one to another. But I also make sure they do not get too dry. Bean plants that have dried out produce pods that start out with a few beans and end in a squiggle.

To speed up growth, the plants can be side dressed with a fertilizer such as 5–10–5. This step is more important for long-bearing pole beans and for heavy feeders such as limas. I do not feed bush beans at all after planting.

PESTS AND DISEASES

Beans can get anthracnose, bacterial blight and mosaic, but these are rarely a problem if you use purchased seed and rotate your crops. If diseases still recur, seek out resistant varieties.

About blossom time you might be

WAYS TO GROW POLE BEANS

Fig. 44

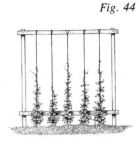

On a trellis: A wooden frame made with pressure-treated 2-by-4 posts is sunk 2 feet into the ground at each end; smaller pieces of lumber are nailed horizontally to support vertical wires 4–6 inches apart. Grow one plant per wire.

On poles: Sink pieces of lumber or saplings, 8 feet long and 1 inch in diameter, a foot apart. Plant several seeds at the base of each.

On a tepee: Use three poles for each tepee. Tie them together at the top and plant six seeds per pole, thinning to three.

visited by Mexican bean beetles, which look like large brown ladybugs. Pick off the adults, the fuzzy yellow larvae, and the yellow egg masses under the leaves. You can also pick off any Japanese beetles that arrive, and you can hose off aphids with a stream of water.

HARVEST

When should you pick? For snap beans, wait until they are about pencil size, but harvest before the beans inside the pods have become lumpy. Then keep picking! Otherwise they will stop producing. I can still remember my mother complaining, every summer, about "keeping up with the beans." But she did it, and there were never any complaints from us about her freezer full of 'Kentucky Wonder.'

For fresh shell beans, let the lumps in the pods get good and fat. For dried shell beans, let the pods get brown and dry on the plant, then pick them before they can split open and spill out the beans or before they can mildew. If it is getting ominously near frost time, you can pick the pods and finish off the drying process indoors. When dry, the beans can be shelled by hand or threshed by putting them in a bag, pounding them, then spreading them out in a windy place. I think shelling is easier. Before storing dried beans, it is a good idea to put them in the freezer for a few hours to kill any lurking bugs or their larvae.

VARIETIES

For flavor in a green bean it is hard to beat 'Kentucky Wonder,' a very old pole bean that needs some stringing. 'Blue Lake' is also an old favorite. 'Scarlet Runner,' with its red flowers, and the Italian flat-podded 'Romano' are both pole beans with ardent followers. 'Burpee Golden' is a good pole wax bean.

'Kentucky Wonder,' 'Blue Lake' and 'Romano' also come in bush form. Other bush beans are 'Tendercrop,' 'Top Crop,' 'Contender' and 'Improved Tendergreen.' You also might try

bush beans

pole beans

'Triomphe de Farcy'—a bush form of the tiny, tasty French *haricot vert.* Good bush wax beans include 'Pencil Pod' and 'Brittle.' 'Royalty,' a purple pod that turns green when cooked, looks pretty in the garden and is a hardy bean.

'King of the Garden' is a good pole lima. Good bush limas include the Fordhook varieties and 'Henderson Bush Lima,' a good baby lima or "butter bean."

Shell beans are so varied and numerous that my best advice is "explore at will," consulting some of the specialty catalogs noted in the list of Mail-Order Sources beginning on page 618. But here are a few to get you started: 'Dark Red Kidney' for chili; 'Navy' for Boston baked beans; 'Jacob's Cattle' ('Trout'), a large white bean flecked with red; 'Black Turtle,' a good soup bean for cool climates; chick peas (garbanzo beans) for hot, dry climates; the old-fashioned types with pods streaked red and white; and the luscious French *flageolets* if you have a reasonably long growing season (they take at least 100 days to mature). Among soybean varieties try 'Vinton,' or 'Verde,' which is good green as well as dried.

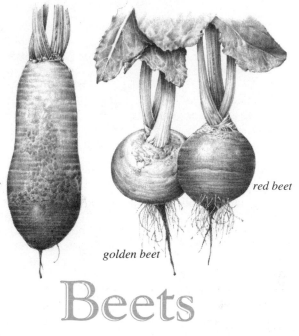

cylindrical beet

red beet

golden beet

Beets

T he best reason to grow beets is to make homemade borscht. But you can also boil them and serve them with butter or one of those gooey sauces, you can pickle them, or you can eat the green tops in salads or as a cooked vegetable.

Beets can be savored from the first tops in spring to the last-dug roots in December, just before the ground freezes. And it is easy to preserve them long after that by canning, freezing or storing in the root cellar. To top it all off, they are an easy, fairly quick-maturing crop. Few bugs or diseases bother them, and almost any climate suits them.

The seedlings are frost-hardy and can be grown in spring, summer and fall in cold climates, and in fall, winter and spring in hot ones. Most varieties mature in about eight weeks.

SITE

Beets are easy to find a place for. They will tolerate some shade, so that if part of your garden gets dappled or half-day sunlight, put them there, or between rows of tall crops such as Brussels sprouts. They do not take up much room. You can even grow an extra-early or extra-late crop in a small cold frame.

SOIL

The best soil for beets is a sandy loam lightened and enriched with compost or aged manure (fresh manure makes the root grow side shoots instead of forming one nice round beet). If the soil is acid, dig lime in to raise the pH to at least 6.0. Give beets a luxurious soil, lightening and enriching it to a depth of at least 8 inches, and pulverizing it and ridding it of rocks, roots and other obstacles.

PLANTING

Sow the seed as early as you can work the soil. For summer and fall crops soak the seeds to help them germinate if the weather is dry. Plant the seeds ½ inch deep in rows a foot or so apart, or plant them in a wide row. In either case try to sow the seeds about an inch apart. If they are any closer they will be hard to thin later; but if they are too sparse you'll have gaps in the rows. Water the seed bed with a fine spray and cover it with a light layer of straw or salt hay to keep it moist. Plant every two weeks if you want fresh beets all summer; let up in August if it is hot and dry, then make a few sowings in fall (or later, in a cold frame).

GROWING

When your seedlings emerge, remove any straw or hay mulch that is covering them. If you have planted in rows add mulch between the rows. It is important to keep the soil moist around the seedlings. When they are about 2 inches tall you will have to thin them. Unfortunately nature produces beets in small, inconveniently designed clusters, and several seedlings will come up where each cluster falls. Pull out seedling groups so that the ones remaining are about 4 inches apart, then snip the extras in each cluster so that just one remains. If you get behind and don't have a chance to thin until the seedlings are taller, it is no big problem; those taller thinnings will be good in salads. Just be sure to give maturing roots space in which to grow without crowding.

The main idea in growing beets is to get them to mature quickly so that they are tender and not hard and woody. This is done by giving them the kind of soil described above, a steady water supply, no weeds to compete with, and proper thinning. If I lived in a warm, dry climate I would probably use the mulched-row technique, especially if I were busy and might forget to weed and water

enough. Beets are fairly heavy feeders and appreciate a top dressing with compost or a balanced fertilizer when about half grown.

PESTS AND DISEASES

A few flea beetles might show up but probably will not decimate the crop; neither will the small yellow leaf miner. Apply rotenone for the beetles if necessary; if you get leaf miners just pull off the whitened, damaged leaves.

Beets occasionally get a fungus disease. Prevent it by keeping the leaves as dry as possible. If it gets started, destroy the affected plants.

HARVEST

While the beets are growing you can pick up to a third of the leaves off each plant and use them as cooked greens. (If you are a real beet-green aficionado you can just pick all the greens and forget the roots.) When your fingers tell you that the beet roots are 2–3 inches in diameter, it is time to harvest them. Pull or dig them up, and cut off the stems. Leave on an inch or two of stem if you are storing the roots.

VARIETIES

The basic tried-and-true red beet is 'Detroit Dark Red,' good for spring or fall. Good early varieties include 'Red Ace,' 'Early Wonder' and 'Little Ball'—a small, sweet one. The popular 'Ruby Queen' gives a bountiful yield. 'Cylindra' is long instead of round. 'Burpee's Golden' is a beautiful red-orange beet root that does not turn everything purple when cut. This is a plus if you are making potato salad, unless, for you, beets should be like real madras—guaranteed to bleed. Especially if you are making borscht.

sprouting broccoli

broccoli raab

Broccoli

I have a great respect for broccoli because it appreciates the cool climate in which I live. In a long, cold spring, a summer with little sun, or a fall with no Indian summer, there is always broccoli, and all it asks is that I keep up with the picking. Gladly. I can make a whole meal out of broccoli, olive oil and garlic.

Our basic green broccoli, sometimes called "sprouting broccoli" and *calabrese* in Europe, came originally from Italy. It makes a big plant with deep, spreading roots. The big broccoli "bunch" that you buy in the grocery store, really an immature flower head, is usually only the beginning for the home gardener. After the central cluster is cut back, side shoots develop that can be harvested for a long time if the summer is not blistering hot. In warm-summer climates the tight buds will "rice," or open as flowers too soon, thus ending the crop, so southern gardeners plant a fall crop that will bear well into the winter instead.

SITE

Choose a spot with good drainage and air circulation where broccoli and other members of the genus *Brassica* (page 184) have not grown for several years. Full sun is nice, but partial shade will also sustain broccoli and can even retard bolting. The plot need not be large. Even though the plants get fairly sizable (2–2½ feet tall and spready) each one produces a lot of broccoli. Six plants in a 4-foot-by-6-foot plot is a good number to start with. Passionate broccoli eaters will want more.

SOIL

Soil should be fairly rich to begin with. As a leaf-and-stem crop, broccoli needs plenty of nitrogen. I dig in a shovelful of well-rotted manure for each plant. You could substitute a shovelful of compost or a small handful of 10–10–10.

Calcium is important; you can make sure it is there by adding crushed limestone. Keep in mind that this will also raise the pH—something you would want to do anyway if your soil is acid. The ideal pH for broccoli is a neutral 7.0. It is even more important to add organic matter to the soil, to help it retain the steady moisture supply that broccoli needs.

PLANTING

In planting broccoli there are several schedules you can follow. Start seeds indoors in a sunny but cool place, six or seven weeks before the last average frost date, and set the seedlings out as 5- to 6-inch plants, two or three weeks before the last expected frost. Or you can sow directly in the garden; in a cool climate do this a month or two before the last frost; in a warm one do it in very early spring.

Usually broccoli is grown from seedlings transplanted into the garden, either ones you grow yourself or ones you purchase in a nursery. After preparing the planting holes as described above, set the transplants an inch or two lower in the ground than they were in their pots or flats, watering them and firming the soil around them. Cover the young plants if you think there might be a really hard freeze. Space seedlings about 18 inches apart each way if you are using a grid, or 18 inches apart in rows with 2–3 feet between the rows.

For direct seeding in the garden, sow several seeds in hills (page 48) and later snip off all but the strongest plant in each. Space the hills the same distance apart as you would transplants. Cutworms like young broccoli plants, so it is a good idea to use collars to foil them (page 72) whichever planting method you use.

Where summers are hot, people seed in a second crop in late spring or early summer that will mature after dan-ger of ricing is past, or they sow a fall crop in July or August. A crop can even be sown in fall and wintered over for a spring harvest if winters are mild. To save space the early crops can be inter-planted with something else if the plants are wide enough apart. Fall crops are seeded in July or August.

GROWING

A good mulch will help the plants retain moisture, but in times of drought give them a good long soaking with a hose if the soil is dry. Extra enrichment is really needed only when you're trying to hasten maturity to beat the heat. In this case a side dressing of blood meal or fish emulsion soaked in (not dug in) helps.

PESTS AND DISEASES

The only pest that ever bothered my broccoli was the small green cabbage worm, which is very common. It never did much damage to the plants, but it had a way of turning up as a surprise garnish at the dinner table. Well camou-flaged by its color, even after picking, the worm turns white when cooked. "Good protein!" a well-brought-up din-ner guest may exclaim diplomatically, but unless your diners have an unusually good sense of humor, you'll want to check carefully for worms before cook-ing or soak the broccoli in salt water to kill and dislodge them. If they really chew up your plants, catch them early next year by applying rotenone or BT (page 73) when you see the cabbage white butterfly fluttering above them, though you might prefer author Catherine Osgood Foster's method. She goes out and swats the butterflies with a tennis racket.

Spray off aphids, and foil root mag-gots with tar-paper mats. Most bugs won't bother your late crops. Diseases like blackleg, black rot and clubroot are best prevented by crop rotation. In the case of clubroot (puny, yellowed plants with misshapen roots), boost the pH to 7.0 with some lime.

HARVEST

When the first nice bunch has formed in the center of the plant (it won't be huge, like the one in the store, unless it is a large-head variety), cut it off at 4–6 inches with a sharp knife. New ones will form in the leaf axils around it, and all over the lower stalk. If you don't keep picking, the green heads will send up tall yellow flowers. A row of blossoming broccoli looks beautiful, but is embarrassing to a good gardener, for it means that the plant will stop producing edible stalks. So keep up with the picking, even if you cannot keep up with the eating and freezing. You can cook and eat stalks with flowers that have started to open, but the opened buds turn brownish when cooked and look almost as unappetizing as cooked cabbage worms.

VARIETIES

The popular broccoli varieties are 'Waltham 29,' the early 'DeCicco,' and 'Calabrese' ('Green Sprouting'). Most people prefer the ones with good side-shoot production, not the ones that produce just a one-shot head like the ones sold in stores, although sometimes this is exactly what you want, either for a quick spring crop before a hot summer, or to make freezing the crop more efficient. 'Green Comet Hybrid' is a good fast-maturing variety for this purpose. 'Premium Crop' is a good single-crop variety. 'Green Duke' is a good variety for the south. Another kind of broccoli that is recently very popular is broccoli raab or raaba or rabb or di rapa, depending on how you spell it. This is grown by direct seeding in rows or blocks. It never forms a head at all, just small branches. Both these and the young leaves are tender and delicious.

Brussels Sprouts

S ome vegetables, like lettuce and asparagus, are grown for the thrill of an early harvest of fresh-tasting produce for the table. Brussels sprouts are a late thrill. The ultimate cool-weather crop, their flavor is actually improved by a touch of frost. So plantings are timed to mature just when days are still warm and sunny but night frosts are just beginning. The plant is slow growing but makes up for it by being frost-hardy. Picking continues well into fall and even winter. The mature plant looks like a palm tree with big floppy leaves on top and little round sprouts growing tightly all up and down the "trunk." Each plant yields about a quart of sprouts; they freeze well.

SITE

Grow Brussels sprouts in a sunny, well-drained plot. Since it takes a long time to mature, reserve it a spot for the whole season. You can interplant small and/or early crops between the rows. If there is a way to shield it from the wind without shielding it from the sun, do so. The tall mature plants can blow over.

SOIL

Brussels sprouts have the same soil requirements as broccoli and the other "cabbage" vegetables: average pH; and a deep sandy loam, well worked and rich but not overloaded with nitrogen. Organic matter in the soil will help it to retain the steady moisture the plant needs. Traditionally Brussels sprouts are grown on a compacted soil, but just a moderate firming with the feet after planting should be sufficient. (Do this even if planting in raised beds.) "Firm" soil doesn't mean "heavy" soil, however; good drainage is important.

PLANTING

How you time your planting depends on your climate. In a cold-winter area you grow one crop, starting seeds indoors and setting out the transplants so that they have 90 to 100 days to grow before hard frosts. By contrast, if you live in a warm climate where the plants would have trouble getting through the hot summer, you are better off planting an early-spring crop, a late-fall crop—or both! Sow seeds directly in the ground in February, water well, and even rush them a bit with some extra fertilizer, then harvest in May. Sow again in mid-summer, watering religiously.

It might take you a season or two to work out the right Brussels sprout schedule for your area and for the varieties you want to grow. Be aware that the plant can take frost, but not hard freezes. And in a totally frost-free area you might not have luck with it at all.

Plants should be spaced about 2 feet apart each way if you are using a grid, or 2 feet apart in the row, 3 feet between rows. Dig a shovelful of compost or a small handful of 5–10–5 into each hole, and water very thoroughly. Make collars to foil cutworms. If you plant seeds, fertilize the whole row, moisten furrows well, and thin to the above spacing.

GROWING

A mulch will help keep the soil evenly moist, and an occasional side dressing of liquid fertilizer will be helpful. Since the plant is tall but shallow rooted, it tends to be a little tippy, and it is wise to make a soil mound around the plant as it grows, firming with your foot or the back of a hoe.

PESTS AND DISEASES

Pest control is the same as for broccoli. Diseases are best controlled by crop rotation.

HARVEST

Each sprout grows in a leaf axil and matures from the bottom of the stalk upward, so start picking at the bottom. I prefer to pick them small, like large marbles—not like the golf balls you get in the market. To make detaching them easier, pick the leaf below the sprout first, then the sprout, with a twisting motion.

You can extend the season a long time by piling straw or other loose mulch around the plants as high as possible and covering plants and mulch with clear plastic. You can even pull them up, roots and all, and heel them into soil in a dirt-bottomed shed or cellar or in big pots like the ones shrubs come in. Or hang them upside down in a cool place, picking for a few more weeks. Another trick to hurry things up, if frost seems to be coming and the sprouts are still tightly closed, is to pinch off the top of the plant. The bottom ones will start to open faster, though the yield will be diminished to some degree.

VARIETIES

The two most commonly grown varieties of Brussels sprouts are 'Jade Cross Hybrid' and 'Long Island Improved.' Both are dwarf and short season (roughly ninety days to harvest). Or try the early 'Prince Marvel' or 'Captain Marvel' (earlier still). Less available but worth trying are the European varieties such as 'Valiant' or 'Fieldstar Number 1.' These have a very long season, though—between 175 and 185 days to harvest—so you'd need to be able to start early and grow them well into the fall. But the flavor is said to be worth every bit of the effort.

savoy cabbage

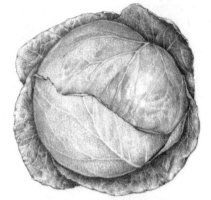

green cabbage

ornamental cabbage

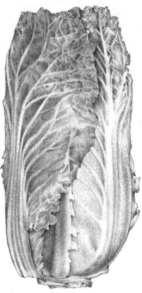

Chinese cabbage

Cabbage

Cabbage isn't grown as much as it used to be. Why? Perhaps it's because in gardening big is no longer beautiful. Long rows of huge cabbage heads to be stored in cellars, then boiled up in soup caldrons for large families no longer have their place in the backyard plot—which is nowadays a tidy cross-stitch sampler of baby zucchini, miniature eggplants and finger-sized carrots. Perhaps it's because of the strong smell cabbage has when it's cooking (an honest vegetable smell if there ever was one). Perhaps it's because by the time gardeners finish reading up on cabbage diseases like blackleg, clubroot and the yellows they've lost their appetites altogether.

But for the same reasons that cabbage has always been such a good staple, it will always be grown. There will always be a sauerkraut, a cole slaw, a hot buttered savoy or a red cabbage simmered in bouillon and laced with sour cream. And for those who must seek panache, there are the succulent Chinese cabbages—*pak choy* and *pe-tsai* (also called *bok-choy* and *wong-bok*). Cabbage is also easy to grow, hardy in the colder climates and storable for months without the boiling-and-canning, blanching-and-freezing marathon you must run with some vegetables.

Two crops are possible with cabbage, an early one started indoors to mature before the heat of summer, and a late one started in summer to mature in the fall. In warm areas cabbage can be grown through the winter. If you only want to grow one crop, I suggest growing the fall one to take advantage of a time when the lush, quick-growing spring and summer produce has been cleared out, and the relatively bug-free days are upon you. For the early crop you'd choose a fast-maturing variety (65 days to harvest, or even less); for the second one, the larger, tight-headed kind that takes a longer time to mature (100 days or more) but keeps better in storage.

SITE

Most kinds of cabbage prefer a sunny site but will tolerate some shade. Grow them in a spot where other cabbage-family plants have not grown for three years. Allow 2–3 square feet for each head of cabbage you want to produce, less for Chinese cabbage. If you are serious about storing them for the winter, plant more for your late crop than for your earlier one.

SOIL

Cabbage is a heavy feeder and likes a rich soil with plenty of organic matter dug in. Manure fills the bill if it is well rotted and dug in at least several weeks before planting. But do not make the soil excessively rich or the heads may crack. Early crops can tolerate more richness, late ones can tolerate a heavier soil. Add lime if the pH is much below 6.5. All this sounds as if cabbage is fussy. It's not. But if your crop's performance could stand some improvement, these are the guidelines to remember in the future.

PLANTING

For an early crop, you need to set out plants three to four weeks before the average last frost date, so start seeds indoors four to six weeks before that in a cool, sunny place. Young plants should be still small, and never leggy for lack of light. Harden them off outside with protection before planting. After what you hope is the last *hard* freeze, set them out deeper than they were in their pots, right up to the first leaves, and firm the soil around the plants. Early cabbage can be set as close as 12 inches apart.

For the late crop, start in July (later for winter crops in the south) and either sow seed directly in the garden, to be thinned later, or sow it outdoors in flats or a seed bed. Doing this saves precious garden space when you are overlapping crops. Late seedlings should be spaced a little farther apart than early ones and should be shaded from very hot sun with lath as needed (Figure 42) or by a tall neighboring crop like pole beans. Chinese cabbage is usually grown as a fall crop, planted ten weeks or so before the first average frost date.

GROWING

Moisture, for cabbages, needs to be steady—always enough, but never so much that drainage is poor. As the cabbages grow, watch for signs of cracking down the middle. It happens when the inside of the plant grows faster than the outer leaves, then splits, intending to send up a seed stalk. This sudden growth can be caused by either overrich soil or by heavy rains or heavy watering after a drought. Keeping the soil evenly moist during the drought can help to prevent it, but if a cabbage does start to crack, there are three seemingly violent acts you can commit that will benignly slow down its growth: either twist the plant in a half turn, pull it part way up with a yank so that the roots are slightly dislodged, or plunge a spade into the soil 6 inches from the stem in one or two places. These measures prune the roots. If performed conservatively, they will not hurt the plant but set it back on its course of producing a proper cabbage.

If you are trying to hurry a slow crop along in order to harvest it before hot weather or before a hard freeze, a light top dressing of nitrogen-rich fertilizer will help. Be careful when you cultivate or weed around the cabbages, since their roots are shallow. Mulch helps. The Chinese cabbages are grown in the same way, except that they can be planted closer together, they mature more quickly and they are even more fond of nitrogen top dressing.

PESTS AND DISEASES

Pests and diseases, and their treatment, are the same as for broccoli and Brussels sprouts, except for the fungus disease called "cabbage yellows." If this is a problem, grow a resistant strain such as 'Golden Acre' next time around. Try to catch diseases in the seedling stage by watching for blackened stems or lumpy roots. Throw these seedlings out. They are not likely to succeed, no matter what you spray them with, and they will only contaminate your garden soil.

HARVEST

Cabbages are harvested when they look completely formed but while they are still firm to the touch. Leave the big outer leaves and cut the head free with a sharp knife. Store them in a root cellar or other room where the temperature stays above freezing but below 45 degrees. Some gardeners even store cabbages in a pit outdoors, with several feet of straw mulch piled over them and topped with a layer of soil.

Chinese cabbage can be stored whole, though for a shorter length of time. But you can start harvesting it much earlier, picking its outer leaves for soups, salads or stir-fries and letting the rest of the plant keep right on growing.

VARIETIES

There are a lot of cabbage varieties to choose from. The best-known early green one is 'Early Jersey Wakefield.' Others are the yellows-resistant 'Golden Acre,' the compact 'Stonehead' and the new super-early ones such as 'Salarite.' Later ones include 'Danish Ballhead' and 'Late Flat Dutch.' 'Red Acre' and 'Ruby Ball' are good red cabbages; 'Savoy Ace,' 'Chieftain' and 'Savoy King' good savoys (crinkled ones). Among the Chinese varieties are 'Lei-choi' (a pakchoi), 'Seppaku' (a spoon-shaped type of pak-choi) and the heading types, chiefly the *michihli* varieties such as 'Jade Pagoda'.

Carrots

If you pull up a Queen Anne's lace plant growing along the side of the road, you will find that its root is a little white carrot. This wild carrot is the species from which our modern hybrid carrots were developed. Indians ate the wild ones, and so can you. But for most gardeners—and cooks—carrots have come a long way. The main goal in breeding has been to develop better flavor and sweetness by reducing the size of the pale core in the middle, where less sugar and vitamins are found. As a result the best ones are a good rich orange-red, crunchy and sweet.

Carrots now come in all shapes and sizes: the traditional long, tapered ones; short stubby ones; tiny fingerlike ones; even little round ones. Such variety does more than just make life interesting. Carrots of different lengths are suited to different soils and different lengths of season.

Carrots do not grow well in very hot weather. Coolness keeps them from turning woody and seems to bring out their color and flavor, too. So in warm areas you must grow them during fall, winter and spring. In the north you can plant them in early spring, then start more every few weeks until August 1 or so, so that there are carrots in the ground even in early winter. They are one of the few vegetables that you can actually leave growing straight through the hard freezes of winter, to pick them in early spring. To a northern gardener in mud season these seem like a real prize.

SITE

The best site would be sunny and well drained, but carrots will grow in partial shade. I have grown carrots in raised beds with great success—it is the best way to maintain the fluffy soil they like. But I find that I have to be extremely vigilant with my hose, since carrots need consistent moisture, and these beds dry out quickly.

SOIL

Carrots like a deep, loose sandy loam— the classic Beautiful Soil. But there is some latitude here. If your soil is a little heavy, even after adding organic matter, you can still grow the shorter carrots (usually an early crop). If your good topsoil is shallow, these shorter ones are also the right choice. For late-season crops you can get by with poorer soil, and a little less moisture and coolness, by growing the longer carrots that root well below the hot, dry soil surface. But for the carrots to get down that far with any kind of grace, the soil has to be light and airy to the full depth of the carrot root. If the soil is not free of obstacles— stones, roots, clay lumps, old horse-shoes, etc., the carrot will bend, fork, twist or even stop cold. The closer to the surface, the more the soil should be pulverized, even sifted.

The second most important soil factor is moisture. Digging in organic matter such as compost or manure will help the soil to stay moist. Well-rotted manure will improve the texture and will add nutrients too, but if you use manure, dig it in at least six months before you plant the seeds. (Fresh manure, or even rotted manure if recently applied, can cause carrots to fork and send out little side roots.) Mulching will also help to keep the water content steady.

Since carrots are a root crop, the soil should be relatively low in nitrogen, higher in phosphorus and potassium. Potassium is especially important to carrot health, and adding wood ashes is a good way to provide it (but screen out chunky cinders that might impede root growth). The ideal pH is around 6.5.

PLANTING

Carrot seeds are sown directly into the garden. The first ones can go in about three or four weeks before the last expected frost. I prefer single rows because they are much easier to mulch, for maintaining the moist soil surface carrots need. I wet the seed bed or furrow very thoroughly before I plant, to speed up germination. I try to space the seeds about an inch apart, although this is virtually impossible to do because they are so tiny. Some people say that mixing them with sand or coffee grounds makes distributing them evenly easier. You can also buy pelletted seeds of some varieties; these are easier to plant. I cover the seeds with a half-inch of loose, pulverized soil made airy with organic matter (a whole inch for summer plantings); the seedlings won't come up through a hard crust. You can cover them with sifted compost, a nonsoil medium such as vermiculite, or whatever mixture suits you, as long as it is very light.

When the seeds are in, I water the bed with a fine spray and lay a layer of salt hay over it to shade it and keep it moist. Some gardeners even lay wet burlap over the seeds, especially if they plan to be away for a few days and won't be able to water. The burlap must be removed as soon as the seeds have germinated. Others sprout the seeds between wet paper towels in the refrigerator. Another trick is to sow them together with a fast-growing radish variety. The radish seedlings will emerge first and shade the slow, spindly carrot seedlings. They will also mark the rows and help break the soil crust, if any. The radishes will be harvested long before the carrots produce their major root growth. But like it or not, carrot seeds just take a long time to germinate, and the best thing to do is keep them moist (without washing them away) and be patient.

GROWING

It is best to thin carrots several times, first when they are 1-2 inches high, then later on whenever they are starting to look crowded. In the first thinning eliminate any seedlings that are closer than half an inch to another seedling. Snipping them off with scissors is one way to do it without damaging the seedlings still growing. The second thinning is more fun, because you are pulling up tiny carrots to toss in salads. When you are finished thinning, each plant should have a space to grow in that is at least the size of a mature carrot, plus a bit more.

So far I have probably made carrot culture sound like pretty picky work. It is at first, but once the carrots are off to a start they take care of themselves quite well. The only supervision they might need is a soaking in dry weather, a loose mulch around the plants, and perhaps a liquid fertilizer when they are about 6 inches tall. The last succession crop really repays you for your trouble. Mulch it heavily and leave it in the ground for a spring harvest. If you see flowers resembling Queen Anne's lace in your carrot patch, it means that the carrots have bolted (produced flowers in order to make seeds). This has never happened to me, but if it happens to you, plant bolt-resistant varieties and stick to cool-weather plantings.

PESTS AND DISEASES

Carrot problems are usually minimal. Carrot diseases are not common, but most, including "carrot yellows," can be avoided by crop rotation. Rotating the crop will also deter the one serious pest, the carrot rust fly. And the fly will not bother your late plantings. Flea beetles may bother your late ones, but not the early ones.

HARVEST

Give carrots a good twist when you pull them up so that the leaves do not break off in your hand, but once they are up, cut off the leaves right away. Carrot tops may look pretty on carrots, but they keep growing and draw moisture and nourishment out of the roots, leaving them limp, wrinkled and tasteless.

VARIETIES

Stored in boxes in mulched pits or trenches outdoors, in moist sand in garbage cans in the cellar, or just in the refrigerator, carrots keep a long time. Freeze the small, tenderest ones, but use the heavy-duty "keepers" in soups and stews or simmered in butter and a little brown sugar until all the cooking liquid has evaporated. Good short, early varieties are 'Danvers Half-Long,' the Chantenay varieties such as 'Red Cored Chantenay' and the sweet Nantes types such as 'Scarlet Nantes.' Good long carrots are 'Imperator' (a great keeper), 'Gold Pak,' 'Orlando Gold,' which resists bolting and cracking, and 'A-plus,' which is especially nutritious. Ball-shaped carrots include 'Kundulus' and the old-fashioned 'Oxheart.' Good midgets are the 3-inch 'Little Finger,' 'Lady Finger' and 'Short 'n' Sweet.'

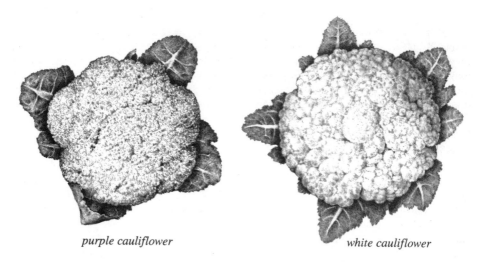

purple cauliflower   *white cauliflower*

Cauliflower

auliflower really is a flower. The big, lumpy white "head" that we eat is a cluster of flower buds nested inside a cabbagelike plant. I think that cauliflower is the sweetest, mildest-tasting member of the cabbage family, but home gardeners grow it far less often than the other brassicas. Why? Probably because it won't tolerate either very hot or very cold weather, so there is only a short season before and after the summer heat in which you can grow it. Or because most varieties need to be "blanched"—their heads covered with leaves while they are maturing. Unblanched heads turn green and don't taste as good as white ones.

Yet cauliflower certainly has its place in the garden. It is a good source of calcium and other vitamins, it freezes well, it is expensive to buy in the store, and it is not difficult to grow if you know and respect its need for a steady supply of water. There are even purple-headed varieties that look like broccoli when cooked but taste nonetheless like cauliflower and do not need blanching.

SITE

Choose a sunny, well-drained spot where other cabbage-family vegetables have not grown recently. Space requirements are the same as for cabbage.

SOIL

Provide the same soil conditions that you would for other brassicas. The soil should be fairly rich, especially in nitrogen and potassium. The pH should be 6.0–7.0. And plenty of organic matter should be incorporated into the soil, so that it will retain moisture. It is best to dig compost or well-rotted manure into the soil the fall before planting.

PLANTING

Cauliflower can take a little frost at the very beginning and the very end of its life, but not much. It really needs at least two months of cool-but-not-frosty weather to come to maturity. This means you can plant it in fall or late winter in warm climates. In cold ones it is usually a fall crop of which there can be several successions, each a week or two apart. Plant fall crops from late May to early July, depending on how cold your climate is. The idea is to allow two to three months between the time you set it out and the first frosts. "Purplehead" cauliflower takes longer—about eighty-five days to harvest.

For spring crops start seeds indoors, four to six weeks before setting the plants out. Keep the seeds at about 70 degrees if you can, with a steady supply of moisture. The roots do not like to be disturbed in transplanting, so use peat pots. When they are about 6 inches tall they can be planted outside, as long as it is no earlier than three or four weeks before the last expected frost. You can set the plants outside to harden off several weeks earlier.

Set the plants about 18 to 24 inches apart. Build a saucer of earth around each plant to help it to hold water (page 52), and use cutworm collars (page 72). Fall crops of cauliflower can be sown directly in the garden, but to save space use a cold frame or the "nursery bed" section of your garden (page 49) to get late plants started, and then transplant to their growing place. Otherwise sow them in hills and thin them to one seedling per hill.

GROWING

The most important thing about raising cauliflower is to keep the growth going. It cannot sit out a hot dry spell. If it is dry, give the soil a good soaking to the depth of about 6 inches. A mulch will also help keep the soil moist. If the heads still are not growing bigger, top dress the plants with liquid fertilizer.

The white flower head that emerges is called a "curd" or a "button." When it is egg-sized, blanch it by bending over the big leaves that surround it so that they cover the curd; then tuck them in on the opposite side, breaking the ribs of the leaves to keep them from springing back. If the head still doesn't stay covered, tie some leaves together at the top with a string or rubber band. The idea is to keep light and moisture out but let some air in, and also leave some space in which the head can grow. The heads should not be covered when the plant is wet, or they may rot. Water the ground *around* the plants and keep the soil water constant.

PESTS AND DISEASES

For pests and diseases treat cauliflower the way you would broccoli, cabbage or Brussels sprouts. Root maggots are sometimes a problem in the fall crop.

HARVEST

Check the heads from time to time to see if they are large enough—about 6 inches across but still tight, with the buds unopened. Some varieties have larger heads—up to 12 inches—so consult the information on the seed package or in the catalog.

When they are ready, cut them right away, just below the head, and either use them or freeze them. If you pull up the plant, roots and all, it will keep in a cool cellar for at least a month.

VARIETIES

The Snowball varieties, such as 'Snowball' and 'Snow King,' are large-headed late crops. But 'Super Snowball,' 'Snowball Improved,' 'Early White Snow Crown Hybrid' and 'Snow King Hybrid' mature faster. 'Self-blanche' has leaves that curl over the head by themselves. 'Purple Head' is a popular purple variety.

Celery

Few gardeners try to grow celery because it is cheap to buy and fussy to grow. But it does taste good and fresh if you grow your own, and frankly, traditional methods of growing celery are fussier than they need to be. Blanching the celery to produce a white stalk is no longer considered to be a necessity. All that mounding of soil, shoring up of plants and tying of collars and what have you got? A plant with fewer vitamins. The green celery we buy in the store is proof of the fact that today's green varieties do not need blanching to taste good.

You can grow celery in any climate if you time it right. It does take a long time to grow—up to six months from seed to harvest—and dislikes hot summers. So start it in the fall in hot areas, and in early spring in cold ones. The short frost-free season in very cold states is compensated for by relatively cool summers. Celery likes those.

If growing celery still seems ho-hum to you, consider celeriac, also called "celery root" or "celery knobs." This gourmet celery makes a delicious,

turniplike root that is hard to find in stores and is easier to grow than ordinary celery. It is tasty in soups and stews and makes a great cooked purée. My favorite way to use it is raw, marinated in a vinaigrette or rémoulade dressing.

SITE

If you have mucky soil, or a high water table, you have an ideal place for celery, and you owe it to yourself to grow it. Celery by choice grows in marshes. But if you don't have wet soil you can still grow it. It will also tolerate partial shade.

You do not need a lot of space for a celery crop. An 8-foot row will grow at least a dozen bunches of celery, or the same number of celery knobs.

SOIL

Celery is a heavy, even gluttonous feeder; it needs very rich soil. It is an equally voracious drinker. Spread a 4-inch layer of well-rotted manure or compost over the soil and dig it in well to a depth of 6–8 inches, to give the soil fertility and help it retain moisture. (I would add some bone meal and wood ashes as well.) Or use another kind of organic matter, such as peat moss, and dig in a handful of 10–10–10 for each plant. The ideal pH is 6.0, but 5.5–7.5 is usually tolerable.

PLANTING

Given a choice, it is easier to buy seed-

celeriac

lings than grow celery from seed. The seeds are tiny, take about two weeks to germinate, and are fussy about light, warmth and moisture. But local nurseries seldom have a good range of varieties, and they may not have celeriac at all. So you may want to raise a seed crop anyway. For a late-summer crop, sow the seeds indoors four weeks before the last average frost date; for a fall crop, sow in May or June. Sow in flats of light sandy soil, ⅛ inch deep. Cover with damp sphagnum moss and keep out of direct sun in a spot that is 70–75 degrees by day and about 60 degrees by night. Transplant seedlings to peat pots when they are 1½ to 2 inches tall.

Spring transplants go in around the time of the last average frost. The plants should be 3–5 inches tall, and spaced 6–8 inches apart. Set the crowns a bit below soil level, or in a deep trench if you're blanching, filling the trench as they grow. Even if you have enriched the soil, give each seedling a cupful of liquid fertilizer on planting, mixed according to the directions on the container; give them another in two weeks or so.

GROWING

Water well, especially in drought. Mulch, and protect the young plants if night temperatures are below 55 degrees consistently, so that the plants will not form a tough flower stalk but a nice head of tender leaf stems instead. Keep the bed weeded. The finely branched, hungry roots will not tolerate competition. Celeriac is grown the same way.

PESTS AND DISEASES

Good seeds, good soil and steady watering will ward off most diseases. "Early blight" and "late blight" of celery are fungus diseases best fought with a tidy, debris-free garden, and if necessary, a fungicide. Celery worms can be picked off, but do consider that they will turn into the black swallowtail butterfly if not destroyed. I would spare these lovely creatures, even if it came to a choice between them and my celery!

HARVEST

Pick outside stalks as you need them, or harvest a whole plant, cutting it off at the base when it looks like a mature bunch of celery. Sometimes you can prolong your harvest past the first frosts in fall by mulching heavily with straw. Celeriac roots can be dug when they are 2–4 inches in diameter. Unlike regular celery they store well in a cool cellar.

VARIETIES

Good green varieties are 'Giant Pascal,' 'Summer Pascal,' 'Florida 683' and 'Utah 52–70.' 'Golden Self-Blanching' is a yellow celery that people seem to like. The most common celeriacs are 'Alabaster' and 'Giant Prague.' 'Giant Smooth Prague' is a bit earlier.

Cooking Greens

A "cooking green" is usually a leafy vegetable that is too tough to be eaten raw: Swiss chard and kale are examples. Lettuce, however, the classic raw salad green, can also be cooked. It is braised by the French and stir-fried by the Chinese. And sometimes cooking greens are eaten raw when the leaves are young and tender. Actually eating raw greens is a relatively modern practice. In colonial times almost all greens were called "pot herbs" because they were served cooked. A colonial salad, or "sallet," was usually a dish of boiled greens.

I happen to think cooked greens are sorely underrated these days. They do not have to be overcooked, bitter or boring. Try Swiss chard cooked in bouillon and served with lemon wedges, or collards simmered with small cubes of good slab bacon. And remember that all sorts of surprising things can become cooked greens. For instance I once grew a long row of borage in my garden. I enjoyed the brilliant blue flowers but forgot what you were supposed to do with the leaves (make a broth to instill courage in the soul). I boiled them and ate them and found them delicious; if you don't mind eating leaves that are slightly furry, give borage a try. My sister Anne cooks lambs' quarters, a rampant weed most gardens have whether they like it or not. She makes them the way you would make creamed spinach, and they have a fresh taste.

The following greens are more

curly kale

Swiss chard

flowering kale

mustard greens

collard greens

usual choices. All are very easy to grow and outrageously nutritious, with high levels of vitamin A, vitamin C, calcium—you name it. Furthermore they are cool-weather crops that you can really appreciate after the avalanche of summer harvests is over. The tomatoes have been canned, the beans are all in the freezer, but kale, collards, mustard and Swiss chard are still fresh in the garden and just starting to taste their best. Some even winter over!

Kale

K ale is a green in name only. The type we call "Siberian kale" is more blue than green. "Scotch kale" (also called "curly kale" or "vates") is almost gray. Flowering kale can be anything from white to vivid pink.

Kale is conspicuous these days as a garnish, because it is so attractive to look at and because it doesn't wilt. Unless it is very young, it does not taste good raw, so use it as a cooked green. Flowering kale, so named because of its leaves' flowerlike color, is as edible as the more subdued varieties. It is a fine accent plant for a flower garden, an herb garden, or a bright spot among the greener vegetables.

Kale matures in two months or less, so theoretically you can grow a spring crop before summer weather toughens the leaves. I say, why bother? I like having some crops that I can plant at my leisure, after the great spring rush. Start kale anytime from June till six weeks before the first frost (frost will actually improve the flavor). Give it a rich, humusy soil and side dress it with "manure tea" (page 32) or liquid fertilizer if growth slows down. Kale, collards and mustard like a pH above 5.5, so add lime if your soil is quite acid; ground limestone is a good way to provide it,

because limestone also contains calcium, which kale needs.

Sow the seeds directly in the garden ½ inch deep. When the seedlings come up, thin them so that they are at least a foot apart. Don't crowd them. If you are growing them from transplants, set them in the soil a few inches deeper than they were in their pots.

Keep the moisture constant by mulching and/or watering, because the roots are shallow and the plant can easily dry out. A good mulch will also help to extend your harvest into the winter. In the south you can even sow some seeds in late summer to winter over. Pests and diseases are the same as for cabbage.

Pick the outside leaves while they are still tender, and the plant will continue to produce from the inside out. Even in the north, you can pick long after frost. Kale also freezes well.

Some good varieties to try are 'Dwarf Blue Curled Scotch' ('Vates'), 'Siberian Improved' and 'Dwarf Green Curled Vates.' I lean toward the curly varieties and the blue and pink 'Ornamental Flowering Kale.' Admittedly I grow kale partly for the way it looks in my garden.

Collards

C ollards belong to the same genus and species as kale, but the two plants grow differently. Collards look like cabbages that have failed to form a head, sitting on top of an upright stem. They are especially popular in the south, where they are grown as a winter crop, usually from transplants, but I have grown them from seed in Connecticut as a summer-to-fall crop and found them very easy. They can take some heat and some early frosts. They like the same growing conditions as kale but can be planted a little closer together. Harvest them the same way you do kale, and treat them for the same pests and diseases as cabbage.

'Georgia' and the shorter 'Vates' are standbys; 'Georgia' is tall and might even need staking. And try the new, even more compact version 'Champion,' or 'Hicrop,' which is also compact and tolerates heat.

Mustard Greens

The mustard seed from which hot-dog mustard is made comes from several different plants. This green is not one of them. Sometimes called "Chinese" or "Indian" mustard, this one is grown for its green leaves, which have a sharp flavor when raw, a milder one when cooked. The young leaves are good raw, to pep up salads.

Mustard greens mature fast— sometimes in as little as thirty days! But they need a fairly light, rich, sandy loam and constant moisture to perform this neat trick. A cold-weather plant, mustard is a good bet for spring or fall—easy to do with such a quick crop. Sow the seeds as early as possible, ½ inch deep; I think sowing in blocks works better than sowing in rows. Thin the seedlings to 4–6 inches apart, eating the thinnings as you go. Harvest the plants before they go to seed. You can plant a succession of mustard crops, or you can cut the whole plant to just above the soil surface and wait for it to put out a whole new set of leaves.

Mustard has no serious pests or diseases to speak of. Good varieties are 'Giant Southern Curled' (for fall), 'Green Wave' (a bolt-resistant variety for spring) and 'Tendergreen' (an especially quick, mild crop). 'Florida Broadleaf' is also bolt-resistant.

Swiss Chard

This green does not belong to the cabbage family. It is a beet. But its root is a beet gone haywire, branching into long, deep taproots and long, meaty laterals. It is grown for the leaves, which are something like those of spinach. Sometimes the large midrib of the leaf is cooked and eaten separately like a stalk of celery.

Swiss chard does not bolt in hot weather the way spinach does. It also wins the prize for cold-tolerance—mine makes it through the winter and re-sprouts in spring with no help from me. But since it is a biennial that will go to seed the second season, you really need to sow a new crop each year.

Swiss chard is not fussy about soil, but given carte blanche it would choose a loose, rich loam with a pH between 6.0 and 7.0. For a summer crop, sow it directly in the garden in spring—two or three weeks before the average last frost. Sow in late summer for a fall crop and in fall for a winter crop in warm areas. The "seeds" are actually little pods containing several seeds, as with beets. This makes them easy to space an inch apart when you plant them. Later you will need to thin them gradually (eating the thinnings) until the plants are 8–10 inches apart. You can pick the outer leaves and let the inner ones keep growing, or you can chop off the whole plant, just as for mustard, and let it regenerate. Few pests bother it.

'Lucullus' and 'Fordhook Giant' are tried-and-true varieties, as is 'Large White Ribbed.' 'Perpetual Chard' regrows well when cut back. I usually grow 'Rhubarb Chard' (also called 'Ruby Chard'). It is dark green with brilliant crimson stems and veins, and I am always a sucker for plants that look beautiful in the garden.

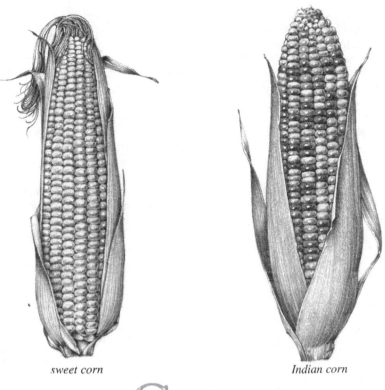

sweet corn   *Indian corn*

Corn

W hen I was a kid, harvesting corn was a triathlon. First you picked the ears, then you ran back to the house from field or garden at full speed, then you husked the ears quickly so that they could be plunged into the waiting pot of boiling water. Total time from stalk to serving plate was not supposed to exceed twenty minutes, lest the sweetness be lost as the kernels' supply of sugar turned to starch. Nowadays, with improved varieties that keep their sweetness and flavor longer, the triathlon is far less frenzied. But the freshest corn is still the best.

Growing corn is so much a part of our heritage that our folk wisdom is full of advice about it. "Put one fish head in each hill, as the Indians did," we are told. "Plant the seeds when the oak leaves are the size of a squirrel's ear." The corn should be "knee high by the Fourth of July." Corn culture is now far more scientific than it used to be, but no red-blooded American gardener should have much trouble producing a crop.

There are so many different corn varieties that it is hard to know which to choose, but this leads the gardener to experiment. A popcorn patch is fun, especially if you have children. I have enjoyed raising flint corn to make cornmeal for real homegrown cornmeal muffins. Most gardeners would choose sweet corn, for that great fresh-picked taste they can't get even at the local roadside stand. Some people think the new genetically altered "super-sweet" kinds are a bit much. They stay sweet for days after being picked or cooked. Even if they have gotten so old they are tough as cow corn, the super-sweets still taste like sugar. And even the yellow varieties, which are the most vitamin-rich, are sweet, while in the old days it seemed only the less nutritious white ones were. I happen to think the super-sweets are wonderful, especially since I like to have leftover cooked corn that stays sweet when I reheat it in milk or cream.

Indian corn, with its multicolored kernels, is rewarding to grow for fall centerpieces and house decorations. The dwarf corn varieties might be the best choice if your space is very limited. You can even find Oriental "baby corn"— those tiny ears you eat whole, cob and all. They grow on little short stalks, but there are five or six ears on each one, as opposed to the one or two that most corn stalks bear. But all the varieties are about equally easy to grow, so it is mostly up to your own taste buds. If you have room, you can grow several kinds. If not, try a different one each season.

SITE

A corn plant is really just a huge stalk of grass. It takes up a lot of room vertically but not horizontally, so even a fairly small vegetable garden can have a place for it. All it needs is a sunny spot where it will not shade what is next to it (unless you are deliberately using corn as a screen to protect a crop from hot sun or wind). In very windy climates, find a sheltered spot for your corn if you can, because it can blow over.

If you have the space to really make a project of corn, you can span a long season with it. Instead of planting one variety that you pick for a week (or all in one day, in a race with the raccoons), plant some early-, middle- and late-season corn. Or plant one variety in several plantings, two weeks apart. Most varieties take two to three months to grow from seed to harvest, so there is usually time for several overlapping crops between the last spring frost and the first fall one.

But this is where site selection comes in. You cannot put different varieties next to one another while they are pollinating. As an annual grass, corn is wind-pollinated, and even the slightest breeze brings the pollen from the male tassels down to the female silks, each of which, when pollinated, grows a kernel. Pollination will occur whether the pollen falls on the silks of the same plant or on those of one near it, and cross-pollinating can be a problem. With "open-pollinated" varieties it does not matter what kind of corn the pollen comes from, but with hybrid varieties it does. The flavor of hybrid sweet corn can be ruined if sweet corn is pollinated by feed corn, cornmeal corn, popcorn, ornamental corn. One way around the threat of cross-pollination is to time your plantings so that your varieties mature at different times. Another is to separate them physically by at least 25 feet. This is possible only if you have plenty of room in your garden.

In short, growing several different kinds of corn at once requires some planning. It is not difficult with some practice, but a beginner is better off starting with only one kind of corn and getting a good sense of the plant's life cycle before branching out. One thing you should always do is plant corn in blocks of at least three or four rows, not one long row; otherwise pollination will be poor.

SOIL

Corn is a heavy feeder and needs rich soil that is replenished each year at planting time and also while the plant is growing. Nitrogen is especially crucial—the Indians knew what they were doing with those fish heads. Dig in well-rotted manure or compost, at least a 1-inch covering each spring.

Corn looks like a shallow-rooted plant, because you can see short roots spreading out on the surface around the plant. These side roots exist partly to give the stalk support, though; underneath are deep feeder roots. So tilling fertilizer in deeply will give the plant nutrients in the place where they will be used. Lime should be applied in fall as needed to raise or maintain the proper pH, which is between 6.0 and 7.0.

PLANTING

Corn is traditionally sown in the garden around the time of the last average frost. If your patch is just a small one, you might push up the date of that first sweet harvest by starting some seeds indoors in peat pots, but a better way is simply to take a chance on an early sowing; use salt hay or another mulch to keep the soil warmer at night, and push it back during the day to let the soil warm up. Or cover the seedlings at night with a plastic sheet; the seeds themselves will not be hurt by frost, and even frost-zapped seedlings may resprout. If all this sounds like an absurd amount of trouble to go to, it is; but I am aware that some gardeners really have a fetish about early corn.

There are as many "best" ways to plant corn as there are gardeners. Some plant 6 inches apart, then thin to a foot, with their rows 2 feet apart. Some plant on a grid, dropping two seeds to-gether every 12 inches each way. Others plant six seeds in a circle about a foot in diameter, every 3 feet, then thin to three seedlings. I could go on. What kind of geometry you use does not make too much difference. The main points are that you need to sow some extra seeds because some will not germinate, then thin to the desired spacing. And you need to make sure that stalks are not too close together, to give each plant its share of the light and nutrients. Early and midget varieties that grow 4–5 feet tall could go 8 inches apart, but the tall, late-season varieties that grow 7 feet tall and over will need to be a good foot apart.

Corn "seeds" are just kernels of corn. I plant them by poking my finger in the ground and dropping one kernel into each hole. I make the holes an inch deep if it is very wet weather, because kernels planted deeper may rot. Otherwise I make them at least 2 inches deep, especially for late plantings in warm or dry weather, when it is important to keep the seeds moist. The deeper they are, the harder it is for the crows to find them and pull them up.

For super-sweet varieties, make the seed bed extra moist and keep it that way until the seeds have germinated. If your climate is hot and dry, plant in furrows that will catch and hold the rain or the water from your hose. If your climate is cold, plant in raised beds that warm up quickly. Do not plant past midsummer, since corn does not ripen well in cold weather. If your seeds are bright pink, they have been treated with a fungicide.

GROWING

As the corn grows, the main thing is to keep it fed and watered. Top dress with a high-nitrogen fertilizer when the corn is about 8 inches tall, and again when the stalks have tassels. Liquid fish emulsion makes a good top dressing for corn; water well to soak it in.

Keep an eye on the leaves. If they curl up on the sides, it means that the plants are thirsty and you need to give the bed a thorough soaking. Do not let weeds compete with the corn's big appetite for nutrients. Remove them by cultivating until the corn is about 6 inches tall, then apply a mulch. After the shallow side roots have formed it is easy to damage them by cultivating.

Remove any puny stalks because they will not bear corn and will only take up room. With tall varieties, mounding earth around the stalks will provide some extra support and may help them withstand wind better. Don't let an old-timer convince you to remove either side shoots or tassels; the plant needs both. Not *all* folk wisdom is accurate.

PESTS AND DISEASES

The biggest enemies of your corn are usually your local wildlife, starting with crows. They seem to know that the tasty kernels are buried in your garden, and even the biggest, noisiest, tin-can-laden scarecrow will not deter them if they find out the seeds are there. But a chicken-wire cover, placed a few inches off the ground, will. Remove it when corn shoots reach 6 inches, when you are applying the mulch. I have never had trouble with crows, perhaps because I plant rather deeply. The covers are a nuisance to make, so you might want to just take a chance, then replant if you have to.

Raccoons are the worst. They are ready to harvest your corn for you the minute it is at peak flavor. People put out flashing lights, blaring radios, barriers of thorns to keep the coons out. They smear oil on the corn ears and tie plastic bags over them. They lay plastic sheeting, mesh, and aluminum foil along the ground near the corn on the theory that the coons won't walk on it. Sometimes these work, often they don't. Electric fences do work, but they are laborious to install, can short out if weeds touch them, and can do funny things to people's heart pacemakers. Humane traps that catch the coons are another solution if you keep trapping them and releasing them miles away.

Another deterrent is the trick of growing long-vined winter squash among the corn. If you feed the soil a bit extra and plant the corn a bit farther apart than usual, the squash will not compete. The coons presumably do not like to walk on the leaves, and this interplanting is a good way to use garden space. I have had good luck with this method, but perhaps it was just that—luck.

Squirrels can be a problem, though they have never bothered my corn. I have heard that slipping small paper bags over the ears can deter them.

European corn borers can attack early corn. They make small holes in the base or sides of the ears. You can try BT or rotenone sprayed in the leaf axils. After harvest, destroy or compost corn stalks to prevent the borers' larvae from wintering over; never try brushing the worms off, because they will just lay eggs on the ground. If you plant late corn in order to avoid them, you might be just in time for the corn earworm, which crawls in through the sides of the ears. A dab of mineral oil dropped on the silks of each ear as it starts to brown will make them less enticing.

Corn flea beetles, which are tiny, dark bugs that jump when disturbed, cause wounds that make the corn susceptible to bacterial wilt. Dust with rotenone, or grow varieties such as 'Silver Queen' that are resistant to wilt.

Corn smut is a hideous grayish-black mass that sometimes appears in corn ears. A fungus, it is filled with spores that spread when the mass bursts. Catch it and burn it before it does so, preferably in its earlier white stage.

HARVEST

When do you pick the corn? "Just before the coons do," is the usual country retort. Beat them to their raid by watching for big, dark green ears with brown tassels. The ears should feel firm, and the tip should feel rounded, not pointed. If in doubt, peel back just enough of the husk to reveal a few kernels, and prick one with your fingernail. If it spurts, and the liquid is milky, pick the corn. Don't let it stay on the stalk too long after it ripens, unless it is for cornmeal, for ornament or for popping. Popcorn should dry for a month on the plant,

then a month or so on the picked cob, then in a jar. Only when it is thoroughly dry will it pop. Corn yields vary, but most early corn produces one ear per stalk; most late corn produces two.

VARIETIES

Of the open-pollinated (nonhybrid) types, some old favorites are 'Improved Golden Bantam' (midseason) and 'Country Gentleman.' Open-pollinated types for cornmeal include 'Mandan Bride' and 'Reid's Yellow Dent.' Of the hybrids try the early 'Polar Vee,' the early 'Earlivee' and 'Early Sunglow.' Good midseason varieties are 'Butter and Sugar,' 'Seneca Chief' and 'Merit.' Late ones include the white 'Silver Queen' and 'Iochief.' If you want a sugar-enhanced sweet corn try 'Kandy Korn,' 'White Lightning' and 'Miracle' (all late). And for the super-sweets try 'Early Xtra-sweet,' 'How Sweet It Is' and 'Illini Xtra Sweet' (all late).

'Golden Midget' is an early-bearing dwarf corn with about four little yellow ears per stalk. 'Golden Jubilee' and 'Northern Xtra-sweet' may perform best for you if you live in a cold climate. Indian corns are usually sold as 'Ornamental Indian Corn,' but some named varieties are 'Calico' and 'Strawberry,' which is actually a popcorn. Other named popcorns include 'Japanese Hulless' and 'White Cloud.'

Cucumbers

Cucumbers have come a long way. If you grew them twenty years ago and gave up because you got a lot of scabby, pulpy, disease-ridden fruits, or the fruit never set, or they turned out great but gave you indigestion, try again! Today there are many good disease-resistant varieties, seedless ones, less bitter ones, even "burpless" ones that you don't have to peel. There are also ones with new shapes, such as the skinny "yard-long" cucumbers, and the little yellow ones shaped like lemons.

The sexual problem has even been solved: cucumber yields used to be diminished by the fact that each plant has separate male and female flowers. The males bloom first but bear no fruit; the females bloom about a week later. New "gynoecious" varieties produce more predominantly female flowers than male for a bigger yield, but are sold with a few "male-bearing" seeds to insure pollination. Some varieties do not even need to be pollinated at all.

SITE

Native to the tropics, cucumbers like warm weather but not intense, dry heat. They are not frost-hardy, but since they grow and mature quickly (55–60 days, usually) it is easy to get a crop even with a short season as long as you plant them in full sun.

Before you decide where to put cucumbers, you need to think about how they are going to grow. The plants have long vines that take up a lot of room. They can be allowed to sprawl on the ground as they grow, but this way you will need to allow about 9 square feet per plant—that's a 6-foot-by-9-foot plot if you grow six plants, an ample number unless you are doing a lot of pickling; one cucumber plant can produce a lot of cucumbers.

My favorite way to grow them is to let them climb up the garden fence. Getting cucumbers off the ground not only saves space, but it gives me healthier, cleaner fruits. Also, with the fence method, I do not have to erect a whole separate support structure. Some people grow them up stakes or up string or wire trellises, pinching the growing tip when it reaches the top and pruning side shoots to reduce the weight of the vine. Wire circular cages held up by metal stakes are a good method (Figure 50, page 301). Remember that you'll have a big, heavy vine, so whatever support you provide must be a very strong one.

SOIL

Clay soils with plenty of humus in them give the highest cucumber yields, but sandy loam that warms up quickly will produce an earlier, faster crop. Prepare the soil by adding plenty of organic matter, preferably a rich compost or well-rotted manure, because cucumbers like fertile soil. The pH can be anywhere from 5.5 to 7.0. Add lime to raise the pH if it is lower than that.

PLANTING

Cucumbers are often started indoors to extend the season, but don't bother unless you can keep your seeds at 70–80 degrees by day and no colder than 60 degrees at night. Otherwise it is better to wait until the soil has warmed up. If you do sow indoors, keep the planting medium moistened but well drained. I think peat pots work best because I can later set them out in the garden without even having to disturb the roots—something cucumbers particularly dislike. I sow a few seeds to a pot without firming the soil and thin to the tallest seedling—snipping, not pulling, the discards. They should be started about five weeks before planting time, which is usually the last average frost date. But if the ground and the air are still cold, harden them off for a while before you plant (page 47). Presoaking the seeds will help them to germinate.

If you sow directly in the garden, you can either plant in hills or rows. Rows work better if you are using a vertical support. When the seedlings are a few inches tall, thin to a foot apart in the row, or to three plants in a one-foot hill (page 48). Enrich the hill or row before you plant. A good way to do this is to dig a trench, put a few inches of rotted manure in the bottom, then cover the manure with an inch or two of soil so it cannot come in contact with the seeds.

One other planting note: If the cucumber you're planting is a gynoecious variety, the seed packet will tell you so, and you will find that the seeds producing male flower plants are dyed a distinct color. Set aside two or three peat pots and plant them with only "male" seeds. Then mark the pots containing them, and tie a colored string to the plants when you set them out. You need only one or two plants with male flowers for pollination, but you do not want to neglect to plant those, or destroy them by mistake when thinning.

GROWING

Mulch is especially worthwhile for cucumbers, and for several reasons. Any that lie on the ground are better protected from disease and rot if there is mulch for them to lie on. Also, since the fruits are mostly water, the plants need an extra-big water supply, and mulch will help keep the soil evenly moist. Mulch will also keep down the weeds. This is important because weeding can damage cucumber roots to the point where the whole plant dies. Careful weeding and cultivating are fine when the plant is small, but when it gets to be about a foot high give it a good top dressing of fertilizer or manure, then mulch it.

You will still need to soak the plants in dry weather. If you have planted in hills, you might like to try the coffee-can method described on page 41, putting a can in the center of each hill. For rows, try a soaker hose along the row. But try not to brush against the plants when they are wet either from watering or from rain—this is how disease spreads. And do not confuse "steady moisture" with "standing water." The plants need good drainage.

PESTS AND DISEASES

The worst cucumber pest is also the culprit behind some of the cucumber diseases. The cucumber beetle (striped in the east, spotted in the west) can damage the plants by chewing but does even more harm by spreading bacterial wilt and mosaic. Pick off any beetles you find, checking for them inside the flowers. You can also try hosing them off, covering plants with fine-mesh netting, or spraying both sides of the leaves with a mixture of one handful of wood ashes, one handful of hydrated lime and two gallons of water. If this fails, dust with rotenone. Another safeguard is to make several plantings several weeks apart in case one whole planting is destroyed. If all the plants make it, then you'll just have an extra-large harvest.

Cucumbers are prone to certain fungus diseases such as anthracnose, downy mildew and powdery mildew. Fungicides will help, but the best defense is to buy resistant varieties. Do not use sulfur with cucumbers because it is toxic to this particular crop.

HARVEST

Cucumbers are one of those vegetables that *have* to be picked, whether you have too many of them or not. Feed them to the pig or to the neighbors or the compost pile, but don't stop picking. If they yellow on the vine the plant will stop producing altogether. Check the seed packet to see how big each variety is supposed to get, and harvest them when they reach that size. Twist them off the vines gently or snip them off with clippers, but use two hands, and be very careful not to break the fragile vines.

VARIETIES

Most cucumbers are either "slicing" types (for salads or cooking) or pickling types. The pickling ones are smaller, faster producing, and have little knobs all over them. Good slicing varieties are the open-pollinated 'Marketmore 70' and 'Burpee Hybrid.' 'Supersett' and 'Slicemaster' are gynoecious. 'Sweet Success' is said to be seedless, burpless, disease-resistant and delicious, and it doesn't need pollinating. I haven't tried it but would like to.

Some good pickling cucumbers are 'Wisconsin SMR 18,' 'Ohio MR17' and 'West India Gherkin.' Some bush cukes for small spaces are 'Bush Champion,' 'Spacemaster' and 'Bush Pickle'; 'Patio Pik' and 'Pot Luck' are good for containers. 'Extra Early Express' is a quick crop and a good producer. 'Victory' is a disease-resistant gynoecious variety that is good for northern climates. Try the Armenian 'Yard-Long' and 'Lemon.' And among the burpless, 'Burpless,' 'Tastygreen Burpless' and 'Sweet Slice Hybrid' are good bets.

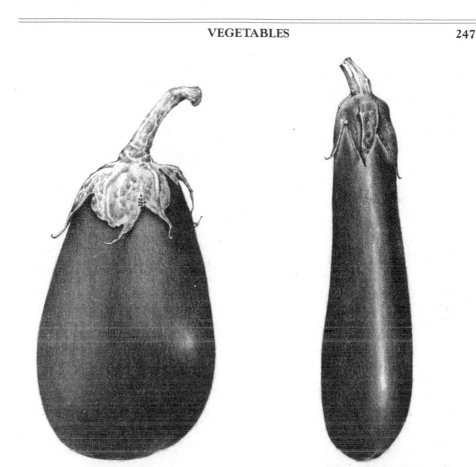

eggplant   *Oriental eggplant*

Eggplant

E ggplant is tough to grow in my climate. Given a choice it would be happiest in a garden with five months of hot weather, which certainly does not describe mine. Why do I even try? Eggplant is not particularly nutritious, having relatively few vitamins and little protein, despite its touted value as a meat substitute. But I love eggplant. I love to fry it, broil it, stuff it, bake it. So I grow it anyway, and the more effort I put into it, the more successful I am.

The plant gets its name from a small white Oriental variety that is seldom grown in this country. We are used to seeing the large, shiny, purple kind. Eggplant is not frost-hardy and demands five months of, if not warm, then at least frost-free weather. So most gardeners buy plants that have been started in a nursery, or start their own indoors when it is still really winter. That means late March, where I live. Sowing eggplant is the first garden job I do in the new year, crossing my fingers that it will be a sunny one, for a certain amount of eggplant-growing is sheer luck.

SITE

Grow eggplant in the sunniest spot you can find, where other plants in the same family have not grown recently (page 184). Growing it in raised beds can help in cold climates, because the soil there will warm up more quickly than in flat beds. Raised beds will also give the plants the good drainage they require; they will not thrive in soggy soil. Garden writer Nancy Bubel even recommends growing them in large containers, to warm up the soil and avoid most pests and diseases. Wherever you grow them, I advise you to start with six plants to begin with and see how you do. For this you will need about 50 square feet of garden space.

SOIL

A heavy feeder, eggplant likes a rich soil a bit on the sandy side, made porous by the addition of humus to promote quick growth and good drainage. Dig in well-rotted manure or compost the fall before, if possible. The pH can be between 5.5 and 7, but 6 is ideal.

PLANTING

Germination will be slow (ten to twelve days) unless you soak seeds overnight and keep the soil very warm—in the 70s or 80s. The only alternative is patience, and if you let the soil get below 50 degrees, your patience will be sorely tried. Sow the seeds in a loose, fine potting medium such as vermiculite, and transplant when seedlings are 2–3 inches tall to peat pots or seed trays filled with loose, rich soil.

Set out plants after danger of frost, but not if the soil still feels cold and the weather is chilly. Hardening them off and bringing them in at night will give them a good start, but do not plant them unless the weather is really starting to warm up. It does help to warm the soil with black plastic before you set out the plants and then put a portable cold frame over them. There is nothing wrong with transplanting them up to larger and larger pots until the weather is more auspicious; this may even forestall some damage from flea beetles, which are an early pest. Some gardeners keep eggplants in big pots till the danger of flea beetles has passed.

When you do set them in the ground, the plants should be spaced about 2½ to 3 feet apart each way, a bit closer if they are a compact variety. Eggplant is not a crop to grow intensively; the plants will be more vigorous and disease-free with ample space, and the fruits will ripen faster if the sun can get in between them. Pour a cup or two of liquid fertilizer into each planting hole, water well, and firm the soil gently. Then put cutworm collars around the young plants.

GROWING

Do not cultivate around the plants, or you may hurt the shallow roots. Pull weeds carefully instead, or use a mulch. You can even plant a quick early crop around the young eggplants, such as lettuce or chervil, or even a flower like alyssum, to provide a living mulch and make use of all that wide spacing. Pour more liquid fertilizer around the plants when they are starting to bloom and at least once a month until harvest. Keep the soil moist.

Some people pinch the stems' growing tips, the bottom suckers, and even some of the blossoms to get better production. I don't know whether it is worth it. The main thing is to get your crop started early, choose early varieties if you have a short, cool season and make sure the plants do not suffer a serious setback at any time, from seed to harvest. They may seem to bounce back after a chilling, a drying out, or a pest plague, but even so you may get little or no harvest.

PESTS AND DISEASES

Watch out for Colorado potato beetles and pick them off; watch for their yellow egg masses on the undersides of the leaves and pick those off too. Tomato worms can also be picked off. Aphids and red spiders can be knocked off with a hose. Flea beetles are the worst pest. They're the ones that suddenly riddle the young plants with tiny holes until there's nothing left of them. Covering the plants with agricultural fabric or screens (page 206), or keeping them in containers for a while (as suggested above) will help, but if flea beetles are still a problem, dust plants with rotenone or diatomaceous earth.

Verticillium wilt, a fairly common eggplant problem, can be averted by using treated seeds, resistant varieties, and crop rotation. Fungi such as phomopsis blight are best avoided by planting resistant strains if you live in a blighted area.

HARVEST

You do not have to wait until eggplant is mature to pick it. It can be only a third its mature size and still taste good. This is its saving grace. If frost threatens and the fruits are still tiny, just pick them and serve up a feast of "baby eggplant." You will be very *au courant*, and no one will be the wiser. If you have brought the fruits to full size, pick them while the skins are still shiny; if they reach the dull-skin stage they will not taste as good. To harvest, cut the stems; don't twist them. You can store eggplants a week or two in a cool place.

VARIETIES

The old, tried and true eggplant variety is 'Black Beauty,' which is open-pollinated and long season. 'Black Magic,' 'Early Beauty Hybrid,' 'Burpee Hybrid' and 'Dusky Hybrid' are earlier. For even earlier crops, grow the long, skinny Oriental type; some varieties are 'Tycoon,' 'Orient Express' and 'Long Tom Hybrid.' 'Black Jack' and 'Super Hybrid' are said to resist wilt. 'Florida Market' is a standby in the south. 'Easter Egg' and 'White Beauty' are small white "egg" types. 'Round de Valence' and 'Small Round Italian' are (you guessed it) small round eggplants.

Boston lettuce

iceberg lettuce

Black Seeded Simpson lettuce

romaine lettuce

Lettuce

S ome lettuces are for lazy cooks; others are for lazy gardeners. Lazy cooks like 'Iceberg,' that classic American lettuce with the big, tight, firm head that needs little washing and keeps for weeks in the refrigerator. It is the joy of the commercial grower, shipper or marketer, and of the bachelor who buys it once a month to eat two leaves at a time in his BLT.

For the home gardener, however, such "crisp-head" or "cabbage-head" types are a tour de force if brought successfully through a hot summer without bolting (going to seed), and few even try. Lazy gardeners choose the fast-growing loose-leaf types like 'Salad Bowl,' the soft, tender butterhead types like 'Bibb' 'Boston' and 'Buttercrunch' or the long, narrow-leaved romaines. As cooks they might complain about having to wash each leaf, dry them, and wrap them to keep them fresh. But as gardeners they give these softer lettuces the prize for easy growing—and for flavor and nutrition too.

There are so many good lettuce varieties to choose from, and they're all so different! Whether planted in contrasting rows and blocks in your garden or blended in a salad bowl, they are beautiful to mix. The colors go from pale green to dark, and there are even some handsome reds. The heads can be spread open, curled tight, or standing upright, and the leaves can be crinkled, ruffled or smooth. Tastes differ just as widely, from mild to strong, and textures from soft to crisp.

In growing lettuce you are not fighting frost; you are fighting heat. To grow lettuce in the summer you need to either shade the plants or find heat-tolerant varieties. In hot climates you cannot grow them in summer at all, only in fall, winter, and spring. Heat makes the plants bolt, each sending up a tall stalk with small, bitter-tasting leaves and a seed head on top (Figure 45). Bolted lettuce looks almost as embarrassing as blooming broccoli—but not quite. And at least with lettuce you can partly blame the weather.

SITE

Finding a spot for lettuce is easy because you can harvest it so soon after you plant. This means that you can grow it in the spaces between slow-maturing crops such as cabbage, cauliflower, eggplant and peppers, harvesting it before the slow crops get big. It doesn't even need full sun and will appreciate the shade cast by stands of corn, staked tomatoes, pole beans or cukes, thus utilizing space that would otherwise go begging. You can grow it in containers on the terrace or indoors. Better yet, build an insulated cold frame and harvest it outdoors, even in the winter.

SOIL

Soil for lettuce should be rich, especially in nitrogen. For once, it doesn't matter if the nitrogen makes the crop "all leaf"; that is exactly what you want lettuce to be. Tilling in well-rotted manure or compost is the first step to provide an airy, moisture-retentive texture as well as richness. Later on, top dressing with blood meal, cottonseed meal or fish emulsion will sustain the quick, steady growth lettuce needs. The ideal soil for a spring crop would be a little on the sandy side, because sandy soil warms up quickly, but heavier soil is fine for later crops. Lettuce also likes soil that is rather pulverized, just as carrots do, so you might follow an early lettuce crop with a carrot patch. The ideal pH is between 6.0 and 7.0, so lime is sometimes needed.

PLANTING

I must admit I never start lettuce indoors early and transplant it outside, just because where I live, so many other things *have* to be started indoors and then transplanted that I am grateful for the few crops I can sow directly in the garden. If you have a lot of time and space for indoor sprouting, though, you can get a jump on the lettuce season this way, especially if you grow the crisphead types that need a long, cool season. Iceberg lettuce will bolt if temperatures are much above 70 degrees for a few days and can take up to 95 days to mature, so you have to start it early. Even the butterheads (55–75 days) and romaines (70–75 days) can benefit from this treatment. Loose-leaf types need it the least, because they mature in 40–50 days.

To start lettuce indoors, sow eight weeks before the last frost, keeping the flats cool (below 70 degrees) and moist.

Hardening off for a few days outdoors is worthwhile. Then set the young plants out in the garden when they are 3–4 inches tall, spacing them a foot apart, more or less, depending on the variety.

Lettuce seeds can be sown directly in the garden as soon as the soil can be worked. Plant them in either rows or blocks, but try to sow as thinly as possible. Lettuce is a nuisance to thin. It must be done anyway, though, because crowded lettuce is more susceptible to disease and rot. (Buying pelleted seeds that are easier to space widely will make life simpler.) The first thinnings will be a size just big enough for your salads. To sow, first moisten the area well, then

BOLTED LETTUCE

Fig. 45

cover the seeds with only a fine sprinkling of soil. I rarely sow a whole seed packet; instead I divide it into halves or even less. I do plant several varieties at once, though—say, 'Black Seeded Simpson,' 'Summer Bibb' and 'Red Sails'—so I can have mixed salads. Then I plant all of them in succession throughout the season. During the summer you might want to plant a few heat-tolerant varieties such as 'Slobolt,' 'Salad Bowl' or 'Green Ice,' then at summer's end sow some more quick-growing, cool-weather types like the ones you sowed in spring. Some years you will get lettuce well into late fall, even in cold climates, but it is wise to sow some in a cold frame too, for a sure-fire late harvest.

GROWING

While lettuce is growing, try to maintain constant moisture. A mulch not only serves this purpose, but also keeps down weeds, keeps the lettuce leaves cleaner, and helps ward off fungus diseases that can rot the lower leaves. Even if you have used a mulch, you should soak the ground (not the leaves) if the plants seem limp, for the roots are shallow and dry out easily. Lettuce that is watered well also tastes less bitter.

Top dressing from time to time with a nitrogen-rich fertilizer like blood meal, fish emulsion or manure tea will help keep growth going. And be sure to keep the soil moist. To keep lettuce from bolting in warm weather, some gardeners screen it with netting, cheesecloth or lath stretched across frames and placed on vertical supports (page 206). The same apparatus could double as a frame for clear plastic covers for frost protection in fall. You can also sow warm-weather lettuce in a part of the garden that gets dappled shade.

PESTS AND DISEASES

Not much bothers lettuce. Occasional pests include cutworms (use collars if necessary), aphids (hose them off), slugs (trap them or repel them with a mulch of sawdust and wood ashes) and leafhoppers, which spread disease (keep nearby weeds to a minimum and use a garlic spray). Several soil-borne fungi can cause leaf rot. Prevent this by mulching, rotating your crops and cleaning up all debris promptly. If mildew is a problem, plant resistant varieties. Certain varieties will also resist mosaic, though since this disease is spread by aphids and leafhoppers you can also control it by dealing with them. "Tip burn" of the leaves is simply the curse of hot weather; prevent it by giving the plants moisture and some shade.

HARVEST

Lettuces are harvested in different ways, depending on the type. You can pick leaf lettuce from the outside, letting the inner leaves continue to grow, or you can crop the whole thing an inch above the soil and let it regrow. Heading types are usually pulled up whole, head by head, as needed, but these can also be picked outer leaves first. And frankly any lettuce is worth cropping, if you have the space. There's always a chance you'll get a few tender leaves for salads when there's no other fresh-picked lettuce around.

VARIETIES

There are a great many new lettuce varieties appearing each year, some of them improvements on the old standards, others more exotic. In the crisphead category the old favorites are 'Ithaca,' 'Burpee Iceberg' and the heat-tolerant 'Great Lakes.' Newer ones include 'Vanguard' and 'King Crown.' Popular butterheads are 'Buttercrunch,' 'Dark Green Boston,' 'Bibb' and 'Summer Bibb,' 'Tom Thumb' and the bolt-resistant 'Kagran Summer.'

Favorite loose-leafs are 'Salad Bowl,' 'Prizehead,' 'Slobolt,' the reddish 'Four Seasons,' 'Oakleaf' (green or red), 'Ruby Red,' 'Red Sails' and the compact 'Black Seeded Simpson.' I try to grow a few of each, but the last is so reliably good that I always include it. The most popular cos or romaine type is 'Parris Island Cos.'

In very cold climates, find a cold-tolerant lettuce variety like 'Frosty' for your early and late crops. In hot ones try 'Green Wave.' On the west coast grow varieties marked MI, which are mosaic resistant. For small spaces, a good bet is 'Little Gem.'

Okra

Grown for its edible seed pods, okra is a handsome plant to have in the vegetable garden. It has showy pale yellow flowers with red centers—not unlike a hollyhock. Okra haters are not impressed by this. They claim that the pods are prickly on the outside and slimy on the inside, and that if they want showy flowers they can grow petunias. Okra lovers, most of whom live below the Mason–Dixon line, point out that modern "spineless" varieties aren't prickly at all, and that the viscous inside is the magic ingredient that thickens a good gumbo—a hearty stew. ("Gumbo" is also another name for the plant itself.)

Okra is popular in the south because it is a warm-weather crop that won't bolt, yellow, die, or otherwise misbehave in midsummer. It just gets taller, lusher and more productive. It is a little hard to get started up north but redeems itself by being, unlike eggplant, a fast-maturing crop once warm weather settles in. So even if you don't plant until late June, you can still pick okra two months later if you urge it along a little. You only need a few plants for the home garden, though any extras can be frozen sliced or whole. Dwarf varieties are available for small spaces. It is disease-free and rarely decimated by bugs.

SITE

Choose a sunny site where the ground will warm up quickly (or even raised beds in the north). The more okra you want to eat or freeze, the more space you need. The first time you grow it, start with six plants in an area of about 40 square feet. You might put an early lettuce crop in with it, but otherwise assign the whole plot to okra for the season. If you grow it each year, rotate the crop.

SOIL

Okra prefers a light, well-drained loam with plenty of organic matter. Avoid heavy soils that warm up slowly, especially up north. A pH of 6.0–7.0 is best, and moderately high fertility. I suggest a healthy shovelful of compost or aged manure worked into each planting hole.

PLANTING

Buy new seed each year and speed up the normally slow germination process by soaking or freezing the seeds overnight, or nicking the seed coat with a file. Wherever you live, make sure that the weather is consistently above 60 degrees and not too wet when you sow. The seeds will just sit and rot in cold, wet soil. In the north start them a month or two earlier indoors in peat pots.

Sown outdoors, seeds should be planted an inch deep in hills or rows and thinned to at least 18 inches apart. Bear in mind that the plants get tall—5 or 6 feet in warm climates. Dwarf varieties that grow to 3 or 4 feet are more convenient for the home garden. In the north space them far enough apart so that the sun can shine on all the pods to ripen them. Plant either 18 inches apart, with 3 feet between rows, or on a grid, with plants 2–2½ feet apart each way (a little closer for dwarf kinds).

GROWING

It is important not to let growth lapse. Gardeners use various warm-up devices to bring the young plants along if it's chilly—raised beds, hot caps, grow tunnels, portable cold frames and sheets of black plastic slit to allow the plants to grow up. Keep plants well watered if it is dry. A mulch is a good idea. And top dress every few weeks with a balanced liquid fertilizer.

PESTS AND DISEASES

Use collars around transplanted seedlings to protect against cutworms. Occasional pests such as corn earworms, cabbage loopers and stinkbugs can be picked off. Aphids and flea beetles can be knocked off with a hose. Diseases such as fusarium wilt and verticillium wilt are best dealt with by crop rotation.

HARVEST

Okra pods are ready for picking several days after the flowers drop but before they are fully mature. If you wait until the pods reach full size, they will be tough. The stems should still be soft and easy to cut, the pods 2–3 inches long. Some varieties can be picked at 4–5 inches. When the plant is in full production it needs to be picked every other day. If some pods have gone too far, pick them anyway and feed them to whatever will eat them, even if it's the compost pile or the garbage can. Otherwise the plants will stop producing. Use gloves when you pick if your skin is sensitive to the prickles on the pods.

Okra plants, if picked regularly, will continue to produce until frost. In the south growers sometimes cut the plants back almost to ground level in midsummer, top dress them, and let them resprout for a whole second crop.

VARIETIES

Good varieties are 'Clemson Spineless,' the old standby, and 'Clemson 80,' an earlier, more productive version. 'Emerald' is a tall, spineless, very productive variety. 'Annie Oakley' is a tall early producer. 'Dwarf Green Long Pod' is a good short variety. 'Blondy,' an All-America selection, is short and bushy with light green pods. 'Red Okra' has red pods; 'White Velvet' has white.

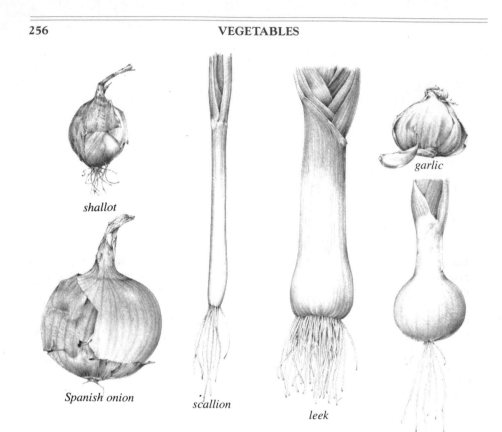

shallot

garlic

Spanish onion

scallion

leek

pickling onion

Onions and Family

The onion tribe are thought of as nature's great repellers. Depending on whom you talk to, you'll learn that they will ward off garden bugs, vampires, heart disease and (if you eat them raw) your friends. I'm willing to keep an open mind about all of these, but I know the onions that come out of my kitchen win me more friends than they send away. They are the cook's greatest ally, whether they are yellow storage onions, big red salad onions, little white boiling onions, scallions, leeks, garlic, shallots or chives.

Most of them are raised for their bulbous roots, which are pungent or sweet in varying degrees, and some for their green tops. And though they are grown in somewhat different ways, all onions like pretty much the same conditions: a sandy, fairly fertile loam; plenty of moisture but good drainage; cool weather to grow the tops; and warm weather to ripen the bulbs. They do not require much space, are easy to grow, and are relatively disease- and pest-free as vegetables go.

Onions

Some gardeners find onion culture a bit confusing because there are so many kinds of onions and often several different ways to grow each one. But choosing the right onion and the right method really is not that hard once you know a few simple things about onions.

There are three ways to grow them: from seeds, from purchased seedlings and from sets. Growing from seed can take a long time and in northern gardens may not bring onions to the bulb stage in time for warm, bulb-ripening weather. So some people start seeds indoors and transplant the seedlings. They also buy started seedlings either from local nurseries and feed stores or via mail from the south and transplant these into their own gardens in early spring to mature at summer's end. Or they buy onion sets— tiny, immature bulbs (or side bulbs attached to mature bulbs) that have been harvested and dried and are ready to plant in early spring. This last is the easiest way to grow onions, but unfortunately very few varieties are available as sets. So unless you just want basic yellow storage onions, it is tempting to try seedlings or seeds.

Which onions you grow depends partly on your cooking and eating needs. If you want long-storing, pungent onions, grow the small, firm "American" type, either yellow, white or red. If you want the tiny, round white type, grow "pearl" or "pickling" onions. If you want the very large, sweet type that are sliced for hamburgers, grow "Bermuda" or "Spanish" onions (also yellow, white or red). If you want scallions you can either harvest other onions while they are still scallion-sized (before they form a bulb), or grow "bunching onions," which don't ever form a round bulb but keep the scallion shape even when mature.

Different parts of the country favor different varieties. If you have never grown onions before, I'd suggest starting with the most standard variety for your area. Ask around to see what grows best where you live. The major regional distinction is between "northern" and "southern" onions. With most vegetables this simply means a short, cool versus a long, hot growing season, but with onions there is yet another factor. The point at which onions start producing bulbs is a function not only of temperature but also of day length. In the north days are much longer in summer than in winter. In the south day length varies less from season to season. "Short-day" onions are suited to the south; they bulb too soon in the north as days lengthen. "Long-day" onions are suited to the north; they don't bulb properly in the south because the days don't lengthen enough. When shopping for seeds, seedlings or sets, try to find out whether the varieties are recommended for north or south.

Storage onions are best grown in the north from sets, Spanish or Bermuda types from purchased seedlings, and smaller types, such as pearl onions or scallions, from seed. In the north begin by growing a yellow storage onion grown from sets, and perhaps some bunching onions for scallions from seed; then in later years if you want to start experimenting, try other types from seeds or seedlings.

SITE

In choosing a site for onion beds, look for a sunny spot and one that is the least likely to sprout a crop of weeds, either from pieces of perennial weed roots or from dormant annual weed seeds. Often this is a patch that had either a thick mulch or a thick weedless crop on it the previous year. Some gardeners divide their crop into several plots here and there in the garden to protect their other crops with the onions' bug-repelling powers.

SOIL

Lime the soil if the pH is below 6.0, and dig plenty of organic matter into it. Well-rotted manure is fine as long as it has been dug in the previous year. A balanced organic fertilizer with all the necessary trace elements is probably the best insurance for good growth. The soil needs to be fairly well pulverized, but not to any great depth, since the plants are shallow-rooted.

PLANTING

Onion seeds should be new and fresh, since they usually are not viable for more than a year or two. If you are starting seeds directly in the garden, sow them in very early spring or else in fall for a wintered-over crop. Make a wide furrow, soak it thoroughly, sow the seeds, and then cover them with ½ inch to an inch of fine soil. As the plants come up, gradually thin them to 3–5 inches apart, depending on how big the onions will be at picking time. Eat the thinnings as scallions.

If you are starting seeds indoors, plant them very early. Keep them at a temperature of about 60 degrees and keep them moist. When they are about 6 inches tall, trim the tops to 3 inches and set them in a moistened furrow in the garden, poking a hole for each one with a pencil or your finger, and allowing the same spacing as for thinned onions (above). Scallions can be sown in the garden as a spring crop, a fall crop, or a wintered-over crop; they do not need thinning.

Onion sets are purchased by mail or at a nursery or feed store by the pound. Common varieties are 'Stuttgarter,' 'Ebeneezer,' 'Yellow Globe' and 'Yellow Danvers.' If you have a choice, pick the smallest ones in the bin. Plant them 2–4 inches apart with the tip up and just barely showing (or just barely beneath the surface if you have trouble with hungry birds) and water them well. If you are really ambitious and want to grow your own sets from seed, sow the seeds thickly in midsummer so that the tops die down while the onion bulbs are still very small—under ¾ inch—and don't thin them.

GROWING

While the onions are growing, you need to keep the soil moist and free of weeds that can choke them out. A mulch, applied when the plants are about a foot tall, will help with both. If you do mulch you may find that planting in rows is best because it is hard to get a mulch in between the plants otherwise—unless it is a very fine mulch.

Side dress with fertilizer every now and then unless the soil is rich; but try not to go overboard on the nitrogen or you will get all tops and no bulb. Cut off any seed heads that threaten to develop and watch for signs that the tops have matured. They will yellow and start to fall over. Do not mistake this yellowing for signs of drought—it happens only when the bulbs are pretty much grown. A common practice is to bend over the onion tops manually to hasten ripening, but it is not a necessity, and you can harm the plants if you do not do it carefully. Better to let them fall naturally unless you are trying to hasten maturation for a special reason such as imminent frost or wet soil that you fear might rot the bulbs.

PESTS AND DISEASES

Onion thrips can be a problem in the south, where they suck onion leaves. They can be hosed off with a stream of water or washed off with a soap spray. The onion maggot can rot the bulbs; an oil or soap spray applied to the ground is said to be effective. The smell of onions is thought to repel most other pests. Diseases are rare.

HARVEST

After the tops have fallen, I pull up the onions to dry and cure them. If the weather is dry and sunny, I let them cure right there on the ground, but if it threatens to rain I move them to a warm, dry place. Some people dry onions on screens for better air circulation. When I visited Plimoth Plantation, in Plymouth, Massachusetts, I saw how the Pilgrims cured their onions—on the roofs of low sheds and chicken coops. You might give that a try.

Don't cut off the tops! They should be left to dry too, until the necks of the onions are thin and no longer green. I like to braid these dried tops together in a French braid, weaving a strong piece of twine through the braid (otherwise the weight of the braid would eventually cause it to break). All types of onions can be harvested and stored this way, or in mesh onion bags like the ones used in stores. Do not put them in a moist cellar with your other storage crops. Scallions are usually not cured but used green, and a few are left in the ground to go to seed for next year.

VARIETIES

Good storing onions are 'Yellow Globe,' 'Early Yellow Globe,' 'White Portugal' and 'Sweet Spanish' (the yellow or white kind). 'Sweet Spanish' is mild. Good red onions are 'Granex,' 'Southport Red Globe' and 'Red Wethersfield.' Large sweet onions are 'Sweet Sandwich,' 'Giant Red' and the Bermuda types—both white and yellow. Good pickling onions are 'White Portugal' and 'Crystal Wax Pickling.' Popular scallions are 'White Bunching,' 'Beltsville Bunching,' 'Japanese Bunching' and 'Evergreen White,' which winters over.

Leeks

These onion relatives look like overgrown scallions. They do not form bulbs but are usually left to grow to an inch or more in diameter at the base. They are a wonderful, flavorful vegetable—cold-tolerant, easy to grow, and for some odd reason, expensive to buy. All the more reason to produce your own. Unless they are dug at scallion-size they are eaten cooked. They like everything that other onions like—perhaps a bit richer soil. I like to grow two separate crops in two separate ways. I buy some started ones that will mature into proper-sized leeks by summer's end. (If I had a greenhouse, I would start some from seed indoors in March.) I also sow some thickly in the garden and don't thin them. These I harvest while they're still ½ to 1 inch thick and very tender, for some really luxurious baked dishes.

I allow my other crop to mature to full size. These big ones are best blanched. Blanch either by planting them in a moist trench that is gradually filled, or by banking them up with soil above the surface—or by a combination of both ways. Leeks are harder to dig up than bulb onions—I never try to pull them but dig them up with a spade or fork. They do not store well indoors, so I harvest them only as needed. I have wintered them over in northern Connecticut with great success. Others in my area even dig them up in midwinter during thaws. Good varieties are 'American Flag' and 'Giant Musselburgh.'

French Shallots

This is another "onion" vegetable that is inexplicably expensive to buy. Few plants are easier and cheaper to grow. All you do is buy a few shallots (the *last* you will ever have to buy) and pull the clusters apart to make sets. Plant them with their points up as you would onion sets, but a bit deeper, and 4–6 inches apart. Plant in early spring in the north, fall in the south. Instead of forming big bulbs like onions, each set will form a whole new head of shallots. The crop takes three to four months to mature. Harvest them when the leaves die down; do not leave them in the ground or they may resprout. Braid the tops and hang them up, or store them in mesh bags. Save a head or two for next year's crop. Be sure you've bought the true French shallots, not "multiplier onions," which have their virtues but do not taste like shallots.

Garlic

This strong bulb will surely finish off any vampires—or fastidious company—that the other onions may have left unscathed. It is planted in early spring in the north, fall or winter else-where, and is grown the way shallots are—but it has deeper roots. Sometimes garlic is overwintered even in the north.

To plant just buy a head of garlic, separate the cloves, and plant each one, pointed end up. They should be 2–3 inches deep in the north, 1 inch in the south. There are white heads, pinkish heads and some huge heads called "elephant garlic." Garlic dislikes very hot weather, overfertilizing and overwatering. To harvest, dig up the heads when the tops have died down; braid or tie the tops, or store the heads in mesh bags.

Other Onions

Chives, the tiniest onion, are considered on page 317. In addition there are a number of unusual onions that you can explore, but frankly I have had no experience with them myself. White "multiplier onions" and yellow "potato onions" form clusters underground. Mild-tasting Egyptian onions (also called "tree onions" and "top onions") form exotic-looking plants with clusters at the tops. All of these can be used as green onions or in cooking as shallots are. Welsh onion (*Allium fistulosum*) is a nonbulbing type.

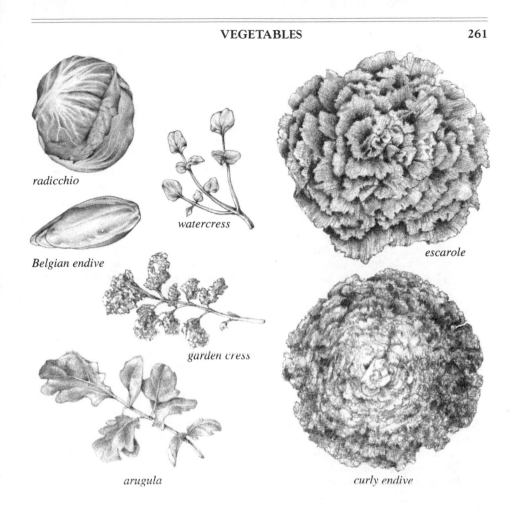

radicchio

watercress

Belgian endive

garden cress

escarole

arugula

curly endive

Other Salad Plants

With all the thousands of green leaves growing in the world, what makes some of them salad-worthy? They need to be flavorful, somewhat crisp, not too bitter and of course nontoxic. For commercial production, they must be economical to grow, ship and store. Lettuce is the standard by which we tend to measure them, but lettuce can get boring after a while, and some greens are favored precisely because they are not like lettuce, such as the peppery arugula or the re-

cently popular radicchio, which is not even green. Gardeners are expanding their salad repertoires, rediscovering some old-fashioned greens and trying new and unfamiliar ones, often from other countries. Here is a sampling of those worth trying.

French Sorrel

This is one of the easiest plants you can grow—a stalwart perennial that usually takes care of itself. I put the young leaves in salads, but my favorite way to use the plant is in sorrel soup in early spring when fresh garden tastes are so well appreciated. Since it spreads so readily, I keep it in a patch off by itself. All it needs is a good loam with moderate fertility and a pH of 6.0–7.0.

To start a new crop, sow sorrel in early spring and eat the thinnings. Keep cutting the plant back to prevent it from growing to its full 3-foot height; when it sends up flower stalks, the leaves become tough and bitter. Clean up the debris in fall and look for the new young leaves as soon as winter is over. Divide the plants in the patch every few years and give the extras to friends who are not, as yet, inundated with sorrel. 'Mammoth Lyon' is a good variety.

Arugula

Also called rucola, rugula, ruchetta, rocket and roquette, this is a traditional European green that is now becoming available in some produce markets. But if you want it fresh for picking right before dinner, grow your own, even if you have only a big pot on the terrace or in a very sunny window. Arugula leaves have a very sharp pepperlike tang to them, and a unique flavor. Some use it sparingly as a salad seasoning; some mix it generously with other greens. I am one of those who can eat it all by itself, by the bowlful. It has no unusual problems or requirements, and is grown like lettuce.

Sow arugula in spring or fall when the leaves taste best. In summer it is not quite as tender, but I eat my spring crop all summer anyway and even into fall if I have neglected to plant a second one. I keep cutting it back, especially if it is forming flower stalks, to help the flavor stay good, though frankly, even gone-to-seed arugula is better than no arugula at all. And if seeds fall in your garden you may get a volunteer crop the next spring.

Escarole and Curly Endive

These closely related plants are the true endives, botanically speaking, not the "Belgian endive" that you find in stores (below). They are easy to raise, frost-hardy, and grown much like lettuce, except that they are more heat-tolerant. Curly endive has light green leaves with thick, crisp ribs and narrow, frilled edges. It is a little bitter for my taste, but many people must love it because I always see it in stores. Escarole has darker leaves that are not curly; it is good raw, but I prefer it cooked Italian-style with garlic and olive oil.

Both taste best as a fall crop sown in midsummer. The plants should be thinned to at least a foot apart, since they grow quite big. Though the centers will be somewhat pale and tender naturally, some gardeners blanch them during the last two or three weeks of growth by tying the tops (as with cauliflower, page 233) or by covering them with flat boards resting on a couple of bricks. Do this on a day when the leaves are dry, and look under the boards from time to time for signs of rot. If you find it, remove the boards. Plants are cut at ground level when full sized. Curly varieties are 'Green Curled' and the bolt-resistant 'Salad King.' The most popular type is 'Florida Deep Heart.'

Belgian Endive

Also called witloof chicory, this is the expensive little white pointed

BLANCHING BELGIAN ENDIVE

Fig. 46

Belgian endive can be blanched by simply planting the roots in a flower pot and keeping them in the dark. But by using a box filled with soil to the top of the roots and 6 inches of sand on top, you do not have to worry about the light. The little heads will grow up through the sand, to be harvested when the tips show.

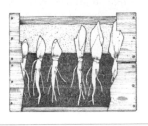

thing you sometimes see marketed as French endive. You will not get those little heads in your garden simply by planting their seeds; the process is a bit more elaborate. But they *are* tasty, and expensive, and so here's how to grow them:

Sow seeds outdoors around the date of the last average frost in the same kind of pulverized soil you'd use for carrots, only much deeper. Do not worry about the top layer being very finely pulverized, because germination is not as difficult as it is for carrots. Long carrotlike roots will grow, which need to be carrot-distance apart or a bit farther, about 6 inches. With no attending to beyond weeding and adequate water, they will sprout some rather poor-tasting greens, then send up long stems with pretty, long-blooming flowers on them, exactly like the blue chicory flowers you see by the roadside in summer. Picking these flowers will give you a better harvest, if you can bear to do it (they lose their color when picked). After the foliage dies down in fall, or when the roots are 1½–2 inches in diameter, harvest the roots by digging them up carefully with a spading fork.

These roots are sometimes used as a coffee substitute or additive. But to get the little pointed shoots, or chicons, you have to take these roots indoors, force them and blanch them. To do this, cut off the side roots and the bottom part of the main root so that you have one thick root 8 or 9 inches long, then cut the stems off about 2 inches above the root. If possible chill the roots in a cold place for a week or more. Then plant them upright in a wooden or plastic container (Figure 46), a bucket, or whatever container you have that is at least 14 inches deep, filling the container with soil up to the root tops, and adding 5–6 inches of sand, sawdust or peat moss above that. The roots can be quite close together, as long as there is a little soil between them and it is firmed gently so there are no air pockets.

Put the box in a cool room or basement and water occasionally, but don't let the roots sit in very wet soil. The best way to water is to poke a stick into each corner of the container and pour water into the holes you have made, so that you are just adding a little moisture to the soil at the bottom.

In about four weeks the tops should sprout tall enough to show at the surface. They will be snow white from growing in the dark growing medium, and they'll have a nice compact shape if this medium is sufficiently light and airy. Pull the roots up and cut off the sprouts where root and sprout join. You can stagger the crop in various ways. You can dig some roots up and leave the rest in the garden for a while, as long as you remove them before frost. You can blanch in several boxes, keeping some at just above freezing, and bringing them into a 60-degree room one at a time. Or you can cut off the tops when they have matured but leave the roots in the box to resprout once or twice more. If you have mice, watch out! Keep them from eating your crop by surrounding it with a cage made of fine-mesh hardware cloth or screening.

Radicchio

This Italian salad plant is also a form of chicory; in fact its British name is "red-hearted chicory," since it sometimes resembles a small green cabbage head with a red center. Other varieties are red all the way through, with striking white veins in the leaves. Radicchio is equally good cooked or raw. It works best as a fall crop in areas with cold winters, and as a spring crop in areas with mild ones where you can sow very early. This is because it should really have up to five months to grow, with a cool stretch at the end. It is not fussy about soil fertility, soil texture or even water, though it should not get either waterlogged or bone dry.

Sow outdoors or indoors. When the seedlings are about 4 inches tall, thin or transplant them to about a foot apart. When the plants are mature, you can harvest the outer leaves or cut off the whole head, which will sometimes regenerate. You also might experiment with indoor forcing, as for rhubarb (page 285). In mild winters heads may winter over. 'Giulio' is the best one I know for home growers.

Watercress

Watercress is one of the few greens that will grow right in the water. If you have a cool, slow-flowing, unpolluted brook or can dam up your fast-flowing brook to form a slower one, you can grow watercress as a spring crop. It likes a spot in semishade and will withstand light frosts. If your winters are fairly mild, you can establish it there as a perennial by planting seedlings shortly before the last frost, just above the water line. But you may find that a very wet garden site is the easiest route, especially if your brook is in an acid soil.

The soil watercress likes is fertile and humusy, with a pH of around 7.0. You can also grow it in pots set in pans or saucers of water. Start it either from seed or by rooting the watercress bunches you buy at the food market. Just put the stems in a container of water with the leaves above the surface, and change the water often. Wherever it is growing, keep it well fed with a liquid or readily soluble high-nitrogen fertilizer, and keep picking it for your salads or garnishes to encourage it to produce more. 'Improved Broad-Leaved' is a good variety.

Garden Cress

Also called curly cress or peppergrass, this dainty green is so quick, easy and satisfying that it is a good first crop for a child to grow. You can even grow it in a window box, indoors or out.

Sow the seed in spring, or anytime indoors. When it is 3 inches tall, thin the seedlings to 3 inches apart, using the thinnings to spice up your salads. Harvest it when it is about 6 inches tall and it will regrow, but meanwhile start another row or pot. You will have cress to pick in as little as two weeks, and a mature crop in five or six. It is sold as 'Moss Curled,' 'Fine Curled' and 'Peppergrass.'

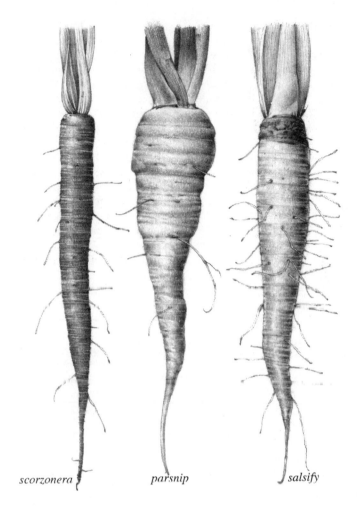

scorzonera   *parsnip*   *salsify*

Parsnip, Salsify and Scorzonera

P arsnips take some patience. The seeds are slow sprouting, the plants are slow growing, and the whole crop can take a good year to produce if you do it right. But they are easy, pest-free, and well worth the wait. They look like white carrrots but are fatter on top and skinnier on the bottom. Parsnips' texture is somewhat potato-like, and they are rather caloric as vegetables go, especially since they absolutely demand, in my mind, to be smothered in large amounts of butter. They are also sweet and flavorful in soups and stews.

Parsnips are biennials that would send up flower stalks and bloom the second season if you let them, but you don't. You plant them very early in the spring, pick some in fall after a few freezes, and winter them in the ground for an early-spring harvest. Parsnips actually turn sweeter after they have been frozen a few times, since the starch in them turns to sugar. So while they may look ready to dig, it is best to leave them in the ground for a while. As I said, patience with parsnips pays off.

Salsify, or "oyster plant," is often grouped with parsnip because it is closely related and is grown the same way. It looks like a slightly shorter, thinner parsnip. "Black salsify" or "scorzonera," is not even closely related to either, though it looks like a black-skinned, white-fleshed salsify. It is grown like salsify, and it is convenient to put it next to parsnips and salsify in books and seed catalogs as well as in gardens. All three are more popular in cool climates than hot ones, but you can grow them in the south by planting them in early summer and wintering them in the ground.

SITE

The site and space requirements for parsnips, salsify and scorzonera are the same as for carrots, except that they will occupy their plot for the whole growing season.

SOIL

The soil should be deep, moderately rich, and not too sandy, heavy or stony—exactly what you would prepare for carrots except that you should pulverize the soil a bit deeper. Obstacles will cause distortion of the roots. Very sandy soil will encourage large, useless side roots to form, and heavy clay soil will be hard for the roots to penetrate. To correct either condition, add plenty of organic matter until the texture is that of a good average loam (page 22). If you still suspect the soil is too heavy, make a large, parsnip-shaped planting hole for each plant by plunging a crowbar into the soil, waggling it back and forth, and filling the hole with a more hospitable material such as aged compost or light rich soil. Avoid too-fresh manure or soil that is too rich in nitrogen, which will cause branching of the roots.

Being taprooted, these vegetables will accept slightly dry soils better than most, since they will dig down for water beneath the surface; they will also tolerate slightly poorer soils. But do not ask the impossible from them. What you want to give them is a moderate but consistent supply of water and nutrients, for a long, slow, steady season of growth. The pH can be anywhere between 6.0 and 8.0.

PLANTING

Sow the seeds outdoors in the garden as soon as the ground can be worked, usually early April where I live. If you wait too long, the plants may not get the full growth they need before cool weather slows the growth down in fall. Parsnips and salsify take about three and a half months to mature, and scorzonera takes four.

I recommend planting by the traditional row method to make mulching easier. Make the rows 12–18 inches apart. You can make this crop better pay for its year-long stay in one spot by interplanting the rows with an early crop such as spinach or lettuce.

Use fresh, new seeds, and soak them overnight in warm water to shorten the two-to-three-week germination period. They can be mixed with sand or coffee grounds for easier planting. Make a furrow and moisten it well, then sow seed thickly because germination of parsnip and salsify is notoriously poor, even with brand-new seed (this is generally not a problem with scorzonera). Cover the seeds with a half-inch of very light, fine soil, or even vermiculite, because they will balk at a surface crust just as badly as carrots will. Pat the soil lightly and water it well with a fine spray.

Keep the seed bed moist during the germination period. If you are like me, you can very easily forget to do this, but there are some tricks to make up for lack of vigilance. Put wet burlap, sphagnum moss or even wooden boards over the seeds till they come up. An even better trick is to plant radish seed mixed in with the parsnip seed. When the fast-sprouting radish seedlings break the surface, they will mark the spot where you have planted so you can cultivate confidently. They will also shade the spindly young parsnip seedlings, keeeping them from drying out. By the time you're pulling the radishes, the parsnips should be tall enough to thin—4 inches tall or more. If you have made crowbar holes, thin each cluster to one plant, snipping the extras with scissors.

GROWING

While they are growing, the plants cannot take much competition, so cultivate and weed often unless you have a good thick mulch that is keeping the weeds at bay. Make sure the soil does not get too dry, especially if the bed is not mulched. Unless you have used pretty rich soil, or a slow-release fertilizer, an occasional light top dressing during the summer will keep growth going, but do not overdo it.

PESTS AND DISEASES

Neither insects nor diseases should be a problem. You might get celery leaf miners that tunnel into the leaves; if so, scrape off the little blisters you will find on them. If your plants get canker, making the roots rot, combat it next time by planting a later crop, using no manure and checking the pH. If your soil is very acid, raise it to pH 7.0 by adding the appropriate amount of lime (page 33).

HARVEST

If you are harvesting in fall, dig the roots and store them as you would carrots. For overwintering in the ground, pile on at least a foot of leaves or straw or some other loose mulch, as soon as the ground threatens to freeze in earnest. During winter thaws you can pull a few up, but as soon as the ground has really softened in spring, harvest all of them. Do not let the tops start growing again or you will ruin the roots' flavor.

VARIETIES

Shopping for parsnip varieties is easy. The best variety is 'Harris Model.' 'Hollow Crown,' a faster crop, is also good. The standard salsify is 'Sandwich Island Mammoth.' The one named scorzonera variety I have seen so far is 'Gigantea.'

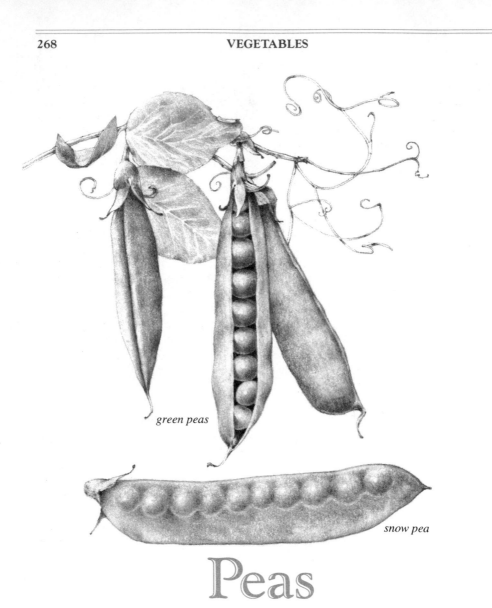

green peas

snow pea

Peas

A pea crop is a lot of vines and a lot of pods, but when you come right down to it, not very many peas. Sweet, succulent and welcome, to be sure, if you can harvest them in May for the first feast from your garden. But high volume they're not.

On the plus side, they are easy to grow, they are good for your garden's soil, they don't take up much space, and they are an early, quick crop that can be over and done with in time to free up space for a fall crop such as cabbage. They also freeze very well if processed just at the point of sweetness. And you take your pick from a wealth of varieties. There are the super-early smooth-skinned peas; the early-, middle- and late-season wrinkle-seeded ones; and even a few heat-resistant ones to take you into the summer. You can choose between the dwarf kinds that need little or no support and the tall climbers that do need trellising but earn that right by producing far more peas. There are also, increasingly, varieties that resist the diseases that peas are sometimes plagued by. All these types fall into the category of "green peas" or "English peas"—to distinguish them from peas grown for drying, which are considered in the section on beans.

Best of all, there are the "snow-pea" types, whose tender pods taste as good as their contents, raw or cooked. We can thank the Chinese for this Great Leap Forward in pea culture—not only for developing them but for putting them into dishes at Chinese restaurants so we'd know what they were for. Some varieties are harvested when the pod is flat; others, such as 'Sugar Snap,' are just as good when the peas are fully round. Some of them, 'Sugar Snap' being one, have strings running down each side of the pods that must be removed before you eat them. Others are "stringless." Some are tall, some are dwarf, but whichever one you choose, you can count on a much bigger harvest volume than you would get if you had to throw away the pods. As a result, many gardeners now grow only the edible-pod kinds.

The most important thing to know about growing peas is that they cannot stand hot weather. If temperatures are consistently above 70 degrees the plants slow their growth, get dried out and brown, get more bugs, and die. Even pollination can be iffy. Since the seeds will tolerate frost well, they are an ideal early-spring crop, but don't think this makes them an ideal fall crop also. The mature plants do not tolerate frost well, so unless your climate affords you a two-month stretch between muggy summer and frost, a fall crop is not dependable. But peas are—face it—so little trouble that it is sometimes worth the

gamble if you can shade them behind the corn or pole beans while it is still hot. Before I knew any better I once planted a second crop of snow peas in late summer and I got a fine harvest.

If you live in a warm climate, fall and even winter planting can be fine. Some southern gardeners sow in fall and let the seeds lie dormant in winter so that they can sprout as early as possible in spring in order to beat the heat. Do keep your climate in mind when you choose your varieties, though. If your spring is short, plant an early, fast-maturing variety or a heat-resistant one. If you have a cool growing season, you can plant several varieties at once that mature at different intervals (early-, mid- and late-season) so you can pick peas over a longer period.

SITE

Peas will grow in a partly shaded location. In choosing the right spot, take into account the need to support long-vined varieties. I like to grow snow peas on the garden fence. Early peas, especially, appreciate raised beds that warm up quickly in spring. Pea crops should be rotated from year to year, both to avoid disease and to benefit other crops by nitrogen fixation (page 215).

SOIL

What kind of soil texture you give your peas depends on whether you are planting an early or late crop. In the cold, wet days of early spring the soil should be a light sandy loam that warms up quickly. For a later crop a clay soil will help keep the plants' roots cool—though it should not be so heavy that it slows the plant's growth and delays the harvest till hot weather. Either soil type should have plenty of organic matter in it because peas always need a good supply of moisture to make their seeds germinate and keep the plants from drying out. At the same time, good drainage is necessary to keep the seeds and plants from rotting. If you have either very sandy or very heavy soil and cannot easily change its composition, choose the appropriate pea variety.

The soil's pH should be around 6.0–6.5, and the soil should be limed if it is more acid than that. Soil fertility is important because peas do feed heavily even though, as legumes, they also return nutrients to the soil. Nitrogen fixation takes a while to really alter the soil. This is especially true with an early crop in a spot that legumes have not occupied recently—and if you are rotating your crops, chances are they have not. Using a bacteria inoculant powder is usually considered necessary to start the process working, and some people coat pea seeds with it. But it will not work if the peas have been treated with a fungicide—and they usually are. This is why the pea seeds are often bright pink when you take them out of the packet. It is a signal for you to be careful not to let your children or pets eat the seeds, for the fungicide can be harmful. I think it is more important to use treated seeds with fungicide on them than it is to treat them with inoculant, because peas are prone to fungus diseases that can ruin the crop and linger in the soil. So I plant peas in soil that has been enriched with well-rotted manure, compost or a balanced fertilizer—and they seem to do fine.

PLANTING

A standard-sized packet of peas doesn't amount to much, since the seeds are so big, so I buy them the way I do corn seeds—in 1-pound packages. There are so many different ways to plant peas that you may want to try several before you decide which you like best. My choice of growing them on the wire fence around my garden is made for simplicity's sake; the fence is already there, and I don't have to erect another structure. Even dwarf varieties appreciate its support. But if I do this I make sure that I weed a strip a foot or so wide along the *outside* of the fence and cover it with mulch as if it were a part of the garden. If the weeds that normally border my garden were to start encroaching (as they always do), along the fence would not be a very choice spot. (In fact it is not a bad idea to have a cultivated, mulched strip along the entire outside of the garden fence, whatever you are growing.)

One thing to bear in mind with peas is that the vines are rather delicate. You do not want to step on them or fool with them in any way until it is time to pick them. Even cultivating and weeding can hurt the vines. A wide row or block is a good way to grow a lot of dwarf peas together. You will get a big harvest, while the peas help to support one another and also shade the ground so that few weeds can grow. You can make this row or patch as wide as you want it to be. If it is no more than 4 feet wide you can reach into the patch from either side to pick; but veteran gardener and writer Dick Raymond has a good pea-picking trick with his extra-wide rows: he puts a stool in the middle of them and sits on it to pick, doing no damage to the crop.

If you are growing tall peas, this planting pattern is impractical. You need something tall for them to grow on (Figure 47). My father has always grown them on brush—well-branched sticks he places in the ground so that they are at least 4 feet high. It gives his garden a more natural look than stakes and trellises would, and he just discards the brush at the end of the season. Another popular method is to plant one or two rows on either side of a vertical support. This can be wire fencing stretched between wood or metal posts, nylon mesh, or just horizontal strands of wire with perhaps some twine criss-crossed among them for extra support. Some people build rather elaborate wood or metal frames—single vertical types or double-A-frame types—that can be reused each year. I don't have much storage space, so I prefer the simplest possible structures. If you use a fine mesh such as chicken wire, it may be impossible to remove the vines at the end of the season and reuse it. A wide-spaced mesh is easier to reuse.

The method of support or nonsupport you use does not determine your method of planting the seeds, but other factors do. In wet soils, and for early crops, a raised bed is a good idea for peas to secure good drainage and warmer soil. Plant the seeds 1 inch deep. In warmer weather or drier soil trench planting is best. Make a trench about 4 inches deep with a spade or wide hoe, moisten it thoroughly with a hose, and plant the seeds in it, covering them with 1½ to 2 inches of soil. (The later the date, the deeper they go.) As the seedlings grow, you can either leave the trench partly unfilled to catch water or gradually fill it with soil, mounding some around the plants to keep the roots cool and help support the stems.

The seeds should be 1 to 2 inches apart, whether in rows or patches, and they should be planted at the depth specified above. I plant them by poking them in with my finger, then patting soil over the hole. Unless it is very wet I always moisten the bed or furrow thoroughly and keep the peas moist while they are sprouting.

GROWING

Once peas are planted there is not much

you need to do with them. A top dressing when seedlings are about 6 inches tall can be beneficial if you feel the soil is not sufficiently rich, or if you are trying to hurry up the crop before hot weather. Do not give them excessive nitrogen or the crop will be very leafy without many pods. At about this time you should mulch if you're trying for a spring crop planted in rows, since the weather is now warmer and the soil is apt to be drying out. Don't mulch earlier, though. If you mulch spring crops at planting time, you will keep the soil from warming up. Fall crops can be mulched lightly as soon as they are planted and more heavily as soon as the seeds are up an inch or two. Broad rows or blocks are not mulched at all.

PESTS AND DISEASES

There are a lot of things that *can* bother peas, but often nothing does. So don't let this list discourage you. Pea aphids can suck juice from the plants and spread mosaic disease. Hose them off and apply rotenone or pyrethrum if necessary. Pea weevils, which are tiny, brownish, black or white worms, burrow into the peas themselves and are common in some parts of the country. If you have them, dusting your crop with lime can help; or use rotenone. Any debris from infected plants should be destroyed, not tilled under. Even seed saved can contain weevils.

Birds sometimes eat the seeds or young seedlings. If your birds are this hungry, cover the bed or row with nylon mesh or chicken wire stretched over small stakes or hoops or with the wooden frames shown on page 205.

Mosaic virus, which makes the plants yellow and stunted, is best fought by curbing the aphids that spread it. Mildews occur in damp, warm weather and are curbed by dusting with sulfur and keeping leaves dry; destroy infected vines after harvest. Root rot is a fungus that makes the leaves turn yellow and the stems rot. Fusarium wilt distorts the leaves and stunts the plants. Both are best controlled by rotating the leguminous crops and growing resistant varieties.

Garden hygiene is especially important with peas. Even though it is a common practice to turn under pea crops because they enrich the soil so well, this should only be done if you are sure the crop does not have any viruses or fungi lurking in it.

HARVEST

Pick peas promptly! If you wait even a day too long they can lose their sweetness and flavor because the sucrose in them will turn to starch. If you wait several days too long you can also slow down production. Pea vines produce from the bottom up, so look for mature peas at the bottom first.

Traditional green peas are picked when you can feel full-sized round peas inside the pods but the peas do not feel hard. You can also open up a pod, look at the peas and taste them. Most edible-pod peas are picked before the peas form, when the pods are full-sized but still flat. 'Sugar Snap' peas can be picked when the peas are formed and will still be sweet and tender.

As soon as you pick garden peas, the sugar in them will start to turn to starch. So pick just before dinner. If you are not eating them right away, at least refrigerate them promptly, or freeze them right away. They will stay sweet when frozen. If you let any kind of peas go too far, you can leave them on the vine to harden and dry, then harvest, thresh and store them as dried peas.

VARIETIES

For early peas try 'Freezonian' or the very productive 'Little Marvel.' Good late varieties include 'Alderman' ('Tall Telephone'), an old favorite, and the heat-tolerant 'Lincoln' and 'Wando,' both good choices for the south or for summer crops. 'Dwarf Grey Sugar' is a bush snow pea, 'Sugar Daddy' is a stringless bush snow pea and 'Sugar Snap' is the tall one that tastes good even when mature. 'Sugar Ann' is a good bush snow pea for the north.

WAYS TO GROW PEAS   *Fig. 47*

On brush: Tall varieties need support. Cut some twiggy branches and "plant" them in the ground alongside your row. The plants will twine around the brush, which can be discarded after harvest.

On a trellis: Make lightweight wooden frames or use old window frames. Cover with wide-mesh wire and lean two together, joined at the top with wire or hinges.

Large Cherry pepper

bell pepper

Hungarian
Wax pepper

Gypsy Hybrid pepper

Long Red
Cayenne pepper

Peppers

I used to think of peppers as a slightly boring sidekick to tomatoes. I would buy the started plants along with tomatoes and plant them exactly as I planted tomatoes, at the same time, in the very next row. At harvest time I'd pick them together and try to think of things to cook with both tomatoes and peppers in them. That was fine, but I did gradually learn that peppers have their own needs and are fun on their own, especially if you experiment with the many different kinds you can grow from seed.

Not that there is anything wrong with the fat green peppers usually sold by nurseries. They are versatile as vegetables for stuffing, sliced for salads, and diced up for use in numerous cooked dishes. Some people automatically pick them while the peppers are green. This

is fine for those first early harvests or for when you want them to keep longer in the refrigerator. But let them get red on the plants and you will have sweeter, prettier, more vitamin-rich peppers (though fewer of them, since the fruit's ripening slows the plant's production). The sweetest of all are the bell peppers that turn yellow when ripe. There are also brown and purple bell peppers, and other sweet types such as pimientos or the sweet wax kind. Most interesting of all are the hot ones, which come in numerous shapes, sizes, colors and degrees of fieriness. Those who can tolerate the real firebombs claim that the more apparent damage to the tongue, the more harmful bacteria they will destroy in the rest of your body. But it's *your* stomach lining, so you decide whether to heed this counsel or not.

Peppers are easier than tomatoes in one sense: they rarely if ever need staking. But they are even fussier than tomatoes about needing warm weather to grow and ripen, and they are harder to bring to maturity before frost in cold climates. You can do it easily, though, if you pay attention to a few details. And the hot ones, which are warm-weather plants, have produced abundantly in my northern garden.

SITE

Give peppers a very sunny spot that they can occupy all season long, where peppers or other members of the same family have not grown recently. Raised beds are suitable. If you are growing both sweet and hot peppers, plant them in separate parts of the garden so that they cannot cross-pollinate. Otherwise you might find your sweet peppers have a zing you hadn't expected.

SOIL

People make outrageously disparate claims about what kind of soil peppers "demand": rich soil, not-so-rich soil, acid soil, sweet soil. I suspect that those stringent soil requirements are described by gardeners who have had to correct unusual imbalances in pH or fertility, and that common sense is the best approach. I have not found that peppers demand anything in particular when it comes to soil. They appreciate a nice sandy loam of moderately high fertility. A neutral pH is probably ideal. But the really crucial factors are temperature and water. You should not disrupt the growth process by suddenly transplanting peppers into cold soil or by letting them dry out. Start with a soil moderately enriched with manure or compost or 10–10–10. Magnesium is important

to peppers. This can be added by dusting the bed with a very fine layer of Epsom salts and digging it into the soil.

PLANTING

Seeds should be started indoors about eight weeks before the last average frost date. Since the seedlings do not like to be transplanted, I prefer to start them in peat pots, several seeds to a pot, then thin to the strongest one. It is important to keep the soil warm, at least 75 degrees if possible. Do not set out the plants in the garden unless it is warm—around 65 degrees by day and 55 degrees at night. Even if the danger of frost has passed, it is better to wait a week or two, even three if it is chilly, so growth will not be checked. If the plants are getting too big for their pots (they do not like this either), you can slit the sides of the peat pots and set them in larger pots of soil.

A good planting distance for peppers is 15 to 18 inches apart, depending on variety. Hot pepper plants are generally smaller than sweet ones and can go closer together. Collars are good insurance against cutworms. Some liquid fertilizer in the hole will help to start them off. Water well when planting.

GROWING

Top dress each plant with about a cupful of liquid fertilizer if the plants' leaf color is too pale or growth seems to be slow. Repeat this again in two weeks. Keep the soil evenly moist. After the ground has really warmed up you can use a mulch to accomplish this purpose.

Warm but not beastly hot weather will ripen the fruits properly, and there is not much you can do but wait for it. If the weather is too hot or cold, flowers may drop, but if you wait for the weather to change you will notice that more flowers form and set fruit.

PESTS AND DISEASES

Pests are rarely a problem. Aphids can damage pepper plants and slow down growth as well as spread mosaic virus. But they can be hosed off. 'Yolo Wonder' and many of the newer varieties resist mosaic and other viruses. Bacterial spot is best avoided in the future by rotating the crop. If whole peppers rot, you may have corn earworms. Find these borers and kill them so that they will not breed in the soil.

HARVEST

Picking can be done any time you have something that looks like a pepper. Pick them little or big, green or red, but don't stop picking or the plant will stop making peppers. And cut carefully with a knife or clippers rather than yank the pepper off the plant, or you may damage the stems.

VARIETIES

There are far too many good varieties of peppers to name them all here, but good bell pepper standbys include 'Yolo Wonder,' 'California Wonder,' 'Early Calwonder' and 'Bell Boy.' Among the good yellow-pepper varieties are 'Golden Bell,' 'Golden Summer,' 'Sweet Banana,' 'Gypsy' and the very sweet 'Quadrato D'Oro.' 'Cubanelle' is a popular frying pepper.

There is even more variety among hot peppers. 'Hungarian Yellow Wax,' good for the north, is medium-hot. 'Red Chili' is a medium-hot red, as is 'Tam Mild Jalapeno.' If you want to play with fire, grow 'Serrano Chili,' 'Large Hot Red Cherry' and 'Jalapeno.' For others consult specialty catalogs beginning on page 618.

Peppers are an important part of the "rainbow revolution" now going on in vegetables. You can get them in all sorts of odd colors, from the dark brown of 'Chocolate Bell,' to the bright purple of 'Aurora.' Many are both pretty and productive when grown in containers.

red potato   *white potato*   *fingerling potato*

Potatoes

I do not grow potatoes every year, even though I like them. For a humble root vegetable available for 29 cents a pound at the supermarket it has an awfully delicate constitution, with a host of diseases and Lord knows how many insects lying in wait for it in the garden. On the other hand, if I do bring a crop through the plagues, I will have done it with less chemical warfare than goes into the raising of commercial potatoes.

For some reason, I find all root crops fun to grow. They are like buried treasure; you do not know what you have until you harvest them. With potatoes I enjoy fishing around the soil at summer's end to see how many each plant has produced, though I have usually stolen some baby ones early on for "new potatoes."

Many people think that new potatoes are a specific type of potato, and in fact some varieties, especially the red-skinned ones, are best harvested as new potatoes. But actually a new potato is any early, immature one. When I was a child our local farm stand used to sell these in "small," "medium" and "large" sizes, ranging from pea-sized to mothball-sized to golf ball-sized. You rarely see such luxury as that today, but you can have some wonderful early meals either by digging up one whole plant before its prime or by robbing here and there around the edges of your hills. Simmer them in butter, covered, with no liquid; or steam them and make a salad with the first sweet raw early peas, an oil-and-vinegar dressing, and some fresh herbs—the taste of spring itself!

There are also some very exotic potatoes out there, though they can sometimes be elusive. I once drove all over Vermont asking farmers about a wonderful local potato I had tasted. It had a very crisp skin when baked and an unusually flavorful, good-textured inside. I never did find it or learn what variety it was, and I would welcome any clues. Nor have I ever seen, in American markets, the mealy, yellow-fleshed potatoes I enjoyed eating in South America. But I have been able to buy seed potatoes for German "fingerling" or "ladyfinger" potatoes, which are tiny, yellow and shaped like fingers, and I have grown them successfully. They are a delicious gourmet crop for a small garden.

(Sweet potatoes are not closely related to regular potatoes. They are vine plants of the morning glory family and while the two have some things in common, they are grown rather differently, so I will discuss them later.)

When we talk of potato "seed" we do not mean seed in the usual sense, though potatoes have these too. Seed potatoes are mature potatoes that are planted in the ground, sometimes whole but usually cut into pieces. You know what happens to a potato when it has been in your kitchen too long. Its "eyes" send out long white stems, which if left to grow would produce leaves and flowers. A potato, if planted in the soil, will produce these too, but it will also produce long roots underground, from which more potatoes, or "tubers" will grow. The foliage grows first, when the weather is warm, then as cooler weather approaches the tubers start to form. They are dug up after the rest of the plant has finished growing and died down.

In the north potatoes are a summer crop, but in warm climates they're planted in late winter or late summer so they will not mature during very hot weather. The crop can take two and a half to four months to mature, depending on whether you are growing it for early new potatoes or a high-yield storage crop. In any climate you can do both with one planting, harvesting some potatoes early and letting the rest grow. You can also plant two separate varieties, early and main-season. Or you can make two separate plantings in suc-cession, both for early potatoes, if you have not much interest in storing them.

SITE

Choose a fairly sunny spot where potatoes, tomatoes and other related crops have not grown recently. You also want a spot that has not been limed heavily and recently, since potatoes like a more acid soil than most vegetables (between 5.0 and 6.5). Alkaline soils are more conducive to a disease called "scab," which produces rough spots on the tubers but seldom really ruins the crop. So it is not something to lose a lot of sleep over.

SOIL

Good soil is important to potatoes, though, since they are a root crop. Potato soil should not be extremely rich but should be very well drained and well aerated. Heavy clay soils not only make it hard for full sized tubers to develop, but they drain poorly and cause tubers to rot. As usual, plenty of organic matter is the best medicine. Beware of fresh manure, though. A well-rotted compost is best, with bone meal or superphosphate and potassium, preferably from greensand or granite dust—not wood ashes, which are alkaline.

PLANTING

Always buy *certified disease-free seed potatoes* each year. I once grew a crop by simply cutting potatoes I bought in the supermarket and planting them, but I was probably just lucky. Besides, store potatoes have often been treated with a chemical that keeps the eyes from sprouting, and this may take weeks to wear off.

The conventional way to grow potatoes is to plant them in a shallow trench that is filled part way with soil. Then as the plants grow you gradually mound soil up around them to give them more and more underground space in which the tubers can grow under cover and away from the light. Light turns potatoes green, and these green areas are poisonous (as are the white sprouts from the eyes). But some gardeners grow potatoes right on top of the soil, covering them with layers of mulch as they grow, instead. They claim that pests and diseases are avoided this way. But I would worry about mice, who eat potatoes and often burrow in mulch. Another good method is to grow the plants in large containers that you gradually fill with soil. Gardeners talk of bounteous harvests in garbage cans, plastic tubs and barrels.

You can plant potatoes several weeks before the last average frost date but not if the ground is still wet. Potatoes rot easily. Shaking them in a paper bag with a fungicide will kill some disease-causing fungi. Do this after the potatoes have been cut up for planting,

making sure all the surfaces get dusted. Another good way to fight rot is to "cure" the surfaces of the cut pieces by letting them sit for a few days in a fairly cool, dry place so their cut surfaces will harden.

The potatoes should be cut so that each piece has one to three eyes on it and enough potato flesh to give the young sprout some nourishment to grow on for a while. A quarter of an average-sized potato is a good size. It is said that chunks with only one eye will produce bigger potatoes; those with more eyes will produce them in greater numbers.

Dig your trench about 6 inches deep and place the pieces of potato a foot apart. Cover with 4 inches of soil, with the eyes facing up. The rows should not be too close together, because you will need plenty of extra soil between the rows for hilling. Some compost in the bottom of the trench will get them off to a good start.

GROWING

In a few weeks you will see green foliage. Let it get 4–6 inches tall and then start hilling with a wide hoe, bringing soil almost to the top of the leaves from both sides of the row. Keep hilling till the plants are at least a foot tall and flowers start to appear, bringing in extra soil as needed. Do it very carefully so that you don't chop up any of the roots or young tubers. Water during drought to keep the tubers growing but not after the foliage has died down. Top dressing should not be necessary unless your soil is very sandy.

PESTS AND DISEASES

You may play host to Colorado potato beetles, flea beetles, leafhoppers, aphids or wireworms, but the first is the main pest to watch out for. It is yellow

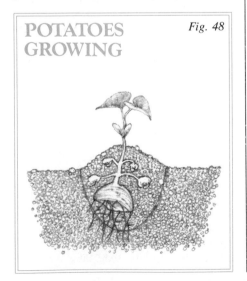

POTATOES GROWING   *Fig. 48*

with black stripes, and the larvae look like bloated pink ladybugs. Almost every pototo patch has them sooner or later, but they are not hard to hand pick. You can also scrape off the reddish egg masses that you find under the leaves. Aphids and other insects can spread disease and should be hosed or picked off or, as a last resort, dusted with a safe insecticide.

The worst disease of potatoes is "late blight," the cause of the great Irish potato famine that brought waves of immigrants to our shores in the nineteenth century. Alas, the Irish are no safer from potato blight here. If your potato foliage becomes blackened, then moldy, it has this blight. Burn it, then wait a few weeks to dig any potatoes that are under the soil. Fight blight with clean seed, fungicides and crop rotation, and hope that you do not run into long spells of the cool, damp weather that seems to foster it.

HARVEST

After the potato foliage dies, you can leave the potatoes in the ground for a few weeks, but dig them if you are expecting a heavy frost or if you are having a warm, wet spell that might start new foliage sprouting. The sprouts will use the food supply in the tubers, making them soft, just as they would in your kitchen.

As I said above, immature potatoes for immediate consumption can be dug at any time, but for good storage potatoes, wait till the skins are mature enough that they do not peel easily. Dig—*carefully*—with a digging fork or potato hoe, starting from the outside of the hill and getting down under the potatoes so that you don't spear or scratch them (the potato hoe, with its curved tines, does this just right). Dig on a dry day, if possible, when the soil is also rather dry, and let the potatoes dry for a day or so before you store them.

Ideal storage conditions are dark and cold but not freezing, just slightly humid but not damp, and well ventilated. Do not wash the potatoes before storing, and do not pile them more than a foot or so deep.

VARIETIES

The standard red early potato is 'Red Pontiac,' but 'Red La Soda' is also good, and both are heat-tolerant for southern gardens. 'Red Norland' is also a fine potato. Favorite white potatoes are the early 'Irish Cobbler,' and the later 'Kennebec' and 'Katahdin' for storing. 'Russet Burbank' is a good white baking potato for north or south, 'Sebago' for the north. 'Viking' and 'Norgold Russet' are good baked or boiled. 'Crystal' is a productive northern variety. 'Fingerling' or 'Lady Finger' is the luscious small, thin, yellow one.

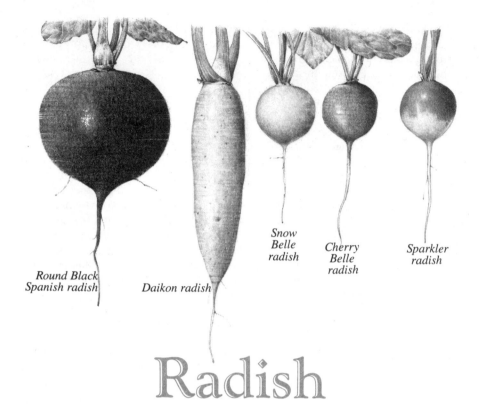

Round Black Spanish radish

Daikon radish

Snow Belle radish

Cherry Belle radish

Sparkler radish

Radish

Radishes earn their keep better than any vegetable in the garden. They germinate faster, mature faster and take up less space than almost anything you can grow, and so they are an ideal companion plant and space filler between rows of slower crops. They are so compact they can be grown easily in containers, even indoors in a sunny window. Sown in the garden as a "nurse crop," with slow-sprouting parsley, carrots or parsnips, they help mark the row and shade these more delicate seedlings from the hot sun until they are tough enough to make it on their own. A "sacrifice" radish row will reportedly lure root maggots away from the more time-consuming, less expendable plants in the cabbage family, of which radish is a member. And the plant is even seen as a deterrent against bugs such as cucumber beetle.

For such a hard-working vegetable, the radish is, unfortunately, not versatile in the kitchen. But if you have run out of ways to cook or serve radishes, you can also experiment with some of the lesser-known radish varieties. The familiar little round red balls are great, but have you ever eaten the long white radishes? Or tried "winter" or "Chinese" radishes? These are usually long and white or big, black and round. They are good cooked in stews or stir-fried as well as raw. You can even let some of your radishes go to seed and eat the little seed pods, peppery when raw, mild when cooked as a green vegetable.

If you did any gardening as a child, you were probably handed a packet of radish seeds. This is a perfect crop for kids, because the seeds are just big enough to plant singly, and they germinate in about five days. An impatient young grower can check the row from time to time, watching the little red roots become more and more like radishes, then eat his or her prize crop in as little as three weeks.

Since radishes are a cool-weather crop and can stand a touch of frost, early spring is the best time to start them, but succession plantings can be made for most of the growing season. Very hot midsummer weather is the least kind to radishes, but fall produces fine ones, especially the "winter" kinds that take up to two months to mature but keep well for months of fall and winter eating. In the south, radishes are often a winter crop.

SITE

Radishes will tolerate some shade, but I still try to give then plenty of good sun if I can. The main goal is to get them to grow quickly so that they will be mild in flavor, tender, and crisp in texture. A crop that sits in the ground and matures slowly is apt to taste too strong and have a tough, woody texture.

It is easy to find a spot for radishes, though, because they take up so little room. Just 1 or 2 square feet will grow as many radishes as I need in one harvest. Succession crops (see below) help to spread the supply out over the season.

SOIL

Soil should be a sandy loam that warms quickly and presents no obstacle to root development, with plenty of humus for moisture retention. If you have a clay soil you will have better luck with winter radishes than with the early ones. The late ones also like a deeply cultivated, deeply enriched soil. Fertility is important for both, especially phosphorus and potassium; nitrogen should be there in sufficient quantity for quick growth, but it shouldn't be present in excess or you will have big leafy tops and skinny little radishes. Wood ashes are a good potassium source that will also help keep root maggots at bay if sprinkled on top of the soil or dug in an inch or two.

PLANTING

Radishes are sown directly in the garden, not transplanted, but they may be grown very early in a cold frame or hotbed if you like. Sow early varieties as soon as the ground is workable, but don't sow when your soil is still mucky, or the roots might crack. Successive plantings can then be made every week or two to ensure a steady supply, since radishes don't store well either in the ground or after harvest. Fall radishes started in early or midsummer can be either the fast-maturing types or "winter radishes." Usually the big black ones are the last ones to mature; they also keep best in the ground.

If you have found one radish variety that is definitely "your radish," buy several packets of the seed and plant it in succession. But if you are still exploring, it is more fun to buy several different kinds, especially if you are not sure which ones are the best for your region. Trial and error is painless if you are growing something this easy and quick.

Work a little fertilizer into a single row, a wide row, or a broad patch, bearing in mind how deep your roots will go, depending on the variety. Moisten the soil and sow the seed ½ inch deep, a bit deeper in warmer weather. Single rows can be anywhere from 6 to 18 inches apart depending on the variety and your space requirements. Space the seeds about an inch apart if you can, though they will be thinned to this distance later when the plants are 1–2 inches tall. Thinning distance is 3–6 inches apart for the large late types. If you are sowing along with a late crop such as carrots, you should sow fewer radish seeds than carrot seeds so you might want to plant another row of radishes by themselves, depending on the size of both the carrot patch and your appetite for radishes.

GROWING

Mulch if possible and keep the plants watered for the best mild flavor. They should not need top dressing unless your soil is very poor or sandy. Cultivate very carefully to keep weeds down if you have not used a mulch.

PEST AND DISEASES

Root maggots may bother radishes, but not much else will. To fight these, rotate your cabbage-family crops and use wood ashes as a deterrent. Some gardeners also swear by putting screen cages over the plants, or placing tar paper on the ground around them or sprinkling coffee grounds. Since maggots are a spring insect, you won't have to worry about them with later crops.

Flea beetles love them.

HARVEST

Harvest spring and summer radishes as soon as they are full grown. Do not let them go too long or they will be tough and tasteless. Winter radishes can be stored in damp sand, sawdust or peat in a root cellar or another area that can be kept around 40 degrees. They will last up to two months.

VARIETIES

Good quick red varieties include 'Cherry Belle' (small, round and bright red), 'French Breakfast' (more oval), 'Scarlet Globe,' 'Sparkler' and 'Champion.' 'All Seasons' can be held in the ground longer than most. 'Crimson Giant' and 'White Icicle' (a 4- to 5-inch cylinder) thrive in summer. 'Easter Egg' hybrid is round, in mixed shades of pink, red and white.

Good winter radishes are the mild 'White Chinese' (6–8 inches long), 'China Rose' (like a small, stubby pink carrot) and 'Round Black Spanish' (a large, round, hot radish). 'Sakurajima' is a very large mild Japanese one, and 'Daikon' is a long white Japanese radish served pickled as an appetizer.

Rhubarb

E ven if you are not a big rhubarb eater, it is nice to have a plant or two because they are so undemanding. One of the few perennial vegetables, rhubarb just keeps coming up every year, sending out long, celerylike stalks for rhubarb pies, steamed rhubarb, rhubarb jams, jellies, syrups, juices—even wine. If you did absolutely nothing nice for it at all, it would still give you some good pies each season. With a little extra attention it will produce all the more; and indeed, you might well become a big rhubarb eater if you have such a handy supply. It freezes well for winter use; you can even force a plant indoors, for fresh winter rhubarb. And it also provides a fruitlike dish in spring and early summer when other fruits are not yet bearing. If you do become so addicted, you can divide and replant rhubarb to increase your supply.

A rhubarb plant is a big mound almost 3 feet wide and almost as tall. Its huge leaves are supported by stalks that are usually crimson, but are sometimes green like a thick stalk of celery. I prefer the red because it is more tasty, more tender and more beautiful, both in the garden and on the plate. The poisonous leaves are never eaten, but the stalks are rich in vitamins and flavor. They are very acid, and so are cooked with sugar. Thus they are classified with fruits, even though the fruiting part of the rhubarb plant is never allowed to mature.

Rhubarb is not suited to hot, dry climates. The plant will grow, but not vigorously, and it will go to seed too easily. Rhubarb also likes to have its roots frozen in the winter, at least a few inches down, so that it can go through the necessary period of dormancy. But certain varieties will grow well in relatively mild climates such as that of northern California.

SITE

Choose a spot that is out of the way—the back row of the garden. Since the planting is permanent, it will not be part of your annual tilling-under or crop-rotation program. Planting it on the sunny side of your asparagus patch is a good idea. The two crops are planted, grown and harvested in much the same way, and it is convenient to work on the two together. In my garden the rhubarb is right next to the sorrel, another perennial crop. A sunny location is important for red-stalked varieties; otherwise the plants will stay green.

SOIL

Like asparagus, rhubarb needs a deep, fertile, well-drained soil. The large roots will spread several feet out and several feet deep, so cultivate the whole area. If you can, dig in a half-bushel or so of well-rotted manure or compost for every plant you expect to grow. The pH should be slightly acid—between 5.5 and 6.5.

PLANTING

Rhubarb is not generally grown from seed, but from divisions of existing clumps. Divisions have one or more buds ("eyes"). Rhubarb seeds cannot be trusted to breed true and they also take a long time to produce mature plants. If you already have an established clump of rhubarb, divide it in half where it grows. Hold a sharp spade over the clump with two hands and plunge it straight down the middle. Leave one half in the soil, where it will keep growing, invigorated by this pruning. Divide the rest into many one-eyed pieces if you want many immature plants, or several larger pieces if you want only a few plants that will bear soon. If you do not have a plant to divide or a friend who is dividing theirs, buy your divisions from a nursery or a mail-order company.

Plant in early spring as soon as the ground has dried out enough to be worked (in milder climates plant in fall). Make a deep, wide trench as for asparagus and dig rich organic matter into the bottom. If you are planting only one

division, just make one deep, wide hole about 2 feet in diameter. Rhubarb has big, thick, hungry roots that will spread out farther than the circumference of the part above ground and deeper than the plant is tall. Also remember this is a permanent bed that you will not redig each year, so make sure a large enough area has the proper enrichment and good soil texture. Place the root so that the crown is 2 inches below the soil surface.

The rhubarb division will take hold faster if there are some roots dangling from the crown. If so, make a mound of soil in the bottom of the trench and spread the roots over it. I think 3 feet apart is a good distance, but bear in mind that some varieties produce larger plants than others. Try to find out from the person who sold or gave you the plant how large it will grow to be.

GROWING

The next spring after planting you should top dress the young rhubarb plant with manure or a granular or liquid commercial fertilizer. The more food and water you give rhubarb, the more stalks it will produce and the thicker they will be. There is little danger of overfeeding. But make sure that water can drain into the soil around the plant, not collect around the root, stems and leaves, because standing water can rot them. Mulch after the ground has warmed up, drawing the mulch away in early spring to let the sun warm the soil around the crowns and coax them into early-spring production.

Later on in the summer, the plant will send up very tall, thick, round stalks that look different from the leaf stalks and produce whitish, plumelike flowers. Cut these stalks near the base, before the flowers form if possible. If the plant sends up a lot of these, it will produce fewer and thinner leaf stalks, or even stop producing altogether.

To force a rhubarb plant in your cellar for winter eating, dig one up before the ground freezes in fall, trying to get as many of the roots as possible and leaving as much soil around them as you can. Put it in a large container and fill in around it with light soil, moistened peat moss, or moistened sawdust. The crowns should be cut back almost to the roots and covered with several inches of whatever potting medium you are using. Leave the container outdoors and let it freeze at least once. A month to six weeks outdoors is even better. Then bring it into a cool, dark place (about 40 degrees) if you are going to keep it dormant for a while. Keep the soil moist but not soggy wet. When you want it to start growing, bring it into a somewhat warmer area (about 60 degrees) and the plant will start sending up nice edible stalks. When it has finished producing you can either throw it away or replant it in the spring. Production may be set back for a while, but the plant will regroup eventually.

Rhubarb plants are not easily discouraged! A clump will thrive almost indefinitely without being divided, though dividing will benefit the plant. When a plant is old, the stalks will be very numerous but thinner.

PESTS AND DISEASES

If you see black spots on the stems of your plants, they probably have rhubarb curculio, also known as rusty snout beetle. It bores into the stalks, crowns and roots and can be kept in check by constant picking off; or you can spray in midspring with rotenone if you anticipate their arrival. They are very attracted to dock, a common weed. So make sure you do not have any of that growing in or around your garden.

Occasionally the plants get "foot-rot," causing the stalks to rot at the bottom. Dig up the whole plant and burn it if this happens, and if you have been mulching the rhubarb patch, stop. Give the plants plenty of air circulation, and if they are in a shady location, find them a sunnier one. Moving the whole row will help to avoid rot the next year, too.

I always notice a few dead leaves at the bottom of my rhubarb plants from time to time throughout the summer. This is normal, not a sign of a grave disease; the leaves rot because they're resting on the ground. I just pick them off and get rid of them, the way I would any garden debris.

HARVEST

The first year you plant rhubarb you should not harvest any of the edible stalks, but do cut back the flower stalks. The second spring you can pick the ones that are at least an inch thick, but most of them should be left on the plant to form leaves so that the roots can grow. (Keep removing the flower stalks, though.) The third year you can pick the thick stalks for about a month. From the fourth year on, pick as many of the thick ones as you like. I have cut near the base with a knife without any problems, but the usual way is to twist the stalk and give it a tug. This is said to leave the stalk less receptive to disease and rot. I pick mine until midsummer or so, and stop when the stalks are coming in thin.

VARIETIES

The standard green rhubarb is 'Victoria'—a big, vigorous plant. Favorite red varieties include 'Ruby' and 'Valentine,'' the last especially resistant to disease. 'Cherry' and 'Giant Cherry' are good choices for areas with mild winters such as California.

Spinach

Spinach is regaining its popularity as a garden vegetable because more people are using it in salads. I still love it best cooked just long enough to wilt it, with some olive oil in which I've crushed a clove of garlic. It also freezes well. It is not hard to grow, and it is also a quick crop—forty to fifty days to harvest, and even less if you eat the thinnings when you thin your rows.

The problem most gardeners have with spinach is that they try to treat it like lettuce. It is a cold-weather crop, like lettuce, but even more so. It bolts in hot weather just as lettuce will but does so more quickly. Spinach is really a spring or fall crop, though you can edge a bit into the summer months if you grow a "long-standing" type. Though heat and dryness are factors, it is the lengthening days that cause spinach to bolt, or to send up a tall, useless seed stalk and stop producing. The lengthening days approaching midsummer signal the spinach to go to seed. In warm climates it is grown in late fall, winter and early spring. Even in the north, some gardeners sow seeds in late fall that come up in the spring—not foolproof, but worth a try.

There are two kinds of spinach. The most familiar is the dark green, crinkly leaved sort; the other is a lighter colored, flat-leaved version. "New Zealand spinach" and "Malabar spinach" are not really spinach, though both taste something like it when cooked and are sometimes grown as spinach substitutes in warm climates or warm weather.

SITE

Plant spinach in full sun or part shade—the latter if the crop will be growing in warm weather. You might start a fall spinach crop between rows of a tall crop such as corn or beans, which will have been harvested once cool weather comes. Spinach for salads needs only a few square feet of space for the whole crop. For growing spinach to cook, however, I recommend a good 40 square feet at least, because it loses so much volume in cooking (or freezing).

SOIL

Spinach prefers a light soil, but with plenty of organic matter. Otherwise the soil will not retain the moisture the plant needs. As a leafy crop it thrives on very fertile soil, and it is almost impossible to overfeed it. Nitrogen is especially important. If you are using commercial fertilizer for it, 10–10–10 is a good choice. You do not need to fertilize the soil to a great depth, though, because the plants are shallow-rooted. They are a little fussy about pH, preferring the 6.0–7.0 range, so add lime if your soil is acid, but don't go overboard because it doesn't like very alkaline soil either.

PLANTING

Spinach is sown directly into the garden or cold frame. Purchase new seed each year because it does not stay viable for very long. For spring planting you can start as soon as there is some ground in your garden that has thawed. This might be as early as eight weeks before the last frost. Some gardeners even get the furrow ready in the fall, so all they need to do the following spring is drop the seeds in and not worry about working the soil while it is still muddy.

Plant single rows 12 to 15 inches apart, or plant several rows close together (about 6 inches) with a space of 1½ to 2 feet on either side, or plant in a block so that plants will all be 1 foot apart each way after thinning. Seeds should be ½ inch deep and if possible 1 inch apart. They will germinate in five to nine days, or a bit more if it is very cold. When there are two true leaves on the plants, they should be thinned to 4 inches apart, then thinned again so that the plants are 8 to 12 inches apart. Use the discarded young plants in salads.

Unless you want a great deal of spinach all at once for cooking or freezing, it is best to save half a packet or so, then sow one or more extra crops at intervals of about ten days. But stop sowing around mid-May; the idea is not to have spinach maturing during the long, warm days of July and August. May sowings should be of a long-standing type, as an extra safeguard against bolting.

Start fall sowings in late August, even later in warm climates. These should be sown a little thicker and deeper than spring crops, because germination is less reliable in warm weather. It helps to keep the soil moist with frequent watering and/or a light layer of salt hay.

GROWING

Mulching will help to keep the soil moist, but I would avoid a very acid mulch such as sawdust, bark or peat moss because these can lower the pH below the plants' tolerance. Salt hay or straw is better. If you are overwintering a crop by keeping young plants dormant, it is best to mulch them heavily after the ground freezes to keep it frozen evenly. Alternate freezing and thawing can damage the plants.

Cultivating or weeding is important if you do not mulch, but do it carefully so as not to harm the spinach plants' shallow root systems. When the plants are 4 to 6 inches tall, a top dressing with a high-nitrogen fertilizer such as fish emulsion or bone meal will spur growth. With spring crops remember to keep the growth going to bring the plants to maturity before they can bolt.

PESTS AND DISEASES

Home gardeners generally do not have many problems of this sort. Spinach leaf miner larvae burrow inside the leaves and produce tan patches. The easiest control is to pick off affected leaves and destroy them. Keeping the garden free of debris and weeds will help. By growing very early or late crops, you might avoid this bug's season. You can also cover young plants with a very fine mesh or cheesecloth so that the fly that lays the eggs that produce these larvae cannot land on the plants.

Spinach blight, or "yellows," is a mosaic virus spread by aphids. The leaves turn yellow, and the plants are stunted. You can control the virus by controlling the aphids, or you can grow resistant varieties. Also practice good garden hygiene. If there are yellow spots on the leaves and a moldy substance underneath, the problem is the disease called blue mold. It appears occasionally in very wet weather. Best defenses are weed control, good drainage, and vigorous, well-fed plants. If they still get blue mold, throw them out and try again in better weather. Fusarium wilt can affect spinach, but there are resistant strains you can grow.

HARVEST

You can reap your spinach two different ways—by cutting the outside leaves and letting the centers keep producing, or by cutting the whole plant just at soil level, like a head of lettuce. I think the best approach is to cut some outside leaves as you need them but not to leave the plant growing too long. Always cut the whole plant if you see buds starting to form at the center; otherwise it will bolt and become useless. Sometimes the roots will send up some new leaves after the plant is cut but not enough to warrant leaving them there if you need the space.

VARIETIES

'Long Standing Bloomsdale,' a savoy, or ruffled type, is probably the most popular bolt-resistant spinach. But also try 'Popeye's Choice' and 'America.' For fall crops grow the cold-resistant 'Winter Bloomsdale.' 'Melody' and 'Hybrid Number 7' are more disease-resistant than most. 'Giant Nobel' is a good smooth-leaved spinach.

Sweet Dumpling squash

acorn squash

patty pan squash

zucchini

yellow crookneck squash

butternut squash

Squash, Pumpkins and Gourds

These members of the cucurbit or cucumber family are all closely related and like most of the same growing conditions. They all look very different; in fact their odd assortment of shapes is one of the fun things about growing them. Gourds are actually hollow, hard-shelled squash, and zucchini are actually a kind of pumpkin. The American Indians were growing gourds, squash and pumpkins when the European settlers arrived. Wherever you live, there are a number of excellent ones that you can grow.

Summer Squash

This group includes the familiar green zucchini (called "marrow" in England and *cocozelle* elsewhere in Europe), the equally familiar yellow crooknecks and straightnecks, and the less familiar but delicious scallop squash or 'Patty Pan.' All are extremely easy to grow, unless your summers are very cold and rainy. All you need is fifty to sixty days of good warm weather.

A few summer squash plants do not take up much room in a small garden, since they are all bush type, but some people are slow to realize that they only need a few plants. I once fed three families from one zucchini plant, though one or two plants per family is a more realistic number, especially if you intend to freeze some. Some people think that summer squash does not freeze well, but my mother freezes them sliced with diced onions, and they taste wonderful cooked together. With more than three plants you will find yourself making squash soup, squash bread, squash ice cream, squash compost. I would rather plant just one green, one yellow and one scallop, and leave the rest of the seeds in their packets where they will keep nicely for four years, than have people say, "Uh oh, here she comes with all her extra zucchini."

SITE

Find a sunny spot with good drainage, where other cucurbits have not been growing recently. Allow 10–16 square feet per plant.

SOIL

All squash like fertile soil with plenty of organic matter to retain moisture. They are heavy feeders and drinkers, because they produce big stems, big leaves and for the most part big fruits. Their ideal pH is around 6.0–6.5. The old bushel-of-manure-per-plant trick is great for them but could be a little expensive unless you keep horses, cows, chickens or other resident manure producers. Otherwise, dig in a lot of moistened or composted peat moss and a generous handful of 5–10–5 per plant, and they will do fine. Distribute this enrichment throughout the planting area, and the plants' far-ranging root systems will find it.

PLANTING

With summer squash I always plant seeds directly in the garden as soon as danger of frost has passed, but you can also start them inside if you really want to get a jump on the season. Squash and pumpkin seeds should be purchased, not saved from previous crops, unless you can be certain they have not cross-pollinated with another variety. Otherwise you will get some very odd-looking, inedible fruits. I plant the seeds six to a hill (page 48) and 1 inch deep, thin to the best three seedlings, then thin to one seedling when the plants are fairly big. I put summer squash plants 3–4 feet apart. Closer planting will lead to lower yields, and I would rather have a few big bushy plants with space around them. I like to be able to walk around them easily and peer under the big leaves to look for ripening squash.

You do well to protect the young seedlings with something to keep off the cucumber beetles, especially if you are growing only one plant of each variety. It is when the plants are very small, with few leaves to spare, that you are apt to lose them to beetles. This can happen before you even know the bugs are there. You need a material such as agricultural cloth (page 206) that will let in light and water but not the beetles. Anchor it with rocks and remove it when the plants grow larger, or leave it in place to ward off borers if these are also a problem.

GROWING

The first pretty yellow flowers that appear are male. You should eat them— seriously. Squash blossoms are good in salads, good sautéed, and good deep-fried as fritters. There will be plenty of them to spare, because you only need a few male ones for pollination. The female flowers follow a week or so later and can be recognized by a small bump of "squash to be" just behind them on the stalk. You can eat some of the female flowers too, and the plant will just keep producing more.

Weed the plants when they are young; later the big leaves will shade the ground and keep most weeds from growing, especially annual ones. A mulch will help to conserve moisture, keep weeds down, and even discourage cucumber beetles. But water the plants anyway if the ground is very dry, and top dress from time to time if your soil is poor.

PESTS AND DISEASES

Cucumber beetles may still appear on older plants. They are yellow with black stripes, and they can spread mosaic and bacterial wilt as well as eat the plants (see pages 69–74 for forms of control). Another pest, the squash bug, lays red eggs on the underside of the leaves. Scrape these off and destroy them, and spray with rotenone or pyrethrum late in the day if they are a serious problem.

Squash can contract a number of diseases: fusarium wilt, powdery and downy mildew, bacterial wilt, mosaic virus, and blossom-end rot. The best defense is to keep the plants as vigorous as possible with plenty of water and fertile soil. Burn any debris, rotate your crops, and use fungicides as needed.

HARVEST

When my summer squash are really producing I try to pick them every day. They taste best when they are very small—about 6 or 8 inches long, or 3 to 4 inches in diameter for the scallops. Large, mature squashes can be stuffed and baked, but frankly the plants' energies are best put to use in making lots of delectable little ones. If you forget to pick, or go out of town for a week, you will find huge green zucchini monsters hiding under the leaves—and believe me, the green ones are good at hiding (an argument for choosing yellow squash). Making big squash causes the plant to slow down its production. When I pick summer squash I cut them off with a grapefruit knife; pulling or twisting them may damage the plant.

VARIETIES

Good zucchini varieties include 'Aristocrat,' 'Ambassador,' 'President Hybrid,' 'Gourmet Globe' (a round one) and 'Gold Rush' (a compact bush that looks like a yellow straightneck but is actually a yellow zucchini). Good yellows are 'Early Prolific Straightneck,' 'Goldbar,' 'Early Summer Crookneck' and 'Seneca Prolific.' Scallops include 'Peter Pan,' 'Early White,' 'Bush Scallop,' the yellow 'Sunburst' and the green 'Scallopini.'

Winter Squash

Fewer people grow winter squash than summer, which is a shame because they are richer in vitamins and, to my mind, tastier. They also keep a long time in storage, for those who like to eat their own produce most of the year. But since winter squash are eaten mature, not very young like summer squash, they take almost twice as long to bring to harvest, and you need a good, long, warm season in which to grow them. They are mostly vine types, too, and as a consequence need a good deal of space. Squash vines can grow 20 feet long, though 10 or 12 is more usual. Nonetheless I have enjoyed growing them in the north, especially the early-maturing varieties, and there are ways of managing them in relatively small gardens. Some varieties come in bush form, though not necessarily the best-tasting ones.

Butternut and buttercup are good traditional garden types that are still popular; buttercups are especially good for cool summers. Hubbard squash are quite enormous, but great keepers. And there are several smaller, earlier-maturing winter squash, such as 'Delicata' and 'Gold Nugget' that are a joy to grow. I have had good luck especially with 'Delicata,' a small, cylindrical squash with green and cream-colored stripes that I have never seen for sale in produce departments, and with 'Sweet Dumpling,' a very small pumpkin striped in green and white.

SITE

Choose a sunny site if possible. I have grown winter squash between rows of corn to save space and to help keep raccoons out of the corn patch. (They do not like to walk on the prickly squash leaves.) But the crop was probably not as prolific as it would have been without the shade cast by the corn stalks.

The other site requirement is plenty of space. Winter squash production will not run away from you in terms of sheer numbers of fruit the way that of summer squash will, but the vines will run across the garden and beyond. There are several solutions to this problem: to let them run out of the garden into the weeds or the lawn if they will not be in the way; to turn the tips of the vines gently back the way they came, so that they double back just as if returning to the garden were their idea in the first place; and to snip off the fuzzy tips of the vines once they have produced a few squashes. (This will make them mature faster anyway.) Some people trellis winter squash, but the supports have to be something resembling steel girders to hold the vines, and the squashes themselves need to be supported by slings unless they are very small types. I draw the line at that. The thought of a wall of squashes reclining in old rags or panty hose would send me into my stack of seed catalogs in search of a "good, compact bush variety," which I would then grow more or less like zucchini.

SOIL

The soil should be the same as for summer squash.

PLANTING

Winter squash seeds can be sown the same way as summer squash, but in cold climates it is probably wise to start them indoors or in a cold frame four to six weeks ahead. Using peat pots will make transplanting more painless; the seedlings do not like to have their root systems disturbed. If your soil is dry, put seeds or plants in a shallow basin; if it is very damp, put them in a low mound. If sown directly in the garden, seeds are usually sown in hills of several seeds and thinned to one strong seedling. The plants should be placed 4 feet apart in rows 6 feet apart, or in a grid pattern with plants 5 feet apart each way. Compact varieties can be planted closer together.

GROWING

Winter squash generally lie on the ground a long time while they are maturing, and consequently they can rot on the bottom. It helps to put mulch under them, or something you can slide under each fruit such as a piece of wood, or plastic, or a shingle. Keep an eye out for wilted vines caused by vine borer (see above). If your growing season is short, cut off the late-appearing flowers after you have some nice fruits on the vines—anywhere from one to six per vine, depending on how prolific the variety. All the plants' energy will then go into the production of those fruits.

PESTS AND DISEASES

Squash-vine borers generally do the most damage to winter squash, which grow on vines—a nice long vine will suddenly die, wiping out all the fruits on that vine. Look for a little telltale pile of excrement (it resembles sawdust) and find the little white grub inside the stem by making a lengthwise slit. Remove the grub and bury that section of the vine. It may reroot and allow the fruits on it to mature. Preventive measures that some gardeners use include dousing squash stems with rotenone, mounding soil around the stems or wrapping them with aluminum foil.

HARVEST

You should leave the squash on the vines till they are mature. Squash will not ripen after picking the way tomatoes will, and unlike summer squash, winter kinds do not taste good young. How do you know when they are mature? Some varieties, such as the buttercups, are ripe when their stems turn dry. But the only really sure way to tell with most of them is to see what the ripe ones look like in the supermarket or in pictures on seed packets or in catalogs. If you are trying a new variety and you can't find a picture of it, you may have to simply use trial and error. Eat one early, let another one go late; you'll figure it out. But be sure you harvest them before frost. If the "frost is on the pumpkin" your pumpkin—or squash—has no business being in the garden. If some of the squash are still unripe and a frost is coming, pick all the ripe ones and cover the unripe ones with something like a heavy straw mulch. Or very carefully gather all the vines together without breaking them and spread a large blanket or tarp over them. Newspapers anchored with rocks might also work. But remove any of these covers in the morning so that the fruits can get sun.

When you pick winter squash, cut off a few inches of stem along with the fruit, using a sharp knife. Tearing the stem leaves a jagged wound that is more open to rot than a clean cut is. Do not use this stem as a handle for picking up the squash. Winter squash look like hard, tough fruits, but actually they need to be handled carefully. Nicks and bruises will prevent them from keeping well. Before storing them, you are supposed to cure most varieties (not acorns) for a few weeks in the warm sun or in an 85-degree room to toughen the skin. Then place them in a cool, permanent storage place. In my cool climate no place is 85 degrees in fall unless we are in the midst of a freak Indian summer. But 70 degrees will do the trick if necessary. Besides, if you live in a cool place you are apt to be blessed with a good storage area where you can keep them below 60 degrees and above 40: a *dry* root cellar, an attached garage or shed. Winter squash may mildew in storage and won't look very appetizing if they do. Wiping them with a weak chlorine solution (one part chlorine bleach to ten parts water), then drying them and rubbing them with salad oil can help prevent mildew.

VARIETIES

If your space is limited or if you are new to squash growing, I recommend that you grow one of the smaller, earlier varieties such as 'Buttercup,' which matures in about 100 days; or 'Emerald,' a bush version of the same; or 'Delicata,' mentioned above. The old standby 'Butternut' is fairly early, 'Early Butternut' (a semibush) earlier still; 'Burpee's Butterbush' is a bush version, 'Waltham' a good standard butternut—and nothing beats the butternuts for soups. 'Sweet Mama' probably has the best flavor of the small, early buttercups. Acorn squashes are quite early (seventy to eighty days) and are usually bush types. Grow 'Ebony Acorn,' 'Table King' (vine or bush), 'Table Ace' or the semi-bush 'Jersey Golden Acorn.' For small spaces grow 'Sweet Dumpling.'

You might also try 'Spaghetti Squash' (also called 'Vegetable Spaghetti'), whose flesh separates into spaghettilike strands when scooped out of the skin. (I love it baked and buttered but find it overrated as a spaghetti substitute; it may be shaped like spaghetti, but it tastes like squash.)

If you want a good big squash that keeps for most of the winter, grow the hubbards—'Blue Hubbard,' 'Green Hubbard' or 'Golden Hubbard.' For more variety, experiment with 'Banana,' a big, pink-fleshed, long-season squash, or the huge 'Tahitian' or the tiny 'Little Gem.' And try 'Turk's Turban,' a red-and-green turban-shaped squash so beautiful you can use it as a centerpiece.

large pumpkin   pie pumpkin

Pumpkins

Pumpkins are simply one kind of tough-skinned winter squash, but they have earned a category of their own because of Halloween and Thanksgiving. Once a kitchen staple for soups,

stews and puddings, they appear now in time for jack-o'-lanterns and pumpkin pies, then fade back into obscurity. If you grow them, no doubt you will find other uses for them. You can serve a stew or soup inside the pumpkin shell, for instance. And some varieties now have edible-shelled seeds that are more rewarding to eat than the usual hard-shelled kind.

Grow pumpkins exactly as you would any other winter squash. The only thing you might do differently is try to get some huge ones for Halloween. The best way to do this is to space the plants widely apart in extra-fertile soil, then pinch off the tips of the vines when they have a few small pumpkins on them. Pick all but one pumpkin per vine when they are pie-sized, and let the remaining one get all the plant's energy. Remove all flowers as well. Water the vine often, and top dress it every two weeks or so, not only at the base, but also wherever it may have touched the ground and rooted. Turn your prize gently from time to time so that one side does not get flat from lying on the ground.

Your chances of growing the biggest pumpkin around will be increased if you have chosen a big variety such as 'Connecticut Field,' 'Big Moon' or 'Big Max.' For small jack-o'-lanterns grow 'Jack-O'-Lantern' ('Halloween') or 'Spookie.' For pies grow 'Small Sugar' ('New England Pie') or 'Spirit'—both small bush-type pumpkins. The one with the tasty seeds is 'Lady Godiva.' There are also miniature varieties such as 'Jack Be Little' and 'Munchkin.'

Gourds

You cannot eat gourds, but you can do almost anything else with them. I loved to grow them as a child. We used

gourds

the dipper type to make birdhouses, with a small hole cut in the fat part. Sometimes the skinny "tail" curved around in curlicues, and we just hung them on something as ornaments. We had a huge round one several feet wide that our grandmother had grown in her long-season Louisiana garden. We used round gourds as various kinds of containers, with a circle cut to make a lid and a bit of stem left on for a lid handle. All these types were the tan-colored *Cucurbita lagenaria.*

The small multicolored gourds belong to the family Cucurbitaceae. They are grown for fall decorations, and sold in mixed-seed packets. This makes growing them more fun because you never know what shapes or colors you will end up with. You can also grow luffa gourds, which make fine home-grown sponges.

Plant and grow gourds just the way you would winter squash, but soak the seeds for a few days first, and allow a long maturing period for the biggest ones—up to 140 days. The best way is to start them indoors in peat pots; set the seedlings in the garden while they're still in the peat pots, since they dislike being transplanted. Since gourds weigh less than other squash, trellising is very successful, and it keeps them from flattening on one side. (Of course you might want to flatten one side to grow a container that won't tip over. Round-bottomed gourd bowls work fine only if you are living in a hut or tepee with a sand floor.)

Gourds are heavy feeders, so top dress them in midsummer. Ripen them on the vine until the stems are brown, but pick them before the first frost or they will go soft and not keep. Handling them very carefully, wash them in a mild chlorine solution or with rubbing alcohol, then dry them very thoroughly in a warm, dry place with good air circulation. This may only take a week for the little ones, but large gourds may have to sit for months before the sound of rattling seeds tells you they are done. The outsides can be coated with paste wax or clear shellac, but only if thoroughly dry.

Pick the club-shaped luffas when they are young and green if you want a soft sponge, when they're brown and mature if you want a very scratchy one for scrubbing. (They also peel more easily when mature.) Soak the luffas in water for several days, then peel off the skin. Cut off one end and shake out the seeds, then wash in soap, water and bleach, squeeze them thoroughly, and spread them out to dry.

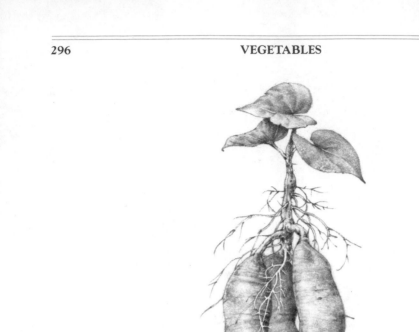

Sweet Potatoes

Sweet potatoes are tubers that grow under the ground just as white potatoes do, but there the resemblance ends. Above ground the plants are sprawling vines that can take up a lot of room in the garden. Sweet potatoes are also a warm-weather crop, needing four or even five months of fairly high temperatures to mature. Nonetheless gardeners can grow them in northern climates. You can also adapt them to small gardens, either by choosing bush-type varieties or by growing them in containers.

SITE

Choose a site in full sun where sweet potatoes have not grown recently. They need warm soil and good drainage, so raised beds are appropriate.

SOIL

The best kind of soil for sweet potatoes is a light, sandy loam, slightly acid, with plenty of phosphorus and potassium. Too much nitrogen can produce rampant vines and distorted tubers.

Sweet potatoes are not cut up and planted but grown from "slips"— sprouts from the tuber. These slips are produced by placing the tuber, or just the round end of it, in moist sand, or by suspending it in a glass of water (three toothpicks will hold it there). Perhaps you did this when you were a child, just to see the sweet potato sprout. Change the water often, and when the slips are about 8 inches long, pull them off the tuber with a twisting motion. They are then ready for planting.

PLANTING

Southern gardeners save sweet potatoes from their fall crops and sprout them during the winter, or else they buy the slips and plant them in early spring. In the north it is hard to find tubers to sprout that are good cold-climate varieties, so gardeners often order them by mail. They then wait for the soil to warm up—usually about two weeks after the last frost. The process can be hastened, however, by using raised beds or just mounded-up rows. (These improve drainage, too.) The soil may also be warmed by laying black plastic over it; the slips are then planted through slits cut in the plastic. Still another short cut is to root the slips in sand or some other potting medium so that they will have developed good root systems by the time they are planted. This is also a handy way to hold them if they arrive in the mail before the soil is warm. They should be planted about a foot apart, with about 3 or 4 feet between rows. Make sure that at least 4 inches of each slip is in the ground.

GROWING

Once in the ground, the slips should be kept well watered to keep them from wilting. A cupful of liquid fertilizer per plant, especially one high in phosphorus that is designed for transplanting, will also help get them off to a good start. You will not see lush foliage immediately; the plant is working on its root system.

While the tubers are developing they do not need a great deal of water, since their roots go deep into the ground. The water supply should be moderate and steady. Heavy soaking during drought can cause the tubers to crack.

PESTS AND DISEASES

If your sweet potatoes contract any of the rot diseases to which the plants are prone, dip the slips in a fungicide next time you try growing them, and rotate the crop. But do not expect a lot of problems from them, especially with northern crops.

HARVEST

Dig sweet potatoes when the foliage turns yellow and dies, or when frost cuts it down. The tubers should not be allowed to freeze. Use a digging fork, and lift them very carefully. Any that are nicked or bruised should be used right away. But the rest will store well, especially if cured for a week or two—if possible at around 85 degrees—to harden the skins. Then store them at 60 degrees or so in a moderately humid environment. Keep a few for sprouting if you want to repeat the same crop next year.

VARIETIES

Some good early varieties include the early 'Porto Rico' or 'Bunch (Bush) Porto Rico'; and 'Jewel.' 'Vardaman' is a bush type, and 'White Yam' is white-fleshed. A good variety for the north is 'Centennial.'

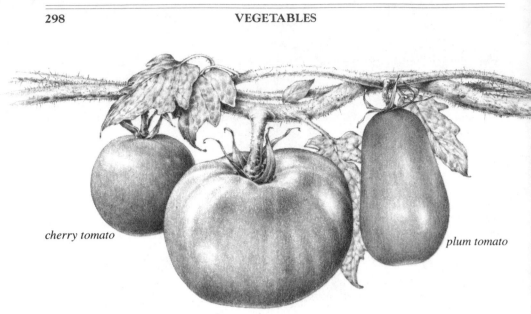

cherry tomato

plum tomato

large red tomato

Tomatoes

Tomatoes are the seductive vegetable—bright red, bursting with juice and flavor, fruitful to a fault. Had they been native not to Peru but to Asia Minor, a tomato—not an apple—surely would have caused our fall from grace. Tomatoes, it seems, have always engendered strong emotions. In the Renaissance they were called "love apples" and thought to be deadly poison. But now they are America's undisputed favorite vegetable (not to mention Italy's), and the gardener's pride and joy. My father once grew a tomato so enormous that he placed it on a platter and carved it as if it were a crown roast. At harvest and canning time they are so bounteous that they are almost too much of a good thing, as the poet Marge Piercy noted in her poem "The Engulfing Garden":

> . . . tomato seeds
> in my hair, tomato skins
> in my teeth, the surfaces
> of the kitchen heaped with
> tomatoes, tomatoes in buckets,
> tomatoes lined up on the window
> sills. . . .

Even if you do not reap buckets, tomatoes will reward you in flavor, versatility, and vitamin C that lasts long after picking, especially if the fruits are ripened on the vine. If I could choose only one vegetable to grow, it would be tomatoes; and I suspect many gardeners feel the same way.

Success with tomatoes depends in part on choosing varieties that are right for your climate. Sometimes the names give you the clues you need, as with 'Seattle Best of All' or 'Frisco Fogger,' both suited to cool summers on the west coast. If you live in a climate with a very hot summer, you would choose other varieties. One way to locate varieties suited to your region is to find a local nursery with a good reputation. Chances are the seedlings it sells have been chosen with your area in mind. Also read the descriptions in a variety of seed catalogs; many make recommendations for your region. Better yet, find a mail-order nursery that grows its own seed in and for your area. For example, I have grown tomatoes sold by Johnny's Selected Seeds in Albion, Maine, on the theory that if they will ripen in the brief Maine summer they will ripen in mine in Connecticut. And indeed they do.

Climate is not the only factor in deciding which varieties to grow. You can choose between "determinate" tomatoes, which are shorter, bushier and set fruit once, then stop, and "indeterminate" ones, which have sprawling vines and keep fruiting until frost puts a stop to them. Determinates are easier, because you do not have to deal with all those long vines. They're handy if your goal is canning tomatoes and you would just as soon process them all at once. But I like to have at least one indeterminate plant for fresh summer eating, spread out over more of the season. You can also choose among the "early" varieties such as 'Pixie' and "main-season" varieties such as 'Supersonic.' The only way to find your favorite tomatoes is to try new ones each season.

One I keep coming back to year after year is a smallish tomato called 'Moira,' which is deep red and rather firm, with a wonderful rich taste. I also like 'Roma,' a "plum" tomato, for cooking and canning. And I always grow at least one cherry tomato such as 'Sweet 100' or one of the little, sweet, oval yellow varieties.

Now this is where seduction comes in. Looking over the seed catalogs at all those enticing choices, you are bound to order—and grow—too many tomatoes. Even those of us who know better usually have too many plants. Unless you do a lot of canning, six is ample. You can still grow several varieties—just save part of the packet for next year— tomato seeds are remarkably long-lived and resilient. If you feed tomatoes to your chickens, the seeds can go through the chickens' digestive systems intact, survive in the manure, survive in the compost bin where the manure is placed, survive in the soil after the compost has been spread in your garden, and come up as volunteers among your eggplants two years later. If they can do this, surely they can survive in a seed packet stored in a cool, dry place. If you buy started plants from a nursery, try to buy them singly or in packs of two so that you can try more varieties.

SITE

Choose a very sunny spot where tomatoes and related plants have not grown recently. Tomatoes do very well in the raised-bed section of my garden, because the soil there warms up fast and gives the young plants a good start. But when growing them this way I have to make sure I give them plenty of room— 6 square feet per plant or more— otherwise the vines flop all over the paths between the beds.

SOIL

The soil should be loose, friable and full of organic matter. Tomatoes feed rather heavily, so it should be rich, with a pH of 6.0–7.0. I incorporate peat moss or other organic matter throughout the bed but also add a shovelful of well-rotted manure and a handful of bone meal to each hole when I plant the seedlings, mixing in thoroughly and watering them in well. The soil should stay moist but not soggy; good drainage is important.

PLANTING

I usually start tomato seeds indoors on a very warm, sunny windowsill. Another good method is to put a heating coil under them that will keep them 75 or 80 degrees, and suspend a fluorescent light over them, especially if your windowsill is not warm or sunny enough; it is important that they not get leggy as they grow, for lack of light. Sow the seeds ¼ inch deep in flats, and transplant to peat pots when they have four leaves. Or start right off with peat pots, sowing several seeds in each and thinning to the best plant. Then either plant them out in the garden in the peat pots, setting the top of the pot a few inches below soil level, or first graduate them once more into larger pots or cut-off milk cartons so they develop even bigger root systems before planting time. But do not let the plants get too mature; you want your seedlings to be short bushy plants with good dark foliage and no flowers.

Since tomatoes take a long time to ripen it is tempting to set the plants out as early as you can. But there is no sense in setting them out much before the last average frost date, when the weather is starting to warm up. Covering them with cloches to ward off frosts or warm the soil around them might help some, but for the most part they tend to just sit there and not do anything. I find that later-planted tomatoes always catch up to the earlier-planted ones anyway!

Tomatoes suffer more shock in transplanting than do most vegetables, but you can minimize this by hardening them off for a week or two first. This means setting them outdoors in their pots in a protected place so that they get some warm sun, a little gentle wind, and even some cool (not freezing) nights. Then they will have adjusted to some of the stresses of real life in the garden before they are hit by the additional stress of having their roots set in the cool ground.

If your tomatoes are the long-vined, indeterminate type, you will need to decide whether or not to give them a vertical support. Just letting them flop on the ground is easiest; you will get a large yield this way and often less sun scald or blossom-end rot. They may also ripen faster on the ground in cool climates. But the plants will take up more room, and lying on the ground leaves them more susceptible to dirt, certain other diseases, insects and assorted small scurrying predators. I have grown tomatoes on the ground successfully by using a salt-hay mulch that keeps them dry while they ripen, and the number I lose to the devilish critter that takes one bite of each and then moves on is balanced by the greater yield.

I suggest you do try a vertical method of growing, however, to see how you like it. Some of the different supports—stakes, cages, trellises—are illustrated in Figure 50. I think the circular cages are the most efficient system for the home gardener, because they

PRUNING TOMATOES

Fig. 49

Using pruning shears or scissors, remove the "suckers," or small shoots that grow in the angle between the leaf stalks and the main stem to get a plant with just one main stem.

hold up the plants without the fuss of tying them to anything; the side shoots that protrude through the mesh hold the plants up. Concrete reinforcing wire is often recommended, but you can use any sturdy wire mesh that has holes big enough to let you put your hand through and pull out a tomato. Do support the cylinder with strong stakes, though; tomato-laden vines are very heavy. Try using two or three 5-foot metal stakes (one foot goes below ground) if you have some lying around. There are also ready-made tomato cages, but they are expensive and often not tall enough.

If you grow your vines vertically you need to prune them to one stem and cut out the suckers that grow in the leaf axils (Figure 49). If you are using stakes or string trellises, be sure to use a strip of cloth or soft twine and tie them loosely in a figure eight (Figure 51) so you do not break the stems.

GROWING

Tomatoes need a steady water supply to help them ripen well. Drought will slow them down, and an excess of water after drought can cause them to crack or develop blossom-end rot (recognized by round black spots on the fruits). A mulch, plus a moderate watering during drought, usually does the trick. I have never had to top dress tomatoes, but you might apply some liquid fertilizer once or twice in the season if growth seems unusually slow. The main thing you have to do is supervise the vines.

It seems to take forever for tomatoes to get red. Some people spray them at the flower stage with a fruit-setting

WAYS TO GROW TOMATOES

Fig. 50

Letting them sprawl: Vines, especially determinate varieties, may be grown without staking. Mulch helps keep fruits dry and disease-free.

Staking: Use metal or 2-by-2-inch wood stakes, 6 feet tall. As vines grow, tie to the stakes with soft twine, strips of cloth or old stockings.

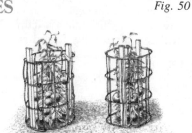

Caging: Wire cages, held up by two or three stakes, will support tomato vines without tying. Use wire mesh with openings large enough to put your hand through for picking.

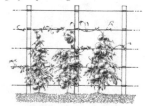

Trellising: Use horizontal wires or wire mesh attached to stout stakes. Tie vines to the trellis with soft twine or cloth.

hormone spray. But ripening is largely up to the weather. If it is a cold, cloudy summer, well, everyone else will be staring at green tomatoes too. The best remedy is to plant a few early varieties to assuage your impatience.

PESTS AND DISEASES

In addition to blossom-end rot, described above, tomatoes get several diseases, notably verticillium and fusarium wilts and mosaic virus. The solution to both is to choose resistant varieties, which will have a "V," an "M" or an "F" next to their names, or all three. "N" means that the variety at hand also resists nematodes, small wormlike organisms that inhabit the soil and can injure plants. Rotating crops and removing debris is also important.

Aphids, tomato hornworms, and other insects bother tomatoes but do not usually do much damage. Far more serious are raids by chipmunks and their ilk; vertical growing usually foils them.

HARVEST

And when is the romance finally over? You can protect the fruit from the first light frosts by covering the plants with tarps or sheets. If it is really going to freeze, however, you'd best get everybody out there and pick all the tomatoes. Put a few on the kitchen table, and let the rest ripen in a cooler, darker place. Arrange them in one layer, and check often to see if any have holes, cracks or even a small spot of rot. Remove these before they start to go, for go they will, transmitting moisture and rot to any that they are touching.

If you have taken a few suckers from a healthy, small-vined plant before the freeze, you can root them and grow them indoors. Several varieties are suitable (see below). A few gallons of soil each will sustain potted plants in a warm, sunny spot. This way you may have vine-ripened tomatoes even in winter.

VARIETIES

Some of the best indeterminate varieties are 'Early Girl V,' 'Better Boy VFN,' 'Burpee's Big Boy,' 'Marglobe VF,' the large pink 'Ponderosa,' 'Rutgers' (for canning), the early 'Fantastic' and 'Beefmaster VFN,' which is late. Good determinates include the early 'Pixie Hybrid,' with compact plants and 2-inch fruits, the medium-sized 'Moira,' 'Floramerica' and 'Celebrity,' both very disease-resistant, and 'Heinz.' Good indeterminate cherry tomatoes are 'Sweet 100' and 'Yellow Pear'; determinate ones are the early 'Small Fry VFN' and 'Tiny Tim.' For paste tomatoes try the determinate 'Roma VF' or 'Nova VF' (earlier); if you want a determinate variety try 'San Marzano.' In cold climates grow early-maturing varieties such as the determinates 'Subarctic Plenty' and 'Siberia.' For terrace or indoor growing, even in winter, try 'Pixie Hybrid,' 'Patio Hybrid' and 'Goldie Hybrid' (a gold cherry type).

HOW TO TIE A STEM TO A STAKE

Fig. 51

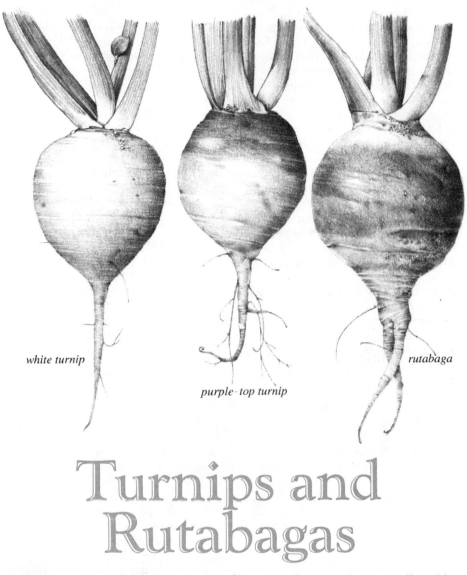

white turnip

purple·top turnip

rutabaga

Turnips and Rutabagas

T here is nothing in the garden quite as unromantic as a turnip, unless perhaps it's a rutabaga. Strong-flavored, good-storing root vegetables, they are rarely invited to sit at formal tables. But they are good earthy peasant food. Most people insist on a bowl of buttered mashed turnips at Thanksgiving dinner, and they are also good cut up in soups.

Turnips are small, usually white, and have no necks (rather like the children in *Cat on·a Hot Tin Roof*). The leaves, which are green and fuzzy, sprout right from the root itself and are an excellent, nutritious cooked green (especially tasty with pieces of ham, salt pork or slab bacon added). Some turnips have yellow flesh, others have white. Some varieties are grown for the root, others for the greens, still others for both.

Rutabagas, sometimes called "Swede turnips," are 5 or 6 inches in diameter and purplish in color. They look somewhat like a rounded sweet potato. The flesh inside is usually yellow. There is a neck or crown 1 or 2 inches long, from which sprout smooth bluish leaves. I once got through a rather lean winter on my rutabaga crop; the tubers, coated with paraffin and stored in the basement, lasted all winter long.

Both turnips and rutabagas are cool-weather crops that get tough and woody and go to seed in hot weather. Which to grow? If you want an early spring crop, or want to grow cooking greens, choose turnips. For a fall crop that will keep a while in the ground and for a long time in your cellar, rutabagas are a better choice, and to some palates they're sweeter tasting. But turnips are twice as fast to mature: 35–60 days compared to rutabagas' 90.

SITE

A sunny location is appreciated, but not essential. A 4-foot-by-4-foot bed will give you up to twenty-five rutabagas and up to thirty turnips. Since both are members of the cabbage family, try not to plant either where other cabbage vegetables have recently grown.

SOIL

Soil texture is important for both turnips and rutabagas, as it is for any root crop. Make the soil loose, well drained, and well ventilated by incorporating plenty of organic matter into it. Use rotted manure, compost or a commercial bagged humus, and dig it in to a depth of at least 7 inches, especially for rutabagas, whose tubers are larger and whose root systems go down several feet. Both like a neutral pH but will tolerate a pH as low as 5.5. Lime the soil if it is more acid than pH 5.5.

Turnips are not very heavy feeders as vegetables go; soil of moderate fertility is adequate—with one exception. If you are trying to grow a spring turnip crop before hot weather comes, you do want fast growth. So give spring turnips a good dose of 5–10–10. Rutabagas like slightly richer soil than fall turnips. And make sure your soil has adequate phosphorus for root development, no matter when you plant.

PLANTING

Spring turnips should be planted as early in spring as you can work the soil (late winter in warm climates)—or set into predug furrows even earlier than that. For fall turnips, wait until mid or late summer in the north, and even until late fall and winter in the south. Plant rutabagas in spring when the ground has warmed, or early summer in the north, allowing three months before the first average frost. You can plant them in mid or late summer farther south, to be sure the tubers are forming in cooler weather.

Seeds are sown directly in the garden. They are very tiny, but try to get them about an inch apart. They should be sown ¼ inch deep in spring, but ½ inch deep in warm weather, in well-moistened furrows. The seeds germinate quickly but do not like to come up through a crust, so just sift some compost or fine soil over the furrow and then keep it moistened.

Rows should be at least 15 inches apart for turnips, and at least 18 inches for rutabagas. When the seedlings are 5–6 inches high, thin them to 3–4 inches apart, eating the thinnings as greens (young turnip leaves are even good raw in salads). Thinning is not as important if you are growing just for greens; but tubers of both turnips and rutabagas need ample room to reach full size undisturbed, so be sure to thin if you want to harvest those. Rutabagas should be thinned to at least 6–8 inches apart to permit good root development.

GROWING

Both crops need careful but frequent cultivation to keep the weeds down. A mulch will help, but be sure to sprinkle some lime on the soil first if the mulch is an acid one like bark. Turnips appreciate a good, deep soaking with water once a week if the weather is dry. Rutabagas are drought-tolerant within reason, since the roots go so deep. Top dressing should not be necessary with either turnips or rutabagas as long as your soil is moderately fertile, except perhaps with spring turnips. But if you do top dress, use a fertilizer that is high in phosphorus, and one that is high in nitrogen only if you're growing turnip greens, not tubers.

PESTS AND DISEASES

For the most part the same ills that beset cabbage and other members of that family afflict rutabagas and turnips. Control root maggots by dusting the soil with wood ashes, and if necessary by covering seedlings with cheesecloth to keep off flies that lay the eggs from which the maggots hatch. Small holes in the leaves indicate flea beetles, which can be hosed off or dusted with rotenone. Treat aphids the same way.

Clubroot and blackroot are occasional problems. Rutabagas can rot in the center from insufficient boron in the soil, an affliction known as 'brown heart.' If this condition appears, dig a little Borax into the soil and soak it thoroughly with a hose.

HARVEST

Dig turnips when they are 2 or 3 inches in diameter. A few light frosts may improve the flavor of both tops and roots, but do not let them freeze solid. Cut off the tops and store the tubers in a cool place, just above 32 degrees. Harvest rutabagas while the ground is still soft enough to dig, and cut off the tops and any long roots projecting from the tuber. Store them the same way you do turnips (burying them in a container of barely moist sand will help keep them from drying out). Dipping them in paraffin will also prolong their keeping time, as it will keep moisture from escaping from the tubers. Just scrape off the paraffin along with the skins when you peel them for cooking.

Turnip greens can be eaten as early as you do your thinning, and as late as a month or so after planting. If you are growing a root-turnip crop, you can still harvest a few outer leaves from the plants occasionally to make a meal of greens. But do not cut off all the greens if you want to harvest the tubers, at least not until it is time to dig the tubers up.

VARIETIES

For early turnip crops, grow 'All Seasons,' 'White Flat,' 'Shogoin,' 'Tokyo Cross,' 'Just Right,' 'Tokyo Market,' 'Jersey Lily' or 'Extra Early White.' For greens, grow 'Seven Top,' 'Shogoin,' 'All Top Hybrid' or 'Just Right.' 'Purple Top White Globe' and 'Aberdeen' (yellow) are good for fall and for storage.

The standard rutabaga varieties are 'American Purple Top,' 'Laurentian,' 'Long Island Improved' and 'Macomber,' a white-fleshed type that keeps very well.

CHAPTER 8

HERBS

It is easy to get the wrong impression about herbs. Leafing through all those gorgeous books full of glossy color pictures of English or American herb gardens, you might assume that herbs are exceptionally tidy plants that grow in little mounds, hummocks and intricate knot patterns, respecting the careful geometrical shapes and ornamental edgings in which they are confined. What you are seeing in these handsome gardens, however, is herbs on their best behavior. Left to their own devices herbs are the anarchists of the garden. To produce those elegant geometries someone has worked very diligently.

Like many gardeners I learned the lesson about herbs the hard way. Planted in little square raised beds, each 4 feet to a side, some of my herbs after a few years really considered themselves shrubs. My oregano plant had completely usurped a bed of its own, my sage plant and my tarragon plant very nearly. The neat little "chive edging" was a forest so dense I could hardly dig the plants up, its flowers bending over the wooden sides of the beds sowing volunteers all over the sandy path like a guerrilla army. Even the dainty little chervil plants that succumbed so swiftly to heat or frost had infiltrated the walkway with volunteer seedlings.

I don't mean to imply that all this discouraged me from herb gardening. The experience did teach me something about the best way to go about it, however. I think that the formal style of herb gardening probably evolved, in part, as a way of curbing the rampant nature of some herbs. After all, how much do you need of any one herb? If I wanted to dry a lot of tarragon, say, or make a big batch of pesto sauce with my basil, I would raise a large crop of each. But usually I need small herb plants that I can just snip a few leaves from here and there for cooking. I have also found that small, compact herb plants produce leaves with more flavor than large, sprawling ones. Fortunately, using herbs is one way to keep them the proper size: the more you snip them, the more compact, bushy and flavorful they become.

I think you have to be realistic about herb growing and consider why you are growing herbs in the first place. To begin with, how are we defining "herb"? Botanically, an herb is any plant with a soft stem as opposed to a woody one. To the colonial housewife, an herb was any plant that was put to household use—for cooking, for treating illnesses, as an aromatic to sweeten musty drawers or rooms and for a host of other tasks. Herbs were powerful instruments that could heal, kill and even work magic. The proverbial witch throwing assorted herbs into a pot is not a far-fetched concept; she is the old woman with years of experience in the ways of using nature for good or ill, and she is a force that was once upon a time respected.

Some modern herb growers are strongly drawn to this tradition and explore the very real medicinal uses of many herbs. Others grow them for dried bouquets and potpourris. Others simply like to look at them and smell their aromatic leaves in the garden. (Weeding an herb garden is as much a treat as a chore, because you are stirring up so many scents as your hands move among the plants.) But for most herb growers today the prime motivation is to produce fresh seasonings for the kitchen. I enjoy my herbs' nostalgic associations as much as anyone, but not enough to grow herbs that I don't like to cook with, look at or use to attract wildlife—even if they have great old-fashioned names like woad or hyssop. My witchcraft largely consists of tossing chives into my caldron of vichyssoise. I share the sentiments of Elisabeth Morss in this verse from her book *Herbs of a Rhyming Gardener:*

> Monarda (Beebalm, Oswego Tea)
> Monarda, or Oswego tea
> First gladdened Indian and bee.
> Then came the English, French
>   and Dutch,
> I wonder if they liked it much.
> It paid no tax to King and Crown,
> And so our forebears gulped it
>   down.
> To patriotic zeal I bow,
> Delighted not to drink it now.

With the need to avoid the British tea tax now well behind me, I grow monarda not to make tea but for its handsome flowers, which lure bees, hummingbirds and butterflies. You'll find it in the chapter on perennials rather than here. I love the way many other herbs look, too, and I have grown them in many different kinds of gardens, always being a bit more vigilant with my pruners than I was in that first herb garden. And while I have narrowed down the list of herbs in this chapter to a modest dozen that are basic culinary herbs, I like to experiment with new ones now and again—and I urge you to do the same.

Ways to Grow Herbs

You do not have to grow all your herbs in one spot. For one thing herbs vary in the way they grow. Some, such as dill, basil, chervil and coriander, are annuals. Some, such as tarragon, sage, chives, mint, oregano and thyme, are perennials. Others, such as parsley, are biennials. Some are hardy, and some, like rosemary and bay, do not survive cold winters even though they are perennials. Some you want a little

of, some a lot of. So you may wind up choosing several of the following options for growing herbs.

HERBS IN THE VEGETABLE GARDEN

I always have a few herbs growing with my vegetables, usually annual herbs I grow in quantity, such as basil, dill and parsley. I plant these crops in rows or blocks, to snip as needed during the summer; and I harvest them before frost for pesto or herb vinegars.

I used to grow all my herbs in the vegetable garden, making separate, defined areas for the perennial herbs such as sage, so they wouldn't get tilled under along with the rest of the garden at the end of the season. But now that the garden is a long way from the house, I prefer to keep my herbs close at hand for snipping while I am making dinner. While I might be willing to make a daily foray to the main garden to pick vegetables, I know I won't go out there in the midst of cooking, so I grow most of my herbs in pots near the kitchen.

If you have the same dilemma, another compromise might be to have a large vegetable garden for space-consuming crops like corn and beans, and a smaller kitchen garden or salad garden closer to the house. The kitchen garden might combine herbs with an eye-catching array of lettuces in different colors, a few pepper plants with fruits in some of the "new" colors and even some compact tomato plants.

GROWING HERBS WITH FLOWERS

It is also possible to grow some, or even all, of your herbs in the flower garden. Most of them have at least one ornamental feature, whether it is the tall, lacy yellow flowers of dill, the purple flowers of mint, or the blue flowers of borage and sage. Herb foliage is often decorative too—the leaves of common sage are a handsome gray-green; other kinds have leaves that are yellow or even a red-green-white combination. 'Dark Opal' basil, a wonderful purple color, is a cultivar specifically developed to look pretty in gardens. It works especially well next to blue flowers and plants with silvery leaves such as artemisias, which are themselves aromatic herbs. Low-growing herbs such as thyme make good edging plants. And many herbs are particularly effective in the rock garden, their various foliage colors and textures blending beautifully with the colors and textures of stone. You can even tuck them between the flat stones of a terrace or in the chinks of walls. Many actually appreciate the relatively dry, well-drained soil that you find in such situations. These examples really only begin to describe the ornamental uses of herbs, and you will enjoy coming up with your own. In planning these gardens, however, pay attention to the design principles discussed in the chapters on annuals and perennials.

HERB GARDENS

If you want to put together a garden just for herbs, there are a number of ways to go about it. Your garden might be an entryway planting, for example—a formal one for the front door or a more casual one for the door leading into the kitchen. Areas around kitchen doors are particularly good sites because the herbs are then easily accessible for cooking. Another good spot might be along a fence in a back or side yard, especially if you want to grow a lot of tall herbs such as dill, angelica and tansy and if you want to produce large bunches of them for drying. There you can give

them plenty of room to grow tall and broad, and to flop to their hearts' content. Herb gardens are not hard to plan (see Figure 52 for an example of one). Put tall herbs in back, medium-height herbs in the middle and short ones along the border for edging—or plant an edging of annual flowers or alpine strawberries. You don't have to think about what blooms when with herbs, because bloom is incidental; you may be cutting most of your herbs just before they bloom, when their flavor is at its peak. Give vigorous plants like mint plenty of room, or grow them in a container in the ground to keep them under control. An old bucket or plastic tub with holes punched in the bottom for drainage can be sunk in the ground and used as a barrier to keep rampant herbs within bounds.

In choosing the site, do keep in mind several things. First, most herbs need plenty of sun (though a few, such as chervil, parsley and mint, will grow well in partial shade). Second, most herbs absolutely require good drainage, and you may have to provide it by growing them in raised beds. And third, most won't tolerate competition from tree roots (again, raised beds might be the solution).

GROWING HERBS IN POTS

I always have herbs growing in the house in winter. Not only does it spare me the work of drying or freezing them in the summer, but they taste better when freshly picked. In recent years I have even taken to growing almost all my herbs in large pots or boxes all year long. Annual herbs I sow in long window-box-type containers, and perennials go into attractive pots, one plant to a pot. I keep them on a terrace next to the house, where they are not only handy but decorative, grouped with pots of geraniums, portulaca and other flowering plants. I find that perennial herbs grown in pots need to be divided less often than those grown in the ground. Constraining their root systems keeps them compact and flavorful. The annuals must be resown two or three times a year; I pinch off the flowers to keep them from going to seed, but sooner or later the crop starts to peter out. By then I have another crop of seedlings started in another container. And after the second crop has finished there are sometimes fresh volunteers coming along in the first one!

I still like to grow certain herbs in great quantity in the vegetable garden, and someday I may have a little herb garden like the one depicted in the plan in Figure 52; but right now I am enjoying my pot system. If it were not for the convenience and attractive appearance of herbs on the terrace, I might sink the pots in the vegetable or flower garden, as some people do, to avoid having to worry about keeping them watered. Now I have to water every day in hot, dry weather, especially the herbs in clay pots, which, though they are the nicest to look at, dry out very quickly.

GROWING HERBS INDOORS

Even if you live in an apartment, you can grow most of the herbs discussed in this chapter in containers (dill and coriander are a bit too leggy). All you need is either a very sunny window (one that gets at least five to six hours of sun a day) or else a growing light (page 44). In fact, if the only outdoor space you have is shady, herbs are better off indoors in a sunny window or under a light. And herbs are attractive indoors, not only to the eye but to the nose as well. Trailing herbs such as thyme and sweet marjoram can even be used in hanging baskets.

A PLAN FOR AN HERB GARDEN

The herb garden shown in Figure 52 is my idea of a somewhat formal one in an old-fashioned style—a garden that is decorative yet practical, supplying you with the basics for cooking with herbs. I have organized it in a logical way to make it easy to tend. The 6-foot square in the middle is a permanent bed that has only perennial herbs in it: tarragon, oregano, sage, mint, chives and thyme. At the center is a large, attractive pot with a rosemary plant in it, to serve as a focal point. (I put the rosemary in a pot because in my climate I must always bring my rosemary indoors for the winter, but if your winter temperatures do not go much below freezing you can grow yours right in the ground. (You could also bury the pot, then dig it up in fall to bring it in.) The centerpiece for the garden might be a statue, birdbath, sundial or some such ornament.

All the herbs in the center plot will be dug up and divided from time to time as they get large, sprawling and woody, but probably not all at once. They do need to be cut back, though, and sometimes twice a year. For example I might make one cutting of the tarragon in midsummer for drying, another in early fall for tarragon vinegar. The mint would have to be in a sunken container, as described above, or it would take over.

The four beds at the corners are all planted with annual herbs. Some particularly ornamental annual flowers are added for color. The bed at the upper left has a big stand of sweet basil, flanked on either side with 'Dark Opal' basil for contrast. Next to that I would put a low, white-leaved plant—perhaps one of the annual dusty millers such as *Cineraria maritima*.

In the upper right bed is a big planting of dill, with nasturtiums on either side. I love this combination because the dill's bluish foliage and yellow flowers are beautiful next to the bright colors of the nasturtium flowers, and the feathery leaves contrast with the flat, round leaves of the nasturtiums. Another reason for that combination: you can eat the leaves and flowers of nasturtiums in salads along with the dill leaves.

In the lower left bed is parsley, which I would let overwinter as a biennial, then plant again for a late-summer crop. Yellow and orange calendulas grow at either end—their flowers are edible and can brighten up salads just as nasturtiums can.

The bottom right bed has coriander, flanked by chervil plants, which are shorter and have lacy foliage. Some intensely blue lobelia provide an accent at the ends.

The corner beds are partially dug up and replanted each year. But I would leave the parsley alone, as well as the places where chervil and dill have been growing, since these will self-sow for the following year.

The paths between the beds are 3 feet wide—any narrower and you'd be dodging wayward herbs that flop in your path. I think brick paths look best, but flat stones, gravel or simply grass would also be attractive. You might also plant the paths with a carpeting herb such as chamomile or thyme. The outside of the garden could be edged with another path, with a fence or with a lawn.

Growing Tips for Herbs

How you grow your herbs depends in part on where you decide to grow them.

OUTDOORS

Once you have found the right site you will discover that most herbs are not fussy about growing conditions. Some people will tell you that herbs like poor, dry soil, and it is true that many of our favorites come from the Mediterranean region, are relatively tolerant of drought and may lose flavor if grown in very rich soil. But frankly, I grow herbs the way I grow most everything else, in a well-drained soil of average fertility that has been enriched with organic matter, with a pH of about 5.5 to 7.0. I give them water when they seem to need it. The recommendations in the list of herbs in this chapter will give you some special pointers about which need that extra little dose of fertilizer and which shouldn't get too much, or which ones benefit from a sprinkling of lime now and again. But basically, if your soil is good, and if it's well drained, the only real problem I think you will encounter is that herbs often succeed *too* well.

Seeds of hardy annual herbs like chervil are sown as soon as the ground can be worked in spring, or even in fall for spring crops. Tender annuals like basil are sown after danger of frost has passed. Some perennial herbs that are easy to grow from seed are sweet marjoram, oregano and thyme, but you'll probably want to start these quite early indoors. Perennial herbs are planted and divided like any perennials (see Chapter 6).

INDOORS

If you are growing herbs in the garden and want to bring some indoors, you have several options. Many herbs can be dug up and brought inside, to be potted in a container of ample size in a good potting medium for houseplants (page 584). Perennial herbs respond especially

PLAN FOR AN HERB GARDEN (21' by 21')

Fig. 52

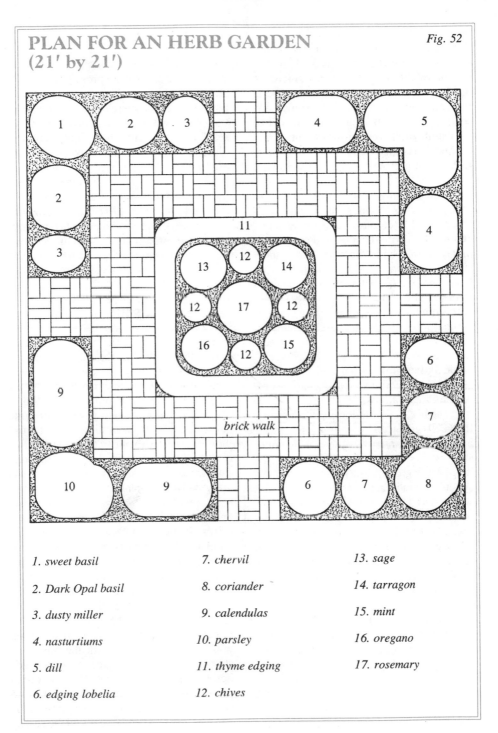

brick walk

1. sweet basil	7. chervil	13. sage
2. Dark Opal basil	8. coriander	14. tarragon
3. dusty miller	9. calendulas	15. mint
4. nasturtiums	10. parsley	16. oregano
5. dill	11. thyme edging	17. rosemary
6. edging lobelia	12. chives	

well to this treatment, though some do best if you give them an artificial "winter" by letting them go through a few weeks of freezing night temperatures outside. When brought indoors, these will end their period of dormancy by sending up fresh new growth. (This trick will often revive housebound perennial herbs that have not been doing well; even putting them into the refrigerator can help, if you have the space.)

But bringing entire herb plants indoors may not always be worthwhile. The annual ones may be at or near the end of their growth cycle, and the perennial ones may be at the point where they are too old, too woody and—unless you have a pot the size of a small armchair—too big to be potted. Often it is better to take stem cuttings (page 594) or to layer plants (page 499) in the garden and then pot up those that grow where the layered stem takes root. To learn which technique is best for which herb, read the growing instructions in this chapter under individual herbs.

Herbs grown indoors will usually thrive if given enough light and water and an occasional feeding (fish emulsion works well). Humidity not only helps their growth but keeps the foliage succulent and tasty. If the air is dry where you live, place the pots in a tray of stones and keep the tray filled with water just up to the bottom of the pots; this helps to keep moisture in the air. Except for rosemary, which appreciates it, I don't like to mist herbs; it encourages fungus disease.

Neither indoor nor outdoor herbs are much bothered by pests (though you might sometimes find mealy bugs on your indoor rosemary or whiteflies on your chives or basil), and I don't like to spray anything that I will eat. Use the soapy-water treatment (page 73) and other safe pest repellents described in Chapter 2.

Harvesting Herbs

I don't have a fixed program for harvesting herbs. When I need some of the leaves I pick them. I go easy on very young plants, because I don't want to set them back. But when plants get very big and bushy I try to think of ways to use the leaves, such as making up a batch of herb vinegar or drying some bunches. The basic idea behind preserving herbs is that their leaves contain volatile oils that produce the scents and tastes we prize; herbs should be preserved in a way that keeps these oils in their potent state. There are several ways to do this.

DRYING HERBS

When herbs are dried, the moisture leaves the plant, but the oils do not, so that dried herbs sometimes have a more concentrated flavor than fresh ones. The trick is to dry them quickly and thoroughly, but not in such a way that you cause the oils to volatilize. Pick herbs you want to dry on a day that is not rainy or humid, just after the dew has dried on the leaves. The ideal time is immediately before the plant blooms—then the oils are at their strongest. With most herbs you can cut back as much as two-thirds of the plant, but you'll probably want to discard parts of the stems you have cut where there is sparse foliage (stems also retain too much moisture). To dry the plants you can hang them upside down to let the oils run down into the leaves, putting them in a paper bag to catch the leaves and seeds that fall. If you keep them in the dark the oils stay stronger. Another method is to lay the herbs on trays or screens. You can even put them in a warm oven for a few hours, but don't turn it up past 180 degrees or the plants' oils will be lost).

After the leaves are dry and crumbly, strip them off the plant and put them in airtight jars. Check every now and then to make sure no moisture is accumulating on the jars' lids; if it does, take out the herbs and dry them some more.

Herbs grown for their seeds, such as dill, caraway and coriander, should be harvested when the seeds have turned light brown or gray. Hang the branches in bags (as above) or spread them out to dry; then after they've dried somewhat, shake the seeds out of the plants and dry them some more. Thresh away the hulls by blowing on them gently, by using a fan, or by letting the seeds fall through a colander or a screen made of hardware cloth.

OILS AND VINEGARS

The most decorative way to make herb vinegars is to put sprigs of fresh herbs in glass bottles filled with wine vinegar. I like to make several kinds: tarragon (always), lovely rose-colored basil vinegar if I have grown 'Dark Opal' and also some bottles with mixed herbs. They make great presents. You can also warm herbs in the vinegar and put it through the blender or food processor for an even stronger brew, *then* add a few sprigs for looks.

Herb oils are made the same way. I use good olive oil, and I whiz the herbs and oil in a blender, because sprigs that float to the top of the oil can turn moldy.

FREEZING

There are several ways to freeze herbs. One is simply to put them in plastic wrap or plastic bags and stick them in the freezer. Another is to put them in oil, butter or water, purée the mixture, and freeze that. The oil-and-butter mixes don't freeze quite solid, and some can be easily scraped off as needed if you freeze them in jars or plastic boxes. Another great method is to freeze either of these puréed mixtures in ice-cube trays, then put the ice cubes in a plastic bag in the freezer. You then have handy little portions you can drop into a soup, a sauce or some other dish whenever you need them.

LIST OF HERBS

The herbs listed here are all good for cooking and are handsome to look at. They are only a snip and a taste of the vast world of herbs, however, a world you can learn more about from the specialty herb catalogs listed on page 621. But these twelve will give you the makings of a kitchen herb garden. Add to them any special favorites you might have.

BASIL
Ocimum basilicum

DESCRIPTION: Every summer the basil in my garden produces tall, lush plants with big bright green leaves. I put the leaves, whole, into salads, especially salads of sliced ripe garden tomatoes. I chop the leaves and put them into sauces, soups and eggplant casseroles. And I purée great handfuls of them in the food processor along with Italian parsley, olive oil, pine nuts, garlic and Parmesan cheese to make pesto—that glorious Italian sauce that turns a simple bowl of pasta into a delicacy.

Every fall the basil in my garden gives me the first unmistakably dismal sign of winter's approach. A few maple leaves just *might* be turning orange because the trees are diseased or it's been dry lately; the geese just *might* be flying south to escape encroaching suburbanization of the county. But there's no mistaking the blackened mess that is my basil after the first frost. Basil, for all its summer bravado, is a tender annual, and if frost is predicted for the night you can find me out there in the dark, picking basil by the armful and making emergency batches of pesto till the wee small hours.

The commonest kind of basil is called "sweet basil" and can grow as tall as 6 feet in warm climates. Mine approaches 3 feet. It has small white flower spikes, beloved of bees. There are other, exotic basils such as anise basil and cinnamon basil, and a bush form (*Ocimum basilicum* 'Minimum') that is recommended for indoor culture. The only other one I've grown is the wonderful purple 'Dark Opal,' which has pink flowers; but a friend of mine recommends 'Spicy Globe.' She says it "makes a little round ball, like a topiary" and is very spicy. I'm dying to try it.

HOW TO GROW: Grow basil in full sun if possible, in rich, loose, well-drained soil a little on the limy side. Sow seeds outdoors after all danger of frost has passed, thinning plants to about 10 inches apart. When the plants are about 6 inches tall, pinch them to make them bushy; if they start to bloom, pinch the flowers off to keep leaf production going, leaving a few to feed the bees, or to self-sow if you live in a warm climate. To grow an indoor crop in winter, either sow seeds or root some stem cuttings from your summer garden before that first frost. Give the plants plenty of warmth and light. Indoors or out, your basil will tell you whether its soil is rich enough: if so, the leaves will be a rich, dark green; if not, they will be pale green.

HARVEST: If you want to dry the leaves, cut before bloom and dry on trays or screens in a dark, well-ventilated place. Freezing or packing them in oil, however, preserves more flavor. Basil also makes an excellent herb vinegar.

CHERVIL
Anthriscus cerefolium

DESCRIPTION: Chervil looks like parsley but is even more feathery. It has a very mild, subtle flavor that tastes like spring itself in a green salad, as long as you don't overpower it with stronger herbs. It is also sublime in an omelet. Rarely more than a foot tall, chervil is nonetheless a survivor. A hardy annual, it will withstand some frost, and though it germinates slowly, it self-sows with abandon. Much of my chervil-harvesting consists of plucking little clumps that have come up in the wrong place (but at just the right time for dinner).

HOW TO GROW: Chervil will grow in full sun but prefers part shade, especially in hot climates. Grow it in nice, light, moderately rich soil. Direct seeding works best. Sow seeds outdoors as soon as the soil can be worked in spring, thinning to 4–6 inches apart. My chervil goes to seed and succumbs to hot weather in midsummer, but by then it has either self-sown its replacement or I have sown a succession crop in a semishaded spot or under a lath cover such as the frame described on page 205. I grow chervil indoors in winter by sowing it in a long box, then sowing a new crop in another box before the first crop peters out.

HARVEST: To dry chervil cut it before the flowers open. It also freezes well in plastic bags.

CHIVES
Allium schoenoprasum

DESCRIPTION: Almost everybody likes chives. If you have grown only one herb in your life, it was probably chives. If you have eaten only one herb in your life, it was probably chives. When my son Chris was little and my mother complained about the fact that he did not like a single vegetable, he replied, "That's not true. I like chives."

Chives are hardy perennial bulbs that belong to the onion family. A clump of chives is simply a dense mass of tiny onions. In addition to the common kind there is one called "Chinese chives" or "garlic chives" (*Allium tuberosum*), which tastes stronger, grows about 2 feet tall, and is often grown as an ornamental plant because of its attractive, flat gray-green leaves and fragrant white flowers. I always have a pot of plain old chives indoors or on the terrace for whenever I want a fresh, oniony but not overpowering taste in something, but I like to grow Chinese chives outdoors in the garden.

HOW TO GROW: Grow chives in full sun or part shade, in rich, fairly moist but well-drained soil. You can grow them easily from seed sown in early spring, but chive plants are so readily available that they are usually grown from a piece of someone else's clump—either a neighbor's or the supermarket's.

If well mulched, chives will often stay green outdoors all through the winter. I seem to remember that when I was living in frigid Vermont, where 4 feet of snow kept them well blanketed, I had lovely fresh green chives as soon as I was able to dig the snow away from them. They are a good herb to winter oudoors in a cold frame, too.

Aside from the occasional aphid plague, chives do not have many problems, but sometimes an *indoor* clump will start to look very dried out and not very productive. If this happens, cut the plant way back and try to pull out some of the dead leaves. Then put it outdoors for a week or two if it is freezing outside or in a cold spot if it isn't. This artificial "winter" should shock the clump into new "spring" growth. Then start feeding it gradually with a liquid fertilizer.

HARVEST: Chives are best fresh; frozen is second best; dried chives are better than nothing but definitely in third place. If you can't keep a fresh pot indoors, grow them in the garden, then chop them up and freeze them in plastic bags or boxes, or freeze chive butter.

CORIANDER
Coriandrum sativum

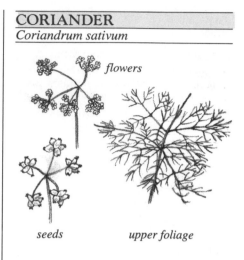

flowers

seeds   upper foliage

DESCRIPTION: This hardy annual herb has upper leaves that look like dill and lower ones that look like parsley, but it also has a pungent flavor all its own. The seeds are also very flavorful. Coriander is widely used as a seasoning around the world, and is called *cilantro* in Spanish-speaking countries and *dhania* in India. It figures in Oriental cooking also and is sometimes known as "Chinese parsley." There has been something of a coriander renaissance of late because there is so much interest in the cuisines of foreign countries and, chances are, if you scratch a foreign cuisine you'll find coriander. The flowers are flat umbels, usually white but sometimes pale pink or lavender.

HOW TO GROW: Grow coriander in full sun or part shade, in very well drained, moderately fertile soil. Sow seeds after danger of frost is past, or in late summer or fall in warm climates. Thin to about a foot apart. Like all the *Umbelliferae* (page 185), it has a long taproot and does not like to be transplanted. But unlike some members of this family it germinates fairly quickly, and you can make successive sowings throughout the summer. To grow indoors, sow seed in deep pots that will accommodate the roots.

HARVEST: Leaves can be cut any time for seasoning. For drying cut them just before bloom. To dry the seeds cut the plants when the seed pods start to turn brown and will crack if you pinch them, but before the seeds start to drop. Hang the bunches in paper bags to catch the falling seeds. Rub the pods between your fingers to get them all out.

DILL
Anethum graveolens

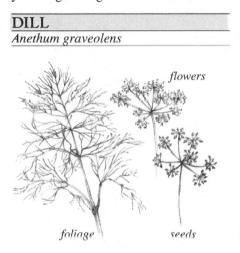

flowers

foliage   *seeds*

DESCRIPTION: Dill has very pretty, wavy, threadlike leaves that are bluish in color, and its flat, umbrella-shaped yellow flowers produce pungent seeds. I use the leaves in many dishes, especially in salads and with fish. Dill is a tall plant, sometimes growing to 4 or 5 feet. A half-hardy annual, it self-sows readily and is very easy to grow.

HOW TO GROW: I grow dill indoors sometimes, so I can always have a bit of its fresh-tasting leaves for seasoning, but the plant does get very gawky in a container, even when snipped regularly. The best solution is to always have a few new pots going. Outdoors it makes a big stand of attractive plants. When it starts to go to seed I cut the big flowers to lend

an airy touch to bouquets.

Dill needs full sun and a steady water supply, but the soil should be well drained—also slightly acid and moderately fertile. Seeds can be sown in early spring, or in late summer for next year's crop. (My plants usually do this themselves, by self-sowing.)

HARVEST: Dill leaves taste best fresh, but can be dried or quick-frozen in plastic or as ice cubes. The seeds hold their flavor better than the spidery leaves do. Cut the flowers when the seeds are brown but not yet dropping, then hang them in a paper bag till the seeds drop.

MINT
Mentha

DESCRIPTION: Mint is such a strong flavoring that I don't use it for very many things; but when I need it I am very glad I have some around. I stuff large handfuls into jugs of iced tea (*before* it's iced, so the tea will absorb more flavor) and sprinkle small snippings of it into cold mixed fruit or in homemade ice cream, sherbet and ices. It is said to be excellent for settling the stomach.

Mint is a very hardy, vigorous perennial that grows 1–3 feet tall depending on the species and conditions. Most species of mint have crinkly leaves, an upright growth habit and attractive purplish flowers. Spearmint (*Mentha spi-*

cata) has the strongest flavor. Other popular garden mints include peppermint (*M. piperita*), with dark, pointed leaves, and apple mint (*M. rotundifolia*), whose leaves are rounded, gray-green and somewhat hairy. (The last is more compact and best for indoor growing.) Most mints grown as herbs are hybrid varieties that do not breed true to seed. There are many other good hybrid mints that you can explore.

HOW TO GROW: Having *some* mint around is never a problem; having just a *little* mint is harder. If you do not restrain the plant in some way, your herb garden will simply be a mint garden. Gardeners devise their own schemes, the more successful of which will involve a barrier not only around the mint, but under it—generally a stout container such as a bucket, with some holes for drainage. Mint roots will, eventually, snake themselves over the top and through the holes, but you can buy yourself a lot of time this way.

Mint will grow well in full sun but prefers partial shade and a rich, moist soil. Pinching back the stems and snipping off flowers as they form will make the plants bushier. Even if cut right to the ground, it will regrow. Mint may be easily propagated to increase your supply. ("Why?" you ask. Answer: to give some to a friend or bring indoors.) Just dig up a plant with runners attached, cutting the stems back, or root a runner or stem in moist sand. Before bringing a pot of mint indoors, cut it back and keep it outdoors for a few weeks of freezing nights.

HARVEST: Snip as needed. To dry, keep the leaves on the stems until they are dry, crumble them off and dry them some more; then store in airtight jars. The leaves may also be frozen.

OREGANO
Origanum

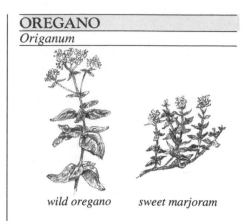

wild oregano   sweet marjoram

DESCRIPTION: I have always felt a bit confused on the subject of oregano verses marjoram, but I don't feel too badly, because so are the botanists. Wild oregano (*Origanum vulgare*) is the available plant that most closely resembles the stuff they put on pizza, though I am told the jars of oregano you buy in the market are really a blend of several different "Italian" herbs. Sweet marjoram has a milder flavor, and its botanical name is *O. majorana* or *Majorana hortensis*, depending on whom you talk to. The difference between the two plants is quite clear, though. Wild oregano is a big, sprawling thing that will make it through the harshest winter; sweet marjoram is a lower, more trailing plant which, though perennial, is not hardy except in warm climates. It has oval leaves and knotlike nodes along the stems, which is why it is sometimes called "knotted marjoram." I grow wild oregano in the garden, mainly because bees and butterflies love its lavish display of pinkish flowers. For kitchen seasonings I am more apt to use my sweet marjoram, which does better as a potted herb than oregano.

HOW TO GROW: Both oregano and marjoram prefer full sun and light, well-drained, slightly alkaline soil. Both benefit by being cut back, especially wild oregano, which should also be divided every few years after it becomes very woody. In addition to division, you can propagate from stem cuttings—or from seed, though germination is fairly slow.

HARVEST: Both oregano and marjoram have better flavor if cut just before they bloom. They dry very well hung upside down in a paper bag or in a dark, airy place. Crumble the leaves off the stems when they are completely dry.

PARSLEY
Petroselinum

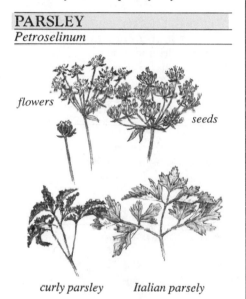

flowers

seeds

curly parsley   *Italian parsely*

DESCRIPTION: Through history, parsley has had powerful symbolic connotations, death and fertility among them. What a come-down to wind up in the twentieth century as the world's most boring garnish. I do remember that among my girlhood classmates, eating parsley was believed to increase the size of the breasts, and nary a plate was sent back to the kitchen at lunch hour with parsley still on it. And health-conscious folk always extol parsley as a source of vitamins A and C, as well as iron. Some of its aura has also returned with the recent resurgence of Italian broad-

leaved parsley, which is actually cut up and used in food instead of merely sitting next to it. But gone are the days when you could just wave parsley in front of an advancing army and cause the soldiers to retreat in terror (if you believe Plutarch).

I would not be without it, nonetheless. A hardy biennial, parsley self-sows dependably in my garden, and new plants await me in early spring. In warm climates you can harvest it all year. I grow both the foot-high curly parsley (*Petroselinum crispum*) and the slightly taller Italian (*P. neapolitanum*). Parsley is an important butterfly plant. Watch for some particularly gorgeous caterpillars on it, green- and black-striped with yellow spots. In return for a small share of your parsley crop they will turn into black swallowtail butterflies that will hover around the flowers of your other herbs, especially the pink and purple ones.

HOW TO GROW: Parsley likes full sun or light shade. Soil should be rich, well lightened with organic matter and moist but well drained. Sow early in the spring or in fall, soaking the seeds overnight to speed up germination, which can take up to three weeks. Or buy started plants for an earlier harvest. Thin to about 6–8 inches apart. The plants regrow beautifully if cut back, even to the base. If you are just snipping, take the outer leaves. Plants can be dug up in fall and brought indoors for winter use, but I think it's also a good idea to start some from seed indoors at the same time so that you will have some fresh plants by the time the old ones start to go to seed.

HARVEST: The leaves are good fresh, frozen or dried. Dry hanging upside down or on screens in a shaded, well-ventilated place.

ROSEMARY
Rosmarinus officinalis

DESCRIPTION: Rosemary is an evergreen perennial in Zones 8 through 10. In cold climates it could, I suppose, be grown as an annual, but a far more satisfactory method is to keep it as a potted plant. It will never achieve the grand scale of the 6-foot hedges you find in the south, but it will become a 2- or 3-foot woody shrub with handsome, dark green, needlelike leaves that smell pungent if you so much as touch them. I use rosemary a lot in cooking, particularly in Mediterranean meat dishes. I may not be able to smell the rosemary miles out from shore, the way sailors do in Greece, but I can smell it all through the house (mingled with the scent of garlic) when I am cooking roast lamb or veal chops.

HOW TO GROW: Grow rosemary in full sun. It will tolerate soil that is slightly dry, rocky and poor, but drainage needs to be excellent (use a raised bed if necessary). A slightly alkaline soil is preferable, so if yours is very acid, plant it with a handful of lime.

Rosemary is rarely grown from seed. It is easier to just buy a small plant from a nursery, or to get a friend to layer some for you (page 499) or to root a soft stem cutting in wet sand. Grow it right in the ground in warm zones; in borderline ones, try mulching the plant heavily and you might be able to overwinter it. I simply set my potted rosemary out in spring and bring it inside in fall, being careful not to let the soil in the pot dry out.

HARVEST: I prefer to use rosemary fresh, but it also dries well. Cut some stems and dry them on screens or hang them in a paper bag. Then strip the leaves from the stems and store them in jars.

SAGE
Salvia officinalis

DESCRIPTION: Sage has long, pointed, pebbly-textured leaves. Usually they're gray-green ("sage green," no less, like all those sweaters) but there is also a wonderful yellow variety called 'Golden Sage,' and one called 'Tricolor,' which is purple-red, green and white. Pineapple sage (*Salvia rutilans*) has bright red flowers; those of clary sage (*S. sclarea*) are very fragrant. Most plants are 1½– 2½ feet tall and get rather broad and woody after a few years. (My 'Golden Sage' stays quite compact, however.)

HOW TO GROW: The plants like full sun and very well drained soil that is not over-rich. Most gardeners just buy a plant, but you can grow sage from seed, starting it indoors in very early spring. You can also take stem cuttings or divide or layer an established plant. These are good ways to obtain an indoor sage plant, or to renew an overgrown one that has a lot of dead wood in the center of the clump. Cutting back sage plants once or twice during the season keeps them from taking up the whole garden and produces nice fresh growth. It also rejuvenates tired house-grown plants.

HARVEST: Pick fresh sage leaves whenever you need them; cut sprigs for drying just before the plant flowers. It is sometimes hard to get enough moisture out of sage leaves to store them in jars; if so, you can just leave them hanging in bunches.

TARRAGON
Artemisia dracunculus

DESCRIPTION: This hardy perennial becomes a woody shrub, usually about 3 feet tall. Its long, slender, dark green leaves have a strong, slightly licorice-like flavor that you either enjoy or you don't. I love it—in salads, in sauce béarnaise, in vinegars and many other ways, too. Ideally I like to have a big tarragon plant in the garden so that I can harvest great gobfuls of it in summer, plus one or two potted plants inside for winter. You should buy only plants labeled "French tarragon." The tarragon market has been infiltrated by a Russian variety that, while a vigorous plant, has little or no real tarragon flavor.

HOW TO GROW: Tarragon prefers full sun but will take some shade. It grows best in very well drained, slightly sandy, alkaline soil. If your soil is heavy and wet, make a raised bed and mix plenty of organic matter into it. In very hot climates the plant may go dormant in summer. In cold climates cut the plants back in fall. If it gets extremely cold where you live, mulch with evergreen boughs or salt hay. Unlike Russian tarragon, French tarragon is not grown from seed. Purchase a plant or obtain a division or a stem or root cutting from a friend. Dividing your plants every few years will keep them vigorous and also keep the flavor strong. To bring tarragon plants indoors, pot up and let sit in freezing weather for a few weeks.

HARVEST: Cut leaves for drying at a time when it is not rainy or humid, by hanging them upside down in a paper bag or in a dark, airy place. Store the leaves in airtight jars. Freeze in plastic bags or containers or as tarragon butter. Make tarragon vinegar. But *try* to keep a pot of fresh tarragon around all the time if you are a tarragon lover, because it tastes best fresh.

THYME
Thymus

DESCRIPTION: Thyme is a low, woody plant, sometimes shrubby, sometimes prostrate. It has tiny little round leaves with a beautifully aromatic scent—if you walk across a bed of thyme, you scent the air around you. Its flowers, usually borne in early summer, are shades of pink and purple and attract butterflies and bees. Thyme is an excellent landscaping plant, especially useful for filling in cracks between paving stones. It is one of the most useful culinary seasonings, too. There are also dozens and dozens of different thymes you can collect, with different scents and often with strikingly different foliage colors. All are hardy perennials. No wonder there is a sort of thyme cult out there, and herb nurseries that take pride in having long lists of thymes in their catalogs.

Cooks generally grow *Thymus vulgaris,* variously known as "common thyme," "garden thyme" and "black thyme"—because it has the best flavor. Within this species you can choose among German thyme, with broad leaves, French thyme, with narrow ones, and English thyme, which is variegated. There is also lemon thyme (*T. citriodorus*) and creeping thyme, also known as "wild thyme" or "mother-of-thyme" (*T. serpyllum*). Both common thyme and creeping thyme have yellow and silver forms that are beautiful in the garden.

HOW TO GROW: Thyme needs full sun and prefers sandy, very well drained soil. If your soil is heavy, lighten it with organic matter. Gardeners usually start thyme from divisions; they propagate it by dividing when the center of a clump dies, or by layering. In cool climates it is better to cut plants back in spring than in fall (heavy cutting in fall produces tender growth that will only be winterkilled), and sometimes a mulch is needed to protect against ice damage. In addition, don't let the soil around the plants get too soggy in winter.

HARVEST: Just before the plant blooms, cut sprigs and hang them upside down in the dark. Strip off the leaves when dry and store in a jar.

CHAPTER 9

FRUITS

When I think about growing fruits I think of the walled "paradise" gardens of ancient Persia, filled with pomegranates. I think of my southern grandfather plucking ripe persimmons off a tree and eating them. I picture a sybaritic California garden filled with avocados, loquats, lemons and figs, or a place in the tropics where really exotic fruits like cherimoyas are grown. My idea of luxury is an orangery in which I could grow fruits like these indoors.

Such things are possible—but, for most of us, unaffordable. As a northern gardener I must be content with sweet strawberries and raspberries in early summer, followed by blueberries and dark 'Concord' grapes, then crisp apples in fall. But after all, that's a rich harvest! Wherever you live, there are fruits that do best not in some faraway place but in your own backyard. You just have to figure out which fruits are your favorites, and you have to learn which varieties of them feel at home where you live so that you can grow them without a struggle.

Fruit crops vary a great deal. Small fruits such as grapes and berries are grown quite differently from tree fruits. Since most fruit crops take up more space than flowers or vegetables, however, they are alike in that you have to plan for them carefully. Hence "the vineyard," "the orchard" and "the berry patch." Fruits are almost all perennial crops, so they must be planted in a place that has been carefully chosen for their needs—and then left there. "But wait," you may say. "I can't have an orchard or a vineyard. I own a third of an acre in suburban Minneapolis." No problem. Most fruits can be grown on a small property in a way that not only fits the space but also provides visual interest. For gardeners who plant grapes on arbors, apples as small shade trees, or cherries for the sheer beauty of their blossoms, the fruits are often extra.

The following pages give an introduction to some popular fruits for home planting. Refer to Chapters 2 and 15 for more information on topics such as planting, growing, protecting and pruning trees, and to Chapter 2 for advice on how to deal with pests and diseases. Refer to the first section of this chapter, on apples, for some specific topics that concern fruits in general, such as training and pruning for a better harvest, thinning fruits, the advantages and disadvantages of dwarf trees, the best site for an orchard and why some fruit trees bear only in alternate years. You should also keep in mind when dealing with any fruit that some are "self-fertile" and can pollinate their own flowers, whereas others need a second variety of the same fruit to ensure pollination—one that comes into bloom at the same time. Espaliering fruits—training them so that they grow in a two-dimensional plane such as flat against a wall—is unfortunately beyond the scope of this book. But it is not a skill beyond the grasp of the beginning gardener. If you are growing fruits in a small space and wish to try some espaliers, refer to the books listed on page 630.

Most of the important lore about fruits is local. Talk to people in your area—friends and neighbors, owners of orchards and berry farms, nurserymen, and people at the Extension Service or local agricultural research stations run by the state or by colleges and universities. And try to give the fruits you grow the taste test first. No matter how highly rated a fruit is, it is important that something you spend so much time bringing to bear be tasty to you and worthy of inclusion in your own backyard "paradise."

McIntosh apple

Red Delicious apple

crab apple

Apples

The poet D. H. Lawrence, who wrote much about country matters in general, had much to say about apples. In "Beautiful Old Age" he compares people who have had rich, full lives "unsoured with accepted lies" with mature apples hanging on a tree:

> If people lived without accepting lies
> they would ripen like apples, and be
> scented like pippins
> in their old age.

This might not be quite how you picture growing old gracefully, but you must admit that Lawrence's image is apt: apple trees are particularly good at aging. We talk of the grandeur of "mature" oaks or spruces, but apple trees look their best when they are *old*. Each old tree acquires a shape all its own, the branches gnarled and craggy, the trunk thick and covered with rough bark. In spring old apple trees still cover themselves in a froth of pink-and-white flowers, like six-year-old-ballerinas, but under a heavy, wet snow they're like old men with white hair, beards and eyebrows. Probably a few frozen apples are still hanging high up where nobody can reach. Ever pick one? Sometimes there's fermented syrup, like a sweet applejack, inside those dark red frozen globes. And the trees' old limbs make the best firewood, perfuming the room with a faint apple scent.

Though I admittedly have a special liking for the way apple trees look, their enormous popularity is a result of their usefulness, not their beauty. No fruit is more versatile for both cooking and eating fresh, and few fruits grow as vigorously and in so many parts of the country. Though apples generally do best in areas where the winter temperature does not stay below 20 degrees for long and is not above 40 degrees for more than forty days throughout the winter, there are varieties that can be grown even under these conditions.

Apple trees live about thirty-five

years; at ages ten to thirty they are at their most productive. The traditional way to grow them is in an orchard with other apple trees. This is because most are not self-fertile, so several varieties are needed to ensure pollination. Varieties that are particularly good pollinators are called "rooster trees"; these include 'Golden Delicious,' 'Cortland' and 'Jonathan.' Notoriously poor pollinators include 'Gravenstein' and 'Winesap.'

Since different kinds of apples mature at different times, you'll also need several varieties for each season, all of which will bear pollen at the same time. Generally the early-bearing apples are eating apples: they are sweet and tasty but don't keep well. Late-bearing apples are the good winter keepers, usually best for cooking. Midseason apple varieties can be either good eating or good cooking. So with roughly three seasons and several apple varieties maturing at each season, it's easy to fill a small orchard. That is fine if you have the space. After all, there are so many ways to use apples—in pies, apple crisp, applesauce, apple butter, apple jelly, cider, apple wine, or eaten fresh—and there are so many fine apple varieties to try, that you might well want an orchard full of them.

Even if you don't, however, apples make good landscaping trees, meaning that placed in the right spot they can grace your yard as well as provide fruit. Since the tallest ones rarely exceed 40 feet, apple trees—and especially the crab apples—make excellent small ornamental or shade trees. They also look lovely lined up along a fence or next to a driveway, providing an attractive welcome in any season.

So much for the good news about apples. The bad news is that while the trees themselves are easy to grow, it is not all that easy to get a big harvest of perfect-looking fruits like those that come wrapped in plastic at the supermarket. A number of diseases and insect pests plague apples (as well as many other tree fruits), and while few do much harm to the general health of the tree, the fruits you grow yourself will probably be blemished unless you live in a part of the country where problems are rare or unless you take measures to combat them. The traditional advice to home apple growers was to embark on a massive spray program that had you in a gas mask all summer, spraying poisons all over your property—something I do not advise. I think you can enjoy home apple production if you set your sights on less than total perfection and employ a few effective and safe means of dealing with apple problems (more about this below).

Standard-sized apple trees are generally between 25 and 40 feet high at maturity. That's small for an ordinary tree but large for a fruit tree. Unless you are growing apples as shade trees or want a very large apple yield, you may not want a tree that big. Maintenance tasks such as pruning, thinning and spraying, not to mention harvesting, will be more difficult the larger the tree; and you will not be able to plant as many trees if you grow big ones. Fortunately for the owner of a small property, apple trees don't have to be so large. They can be grafted onto dwarfing rootstocks to produce trees as small as 6 feet tall in the case of miniatures, though most dwarf apple trees are about 8–12 feet, and most semidwarfs 12–20. All apple trees are grafted, mind you, even the standard-sized ones, because they rarely breed true to seed. Standard-sized trees are grafted onto the rootstock of a particularly vigorous variety that will put out a strong root system and resist the diseases that apple roots might otherwise get.

Dwarf trees have other advantages over standard-sized varieties, as well. Fruit that drops from a dwarf does not fall far and is less apt to bruise. And best of all, dwarf trees take up much less space. You can grow as many as nine dwarf trees in the space it would take to grow a standard-sized one.

A drawback to dwarfs is that they have relatively shallow root systems. As a result they usually need to be staked heavily and permanently, or espaliered—trained flat against a wall—or grown in rows supported by horizontal wires. Dwarf varieties are not suitable for very cold climates where the roots can be winterkilled. Semidwarfs fare better in cold and need less staking, but even they cannot take very cold winters. From Zone 4 northward it is best to stick to standard-sized trees.

The delicacy of dwarf apple trees can be overcome by complex grafting. Sometimes dwarf trees are grown on an "interstem" graft—a double-grafting technique whereby a piece of main stem imparts the dwarfing habit but is in turn grafted onto sturdier roots. These trees will often withstand harsher conditions that single-grafted dwarfs can. Also bear in mind that trees can be kept smaller by other means, such as pruning. Soil conditions will also make a difference; trees grown on soil that is very rich may grow larger than you'd like even if they are on dwarf rootstocks. There are also trees in which the scion (the main part of the tree that is grafted onto the rootstock) has a dwarfing habit. An example of this would be a "spur-type" strain, which has very plentiful fruiting spurs—the twigs on which the apples grow. These put their energy into the buds that produce fruit, not those that produce growth. There are spur strains of many popular varieties, and often it makes sense to buy them so you will have a large harvest of fruit that

is also close to the ground and thus easy to pick.

Another thing you need to know about apples is that some bear heavily only in alternate years. (This can happen with other tree fruits as well.) This is because apples form buds at the tips of the fruiting spur for the new crop the year before the spur bears. A heavy crop takes much of the tree's stored food, so that new fruiting buds cannot form, and the tree must rest a year before it has the resources to produce a full crop again. Some varieties bear quite consistently each year. Others will bear annually if soil conditions are particularly good. Those that do not can be made to bear annually by thinning the fruit, an option that gives you a choice between a bumper crop every other year and a smaller one annually.

SITE

Apples like a sunny site with good drainage, preferably a south- or southeast-facing slope, with no more than a 20-percent incline. (On a steeper slope the trees are hard to tend.) If you have a slope like this, don't plant the trees near the bottom. Despite the fact that valleys are sheltered from cold winds and tend to be warmer than higher areas in daytime, cold air can flow down into them at night so that they become "frost pockets." This is a problem in spring when the trees are setting fruit, because buds or flowers can be nipped by frost before pollination can take place. Planting in a frost pocket can also hurt trees in late fall when apples can freeze before ripening. On the other hand, trees growing at the top of the hill may be exposed to harsh, cold winds that can break branches, cause fruit to fall, or winterkill the trees. If you have a choice, partway down the hill is best.

If a site needs wind protection,

planting a windbreak of other trees (page 528) can help. As a rule apples do not do well in seaside areas where the winds are strong and salt-laden.

When you plan your orchard, even if it's only the two or three trees necessary for pollination, be sure to allow enough space between them. Though apple trees are often planted closer than this, I recommend leaving about as much space between them as the ultimate height of the tree. (Try to find out what this is expected to be.) If you plan to have a large number of trees, plant them in rows with enough distance between them so that you'll be able to remove limbs you have pruned out, bring in a pickup truck for harvesting or mulching and do any other tasks that need space. The more room between trees, the more sun they will get, too.

SOIL

Soil for apples should be deep—that is, unobstructed by bedrock or other obstacles. If you are planting on land that has been cleared of trees, the stumps and major roots should be pulled out. Though apples do not require an extremely fertile soil, which in fact can even cause tall, gangly growth at the expense of fruit, they do appreciate some richness, and they need plenty of organic matter to hold moisture and at the same time facilitate drainage. If you have a heavy clay soil, don't just dig pockets and fill them with lightened soil—water will collect there. Try to improve the soil throughout as deeply as possible. A pH between 5.5 and 7.0 is the most suitable for apples.

PLANTING

Apple trees are best planted in early spring in the north; in warm climates they can be planted any time they are dormant. You can buy them by mail order or at a local nursery. Buying by mail will give you a wide choice of varieties, but by shopping locally you may be able to get advice from the seller about varieties that suit the climate, your particular site, and your particular needs.

When you buy a fruit tree it is best to buy it young. Not only will it establish itself better, quickly catching up in size to trees that were older when planted, but you also have more control over the way the tree grows and can give it that very important early pruning that will determine its final shape. It's probably best (and least expensive) to start out with a one-year-old "whip," also called a "maiden." This is just a central stem that has not branched yet. Most mail-order fruit trees are sold bare-root as whips. If you are buying locally you can also start with a two-year-old tree. A whip should be about 4 feet tall. A two-year-old tree should have three or four horizontal branches spaced well apart on a nice straight trunk; the branches should come out at wide angles, not narrow ones, and should be well distributed around the trunk's circumference like the spokes of a wheel. If you are shopping in a nursery you should also check for signs of disease, damaged branches and a poorly developed root system.

Before you plant, trim off any damaged roots. Heel the tree into a spot with well-drained soil if you cannot plant it right away. All the information on planting trees in Chapter 2 applies to apples, and note page 77 and page 530 about protecting them from animal damage. Plant apples so that the graft is at least 2 inches above the soil surface, especially if the tree is a dwarf or semidwarf. Otherwise the wood just above the graft may root, thus circumventing the dwarfing effect created by the rootstock and causing the tree to grow tall. Since dwarf trees are very shallow-rooted, they need to be staked to keep them from blowing over. It's best to do this in a permanent manner when planting. Use a pressure-treated 2-by-4 or a cedar or locust post 6 to 7 feet tall and sunk at least 2 feet into the ground. Then tie the tree loosely to the stake using wire threaded through sections of garden hose.

The young tree should be cut back when it is planted. By doing this you accomplish several things. You compensate for the loss of roots the tree has suffered when it was dug, you encourage the tree to start branching low enough on the trunk so that harvesting will be easier, and you start to create a scaffold of branches that is shaped in such a way that the tree will look good and bear well. If you have planted a whip, cut it back by about a third, just above a bud. If it has branches, cut these back by about a quarter of their length to an outward-facing bud. Save only the three to five branches with the best placement and crotch angles, rubbing off buds between them with your thumb. Branches that are growing vertically, with narrow crotches, should be removed. The uppermost branch that you keep will become the central leader. If all the branches are too high up, beginning three feet or more above the soil surface, you can start over again by removing all of them to make a whip and cutting it back just above a bud.

Be sure that you water your young tree well when you plant it, building an earthen saucer to contain the water. Spread a circle of mulch 3 feet in diameter around the tree, leaving 6 inches between the mulch and the trunk.

GROWING

While the young apple tree is growing, keep it watered and mulched, enlarging the circle of mulch so that it reaches at least as far out as the branches. A mulch is especially important with trees that are young or dwarfed and thus have shallow roots. It protects the trees from winter injury, loss of moisture and competition from grass and weeds. Thick straw is a good mulch; so is about 4 inches of shredded bark. Some growers just let grass grow around the trees, and many an apple tree has done perfectly well with this treatment, but they do better with the mulch. Don't have either grass or mulch right near the trunk, since both can encourage mice.

Avoid feeding your young tree until at least a year after planting, but after that some top dressing will help it to grow, to bear earlier, and even to produce more fruit on its "off" years if it is an alternate-year bearer. I think spreading an inch or two of rotted manure or compost on top of the soil under the tree's whole canopy works wonders—you'll have to rake aside the mulch to do it, but it's worth it. Wood ashes and a phosphorus source like bone meal can also be beneficial if you dig them into the top few inches of earth to help them get down to where the roots are. Most of all, however, apple trees need a good supply of nitrogen. If you don't have manure handy, purchase some cottonseed meal or blood meal and water it into the soil thoroughly, or apply a pound of a balanced fertilizer such as 10–10–10 throughout the root zone for every inch of the trunk's diameter. Feeding is best done very early in the spring so that the new growth it produces can harden off before winter. This treatment can be continued throughout the tree's life and is especially helpful for reviving an old tree that has slowed down in its bearing but still has a few good years to go.

TRAINING AND PRUNING APPLE TREES   *Fig. 53*
(green lines indicate pruning cuts)

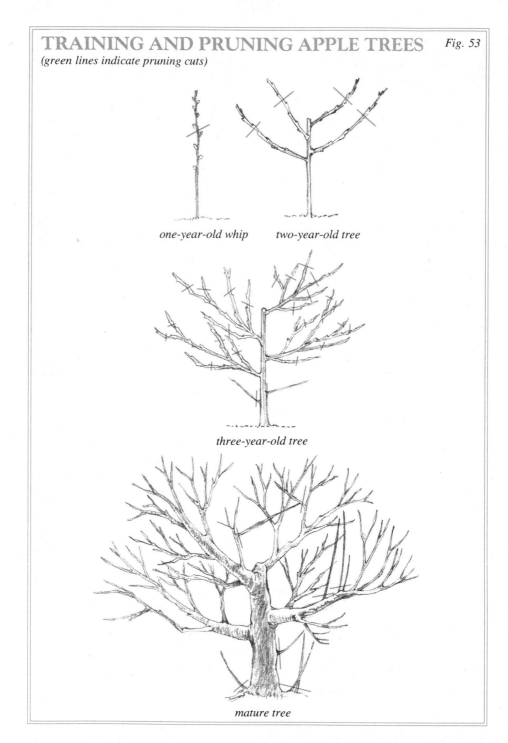

one-year-old whip   two-year-old tree

three-year-old tree

mature tree

During the tree's early years keep your pruners handy, and continue the training program that you began when you planted it. If it started as a whip, prune it the second year as described above for a new two-year-old tree. In the third year of its life you will be encouraging some more well-placed lateral branches to form from the main trunk, creating more of a framework, and you will be choosing the best side branches that form on them. Keep the ones that grow outward rather than back toward the center of the tree. The more vigorous the side branch, the more it is cut back; this will keep all the branches in balance.

Your goal in pruning apples is to let light into the tree from above so that more fruits will be produced and ripen well. Everything I say about pruning trees in Chapter 15 applies to fruit trees, but the need for pruning is greater with them than with the others because you are producing not only a pleasing shape, but also a shape that will help the trees to bear fruit. Eliminate branches that cross one another or grow right under the branch above. Imagine the spokes of a wheel ascending like a spiral up the trunk of the tree, letting in light and air.

Some growers simply remove the top third of an apple tree to let in sunlight. Even if you don't want to take such drastic measures, at least keep the center fairly open, and head back branches so that those on top are short and those below them increasingly long. That way, the tips of all branches receive light.

Regular maintenance pruning also entails removal of water sprouts, which come up from the branches and suckers, which come up from the base of the trunk. Overpruning a tree may lead to the formation of many water sprouts and may dwarf the tree and reduce the fruit yield (though that may be just what you

are trying to accomplish). This is where experience comes in; as you work with your trees you'll learn to balance growth with fruitfulness and achieve just what you want from them.

Spur-type strains of apple tree, because they put more energy into fruiting than growing upward, need less pruning than other types but profit from thinning. Thinning the fruit to one per cluster, or about 6 or 8 inches between fruits, will make each fruit larger and relieve the branches of the weight of too much fruit. It will reduce insect and disease problems and often induce an alternate-bearing tree to produce an annual crop. Thinning fruit is usually done six to eight weeks after flowering, while the apples are still small.

Crab apples also need less pruning than most other apple trees and can become covered with water sprouts if overpruned. Thinning them is rather impractical too, since the fruits are so numerous and tiny. If they are alternate bearers, and many crabs are, you can try top dressing them with manure, but usually you just have to be content with blossoms and fruit in alternate years.

People often have old, neglected apple trees on their property. Lovely as they are, you may decide to give them some reconstructive surgery to improve their health, prolong their lives and encourage them to bear, and as long as the trunk is not hollow or many of the limbs lost to breakage or disease, they may well be worth saving. Even if they are bearing, chances are all the fruit is way up at the top of the tree where you can't reach it, and the lower branches are too shaded to bear. If the tree is tall, you may want to enlist a professional's aid for safety's sake.

The best way to tackle the job of restoring an old tree is in stages. The first year remove any dead branches, suckers and watersprouts. The second year remove the worst of the crossing or inward-leading branches and some of the top branches, to let in light. The third year do the same thing, but more completely. Work from the bottom of the tree up, and from the trunk outwards, thereby opening up some room for you to work in, and taking care of the major cuts first.

The traditional time to prune apple trees is in winter or very early spring when they are dormant. It's also a convenient time because it gets you outdoors when nothing else is going on in your gardening life except misting your indoor ferns or bringing pots of forced spring bulbs out of the darkness. Be aware, however, that winter pruning has the effect of producing vigorous new growth, because when spring comes the tree will respond to your stimulus with gusto, and you may end up with a lot of thick new growth toward the inside of the tree where you don't want it. If you are renewing an old tree in stages or trying to keep a rapidly growing younger one within bounds, you might try pruning in midsummer instead, when growth is slowing, especially in a warm climate where new growth can be particularly rampant. Then when you have the tree tamed, so to speak, do some winter pruning toward the end of the branches to encourage fruiting.

PESTS AND DISEASES

Unfortunately, not much of what I have to tell you in this section is cheering if you are as loath as I am to use poisons when you garden, especially on food crops. What discourages gardeners from apple growing is not the intricacies of pruning, pollinating and picking. These are all pretty simple tasks, really, and if you follow even half the advice I've given you'll probably do satisfactorily. Most discouragement is due to attacks by critters that gnaw and girdle the trunks, and by insects and fungus diseases that disfigure the fruit and make it unappetizing. The trunk-nibblers are the most deadly—a baby rabbit can decimate your prize young apple tree in minutes—but fortunately they are also the easiest problem to deal with. Just follow the advice for protecting trunks on page 77. The fruit spoilers are less of a problem if you're growing cider apples and perhaps some for baking—the ugly parts can be cut out and discarded. Some pests, however, such as apple maggots, do so much damage that often there are no good parts to keep at all. Furthermore, most of us like to have some "pretty" apples, too, to put in a bowl on the kitchen table and bite into confidently without fear of bad surprises.

If you live in a part of the country where apple plagues are rampant I can only offer you protective measures that will help to give you *some* pretty apples, while urging you to settle for less than perfection. Let's start with the dastardly apple maggot, also called the "railroad worm" because in its larval stage it tunnels through the fruit leaving little brown tracks. The maggot is also called the "apple fly" because it's not unlike a housefly in the adult stage. It starts its fruit-tunneling journey in mid-June in warm climates, early July in colder ones. Planting late-maturing apple varieties will help to outfox the apple maggot; but for your early crops be ready for him with the red sticky ball traps described on page 73. Hang the balls throughout the tree, about six per tree for standard trees, three or four for semidwarfs, one or two for dwarfs. You won't get all the maggots, but enough will be gummed up on your ersatz apples that you'll probably reduce the damage quite a bit. Hanging out jars of molasses and water spiked with ammonia and soap (which lure and then kill the flies) also works. Picking up apples that fall to the ground and removing them far from the tree will also help minimize infestations from one year to the next.

The codling moth, which makes a larger hole than the apple maggot and goes straight to the core of the fruit, is another serious apple pest. Long ago the remedy was to build a bonfire in the orchard to lure the moths. The customary bonfire—probably an excuse for a good party on a summer evening—was later displaced by the use of insecticide sprays. Modern nontoxic methods of control include wrapping the trees in collars of corrugated cardboard with the bumpy side next to the tree, letting the moths spin cocoons in the collars, and destroying the cocoons regularly until after harvest time. You can also scrape loose bark from the trees—this also dislodges cocoons. (Scrape carefully, lest you injure the tree.) Pheromone traps may also help control codling moths.

Using a dormant-oil spray on your apple trees can be effective against a number of problems including scale, leaf rollers, mites, aphids and even apple-scab disease. It should be applied just before the flower buds open (page 73). A blast of insecticidal soap spray may help to control some insect pests. Using a device that attaches to your garden hose will make spraying your trees a lot easier. Some of the sources listed beginning on page 620 will give you more details about coping with individual pests, but keep in mind the importance of cleaning up debris such as fallen fruit, fallen leaves, and rotted portions of the tree, which may harbor insect larvae from one year to the next.

Diseases are a bit less discouraging to the home apple grower than insects because of the development of so many disease-resistant varieties. While some are suggested below, I recommend that you research the subject further, finding out from your Extension Service what diseases you can expect in your locality and what apple varieties that do well in your area can best resist them. Beyond this the best prevention, as always, is tidiness—raking up dropped fruit and dead leaves and cleaning out any infected parts of the tree according to the method described on page 536.

The most annoying and prevalent disease of apples is apple scab, which causes dark spots to form on the leaves, twigs and fruit. It overwinters in fallen leaves and is especially active in rainy weather. Clean up all debris, plant resistant varieties whenever possible, and if these measures fail, try dormant-oil spray.

Cedar apple rust, which produces rust-colored spots on the leaves, especially during wet spring weather, occurs only when you have red cedar trees (*Juniperus virginiana*) nearby. The disease spreads from the junipers to the apple trees and back again but not from juniper to juniper or from apple to apple. Break up the team by growing junipers or apples but not both. If your neighbors won't part with their junipers, grow resistant varieties.

If your trees get fire blight (the ends of the branches will look blackened and burned), prune out the diseased portions and burn them, sterilizing your tools after every cut you make, and grow resistant varieties. A wettable sulfur spray applied weekly in warm weather may help save disease-prone apple crops, but the best prevention is removal of all debris and the selection of disease-resistant varieties.

HARVEST

How do you know when an apple is ripe? A ripe apple looks and tastes the way it is supposed to look and taste. It picks easily, hanging onto its own little stem but severing without resistance from the fruiting spur, which must remain on the tree to produce more apples next year. Some apples, notably the late-maturing ones, can be picked a bit before they are ripe so that they can ripen off the tree without danger of freezing. Always pick the early ones right on time, though.

If you've just planted your first collection of apple trees, you'll no doubt be impatient for your first harvest. It may take a good six or seven years, though, before you have a respectable crop. When your trees are mature, expect anywhere from seven to twenty bushels for a standard-sized tree but as little as one bushel for the smallest dwarfs.

"Keeping apples" (the later-maturing ones) should be stored at a temperature just above freezing, if possible, in a fairly moist atmosphere, and they should not be piled too deep. More than half a bushel deep invites rot. Inspect them from time to time; one rotten apple can, as they say, ruin the whole barrel. You should not try to store apples that are nicked or bruised. Those that are not keeping apples should be eaten or made into jelly, applesauce or apple butter right away.

VARIETIES

Choosing apple varieties can be daunting because there are so many good ones and because you want to be sure the ones you've selected are worth the wait—and the work. First, order some catalogs (page 618) and see what varieties exist. Read the descriptions carefully—not just phrases like "irresistibly flavorful and juicy," but remarks about suitability for different purposes, how the tree grows, what climates it is appropriate for, what time during the season it bears, and which diseases it is resistant to, if any.

The nursery catalogs will help narrow down your choices somewhat, but what tastes wonderful to some may seem uninteresting to you. Therefore, I suggest you also try to find a pick-your-own orchard located nearby, where you can taste a number of different apples, observe how they grow and even get advice from the owner about their culture. (See the listing for "Applesource" on page 619.) In the meantime here is a brief rundown of what is out there.

Old standbys. While many of these apples have been improved upon by hybridization, they have nonetheless stood the test of time and are still grown. Look for "improved strains" with superior characteristics such as better keeping ability, color, flavor or disease resistance, as well as a "spur-type," dwarf or semidwarf habit. These are among the standards by which the newer apples are measured.

'Delicious.' This is the popular variety's original name, though it is often called 'Red Delicious' to distinguish it from 'Golden Delicious.' Still the most popular eating apple in America, it is very red, very sweet and a good keeper. Not for the far north.

'Golden Delicious.' Also called 'Yellow Delicious,' it is like 'Delicious' only in that both are very sweet. This one is much rounder and grows on an extremely vigorous tree that bears while young; it is a late-season apple. It is one of the few apples that does not need a pollinator. Not for northern zones.

'Jonathan.' A red midseason apple that is good for eating fresh or for cider, less good for pies or storage. Popular in the Midwest.

'McIntosh.' Best for eating fresh, with outstanding flavor, it grows on a hardy, vigorous tree but is susceptible to scab and other diseases. Early.

'Yellow Transparent.' A very early, hardy and vigorous yellow apple that does well most anywhere.

'Baldwin.' A large, red, midseason apple, long considered a good all-purpose apple for cooking or eating.

'Granny Smith.' An old-timer that has had an overwhelming recent resurgence in popularity, this green apple is a classic late-bearing one, excellent for storage. Although it's rather tart, it is popular for both eating and cooking. Not for northern zones.

'Wealthy.' A crisp, hardy old-timer that bears early in the season and is popular in the Midwest.

'Cortland.' A good all-purpose, midseason apple that doesn't turn brown when cut.

'Rome Beauty.' Also called 'Red Rome Beauty,' this very large red apple is excellent for baking, bears young, and is quite disease-resistant. A late-season apple.

'Grimes Golden.' A hardy, disease-resistant and tasty late-season apple that is yellow inside as well as out.

'Winesap.' A classic, all-purpose late red apple, good for cooking, cider and storage. It bears young.

'Northern Spy.' An all-purpose midseason apple and a great keeper.

'Winter Banana.' A large midseason apple with a unique flavor. Yellow blushed with pinkish red, it does well in warm climates including that of southern California.

Newer apples. Some of these are brand-new and excellent, others have been around somewhat longer and have acquired a fine reputation.

'Mutsu.' This Japanese introduction is a big, yellow-green, midseason apple, slightly tart but tasty and a good keeper.

'Red June.' This very early apple is deep red and great for cider or eating.

'Black Arkansas.' This late apple is very dark red, a fine cooking apple and a good keeper.

'Empire.' This very popular new apple is a cross between 'McIntosh' and 'Delicious.' It is a midseason apple with excellent flavor for eating.

'Jerseymac.' A dark red, early apple, fine for cooking.

'Macoun.' This is one of my favorites. It is a midseason apple rather like McIntosh but larger, and it has a very fine flavor.

'Idared.' A late, very red apple with white, crisp flesh, fine for both eating and cooking; an excellent keeper.

Disease-resistant apples. One of the best recent developments in apple culture has been the breeding of apples that resist the major apple diseases. Here are some of the best.

'Liberty.' An early to midseason, all-purpose, sweet apple. Crisp and juicy, stores well.

'Freedom.' A hardy, all-purpose, early to midseason apple.

'Prima' and 'Priscilla.' Both are early and slightly tart.

'Macfree.' Similar to McIntosh. Grows on a vigorous tree. Keeps well and tastes best when stored awhile.

Low-chill apples. Apples suited to the cold winters and short growing seasons of the northern states and Canada are noted above as "hardy." There is also a special group, low-chill apples, developed for areas that never get cold enough for most apples to set fruit.

'Anna.' A big pie apple developed in Israel, it is a heavy producer and will grow even in Zone 10.

'Ein Shemer.' Also from Israel, it is similar to 'Golden Delicious' but more tart.

'Dorsett Golden.' A good yellow that will grow in Zone 10.

Crab apples. Crab apples are most often planted as ornamental trees, but many have fruits that are both beautiful and fine to eat or to use in jellies. Here are some good ones.

'Snowdrift.' Disease-resistant variety with white flowers and small, red-orange fruits.

'Dorothea.' Semidouble, deep pink flowers and yellow fruits.

'Profusion.' Vigorous, disease-resistant, with red flowers and fruits.

'Radiant.' Popular ornamental variety with red flowers and fruits.

'Van Eseltine.' Double, pale pink flowers, fruits yellow streaked with red, on a handsomely shaped upright tree.

'Royalty.' Single red flowers, purplish red fruit and maroon foliage.

'Dolgo.' Early red fruits on a vigorous, hardy tree make exquisite jelly.

'Bob White.' White flowers, and fruits that stay on the tree a long time.

Historical Apples

Though many popular apples are very old, there are many other old-time varieties that are less apt to be in general circulation. These have been the subject of historical preservation in recent years—some for nostalgic reasons, others because they really are fine old apples. Some have been passed by because they don't ripen as uniformly or ship as well as modern varieties do, but for the home gardener these drawbacks are not important. Some have skins that might appear funny-looking to the average supermarket shopper; they might have a strange color inside or out, or they might show a rough brownish speckling, called "russeting," a trait that is actually a sign of a good keeper. Here are some apples that have stood up best over the years. They are available in the specialty nurseries listed in the back of the book and now even in some more general nurseries.

'Wolf River.' This large midseason apple is very hardy, grows on a strong tree and is valued for pies.

'Snow Apple' ('Fameuse'). A dark red apple with very white, juicy flesh. Exquisite, but not a keeper. Midseason.

'Esopus Spitzenburg.' A late-midseason Baldwin type that Thomas Jefferson considered the tastiest eating apple. Many still agree. It is yellow-fleshed and an excellent keeper.

'Cox's Orange Pippin.' A very flavorful yellow-fleshed midseason apple, long a favorite in England.

'Golden Russet.' A very sweet russeted apple that bears late and keeps extremely well.

'Westfield Seek-No-Further.' This late-fall apple is very hardy and has especially fine flavor for eating.

'Pound Sweet.' An enormous midseason apple—one is said to be enough for a pie. It is yellow, very sweet, hardy and vigorous.

'Calville Blanc d'Hiver.' A late-bearing European apple especially rich in Vitamin C.

'Sops of Wine.' A medieval variety, good for all purposes, it is dark red with streaks of red running through the white flesh, and it bears early in the season.

'Lady Apple.' This tiny apple dates back to Renaissance France. It has red-and-yellow skin and tasty, crisp white flesh. It bears late in the season.

Apricots

pricots are native to the mountains of Asia and need freezing weather during their dormant period. Though quite cold-hardy, they are happiest in long-summer areas in Zones 6–8, especially the west coast. Since they bloom very early in spring, they don't thrive in areas such as New England where spring weather is erratic and can kill the tender flower buds, thus keeping the trees from fruiting. The tangy fruits are very rich in vitamins and are grown on 20-foot trees that are very long-lived in favorable climates.

SITE

Though southern slopes are good in mild climates, avoid them in areas where early bloom can be frost-nipped, choosing a northern exposure so bloom will be delayed. Don't plant apricots near tomatoes or any other members of the *Solanaceae* (page 184), or near melons, raspberries or strawberries, all of which can transmit disease. (It is even best to avoid places where these plants have grown within five years.) Plant the trees a good 25–30 feet apart unless they are dwarfs. The branches spread wider than the tree is tall.

SOIL

Soil should be deep, with no interference from subsurface rock. Fertile, well-drained loam is ideal; clay soils are all right if not too heavy; sandy soils, because they warm quickly in spring, can cause too-early bloom.

PLANTING

Buy one-year-old trees and plant in early spring while dormant (fall in mild climates). Cut the top back to 2 to 2½ feet.

GROWING

Since apricots are deep-rooted they need to be thoroughly watered, especially when the fruiting buds are developing. Don't overfeed them, though, and avoid high-nitrogen fertilizers that can produce soft fruit with pit burn. Too much growth too fast can also produce weak branches.

Thinning helps produce larger fruit, reduces strain on the branches and keeps the fruits free of disease. Often late frosts will thin the tree for you, or the tree will drop some fruit on its own later on; but if it doesn't, thin fruits to about 3 inches apart when they are thumb-sized. Prune apricots as you would apple trees, heading back the top when it reaches the desired height and keeping it open enough to let in sun to ripen the fruit. Fruiting spurs will stop producing after a few years and should be pruned out to favor new growth.

PESTS AND DISEASES

Several diseases can plague apricots. Brown-rot fungus covers the flowers with gray spores; if you can catch it at this stage and prune out affected areas it may not injure the fruit later. Bacterial canker (black spots on fruit, purplish spots on leaves) should also be pruned out. Black heart, a verticillium fungus, may appear as wilting leaves in early summer and as black streaks within the wood. Avoid growing apricots with the plants mentioned above. Pit burn makes the flesh near the pits turn mushy. Keep the roots cool with mulch in hot weather, and avoid overfeeding. Wounding trunks can cause crown gall, so protect them.

Cankerworms that attack the trees may be deterred by a sticky material wrapped around the trunk (commercially available). Fight borers by promptly removing all dead or diseased wood, including any lying on the ground. Some pests that bother plums and peaches, such as plum curculio and peach-tree borer, also affect apricots.

HARVEST

You can expect to start harvesting some fruits three or four years after planting. A healthy, mature tree can produce as much as 250 pounds of apricots. Pick when fruit is ripe and can be picked easily, but before it loses its firmness.

VARIETIES

Most apricot trees are self-pollinating, so the time of bearing is less important in selecting varieties than is the area in which you live. The late-bearing 'Moorpark' and the early 'Goldcot' are the most popular varieties in prime apricot country. Other good varieties include 'Hungarian Rose,' 'Early Golden' and 'Perfection' (the last is not self-fertile). In colder climates you will do better with 'Moongold,' 'Alfred,' 'Chinese,' 'Sungold' and a series bred for both hardiness and disease-resistance that includes 'Harcot,' 'Harglow' and 'Hargrand.' There are also varieties such as 'Erligold' developed for low-chill areas like southern California.

Blueberries

Blueberries are wonderful plants. Not only do they live for decades and bear delicious fruits that need almost no care, but they also are beautiful in themselves, with white, bell-like flowers in spring and handsome oval leaves that turn orange-scarlet in fall. The berries are pretty, ripening slowly so that clusters are green, red and blue all at once. Even the bare reddish stems are eye-catching in winter. I often use blueberries in landscaping a home whether the owners want to eat the berries or not (if they don't, certainly the birds will). The plants look good as hedges, at the edge of a pond or even near the house as specimen shrubs.

There are several different blueberry species. The one most commonly grown for fruit and for ornament is highbush blueberry (*Vaccinium corymbosum*). It is the hardiest of the lot and usually grows to about 8 feet tall if unpruned (sometimes twice that). Lowbush blueberry (*V. angustifolium*) stays under 2 feet tall and makes a fine ground cover. Rabbit-eye blueberry (*V. ashei*) is a highbush species that, unlike *V. corymbosum*, does not need to be thoroughly chilled in winter and will bear well in the south. (It does not thrive north of Zone 7.) *V. ashei* is a very tall, vigorous shrub that ripens later than northern blueberries; the fruits are generally not as sweet but are large and good for baking. In Connecticut, where I live, both highbush and lowbush blueberries grow wild. I think the wild berries are the best of all if you judge by flavor, even though they are smaller and "picking a pie" may take hours. But what better way to spend a few summer hours on a sun-baked hillside?

SITE

Selecting a blueberry site by observing the plants in the wild can be misleading. The highbush ones often grow in swamps, and while it may look as if they are growing with their feet in the water, they are actually perched above it, with the ground they grow in soaking up water from below. The lowbush blueberries appear to scramble over bare, rocky mountaintops where there seems to be hardly any soil at all, let alone water. But their long roots are actually snaking down into fissures in the rocks, finding both. (The roots of both highbush and lowbush blueberries spread vigorously underground.) You should give your blueberries a site where moisture is ample but doesn't just sit around the roots. Other important factors are full sun so they'll ripen, and good air circulation to prevent disease.

SOIL

Soil should be loose and light, but the most important factor in growing blueberries is acidity. Blueberries like a pH of about 4.5 and will grow in anything from 3.5 to 5.5. If you are not sure whether the soil is acid enough in your area or in the spot where you want to grow them, have it tested. If the soil is alkaline you may want to grow something else instead, but if you are hell-bent on blueberries there are ways to make your soil more acid. You can add aluminum sulfate purchased from a garden center, following the directions on the package or the recommendations of your soil test, but in most cases you can

lower pH simply by digging a lot of acidic organic matter into the soil: rotted leaves, wood chips, peat moss, shredded bark, sawdust—any of these will do the trick and will also help the soil to retain the moisture that blueberries need.

PLANTING

Buy dormant plants that are two or three years old—those any older are difficult to transplant. You can order them by mail or pick them up locally. Planting bare-root is fine and gives you a chance to see whether the plants have a good, healthy, fibrous root system rather than just a few stringy roots. But be sure to keep the roots moist up until the time they go into the ground; this is crucial.

Plant blueberries in early spring in cool climates, late fall in mild ones, in holes 18 inches deep and equally wide, well enriched with organic matter. If the planting area has poor soil, enrich it throughout. Don't add fertilizer or manure directly to the hole, however, though you may spread some on the soil surface. Highbush berries are best planted at least 6 feet apart, or even a bit farther (especially for rabbit-eyes), so the whole bush can be sun-ripened, but if you are making a hedge, then 3 to 4 feet apart is acceptable. Dwarf highbush varieties can also go this close, or they can be planted in containers. Plant lowbush berries about 2 feet apart. These can be dug from the wild if you have a source, by removing large pieces of sod along with the bushes.

Plant blueberries at the same depth at which they were growing previously or an inch or so deeper, spreading the roots out in the soil, firming lightly and watering well. Cut back the tops by half and apply a thick mulch (6 inches is about right) of an acidic organic material such as shredded bark.

GROWING

It is very important to keep the plants moist the first year they are growing and any time that fruit is forming. They should be fed fairly heavily each year at blossom time by top dressing with an acidic compost, well-rotted manure, or a commerical fertilizer designed for acid-loving plants such as azaleas. You can also use cottonseed meal, blood meal, fish meal, ammonium sulfate, rock phosphate, bone meal or just about anything else you like—except materials, such as wood ashes or lime, that will raise the pH. And don't fertilize excessively with nitrogen or you may get vigorous plants with sparse fruit. You can feed again as fruits are forming, but don't feed past June in climates where late new growth may be winterkilled. Don't try to dig fertilizers into the soil since the plants are shallow-rooted; just remove the mulch, apply nutrients to the soil surface, water well, and replace the mulch. The mulch will break down and do its part in acidifying and lightening the soil; add some more each year.

Blueberries, especially highbush species, benefit from pruning to keep the plants a size you can pick easily, to let sun into the bush to ripen fruits, and to keep a good supply of fresh new growth coming along. Berries develop on fruiting spurs produced the previous season on side branches of old main stems. You probably won't have to start pruning until bushes are three or four years old, but then start thinning them once a year while they are dormant. Just when they are about to leaf out is a good time because you can then remove any winterkilled wood. Thin out old, gray canes with lots of little twigs that have grown beyond bearing age and have no fruiting buds visible, cutting them at the base of the plant. Favor the newer, red-der canes, keeping six or eight good bearing canes on the bush. Tall, straggly canes can be headed back, and weak, short, twiggy growth can be removed from tips. Note, while pruning, that fruiting buds are fatter than leaf buds; avoid removing twigs with a lot of these.

PESTS AND DISEASES

If you buy healthy bushes and take good care of them, you will probably have very little trouble with blueberries. There are some diseases, but most modern cultivars have been bred for resistance. If you live in an area where the berries are more disease-prone, apply fresh mulch each year, prune out debris promptly (disinfecting your clippers between cuts) and go easy on the fertilizer. If bushes succumb to botrytis in wet weather (the berries shrivel and the tips die) or stunt diseases (which are spread by leafhoppers and stunt the plants), destroy them and start over in a new place. They might occasionally get yellows disease if drainage is poor and the pH too high. Mummy berry, a fungus that makes the berries shrivel and harden, is often caused by wet weather and poor air circulation. Remove all debris, especially dead berries, hold off on fertilizer, and turn over or replace the mulch in early spring.

The most troublesome pests of blueberries you'll have to deal with will be birds. You will probably have to cover the bushes with plastic netting or cheesecloth extending clear down to the ground to avoid losing much of your crop. Spreading the netting on a lightweight metal or wooden framework with a flap you can lift to enter the "cage" will make picking easier. Other pests include blueberry maggot (the larva of the blueberry fruit fly), which enters the fruit and rots it. Clean up dropped berries and fight the critter by catching it in the fly stage with yellow sticky traps (page 73) or by using rotenone. If blueberry stem borers get into the stems in early summer, causing them to wilt, remove the stems and burn them. Pick off Japanese beetles or use milky spore disease (page 73).

HARVEST

If you can bring yourself to do it, you should rub off developing berries on young plants until they are three or four years old, to let the bush put its energy into growth. You'll start to get abundant crops when the bushes are about five years old—probably about six quarts per bush. You should pick at least twice a week, just rubbing your thumb over the berry cluster and letting the ripe berries fall into your hand or a container held under them. Picking this way is important, because berries that look blue are not always ripe. They should really sit on the bush for a week after they are blue, until they fall off easily. The fact that the clusters ripen a little at a time means that you can pick from a single cluster for up to a month and enjoy the berries over a long period. If you plant early, middle and late varieties, you can harvest berries from June to September.

VARIETIES

Most blueberry varieties do not self-pollinate well, so it is best to plant several. Popular early varieties include 'Earliblue,' the short-growing 'Northland,' and 'Collins,' which bears in long, uniformly-ripening clusters. For midseason grow 'Blueray,' 'Bluecrop' and 'Berkeley,' all of which bear abundant crops of large berries. For later berries grow 'Jersey' (the shrub is especially handsome), the sweet, dark 'Herbert' and, to wind up the season, 'Coville.' Good varieties for the north are 'Northland,' 'Earliblue,' 'Blueray,' the early 'Patriot,' the late-bearing 'Elliott' and 'Northblue,' which is a self-fertile dwarf variety. 'Tophat' is a hardy dwarf that can be grown in tubs. For rabbit-eye varieties the standard favorite is 'Tifblue,' a vigorous, upright bush that bears fairly late. For an early one try 'Climax' or the lower-growing 'Woodward.' For midseason try the compact 'Southland' and for late season the sweet-tasting 'Delite.'

Cherries

C herries are beautiful trees to have on your property, whether you grow the purely ornamental kinds or those bred for their fruits. Cherry trees have a pleasing shape and distinctive smooth, shiny bark, and they bear clouds of delicate pink blossoms in spring. The tasty fruits are among the earliest tree fruits to appear—usually in June or July.

There are two basic types of edible cherries: sweet and sour. The distinction seems to blur at times, because some of the sour cherries can taste quite sweet if left on the tree long enough to fully ripen, and some of the sweet ones are a bit tart. But in general, "sweet cherries" are best for eating fresh and "sour cherries" are used mostly for cooking or preserves—in fact the latter are often called "pie cherries."

Sweet and sour cherries are two distinct species and differ quite a bit. Sour cherries are much the easier to grow; they are hardy, generally speaking, from Zone 4 to Zone 7, and they are less bothered by insects and diseases than sweet cherries. They are also more compact trees (most attain about 15 feet) and thus better suited to small properties or intimate landscape settings. Most sweet cherry trees are hardy in Zones 5 through 8; they do well in roughly the same climates where peaches thrive. Most grow to about 25 feet, but some get much taller than that. Dwarf varieties of both sweet and sour cherry trees are available, as well as bush types such as Nanking cherry. Some dwarfs and bush types are so small they can even be grown in tubs for terrace gardens.

The purely ornamental cherries are sold as "flowering cherries," despite the fact that those grown for their fruits also bloom beautifully. They are very fine small landscaping trees bred mainly for their showy flowers, and they require the same growing conditions as fruit cherries.

SITE

Cherries like a sunny spot, and those grown for fruit are often planted on south-facing slopes. Avoid cold valleys where trees can be winter-injured and the early blooms nipped by late frost. Allow enough room between trees to permit ripening—about 12 feet for most dwarfs, 20–25 feet for sour cherries and 25–40 for sweet, depending on the size of the variety.

SOIL

The most important requirement is that the soil be very well drained. Cherries will not thrive in soggy soil, especially in cold climates where it can contribute to winter injury. Both sweet and sour cherries prefer a light, rather sandy soil, though sour cherries can take soil a bit heavier than sweet ones can. Soil for cherries should be reasonably fertile and also deep, especially if the ground is dry. Cherries need moisture at flowering and fruiting time but can get by with a dryish soil even at these times if the roots can get down deep enough to find moisture. The ideal pH for cherries is about 6.5, but a range of 5.5–8.0 is acceptable.

PLANTING

Almost all cherry trees you buy are grafted, usually on cherry rootstocks. Buy one- or two-year-old dormant trees 4 to 5 feet tall, and cut them back by a third. Cherries are best planted in early spring before buds swell, except in warm climates, where fall planting is fine.

It is very important when planting cherries not to let the roots dry out at any time; cut off any that are either damaged or long and straggly. The soil should be well loosened in the bottom of the planting hole and for several feet around the hole, and organic matter such as compost or moistened peat moss should be dug in. Set the young tree at the depth at which it grew in the nursery or just a bit deeper, and be very sure to firm the soil around the roots to avoid having any air pockets, which might cause the roots to dry out. Apply a mulch, especially if you are planting in the fall, to protect roots in winter and conserve moisture in summer. Protect the trunk against mice with hardware cloth or a plastic guard. It is also helpful to paint the trunk with white tree paint to prevent sun scald.

GROWING

Water cherry trees deeply if the weather is very dry at flowering time or just as the fruits are ripening. The trees do not need a lot of feeding, in fact too much can lead to diseases and a sparse harvest. Nonetheless an annual top dressing with manure or a nitrogen source such as blood meal can be beneficial, especially if your soil's fertility is okay but not great. Don't feed trees after early summer, though, or they may form new growth that will not harden sufficiently before winter. Weed control is important; again, a mulch will help.

Cherry trees need only a little pruning. Prune them as you would an apple tree, opening up the top to encourage the fruits to ripen well. Take care to eliminate narrow crotches when you are selecting lateral shoots for the main structure. Narrow crotches are characteristic of cherry trees and can produce a tree with very weak branches, especially if cropping is heavy. Sweet cherries are more upright in their growth, while sour cherries are more open and spreading, making them much easier to pick. Sweet varieties can be cut back hard on top to make them more manageable. Pruning is best done when the trees are dormant.

PESTS AND DISEASES

The biggest problem with cherries, especially sweet cherries, is beating the birds to the crop. Hanging noisy objects like pie tins in the trees is of limited value. About the only thing that really works is netting. Covering a small tree with netting may well be worth the effort; for a tall tree you might try to cover the bottom branches and let the birds have the cherries on top, which are hard to pick anyway. If you have a large number of trees, there may be enough fruit to go around. Or you can plant mulberries as a "trap crop": the birds like them better than cherries. Make sure, however, that the cherry varieties you've chosen ripen at the same time as the mulberries—otherwise the birds will just get a two-course meal.

The other serious pest of cherries is tent caterpillar, described on page 73. Breaking up the caterpillars' nests at night when they're inside is the best remedy; but you can also spray the larvae with insecticidal soap when they are crawling on the tree and chewing its leaves. BT (page 73) can be used if these methods fail. Another pest is the cherry fruit worm, which can give you wormy cherries. BT can be used on the fruit worm as well. Wormy cherries can also be the work of cherry fruit fly larvae. If you're not sure which worm you have, get your Extension Service office to identify it for you. Cherry fruit flies can be foiled in the adult, flying stage by the red sticky-ball traps described on page 73. Another common pest is cherry aphid. (Doesn't it sometimes seem as if every plant has its own special aphid?) Fight it with soap spray and dormant oil. Since cherries and plums are close cousins you also might encounter plum curculio and black knot (page 374).

Cherry leaf spot is a typical leaf-spot disease in which purple-edged spots develop on the leaves and often fall out to produce a shot-hole effect. Leaves then turn yellow. Bordeaux mixture (a concoction of hydrated lime and copper sulfate) applied at the time blossoms drop may help. It is also important to clean up fallen leaves in autumn. Cherry fruits can also crack in rainy weather; if that's a problem in your area, seek out resistant varieties.

HARVEST

From a good, vigorous sweet cherry tree you might get 3 bushels of fruit; from a sour cherry, 2 to 2½ bushels; from a dwarf of either, perhaps 1 bushel. Pick when the cherries seem to be the right size, color and taste and are easily picked. If you're going to use them right away, it is best to pick them without the stems; otherwise pull the stems off the spur gently with a twisting motion. Sweet cherries might keep a few weeks if refrigerated; sour ones should be made into rich jams or pies as soon as possible.

VARIETIES

Most sweet cherries need another variety growing nearby to ensure pollination. The exception is the popular sweet cherry 'Bing.' It is vigorous, productive, tasty and moderately hardy, and unlike most sweet cherries it can pollinate itself. On top of that, Bings grow into compact trees. Unfortunately, like many sweet cherries Bing is disease-prone. Other dark sweet cherries include 'Schmidt's Bigarreau,' 'Windsor,' 'Black Tartarian,' 'Lambert' and 'Sweet Black Kristin,' which is hardy even in cold climates. Of the dark sweet type, 'Hedelfingen' and 'Van' are especially crack-resistant. Some other interesting sweet cherries include the compact-growing, self-pollinating, dark red 'Stella' and the yellow cherries, which fend off cherry diseases much better than their red relatives. Try the classic 'Royal Ann' (also known as 'Napoleon'), the very hardy 'Yellow Glass' (perhaps the best sweet cherry for cold regions) and 'Gold,' which resists both disease and cracking. Don't try to pollinate 'Bing' and 'Lambert' with each other; it won't work. But 'Black Tartarian' and 'Windsor' are good pollinators for other sweet cherries.

Sour cherries are usually self-pollinating. The classic is 'Montmorency,' a big, red, all-purpose pie cherry that is crack-resistant. 'Early Richmond' is a good early variety. If you live in a very cold climate—even Zone 3—try the semidwarf 'Meteor' (under 15 feet) or the dwarf 'North Star' (well under 10 feet). Also worth noting are the "Duke" types, such as 'Royal Duke,' 'May Duke' (early) and 'Late Duke' (late); these are sweet-sour crosses and bear big, dark fruits in Zones 5 through 8.

There are a number of fine ornamental flowering cherries, too numerous to list here. Of special note are Kwanzan cherry (*Prunus serrulata* 'Kwanzan'), which bears heavenly double pink blossoms on a compact tree (usually about 15 feet), and the elegant weeping Higan cherry (*P. subhirtella* 'Pendula'), whose willowlike branches brush the ground.

lime

lemon

orange

grapefruit

Citrus Fruits

I f you live in the right part of the country, you'll probaby want to have some citrus trees on your property. Not only do they bear tasty, vitamin-rich fruits, but the trees themselves are beautiful—compact broad-leaved evergreens with a pleasing, rounded shape and waxy white flowers that fill the air with fragrance. You can grow some citrus fruits outdoors year-round in California, Florida, the Gulf Coast and parts of Texas and Arizona, but if you have a warm, protected spot on your property, you just might get away with some varieties farther north. And citrus trees on dwarfing rootstocks also make fine container plants in cooler climates. Chapter 17 tells you how to grow them as houseplants, but you can also grow them as small trees in tubs on your terrace in the summer, moving them to a spacious, sunny spot inside the house to spend the winter.

Citrus fruits vary in their hardiness. Limes can't take any frost at all and can be grown only in Zone 10. Lemons are almost as tender but can survive in the warmer parts of Zone 9. Sweet oranges, the kind most commonly grown, can survive temperatures as low as 20 degrees Fahrenheit. Grapefruits have the same hardiness as oranges, though they produce the tastiest fruits where it is hot. They are grown the same way oranges are in most respects.

Conditions in the "citrus regions" are not at all uniform; for example, Florida can be quite moist and humid, whereas the southwest and the west coast can be very dry. Each locality has citrus varieties best suited to it, and while many popular ones do well anywhere, it is advisable to get some advice from local experts about what thrives best where you live. (At the present time in Florida, citrus canker threatens all citrus crops, and sale of the trees may be restricted. Check to make sure they can safely be planted in your area.)

Lemons and limes bloom and fruit at the same time, year-round. Oranges and grapefruits are spring-blooming and experience a dormant period in winter if temperatures go down into the 50s, but the fruits keep well on the tree for so long that oranges and grapefruits may often seem like all-year crops. Valencia oranges can take more than a year to ripen in some climates. As a result you may have the crops of two separate years on the tree at the same time. Orange trees can grow as tall as 25 feet (sometimes Valencias grow even taller), and are rather upright; grapefruit trees are a comparable size but more spreading. Lemons and limes grow on open, spreading trees up to 15 feet tall for limes and up to 20 feet for lemons. One of the nicest things about all citrus trees is that they are self-pollinating, and while you might well want a number of varieties, one is all you need to get fruit.

SITE

Where you grow your citrus fruits depends on local conditions. All citrus like plenty of sun and heat, so if you live in the cooler edge of their range make sure they get your sunniest, warmest, most protected exposure. If your area is very hot, however, some partial shade will be appreciated, especially at midday and especially if you live in the desert. Drying desert winds can also be a problem, and a windbreak should be provided. In Florida you need to make sure that the site where you plant a citrus tree is very well drained. Container-grown citrus trees do best on a sunny terrace. Containers should be at least a foot tall and a foot wide, larger if you are letting the trees grow over 4 feet tall. But if you are wintering the trees indoors, don't make the containers too heavy to move.

SOIL

Citrus fruits are not too fussy about soil, but the moisture level must be right; there should be sufficient moisture for growth, but drainage must be good—in fact it is best if the soil gets slightly dry between soakings, especially in heavy soils. Oranges like a light, sandy loam; heavy soils should be lightened with plenty of organic matter. Lemons have more tolerance for heavy soils (but only if they're well drained). The pH should be slightly acid—between 5.5 and 6.2 if possible. In the dry areas of the west, soils are often too alkaline and must be corrected. Salty soils will not grow most citrus fruits.

PLANTING

Lemons and limes can be planted at any time of the year; oranges and grapefruits are best planted in cool weather. Plant citrus trees bare-root in moist climates, balled-and-burlapped in dry ones. Oranges and lemons should go 20–30 feet apart, depending on the size of the variety, lemons and limes 10–15 feet apart, dwarf trees 6–10 feet apart.

Citrus trees are almost always grafted, and it is important that the graft be about 6 inches above the soil level. This often means planting the tree a bit higher than it was growing in the nursery. Water thoroughly and keep the soil fairly moist after planting and during the tree's first season.

GROWING

The roots of citrus trees are fairly shallow and extend quite a bit beyond the spread of the branches. Keep this in mind when you are feeding and watering. In dry climates you'll probably need to irrigate them, giving them a deep soaking, not a steady trickle. The same applies to watering in dry weather in other regions. They like a good nitrogen supply—top dressing with compost, well-rotted manure, blood meal or cottonseed meal works well, or you can apply a slow-release organic fertilizer several times a year. Trees will need heavier feeding in sandy soils where nutrients leach out easily, but in dry climates they may not leach out fast enough, so avoid using inorganic fertilizers whose residues can accumulate and make the soil too alkaline.

Keep the area around the tree free of weeds that can compete with the shallow roots; even mowed grass can rob them of nutrients. Using a mulch is best, but keep the area right around the trunk free of mulch to avoid brown-rot gummosis. Citrus bark is thin, and the trunks should be protected against sun scald with white latex paint or tree wraps, especially in the desert.

Your trees won't need much pruning—in fact it's best to keep pruning to a minimum; ample foliage will protect the fruits and lead to greater yields. While they are young, train the trees to have a nice, balanced scaffold shape, just as you would any tree, removing excessive watersprouts. Then in future years just cut back the occasional overvigorous limb that unbalances the shape of the tree, and remove branches that grow too low on the trunk. Lemon trees may need a bit more cutting back to keep them round and compact and thereby protect the fruits from sun, wind and cold. Old citrus trees can be rejuvenated by heavy cutting in early spring after danger of frost has passed. And always remove any dead, damaged or diseased wood as soon as you notice it. Container-grown trees should be root pruned every few years (page 497).

PESTS AND DISEASES

Aphids, mealybugs and red spider mites can all attack citrus trees. All can be controlled to some extent by spraying with a strong stream of water or with insecticidal soap. An oil spray may also be needed for these insects, as well as for scale infestations. (Consult your Extension Service for advice about types of oils and the proper timing of their use in your area.) Gophers can destroy citrus trees by girdling the roots. Avoid mulch if gophers are a problem, because it gives them a good hiding place. You may need to resort to trapping them.

Citrus trees are much more prone to diseases in humid areas such as Florida than they are in the drier western regions. Lemons in humid climates can get scab, which makes the leaves and fruits scabby and distorted. Fight it with good sanitation: destroy all plant debris, and cut off suckers that grow from the roots; these can harbor the scab fungus. Spray with benomyl in early spring if necessary, and seek out resistant varieties. Benomyl will also help against greasy-spot fungus. This disease produces greasy spots on the leaves, which then fall off. Brown-rot gummosis (also called "foot rot") is as distasteful as it sounds; the bark on the lower trunk gets gummy after a stretch of wet weather, and a bad case of it can girdle and kill the tree. Seek out plants with resistant rootstocks, plant the tree a bit high, keep the trunk as dry as possible, remove any mulch and even the top few inches of soil. Destroy all plant debris, and make sure soil drainage is excellent.

HARVEST

Pick lemons, limes and Valencia oranges year-round, navel oranges and grapefruits in winter and spring. All citrus fruits must be fully ripe on the tree before you pick them. It is sometimes hard to tell if they're ripe, because color depends more on the time of year than on ripeness; best cut one open and taste it to be sure. Pick carefully with a gentle twist or snip off with shears, being careful not to damage the twigs.

VARIETIES

The most popular oranges are 'Robertson Navel,' 'Washington Navel' and 'Valencia.' You might also want to try blood oranges, which grow on small trees and are pink inside if grown in sufficiently cool parts of the orange's favored temperature range. Blood orange varieties include 'Moro' and 'Sanguinella.' 'Calamondin' oranges are described on page 602 and are often grown as houseplants as well as outdoor trees.

'Eureka' is the standard lemon variety. 'Lisbon' is slightly more cold-hardy, growing on a large, vigorous tree. 'Meyer' lemon is a dwarf variety, hardy to 15 degrees Fahrenheit, and 'Ponderosa' bears huge fruits; both are described on page 602. For a good grapefruit variety, try the seedless 'Redblush.' For limes you have a choice between the 15-foot 'Bearrs' (also called 'Tahiti' or Persian lime) and the more compact, fine-leaved key lime, which grows in the Florida Keys and is the essential ingredient in key lime pie.

Grapes

Grape growing isn't what it used to be. No more do voluptuous *bacchantes* run madly through the forests of Greece to celebrate the fruits of the vine. No more do the village lads and maidens of the French countryside roll up their pantaloons and hitch up their petticoats to tromp on the newly picked grapes. The tales told of modern grape culture have to do with calculating how many buds to leave on the vines and interpreting pruning diagrams complex enough to drive anyone back to peas and petunias.

Even in our scientific age, however, grape growing is not that difficult—especially if you choose the right kind of grapes for your region. And to my eye grapes are among the most beautiful of plants: the vines, the broad leaves, the tendrils, the ripe bunches of fruit. Fur-

thermore, your grape harvest can give you so much: jams and jellies, juice, grapes for fresh eating, and even wine if you are adventurous. Grapes grow on immensely vigorous and sturdy plants which, if you plant them correctly and give them good basic care, will probably outlive you.

The most famous wine regions of the world are warm, sunny places with long growing seasons, but there are grapes native to cold, short-season areas as well. After all, when Leif Eriksson landed in North America, he named the new continent "Vineland" because of the abundance of wild grapes he found growing there. These were native species such as fox grapes (*Vitis labrusca*), grapes whose skins slipped off the flesh easily, quite different from the grapes brought over in colonial times, hybrids of the European species *V. vinifera*. The European imports failed to thrive in the New World but were eventually crossed with American grapes to produce the fine hybrids such as 'Concord' that we grow today. In return, American grapes have been bred with those growing in Europe to impart resistance to grape phylloxera (below), so most grapes now grown have some parentage on both sides of the Atlantic. The predominantly American types are the best for cooler climates, but the European types are grown very successfully in California. Gardeners in the southeastern and Gulf states can grow hybrids of the native muscadine grapes (*V. rotundifolia*), which are tasty and grow on extremely vigorous, heavy-bearing vines.

Most grapes are self-pollinating. For those that are not, you must plant a suitable variety as a pollinator. (The nurseryman or catalog that sells you the variety should advise you here.) Since grapes are pollinated by wind, not by bees, the two varieties should be no farther than 50 feet apart.

SITE

Where you grow your grapes depends partly on what you are growing them for. Two vigorous vines are probably ample for the table-grape consumption of most households, since each can produce up to 15 pounds of grapes. Vines grown for table grapes can be made part of your landscaping plan. They might be trained against an existing wooden fence, along a garage wall or even across the top half of a window so that the grapes dangle down and are visible from indoors. You might also grow a vine or two on a sturdy arbor over a terrace or grassy area, forming a canopy that you can sit under in summertime when it's hot, watching the clusters of grapes ripen as summer progresses. You

should be aware, though, that grapes grown on an overhead arbor are difficult to take care of, and if your goal is strictly grape production, not decoration, you had best use a trellising system closer to the ground, such as the one shown in Figure 54. If you are making a lot of juice or wine, or if you just want to try a lot of different varieties, you'll also want more vines than you can put on an arbor unless it is an extended pergola, and you'll probably want to create a small vineyard. This means finding a cleared area with plenty of space.

Grapes need full sun to ripen, so the best spot for them is a gentle slope that faces south, southeast or southwest. Sometimes grapes are planted on a north slope so as to delay spring growth and thus forestall damage from late frosts. The site should also have good air circulation. Air circulation is very important for grapes and can often mean the difference between a disease-ridden and a healthy crop. You should also protect vines from strong, cold winds. Having the rows run in the direction of the prevailing winds will cut down on their impact and will allow the winds to blow down between the rows to circulate the air freely.

SOIL

In many parts of the world grapes can be seen growing in perfectly dreadful soil—dry and gravelly. Their long, deep roots do allow grapes to adapt relatively well to conditions such as these, but for your own grapes you'll probably want to do a bit better. A soil on the sandy side that warms up well in spring is preferable; it will also give grapes the good drainage that they require. But it must be deep, and, if possible, well supplied with organic matter to retain the moisture the vines need when they are getting established. In general grapes like a fertile soil, but too much richness can weaken the vines and make them more vulnerable to disease. The ideal pH is 6.0–6.5, but 5.5–8.0 is acceptable.

The soil must be well prepared, preferably starting in the fall before spring planting. Since grapes are a permanent crop, be sure to remove rocks and any perennial weeds that will compete with the vines and be difficult to remove after the grapes start growing. And prepare the soil with organic matter dug in throughout the planting area, not just in the spots where individual vines will be planted. The roots will soon spread out in a radius of at least 8 feet from each plant.

PLANTING

Buy first-grade, one-year-old stock (older plants will not produce grapes any faster) and plant them while they are fully dormant in early spring, as soon as the ground is workable. Fall planting is done only in areas where there is no danger of winter injury. The root system should be healthy and fibrous, and should be cut back to 6 to 8 inches long. The top of the plant should be cut back so that only two nodes are left on the stem (Figure 3).

Even though your vines will be quite small the first year or two and will need fairly minimal support, it is a good idea to figure out at the beginning how you are going to support the mature vines and set up the appropriate structure then, so you don't have to disturb the plants and their roots with future construction. There are many ways to train and support grapes. (See Chapter 13 for methods of supporting vines.) The four-arm Kniffin system shown in Figure 54 is probably the support used most universally for grapes as a food crop and the easiest for you to start with.

At each end of the row, set a stout 4-by-4-inch post at least 2½ feet into the ground. Brace these end posts with a diagonal piece of wood, or even set them in concrete, especially if you cannot sink them very deep. Then set posts in a row between the end posts, spaced 24 feet apart. You'll need 24 feet to grow two grape vines, so if two are all you are planning to grow, you'll only need the two end posts, spaced 24 feet apart. The posts set in between need not be buried more than 2 feet, but all the posts should extend about 6 feet above the ground. Then string two strands of heavy wire (at least 10-gauge) tightly along your row of posts, stapling it securely at the ends and running it through screw eyes attached to the row posts. Put the first strand 2½ feet, the second 5 feet, above the ground. You can install a turnbuckle on each wire near an end post so that wires can be tightened as needed in years to come. If you are planting more than one row, make the rows at least 10 feet apart.

Now you're ready to plant. Space vines 8 feet apart; this gives you room for two vines between posts (less vigorous varieties might go as close as 6 feet; highly vigorous ones as far as 12; muscadines need about 20 feet for each vine). Dig a hole a foot deep and a foot wide, adding some well-seasoned compost or moistened peat to the hole. Place a 2-by-2-inch stake about 4 feet tall in the hole as a temporary support for the young vine—if the vine grows upright it will produce better laterals. (An alternative method of encouraging upright growth is to tie a string from the young plant to the first wire.) Then spread out the roots in the planting hole and fill it with soil, watering when the hole is half full and setting the vine at the same depth at which it originally grew, or an inch or so deeper. Then you may spread some compost, rotted manure or fertilizer (say, 2 ounces of 10–10–10) on top of the soil in a circle about a foot from the plant's stem. If rabbits are a problem in your area, either fence the whole planting or use the guards described on page 77. Then mulch the whole planting with an organic material like straw, salt hay or shredded bark to keep weeds down and conserve moisture.

GROWING

While the grape vines are growing they will not need much feeding or watering. You may find that a good mulch takes care of your watering needs, though if you need to warm up the soil early in spring to promote growth you may want to pull the mulch aside at that time and replace it in early summer. Although some growers never feed their grapes at all, grapes do in fact like some nitrogen. Top dress the soil with well-rotted manure or a fertilizer in early spring, gradually widening the dressed circle to about 8 feet for a mature vine. I can't give an exact formula for feeding, not knowing your soil or which grapes you are growing, but try working in up to one bushel of manure (and perhaps a pound or two of granite dust) or half a pound of 10–10–10 for each mature plant, increasing the amount only if the foliage lacks a good green color or the vines are not growing as vigorously as they should be.

The most important things to do for your grapes are the initial training and, after that, annual pruning. Grapes that are left untrained and unpruned turn into a mass of tangled vines that are mostly old and unproductive wood. You'll get a much better crop if you prune regularly; even a vine grown on an arbor for ornament will be healthier and more attractive and will put less strain on its support structure if it's pruned each year. Pruning is always done while the plants

are dormant; if you do it after the buds start to swell you may break off the buds. In warm areas, prune any time the plants are dormant; in cold ones you must wait till after the dormant vines are no longer frozen and hence breakable— late winter or early spring. Spring pruning will also let you see wood that has been winterkilled, so you can remove it.

Essentially in pruning a grape vine you maintain a sturdy main stem, called the "trunk," from which new lateral fruiting canes are allowed to develop each season. Since the grape crop will be borne on these canes the second year, you need both a supply of bearing canes, trained along horizontal wires, and some renewal canes coming along for next year.

The initial training is done in the winter following the first summer's growth. That little stick you planted will have grown canes from those two nodes and probably some other side shoots as well. Pinch off all but the strongest cane—this will be your trunk—and tie it loosely to the supporting stake. When the trunk is tall enough to reach the first wire, let two good canes (with at least four nodes each) develop at the height of the wire. (If the trunk doesn't get as high as the wire the first season, prune it back to two or three nodes the following spring and let it start over.) When it's time for the first spring pruning, remove everything but those two horizontal canes and the central trunk, which will continue to climb upward. Tie the two canes (or "arms") to the wire, one to the left, one to the right, as shown in Figure 54. During the next spring pruning, cut each arm back to three nodes. When the trunk reaches the second wire (possibly during the first season, but possibly not till after the second growing season), select another pair of good canes and train them to left and right the same way. Then cut off the top of the

TRAINING AND PRUNING GRAPES

Fig. 54

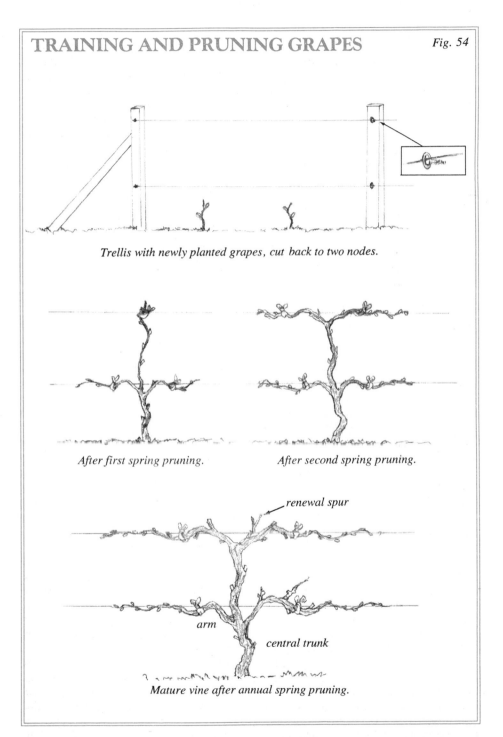

Trellis with newly planted grapes, cut back to two nodes.

After first spring pruning.

After second spring pruning.

renewal spur

arm

central trunk

Mature vine after annual spring pruning.

trunk just above them. All other canes coming off the trunk at this point, and any suckers coming up from the base, should be removed during spring pruning.

During the second growing season it is best to remove flower clusters so the vine will put its energy into growth, letting the lateral branches produce a number of long canes. During the third spring leave one long cane from each side of the trunk for both the top wire and the lower wire—four in all. These will become the first "fruiting arms" and should be cut back so each has about ten nodes. Also leave four more canes close to the trunk. These, which are pruned back to two nodes, are your renewal spurs; they will produce fruiting arms for the following year. During the third growing season you can let the arms produce clusters of grapes from shoots that form at the nodes, and the renewal spurs will grow to form a nice long cane for next year's crop.

In future years all you need to do each spring is remove each old cane that has borne fruit and cut the new ones back to about ten nodes, although you can leave the canes longer if the vine is a vigorous one. A few years of experimental pruning with each variety you grow should set you on the right track.

PESTS AND DISEASES

If you give your grapes good air circulation, keep them well pruned, clean up all prunings, fallen leaves and fallen fruit, and don't overfeed them, it's quite likely that you won't have any disease problems at all. Nevertheless you might encounter some of the following troublemakers. The black-rot fungus turns the fruits hard, black and shriveled. It can be a problem in warm, moist areas and is best fought by good air circulation. There are also rot-resistant grape varieties available. Anthracnose, which produces spots on the fruit, can occur in wet spring weather and is best prevented by the sound grape culture summarized just above. Downy or powdery mildews most often affect the European-type grapes, but any grapes can get them in areas where mildew is a problem. You may have to resort to fungicides such as benomyl or copper sulfate to get rid of mildews.

The grape berry moth is best identified by the little silken webs with which it ties leaves or grape clusters together. If you spot these, be sure to clean up all fallen leaves or fruit in fall, then from mid- to late spring cultivate the first inch or two of the soil (carefully, since grapes have roots near the surface) to expose overwintering pupae to the air. Japanese beetles love grapes; they can be controlled with milky-spore disease, but in cool climates this takes a few years to work. In the meantime, it may be necessary to pick beetles off by hand to save your crop. Grape leafhoppers can also do considerable damage; control them with insecticidal soap or by planting blackberries among the grapes—these harbor a tiny parasitic insect that attacks the leafhoppers. Grape phylloxera is a serious insect pest that sucks the juices from the roots. You can see pea-sized galls on the roots and on the undersides of affected leaves. Phylloxera almost destroyed the entire European wine industry many years ago. The grapes were saved by the introduction of American species into the breeding—these are immune. You can avoid phylloxera by growing American grapes or by growing European grapes grafted onto American rootstocks.

HARVEST

Grapes must be fully ripened on the vine in order to reach the peak of flavor and sweetness. Don't go by looks; taste a grape near the tip of the cluster. If it tastes ripe and the seeds have turned brown, you can pick. Grapes should be cut off the vine with a sharp knife or a pair of "grape shears," not pulled off. Pick them on a dry day and they'll store better. They don't keep a long time but can be held for a few weeks at just above 32 degrees Fahrenheit. The European types store better than the American.

VARIETIES

The varieties of grape you will find listed most often in catalogs are of predominantly American parentage. Among these, some of the most versatile and easy to grow are 'Concord,' the classic blue grape, which matures fairly late in the season on a vigorous, healthy vine; 'Niagara,' sometimes called a "white Concord," which is white and a bit earlier; 'Fredonia,' a big, early blue-black table grape on a vigorous, disease-resistant vine; 'Golden Muscat,' a late white; 'Steuben,' another good blue-black table grape; 'Delaware,' a good midseason red grape; and 'Catawba,' an excellent late red. In general these grapes do well in both warm and cold regions. Others do well only in the south, such as the sweet red 'Flame' and the muscadine types. Southern grapes include 'Scuppernong,' the classic muscadine that is bronze-green colored and tart-sweet. Most muscadines need a male and a female plant for pollination, but 'Carlos,' a big bronze-colored grape, and the large blue-black 'Cowart' are both self-pollinating.

Seedless grapes do not always have the richness of flavor that the seeded, slip-skin types have, and so are not as good for cooking and preserves, but they are popular for easy eating. The hardiest are the white 'Himrod,' the pinkish 'Reliance' and red 'Canadice.' Other good ones are 'Seedless Concord,' which is like 'Concord' but smaller, blue-black 'Venus' and 'Glenora,' and the moderately hardy red 'Suffolk' and white 'Interlaken.'

Wine can be made from any grape, but there are varieties bred expressly for wine. Wine grapes are a rather specialized topic about which much has been written. In general, gardeners in climates like that of California can grow just about any wine grapes, including the European ones; in colder climates you can grow the newer "French" hybrids, such as the red 'Foch' and 'Baco Noir,' or the white 'Aurora' and 'Seyval,' which are more suited to climates such as that of New York State.

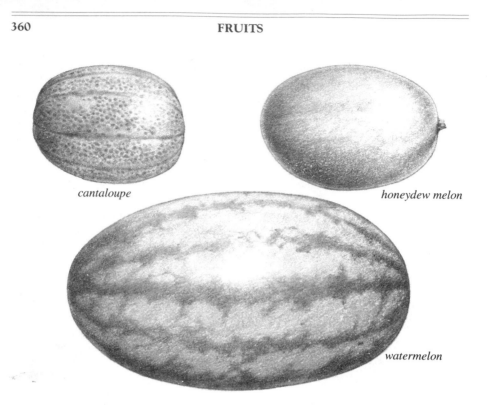

cantaloupe

honeydew melon

watermelon

Melons

When I was a little girl my grandfather took me out into his Louisiana melon field and taught me how to thump watermelons. You flicked your middle finger against the pad of your thumb so that it struck the melon hard, then listened for the sound: if it was a resounding hollow thump the melon was ripe. When I found a ripe melon I took it back to my sisters, and we sat on the lawn eating it, where we wouldn't make a mess, shooting the seeds at each other from between those same two fingers. (No one needed to teach us how to do that.)

Even if I had a space big enough for a watermelon field now I'd have trouble growing most varieties in New England (though I still consider watermelon thumping a useful skill to possess). In fact it's pretty hard to grow any melons here at all. Most need at least three or four months of genuinely warm weather to produce well, especially watermelons and the "winter melons," so called because they ripen as it's starting to get cool, and including honeydews, crenshaws and casabas. Cantaloupes (more correctly called "muskmelons") can be grown up to Zone 4, but only with a lot of effort. Northern melon growers tend to have an almost heroic pride about the endeavor—every bit of it justified. Their success is partly a matter of choosing early-ripening varieties and partly a matter of learning some handy tricks described below.

Even watermelons and the winter melons can be worth a try if you grow short-season varieties. But if your garden space is limited and you don't live in melon country, I'd think twice about whether to give melons the large space they need.

SITE

A site that gets full sun is crucial for melons, wherever you grow them. If it is also protected from chilling winds in spring and fall, all the better. But there should be plenty of air circulation to dry the plants quickly after rain and help ward off the diseases melons are prone to. A gentle south-facing slope is ideal. Many gardeners grow melons in the vegetable garden because, unlike most fruits, they are annuals and so are replanted each year, as most vegetables are. In fact they are grown very much like squash and pumpkins, with similar space requirements and pest problems. For these reasons you may want to make melons part of your garden-rotation scheme (see page 197), rotating them along with the squash. But bear in mind that a single melon plant needs at least a 4-by-4-foot space, and usually much more a watermelon plant might need as much as 100 square feet. If space is limited you can try the compact "bush" melon varieties or even try growing the standard types vertically on a fence or strong trellis. But if you do this you must support the ripening fruits or they will fall. Use slings made from pantyhose, mesh onion bags or, less conspicuously, pieces of black nylon bird netting. Tie the vines loosely but securely to the support with soft strips of cloth.

If you have plenty of space on your property you may well find it easier to have melon patches away from the garden, rotating the melons with other space-consuming crops like corn, or with cover crops that will add nutrients to the soil when tilled under (page 27).

SOIL

Melons like a light, sandy loam. They won't do well at all in heavy, clay soils, so if that's what you have, be prepared to lighten it with a lot of organic matter. In fact, adding organic matter is a good idea regardless of what kind of soil you start with, because it will help retain the steady supply of moisture that melons need and it will provide good drainage at the same time. The soil should also be high in nutrients in order to produce the fast, steady growth that will ripen the fruits before cold weather. If possible dig in some compost or well-rotted manure, supplemented with a phosphorus source such as bone meal or rock phosphate, and a potassium source such as greensand or granite dust.

Having a deep, obstacle-free soil will cause the plants to root deeply, which is important in helping them to resist drought. Soil pH should be about neutral for cantaloupes; a range of 6.0–8.0 is acceptable. Watermelons can take greater acidity—a pH as low as 5.5.

It might seem from all the cautions I've given you that melons are delicate plants in need of coaxing. Quite the contrary: they are big, vigorous vines. The problem is rather that they must be planted when the weather has warmed up, and that for the most part they won't ripen if the weather turns cold. So you need to give them good soil as well as the extra care described below so they'll mature within the limits of the season. This is sometimes true even in very hot climates, where it's preferable to ripen melons before the intense, drying heat of summer since the heat can be almost as hard on melons as the cold.

PLANTING

Young melon seedlings will not grow if the temperature drops below 50 to 55 degrees Fahrenheit; in fact the vines may not even set fruit later on if they've been chilled in infancy. So you need to wait longer than until "after danger of frost has passed" to plant them. The weather must be warm and the soil about 70 degrees. If this happens early enough to give the plants the number of days necessary to ripen the particular variety you are planting (the catalog or seed packet will tell you how many days this is), you can sow the seeds directly in the garden; if not, you must start them in a cold frame or indoors.

If you're starting melons indoors you may be tempted to do it very early in order to have large plants to set out. Don't. Melons are not easily transplanted, and if the plants have more than four leaves and have started to produce little tendrils, the roots will be difficult to establish. Wait until two to four weeks before it's time to plant them in the garden before you start melon seeds. Sow several seeds in large peat pots, ½ inch deep, and put them in a place where the soil temperature will be between 75 and 90 degrees. When the seedlings are about 2 inches tall, thin to the strongest one by snipping the others at soil level with scissors. Harden them off outdoors (page 47) before planting. To start them in a cold frame, follow the same procedure, but be sure the frame is well insulated against cold nights.

Make sure your soil has been well prepared before you put either seeds or seedlings in the ground. Even if you've enriched the whole area it's a good idea to dig a good shovelful or two of compost or thoroughly rotted manure into an area 2 feet in diameter and a foot deep, where each plant will go, plus a few trowelfuls of bone meal for good root development. I think planting on a grid with all the plants equidistant from each other works best. Most varieties should be spaced 4–6 feet apart, but very vigor-

ous vines, especially watermelons, should go anywhere from 6 to 12 feet apart. Bush varieties can go as close as 2 feet. Seeds planted directly in the garden should be sown in hills (page 48), then thinned. Some gardeners leave two or three vines in the hill, but if you have any doubt about their ability to ripen before frost, plant one to a hill to avoid competition.

A mulch is usually a good idea for melons, in order to keep the ground moist and the fruits clean and less prone to rot and disease. Melons are one crop where a black-plastic mulch makes a lot of sense, even if you don't like the way it looks. It really helps the soil to warm up in the spring and keeps it warmer on cool days in summer, too. Put down big, heavy sheets of it a few weeks before planting time, and make little slits when it's time to sow your seeds or set in your transplants. But anchor the plastic firmly on the sides by burying the edges or laying boards over them, then anchor it between plants with bricks, boards or stone. If the plastic shifts even an inch it will cover up the tiny plants and kill them, so keep checking it every day. If soil warmth is not an issue, use any good organic mulch like straw, salt hay or chopped leaves.

Give the seeds or transplants plenty of water to help them get established. You can also spread some manure or compost on top of the soil in a circle around the plant about 2 feet in diameter, or add a cupful of commercial fertilizer such as 10–10–10. Some people keep the young plants warm and hasten their growth by using hot caps or clear-plastic grow tunnels. Do this only if you check them constantly, as these heat concentrators can bake melon seedlings if you're not careful. A safer technique is to use the agricultural fabric sometimes called "floating row covers" (page 206), which will warm the plants a bit and also keep out aphids and striped cucumber beetles. Guarding the young plants against these pests is important not only because of the damage the insects can cause by feeding on the plants but, even more important, because of the diseases they can transmit. Be sure to remove the fabric when female flowers start to form (recognize them the way you do female squash blossoms, page 290) so that bees can pollinate them. By then there will be less danger from both cold and cucumber beetles.

GROWING

As melon plants grow they need a steady supply of water up until the time the fruits are ripening; but unless it is very dry you should hold off on the water the last week or two to make the melons have better flavor. Try to keep the leaves and fruits dry when you water, to help prevent disease.

If your soil is rich you may not need to feed melons while they are growing. If it is poor or average, or if you are trying to hasten growth along, give them some liquid fertilizer (fish emulsion or manure tea is fine) just before the vines start to take off and just when the tiny fruits are forming. If you're trying to grow very big watermelons, top dress them with a lot of manure.

Don't cultivate the soil, since roots near the surface can be injured; weeds that come up despite the mulch should be pulled carefully. You should also try to avoid walking on the vines. In very hot climates you may need to shield ripening fruits from sun scald; often all you need to do is draw the vines over the fruits so big leaves shade them a little.

If you want your melons to be large, or if you're trying to hurry up the crop, remove all but two to four melons from each vine. Watermelon vines will produce at most two fruits anyway, but if you want a very large watermelon, leave only the one closest to the roots of the vine. After midsummer it is a good idea to remove all blossoms and small fruits that won't ripen in time; this will make the vine put its energy into those that are left. Pinch off the tips of the vines at the same time.

PESTS AND DISEASES

The worst pest to watch out for is the striped cucumber beetle, described on page 246. As I suggested above, using lightweight agricultural fabric will usually keep the beetles off; use rotenone only if necessary, as soon as the seeds have sprouted or the transplants are set out. (But use it only at the end of the day when bees aren't active.) Using agricultural fabric will also control aphids as noted above; or use a soap spray. Squash-vine borers may also be a problem (page 291).

A number of fungus diseases can attack melons, especially in warm, humid climates. That's the bad news. The good news is that many modern varieties are resistant to some or all of these diseases. Find out which diseases are a problem in your area and look for varieties that are resistant (catalogs are usually quite specific about this). Rotating crops is also a big help.

Fusarium wilt is a fungus that lives in the soil. It occurs most often in the north, so crop rotation is especially important there, as is controlling the cucumber beetles that spread the wilt. If a vine suddenly wilts this may be the cause, so unless you can find evidence of squash-vine borer the vine should be destroyed. Mildews are more common in warm climates in wet weather. Powdery mildew, which gives the leaves a dusting of white, can ruin a crop. It is fought by keeping the vines' foliage dry.

Diseased shoots should be cut out and destroyed. You can try spraying the rest of the plant with benomyl; but remember the following year to plant only resistant varieties. Downy mildew (described on page 76) can sometimes be controlled by standard garden fungicides but is best fought by growing resistant varieties. Mosaic virus makes the foliage yellow and mottled and is controlled while the plants are young by keeping away the aphids that spread it.

HARVEST

Melons won't ripen much off the vine, so it is important to know just when to pick them. You can usually smell that great rich aroma when cantaloupes are ripe—better to test with your nose than with your fingers, which can damage the fruit. If the stem slips off easily when you press the base of the stem with your thumb, the melon is ripe. Also watch the color of the background underneath the "webbing" that covers the fruit: as the melon gets ripe it turns from green to tan.

In addition to thumping a watermelon you can turn it over and look at the light-colored patch on the bottom where the melon rests on the ground; when this turns a gold or orange color the melon is ripe. Harvest the thin-skinned "icebox melons" promptly. Keeping time for melons varies. Cantaloupes may last only a week or two, even in a cool place, casabas as long as eight weeks.

VARIETIES

Some of the best cantaloupes to grow are the vigorous 'Burpee Hybrid,' the drought-tolerant 'Hale's Best,' the disease-resistant 'Classic Hybrid,' the high-yielding 'Mainstream' and the very tasty, green-fleshed 'Rocky Sweet.' 'Jenny Lind' is another fine-tasting, green-fleshed variety. 'Ambrosia' and 'Saticoy' are famed for both sweetness and disease resistance. Early varieties to grow in northern areas include 'Earligold,' 'Earli-Sweet' and 'Alaska.' Some small-vined varieties, which take up less space and also ripen earlier, are 'Minnesota Midget' and 'Bush Musketeer.' 'Early Hybrid Crenshaw' will ripen faster than the standard 'Crenshaw,' and 'Earli-Dew' is an early honeydew.

Among the many fine watermelon varieties are the rather rounded, striped, disease-resistant 'Crimson Sweet,' the oblong, uniformly colored 'Charleston Gray,' and its related varieties such as 'Charleston Gray #5' and 'Calhoun Gray,' all of them disease resistant. 'Sweet Favorite Hybrid' is a good oblong variety for cooler areas, but for best success in the north grow a small-fruited, small-vined "icebox" watermelon like 'Sugar Baby,' 'Bush Jubilee,' 'New Hampshire Midget' or 'Family Fun.' The yellow-fleshed 'Yellow Doll' is also fairly compact and early. If you live in a warm climate and want to grow big whoppers try 'Black Diamond,' also known as 'Cannonball,' and 'Florida Giant.' There are a few seedless watermelon varieties, notably 'Burpee Seedless Hybrid' ('Tri X–313'). Seedless watermelons actually have rather inconspicuous white seeds and do best in warm climates.

Peaches

Peaches have the reputation of being hard to grow. It is true that both the trees and the fruits are a bit fragile and that the ideal peach-growing part of the country is not vast. But if you can find a variety that does well for you, and if you manage to get some peaches to that perfect tree-ripened moment, you'll find it was all worth the trouble. There is more of a difference between store-bought and fresh-picked with peaches than there is with just about any other produce. And in some ways they are a more trouble-free crop than apples.

To start with the good news, most peaches are self-fertile ('Elberta' and 'J. H. Hale' are notable exceptions), so that even if you grow just one little tree you'll get peaches. They are also early-bearing as fruits go; you can have them ripening from July to September if you plant a succession of varieties. Peaches grow on attractive trees about 20 feet tall that have pink flowers in spring and bear when they're as young as three years. Many modern varieties are disease-resistant, and while a few serious pests attack them these are less apt to blemish the fruit than pests that attack apples.

The tricky part of growing peaches is temperature. Most of the best peaches won't take winter temperatures colder than –10 degrees Fahrenheit, although many fine varieties have been developed that withstand lower winter temperatures. On the other hand, peaches do better in warm climates than many other fruit trees, such as apples, pears and plums. In warm areas you just need to be sure to plant low-chill varieties or they will break dormancy sporadically and halfheartedly in spring. Consult local growers or your Extension Service office for advice on peaches that do best where you live.

Peaches can be grown from seed but are usually grafted on peach stock. There are dwarf varieties, but I would start with standard-sized ones, which are more reliable and can be kept low and easy to pick by pruning. (You might try some "genetic" dwarfs, however, such as 'Compact Redhaven' or 'Compact Elberta,' which are true dwarf trees, not standard trees on dwarfing rootstocks.) You might like to grow nectarines too, especially if you live west of the Rockies, where they do best. (Nectarines are not a different fruit, but simply fuzzless peaches.)

SITE

The ideal site for peach trees is on a slope above a body of water, which will tend to draw off the cold air and keep the temperature even. Never plant them in a frost pocket where cold air collects at night. Usually a south- or southeast-facing slope is best, but in cold areas you might want to plant on a northern slope to avoid too-early bloom or you might plant on the north side of a building as long as the trees are set out far enough so that they get plenty of sun. Full sun is crucial for the ripening of fruits. The site must also be perfectly well drained—perhaps more important for peaches than for any other fruit, because they can develop moisture-induced problems such as crown rot.

SOIL

Peaches like a light, fertile soil that is sandy or even gravelly, so it will warm up well. It should be well supplied with organic matter, with a pH of 6.0–6.5 (though anything between 5.5 and 8.0 is tolerable).

PLANTING

Peaches are generally planted in spring while dormant. Buy vigorous one-year-old trees and plant them 20–25 feet apart (10–12 feet for dwarfs). The graft should be just above the surface, and the trunk should be protected against rodent damage and sun scald with plastic tree protectors. Cut the tree back to 2 to 3 feet tall, removing any lateral branches that have formed. Water well and mulch, but not right around the trunk.

GROWING

About six weeks after planting you can scatter some compost or 10–10–10 around the young peach tree, then each year feed in spring and again in early summer. It is important to fertilize peaches with a light hand. Too-rapid growth can produce weak-limbed trees. Avoid fertilizing beyond early summer, so as not to stimulate growth that won't harden before winter. For the same reason you should not prune after early summer either, or even water too heavily unless the soil is very dry. If your soil is very rich you might want to grow grass around the trees to slow their growth. Otherwise keep a mulch on the ground, especially if you are trying to forestall early bloom in cool climates.

Peach trees need careful pruning. In warm climates do it when trees are dormant; in cool ones wait until you can tell which wood has been winterkilled, if any. Unless the tree is a strongly upright-growing variety it is best pruned with an open center—i.e., without a central leader. Allow three strong lateral branches to develop. As other laterals and side branches grow in, eliminate downward-growing ones and those that turn back into the center, always trying to let sunlight into the middle of the tree. Fruit is produced on lateral twigs formed the previous season—you want these to be vigorous shoots at least 10 inches long.

Peaches are pruned more severely than other fruit trees, unless they have suffered a lot of winter damage and so need a lot of foliage with which to recover. Yearly pruning should not only eliminate weak or misdirected branches but should also serve to lighten branches, because fruit-laden ones can easily break. (Some may even need to be propped up with posts from below.) Thinning the fruit is also very important with peaches. Wait and see how much the tree will drop by itself in June, then thin to about 6 inches between fruits, eliminating any that have been damaged by insects or other causes. An old, neglected tree can be renewed by cutting back to three-year-old wood: you'll notice that the current year's stems are reddish pink, the previous year's are greenish and those formed the year before that are grayish. Cut back to a side bud on the most recently formed grayish stems.

PESTS AND DISEASES

Among the diseases that plague peaches are brown rot (page 340) and plum curculio (page 373). Nectarines are particularly prone to both. Perennial canker is a fungus that can get into the tree if you prune it while the weather is very cold, so don't prune until spring weather has settled in. Bacterial leaf spot causes spots to appear on the leaves that may

then turn into holes, and it also produces sunken spots on the fruits; but many modern peach varieties are resistant. Yellows causes the tree to turn yellow and eventually die, and since it is contagious you'll have to destroy the tree as soon as it is diagnosed.

The peach-tree borer gnaws into the trunk, usually near the bottom, leaving a gummy secretion. It can girdle the tree and kill it. Time-honored remedies include probing the tunnels with a wire to stab the borer and discouraging it by spreading moth crystals around the trunk in summer, then mounding about 4 inches of earth over the crystals. This may work, but be sure to remove the earth before winter. The peach-twig borer enters the tree through wounds made by mechanical injury, so don't be careless with your tools.

HARVEST

Peaches will bear after three to five years, even sooner if they are dwarfs. They should give you at least ten years of good bearing, but since that's not a very long time, it is wise to keep replanting new peach trees. The two most important things to know about harvesting peaches are that they *must* be ripened on the tree, and they *must* be picked carefully. When you look at most peaches you'll see that they have a background color (usually yellow) and a rosy "blush" on top of that—just like the blush on someone's cheek. A blush does not in itself indicate ripeness—you must wait for the background to lose its green color. Only then will the peach taste ripe and sweet. It should still be slightly firm but should come off the twig with just a slight twist. Picking before this moment will also result in bruises from your fingers as you try to remove the peach against its will. Always handle these delicate fruits with great care and store them in a cool spot so they don't get overripe before you can eat them.

VARIETIES

There are two kinds of peaches: free-stone and cling. Cling peaches, the kind you usually see in cans, have firm yellow flesh that holds its shape well. Though these are good for canning, their texture is not as good for fresh eating, and the flesh *clings* to the pit. Most peaches grown for the home orchard are freestone, with delicate flesh that comes away from the pit easily when you eat it.

There are many fine peach varieties; here is a sampling. The old standby is 'Elberta,' a big, hardy peach that keeps and ships well and grows on a vigorous, disease-resistant tree. 'Red-haven' is probably the best early variety; it's red and almost fuzzless, freezes well and has excellent flavor. The old-fashioned 'Belle of Georgia' is a hardy, sweet peach with white flesh and skin that is also white but flushed with pink. Other good white-fleshed peaches in-

clude 'Champion' and 'Raritan Rose.'

Other favorites are 'Redskin,' a good all-purpose red peach; the disease-resistant 'Cresthaven'; 'Golden Jubilee,' a good early yellow; the hardy, late 'Halehaven'; and the old 'J.H. Hale,' a very fine-flavored peach that does best in warmer climates. In the Deep South grow a low-chill peach like 'Sweetheart' or 'Florida King.' In very cold regions try 'Reliance,' a super-hardy peach that grows on fairly small trees that are handy for small yards. 'J.D.' is a hardy peach that doesn't brown when cut, and 'Polly' is a hardy white one that is sweeter than most northern varieties. If you want to try some great old peaches, grow 'Indian Blood Cling,' which is dark red both inside and out, or 'Slappy,' which is big, yellow and almost fuzzless.

The most popular nectarine varieties are 'Mericrest,' which is red, hardy and disease-resistant, the early 'Nectared' and 'Hardired' (both red), and the sweet 'Nectacrest.' If you live in the Deep South, try the early, disease-resistant 'Durbin.'

Seckel pear

Bosc pear

Bartlett pear

Pears

Pears grow on sturdy, deep-rooted trees that can live and bear for as long as seventy-five years. They will take less cold than apples but more than peaches, and often have fewer pest and disease problems than either. They are not especially rich in vitamins, but no matter. Get your vitamins A and C from the tomato crop and enjoy sweet, juicy home-grown pears for the sheer joy of it.

The pear's brief, early bloom can result in the flowers' being killed in cold areas, and can lead to inadequate pollination. Even if the flowers appear when it is warm enough for bees to be active, they are not as fragrant as those of other fruits, and bees may pass them by. Pear trees are not self-fertile either, though most varieties will cross-pollinate each other well. (The combination of 'Bartlett' and 'Seckel,' which are incompatible, is the notable exception.) Most do badly in very warm zones, since they need a winter chilling to break dormancy.

Pears are upright-growing, usually reaching at least 25 feet. Dwarfs can be grown successfully, usually on quince rootstocks.

SITE

Plant pear trees in a sunny spot except in climates where the sun is very strong. Protect them from winds that are cold or salt laden. In cold climates planting on a northern or eastern slope will help to forestall too-early bloom. It is very important to give pears good air circulation to ward off fire blight, the most troublesome pear disease. Plant standard-sized varieties 20–25 feet apart, dwarf ones 12–15.

SOIL

Pears are deep-rooted and need a deep soil. They will do better in a heavy soil than a light one, since they need plenty of soil moisture. (Sandy soils also warm up too quickly in spring, producing frost-vulnerable early bloom.) Pears growing in dry soil will bear pretty flowers and then drop unripe fruit all over the ground. On the other hand, too-rich soil will make them more susceptible to fire blight and may produce rapid growth that splits the bark. Best pH is about 6.5, but a wide range is tolerable.

PLANTING

Plant while dormant in fall in frost-free areas, otherwise in early spring. Buy one-year-old whips and cut back to 3 or 3½ feet. Set them out at the same height at which they grew in the nursery, but with dwarf varieties make sure the graft is several inches above the soil so the tree won't root above the graft. At planting time dig in organic matter such as peat and perhaps some bone meal, but no nitrogenous fertilizer. You have a vigorous tree, and can kill it with too much kindness.

GROWING

As the trees are growing, you can top dress them lightly with compost or whatever it takes to keep leaf color a healthy green and the tree productive— but you may not need to feed at all. It is more important to make sure the tree has plenty of moisture, especially at blossom time and when the fruit is ripening. A heavy mulch not only will conserve moisture but also may help to forestall too-early flowering. You may also grow grass around the tree to defer flowering and restrain growth. But beware heavy applications of lawn fertilizer.

Pear trees are pruned very much the same way as apple trees, but lightly so as to avoid producing vigorous new growth that will be susceptible to blight. Like apples, they bear for many years on long-lived spurs. It is, however, a good idea to keep the top pruned low

while the tree is young so it will not grow too tall to pick. Cutting it back later is harder to do and will invite blight. Old trees can be renewed in the same way as apples. Thinning will benefit the tree and the crop, though pears are notorious self-thinners, often dropping half their crop in early or midsummer.

PESTS AND DISEASES

The biggest pear plague is fire blight, a bacterial disease that blackens the leaves and twigs so they look burned. They may also curl over in a "shepherd's crook" shape. Cankers (sunken places) can be seen at the base of the blackened parts. The disease is carried by insects that enter the flowers in spring and is best prevented by growing resistant varieties. Also observe the cautions mentioned above. If your trees still get fire blight, prune out the affected shoots at least several inches below the damage, sterilizing your clippers in a chlorine solution between cuts and destroying the debris by burning or burying it. Badly damaged trees may need to be destroyed. There are antibiotic sprays, best administered by a professional, that control fire blight.

Other diseases include brown rot (page 340) and pear canker, a fungus that produces sunken areas on the twigs. You might have trouble identifying the latter, so take twigs to the Extension Service to see if pear canker is the trouble. If so, just prune it out and improve drainage in the area where the tree grows. Pear scab produces olive-green spots on the fruit in warm, wet weather; any infected areas should be pruned out and destroyed.

Pear psylla, a plant louse, is the most serious insect pest, blackening the leaves and fruit in midsummer because of the sooty mold that grows on the

sticky "honeydew," which the lice secrete. Dormant-oil spray, applied in
spring before buds swell, will help to
control it; follow this treatment with
insecticidal soap spray, as needed, later
in the season. Aphids, which also secrete honeydew, are also controlled by
dormant oil followed by soap. Even if
neither psylla nor aphids do great damage, both can introduce fire blight into
the tree. Pears are also injured by the
codling moth (page 335), and by pear
slugs, which are best done in by sprinkling them with lime.

HARVEST

Pears are best picked before maturity.
Left to ripen on the tree they become
grainy and can go very quickly from
ripe to rotten. Pick when the skins are
light green, when the seeds inside are
brown (open one pear to check) and
when the pears can be severed from the
branch easily with an upward-twisting
motion. If possible, store pears in a dry
room where the temperature is just
above freezing; they'll keep this way for
several months. Then bring them into a
warmer room when you want them to
ripen. But handle them carefully at all
stages because they are easily nicked
and bruised. Standard trees bear a good
crop in about six years, on the average,
and dwarfs in three or four. Expect up to
five bushels per tree from standards, up
to a bushel and a half from dwarfs.

VARIETIES

'Bartlett' is the best-known pear, the
standard commercial variety that keeps
and ships well; the tree is vigorous but
prone to blight; fruits are early. 'Clapp's
Favorite' is the standard late variety,
hardier for the north than 'Bartlett' but
also susceptible to blight. So is the exquisite 'Bosc,' that wonderful little
brown, long-necked pear, and the sump-
tuous old-world 'Flemish Beauty.' Less
risky is the wonderful old 'Seckel,' or
"sugar pear," which is small, brown
and very sweet; it grows slowly but
vigorously on a compact tree and is
quite hardy. (Also try its early version,
'Tyson.') Modern choices include the
early and dependable 'Moonglow,' or,
for canning, 'Kieffer,' a big, crisp, yellow pear that matures fairly late and
keeps very well. Another good bet is
'Magness,' a good blight-resistant pear
for the south and west that is very sweet,
keeps well and grows on a nice, spreading tree. (Grow two additional varieties
to ensure pollination.) 'Orient' is a good
round, green canning pear for the south,
also blight-resistant. Also try the great-
keeping 'Red Anjou' or the trouble-free
'Starking Delicious.'

Western gardeners owe it to themselves to try the 'Comice' pear, an old,
choice French pear considered the
crème de la crème; it bears late, has
exquisite flavor and is blight-resistant.
They should also grow the Asian pears
that are starting to become popular.
Huge, crisp pears that are something
like apples in texture, these are good
keepers and grow on large, self-fertile
trees. Good varieties include 'Chojuro'
and 'Twentieth Century.'

The Callery pear (*Pyrus calle-
ryana*) is an ornamental tree worth noting, especially the variety 'Bradford'
(called Bradford pear). It has a nice
shape and makes a good street tree,
resistant to fire blight. It is covered with
white flowers in spring and turns a
lovely dark red in fall. The tiny fruits
are not edible.

Plums

This Is Just to Say

I have eaten
the plums
that were in
the icebox

and which
you were probably
saving
for breakfast

Forgive me
they were delicious
so sweet
and so cold

   —William Carlos Williams

Plums are a good fruit crop for the home gardener. In areas where they do well they have relatively few problems. And they grow on small trees, so that often it is not necessary to grow dwarf varieties. Even if you have only a supermarket education in plums, you know that they come in many sizes, shapes and colors. The big, fat, juicy red ones are Japanese plums. These do best in warm climates—anywhere that peaches thrive. The trees are more delicate, bloom earlier, and require more care than other plums. European plums are the smaller, oval blue or purple ones. They are hardier than the red plums and do well in the north but not in very cold areas. They include Italian plums, prune plums (which are simply plums that have enough sugar content that they can be dried without removing the pits) and the tart but hardy damson plums, which are used for jams and jellies.

There are also a number of native American plums such as the beach plum of the northeastern coast, which tolerates seaside conditions, and the hybrids of *Prunus americana*. These are very cold-hardy and can be grown where other plums cannot. They are not as tasty as European and Japanese plums, however.

Though most plums are self-pollinating, you'll get a better crop if you grow several varieties, provided they are in the same color group. Don't try to pollinate a blue plum with a red, and check your catalog (or ask your nurseryman) to be sure you get at least two varieties that will cross-pollinate.

SITE

Plant plums in full sun and away from any frost pockets. Since plums bloom early it is best to plant them where the soil will warm up slowly in spring. That way, flowers will not appear so soon that they will be frost-nipped. This is especially important if you live in a cool climate and grow the red plums. Allow about 20 feet between trees, less for dwarfs, bush types and damsons.

SOIL

Plums aren't fussy about soil though a slightly heavy soil will suit them better than a light sandy one (except for beach plums). Blue plums need deep soil. All types prefer well-drained, fertile soil that is well supplied with organic matter. Ideal pH is about 6.5, but a range of 5.5 to 8.0 is tolerable.

PLANTING

Plant one-year-old dormant stock in early spring (fall in mild climates). Cut back to about 3 feet tall. Plant trees at the same depth as that at which they grew in the nursery or slightly deeper; protect the trunk (page 77) and apply a thick mulch, but take care to keep the mulch away from the trunk.

GROWING

Top dress plums annually with rotted manure, wood ashes and superphosphate—or use a commercial fertilizer. Make sure the trees have adequate water at the time they are flowering and fruiting. Prune young trees to three strong lateral branches, allowing the trees to develop multiple trunks only if, as some plums do, they have a bush habit, in which case you must train them to an open center. As a rule plums don't demand a lot of pruning, but you should let light into the tree to promote fruiting and ripening, pruning will also encourage the tree to bear annually. Red plums need more pruning than blue plums, because they are more vigorous and because they fruit on wood formed the previous year as well as on older wood. Pruning some of the year-old wood will help to prevent the tree from overbearing. The fruits of red plums are also heavier than others and so are more apt to need thinning.

PESTS AND DISEASES

Plum curculio is a beetle that lays eggs in the fruits when they are small, making a little crescent-shaped cut; the grubs hatch inside the fruits and rot them, secreting a gummy ooze that you can see on the outside. Shaking the beetles out of the trees onto sheets laid on the ground at blossom time in summer is a way of dealing with them without spraying. You should also destroy all fallen fruit containing grubs. (Red plums are not susceptible.) Aphids on plums can be controlled with dormant-oil spray.

The fungus disease called "black knot" produces hard black lumps on the twigs and branches. Prune out by cutting the wood several inches below the knot, then burn the cuttings. Wild cherry and wild plum trees can harbor and spread black knot, so monitor these if you have them on your property, destroying affected trees if need be.

HARVEST

Blue plums generally start to produce in about five years, red ones somewhat sooner. Yield is two to three bushels from a productive tree. Plums are ripe when they come off the branch with a slight twist. Red ones should be ripe when you pick them; the other types will ripen off the tree and so can be picked when they're a bit firmer.

VARIETIES

Popular red plums include the early, purple-red 'Santa Rosa,' the vigorous red 'Ozark Premier' and the sweet, early, yellowish 'Shiro.' Also try 'Elephant Heart,' a very big purple-red plum, 'Burbank,' which grows on compact trees, and 'Methley,' which ripens over a long period. In cold climates grow the hardy 'Superior,' 'Toka' or 'Tecumseh.' In warm ones grow 'Wade.'

'Stanley' is the most popular blue plum; it is good for preserves and grows on a vigorous, productive tree. Also try 'Fellenberg' (Italian) and 'Blue Damson' ('Shropshire Damson'), which is great for jellies. The old-fashioned 'Green Gage,' a greenish, sweet, all-purpose plum, does well in most regions.

raspberries   *blackberries*

Raspberries and Blackberries

If I could grow only one fruit, it would be raspberries They're my favorite to eat, and they're almost unaffordable in the markets, even during berry season. Fortunately they're very easy to grow in my climate, and for the most part they're trouble-free. If I lived in the south where raspberries do less well, I'd grow some gorgeous fat blackberries, which like hot climates.

Raspberries and blackberries are known as "bramble fruits" because they are so thorny—surely a deliberate move on nature's part to make them harder to pick. Like roses, they are an exquisite prize that you earn only by putting up with a little aggravation.

Bramble fruits are perennial plants that bear on biennial canes. This means that the roots live indefinitely and send up canes each year that generally fruit the second season, then die. By removing dead canes that have finished fruiting and letting the new ones grow, you can maintain a berry patch for many years. Since the patch is a permanent planting, it's worth spending some time at the beginning to figure out just which berries you should grow.

Red raspberries appear in early summer, usually in July—although there are some fall-blooming varieties (see below). They bear for a few blissful weeks during which you gobble as many fresh raspberries as you possibly can, since they don't keep well, then freeze the rest or make them into jam. You can stretch this early-summer Nirvana to a month or more by planting several varieties that ripen at slightly different times. Yellow raspberries are excellent for home growing too. They are very sweet but not quite as appealing to birds as the red ones are. You rarely find yellows for sale in markets, since they don't ship well, so they make a special home-grown treat to serve alone or mixed with red and black raspberries. They grow exactly like red raspberries, on sturdy, erect plants, and many are hardy even in Zone 3. Both red and yellow raspberries send up new canes from the crowns and also from the roots as suckers, so even if you plant only a few you will soon have many. Raspberries and other brambles are self-fertile, so you need only one variety to ensure pollination (though some growers maintain that their yield is greater if they grow two).

Black raspberries, also called "black caps," are quite different from red ones. Their canes are arching or trailing and send out vigorous fruiting side branches, whereas red raspberries are borne mainly on the long, slender canes. Black raspberries don't produce the multitude of suckers that red raspberries do. Most are hardy only to Zone 5 or 6, but unlike the red ones, black raspberries will tolerate a fair amount of heat. Their flavor is also a bit more tart and rich, making them a superb choice for baking, for ice cream or for jams. Purple raspberries, a cross between black and red, grow much like the black ones, though they are often more hardy.

You can also plant ever-bearing raspberries for a fall harvest. These don't really bear all summer; rather, they have two crops, one borne on second-year canes at the usual time, and another borne in fall on the tips of new canes produced that season. If you cut these back after the fall harvest you will sacrifice the summer crop, but this means that the fall one will be bigger. I prefer to grow them this way, for a big fall crop. I can always plant a standard summer-bearing variety for the early

crop. Ever-bearing varieties can be either red or yellow.

Blackberries are larger than raspberries and a bit less sweet. They are also less cold-hardy and do best in moderate or warm climates. The plants are extremely vigorous and vary as to their growth habits: some have strong, erect canes; others are trailing and will lie on the ground unless supported; still others are semitrailing. Some varieties are thornless. Boysenberries and loganberries—both of which are large and wine colored, growing on trailing plants—are simply blackberry varieties.

SITE

The best site for bramble fruits is a slightly sloping, sunny hillside where cold air drains away. They will take a bit more shade than other fruits, but a sunny location will provide a better yield, especially in cool climates. Avoid sites where any of the *Solanaceae* have grown in recent years (page 184), since these all share with brambles a susceptibility to the verticillium-wilt virus. It is also best to separate red and black raspberries by 300 feet, if possible, since seemingly healthy red plants can transmit diseases to the less-resistant blacks. Wild raspberries and blackberries can also transmit diseases, so it is wise to eradicate any you have on the property. Be sure to pick a well-drained site; none of the bramble fruits will grow where it's mucky.

SOIL

Most soil types will grow bramble fruits as long as drainage is good. Moderate fertility is sufficient, though the plants will appreciate some bone meal and some rotted manure or compost worked into the soil. The more organic matter in the soil, the better; it will help the soil to hold moisture. The soil should be slightly acid—about 6.0 is ideal, but a range of 5.5 to 7.0 is acceptable. Remember that this is a permanent bed, and all weeds, rocks and other obstacles to good growth must be removed at the beginning. The soil should be enriched, lightened and well tilled throughout the bed before you do your planting.

PLANTING

It is very important to buy certified virus-free plants. Your neighbors will tempt you with offers of free raspberry plants when it's time to weed out the suckers between their rows. Turn them down, or there's a chance you'll start out with diseases you'll never get rid of. Root nematodes can also get started in your garden this way, and the nursery you buy from should be able to guarantee their stock to be free of these, too.

Planting time is early spring, except in Zone 6 and southward, where fall or even late-winter planting is possible. You don't have to buy very many plants of each variety, especially red raspberries. (Keep in mind that in a few years you'll be throwing out extras.) A dozen plants, spaced 3 feet apart, will soon give you a large harvest, with each foot of row producing about a quart of berries. Plant blackberries and black raspberries about 4 feet apart, trailing blackberries 5–6 feet apart. If I'm planting more than one row I make sure that the rows are pretty far apart—a good 10 feet is best. (When I'm pruning or picking I like to be sure that no wayward canes will reach out and grab me from behind.) If you're using a trellis system (below), you can space the rows more closely.

Make sure that the roots do not dry out between the time you buy them and the time you put them in the ground, and moisten your planting holes. Plant rasp-berries a few inches deeper than they were growing in the nursery, blackberries at about the same level. Cut red raspberries and blackberries back to 6 inches, but cut black raspberries back to ground level as a precaution against disease. Then water the plants some more.

GROWING

It is very important to give all bramble fruits a constant water supply while they are growing and especially when they are forming fruit. A good thick mulch of an organic material such as salt hay will help a lot, and it will also keep weeds from working their way into the berry plants' root systems. In addition, mulch will keep you from having to cultivate the soil. This is an important advantage, as cultivating can nick the plants' shallow roots, which, in the case of red raspberries, can promote excess suckering. But even with a mulch, you should watch soil moisture. If it's dry weather and a crop is ripening, laying a soaker hose along the rows will definitely increase your yield. Top dress each year in early spring with at least a shovelful of compost or rotted manure for every foot of row, or apply a handful of commercial fertilizer such as 10–10–10 to the same area.

The most important job in growing bramble fruits is keeping the plants properly pruned so that the bed does not become an impenetrable tangle of thorny canes. Each berry type has a different way of running rampant, but run rampant it will.

Red and yellow raspberries, as I explained above, don't branch much but they do send up lots of canes. Every year in early spring you should go out to the raspberry patch, wearing a long-sleeved shirt and leather gloves, and prune out any winterkilled canes at ground level. Then cut back all the remaining canes at about chest height. After the harvest, cut back at soil level all the canes that have borne fruit. If the plants have just fruited it's easy to tell which these are, because you can see what remains of the little berry clusters after the berries have been removed. If you've let the job go until winter or early spring, you'll still be able to distinguish the old canes because they are darker, with peeling bark. Any part of the plant that looks diseased should be removed at whatever time you spot it.

I don't bother to use any kind of a trellising system with red or yellow raspberries, because the stiff canes support themselves so well. I use the hedge-row method, just letting the row fill in with new plants until it gets about 1½ to 2 feet wide. Any wider than that, and it's hard to reach and pick. Every spring I pull up *all* the suckers that come between the rows (and later in the season too, as they appear). It is also a good idea to thin the plants within the rows, pulling up some of the new canes so that the remaining canes are about 6 inches apart.

Some gardeners do use a trellis system for raspberries, either because they find them easier to pick this way, or because they're short of space. Trellised rows can be as close together as 5 feet. Keep in mind, though, that the farther apart they are the better the air circulation, and the less chance of disease. You can use a system similar to the four-arm system for grapes, pictured on page 357. Or you can box the vines by running wires on either side of a thick wooden post, trapping the vines between the wires (Figure 55). Or nail 2-foot crosspieces to the posts, as on a telephone pole, to make a wider box. You can also just place metal stakes 2 feet apart and string wires along those. Brace the end posts to keep them from bending.

Black raspberries don't sucker freely. Their way of running amok is to bend over their long canes so that the tips root in the soil between your rows. If you let them do this, pretty soon you won't have any rows, just a solid mass of berry bushes. Cut off the new canes to about 2 feet tall in midsummer. This will cause them to form lateral branches, which will bear fruit next year. In early spring cut back each of those lateral branches to about 12 inches long. Then after harvest cut back the canes that have fruited, just as you do with red raspberries. If you prune them this way you can keep the plants fairly short and erect, so you shouldn't need to trellis them. Thin the rows as needed, and pull up any plants growing between them.

Ever-bearing raspberries bear the first year, in fall, at the tips of the canes. If you want a second crop, cut off the tips after harvest; the following season they'll bear on the uncut portion in early summer. Then cut back the whole cane after it finishes fruiting. Both crops will be smaller than that produced by ordinary summer-bearing raspberries. To get one big fall crop instead—and simplify your pruning job as well—cut *all* the canes back to the ground after the fall harvest.

If you're growing blackberries, cut the first-year canes back to 3 feet in midsummer to encourage lateral branches, which will bear fruit. Then in late winter or early spring cut each lateral branch to about half its length. After harvest cut back at soil level canes that have borne fruit. Thin the new canes so that they're about 6 inches apart. Whether or not you trellis blackberries depends on what type they are. If they have erect canes and you prune them well, they can stand alone like raspberries. If they are trailing or semi-

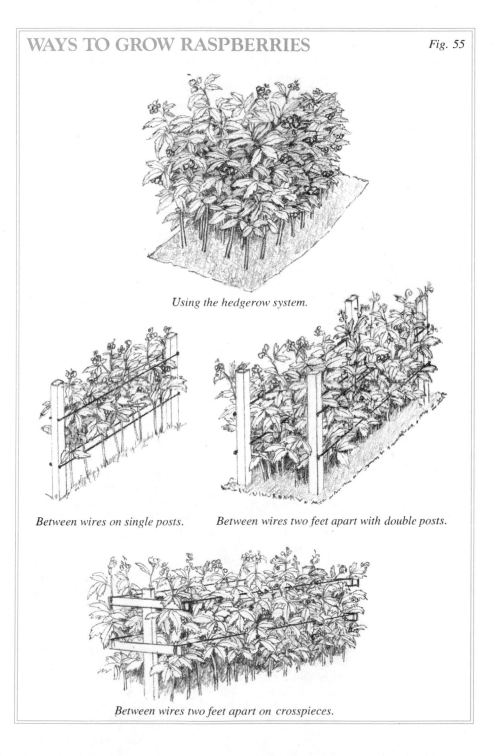

WAYS TO GROW RASPBERRIES

Fig. 55

Using the hedgerow system.

Between wires on single posts.

Between wires two feet apart with double posts.

Between wires two feet apart on crosspieces.

trailing, they'll need some kind of support. You can bunch the canes together and tie them to stout stakes, but they'll enjoy better air circulation if you train them on wires. Either use the four-armed system shown for grapes on page 357, tying a number of canes to each wire and letting a few trail along the ground as well, or use the box system shown in Figure 55. With trailing varieties you'll have to tie the canes to whatever support you use.

Propagating new bramble plants is easy. Do it at the time you would normally plant them in your area. For red raspberries just dig up some suckers and replant them. For black raspberries bend a cane over and bury the tip in a pocket of enriched soil, anchoring the tip with a rock or a bent wire just as you do with a stem you are layering (as shown in Figure 66). Blackberries can be propagated by replanting suckers, by rooting the tips of canes or by digging up some roots on the edge of an established clump and replanting them. With all these methods, cut the stems back to the appropriate height when you replant.

PESTS AND DISEASES

There is a long list of diseases of bramble fruits, though yours may escape all of them, especially in cool climates. Fortunately there are a number of things you can do to keep berries healthy, even in areas where diseases are common. First, buy new, clean stock. Remove all plant debris—winterkilled stems, canes that have borne fruit, and any diseased parts of the plant—as promptly as possible, and either burn the debris or cart it away. Don't leave it lying around the property, even in the compost heap. Remove all wild bramble plants from the property. Try to provide the plants with good air circulation by choosing the right site, pruning and thinning the canes, and trellising them if necessary. Provide good water drainage for the roots. Feed, water and mulch as needed to keep the plants vigorous, but avoid giving them excessive nitrogen. Finally, seek out varieties that resist specific diseases that are prevalent where you live.

Some diseases to watch for are mosaic, which makes leaves yellow and mottled; botrytis cane wilt, which makes new canes wilt; verticillium wilt, which causes canes to wilt suddenly in hot, dry weather; anthracnose, which produces purplish spots on the leaves, then grayish growth on the stems; powdery mildew, which covers the leaves with whitish powder; orange rust, which shows up as bright orange pustules on the undersides of the leaves; leaf-curl virus, which makes the leaves dark green and tightly curled; and spur blight, which produces brown spots on the canes.

Foil hungry birds with plastic netting if they're getting too much of your crop, though if you have lots of berries and pick often you may not find birds a big problem. The netting can be draped over the plants, but it is hard to remove for pruning and picking that way, so you may want to erect a lightweight wooden or metal frame to support it; this can be either box-shaped or constructed like an A-frame house.

Japanese beetles bother raspberries; pick them off or use milky spore disease (page 73). Hose off aphids, or spray them with insecticidal soap; they can transmit diseases. Prune out canes infested with borers (you'll be able to see the little holes where they have entered the cane), and remove plants with galls that indicate crown borers. Fruit worms, which eat the buds and the berries, can be sprayed with rotenone; the soil should then be cultivated around the plants in late summer and early fall to keep the worms from overwintering there as pupae. A few raspberry varieties, such as 'Purple Royalty,' are insect resistant.

HARVEST

Pick berries only when they are ripe, but don't let them sit on the bush too long. Pick at least twice a week when they are bearing. Be careful not to squeeze the berries; just pull them off the stem gently. (Raspberry cores will stay on the stems.) Keep your pail or basket in the shade as you pick, and don't let the berries get more than a few inches deep in the container or they'll squash. Store in the refrigerator until you're ready to use them.

VARIETIES

For summer-bearing red raspberries, the old standby 'Latham' is fine, but there are other good choices too. 'Newburgh' is vigorous, hardy, productive and disease resistant, with a big berry. 'Canby' and the very large 'Thornless Red Mammoth' have practically no thorns, for easy picking. 'Reveille,' 'Sunrise' and the huge 'Titan' are extra-early. 'Taylor' is hardy, vigorous and especially fine tasting. 'Willamette,' a large, dark red berry, is recommended for the west coast, and the vigorous 'Dorman Red' is the one to grow in the south. The everbearing 'Fallgold' is the most popular yellow variety. Of the ever-bearing reds, 'Heritage' is the most universally grown, but the hardy, disease-resistant 'Fall Red' is well worth trying. 'Scepter' and 'Indian Summer' also have good disease resistance.

Popular black raspberries include the vigorous, upright standby 'Bristol,' and 'Black Hawk,' which is both disease and heat resistant. Especially coldhardy varieties are the large 'Cumberland,' 'John Robertson' and the disease-resistant 'Jewel.' 'Allen' is sweeter than most. For purples try the large, sweet 'Royalty,' which is hardy and both insect and disease resistant. 'Brandywine' is a good, fairly hardy, tart variety that people favor for jams. 'Lowden Sweet Purple' is anthracnose resistant and almost seedless.

Good erect blackberries for the south include 'Cheyenne' and the sweet, early 'Rosborough.' 'Darrow' and 'Ebony King' are hardy upright varieties. 'Boysenberry,' 'Loganberry' and 'Lucretia Dewberry' are tasty trailing varieties. Among the thornless blackberries 'Chester' and 'Hull' are especially hardy, and 'Black Satin' and 'Thornfree' especially disease resistant. Also try 'Thornless Boysenberry.'

*woodland
strawberries*

strawberries

Strawberries

I n growing strawberries you must
know what to expect. Yes, you'll
get luscious red fruits for short-
cakes and pies, and in a lot less time
than you'd have to wait for tree fruits.
Yes, strawberries are vigorous perennial
plants that grow like crazy with very
little encouragement. And yes, they take
up relatively little space in the home
garden. But your venture will be disap-
pointing unless. you acquire a bit of
strawberry savvy. Established beds that
are left to fend for themselves will have
all sorts of problems. They may suffer
from bugs, diseases and weeds that
creep in. The plants will become over-
crowded and will overrun the rest of the
garden. Old plants will, over time, bear
less and less heavily; their crowns will
push up out of the soil and be winter-
injured. And what you assumed would
be strawberry fields forever will be
nothing but a strawberry mess. To prevent all this from happening you'll need
to put a little effort into managing those

beds. You may even decide that growing
strawberries as an annual crop is the
way to go.

There are four different kinds of
strawberries, each of them wonderful
for different reasons. The classic strawberry plant bears for a few weeks in
June (earlier in warm climates) and then
quits. Strawberry festivals were inspired
by this kind, because the output during
those weeks is so great that you either
need to bake them, can them, freeze
them, or open up your doors and feed
the whole town.

"Ever-bearing" strawberries, the
second kind, don't really bear all season. They produce two crops, the first at
the usual time and the second in late
summer. Neither crop is as large as that
of June-bearing plants, and ever-bearing
types tend to be a little less hardy, but
for gardeners who want two modest harvests rather than one big one they are
just right.

"Day-neutral" strawberries are a

new development. Because they are less sensitive to the difference between long and short days than the first two types, they bear most of the summer, even as days lengthen, letting up only in the very hottest weather. These are perfect if you're more interested in a steady supply of strawberries than an avalanche. Day-neutral varieties are often planted in fall and harvested the following spring even in relatively cool climates. Give this a try even if you live up north and see how it works for you.

Finally, there are the "Alpine" strawberries, or *fraises des bois*—tiny little elongated fruits from Europe that are similar to the little wild strawberries that grow in the United States, but are bigger and easier to pick. You have to grow a great many plants to have more than a sprinkling of fruit to top a bowl of cereal or a whipped-cream-covered cake or a pie, but a great many Alpine strawberry plants is not a bad thing to have. I have had excellent luck growing them from seed. They do not spread by runners the way other strawberries do and so require less managing. They are also very pretty and can be used as decorative edgings in flower gardens as well as for a food crop. Best of all, they bear all season long.

SITE

First of all, you need a sunny spot for strawberries. It should also be a warm one, to help the plants escape late-spring frosts. These can nip the blossoms, turning their centers black and preventing berries from forming. Choose a gentle, south-facing slope, not a pocket that traps cold air. You also need a spot with good drainage or the plants will rot and get diseases. If your drainage is not excellent, consider growing strawberries in rasied beds.

The vegetable garden is a good place for strawberries if you can spare even as little as 60 square feet. You can also grow them among fruit trees as long as the berries get enough sun. For example, you might plant two rows of fruit trees with an avenue between them and a path down the center, then edge the path in strawberries. Also, if your space is very limited, you might grow a small crop spaced intensively in a raised bed or in one of those strawberry barrels or pyramids you see advertised. While these look charming on a terrace, however, don't expect the kind of yield you'd get from a bona-fide strawberry patch.

SOIL

In addition to needing a well-drained site, strawberries require soil that is fertile and very generously supplied with organic matter. Well-rotted manure, thoroughly dug in, will accomplish both purposes. The pH should be a bit on the acid side—5.5 to 6.5. Removing all weeds from the site is of *utmost* importance, especially if you want to keep a bed going for a number of years. Like many gardeners, I have learned the hard way what perennial weeds, particularly grasses, can do to a strawberry bed. It is best not to plant on a spot where grasses or hay have been growing recently; instead choose a more established garden area. You might even prepare a spot by growing cover crops and turning them under for a year or two before planting (page 27).

PLANTING

Strawberries are usually planted in early spring, although in warm climates they can be planted in fall. (Fall planting will give you a crop the first spring.) Strawberries are available at most garden centers, where they are grown in flats, just like vegetables. But the most inexpensive way to buy them is bare-root, in bundles. Strawberries may carry viruses that will ruin the crop and be hard to eliminate from your garden, so unless you have a very good local source, order strawberries by mail from a reputable company that will certify them as disease-free stock. One-year-old plants will usually bear just as soon as older ones, and they're cheaper.

Start with twenty-five plants. Since you do have to fuss with strawberries a bit it's best not to overextend yourself. In any case, twenty-five plants will probably be all you'll need because each mature plant will produce as much as a quart of berries. (If you find you enjoy strawberry-growing a lot and want to freeze them or make jam, add more plants, of several different varieties, in subsequent years.) If the plants arrive before planting time, put them in the refrigerator with the plastic wrapping open, and keep the packing around the roots slightly moist. Try to plant them as soon as possible, or at least heel them into the ground (page 49). Take special care not to let the roots dry out at any time.

When your soil is thoroughly prepared, mark out some nice straight rows. Although there are several different ways to arrange a strawberry plot, depending on how you want to manage the subsidiary plants that form on "runners," they all start with straight rows.

If you watch the way strawberry plants grow, you'll see that the original plant that you put in the ground, called the "mother" plant, soon puts out long, thin stems; these are the runners. When they get to be about 9 inches long they turn up at the tips and put down roots, forming "daughter" plants. If left to their own devices the daughters send out their own runners and produce granddaughters, and pretty soon what you

have is a thick, unproductive ground cover. So some form of birth control is always needed with strawberries.

If you're a laissez-faire kind of gardener, try the "matted-row" system. The plants are set out about 18 inches apart in rows 3–4 feet apart and are allowed to send out as many runners as they want. To keep the space between the rows from filling up with plants, go to your patch after harvest and get rid of the outermost plants on each side of a row, either by removing granddaughters individually by snipping the runners and digging up the little plants, or just by running a mechanical tiller between the rows. When you're done, the row should be only a foot or two wide. (It is also a good idea to remove some of the mother plants from within the row. Leave the newest ones, which will bear more vigorously the following season.) If you remove as much as 75 percent of the vegetation, your patch will be the better for it.

If you are a meticulous kind of gardener, you'll like the "spaced-row" system. Here, you set the strawberry plants at least 18 inches apart and remove some of the runners from each so that there are only four to six of them, spaced at least 6 inches apart. Some rather compulsive growers even reposition the daughters to make the spacing more even. In future years, keep removing older plants so there is always at least 6 inches of space around each of the remaining ones.

The last method is for tidy gardeners. It is commonly (and rather misleadingly, I think) called the "hill system." No true hills are involved, however: you simply set the plants fairly close together—12 inches apart in every direction is fine, 18 if you have plenty of space—and remove any and all runners that form. This forces the mother plant to put its energy into fruiting rather than making runners, though it will form multiple crowns. You can make single rows, or space the plants equidistant from each other in a grid (page 196), but don't make the patch so wide that you can't reach into it easily from the outer edge. If you have to step into your patch at picking time you'll squash a lot of precious berries. Eventually the mother clumps will get too dense, so if you are growing your own replacement plants you'll want to let just some runners grow and form new plants. This method works particularly well for the day-neutral strawberry varieties, which tend to produce fewer runners anyway.

Whatever kind of spacing you use for strawberries, always set the plants into the ground the same way. The roots should be spread out but pointing downward. The best way to do this is to dig a cone-shaped hole with a smaller cone of earth in the center of it, then drape the roots over the earth-cone, rather like the way day lilies are planted in Figure 29, but with only one plant per hole. Be absolutely sure that the crown (the place where the roots join the stem) is exactly at the soil surface: too deep, and the crown will rot; too shallow, and the roots will dry out. Also be sure to firm the soil well around the roots. Water thoroughly. If your soil is not very rich you can use a weak liquid fertilizer solution at planting time.

GROWING

The first year, little spring-planted strawberries will produce some flowers, but these should be pinched off so that the plant will put its energy into growing and producing a fine crop for next year. A mulch between the plants and between rows will help conserve moisture and keep down the weeds, and a winter mulch laid over the plants may be necessary from Zone 5 northward. You can use the same material for both purposes—something light such as straw or salt hay. Apply the winter covering about Thanksgiving time, or whenever hard frosts are a regular occurrence, then brush it aside to expose the plants at blossom time. Don't take the mulch away, though; leave it next to the plants and use it for a quick emergency cover if late frosts threaten or for covering the ground under ripening berries to keep them clean and rot-free.

Top dress the plants once a year at blossom time with rotted manure, compost, or a balanced fertilizer like 15–15–15. If the weather is dry, make sure the plants get an inch of water per week, especially when flowering and forming fruit. And be sure to keep up with the weeds, removing them while they're still tiny, especially if you haven't mulched.

With June-bearing strawberries it is also a good idea to cut off the foliage right after the harvest. Timing is important: either cut plants down as soon as your crop is finished or not at all, otherwise there won't be enough time for new leaves to grow and nourish the plants for the rest of the season. In a small patch you can cut plants down with shears; in a large one use a scythe, a sickle or a power lawn mower set so that the plants are cut back to 1½ inches tall. Then fertilize and water deeply.

One decision you will have to make no matter what growing method you use is how long to keep a patch going. If there are a lot of disease problems in your area you may find that starting a brand-new crop in a different part of the garden every year will keep the plants much healthier. But you'll always need to have two patches going at once. While one patch is producing, another one will be growing to replace it the next year. It's up to you how you manage your patches. If your plants never get diseases and you're not much interested in trying new varieties, you may prefer to just keep the same patch going by removing the older plants each year.

PESTS AND DISEASES

You will assuredly have some problems with birds eating your ripe strawberries, and possibly with chipmunks as well. If your crop is big you may not lose enough for that to make much of a difference, but if it is a small one you should protect it. Birds can be deterred by plastic netting, cheesecloth or the agricultural fabric described on page 206. These will provide some measure of protection against chipmunks too, as will a series of chicken-wire-covered wooden frames such as those shown on page 205.

White grubs in the soil, especially those of June bugs, can eat the plants' roots. If your plants wilt suddenly, even when it's not dry, pull one up and see if the root system looks damaged. The best way to deal with grubs is to avoid planting in areas where sod has recently been growing. If you still get them, try pouring a weak kerosene solution (one tablespoon of kerosene to a cup of water) on the soil around the plants.

Rotating your strawberries with other crops will help keep both insect and disease problems under control, but take care that you don't plant them where tomatoes and other *Solanaceae* (page 185) have grown recently—or melons, raspberries, mint or roses. These can all harbor verticillium wilt, which wilts plants and stunts their growth. It is also very important when growing strawberries to remove all plant debris from the patch, because it can rot and harbor fungus diseases. This includes berries that you don't pick because they are overripe or have been nibbled or otherwise damaged. Toss these into a separate basket and destroy them.

Another disease to watch out for is red stele, a fungus that rots the strawberries' roots. Both verticillium and red stele are cool-climate, cool-weather diseases. Botrytis fungus and other rot diseases are best fought by good sanitation and thorough picking. Virus-infected plants must be destroyed, and the place where they have grown should not be used for strawberries for a number of years. In fact it's best to wait awhile before growing strawberries anywhere following a virus attack. Virus diseases are difficult to identify, so it is advisable to consult your Extension Service if your plants are doing poorly and you can't pinpoint the problem yourself. Fortunately, there are now varieties that resist strawberry diseases. I have noted below some with good general disease resistance; for more precise information about strawberries that resist specific diseases, consult the tables included in some of the catalogs of nurseries that specialize in berry plants (page 619).

HARVEST

Strawberries can be harvested the second year after planting. With June-bearing ones this will mean waiting for about fourteen months for your first crop, but in climates where fall planting is safe your crop should be ready the following June. Wait for the berries to be fully red, not green at the tip, before you pick them. Resist the temptation to beat the birds to the strawberries by picking them almost-ripe. They will not ripen well off the vine. Strawberries, despite their bright color, can be hard to find; lift the foliage up to see those hiding underneath. Never grasp the berry itself when you pick, because it is easily bruised; instead pinch or snip the stem. Collect and store the berries in shallow containers, in a layer no more than 5 inches deep or the weight will crush those on the bottom.

VARIETIES

There are so many strawberry varieties available that it is sometimes hard to know which to choose, but here are some guidelines. Some of the most popular June-bearing varieties are 'Earliglow' and the large-fruited 'Honeoye,' both early bearers; the drought-tolerant 'Surecrop,' 'Dunlap' and 'Sunrise'; the jumbo-sized 'Guardian,' 'Scott,' 'Catskill,' 'Allstar,' 'Empire' and 'Cardinal.' 'Sparkle,' 'Midway' and 'Redchief' are also fine, tasty berries. If you're looking for a very vigorous grower, you might pick 'Honeoye,' 'Sunrise,' 'Sparkle,' 'Blakemore' (also called 'Tennessee Beauty'), 'Surecrop' or 'Scott.' For good disease resistance grow 'Guardian,' 'Allstar,' 'Earliglow,' 'Surecrop,' 'Redchief' or 'Sunrise.'

Good choices for cold climates are 'Trumpeter,' 'Sparkle,' 'Kent,' 'Surecrop,' 'Catskill' and 'Midway.' In the south grow 'Sunrise,' 'Blakemore,' 'Cardinal,' 'Guardian,' 'Redchief,' 'Tioga' and 'Florida 90'; the last two thrive even in very hot areas. Consult your Extension Service for recommendations about more specific areas.

The most popular ever-bearing strawberry is 'Ozark Beauty,' good for most regions, even the north. Some other cold-hardy ever-bearing varieties are 'Fort Laramie,' 'Superfection,' and 'Ogallala.' Those with more disease resistance than 'Ozark Beauty' include 'Ogallala' and 'Quinault.' The best day neutral varieties are 'Tristar' and 'Tribute,' both fairly disease resistant.

CHAPTER 10

BULBS

S pring bulbs must surely have been invented by some divine marketing expert to make life easy for beginning gardeners. A bulb is like a prepackaged kit, complete with its own stored food. Put it in the ground in fall, and it will simply carry out the growing program that it came with, while you forget about it and go on with the business of winter. Then, lo and behold, in spring it presents you with a flower.

This is not to say that bulbs come with a money-back guarantee. Neither Mother Nature nor the bulb sellers are responsible if a mouse eats your bulb or if you plant it in soggy soil, and there are a number of little things you can do to make your bulb display more spectacular. But as plants go, hardy bulbs are among the easiest and showiest. They are also among the most rewarding. Perhaps it's because they are such joyous heralds of spring, bursting into bloom long after the labor of planting them has become a dim memory.

Usually when we speak of bulbs we mean flower bulbs, as opposed to the kind you eat, such as onions. And when we think of bulbs we think of Holland, where most of the world's hardy spring flower bulbs are grown. As a matter of fact, however, virtually none of the bulbs sold commercially are native to Holland or anywhere near it. Most originated in the Middle East or southern Europe, particularly the area around the Mediterranean. But bulbs, both hardy and tender, have always been world travelers, prized by emperors and kings, traded in commerce, and brought back by soldiers and adventurers from the exotic lands where the bulbs were growing as native plants. Many bulbs were first introduced to Europe by men returning from the Crusades. The fact that they are so easily transported while dormant (such ingenious packaging!) surely has been a contributing factor in the spread of bulbs. Take the ranunculus, truly a citizen of the world. It is variously known as the "Dutch buttercup," the "Scotch buttercup," the "French buttercup" and the "Persian buttercup"; but only the last name is appropriate. *Ranunculus asiaticus,* from which modern hybrids are derived, is native to Asia Minor.

Again, when bulbs are mentioned most people think only of spring bulbs. They don't realize how many excellent summer-blooming bulbs there are, and they forget that there are even a few fall-blooming bulbs.

What Is a Bulb?

A ll the bulbs discussed in this chapter are perennial—that is, they come up every year, assuming they're planted in a climate that they can tolerate. They are also herbaceous—that is, they have soft green stems as opposed to woody ones. But bulbs are distinguished from the fibrous-rooted herbaceous perennials discussed in Chapter 6 by the fact that they come up from a swollen mass of plant tissue of some sort (though these masses generally have fibrous roots at the bottom).

A number of plants that are discussed along with bulbs and are sold by the same people that sell bulbs are not true bulbs but corms, or tuberous roots or tubers. These terms all refer to an enlarged portion of a plant that stays underground and stores food over the winter, for root growth in winter and for leaf and stem growth the following season. A true bulb, such as that of a tulip or daffodil, is a swollen underground stem consisting of scalelike leaf bases. These are filled with food and are tightly wrapped around a bud in the heart of the bulb, and usually are surrounded with a hard protective covering.

A corm, such as that of a crocus or gladiolus, is similar but has a bud on top and is replaced by a new corm each year. A tuber (cyclamen or tuberous begonia) is the swollen part of an underground stem. A tuberous root (dahlia) is a swollen root, not a stem, and must have part of a stem with a bud attached to it in order to produce a plant.

It is not important that you remember all these distinctions, and indeed, in this chapter I will use the word "bulb" to cover corms, tubers and tuberous roots as well as true bulbs. What is important is that you understand in general what all these swollen tissue masses do. Their purpose is to enable the plant to survive the periods of cold and/or drought that it experiences in its native climate, then have enough nourishment to begin its growth properly when the growing season arrives. Bulbs and similar structures go through those cold or dry periods in a state of dormancy. If your climate does not give the bulbs that dormant period, then you must.

There are two major categories of bulbs, spring blooming and summer blooming. There are also a few that bloom in fall, such as colchicums, autumn crocuses, and some of the alliums and cyclamens. Spring-blooming bulbs and summer bulbs are usually handled rather differently. (Fall-blooming bulbs are handled in various ways and are considered individually in the List of Bulbs.)

SPRING BULBS

This group is the most familiar and includes anemones, most crocuses, fritillarias, glory-of-the-snow, snowdrops, grape hyacinths, hyacinths, bulbous iris, daffodils, scillas, tulips and winter aconites. Most spring bulbs, once planted, do not have to be dug up except for propagation purposes or to ease

overcrowding. There are exceptions, however. In the north some, such as Dutch irises, are tender. Gardeners in these areas may elect to dig them up and store them over the winter in a protected place. But usually northern gardeners simply choose from the many hardy bulbs that they can grow without worry.

In very warm climates, by contrast, spring bulbs can be a problem for gardeners because the winters are not cold enough to make many spring bulbs go dormant. They must dig them up in late fall and refrigerate them for a few months to simulate a northern winter—or grow tropical bulbs instead.

SUMMER BULBS

These include such bulbs as alliums, tuberous begonias, cyclamens, dahlias, gladiolus, lilies and ranunculus. Most of these are tender and need warm, frost-free regions. The exceptions, which prefer a cooler, more temperate northern climate, are most lilies, most alliums, and some of the cyclamens. Gardeners in cold zones can grow the tender bulbs very successfully by digging them up and storing them over the winter in spots where they will stay cool but not freeze. (Even in warm areas many of these bulbs are dug up, divided and replanted in order to renew their vigor.)

How to Use Bulbs

As you can see we're talking here about a very diverse group of plants, united only by the fact that they grow from a swollen mass as opposed to a fibrous root. Since, as a group, bulbs span a long blooming season, from winter or early spring to fall, you might conceivably create a bulb garden in which something was always in bloom. This would be an interesting project and could result in a pretty garden, but it is rarely the way bulbs are grown. Usually spring bulbs are grown by themselves or combined with early-blooming annuals and perennials or with bushy later-blooming plants that will hide the bulbs' withering foliage. The summer bulbs are grown in plantings by themselves, in containers, or combined with summer-blooming annuals and perennials. Here are some of the ways I have particularly enjoyed using bulbs:

AN INTIMATE SPRING GARDEN

I think it's very important to have some of the small, early bulbs close to the house where you can really enjoy the encouraging sign of winter's end that their flowers bring. Mine are planted under some old crab apple trees near the back door (the one everyone uses). I have winter aconites, followed by crocus, scilla, grape hyacinths and hyacinths, in that order, but I would like to add some snowdrops, *Iris reticulata,* glory-of-the-snow, miniature daffodils and perhaps some of the small, early tulips.

Planted among these bulbs, in the same bed, are spring-blooming perennials: wild columbines (*Aquilegia canadensis*), foamflower (*Tiarella cordifolia*), wild blue phlox (*Phlox divaricata*), creeping phlox (*Phlox subulata*) in both blue and white, Jacob's-ladder (*Polemonium caeruleum*), *Pulmonaria saccharata* 'Mrs. Moon,' pale yellow primroses (*Primula* 'Moonlight') and some lamiums with both silvery-white and golden-yellow leaves. These are all fairly low growing, and they were chosen not only because they complement the bulbs well, but because they appreciate the dappled shade cast by the crab apples. All are vigorous enough to tolerate some competition from the tree roots; in fact I have to weed out some of the extras each year. I like to stick a few pansies in here and there, too, and I tolerate the violets that volunteer, weeding some of them out when their population starts to get out of control.

The garden is at its best in spring, but for later bloom there are about six different kinds of perennial geraniums, followed by four or five different astilbes, and I also tuck in some shade-loving annuals such as impatiens, coleus and wax begonias. For fall there are hybrid Japanese anemones. Some of the bulbs leave rather untidy foliage, especially the hyacinths, but the perennials growing around them help to minimize the messy effect until the bulb foliage dies down.

A DAFFODIL AND TULIP BORDER

I grow my taller bulbs at the far side of the lawn in a long sweep in front of an old stone wall. The daffodils are a mixture that I have assembled, including many shapes and colors and periods of bloom (see the List of Bulbs) so the display lasts several weeks and overlaps with the slightly later tulip display. The tulips are likewise a collection of different shapes, colors and times of bloom. (You can put together your own collections or buy preselected assortments.)

All the bulbs are planted in small clumps of about four or five, each clump a single variety, but they would also look good completely mixed up. I have tried to make the swath of plants (roughly 6 feet wide and 200 feet long) look as natural and informal as possible. All the bulbs are growing in the lawn rather than in a bed, though admittedly, tulips are usually grown in beds and are probably at their very best that way.

Since I add new tulips each year and sometimes some daffodils, there is al-

ways the problem of how to find planting spots where no bulbs are growing.
By fall planting time the bulbs' foliage
is gone without a trace. I have tried
marking bulb clumps with little plant
labels too short to be chopped up by the
mower, but they are always hard to find
later. You may devise your own system.
One might be to mark the spaces where
new clumps can go just before you cut
down all the foliage in early or midsummer, using small wooden plant markers
dabbed on top with red paint or nail
polish and pushed into the soil so that
only the red top sticks up. With any luck
they will still be there at planting time.

NATURALIZING BULBS

When you naturalize, you group plants
together informally in drifts or patches
and let them multiply by themselves.
Many gardeners find that this is their
favorite way to grow bulbs. The best
bulbs to choose for naturalizing are
those that are the most at home in your
area and have a vigorous habit of
growth, for these will spread despite
competition from grasses and other
plants. Where I live, daffodils naturalize
beautifully. A neighbor of mine planted
ten thousand of them forty years ago,
adding to them over the years, fertilizing them and occasionally dividing them
when the clumps got very thick and the
leaves started to flop over. They now
carpet acres of meadows, lightly shaded
woodland and the shores of a small lake.
People come from miles around each
spring to walk among the daffodils, admire them and photograph them. An
orchard would also be a wonderful place
to naturalize daffodils in this way.

Another bulb I also see naturalized
successfully is scilla (*Scilla siberica*),
which makes lawns around here look
like blue lakes in springtime. Subsequent mowings will not impede the

plant's growth, since the leaves are close
to the ground, and the relatively short
lawn grasses will not hide the 4- to 6-
inch flower stems. Scilla, and many
other bulbs, also are charming when
naturalized in woodland areas. Other
good bulbs for naturalizing are *Anemone
blanda,* colchicums, *Fritillaria meleagris,* glory-of-the-snow, grape hyacinths, bulbous iris, some of the lilies
such as the Asiatic hybrids, snowdrops,
and crocus, which I have naturalized
successfully on a steep, scrubby bank.
Make sure that the bulbs are in a setting
where they will be seen. And remember: just because a plant self-sows,
don't assume that it can hold its own
among all grasses. Winter aconite, for
example, will naturalize in beds or in
rock gardens, but it would not survive in
grass, even lawn grass. And keep in
mind that when you plant bulbs in grass,
you will not be able to mow the grass
until after the bulbs' foliage withers.

BULBS IN ROCK GARDENS

Most of the small and medium-sized
bulbs look beautiful in a rock garden
and can be used to start off the season
there. I especially like to see crocuses,
the small bulbous iris and the species
tulips. Naturalize a number of spring
bulbs on a rocky hillside, and it will
look like a little piece of the Aegean
coast.

BULBS IN HERBACEOUS
BORDERS

You can use spring bulbs to extend the
season of your perennial border, planting some tulips and daffodils toward the
back. The other plants will grow up and
hide the spent foliage while you are
waiting for it to die. I've also enjoyed
using small bulbs with fairly unobtrusive foliage, such as glory-of-the-snow,

in the front of the border. But the best bulbs for the herbaceous border are the summer-blooming ones. I have added gladiolus for vertical accents, dahlias to add color to that difficult late-summer blooming period, and many kinds of lilies just for their spectacular effect. The most successful lilies I've tried in the border have been 'Enchantment,' which forms indestructible clumps, white regal lilies, which are grand and vigorous, and red speciosum lilies, but you may find others that become your favorites.

FORMAL USES FOR BULBS

Naturalizing bulbs is a relatively modern concept. Throughout history bulbs have most often been grown in tidy geometrical beds, whether in the fragrant courtyard gardens of ancient Persia, the carefully measured parterres of European gardens in the Renaissance, or the dooryard gardens of colonial America. In Victorian times bulbs were used in formal bedding patterns—a style that is still used today in parks and other public places.

   In some situations a formal style may be exactly right, even for the average home. Next to a colonial-style home in Virginia, say, I might well choose to plant a courtyard garden in neat parterres edged in boxwood, with pink cottage tulips in every one. Tulips are the bulbs best suited to formal gardening, because they are so regular: all those stems the same length, all those symmetrical globes of color that don't, like daffodils, face every which way or turn toward the sun with their backs to you. Many other bulbs also lend themselves to formal treatment if planted in a regular pattern: hyacinths, irises, and many of the summer bulbs such as lilies, tuberous begonias and cannas. But don't plant bulbs in a rigid pattern unless the design of your garden makes it appropriate. Lines of tulips marching across the front of a curved bed or foundation planting look stiff; free-form clusters would be better.

BULBS IN CONTAINERS

Just about any kind of bulbs can be grown in containers, on a terrace or patio, in a roof-top or balcony garden, or around a swimming pool. This is often a good solution if you do not have plots of land to grow flowers in—or not enough of them. But the most common use of container bulbs is as a way of growing summer bulbs in climates where they are tender. Growing ranunculus or tuberous begonias in pots will make it easier for you to dig them up in fall before frost. And summer bulbs such as these are often such special, showy plants that gardeners don't want them to get lost among the masses of a large planting. Gardening in this way may also encourage you to try exotic tropical or semitropical bulbs that are unfamiliar to you and that I have not had the space to describe in the List of Bulbs—such as montbretia, tigridia, lycoris, crinim lily, lily-of-the-Nile, and hymenocallis.

OTHER WAYS TO USE BULBS

You will no doubt find places for bulbs and ways of combining them that just suit your own needs. You might want to plant them in front of shrubs, or along a fence or wall. Or you might grow them indoors in winter in addition to your spring and summer displays; or, if there is no outdoors to the place you live, you might make spring and summer displays indoors. You will find certain combinations that appeal to you as you start to learn which plants flower at the same time—red tulips planted with blue forget-me-nots, for example, or with blue grape hyacinths. Or try a succession of early, middle and late lilies emerging from a bed of ferns. The tall lily stems will look less gawky with an understory of feathery ferns, yet the matlike roots of the ferns will not interfere with those of the deeply planted lily bulbs. In fact they will help to give the lilies the "cool feet" that they require.

How to Grow Bulbs

S pecific growing instructions for twenty bulbs are included in the List of Bulbs. But a few general comments apply to all of them.

CHOOSING A SITE

Bulbs, as a rule, are sun-loving plants. It is easier to find a sunny setting for the spring-blooming ones than it is for summer bulb plantings because most of the spring bulbs bloom and carry out much of their growth before there are leaves on the trees. Thus you can plant them almost anywhere except under evergreens. Growth will continue for a while after the trees leaf out, but the partial shade will not really affect the plants during that period. Most summer bulbs, however, with the exception of tuberous begonias, need a spot that gets full sun.

When it comes to drainage, bulbs are fussier than most plants. If they sit in waterlogged soil they will simply rot and die. Sandy soil, or soil well lightened with plenty of organic matter, will make life easier for your bulbs, but if the topography itself is causing poor drainage, lightening the soil will not be enough. In that case you'll have to correct the situation with drainage pipes, or grow your bulbs in containers or raised beds.

Another site factor to consider is that the soil warms up faster in spring in a warm, protected location, thus producing earlier blooms. For example the bulbs I have planted in an ell of the house facing southeast bloom a week or two earlier than the very same kinds of bulbs planted around the corner to the northeast, and the very earliest are those in the southeast-facing ell that are closest to the house, because the house itself gives off heat. Bulbs planted in raised beds will also bloom faster. Those growing in a dense ground cover such as pachysandra, or under a thick mulch, will come up more slowly and bloom later than those planted in unmulched soil or along with a sparser ground cover that lets in some sun, such as periwinkle. Of course you may not always want early bloom. I like to have the same plant in several locations with different conditions, precisely because they will not all bloom at the same time and I can enjoy their display longer.

SOIL PREPARATION

Summer blooming bulbs, which are usually grown in beds or containers rather than naturalized, tend to have more specific soil requirements than spring-blooming bulbs. Individual soil requirements are discussed under individual plants. With spring-blooming bulbs, apart from providing a soil with good drainage, there is not much you need to do to the soil unless it is very poor. This is especially true for large-scale, naturalized plantings where you are not digging up the whole area but merely making planting holes here and there and digging in a little fertilizer. When planting in wild grassy areas, try to find spots that are not too rocky and avoid ground filled with extremely vigorous perennial weeds or grasses with dense, matted root systems that will compete too aggressively with the bulbs. For small plantings, or plantings in beds, I like to dig organic matter into the soil.

BUYING AND STORING BULBS

Spring-blooming bulbs become available in garden centers, hardware stores and various and sundry places toward summer's end. It is a good idea to buy them as early as possible to get the best selection and plant them as soon as the days start to get cooler. Planting during extended hot weather can cause bulbs to sprout prematurely. On the other hand, you do want them to start establishing a good root system before the cold and dryness of winter set in.

Often bulbs are sold prepackaged in mesh bags, but I prefer to buy them at a place where I can select each bulb myself and drop it into a bag, just as if the bulbs were onions in the grocery store. This way I can choose nice, solid, fat ones, and squeeze them to make sure they are not mushy and do not have any soft spots. I can check them for visible signs of disease, insects or mildew and smell them to see if there is any sign of rot. With daffodils especially I look for the really big "double-nosed" bulbs, which are really two bulbs joined at the base—or better yet, three.

It is also perfectly all right to buy bulbs through the mail. They may not always arrive as early as the ones you buy in the store, and of course you cannot squeeze, smell or look at them. But mail order enables you to choose from a greater selection of varieties and take advantage of more specials. If you order from a reputable supplier, the risk is generally not too great.

Summer-blooming bulbs become available in nurseries and stores in early or midspring. Order from mail-order companies in mid- to late winter for spring shipping. Lilies are usually available in either spring or fall.

If I obtain spring bulbs before I am able to plant them, I keep them in a dry, dark, fairly cool place. You shouldn't let them freeze, however. To store bulbs in preparation for forcing, see page 399.

Summer-blooming bulbs that arrive before spring planting time, which usually means after danger of frost has passed, can be stored under similar conditions unless you are starting them indoors (see the List of Bulbs for growing specific plants such as tuberous begonias or dahlias).

PLANTING BULBS

I plant bulbs by making a hole large enough for four or five bulbs, digging some bulb fertilizer in the bottom of the hole and then replacing the soil. If they are large bulbs such as narcissus, hyacinths and tulips, I make a square-sided hole by making deep cuts with a sharp spade. If they are smaller bulbs that are planted more shallowly I use a large trowel. If I am planting in grass I really have to heave the spade into the sod (Figure 10, page 56), and it is hard work—something I am inclined to forget when I am happily ordering bulbs by the hundred. But once I have that nice hole, all I have to do is replace the soil and the sod lid, and the bulbs will come up through it.

Gardeners disagree about how deep bulbs should be planted. The rule of thumb is usually three times the depth of the bulb itself. But I tend to favor deep planting, especially with daffodils and tulips. If they are buried deep, there is less chance of their sprouting in fall, being damaged by cold, or getting heaved up by freezing and thawing or being eaten by animals. Deeply planted tulips will produce flowers for more years than shallowly planted ones. I

WHICH END IS UP?

Fig. 56

Planting bulbs right side up will give them a better start in life. Corms and true bulbs are usually pointed on top and flatter on the bottom; often you can see the dried remains of last year's roots on the bottom, too. Round tubers are usually concave on top, round on the bottom. Anemone tubers come in a number of shapes, depending on the species: plant clawlike ones with the claw facing down; if there is a flat side, place it facing up; if there is a circular mark on one side, put that side up.

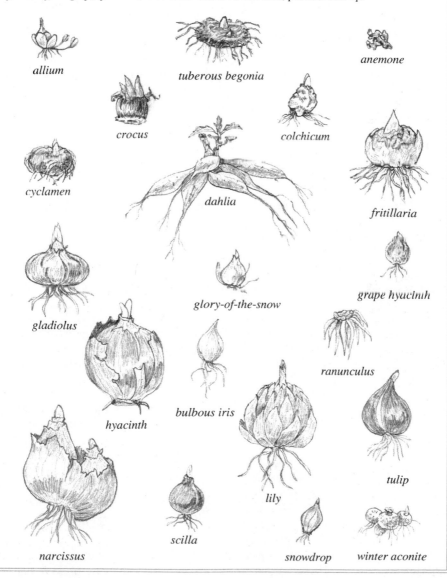

allium

tuberous begonia

anemone

crocus

colchicum

cyclamen

dahlia

fritillaria

grape hyacinth

gladiolus

glory-of-the-snow

ranunculus

hyacinth

bulbous iris

tulip

lily

narcissus

scilla

snowdrop

winter aconite

plant tulips and daffodils a good 10 inches deep if I can, measured from the bottom of the bulb to the surface.

If you have a good supply of compost, dig some into the bottom of the holes, but when planting on a large scale you are usually better off buying a bulb fertilizer. These are high in phosphorus, for root development, but low in nitrogen. I buy bulb fertilizer in large bags and keep it around, because a high-phosphorus, low-nitrogen fertilizer is excellent for other plants too, especially perennials. For specific planting instructions, see the List of Bulbs. If you are nervous about getting the bulb right side up, see Figure 56.

MAINTENANCE CHORES

Usually bulb plantings are low-maintenance gardens that can just be left alone. However, some benefit by being top dressed with compost or 5–10–5 fertilizer in early spring when the tips show, and again in fall, and by being divided from time to time. Deep watering is a good idea if you are going into winter after a long drought. But the most important task is to make sure no one comes along with a lawn mower and cuts off "those messy leaves" before they have turned brown. I find that not only tall grass but annual weeds come up among my bulbs early in the season. I take a sharp sickle to them, just above the height of the bulb foliage, trying to make them look as good as possible in hopes that no one will blitz them in a fit of tidiness.

Deadheading (page 156) is another favor you can do your bulbs, since it keeps the plant from putting energy into seed formation. But don't do it with bulbs that you hope will self-sow, such as scilla or grape hyacinth. Some of the summer bulbs have other maintenance requirements, such as staking.

GETTING READY FOR WINTER

If you have planted spring bulbs in late summer and have an unseasonably warm fall that causes the tips to emerge from the ground, don't panic. I have left sprouted narcissi unmulched, and the little green tips weathered the winter cold and snow just fine.

Summer-blooming bulbs that are not hardy for your region should be dug up, or their containers brought in, when the weather turns frosty. Most can be stored in bags of peat or some other dry, loose material in a dry place where they will stay cool and dormant but will not freeze. Dusting with a fungicide before storing will help keep them from contracting mildew, rotting or becoming diseased.

PESTS AND DISEASES

Pests, aside from the ones that dig up bulbs (like dogs) and eat them (like mice), are rarely a problem. Nor are there many diseases that plague them. Deer sometimes nibble my tulips, but only when the shoots are very new and tender. While the shoots are new, try some of the deer remedies described in Chapter 2. If rodents bother your bulbs despite deep planting, plant them in cages made of wire mesh; the stems will grow up through the mesh. I have read that hyacinths and daffodils are the only bulbs that animals do not find and dig up. But our puppy dug up a hyacinth and chewed it to pieces two days ago. So much for that bit of wisdom.

Forcing Bulbs

In climates like mine, where winters are long and cold, there is a lot of enthusiasm for forcing spring bulbs. Gardeners can get just as much color from flowering houseplants, of course, but it isn't quite the same. Spring bulbs in bloom are, in the gardener's mind, an encouraging reminder that the grayness of winter will end, that the roads will not be icy forever, that the heating bills will eventually stop.

If you have ever been confused about what bulb forcing is all about, think of it as letting the bulb do what it naturally wants to do, but in a time period that you, the gardener, determine by manipulating the bulbs' natural growth cycles. You must start with a dormant bulb, as usual. You must give it a long, cold period in which it *thinks* it is buried in the dark, cold ground. Then, when you bring it out into the light and warmth of your windowsill, it will think spring has arrived, and it will bloom. You can make this "spring" happen at any time during the winter if you plan things right.

Buying and storing bulbs for forcing. While all of the spring-blooming bulbs discussed in this chapter can be forced successfully, some varieties are better than others. Mail-order suppliers will sometimes make recommendations, and local nurseries often will too, displaying bulbs they sell expressly for this purpose. Buy them as soon as they are available, in order to get a good selection, and store them in the coolest spot in your house. When you put bulbs into cold storage, take into account that the bulbs' "winter" has begun. The best way to store them is potted up.

Planting the bulbs. There are many kinds of containers sold for bulb forcing. I buy inexpensive clay pots, with saucers, that are about half as tall as they are wide, in a range of sizes. I fill the pots partway with a soil mix that I make up, consisting of one part ordinary garden soil to one part of a soil lightener such as peat or a commercial potting medium such as ProMix (some gardeners use perlite). I might throw in a small handful of compost or very well rotted manure for each pot.

Then I place the bulbs in the pots and pack my soil mix gently around them so that just the tips are showing, making sure the soil comes up no higher than a half-inch below the rim. I water them well, using a weak solution of high-phosphorus, low-nitrogen liquid fertilizer. Some people will tell you to give your forcing bulbs a lean, no-compost, no-fertilizer diet, claiming that the bulbs can, in effect, live off their own fat. This is true; but I like to really nourish bulbs' root growth and leave the bulbs in a less depleted state when I'm ready to replant them again in the garden. There are a few bulbs, notably hyacinth and crocus, that can be grown in nothing but plain water, either in a special glass container so you can see the roots, or sitting on top of little rocks. If you do this be aware that you will have to discard the bulbs after bloom, because they will be too depleted to be worth much in the future.

How many bulbs you put in a pot is up to you. I plant hyacinths one to a pot, since one makes a big flower that will perfume a whole room and also makes a nice gift. Five daffodils look nice, or seven crocuses. I leave between a half-inch and an inch of space between each bulb. Flat-sided bulbs such as tulips should have the flat side facing out, because this makes the leaves arch out nicely.

Putting them to bed. On the average, bulbs need about twelve weeks of artificial "winter" in order to bloom properly, but this varies a great deal. Crocus, hyacinth and grape hyacinth might get by with as little as six or eight weeks; tulips and narcissus may need as much as fifteen. It is better to give them too much cold time than too little. Logically enough the earlier a bulb flowers outdoors, the less of an indoor winter it needs. On the other hand the longer a bulb is kept in winter storage, the faster it may sprout and bloom when you bring it out (partly because as spring nears there is more light and warmth in the house).

Finding the right spot for this storage period is important. It must be dark, and the temperature must stay between 35 and 50 degrees (40 degrees is ideal). I don't have the oft-mentioned "cool cellar" or "attached garage." I do have a cool attic full of bulb-eating mice. I use the attic, but I wrap the pots with hardware cloth secured with bits of wire. Use a minimum-maximum thermometer to select your storage

spot and check the temperature from time to time as the weather changes. Some gardeners bury their bulb pots outdoors, covering them with sand and mulch to keep them from freezing into the ground, or building cold frames that they fill with various mulching materials such as leaves, shredded bark or hay. They cover the bulbs with wire mesh if mice are a problem. The sooner you can get bulbs into a *consistently* cool environment, the sooner you can start counting the weeks till they are "done" and ready to bloom.

Waking them up. When you are ready to bring out a pot of bulbs, you will see little shoots emerging, just as you would on a 40-degree day in March, April or May. Get these tender shoots used to the light gradually. Put them in a shaded spot for a day or two, then in a spot that gets bright light but not direct sun and stays at about 55–65 degrees. Keep the soil moist but not soggy, and give them a little liquid fertilizer. When the shoots are green and about 5 inches tall, put the pots in a sunny spot that is about 75 degrees, at least in the daytime. Turn the pots every day so that each side gets sun. When the buds start to show color, put the pots back in the cooler spot with the bright, indirect light so the flowers will last longer; or display them wherever they look best.

After blooming. When the show is over cut the flower stalks back, but let the leaves continue to grow, just as if they were in the ground, and feed them occasionally, but start to water them less and less. When the leaves die back, cut them off and store the bulbs in a cool, dry place till the normal planting time. You can even replant them in late spring, just to get them out of the way. Don't expect them to be their old selves for a few years. You'll need to start with fresh ones for the next fall's forcing.

Timing is everything. You will notice that I have not said a word about *when* to do any of these steps. That's because you have to look at the whole sequence together. Forcing bulbs is easy to do, but it takes some careful planning to produce bloom exactly when you want it— Paper white narcissus for Christmas, for instance, or your mother's favorite blue hyacinth for her birthday on February 19. Or you may simply want to have something always in bloom throughout the winter. Just as the length of time needed for dormancy varies with the plants and with the place you store them, so the length of time it takes to bring the plant into bloom varies. If timing is important to you I would suggest keeping records, noting also where you kept the pots and for how long, so that in subsequent years you can manipulate bloom with greater accuracy. Usually it will take between three and five weeks to produce bloom after the pots are in the light. So just count backwards from the desired blooming date, adding together the number of weeks in the light and the number of weeks in the dark. If you put up new pots every week or so, then remove some from the dark each week as they become ready, you should have an overlapping sequence of bloom.

The easiest way to keep it all straight is to write the name of the bulb and its planting date on a little wooden label and stick it in the pot. You can even use these as your permanent record, noting the wake-up date and blooming date on the same marker.

Bulbs that don't need a "winter." Tender bulbs that are native to areas with mild winters naturally don't need such a long cooling period. Paperwhite narcissi, for example, can be purchased when available, potted, and kept in a 50- to 60-degree spot in the dark or low light till they sprout; then they can be moved into the light to bloom. The whole process should take four to six weeks. Since there would be no point in planting them outdoors in a cold climate, where they would not survive, they are discarded after bloom. As a result Paperwhites are usually grown in water. I put mine on top of pebbles or rounded black stones in a low ceramic container, and keep the water level just below the bulbs so they don't rot.

This is so easy to do, and the fragrance of the flowers is so sweet, that Paperwhites and other Tazetta varieties of narcissus are probably the most popular bulbs for forcing. But do try some of the more subtle, less predictable ones too, such as a little pot of snowdrops or some winter aconites (being sure to soak the tubers overnight first). Try to have some different little surprises each winter to bring in out of the dark.

LIST OF BULBS

ALLIUM (FLOWERING ONION)
Allium

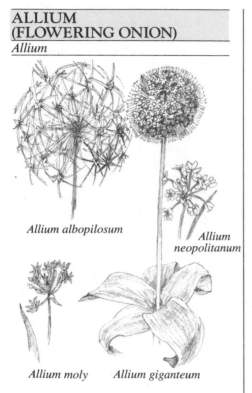

Allium albopilosum

Allium neopolitanum

Allium moly   *Allium giganteum*

DESCRIPTION: If you have ever seen chives blooming you may have been surprised to find that the plant is as ornamental as it is useful in the kitchen. Most gardeners do not realize that many members of the onion family produce flowers pretty enough to grow in gardens. They are a very diverse group, with flower clusters in many sizes, shapes and colors, and blooming times range from spring to summer to fall. The one thing they have in common is an oniony smell when the foliage is rubbed or stepped on, but this does not happen often enough to offend, and some of the flowers are sweetly fragrant. Most of them make fine, long-lasting cut flowers, and some even dry well for winter arrangements.

A wonderful allium to try is *Allium giganteum* (giant garlic). In early summer it sends up long stalks about 4 feet tall, topped with 5-inch balls, perfectly round, made up of tiny purple flowers. By the time they bloom there is little or no foliage around the stems, so grow them together with lower, bushy plants or behind a low wall. If you like big, round purple flowers, you'll *really* love *A. albopilosum* (*A. christophii*), commonly called "star of Persia." Its flower cluster is looser than that of *A. giganteum* and up to a foot in diameter, with star-shaped flowers in late spring. Stems are shorter, about 2 feet. *A. aflatunense* has 4-inch purple balls in May and grows to 2 feet or a bit more. Other handsome spring alliums include *A. moly* (golden garlic), with flatter clusters of yellow flowers, about a foot tall, and *A. neapolitanum* (daffodil garlic), which is roughly the same height and bears fragrant white flowers in April.

For late-summer bloom, *A. tuberosum* (Chinese chives or garlic chives), which has white, fragrant flower clusters. For fall try *A. stellatum* or *A. thunbergii,* both short stemmed and pink flowering. Most alliums are hardy to Zone 4; *A. neapolitanum* is hardy to Zone 6.

HOW TO GROW: Alliums like full sun, though *A. giganteum* will do fine in part shade. Soil can be of average fertility but it should be lightened with organic matter and moist but well drained. They can be planted in spring or fall, from bulbs or from seed (though seed-grown plants may take a long time to reach flowering size). Plant the short ones about 4 inches apart, the tall ones 8 inches to a foot apart.

A few things to watch for: some alliums should be deadheaded to prevent them from self-sowing all over the place. (They also propagate themselves by forming little bulblets on the sides of the bulbs by which you can increase your stock if you so desire.) A friend of mine cautions me that his *A. giganteum* did not produce flowers the second year because its energy had gone into producing bulblets, although by the third year the bulblets were large enough to flower. So if your allium gives you foliage but no flowers, be patient; it may perform better in the future. Also note that many spring-flowering species are summer dormant, so don't be alarmed when the foliage disappears.

ANEMONE (WINDFLOWER)
Anemone

Anemone coronaria   Anemone blanda

DESCRIPTION: These are the tuberous anemones as opposed to the fibrous-rooted types such as pasqueflower (*Anemone pulsatilla*). All are spring flowering. The most familiar kinds are the ones sold by florists, which are hybrids of *A. coronaria*. These have 3-inch, very brightly colored flowers in shades of red, pink, purple, blue or white, often with striking black or yellow centers. They look a bit like small Oriental poppies and grow 12–18 inches tall. Popular strains are the single 'De-Caen' hybrids and the semidouble 'St.

Brigid' and 'St. Bavo.' None are reliably hardy north of Zone 7. *A. × fulgens* is similar in flower and growth, bright red, and a little hardier. *A. blanda* (Greek anemone) is hardier still, though a bit less showy. Daisylike flowers on 6-inch stems in shades of blue, pink, lavender and white carpet the ground and may survive as far north as Zone 5 with a winter mulch.

HOW TO GROW: Anemones like full sun but can take part shade, especially at midday. The soil should be well drained and can be lightened with organic matter for better growth. Add some lime if the soil is acid or if you have used an acid material like peat to lighten the soil. Soak the tubers overnight in water before planting. *A. coronaria* tubers are planted 8 inches apart, 2–3 inches deep; those of Greek anemones, 4–6 inches apart and 2 inches deep. If you live in the north you need not give up on the tender anemones altogether. Either grow them indoors or plant them outdoors in early spring, then dig them in late summer and store them in a cool place in bags of peat.

BEGONIA
Begonia × tuberhybrida

DESCRIPTION: Tuberous begonias are prima donnas compared to the relatively low-key plants in the rest of this chapter, but it is hard to resist them, especially if you are coping with a shaded or partly shaded situation. These are not grown as annuals, like the fibrous-rooted wax begonias described in Chapter 5. They grow from little round tubers that persist from year to year if you take care of them properly.

There are many types of tuberous begonias, all of them gorgeous. The most spectacular are the upright forms, which grow a foot or more tall and

camellia-form

picotee

hanging

begonias

produce flowers as large as 10 inches across in vivid reds, pinks, salmons, apricots, yellows, oranges and white. Flower forms vary: some are shaped like roses, some like camellias; some have ruffled edges, some have edges in a contrasting color. The *multiflora* types are bushy plants about a foot tall with smaller flowers; but they are easier to grow and are more tolerant of sun. The *pendula* types have long, trailing stems that make them perfect for hanging baskets. All types bloom all summer but are hardy only in frost-free zones.

HOW TO GROW: The stems of all begonias are fragile and will not stand heavy dog and cat traffic, so plant them in a safe spot. They can also be grown in containers, indoors or out. The leaves do not like to get too wet (they can mildew) or sit in the sun (they scorch). The worst thing you can do to begonias is to get their leaves wet, *then* let them sit in the sun (the leaves die). The tubers and stems can both rot if the soil is too wet. The flowers also have a tendency to drop off, like reluctant debutantes, just as they are reaching their peak of exquisite perfection. (But wait! You can float a dropped-off blossom in a bowl of water, and it will stay pretty for days.)

Put begonias in a spot where they'll get plenty of bright light to keep them from getting leggy, but don't put them in direct sun. Give them moist, light soil with plenty of organic matter, and make sure it is well drained. They prefer humid air, but it must circulate freely around the plant.

To plant begonias, start the tubers as early as February, setting them in trays of moistened peat moss. I simply press them gently, flat side up and round side down, into the surface of the peat. Water lightly and wait for them to sprout little pink buds if they have not done so already. Shoots will emerge from the buds, and roots will form at the sides of the tubers. When the tubers have sprouted, put each one in a pot about 5 inches wide on top, filled with a light potting mix such as one part loam, one part peat, and one part sand, with perhaps some compost or rotted manure worked in. As the plant grows be sure it has plenty of light or you'll get leggy growth. (Stems should not be pinched.) Use fluorescent lights if you haven't a bright natural source out of direct sun.

When night temperatures are consistently 50 degrees or over and there is no danger of frost, you can move the pots outside or unpot the plants and set them in a bed of nice humusy soil, at least a foot apart. Keep feeding them liquid fertilizer every couple of weeks. A high-nitrogen fertilizer such as fish emulsion will give the leaves the rich, dark green color you want to see. When frost threatens bring the potted plants indoors, but don't try to keep them blooming too much longer. Before fall is too far underway you should let them become dormant by withholding water and letting the foliage die. Then store the tubers in dry peat or sawdust until it's time to plant them again. Some people divide the tubers by cutting them, making sure there is one eye to each plant. I prefer to let each tuber get bigger and fatter each year, making larger, more magnificent plants, and then take cuttings from these if I want to increase my stock. Cuttings should be rooted in moist sand.

COLCHICUM (AUTUMN CROCUS)
Colchicum autumnale

DESCRIPTION: This is a very weird plant, and if you don't know what to expect it can really fool you. Its foliage comes up in spring, just like that of a spring bulb, but it doesn't bloom, and by summer the leaves disappear. In fall, long after you've probably said, "Oh, well, so much for *Colchicum autumnale*," some stems come out of the ground with no leaves on them, just big pink, lavender or white flowers that look sort of like large crocuses.

Nice as it is to have a fall-blooming bulb, or fall-blooming anything, you do have the problem of how to landscape those flowerless spring leaves and those leafless fall flowers. They are supposed to look great planted in front of shrubs, but I think this makes them look all the more gawky. Plant them in a natural setting, in sun or light shade, where there is a permanent, evergreen ground

cover such as periwinkle, which will de-emphasize both the leaves and their absence. They will also naturalize well in grass. Colchicum grows from corms and is hardy to about Zone 4.

Hybrids of *C. autumnale* grow about 8 inches tall. Some colchicums sold are hybrids of *C. speciosum*. These are apt to be a bit taller. *C. speciosum* 'Album' is white. Despite the fact that these all look something like crocuses and are even called "autumn crocuses" in some catalogs, they are not the same as spring-blooming crocuses (below), which are another species altogether and have their leaves and flowers well synchronized.

HOW TO GROW: Colchicum corms are sold in summer. They should be planted in late summer or early fall in sun or part shade, about 8 inches apart. They are not fussy about soil, but add organic matter if yours is sandy or dry because they need a reasonable amount of moisture. Plant the large bulbs with the tops at least 3 inches below the soil surface. Bulbs usually multiply by themselves without human intervention

CROCUS
Crocus

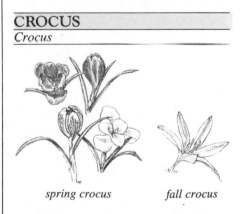

spring crocus   fall crocus

DESCRIPTION: Of all the small spring bulbs the crocus is most people's favorite. It is not the earliest to bloom, but when it does, often poking up out of the snow in such bright colors, it seems to tell you that if it can get through the rest of winter and mud season without looking grim, so can you. Most of the crocuses we grow are hybrids of *Crocus vernus* or *C. chrysanthus* and have showy flowers in shades of yellow, purple, lavender and white. Some are striped, and all have handsome yellow stamens. The large-flowered Dutch hybrids are the most popular, but if you search out other kinds of crocuses you may be able to stretch the blooming period. Some, such as the lavender *C. speciosus,* even bloom in fall. *C. sativus,* which is lavender or white, is the crocus from which the prized spice saffron comes. The bright orange stamens are dried to make this costly seasoning. Most crocuses are hardy to Zone 3 and do best in cool climates. They grow from corms.

HOW TO GROW: Gardeners like crocuses not only because of their spring message of cheer, but also because they are trouble-free, permanent plantings that multiply by themselves and needn't be divided. They can be naturalized in grass, but as with any bulb with foliage that persists after bloom, they should not be mowed while the leaves are still green. Crocuses like full sun or part shade. I advise planting some in a sunny, sheltered spot for early bloom and some others in a cooler, more shaded spot for later bloom. Soil need not be rich but must be well drained. Plant them about 4 inches apart, 4 inches deep in early fall. Plant fall-blooming crocuses as soon as they become available in late summer.

CYCLAMEN
Cyclamen

DESCRIPTION: Cyclamens are beautiful plants. The flowers hover above the leaves like moths, on long wavy stems. The leaves are heart shaped and often

hardy cyclamen   florists' cyclamen

handsomely variegated. Most are dormant in summer. The florists' cyclamen, *Cyclamen persicum,* thrives outdoors in places like California but is grown as a winter-blooming houseplant north of Zone 9. Its flowers are as large as 4 inches across and rather flamboyant, in shades of pink, red, lavender and white; often they are fringed or double. The plant blooms from late fall to early spring and grows about a foot tall.

Several cyclamen species are hardy in the north. They are shorter (4–5 inches tall) with pink, red or white flowers about an inch across and marbled or mottled leaves. Many gardeners find them even more charming than their more tropical relatives. *C. coum* blooms in early spring. *C. europaeum* (C. purpurascens) and *C. neapolitanum* (*C. hederifolium*) are fall blooming and fragrant. They are all hardy to about Zone 5 but may survive farther north with winter protection. I think they look best in an informal, woodsy setting, but only if they are not overshadowed by larger, bolder plants.

HOW TO GROW: Cyclamens grow from corms and are planted while they are dormant, usually in midsummer, about 2 inches deep and about a foot apart. (Plant florists' cyclamens outdoors in fall in Zones 9 and 10.) They like soil that is rich and moist but not cold or wet. Give then part shade outdoors; indoors, give them indirect, bright light.

DAHLIA
Dahlia

DESCRIPTION: Dahlias are one of those plants with endless flower classifications: some are single, like daisies; some are like round balls; others are "cactus-flowered," "orchid-flowered," "anemone-flowered" or "peony-flowered" (why do flowers always have to look like some *other* flower?). The flowers can be as small as an inch across and as large as 12 inches if you are growing exhibition-size ones. Heights range from 1 to 7 feet. There is a large range of colors, roughly the same as that of chrysanthemums. The thing I like about dahlias is their blooming period, which goes from midsummer to the first frost or a bit after. I use them to add some showy late bloom to perennial borders, but they are also very effective grown in beds by themselves. They are colorful and long lasting as cut flowers.

HOW TO GROW: Grow dahlias in full sun or light shade, in a soil rich in organic matter and nutrients, especially phosphorus and potassium. Add some lime if your soil is very acid. Dahlias have tuberous roots that must be dug up

decorative   anemone-flowered

and stored over the winter in zones where there is frost, a chore that is not much of a bother once you get into the routine.

I order new dahlia roots by mail and plant them about a week before the date of the last average frost, laying them horizontally in a hole 6–8 inches deep. If I'm planting a tall variety, I put a 5-foot bamboo stake next to the root and stick it firmly into the ground (if you stake later on you run the risk of piercing the root). The root should be covered with a few inches of soil; as the plant grows, the rest of the hole can be filled. When the stems become tall, tie them to the stakes; if you want shorter, bushier plants, pinch them when they are 10–12 inches tall (page 156). Pinching is less important with the short varieties. Deadhead the plants for more profuse bloom, and water them deeply during drought or they will not bloom.

After the first few frosts, gently dig up the roots with a digging fork, cutting the stems back to a few inches. I have found that storing in a cool cellar (ideally 35–45 degrees) in a tray of peat is a good way to hold dahlia roots over the winter, but only if I protect them against mice with some form of wire mesh. One year I found nothing but trays of peat in spring; the mice had eaten every speck of the dahlias. When it is time to replant them in spring you can divide them to increase your stock. Notice that the buds ("eyes") emerge from the base of the old stem. Slice through the stem vertically with a sharp knife, making sure that each piece of root has part of the stem attached and at least one eye. (Dahlias can also be propagated from stem cuttings.) I have gotten a head start on the dahlia season by starting mine in pots indoors in a rich, light soil; the only problem is that pots large enough to hold the roots comfortably take up a lot of space.

FRITILLARIA
Fritillaria

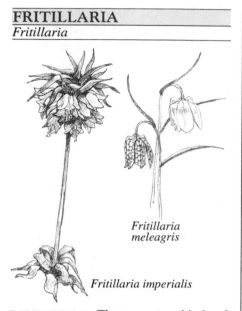

Fritillaria
meleagris

Fritillaria imperialis

DESCRIPTION: There are two kinds of fritillarias commonly grown in gardens, and they're like Mutt and Jeff. *Fritillaria meleagris* (checkered lily) has flowers shaped like little hanging bells, in muted, neutral tones like gray, purple, brownish and white with an odd, checkerboard pattern. They grow, at most, to 12 inches, bloom in midspring, and often self-sow prolifically. They are best seen close up, in a natural setting, and are hardy to Zone 3. *F. imperialis* (crown imperial) sends up a 3-foot stem topped by a huge cluster of hanging bells in shades of red, yellow and orange (often two shades together), and the leaves stick up in a tuft on *top* of the flower. Grow it in a clump by itself or behind shorter bulbs. Combining it with yellow daffodils and red tulips could be interesting (though it doesn't produce the subtlest of effects). It is hardy to Zones 5–6.

HOW TO GROW: Give fritillarias a gritty, humusy, moist but extremely well drained soil. It ought to be fairly rich. They grow well in full sun or light shade. Buy them as soon as they become available and plant them immediately; their bulbs should not be allowed to dry out. Crown imperial bulbs should go at least 8 inches apart and 6 inches deep (measured to the top of the large bulbs). Checkered lilies should be 3–4 inches apart and 3–4 inches deep. Division is possible but not necessary; in fact the bulbs seem to do better if left alone.

GLADIOLUS
Gladiolus

gladiolus hybrids   Gladiolus byzantinus

DESCRIPTION: Gladiolus, or "glads," as they are sometimes nicknamed, are popular flowers. Their tall, brightly colored flower spikes are showy in the garden and last a long time when cut, opening gradually from the bottom of the spike upwards. Since I prefer to make open, relaxed-looking flower arrangements, I don't grow glads for cutting. But I have grown them in a large flower border as vertical accents and in the center of a small round bed filled with a tumble of bright annuals. I can also visualize a fine gladiolus display with flowers growing in a bed by themselves along a fence. You might also grow them in rows in the vegetable garden if your main goal is to have them for cut flowers.

Glads come in all colors but blue, and sizes vary from 6-foot spikes to the dwarf "baby glads." Most baby varieties are hybrids of *Gladiolus* × *colvillei,* but there are also several species of glads you can sometimes find that are less artificial looking. Try *G. byzantinus,* a 2-foot red flower. It is hardy to Zone 5.

HOW TO GROW: Glads grow from corms. They are planted in full sun and in rich soil that should, ideally, be more sandy than heavy. You can start planting as soon as the danger of frost is over, then plant in succession every 2 weeks till midsummer for a longer season of bloom. You should plant glads in groups, digging some compost of 5–10–5 fertilizer into the soil, but add a little soil over it; the corms should not rest directly on the fertilizer. The corms should go about 4 inches deep, but you can plant tall varieties deeper if you like, for better support. Staking, or mounding the stems with soil, may also be necessary. I would plant no closer than 6 inches apart. I would also sprinkle a little more fertilizer around the plants after they come up, and once again after picking. You should leave some foliage when you pick them so the plant can continue to grow and form new corms. Water plants deeply once a week during very dry spells.

As soon as the first frost hits, dig the glads all up with a spading fork and cut the stems back to 1 inch. Dry the plants for a few weeks out of the sun, and then break off and discard the old corm, which will have exhausted itself. Any new corms or cormels (immature corms) should be saved and stored at 40–50 degrees. Even gardeners in frost-free areas dig up glads and store them for a few months in a cool spot; the period of cold dormancy makes them flower better the following season. If thrips are a problem, grow only early plantings and dig them up before the thrips become active. Put moth flakes in the storage bags with the corms to keep thrips from wintering over; dusting the corms with a fungicide is a good idea.

GLORY-OF-THE-SNOW
Chionodoxa

DESCRIPTION: These delightful bulbs have little, bright blue, star-shaped flowers and grasslike leaves. They start blooming shortly after crocuses, which is handy, because the two look good together. They are a good bulb for cool climates and are hardy to Zone 3, but they don't do well south of Zone 8. Naturalize them around a tree, in a rock garden, along a woodland path, or wherever they will best be seen. *Chionodoxa luciliae* grows up to 6 inches tall and is typically blue with a white center, but 'Alba' is white, 'Rosea' is lavender-pink and the large-flowered 'Gigantea' can be blue, purple or pink. *C. sardensis* is dark blue without the white eye.

HOW TO GROW: Full sun is best, but glory-of-the-snow will take part shade and in warm areas actually prefers filtered shade. Plant in early fall about 2–3 inches apart, and 3 inches deep (a bit deeper in warm climates). They like a soil that is rich, moist but well-drained and lightened with organic matter.

GRAPE HYACINTH
Muscari

DESCRIPTION: I can count on this bulb to bloom at the same time as my daffodils and tulips and provide me with some blue accents for my bouquets. The stems are just long enough to be stuck in among the larger flowers, and the small spikes of tiny blue balls are a good contrast to the rounder shapes of the daffodils and tulips. They are best grown in a spot where you can admire them up close, because the flowers are small and because blue flowers are hard to see at a distance. They are lovely in rock gardens.

Most of the hybrids sold are derived from *Muscari armeniacum,* which has large flowers and grows up to 8 inches, or from *M. botryoides,* which is a little taller and usually deep blue. There is also a white variety called 'Pearls of Spain.' *M. tubergenianum* grows up to 8 inches and is light blue at the the top of the spike and darker blue at the bottom. These rugged little bulbs are hardy to Zones 2–4 depending on the variety; those derived from *M. botryoides* are the hardiest. Foliage sometimes appears in fall and winters over.

HOW TO GROW: Grape hyacinths like full sun or part shade and an average, well-drained soil. Plant 3 inches apart, and 3 inches deep, in late summer or as early in fall as possible. You can propagate the species from seed and hybrids from offsets (new bulbs that form next to the old ones). Usually they will multi-ply well by themselves, but if you let them self-sow they may not breed true to color.

HYACINTH
Hyacinthus

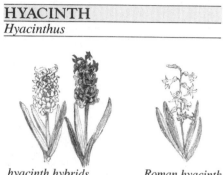

hyacinth hybrids   *Roman hyacinth*

DESCRIPTION: I always grow at least a few hyacinths so I can pick them. I think they look prettier indoors in vases, where they can perfume the room, than they do in gardens. The leaves, which seem to stick around forever, are quite unsightly, and even the flower heads look rather lumpy among the more dainty shapes of the other bulbs. But grown with something to soften them, such as a sea of forget-me-nots or blue-flowering periwinkle, they are not hard to take. The flower heads become less thick as years go by—an improvement, I think.

There are hyacinths you can grow besides *Hyacinthus orientalis,* from which the big Dutch cultivars are commonly derived. Try Roman hyacinth (*H. o. albulus*) in blue, pink and white. Roman hyacinth has a looser cluster but more stems per plant. The common hyacinth is hardy to at least Zone 5, Roman hyacinth to Zone 6, but you can still try it north of there if you give it some winter protection and plant it fairly deep.

HOW TO GROW: In the north plant hyacinths as early in fall as possible; in warm areas refrigerate the bulbs for a few weeks and plant in late fall. They like a sandy loam of moderate fertility that is moist but very well drained. Grow in full sun or light shade. Plant the large bulbs 5 inches deep and 6 inches apart, trying to create the effect of natural groupings to offset the rather stiff bearing of the leaves and flowers.

IRIS
Iris

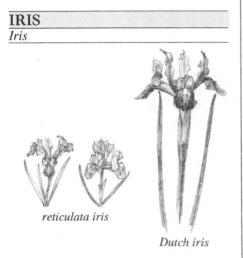

reticulata iris

Dutch iris

DESCRIPTION: Some iris, such as bearded iris, grow from rhizomes; some, such as Siberian iris, have fibrous roots; and others, such as Dutch iris, grow from bulbs. Only iris that grow from bulbs are considered here—the others are treated as perennials and are discussed in Chapter 6. Most of the bulbous iris are small, elegant plants that look particularly good in rock gardens but are effective in any intimate garden spot. My favorites are the "reticulata" types, especially *Iris reticulata* (netted iris), which blooms even earlier than crocuses, is lavender-blue with yellow markings and is about 6 inches tall. Other reticulata types are the deep-purple *I. bakerana,* yellow *I. danfordiae* and the charming blue *I. histrioides* 'Major.' All are about 4 inches tall, have grassy foliage and are hardy to at least Zone 5. The so-called "Dutch iris," which are hybrids of *I. xiphium* (Span-

ish iris) and other species, are much taller—about 18 inches—and bloom in early summer. Colors include blue, purple, lavender, yellow and white. When picked just as they are opening they make very fine, long-lasting cut flowers and are often used by florists. Unfortunately they are not reliably hardy above Zone 7, but if you live in the north and dearly love them you can try mulching them, or even digging them up in late summer and storing them over the winter.

HOW TO GROW: All the irises mentioned here should be planted as early in fall as possible, in full sun. They like a light, moderately fertile soil and need water during their growth period, although they absolutely must have good drainage. I would plant the smaller types 3 inches deep and 4 inches apart, the larger Dutch iris 5 inches deep and 5–6 inches apart.

LILY
Lilium

DESCRIPTION: These are the true lilies as opposed to the day lilies described in Chapter 6, which grow from rhizomes. True lilies grow from big, fat white bulbs that are made up of scales and produce magnificent flowers in a very wide range of shapes, colors and sizes. They bloom at various times, from early summer to late summer and even into fall. (As I write this it is past Labor Day, and my *Lilium speciosum* 'Uchida' is still blooming.)

Everybody who has grown a number of different lilies has favorites—I mentioned some of mine in the introduction above. I haven't the space here to describe many of them in detail, but here is, at least, a run-down of the basic lily groups, more or less in order of bloom:

The Asiatic hybrids bloom in June (some later), in many colors, with heights ranging from 2 to 5 feet and with several different flower shapes. The red-orange 'Enchantment' is typical of the upward-facing flower types and is a particularly vigorous plant that forms clumps. 'Connecticut Lemonglow' has an outward-facing flower; others have a pendent or "Turk's-cap" shape. The Martagon hybrids are a group that bloom in June, have Turk's-cap flowers, and are quite tall—up to 6 feet. Madonna lilies are white (though some of the hybrids are cream or yellow), stand 3–4 feet tall, and bloom in June or early July. The American hybrids, which can grow as tall as 4–8 feet, include the long-lived Bellingham hybrids.

Midsummer lilies include the Easter lily, *L. longiflorum*, which is forced into bloom for Easter display but blooms later in the normal course of things. Regal lilies (*L. regale*) are tall, white and very fragrant. The Aurelian hybrids are an important part of the midsummer lily show. They tend to be fairly tall (4–6 feet) and include such spectacular varieties as the dusty rose 'Pink Perfection,' and 'Black Dragon,' whose large flowers are dark red on the outside and white within. Tiger lilies (*L. tigrinum*), with orange, curled-back petals spotted with black, grow up to 4 feet tall.

The last lilies to bloom, in late summer and sometimes early fall, are the Oriental hybrids, which include the glorious gold-banded lily (white, striped with gold and spotted with red), the Imperial strains, such as 'Imperial Silver' (white spotted with brick red) and, last of all, the hybrids of *L. speciosum*, such as 'Uchida,' mentioned above. Most lilies are hardy as far north as Zone 4 or 5; *L. candidum* to Zone 8.

You have to think carefully about how to use lilies. They have tall stems with rather sparse foliage growing around them, and they may have to be staked, which makes them look a bit like basketball players on crutches. I put some in perennial beds, and I grow the rest in a semishaded spot where a lush nest of ferns hides at least the lower half of the stems. It is often said that lilies like to have "their heads warm, their feet cool." Try to plant something around the base of the plants for their health as well as for looks, but choose shallow-rooted plants that will not strangle the lily bulbs.

HOW TO GROW: The difference between lily bulbs and other bulbs is that lilies never really go dormant—their roots are always growing—and no hard protective covering forms around them. What this means for the gardener is that you must handle them very carefully so as not to break off the roots or the delicate scale-like pieces that make up the bulb, and you should keep them out of soil for as short a time as possible. Local nurseries often sell them potted up. If they are unpotted, or if you order them by mail, keep them in a slightly damp (not wet) packing medium such as peat until you can plant them.

Lilies do not need fertile soil. In the areas where they are native (generally in the Orient) lilies often grow wild in poor, gravelly ground. Overfeeding causes them to have weak stems that always need staking. They need some moisture while they are actively growing, but drainage must be exceptional. Adding organic matter will help to provide both. Soil pH is not much of an issue except in the case of the Martagon lilies, which like soil slightly acid, and Madonna lilies, which like it slightly alkaline. Most lilies will do equally well in full sun or part shade—filtered shade is nice because it keeps the colors from fading. Martagon lilies, wood lilies and a few others really prefer some shade.

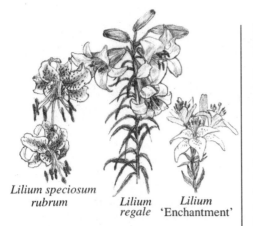

*Lilium speciosum
rubrum*

*Lilium
regale*

Lilium
'Enchantment'

Though lilies may be planted either in spring or fall, I prefer spring—they seem to get established a little better. The only lilies I know of that are always planted in fall are the Madonna lilies. Plant most lilies 4–6 inches down, measured from the top of the bulb; Madonna lilies, again the exception, are planted with only an inch of soil on top of the bulbs; you should start to see some of their foliage sprouting before winter. I think lilies should be at least a foot apart to allow for air circulation.

I hold off staking the plants until I think something might knock them over if I don't. You should also deadhead them, but cut off only the dead flowers, not the stems and leaves, which will continue to make food that the bulbs will store. One other word of caution: lilies can be slow to come up in spring, so be very careful that you don't dig around the spot where they are planted or might be planted. If your memory tends to be fuzzy, mark the spot. Expect to see either clusters of pointed leaves, or an odd little stub with little pointed leaves arranged around it in concentric layers, like a shaggy haircut. These get longer and longer, and are fragile, so try not to step on them and break them off. And don't be disappointed if your lilies fail to reach their full height the first year. Sometimes they just don't.

NARCISSUS
Narcissus

DESCRIPTION: First, let's establish what we're talking about. We all know what a daffodil looks like, right? Well, maybe. When I was a child I called all the yellow flowers of this type "daffodils" and the white ones "narcissus." I also know people who call the yellow ones "jonquils." Well, botanically speaking, they're all from the genus *Narcissus*. But you're welcome to call them whatever you like. These narcissi, like many flower groups in which many different species, and their hybrids, are grown, have been classified into groups. Here are the major ones, which sound at times like a list of bra sizes. Keep in mind that the "cup" is the round, protruding part of the flowers that is surrounded by the petals.

"Trumpet" narcissi produce one flower per stem, in which the cup is at least as long as the petals. The big yellow 'King Alfred' narcissus is a classic example.

"Large-cupped" narcissi have a cup that is as big around as but shorter than that of a "trumpet." I especially like the ones with the pink cups, of which 'Mrs. R. O. Backhouse' was the first, and 'Pink Beauty' is a fine modern example.

"Small-cupped" narcissi are rather flat flowers with a short cup. With any of these, the cup may be one color, the petals another.

"Double" narcissi are any that have more than one row of petals. They tend to be very fragrant, with almost a jasmine scent, and there are often several on one stem. 'Cheerfulness,' which is white with some yellow deep in the center, is a popular double.

"Jonquils" are hybrids of the small, early *N. jonquilla,* and have as many as six flowers to a stem. No longer all-yellow, the colors vary.

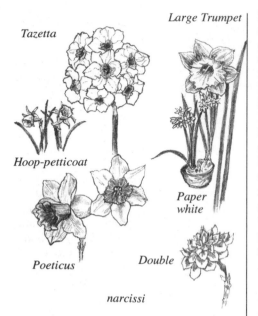

Large Trumpet

Tazetta

Hoop-petticoat

Paper white

Poeticus

Double

narcissi

"Tazetta" narcissi have many flowers on a stem and are fragrant, often with a small, colored cup. 'Paper white' and the yellow and orange 'Grand Soleil d'Or,' both nonhardy narcissi that are excellent for forcing, belong in this group.

Those in the "Poeticus" group are fragrant and have only one flower per stem, which is white with a contrasting, shallow cup. In 'Actaea,' an old favorite, the cup is yellow edged with red. The red-cupped 'Geranium' is another good variety.

In addition there are a number of delightful species, and their hybrids, that produce miniature flowers on short stems, perfect for the rock garden or any other small-scale planting. Among these are *N. bulbocodium* (hoop-petticoat daffodil), which has a big cup and rather wispy petals; *N. triandrus,* which has little drooping flowers with pulled-back petals ('April Tears' is a lovely, fragrant yellow variety); and *N. cyclamineus,* whose petals look as if they were being blown back by the wind.

HOW TO GROW: Give narcissi full sun or light shade. They prefer a well-drained sandy loam. Plant large varieties at least 6 inches apart and at least 6 inches deep. Small varieties can be a little closer and less deep. Work some high-phosphorus fertilizer into the soil. Do not cut the foliage down until it turns brown. Established plantings will increase by themselves but benefit from being dug up every four or five years and divided. To do this, wait till the foliage has died, then dig them up with a digging fork and pull apart the bulbs that will separate easily. Either replant them right away or store them in a cool place until later in the summer.

RANUNCULUS (PERSIAN BUTTERCUP)
Ranunculus asiaticus

DESCRIPTION: Most of the ranunculus available are the showy hybrids that you see in florist shops. The flowers, which are several inches across, are round globes made up of many papery-textured petals in bright, almost electric colors—red, pink, yellow, gold, white and "picotee," that is, with the petals edged in a contrasting color. They grow 18–24 inches tall. They are hardy only in warm climates, blooming there in late winter and spring and going dormant in the summer; both the flowers and the attractive ferny foliage die back. In zones where there is frost they are grown outdoors for bloom in spring and summer—until it gets very hot. They can be grown in beds, but they make a particularly fine show as container plants on a deck or terrace.

HOW TO GROW: The plants like full sun and need moisture around the roots, but they will rot if drainage is poor around their crowns. They are planted in late fall in warm climates; in cool ones they are started indoors two months before

the last frost. Soak the claw-shaped tubers in water for a few hours before planting them. Place them in the soil with the claw facing down. Start with small pots, filled with a light, rich potting soil, and move them up to larger pots as they grow, keeping them cool at night and keeping their soil moist. Bring them outdoors only after danger of frost has passed. After they stop blooming in summer, let the foliage die down and the tubers dry out. Store them in bags of dry peat at about 50 degrees until planting time. Even warm climate gardeners dig ranunculus up and store them over the summer.

SCILLA (SQUILL)
Scilla

DESCRIPTION: Scillas have small bell-like flowers that dangle from thin 3- to 6-inch stems. Most of the ones I see in gardens are blue, but you can get purple, lavender, pink and white scillas too. They are lovely in situations where their delicate beauty can be appreciated: planted in woodland gardens, under the light shade of a deciduous tree, in rock gardens, or naturalized in lawns. Modern hybrids come from a number of species, most commonly *Scilla siberica*. *S. tubergeniana* has fewer flowers on a stem but more stems to a plant. *S. bifo-*

lia, the twin-leafed squill, has more open flowers. *S. hispanica* (*S. campanulata*), Spanish bluebell, is quite tall (usually over a foot) and a good choice for shady locations. The hardiest of all these is *S. siberica,* which will survive as far north as Zone 2 or 3; the others mentioned are for Zones 4–5. All are cool-climate plants. But if you live in Zones 8–10 you can grow *S. peruviana,* which is a foot tall and usually purple. (Like the names of many bulbs, *S. peruviana's* name is a geographical muddle; though both its Latin name and its common name, "Cuban lily," give it a Latin American origin, it is really native to the Mediterranean region.)

Scilla siberica   Scilla campanulata

HOW TO GROW: Plant scilla bulbs in the early fall in sun or part shade in a nice sandy loam, 2–3 inches deep and about 6 inches apart. Give it moisture during the growing season if it's very dry, but otherwise you can just leave it alone.

SNOWDROP
Galanthus

DESCRIPTION: These little white, nodding flowers on stems up to a foot tall are the first bulbs to appear in early spring. Plant them where they will be noticed, or they will just blend in with the snow. Try planting them with yellow winter aconite and blue *Iris reticulata,*

which bloom at the same time, for a colorful early-spring display. Since they like filtered shade, they do well under deciduous shrubs and trees. Plant a lot of them for best effect. Snowdrops will usually self-sow.

Galanthus nivalis is the most common and the best for cold climates (hardy to Zone 3). There is also a double variety, *G. nivalis* 'Flore Pleno.' In warmer areas you can plant *G. elwesii,* which has slightly larger flowers. Snowdrops are sometimes confused with snowflakes (*Leucojum*), which are similar but have flowers that are more bell-like, with little green dots on the points of the bells. Snowflakes also bloom a bit later than snowdrops.

HOW TO GROW: Plant in late summer, if possible, in a humusy, well-drained sandy loam. Bulbs should be covered with about 3 inches of soil and should be spaced 3 inches apart. They can be divided and replanted after blooming if you want to make a patch of them somewhere else, but they are also inexpensive to buy.

TULIP
Tulipa

DESCRIPTION: A yard with a lot of tulips blooming in it looks like a jeweled crown. There are so many wonderful tulips that it is tempting to tuck them in everywhere; but if you do this keep in mind that the broad, straplike leaves will be conspicuous long after the jewels are gone, getting uglier and uglier as they start to turn brown. You'd have to either live with that or treat tulips as annuals by getting rid of the leaves after bloom and ending the plants' growth. When tulips are grown in more compact plantings, their leaves can be deliberately hidden by bushy annuals, perennials or ground covers. My solution is to plant them far enough away that I can see all those bright spots of color but not the leaves.

Buying tulips bulbs can be confusing unless you know the different types. Here are the major tulip groups:

Early-flowering tulips. These start blooming shortly after crocuses. They include single tulips that grow up to 16 inches and doubles that grow up to a foot. The gold-orange 'General de Wet' is a fine example.

Midseason tulips. These include the single "Mendel" and "Triumph" tulips, which grow 16–26 inches tall, and the big "Darwin Hybrids." These grow to 30 inches, stand up well in bad weather and are long-lived as tulips go. They come in many colors; 'Apeldoorn' is a bright orange-red.

Late-flowering tulips. This group includes "Darwin" tulips (not to be confused with the "Darwin Hybrids"), which are shaped like an egg that is slightly squared off at the bottom and grow 22–30 inches tall. The "Lily-flowered" tulips, such as the pink 'Mariette,' are shaped like a vase that comes in at the neck and then flares out again in points, and grow 18–26 inches tall. "Cottage" tulips have a compact egg shape. "Parrot" tulips, which grow 20–22 inches tall, are very showy, with twisted, ruffled or fringed petals (plant the spectacular deep-purple 'Black Par-

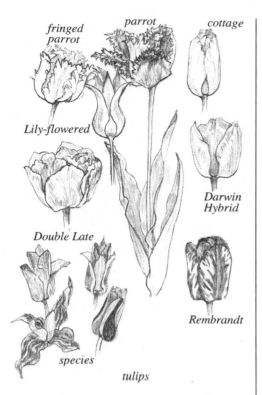

fringed parrot

parrot

cottage

Lily-flowered

Darwin Hybrid

Double Late

Rembrandt

species

tulips

rot' with some white parrots for a striking combination). The "Double Late" tulips also called "Peony-flowered" tulips, have big, many-petaled flowers and grow 2 feet tall or less. "Rembrandt" tulips are "broken," that is, striped or spotted; the colors are combinations of red, yellow or white.

"Species" tulips are actually hybrids of several species, and are, for the most part, short stemmed. They include the early-blooming *Tulipa kaufmanniana* (waterlily tulip) which has open-spreading, pointed petals, is often bicolored and grows up to 8 inches tall; *T. fosterana,* also early, which has very large flowers and grows 12–18 inches tall; *T. greigii,* which is late blooming, is less than a foot tall, and has yellow and red petals. Species tulips, especially *T. kaufmanniana* hybrids, tend to be longer lived than the taller types.

HOW TO GROW: Tulips like sun but will grow and bloom in part shade, in fact they prefer partial shade in warm climates. Be sure to keep the bulbs cool if you are not planting them right away; in hot climates give them a month of refrigeration before planting time. Plant in midfall in well-drained, sandy loam. If you are planting them in a bed, dig plenty of organic matter into it. Scratch some high-phosphorus fertilizer into the soil and plant them at least 6 inches deep; plant in wire cages if rodents are a problem.

WINTER ACONITE
Eranthis hyemalis

DESCRIPTION: This bulb send ups 3- to 8-inch stems in late winter or very early spring, with flowers that are little, bright yellow rosettes, like large buttercups; the leaves are a rufflike collar just under the blossoms. Winter aconites are a welcome sight, and the snow does nothing to discourage them. They look best planted in large drifts and will help add to the effect each year by self-sowing. They do fine in rock gardens but won't hold their own very well if planted in grass. They grow from odd, twiglike tubers and are hardy to Zone 4.

HOW TO GROW: Grow winter aconites in full sun or light shade, such as that cast by deciduous trees and shrubs. The soil need not be very fertile, but it must be well drained. The plants need moisture in spring and early summer; then they go dormant. Plant in late summer if possible, 2–3 inches deep and about 4 inches apart. Soak the tubers in water overnight before planting.

ROSES

I have read a bit about the history of roses, and I am convinced there is a film in it. It has everything: sex, violence, romance, spectacle, intrigue. Cleopatra wading through knee-deep billows of rose petals to receive Mark Antony on their first date. Nero throwing a banquet with petals strewn on the floor, petals hanging in nets from the ceiling, petals in the food, petals in the baths, petals in the beds. Roman politicians hanging a rose from a conference-room ceiling to proclaim that a meeting was secret, or as they said, *sub rosa*. Persian poets or Mogul emperors luring doe-eyed maidens into perfumed rose bowers.

The plot takes a turn in the Middle Ages, when the Catholic Church holds a dim view of wallowing in roses. Medieval ladies are scattering roses daintily among the linens, bathing in rose water, dosing ailments with rose syrups, and weaving roses into garlands ("rosaries") in their cloistered gardens, which were set off like tiny paradises in a violent world. In great cathedrals light is filtering through rose windows in glowing colors. But the rose, once a symbol of luxury and sensuality, has now become symbolic of the Virgin Mary, the unity of creation, and pure Christian love—except when a daring poet like the author of *The Romance of the Rose* writes of stealing into a walled garden and capturing his rose (really a beautiful lady) as a prize.

Fast forward to another rose garden, in the fifteenth century, where Richard Plantagenet plucks a white rose as an emblem of the House of York, and the Earl of Somerset, of the House of Lancaster, plucks a red one. Thus the Wars of the Roses begin. Forward again to the Napoleonic Wars. While Napoleon is off annexing countries, Josephine is raiding them for new rose varieties, trading cuttings with enemy horticulturists, and amassing the most vast and imperial rose collection in history in her garden at Malmaison. Even when French ships are seized at sea, all roses on board are sent to Josephine.

And what great rose scenes can be played for modern times? Perhaps Francis Meilland dispatching cuttings of a hybrid rose on the last plane out of France before the Nazi invasion, then discovering after the war is over that rose growers around the world have propagated it as the great rose 'Peace.' Or U.S. Army Intelligence officers meeting—each wearing an arm patch with a rose surrounded by compass points, to signify secrecy. Or perhaps the best scene is in a film already made, where Charlie Chaplin holds a rose to his nose and smiles shyly at the shop girl in *City Lights*.

Or perhaps it is a scene of you in your rose garden. The late-afternoon sun is backlighting the velvety petals in shades of salmon, crimson and gold. Butterflies hover above the blooms, and there is a background hum of lawn mowers and bees. You are endlessly dropping Japanese beetles, one by one, into a large, kerosene-filled jar.

Two television movie critics debate the meaning of this scene: "It's fraught with irony," one says. "You want to participate in the romance of growing what Sappho called 'Queen of the Flowers,' but the truth is, roses are a pain to grow. The best ones aren't very hardy, you have to prune them constantly and they attract every insect and fungus known to man." "No, you miss the point," says the other critic. "The flower is so sublime that just looking at it makes any struggle worthwhile. Ask Dante. Ask Josephine. Ask anyone who has made a million dollars on a rose patent."

Actually both critics are wrong. Contrary to current mythology, roses are not hard to grow. They are a stalwart shrub, one of the oldest plants known to man, and they even grow above the Arctic Circle. There are a few tricks you can learn that can make you more successful with roses, and you do need to choose the ones that will do best in your climate. You may turn out to be one of those people who must grow perfect roses. Or you may be like me, a grower of perfectly okay roses that are healthy, survive most winters and provide blooms for bouquets all summer long. There is nothing else I can grow in my climate that is as showy and long blooming, and that comes up every year. This is why I grow roses.

Types of Roses

There are many ways to use roses in your landscape, because they have several different habits of growth: as small shrubs, large shrubs, hedges, climbers and even ground covers. Let's take a look at the major types and how they can be used most effectively.

HYBRID TEAS

This is the flower most people picture when they hear the name "rose." A typical hybrid tea flower is large, with many petals and a high center, opening from long, pointed buds (Figure 57). The typical bush (Figure 58) grows about 3 feet tall in cool climates, taller in warm ones. The size range is about 2½–7 feet. The history of the hybrid tea rose dates back to 1867 when the first one, called 'La France,' was developed. This was a real revolution in rose breeding. Up until then the roses grown here and in Europe had red, pink or white flowers and bloomed only once during the season, usually in June. By crossing these with the yellow roses of China that

bloomed all summer long, breeders obtained long-flowering modern roses that bloomed not only in all the old shades but also in yellow and in mixtures such as orange, salmon and peach. These were the forerunners of the hybrid tea roses we grow today.

Since some of the Chinese roses were not native to cool climates, the hybrid teas that were developed from them are not as vigorous there as their European predecessors, nor as resistant to disease. If you grow hybrid teas you must expect to pamper them a bit. I find if I stick to those that are the most reliable in our cold winters, such as 'Peace' or 'Tropicana,' they will survive even if I don't bother to protect them in winter (page 435). But I always like to take a chance on some less hardy roses, and I find it's worth the extra effort.

Hybrid teas are generally compact shrubs that look best, to my mind, in a bed planted only with roses, though they do mix well with roses of other types if you give them their own section of the garden. The garden in Figure 59 shows how this might be done.

FLORIBUNDAS

These have the same color range as hybrid teas, but the flowers are usually less high-centered and are arranged in clusters. The bushes are shorter, generally 2–4 feet high, sometimes taller. Floribundas are easy to grow because they are hardier and more disease-resistant than the hybrid teas and can be useful as landscaping plants—as hedges, for example, or in the foreground of shrub borders. Pink 'Simplicity' and 'Betty Prior' are especially reliable for massed plantings. Other popular floribundas are the red 'Europeana,' white 'Iceberg' and salmon-pink 'Fashion.'

GRANDIFLORAS

These are a group of hybrids bred by crossing hybrid teas and floribundas. The first grandiflora was a pink rose called 'Queen Elizabeth.' They are large bushes, as tall as 8–10 feet. 'Queen Elizabeth' is still probably the best, but I also love the salmon-pink 'Sonia.' If you have the room they are satisfying to grow because they are so vigorous.

CLIMBING ROSES

Climbing roses are not vines and do not climb the same way that vines do. Vines have tendrils or some other means of twining around or sticking to the thing they are climbing, to help them up. They also tend to have flexible stems so they can bend in appropriate directions (Chapter 13). Roses, on the other hand, simply send up stiff woody canes in hopes of reaching the sunny air above the tops of other shrubs and small trees. The only aid they have is their thorns, which hook onto vegetation. Once they are up in the light, they send out horizontal shoots that produce flowers, which is why a climbing rose that is only growing vertically may not bloom much, or at all.

I often wish I lived in a warmer climate where climbing roses were vigorous and I could send them up into the trees (not planting them right among tree roots, however). Apart from the indestructible 'Blaze' and a few others such as 'Golden Showers,' there are not many climbers I can grow at all, and most of the ones I can die back almost to the ground each winter. Gardeners in warmer zones, rejoice! Look at Gertrude Jekyll's book *Roses* to see what she did with climbers in Victorian England. She speaks of camouflaging unsightly tool sheds with them, and judging from the pictures, some of them look as if they might obliterate your house if you turned your back.

There are a number of different climbing rose types, but most of the ones available are called "large-flowered climbers" and have flowers in clusters, in a large variety of shades including the yellows. Climbers do well on walls and trellises, supported in such a way that the branches can be trained laterally.

"Pillar roses" are either roses that don't climb as high as most climbers— about 8 or 10 feet—or ones that are pruned at the top so that they remain at this height. They are traditionally trained vertically on a free-standing pillar, but they also look attractive and natural growing on a post supporting a porch or other structure. "Ramblers" are climbers that have very flexible canes and bloom only once, in early summer: their color range is limited to pink, red and white. "Trailers" are low-growing roses with long canes that are very lax and tend to lie on the ground rather than grow upright. They make good ground covers. Many different types of roses fall into this category; the hybrid rugosa 'Max Graf' is one example.

MINIATURE ROSES

These roses are dwarf in every way: their flowers, their leaves and their bushes. Sizes range from the tiniest micro-minis, as short as 6 inches, to the 3-foot macro-minis. They have a broad range of flower types and colors. Miniatures are charming in small-space gardens where they can be viewed close up, in flower borders, in rock gardens, massed as ground covers, and in containers, both indoors and out. Some look well in hanging baskets.

ROSE FLOWER TYPES

Fig. 57

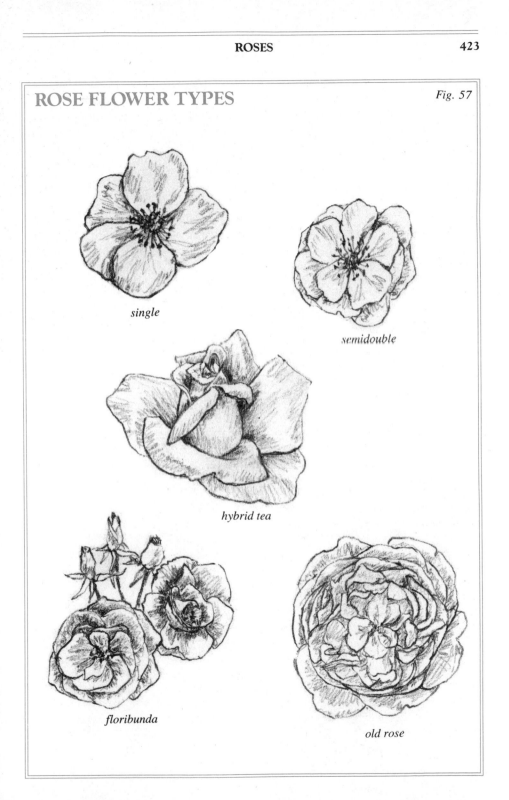

single

semidouble

hybrid tea

floribunda

old rose

OLD ROSES

This vast category encompasses many important types of roses, among them gallicas, albas, cabbage roses, moss roses, bourbons, damasks, hybrid perpetuals, teas, Chinas and noisettes. Despite the fact that color range and blooming period are limited, these "historical roses," as they are sometimes called, have much to offer that modern roses lack, and they are experiencing something of a comeback. They are large plants, grown as shrubs. A number of specialty mail-order nurseries sell old roses (page 624), and at least one garden center near me carries a good selection of them in containers.

Many things attract gardeners to old roses. They tend to be much more fragrant than modern ones, which have been bred for such things as wide color range, large high-centered blooms, stiffer necks that don't nod and bend, stiffer petals that don't crush when shipped, as well as disease resistance and vigor. But fragrance has often been sacrificed, even though there are some notoriously fragrant modern roses (such as 'Mister Lincoln,' 'Fragrant Cloud,' 'Sutter's Gold,' 'Chrysler Imperial' and 'Double Delight'). But in a garden of old roses almost all exude fragrance. And there are wonderful flower shapes

HOW ROSES GROW

Fig. 58

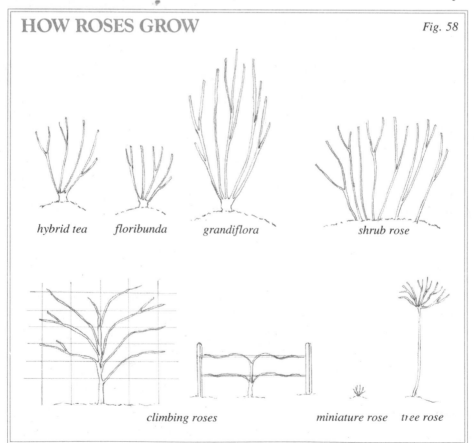

hybrid tea   floribunda   grandiflora   shrub rose

climbing roses   miniature rose   tree rose

in the old ones that you rarely see in new. The heavy, luxurious cabbage roses, or "centifolias" (the name means "a hundred petals"), nod on their stems like sleepy courtesans. These roses and many other old roses have a flat, "button-eyed" flower whose petals all seem pulled in toward the center. On top of that the old varieties are rich in history. Their names alone are enough to seduce some gardeners: 'Reine des Violettes,' 'Souvenir de la Malmaison,' 'Hebe's Lip,' 'Nymph's Thigh.' I hope this has given you a taste of a subject worthy of far more lengthy attention.

WILD OR SPECIES ROSES

These roses are the ones from which all the countless hybrids, old or modern, have been derived. If they are not common to your region, you will probably find them hard to obtain except through a few specialty nurseries. Their rarity makes them alluring. I would love to be able to grow *Rosa eglanteria* (the sweetbrier rose, or Shakespeare's eglantine), *R. spinosissima* (the Scotch rose) or *R. wichuraiana* (the Japanese ancestor of most modern climbers). Perhaps those who have them in their backyards wish they had the *R. multiflora* that grows in mine and in everyone else's around here. If you jog along the roads on a warm June evening, you are almost overpowered with the heady scent of its small white, clustered blossoms. It's lovely, but unfortunately you can't have just one or two multifloras, because birds eat the seeds and spread them everywhere. Local landowners are out there with their tractors and brush hogs every year, trying to stop *R. multiflora* from taking over their pastures.

SHRUB ROSES

This rather amorphous classification in-cludes a number of rose types. Those of early origin, such as the fragrant white 'Blanc Double de Coubert,' are often listed under old roses. Others, such as the newly introduced 'Bonica'—a pink rose—are modern hybrids. Rugosa roses are important members of the group. They are very hardy and vigorous, with wrinkled leaves, and are remarkably tolerant of seaside conditions. Flowers are pink, red or white and usually single, though there are some doubles. Rugosas bloom over a long period. The hips (the fruits that follow rose blossoms) are particularly showy and rich in vitamin C. 'Pink Grootendorst' is a good hybrid rugosa, with pink double flowers.

Some favorites classified as shrub roses are 'Harison's Yellow,' which bears small, fragrant yellow flowers once early in the season; 'Austrian Copper' (*R. foetida* 'Bicolor'), with striking early-blooming yellow and red single blossoms; and 'The Fairy' (actually an old-fashioned polyantha), with thick clusters of tiny, pale pink flowers and delicately cut foliage on a low, sturdy, twiggy plant. It looks as good in a perennial border as it does in a rose bed, and is a pretty accent plant for, say, next to a gate or doorway.

TREE ROSES

These are not really trees but roses grown to look like trees. They consist of three parts: the rootstock; the trunkstock, which is budded (grafted) onto the rootstock; and the top, which is budded onto the trunkstock. Many different types of roses are used for the top. If it is an upright, compact rose, the top will be a round head of foliage and flowers. If it is a long-caned type, the top will hang down and resemble a "weeping" tree. Tree roses require staking and special winter protection for the trunk and upper graft, and are not recommended for cold regions. Generally they are small, exquisite specimens except in very mild climates, where they can become quite large.

Plan for a Rose Garden

In discussing the various types of roses, I have mentioned some ways to use them in the landscape. But if you are really attracted to roses, you may decide that you want a separate garden devoted solely to them. The phrase "rose garden" suggests many things: fragrance, formality, luxury, romance. Assuming that time, space and money were no object, I could conjure up a rose garden in the old style, surrounded by ancient brick walls or boxwood hedges, to enclose you in a secret world of fragrant flowers. Alas, few of us have the means to achieve anything so grand. On the other hand, it is possible to plan a very modest rose garden that echoes the grand style.

The garden shown in Figure 59 is only 20 feet square and contains no elaborate structures, but it captures something of the old-fashioned formal rose garden on a small scale. At the back is a dark evergreen hedge to set off the bright colors of the roses. One good, simple choice for the hedge would be sheared Japanese yew. Others would be hemlock and Hinoki false cypress. In fairly mild climates you can use boxwood.

In the center, just in front of the hedge, is a simple arbor with a seat where you can sit and admire the roses. A climbing rose or pillar rose might be placed to grow on each side—or on just one side if your climber is a vigorous, heavy plant. A simple wooden fence or trellis borders the garden on each side.

Here you could plant more climbers, some ramblers and perhaps some of the taller roses such as shrub roses and grandifloras. Any of the roses could be trained along the fence horizontally as needed.

The central part of the garden consists of two walkways that join in a circle at the bench and are separated by a small central bed shaped like an elongated ellipse. These are easy to mark out: all you do is take a garden line or a screwdriver tied to a string, and, using it as a compass, make two concentric half-circles, one with a radius of 5 feet, the other with a radius of 2 feet. If you are working in bare ground, scratch the lines in the earth; if in sod, mark the circles with small wood or plastic plant markers every foot or so and lay a garden hose along them. Then edge the line with a spade. The side beds are planted with the smaller roses such as hybrid teas and floribundas, the central beds with still smaller ones, including some miniatures. In the very center is a tree rose. I have not suggested specific rose varieties except for the one in the center bed, because I would prefer you to select roses that are just the right ones for your area.

I sometimes mix a few other plants with roses, although if I am growing roses that need winter protection I don't plant anything too close to them; this way there is plenty of room to place winter mulch or soil mounds around them. Certain kinds of plants go especially well with roses—old-fashioned, romantic flowers in shades of pink, red, blue, lavender, pale yellow and white. Flower forms should be subtle and restrained too, and it is nice to find some with airy flowers, such as sea lavender or baby's breath, or spiky ones such as lavender, foxglove and veronica, as a contrast to the round shape of the roses. I would avoid big flowers in hot colors,

PLAN FOR A ROSE GARDEN (20' by 24')

Fig. 59

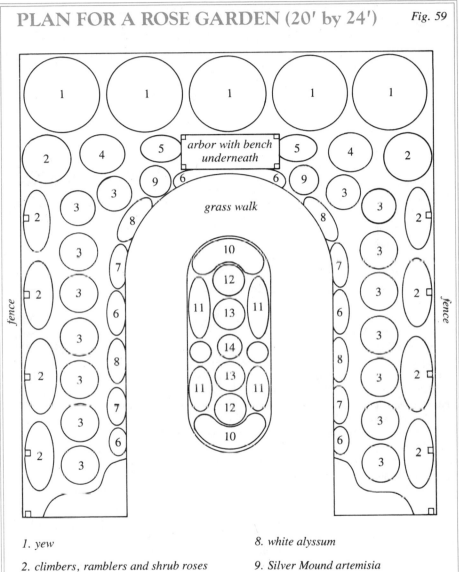

1. yew
2. climbers, ramblers and shrub roses
3. hybrid teas and floribundas
4. grandifloras
5. climbers
6. blue ageratum
7. purple alyssum
8. white alyssum
9. Silver Mound artemisia
10. dianthus
11. miniature roses
12. The Fairy roses
13. Iceberg roses
14. tree rose

such as large-flowered marigolds or glo-
riosa daisies. You want to set off the
roses, not overpower them. Foliage
plants such as silvery-leaved artemisias
or blue-leaved rue can be lovely too.
Use annuals, perennials or a combination. If most of your roses are early
blooming you might plant early-summer
perennials. If it is an all-season rose
garden plant some that bloom later,
mixed with annuals. But try not to let
these flowers steal the show from the
roses. Often, just a low edging is best.

The garden in Figure 59 is edged
with flowers that will neither hide the
roses nor interfere with winter protection of the hybrid teas. The artemisia
'Silver Mound' and the alpine pinks
(*Dianthus alpinus* 'Allwoodii') are perennial. Annuals include violet-blue
ageratum, white alyssum and purple
alyssum. You can vary the choice of
annuals year by year, and naturally you
can substitute plants of your own choosing. Some other plants that might go
well with roses are perennial geraniums,
heather, any of the bellflowers, columbines, coral bells, scabiosa and yarrow
in red, lavender or pale yellow shades
(all of these grown as perennials); larkspur and pansies (grown as annuals or
biennials); and stock, love-in-a-mist, lobelia and Iceland or Shirley poppies
(grown as annuals).

The path in this garden is simply a
grass strip that is an extension of the
lawn; a metal or brick edging should
separate it from the beds. A grass path is
the easiest, but a brick or stone one
would also be lovely. If you want to
make this bed even smaller, you can cut
off some of the bottom area, making the
central bed a shorter ellipse or even a
small circle with one exquisite tree rose
or rose bush in the center.

Choosing a Site

Roses generally like a sunny
location—at least six hours of full
sun a day—but if your only good spot
gets as little as four hours a day, roses
are still worth a try. A southen exposure
is fine, and a western one is all right.
But an eastern exposure is best in most
areas, especially warm ones and those
with a lot of humidity where disease is a
heavy risk. The morning sun will dry
the dew off the leaves promptly, and
you will also avoid the hot afternoon sun
that is apt to fade the color of the
flowers.

In cold climates, try to find a sheltered location out of cold winter winds,
but don't pick a spot where air circulation is really poor; it can lead to disease.
Your site should not have tree or shrub
roots that can compete with the roses.
Above all it should have excellent drainage. Roses will not survive if their roots
are sitting in water. If your only possible
site does not drain well, build raised
beds for your roses, or even have some
drainage pipes installed to lead water
away from the bed.

Preparing the Soil

Roses will tolerate a fairly wide
range of soils as long as they are
well drained. They will tolerate clay
soils better than sandy ones, and acid
soils better than alkaline. Ideal pH is
about 6.0 to 7.0; anything over that may
be a problem correctable by adding peat
or sulfur; add some lime if the soil is
very acid. The soil does not have to be
very rich, but it should have plenty of
organic matter worked in—compost,
well-rotted manure, or moistened peat
moss are all fine. If the soil is quite
infertile, or if your source of organic

matter is one such as peat that is nonnutritive, work a balanced fertilizer into the soil throughout the bed.

Since roses have long, deep roots, I like to dig a rose bed to a depth of almost 2 feet (page 35). For spring planting, it is best to dig the bed in fall and let it settle over the winter so that you will not be working wet soil in early spring. Your bed will be all ready so that you can plant the roses early, while they are still dormant.

Buying Roses

I t can sometimes be frustrating to buy roses, because you cannot always tell whether or not they are the best ones for your garden. I advise sending away for a number of catalogs from mail-order suppliers and going through them carefully. Many companies will make recommendations based on climate. They may be a bit vague—saying only "winter hardy" or "not winter hardy" as opposed to giving hardiness zone numbers—but even such minimal information is a start. Besides, a rose that is not quite hardy enough for your zone may survive fine if you plant it in a warm, sheltered part of the property and protect it well in winter. If you buy plants in a local nursery, they may or may not be the best choices for the area; but if it is a good nursery the staff will be able to tell you which ones people have the best luck with. I would start with some that are fairly safe bets so that a cold winter does not wipe out your new garden completely and discourage you from rose growing forever.

Most mail-order companies ship at the best planting time for your area—in general, early spring for cool climates, early fall where winters are fairly mild, and winter in very warm areas. Some suppliers of old roses ship in fall even to cold climates. This is because old roses are not grafted but are usually grown on their own roots and are thus very easy to establish. When you buy a modern rose you will notice that there is a bulge at the bottom of the stem where the hybrid variety has been budded onto a rootstock of some rose with vigorous growth that will provide a good root system for the plant. The graft bulge is called the "bud union."

Plants that are shipped by mail should be "dormant, two-year-old, Number-1, field-grown plants" (look for this designation). According to the official system of grading roses, "Number 1" means that the plant has at least three vigorous canes at least 18 inches high (15 inches for floribundas). Two other notations that may alert you to a good rose are "AARS" (meaning the rose is an All-America Rose Selection) or a high rating on a scale of 1 to 10 by the American Rose Society, as published in the magazine *The American Rose*. But don't go by these ratings alone, since there may be particular qualities in roses that you will come to prefer, and certain ones that will do best in your particular garden.

Unless they are miniatures, your roses will arrive bare-root (with no soil around them) and should be soaked in water for twenty-four hours upon arrival. Heel them in (page 49) or wrap them in damp sphagnum moss if you cannot plant them right away, but try not to hold them this way for more than two weeks.

If you buy your plants potted in a local nursery, look for Number-1 plants with healthy foliage. I would avoid bargain plants in places like supermarkets; even if you have an eye for a good rose bush and know your varieties, it is better to buy from nurseries you know, whose plants are usually healthy and who will replace the plant if it is not satisfactory.

Potted roses can be held until you are ready to plant them if you keep them in a semishaded location and water them well.

Planting Roses

S̲ome people plant hybrid teas and floribundas very close together, especially in cooler climates where almost all the growth is the current year's, where the bushes never get very large, and where they are not always covered with blooms. It does make for a better show, but I advise keeping plants at least 2 feet apart and preferably 3—even 4 in warm areas. I'd rather be optimistic about the size the bush will attain and keep plenty of circulating air around each one. Of course different types of roses have different spacing requirements. Miniatures can go as close as a foot apart, but many old roses, shrub roses and climbers can become very large, and you need to allow room for their eventual spread. Try to find out about the plant's growth habit before you decide on the spacing.

Planting the roses is easy if you follow a few simple rules. Always dig a large enough hole—1½–2 feet wide, and deep enough to accommodate the roots. When you are planting a rose bare-root, it is important not to let the roots dry out. Don't leave them lying exposed to sun and wind. Better yet, puddle them (page 51) and leave them in their nice bucket of mud until the minute you are ready to plant them.

PLANTING ROSES

Fig. 60

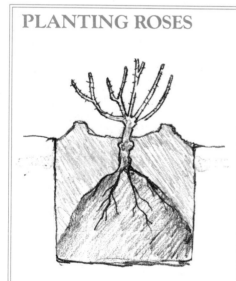

Spread the roots over a mound of soil. The bud union should be above the soil surface in warm climates, and just below it in cold ones. Fill the hole halfway with soil, watering thoroughly and firming the soil gently around the roots.

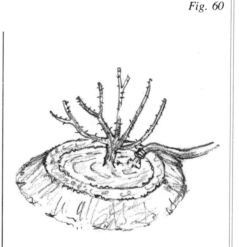

Fill the rest of the hole, then make a saucer of earth around the rose bush and fill it with water. Remove the metal tag from the bush and attach it to a wooden marker stuck in the soil nearby.

On bare-root plants you can see the root system and tailor your hole to accommodate long roots (don't prune them back unless they are damaged). The position of the bud union is important: in warm climates it should be just above the soil so the sun can reach it and cause it to send out new canes, but in cold climates place it an inch or two below the soil to protect it from cold.

Making a soil mound in the center of the hole and draping the roots over it may help, but don't try to crowd the roots into a tidy arrangement or wind them around in a circle. Firm the soil gently around the roots, water them when the hole is half full, then fill it with soil, making sure there are no air pockets. Then make a soil saucer (page 52) and fill it with water.

If your rose is in a container lift it very gently out of the pot, trying to keep as much of the soil around the roots as possible. Some gardeners even cut out the bottom of the pot, holding it in place with their hands, then lower the plant into the hole, slit the sides of the pot and remove it in pieces. Roses that come in cardboard boxes are planted box and all, though you should peel off the part that sticks up above the soil. (Instructions on the box will usually guide you.)

If you have enriched the soil throughout the bed you should not have to feed the roses at the time you plant them. You do not want to encourage a lot of new growth until the root system develops further and can sustain it. In fact, if the rose has canes longer than 18 inches it is best to cut them back to this length when you plant. Your last job is to remove the little metal tag that is usually wired to one of the canes. Attach it to a stake and stick it next to the plant if you want it for identification, but don't leave it on the plant; if you do, it may girdle and kill the stem as the stem grows.

Rose Supports

A small rose bush or a trailing rose does not need any kind of support, but climbing types usually do, to keep them from sprawling awkwardly, getting in the way and falling down (Figure 58). Roses that climb up pillars must be tied to the pillars; those on trellises can be tied and/or woven through the openings. Climbing roses almost always need to be anchored in some way to whatever they are climbing.

Rose supports also serve to encourage lateral branching and more profuse bloom. Roses can be grown completely horizontally along a fence, where they will send up lateral shoots along the canes. Or the canes may be trained upwards to a certain point, then trained sideways along a wall or trellis. Gardeners also construct arbors and pergolas— open wooden structures like the frame of a house without the walls—for roses to climb on. Keep in mind that if a rose is the kind that only blooms well on the horizontal canes, you don't want it to reach the roof before going sideways or you will never see the flowers. With some roses you may have to watch them grow and see how they are going to behave in your yard before you figure out the best way to support them.

Taking Care of Your Roses

Roses are not delicate creatures that must be fussed with every two minutes. If I have an exceptionally crazed summer and don't get to tend mine at all, they are still there in fall and have provided me with enough blooms to stick into flower arrangements for a touch of elegance among such peasant stock as coneflower and yarrow. But there are a lot of small favors that you can do for your roses that will make them not only still there in fall, but there in all their glory. And if you want to, you will be able to gather bouquets that are nothing but roses, roses, roses.

WATERING

With their deep root systems roses will make it through all but the most horrific drought, but will they bloom through it? Hardly. Even if your summer is not a particularly dry one, chances are it is noticeably drier than your spring was or your fall will be. And if you give your roses a thorough, deep soaking a few times a week you will have many more flowers. The best way is to water the soil, not the leaves, using a soaker hose (page 96) or a regular hose with a bubbler attachment that will let water seep out gradually for a few hours. Watering in the morning is best so that you don't go into the evening with a lot of disease-fostering moisture sitting around on the ground or on the plants.

WEEDING

Any garden needs to be kept free of weeds, and roses are no exception. Try to remove all perennial weeds, and their roots, from the bed when you prepare it, then cultivate every now and then to prevent annual weeds from gaining on you. Roses are very sensitive to systemic herbicides, so it is probably best not to use these in the rose garden, even if you are a dead-eye with your sprayer. A mulch will help to keep the weeds down, and will also help to keep the soil moist. I recommend mulching if disease is not much of a problem in your area; but if you live in Mildewville or Blackspot City, a mulch may aggravate rose ills and so may not be worth using.

FEEDING

When it comes to feeding roses I am like one of those mothers who never let their kids eat Twinkies or Froot Loops. "No 'rose food,'" I tell them. "I am never sure what's in it—probably a lot of empty calories. You get a moderately enriched soil to start with and then a wholesome, balanced fertilizer—after unmounding in spring, after the first flush of bloom and in August to promote fall bloom." I would use a liquid fertilizer that delivers food straight to the roots when they need it and does not persist in the soil. Roses should not have food before bedtime: feeding in fall when the plants are about to go dormant will make them put out tender growth that will only be winterkilled. In a warmer climate I would be a bit more indulgent, giving larger portions and perhaps a feeding in mid- or late August. Dry fertilizers should be scratched into the surface, then watered. Liquid fertilizers may be applied to the soil. Rose enthusiasts who exhibit their roses often practice "foliar feeding," a method of spraying soluble inorganic fertilizers onto the undersides of the leaves to promote flowering and give the leaves good color.

PEST CONTROL

I feel the same way about "rose spray" and "rose dust" as I do about "rose food." They are supposed to take care of everything that might possibly afflict your roses. But I don't like all-purpose chemical concoctions that will wipe out everything—including beneficial insects. I would rather diagnose specific problems and treat them individually.

Every area seems to have something that really plagues its roses. In some areas it is a particular disease, such as blackspot or mildew. The first, which you can recognize by black spots on roses' leaves, haunts regions that are rainy or humid. The latter, which turns the leaves a powdery white, seems to be more of a problem in hot weather. Both can be treated with regular applications of a fungicide designed to treat that disease (follow the directions on the label). The same applies to rust (orange pimples on the undersides of the leaves) and rose canker (brown areas on the stems), both fungus diseases. Cut stems just above the dormant leaf bud (see page 434) so you won't leave stubs that will die and invite canker. And try to keep the leaves dry and the garden free of debris that can harbor the spores of fungi. If your plants do have diseases, dip your pruners in a disinfectant such as alcohol between cuts. This avoids spreading diseases among plants.

Every region has its own insect predators, too. If mountain laurel is Connecticut's State Flower, then surely the Japanese beetle is its State Pest. Some years they are very hard on the roses, some years they are not. I don't like to use poison sprays and have found pheromone traps of minimal benefit. Applying milky spore disease to the lawn to kill the beetles' larvae is effective but expensive. I prefer my mother's remedy. When we were children she always kept a quart jar of kerosene in the garden, and the rule was that whoever went outside had to make a pass through the roses and drop and beetles they found into the jar. If you are vigilant about doing this, you can really minimize the damage they cause.

If you see a lot of ants in your rose blossoms, they are herding aphids— literally farming them so that they will secrete a honeylike substance the ants love to eat. Wipe out the ants by wiping out the aphids; just wash them off with a blast of water from the hose. Rose scale (white spots on older canes) can be controlled with a dormant oil spray (page 73) applied early in the season before the plants leaf out. Remove badly infested canes, and clean up all debris. For spider mites, which make webs on the undersides of the leaves, spray with the hose and keep the bed free of weeds and debris. If thrips or leafhoppers are a serious problem use a pyrethrum spray. Rose galls, which are bulges on the stems, are caused by wasps and can be pruned out; crown gall, at the base of the plant, should also be cut out, or the plant destroyed if it is badly affected. (For more information on controlling pests and diseases, see Chapter 2.)

PRUNING

For rose enthusiasts, pruning is a complex topic about which few agree. For the average gardener it is a fairly simple practice aimed at keeping roses healthy, well shaped and free flowering. If you did no pruning at all—letting winter kill off some excess canes, then simply cutting back stems in summer by picking roses for the house—you could get by. But you'll have much nicer roses if these things happen in a more controlled way.

Some people cut their roses back in winter. I just cut off some long tips that get in the way of protective coverings, and I anchor the long canes of climbers to keep them from blowing around and getting broken by ice. Then I let nature take its course.

In spring I prune my hybrid teas and floribundas when I remove the plants' winter covering (page 435) and the plants are still dormant. I can see immediately that some of the canes have died on the less hardy ones, or died partway. I put on some sturdy gloves, take my hand pruners and go to work on anything that looks dead. Rose canes are deceptive: sometimes they look brown and lifeless when they are still alive. So

I start at the tips and start snipping a few inches at a time until the centers of the pruned stems look white instead of brown. Then I cut back any canes that are still longer than about 18 inches. I try to leave the plant with a compact, balanced shape, cutting back long, straggly canes even if they are alive. The goal in pruning back rose bushes is not only to make the bush more compact and to make it flower more but also to open up the center. This will get more sun into the bud union where canes are produced, promote air circulation to ward off disease, and create an open, bowllike shape that displays the flowers well instead of a dense, twiggy one that conceals them. If there are a lot of canes coming up from the bottom, prune out some of the older ones as shown in Figure 61. Cut out any dense, twiggy growth and any canes that cross and rub against each other.

When cutting canes back partway, always try to cut back to an outward-facing dormant bud. Notice that a rose leaf is made up of a number of leaflets—always an odd number, in fact. When you cut the stem just above one of these leaves, a bud will later appear where the leaf joins the main stem; if the leaf is facing outward, the bud will be too, and it will send out a new branch in that direction. Even when you are cutting roses for the house you should count leaflets. Cut back to a leaf with at least five, so that a bud will form, and if you have a choice of blossoms, choose one you can cut above an outward facing bud. Make your cuts on a slant to encourage water to drain off the cut, and coat large cuts with a commercial plant-

PRUNING ROSES

Fig. 61

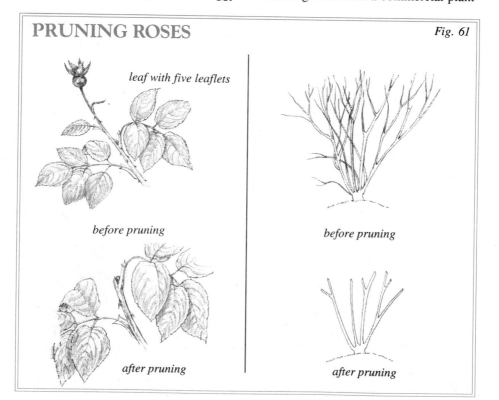

leaf with five leaflets

before pruning

after pruning

before pruning

after pruning

wound sealer, or even shellac or nail polish.

These techniques apply to the types of roses that grow on fairly small plants. But even large shrubs and climbers need to have dead wood removed, old canes thinned out and the center of the plant kept reasonably open. For these you may need loppers (page 93). Ramblers are pruned rather heavily to encourage them to form lateral branches for more flowers, and are often cut back entirely after they bloom; the new branches that grow will produce the following year's flowers. Old roses, and any that bloom just once in early summer, are generally pruned lightly in early spring to remove dead wood, then more drastically after flowering to improve shape and promote growth.

DEADHEADING

Deadheading (page 156) is especially important with roses and should be practiced just as if you were pruning, cutting back to an outward-facing bud above five leaflets as described above. All types of roses benefit from deadheading—if you can reach the flowers. With clustered flowers such as those of floribundas, I even remove faded blooms from a cluster that is still producing flowers. I find this is one job I always remember to do, because when I go out to pick some roses I hate the sight of dead flowers on such elegant plants.

WINTER PROTECTION

In late summer you should let your roses start winding down for the winter, especially in cold areas. You don't want to feed them, prune them or even pick them heavily for fear of promoting new growth. The one thing you do want to do, however, is water them, so that they will have enough moisture around their roots after the ground has frozen.

In cold areas you should then cover any roses that are not hardy in your climate. Even those that are hardy will look less beat-up in spring if protected in some way.

The traditional way of protecting tender roses is to mound soil around the base of the plants, anywhere from 6 to 12 inches of it. The soil will not only protect against extreme cold but also help to keep the roots from drying out. It is applied after there have been several hard freezes; in fact I usually wait until just before the ground is too hard to dig; otherwise the mounding may encourage new growth. The soil must be brought in from somewhere else, like the vegetable garden, not dug up from between the rose bushes (which would make the root systems all the more vulnerable). This method works best with the smaller rose bushes, although tender climbers are sometimes removed from their supports, laid along the ground, and buried. Tender tree roses are sometimes dug up entirely, laid on their sides and buried (or dug on one side and tilted over). If tree roses are left standing, the trunk and top are wrapped in burlap.

In spring, when you think new growth might be starting to appear at the base of the plants, dig away some soil with your fingers. If you find new growth remove all the mounding soil very carefully and haul it back to the place it came from.

A less laborious method of protecting roses is to erect a barrier around the bushes, or around the whole bed, to make a sort of pen that is then filled with leaves, shredded bark, or some other loose material. To hold up the mulch, people use tarpaper, snow fence, wire fence, bushel baskets, even newspapers. If you use the same material you are going to mulch with, you can simply spread all or most of it back over the bed in springtime. This method also helps keep ice and wind from breaking the branches. (Sometimes gardeners mound roses *and* surround them with mulch.) There are also "rose cones" you can buy that fit down over the whole plant, though this method can be expensive if you have a lot of roses. Tall roses such as grandifloras or climbers can also be wrapped in burlap for some measure of protection, if you don't mind looking at mummified rose plants all winter.

Whether you protect your roses, and how, will depend on what you grow and where you live. Sometimes roses winter over beautifully in regions where a heavy snowfall provides a natural mulch keeping soil temperature constant. In climates where there is a lot of freezing and thawing throughout the winter, soil mounds and mulch make for a lot of moisture around the stems and should probably be avoided.

Roses are among the most satisfy- ing ornamental plants you can grow, and many gardeners get totally hooked on them. Since they are such a popular plant it is fairly easy to find opportunities to see them growing and learn about different kinds. The American Rose Society (page 617) can direct you not only to its regional branches but also to public gardens where you can see dozens of different roses on display. If you get involved in the rose world you will meet many gardeners ready to share not only their enthusiasm and expertise but also budwood with which to graft new hybrids you may not have tried, or cuttings of old rose treasures that have nearly passed out of existence. You'll learn which varieties and which techniques succeed in your area and which don't. You may never get to wade knee-deep in rose petals, but as the little chores of rose growing become routine, you'll wonder how you could ever have a garden without at least a few roses in it.

LAWNS AND GROUND COVERS

Like many people, I suppose, I have a love-hate relationship with the lawn. Sometimes I look out at it and picture all the more interesting things that could occupy that vast space: more roses; an orchard; an expanded vegetable garden nearer to the house; an unmowed meadow full of wildflowers. Other times I look at the lawn and admire the way it ties the whole yard together, the way a plush wall-to-wall carpet ties together a room. I like the way it turns a technicolor green in spring and sprouts yellow dandelions throughout the summer, all by itself.

The way I feel about the lawn is not, however, very important. In this household the lawn is, quite literally, male turf. It belongs to the softball players, the football players and the male Labrador retriever. It is maintained not by me but by a platoon of men armed with large noisy machines who swoop down on it for half an hour every Friday as if it were the island of Grenada and leave it tamed and fragrant from cutting. But if anyone *were* to ask me, I would say that the lawn is okay. It is both pretty and practical. The lawn works.

Do You Need a Lawn?

How you make peace with your own lawn depends on a lot of things—including who mows it. But before you decide on an approach to your lawn you should ask yourself whether you want a lawn in the first place, and if so how much lawn you need. In some communities a lawn may be a requirement—I know of a case where a homeowner was sued by his neighbors for growing a wildflower meadow in his front yard instead of grass. I tend to admire someone who does whatever he wants with his yard, even though it is different from all the other, identical yards on the block, but I concede that custom can be a powerful reason for keeping a lawn. Still, you may be able to find other ways to cover the ground neatly and attractively in a way that won't disturb your neighbors, if you're not in the mood to go to court. If you can, and you don't need a lawn for outdoor activities and would just as soon not have to maintain it, there are many ground covers you can use instead, a number of which are described later on in this chapter. Or you may decide that a lawn is appropriate in some areas, and ground covers in others. Before you make these decisions you should understand what a lawn does and doesn't do.

A grass lawn is the most useful, all-purpose ground cover that you can plant, for one major reason: you can walk on it. There are a few other ground covers that will take some foot traffic, such as thyme, but none are as tough as grass, and most of them can't be walked or played on at all but must have paths through them if walking is necessary. There are also few ground-cover plants that have the tidy, uniform appearance that mowed grass has, or that are dappled in the lovely way grass is with the changing patterns of sun and shade cast by trees and clouds.

On the other hand, a lawn is a lot of work. Even if you don't feed it or weed it or do anything else besides cut it, that's a major task in itself, and it must be performed at least once a week when the lawn is actively growing. Ground covers, though more expensive to plant than lawns, require far less upkeep. Another problem with grass is that there are areas where grass is impractical to grow because they don't admit a mower: steep slopes, tight corners, under overhanging branches of trees and shrubs or around their trunks, rocky areas and near pools where clippings can get in the water. There are also places where grass simply will not grow because the ground is too shady or the soil is too wet or too dry. (For all these problem spots, however, there are ground covers that are just right.) Your choice of lawn or ground cover may also be based on visual considerations. Lawns do not provide the varied effects that you can achieve with ground covers. (See the section below on designing with ground covers.) And finally, the chore of lawn maintenance can be a big factor. You need to decide how much lawn you really want to take care of. Don't assume that every spot that *can* have grass *must* have grass. Consider letting some of the property revert to a more natural state as a habitat for wildlife, or nurture a wildflower meadow on part of the lawn area (page 562).

What Makes a Good Lawn

If there is going to be some grass on your property, you might as well have as good a lawn as you can. Notice I said a "good" lawn, not a "perfect" one. Since a lawn is something that just about every home has, and lawn care is often the only form of gardening that a homeowner does, there is enormous peer pressure about the subject. I find that men especially take great pride in having the lawn look good (in other areas of gardening, male and female enthusiasm is usually about equal) and that they talk about their grass the way women talk about their hair. It is never thick enough or the right color. And heaven forbid it should have a weed in it—a blemish worse than a gray hair.

I think wanting to have a lawn that is your pride and joy is fine, and I can also empathize with those who find mowing and raking the lawn a relaxing way to spend a day outdoors. At times I've felt the same way. But too often the quest for lawn perfection leads to lawn madness—a mania that causes people to dump absurd amounts of herbicides, insecticides and chemical fertilizers on their lawn whether these are needed or not. People in the advanced stages of lawn madness even use dyes to make their grass greener and chemical growth retardants to keep it from growing too fast! My own philosophy, as with the other kinds of gardening discussed in this book, is that such perfection is rarely worth the chemical means used to achieve it. I believe that a healthy environment is more beautiful than an unblemished rose, tomato, or lawn. And that safer methods of lawn care can actually keep your lawn in better condition than the chemicals allow. Lawn grasses are very tough, resilient plants that shouldn't need much care beyond mowing if you choose the right ones and give them the right growing conditions. Here are the steps that I consider most important to having a good lawn.

Preparing the Site

If you have no lawn at all and have to start from scratch, you are lucky. You have a chance to start off right. While there are steps you can take to improve an established lawn, they will make much less difference than those you can take at the outset. The following instructions for preparation apply as well to areas intended for ground covers.

MAJOR GRADING

The first thing you need to do is take a look at the whole area where the lawn is to go and see if it needs to have its drainage corrected (page 40). Grass planted in spots where water sits will not grow well and will be prone to disease. At the same time, look at the lay of the land and see what grading you need to do. Your lawn need not be perfectly flat unless you are constructing a very formal area, or one where you'll want to play sports that require a flat lawn such as tennis, badminton, volleyball or croquet. Nevertheless, some major grading is usually necessary, if only to give the lawn a smooth, rolling appearance instead of a lumpy one. Whenever possible try to make your lawn slope away from, not toward, the foundations of buildings so that water drains away from them. Do not plan lawn areas on slopes that look too steep to be mowed easily and safely; either terrace them to make flat sections that are mowable, or plant ground covers on the slopes instead. If you have a large lawn, or if the grade problems are major, you may need to bring in a bulldozer to do it. Otherwise use a shovel and rake to create the grade you want.

REMOVING OBSTACLES

You will also need to remove rocks from the lawn. While lawn grasses are relatively shallow rooted as plants go, and therefore most roots are near the surface, some may go down a foot or more. Besides, soil with large rocks under it dries out much more quickly than unrocky soil and will give you brown patches in the lawn. If there is ledge or large rocks you can't remove that are closer to the surface than, say, 6 inches, you should either spread more soil over them or plant something other than grass in those spots. Even small rocks close to the surface can give the lawn a spotty appearance. I would say any rock larger than an egg in the top 2 to 3 inches of

soil should go. Below this level you only have to worry about removing larger rocks, and the deeper you go, the larger the rocks you can ignore. Most rocks will work their way up in time, but at least you'll have gotten the new grass off to a good start. Remove all debris as well, including buried logs and pieces of wood. Most likely you will remove some of the rocks while grading and the rest later on when you till the ground.

IMPROVING THE SOIL

After you've finished the major grading it's time to go to work on the soil. Everything I say about soil structure and fertility on pages 21–34 applies to the ground where you are going to put your lawn. The topsoil layer should be at least 6 inches deep. If it is less than that, either because it is naturally shallow or because of recent construction or the grading you have just done, it is a good idea to add more topsoil and spread it evenly, getting it as close to 6 inches deep as you can. If possible buy topsoil that has been screened to remove rocks, plant roots and other debris. In a garden you might be able to create topsoil by adding organic matter; but most lawns are too large for this to be practical, so you have to bring it in from elsewhere.

Even if there is plenty of topsoil, it will probably need some improvement. It is a good idea to get a soil test as a first step. The test will tell you not only what nutrients you need to add to help the grass grow well, but also the soil pH, which should be corrected if it departs too much from the pH that most grasses prefer—about 6.5. Remember: a lawn is a permanent planting, and creating good soil is the most important thing you can do to ensure that your lawn will be successful. Incorporate plenty of organic matter into the soil (peat moss, compost, rotted manure, or whatever it is practical for you to obtain), tilling it under to a depth of at least 8 inches. A rototiller is a good aid if you can get hold of one. Remove rocks and debris as you go. Then go over the whole lawn with a heavy metal rake, continuing to remove any rocks or debris in the top layer and smoothing the surface.

The foregoing sounds like a lot of hard work, but believe me, when I've installed a new lawn I've found it very reassuring to know that by doing all this first, I've saved a lot of work for whoever will maintain the lawn thereafter.

When the surface is smooth, it is time to plant. But first make sure that you buy the right kind of grass; this is very important.

Choosing the Right Grass

What grass you plant depends partly on what your lawn will be used for. For example, creeping bent grass is good for golf courses, tall fescue is good for athletic fields, and a quick-growing annual grass such as annual ryegrass is good for temporarily preventing soil erosion. If, as is probable, you just want a permanent, all-purpose lawn that is partly for decoration and partly for play, you will find that different grasses are suitable for different parts of the country and to different degrees of sun and shade. Lawn grasses fall into two major categories: cool season and warm season.

COOL-SEASON GRASSES

Cool-season grasses, used primarily north of Zone 7, are hardy in northern winters; they stay relatively green in winter but are subject to stress in very hot weather and may brown if the weather is very dry. They tend to be fine textured and are mowed relatively high. They can be either grown from seed or started as purchased sod. While you can buy different kinds of seed individually (in "straight" lots), northern lawns are best planted with lawn-seed mixtures that are made up of several grasses. A mixture helps ensure the health of your lawn, since a disease or pest, or some other stress factor, is more likely to wipe out a lawn composed of only one grass species. A mixture also helps a new lawn to become established, because different grasses germinate at different rates. To understand this let's look at the grasses that might be contained in a typical cool-weather lawn-seed mix:

Kentucky bluegrass. Not native to Kentucky, but a European introduction, Kentucky bluegrass is the most widely planted lawn grass in America, and should make up at least 50 percent of any cool-season mixture. It makes a lush, dense, dark green lawn, spreads by rhizomes, and is very hardy. Old varieties, such as the standby 'Merion,' should not be cut shorter than 2½ inches, though newer ones such as 'Fylking' can be cut shorter.

Fine fescues. These are the same as "red fescues" and include the Chewings fescue group. Fine fescues are usually present in mixes because they are more shade- and drought-tolerant than Kentucky bluegrass. They may be 30 percent or 40 percent of the mix. Mow them as you would Kentucky bluegrass, though the Chewings types can be cut a bit shorter.

Perennial ryegrass. Up to 15 percent of the mix can be perennial ryegrass, but any greater percentage than this may keep the other grasses from developing. This grass becomes established much more quickly than the others, and thus it is often included as a "nurse grass" to shade the slower-sprouting species and help hold the soil as the others grow. Improved "turf-type" varieties don't turn brown at the tips after cutting as the old ones do.

Bent Grass. This very fine textured grass is sometimes included in cool-season mixtures as a nurse grass and is a good grass for cool, wet regions such as the Pacific Northwest. It is widely used for golf courses and can be mowed much shorter than most cool-season grasses.

WARM-SEASON GRASSES

These grasses go dormant and turn brown in cool weather, so they are not suited to northern climates, but they keep a good green color during the long, hot summers of the southern zones. They tend to have a coarser texture than cool-weather grasses, and they are mowed short (1 inch for most). Usually they are not planted by seed but as sod, sprigs or plugs (below), and they are usually planted straight, not in mixtures. Here are some of the more common warm-season grasses:

Bermuda grass. This is a vigorous, popular southern grass. Its improved varieties need more watering, feeding, mowing and dethatching than the old kind but are finer textured and do not brown as much in winter. None of them will do well in shade.

St. Augustine grass. I used to love to pull the runners of this grass out of my grandmother's Louisiana lawn because each came up in one seemingly endless strand, unlike the grasses back home. St. Augustine is coarse textured and difficult to mow; its chief value is its shade-tolerance.

Zoysia grass. This extremely durable grass is quite fine textured and tends to have few problems, with the exception of thatch (below). Though it will survive in cool climates it turns brown

in winter and is not recommended for the north.

Bahia grass. This coarse-textured grass spreads by seed and may be hard to eradicate once established. But it is well adapted to hot, dry climates such as that of Florida, and to sandy, poor soil. Mow it high (2–3 inches).

Carpet grass. A coarse but low-maintenance, disease-resistant grass for very warm, moist climates.

TRANSITION AREAS

If you live in an area where the winters are a bit too cool for warm-season grasses and the summers too hot for cool-season ones (generally, Zone 7), you may feel frustrated about finding the appropriate lawn grass. Try either the turf-type perennial ryegrass mentioned above or this one:

Tall fescue. Though rather coarse in comparison with other cool-season grasses, tall fescue makes a very durable lawn in transition states. It withstands hard traffic and playing, and newer varieties are finer textured than the old ones. It grows in bunches, takes some shade, and stays green all year.

Planting a Lawn

How you plant your lawn will naturally depend on where you live and what type of grass you are planting. The best time to plant the cool-season grasses is late summer or early fall. The soil is warmer than it is in spring, helping the grass to germinate and get off to a good start, and annual weeds will soon be killed by frost, whereas in spring they are just starting to marshal their forces. Since these grasses do their growing best in cool weather, you are giving them a good long stretch of it before they have to face the heat of summer, which is more traumatic to them than the cold of winter. Still, try to get the seed in at least four weeks before the average first frost date (six weeks is better yet) to let them establish a root system. Warm-season grasses, on the other hand, are started in spring so that they can enjoy a long stretch of the warm weather they like before they are subject to the stress of winter.

SOWING GRASS SEED

How thick you sow your seed is best determined by the directions on the package (3 pounds per 1,000 square feet is about average for a standard bluegrass mixture). I like to broadcast seed by hand, but many gardeners find it easier to use a spreader, either the kind that drops the seed or the kind that spins it out in a circular motion.

After the seed is sown it will grow even if left alone, but it will grow better if you do something to bring it into closer contact with the soil. Dragging a lawn rake lightly across seeded ground helps to mix seed in, and rolling it with a lawn roller to firm the earth slightly will also help. Don't worry about walking on the new seed; you'll notice that your footprints will be the places where the seed germinates first! Watering is also a good way to work the seed in, and watering helps seed to sprout. The ideal stroke of luck is to have a nice, steady, not-too-hard rain as soon as you've planted. Put down a light mulch to keep water run-off from taking the seed with it. It is very discouraging to see your carefully sown grass seed collecting in puddles. Salt hay, applied thinly enough so that you can see plenty of ground between the stalks, is the best mulch. Don't bother to remove it; when the grass is up you'll never even know the hay is there, and eventually it will rot. If you don't get any rain, keep sprinkling the seed to moisten it so it will germinate quickly.

PUTTING DOWN SOD

Some of the warm-season grasses are best started from sod, and sod is also a good way of starting cool-season grasses. The advantages? One is that you get instant lawn. Another is the fact that sod is easy to lay down on a slope; you won't have to worry about seed washing off. Finally, sod is weed-free. Disadvantages are sod's cost and the fact that it is harder work to lay heavy sod strips than to sprinkle light seeds.

Sod usually comes in a big roll and is less than an inch thick spread out. There is very little soil attached to the grass, so don't make the mistake of thinking you don't have to prepare the soil as deeply for sod as you do for seed. Lower the soil level next to walks or other hard surfaces to allow the sod to lie flush with them when it's laid. Try not to let the sod sit around more than a few days before you plant it, and keep it moist. Once sod dries out it dies; it cannot be revived with water the way established grass can.

To lay sod, water the ground thoroughly, then cut off blocks of sod in a size you can handle easily, laying them in staggered courses the way you would bricks, making sure the edges are fitted tightly together and cutting pieces to fit along curves and odd-shaped corners. Then water again. Keep the sod well moistened until the roots have taken hold and you can no longer pull up clumps with your hands.

PLANTING PLUGS AND SPRIGS

Some grasses are sold as little plugs of sod or individual bare-root sprigs. These can be planted individually, just as you would any small perennial plants. Set plugs out at the recommended distance apart (the supplier should give you guidance about planting the particular type of grass you have purchased) in a grid pattern or in staggered rows. The plugs will fill in the spaces between them fairly quickly, since most of the grasses planted in this manner are vigorous spreaders. Nevertheless it is a good idea to sow some annual ryegrass along with them; it will deter weeds while the soil is bare, and the ryegrass will die out or be smothered out by the grass you have planted. Sprigs, which are individual rooted stems, are best planted in furrows, but it may be tedious to plant them this way if you have a very large area. In this case just scatter the sprigs on the surface, mulch them lightly with a material like shredded bark or straw and tamp or roll them. Whichever method you use, keep the sprigs watered until they take hold.

Maintaining a Lawn

Once you have your lawn properly installed, the amount of work it requires will depend partly on the grass you have chosen (some grasses grow faster than others, for example), partly on your climate (you'll have to water more in dry areas) and in large part on your own requirements: you may be satisfied with having a serviceable lawn that remains more-or-less green, or you may be fussier, insisting for example that all the green comes from bona-fide lawn grass and not from whatever weeds turn up. Though you will decide yourself just how much time or money you want to put into the lawn, do keep your priorities in order. Here's how.

MOWING

The most important thing to know about maintaining a lawn is how to mow it properly. Use whatever type of mower suits you (page 100) and follow these general principles:

Mow grasses to the correct height. Each grass has a height at which it does best. Don't cut it too long or too short. Weather can also influence how high you should mow your grass. Cool-season grasses should be mowed slightly higher in hot weather than in cool, to stress them less; warm-season grasses should be mowed slightly higher in cool weather than in hot, for the same reason. Mow any grass a bit higher if it is in a shaded spot.

Mow the lawn regularly. This helps to control weeds, by cutting annual weeds' stems before they can go to seed and by restraining the vigor of perennial weeds. If you let the grass go too long between mowings you will not only have a weedy lawn, but it will be hard to cut and may turn brown when you do mow it because you will be exposing the part of the blade that has been shaded and can't stand the sun. Cutting tall grass will also leave heavy piles of clippings that can kill the turf. The rule of thumb is to cut no more than a third of a blade's length, so that if you have a bluegrass lawn that grows best at 2 inches, for example, you would mow before it got higher than 3 inches. Cutting too short, on the other hand, can keep grass from forming a good root system.

Often we end up mowing our lawns once a week regardless of factors such as these, simply because weekends are the only time we have to mow or because the person you hire to mow the lawn is on a fixed schedule. But if you or your lawn service can be flexible enough to mow more often when the grass is really leaping up (in spring or after a rainy spell), and hold off when it is growing slowly, the lawn will be better off.

Do not cut the grass when it is wet. Wet grass is not only harder to cut, it cuts raggedly.

Avoid mower damage. Be very careful not to bump up against the trunks of shrubs and trees. (The mulching technique described on page 531 is a good way to avoid this.) Laying down a brick, wood or flagstone mowing strip on which to run one wheel of the mower is a handy way to edge flower beds without chopping up valuable plants or their flowers (page 57). But even with these tricks you will need to use some kind of trimmer on areas that the mower is too large or clumsy to do (page 100).

Leave the clippings. It is not necessary to rake up lawn clippings unless the grass is very high when you cut it. You can, of course, rake clippings up if you are collecting them to use as compost or mulch. But otherwise just let them decompose and return nutrients to the lawn's soil.

Keep your mower sharp. Dull blades will fray and chew up your lawn. You'll probably need to have the mower sharpened several times each season.

FEEDING

If you have prepared the soil well and chosen a grass that likes your climate, you may need to feed your lawn only rarely, if at all. Probably more problems are caused by feeding lawns too much, or with the wrong stuff, or at the wrong time, than by not feeding them at all. Producing too much lush growth by overfeeding can make grass prone to disease and cause a thatch layer to build up (below) because so much plant matter is decomposing. Putting too much chemical fertilizer on a lawn can burn it,

and too-frequent applications can cause harmful salts to build up in the soil because rain and watering can't flush them away quickly. In addition, grass plants that exist on quick-fix fertilizer applications near the soil surface are not encouraged to form deep roots; they are puny plants that need to be fed more often than vigorous plants.

If you do feed your grass, do it on a dry day, but not during drought when there is no moisture to carry the fertilizer down to the plants' roots. More than one or two applications per year are rarely necessary. In cool climates a feeding in late summer or early fall will encourage root growth, for the same reasons given above for fall planting of cool-season grasses. You can also give the grass an early-spring feeding, just as the grass is ready to start greening up. For the warm-season grasses grown in warm climates spring is the best time to feed, though you can feed any time if the grass really needs it. If your soil is very sandy, fertilizer will leach out of it quickly, and despite good soil preparation you may have to feed frequently— as often as once a month during the growing season. If you're not sure what your lawn's nutrient requirements are, a yearly soil test before feeding will be helpful.

For feeding the lawn, I suggest using a slow-release organic fertilizer formulated especially for that purpose: it should be high in the nitrogen that leaf crops such as grass need. Or you might mix up a homemade brew using a nitrogen source such as blood meal, fish meal or cottonseed meal, combined with a phosphorus source such as bone meal and a potassium source such as greensand (page 33). Sprinkle this on the lawn and water it in well.

WATERING

Most of what I've said about feeding lawns applies to watering them as well. If you've built a good lawn with the right grass and plenty of organic matter in the soil, it should survive dry periods. Even if the grass goes dormant and looks brown, there is no need to panic and waste water if it is a scarce resource where you live: the lawn usually revives when wet weather returns.

The most important thing to know about watering is that you should either water deeply or not at all. A shallow sprinkling of water on the surface causes roots to grow toward the surface rather than down deep where you want them to go. It's best to water at the beginning of the day and let the sprinkler soak the lawn for several hours, perhaps watering a different section each day. Allowing the soil to dry out between deep waterings will help the lawn to resist disease.

In some parts of the country dry weather may make it very difficult to keep a lawn green. Some gardeners install underground sprinkler systems that do the job. My advice is to choose drought-resistant grasses in preference to laying out fancy irrigation systems. Then try using some of the simpler watering devices described on page 96 before you resort to more expensive measures. And don't overwater your lawn, either; this can deprive the roots of oxygen and cause disease as well.

DETHATCHING

Thatch is a layer of dead grass parts that forms just above the soil surface of a lawn. There is always a thatch layer in grass, but sometimes it gets too thick and causes problems. Thatch buildup is more common with southern grasses and usually results from feeding or wa-tering too much or from mowing too infrequently and leaving thick piles of clippings on the lawn. If thatch is more than a half-inch thick it can harbor insect pests and keep water and nutrients from penetrating down to the grass roots. Some grasses are more prone to thatch than others. If your grass has a springy, spongy feel, like carpet with a thick foam-rubber pad under it, and if you are able to see the thatch if you poke down among the grass with your fingers, the thatch is too thick.

Try raking the grass with a heavy metal rake or a dethatching rake; you can pull a lot of it out this way. But if the thatch is too heavy or the lawn too large for this to be practical, rent a dethatching machine, also called a "vertical power mower." This machine has tines that dig down into the soil and pull up the thatch. In cool climates you should dethatch in early fall so that you can spread fresh grass seed over the lawn.

LAWN WEEDS

Weeds are not as conspicuous in a lawn as they are in a garden, because they blend into the green. Technically a lawn weed is anything that is not part of the original grass formulation that you planted, but there are usually some extraneous wild grasses and broad-leaved plants in purchased grass seed, and others invariably seed themselves from the wild. Often weeds are not very noticeable. It is only when a lot of broad-leaved plants or coarse-textured grasses start to intrude that the appearance of the lawn suffers. In the normal course of things lawn grasses grow so vigorously that they crowd most weeds out. If anything weakens the vigor of your lawn grass, however, broad-leaved plant species may take over. If there are bare patches due to infertile soil, crabgrass will make itself at home. Compacted soil can also encourage weeds. In these cases the best course may be to renovate the soil as described below, or even to start over again with better soil and new grass, although such drastic measures are seldom needed.

Traditional means of lawn weed control involve the use of herbicides: either preemergent weed killers that keep annual weeds like crabgrass from germinating, applied between forsythia and lilac time, or products that kill only broad-leaved plants without harming grasses. I don't use either. Not only are they toxic to people and animals, they are also apt to drift or wash onto other plantings and damage them. As part of commercially prepared combinations of weeding and feeding formulations herbicides are often applied indiscriminately and excessively.

My approach to lawn weeds is to tolerate many of them, especially those that bloom. Once I was working on someone's perennial garden and took a close look at the adjacent lawn, which the lawn service had abandoned for a week or two. It was starting to look like one of those "flowery meads" that you see in medieval tapestries, where little clumps of flowers are spotted here and there in a sea of green. Though the lawn grasses no doubt suffered from such neglect, I couldn't help but feel that lawn in that state looked just as pretty as the flower bed I was so carefully constructing. Flowers in the lawn encourage butterflies, bees and other desirable insects, too. (Bees especially love the clover, so watch your bare feet!)

Some lawn weeds that bloom nicely are ajuga, veronica, ground ivy, pussytoes, dandelions, violets, English daisies and Quaker ladies—and there are many more. Most are short enough to escape the mower much of the time, though if there is a fine stand of ajuga sending up bright blue flower spikes in the lawn I will mow around it. Clover is another pretty lawn weed; in fact it is considered a weed only by some, and is often included in lawn-seed mixes because of its good green color and small leaves, and because as a legume it enriches the soil.

If there are a lot of less interesting weeds in a lawn, however, and if they really detract from its appearance, I would give hand-weeding a try. This may sound like a crazy proposition, especially if your lawn is a large one. But if you just do a section at a time when you have the energy for it, sprinkling some fertilizer and seed as you go to help the grass rebuild, you can make quite a bit of difference over the course of time.

Also keep in mind that regular mowing helps to keep weeds down. It lops off the heads of annual weeds before they can go to seed and can set back the growth of some perennial weeds.

Lawn Diseases

There are a number of diseases that lawn grasses can contract. Here are a few to watch for:

Brown patch produces roughly circular patches that are purplish and then turn brown, becoming several feet in diameter. It can plague bent grasses, fescues and most southern grasses, especially in hot, humid weather and can be cured by holding back on water and fertilizer and by improving drainage.

Snow mold is a grayish, stringy fungus that lives under the snow and appears as round dead patches in spring. Prevent it by raking leaves off the lawn in fall and avoiding too-late applications of fertilizer in fall. Mow late in the fall, since snow mold breeds in tall grass.

Dollar spot, which afflicts bent grasses, Bermuda grass and others, causes whitish spots the size of silver dollars. Fight it with water and a high-nitrogen fertilizer.

Stripe smut gives the grass blades a black and sooty, yellow or gray appearance; grow varieties that resist it. Fertilizing in fall will also help control it.

Melting-out produces purple-bordered spots on grass leaves, which then die. If drainage is poor, try to improve it, and mow higher.

Fairy rings are caused by fungi, usually from woody matter such as stumps or pieces of wood buried in the soil. Large, dark green circles magically appear on the lawn, often with mushroomlike growths. They are best fought with fertilizer and lots of water, and by aerating the soil to let these penetrate.

Most lawn diseases are caused by fungi and can be eradicated with fungicides. But these are not practical for the average gardener to apply. Diagnosing the disease, finding the right product to treat it, timing the application correctly and applying the agent often enough to kill the fungus are all pretty tricky—and not worthwhile.

My advice is try to identify the disease so you'll know what you are treating, consulting your local Extension Service agent if necessary. Apply extra water and fertilizer if this is indicated, though if you have been feeding or watering *too* much this may have been the initial cause of your trouble. Cutting the lawn higher, or aerating the lawn with a heavy rake or an aerator (below) can also help fight disease.

Usually a disease will simply go away by itself as soon as the weather changes, and the lawn will then recover. Keeping the lawn vigorous by following the advice given above will help it to resist diseases and, if they should strike, to withstand them. Also, more and more new lawn-grass varieties are being developed that resist specific diseases.

Again, your Extension Service can probably direct you to varieties that are the least susceptible to whatever plagues your lawn. If the problem recurs often enough you may want to start over with a new lawn, planting a resistant grass.

But before you do anything this drastic make sure it really is a disease that is making the lawn unsightly. Insect damage, spilled gasoline or other chemicals, road salt, spilled fertilizer, the urine of female dogs, can all cause dead patches that look like disease symptoms, though they tend to be more irregular than patches caused by disease. If you can trace the problem to a spilled toxic substance, flush the spot with water to dilute the harmful agent.

Lawn Pests

A number of insect pests can cause problems in lawns, but usually the damage is not too serious. If you find damage in irregularly-shaped patches and have ruled out chemical spills, look hard and see if you can find and identify the culprit.

Grubs are often found in lawns. These are the larvae of beetles such as Japanese beetles and June bugs that live in the soil and feed on grass roots. You can diagnose the problem quickly by the fact that a dried-out patch of grass peels back like a carpet; the reason is that the roots have been severed. You can also see the white grubs themselves, curled up like commas. Milky spore disease will combat them. (As a side benefit, you will also reduce the local population of adult Japanese beetles.) That treatment may take a few years to be effective in cool climates—if so you'll have to live with the problem for a while. Water the patches to revive the dry grass and get the roots to regrow.

Sod webworms are caterpillars that gnaw off the blades of bluegrass and drag them into little silk-lined tubes just above the soil surface, where they consume them. This causes small brown spots at first, then larger irregular patches in your lawn. The caterpillars turn into little tan-colored moths which you can see fluttering above the grass at dusk, laying eggs. The caterpillars themselves can only be found at night, but you can detect their presence from tiny, green, pelletlike droppings. Since the caterpillars like hot, dry grass, ample water will sometimes be enough to control them, or at least help the grass, dried out by their chewing, to renew itself.

Chinch bugs, which are tiny black-and-white creatures, live above the soil surface, feeding on the grass and creating irregular brown patches. The bugs themselves are found in the green grass on the edge of these patches. One way to see if you have them is to tap a bottomless coffee can into the soil a few inches, fill it with water, and see if any chinch bugs float to the top. Like sod webworms they prefer dry grass, and can be discouraged by watering, which also helps to restore the damaged grass. Some grasses, such as St. Augustine and zoysia, are bothered more than others by chinch bugs.

Most lawn insects are kept more-or-less under control by natural predators: the moles that eat grubs, the big-eyed bugs that eat chinch bugs, the birds that peck out the sod webworms. Gardeners and lawn services that dump insecticides on lawns kill these beneficial predators and also kill the earthworms that aerate the lawn's soil and the microorganisms that keep it fertile. Insecticides also sometimes kill household pets. Even poisons sprayed in large quantities on your neighbor's lawn can drift over to your place and be a hazard, so using them is a practice best discouraged on a neighborhood basis, if possible.

Try to keep your lawn healthy and vigorous, the better to weather these brief insect invasions. If a thick thatch layer is harboring insects, dethatch the lawn. One interesting new development is the marketing of grasses that contain "endophytes"—fungi that repel insects such as chinch bugs and sod webworms and fight some diseases as well. Some tall fescues and perennial ryegrasses contain them; look for other grasses with endophytes as well.

Renovating a Lawn

Sometimes, despite your best efforts, your lawn remains a disappointment. Often it is a lawn you have inherited from a previous owner who didn't plant the right grass or prepare the soil adequately. If only parts of the lawn have problems you can sometimes just fix those, patching dead spots with clumps of new sod, or cultivating the soil there and reseeding it. Rolling the soil will often help if grass roots have been heaved out of the soil by insects or moles. (See page 78 for more information about moles.)

Sometimes the lawn is compacted and needs to be aerated, although this is not often the case in northern lawns, where the action of frost in winter moves the soil and breaks up hard clumps. But where compaction is a problem you might consider renting an aerator—a machine that rolls over the soil and extracts cores of earth, which it then deposits on the soil surface. The best approach is to rake these up and use them to fill in low spots, then fill the holes you've made in the lawn with good compost or some other fertile organic matter.

If the entire lawn is hopeless, use a

tractor or rototiller to till up the whole thing, burying clumps of sod and adding whatever soil amendments are needed. Sod clumps that are lying on the surface should be raked up so that the surface is smooth. Then reseed as you would for a brand-new lawn. If the old grass is a kind that you want to keep from regrowing, strip it off or use a glyphosate herbicide on it (page 57) before you till it under, waiting a week or two until the grass is completely dead.

Using Ground Covers

G round covers are a rather broad category of plants and include just about anything that will cover the ground quickly and thoroughly. They might be shrubs, vines, herbaceous perennials or even annuals that you reseed each year or that seed themselves. Some accomplish their ground-covering feats by means of underground stolons or rhizomes which venture out and send up new shoots, or by above-ground runners that do the same thing. Others spread by branches that trail on the ground and root, yet others simply by being long-stemmed and floppy, like cotoneaster or *Rosa wichuraiana*. Probably the most useful ground covers are low-growing, perennial, and evergreen. Like grass these are grown primarily for their foliage, though if a ground cover were to cover itself in blue flowers, as periwinkle does, who could object? The trick is finding the right one for the spot.

Designing with Ground Covers

I f you want a ground cover that you can look at all year, choose an ever-green one like pachysandra. If year-round good looks are not an important consideration, you can choose among the many fine deciduous ground covers such as epimedium, sweet woodruff, pulmonaria and lily-of-the-valley. Many of these flower so beautifully that you'll forgive them for taking a winter vacation. If the ground cover must be a flat carpet to set off other plantings, choose a very low-growing one such as Irish moss (*Arenaria verna*), dichondra (a broad-leaved plant that is treated like a lawn grass) or one of the prostrate sedums. If you want something with more height, pick a shrub ground cover like 'Arnold Dwarf' forsythia, Andorra juniper or one of the prostrate pyracanthas. If you want a very tidy look for a formal situation, pick a compact, well-behaved ground cover like wild ginger. In a more informal situation you can use a more sprawling plant like crown vetch.

Many vines make good ground covers, crawling along the ground and rooting. English ivy, woodbine and euonymus, all described in Chapter 13, are good examples. But remember that vines, given a chance, will climb, and you must expect them to head upward when they get to trees, shrubs and even small herbaceous plants, none of which is likely to appreciate the onslaught. Also keep in mind that just because a plant is spreading and vigorous, it is not necessarily what you want as a ground cover. Goutweed (page 159) is often sold as a ground cover and makes an attractive one, but it is much too invasive as it can infiltrate your whole property. Bittersweet and Hall's honeysuckle generally fall into the same category.

One of the best uses for ground covers is as a unifying theme. Let's say you have a shrub planting that runs across the front of your house. You've put a lot of different plants into it, either because you like variety or because you want to see something interesting, like foliage, flowers, or berries at different times of year. Planting the same ground cover in front of and around the bases of all the shrubs will tie the collection together visually and give it the appearance of a designed border rather than a hodgepodge. The effect will be even better if you carry out the same ground-cover theme in other areas—around the trees in the lawn, for instance, along the walk that leads to the front door or even in the side or rear areas of the property.

The ground cover you choose might echo the foliage texture or color scheme of the plants it complements. For example, I like to use periwinkle in the foreground of plantings with other broadleaved evergreens such as rhododendrons and Japanese holly. All have smooth, dark green leaves, though in different sizes—those of the periwinkle fall between the long, narrow leaves of the rhododendrons and the tiny, round ones of the holly. In other situations a contrast might be needed instead. I might combine the rounded leaves of wild ginger, densely crowded in a low carpet, with the lacy fronds of ferns.

Often the ground covers themselves are the focal point: a planting of spiky lilyturf next to a patio; a circle of epimedium beneath a maple; or several ground covers combined, like the sweet woodruff, periwinkle and ajuga mingling together under birches in the drawing at the beginning of this chapter. Whether you display these specimens in a formal or informal way depends on the situation. I'd probably make the lilyturf planting a regular shape, edged neatly on the sides and mulched, whereas the planting under the birches would be more random, seeking its own shape. I might weed out some of one species if it threatened to crowd out the others, but I'd be happy if the planting had a free-form look.

Ground Covers for Special Situations

Often a ground cover solves the problem of what to plant in a difficult spot. Here are some examples:

Shady sites. Many ground covers will grow in shade, whereas most grasses will not. So shade is probably the situation where ground covers are most often used. Among the shade-tolerant ones described in the List of Ground Covers are ajuga, epimedium, lamium, lily-of-the-valley, pachysandra, pachistima, periwinkle, pulmonaria, sweet woodruff, wild ginger and wintergreen. But there are many others not on the list including the wild woodland species described on page 561. Do note how much shade the site has, however (see page 37 for different types of shade), and make sure that the light available is enough for the plants you choose. You may have to prune the lower limbs of some trees to let in a bit more light.

Sunny sites. Some sun-loving or sun-tolerant ground covers described in the List of Ground Covers are bearberry, heather, and lilyturf. But also try sedum, perennial candytuft, creeping veronica (*Veronica prostrata*), woolly yarrow (*Achillea tomentosa*), mat-forming pinks such as *Dianthus alpinus* 'Allwoodii,' ornamental grasses such as *Hakonechloa* and blue fescue (*Festuca ovina glauca*), and creeping herbs such as chamomile and thyme.

Dry sites. Some good ground covers for dry places are bearberry, thyme, sedum, pyracantha, lavender cotton (*Santolina chamaecyparissus*), St. Johnswort (*Hypericum*) and any of the prostrate junipers.

Moist sites. In moist soils use ground covers such as sweet woodruff, bunchberry, violets, heather, mint, bog-rosemary (*Andromeda polifolia*) and forget-me-not (*Myosotis scorpioides*).

Banks. To keep a steep bank from eroding you need a vigorous ground cover that spreads quickly, with roots that go deep enough to really hold the soil. Bearberry is a good one, as are spreading cotoneaster, juniper, day lilies (especially the wild *Hemerocallis fulva*), 'Arnold Dwarf' forsythia, crown vetch, English ivy and *Rosa wichuraiana*. It is best to plant perennial ground covers on a bank, so that the soil will be held all year long.

Ground covers with bulbs. Ground covers and spring bulbs are a great combination because the foliage of the ground cover helps hide that of the bulbs once they have finished blooming. This is especially true if small bulbs such as crocuses are used. But be sure to match the ground cover to the bulb: pachysandra is so tall and thick that a short bulb like crocus or glory-of-the-snow would be lost in it. And sweet woodruff is too low-growing to hide the large, conspicuous leaves of hyacinths or tulips. Periwinkle looks good with almost any bulb; I like to use it because it is not a dense ground cover and it lets enough sun come through to warm the ground beneath it and encourage the bulbs to come up early. Ground covers are also excellent in combination with bulbs that bloom with no foliage. Fall-blooming colchicums, for example, look less naked when emerging from a bed of lily-turf than they do when planted all by themselves in bare ground.

Establishing Ground Covers

For permanent ground-cover plantings prepare your soil well to a depth of at least 6 to 8 inches, following the advice given in Chapter 2 and with the needs of the particular plants in mind. Most herbaceous ground covers are sold bare-root, often as bundles of rooted cuttings, and it usually makes sense to buy them in quantity—say, flats of fifty plants each—to make large plantings more affordable. In cold climates try to plant them in spring, so as to avoid having the roots heaved out of the earth by winter freezing and thawing, but if fall planting is necessary I have found that a shredded-bark mulch several inches thick will help prevent this heaving.

How closely you space the plants depends on how impatient you are to have the planting fill in, how quickly your chosen plant is expected to spread and how many plants you can afford to buy. If you plant periwinkle or pachysandra 6 inches apart, you will have a nice thick bed within two years. But if a large area is to be planted you may have to sacrifice patience for economy and set plants as far apart as a foot, waiting three or four years before your bed has a good, lush growth. Most ground-cover shrubs can go between 2 and 3 feet apart. Plant in staggered rows, with all the plants equidistant from one another. The farther apart you space the plants, the more useful a mulch can be in preventing weeds from filling in the gaps. Interplanting with spring bulbs and/or annuals can also tide you over while you are waiting for a ground cover to grow.

If you are planting on a bank, either terrace the slope or erect soil berms that will help the plants retain water. These look just like the water-catching saucers pictured on page 52, except that they are built up only on the downhill side of the plant.

While you are waiting for the planting to fill in, keep it mulched and remove any weeds that crop up. In established beds weeding can sometimes be difficult. For example, it may be very hard to remove weeds with long, creeping roots from plants like pachysandra and lily-of-the-valley, which have that kind of root themselves. Or you might have a bed of junipers so thickly grown that it is impossible to dig down and pull up grass that has worked its way into the soil. In both cases I might use the brush-dipped-in-glyphosate trick described on page 57, being very careful not to "paint" my ground cover at the same time. Even if you don't get all the weeds out, if you keep at it you can sharply reduce their numbers.

Propagating ground covers is usually easy, since they are naturally spreading plants. You can often divide them, layer them, root them from cuttings, or take some from a thick bed and transplant them to another spot where you'd like more of the same. More often than not, your best source will be a neighbor who has "pachysandra as far as the eye can see." "We have a pachysandra *farm*," she'll tell you. "*Please* come and take some." Now, how could you possibly say no?

LIST OF GROUND COVERS

AJUGA
Ajuga reptans

DESCRIPTION: This fast-spreading plant, sometimes called "bugle," has much to recommend it. It can take more foot traffic than most ground covers and is hardy to Zone 4. Once it is established, the rosettes of foliage form mats on the ground that keep weeds to a minimum. Ajuga is handsome: the leaves are a rich dark green that turns to bronze in fall, and they last long past frost. (In Zones 8–10 the plant is evergreen.) Some varieties such as 'Bronze Beauty' are bronze all season. Others are variegated, such as 'Burgundy Glow,' which is marked with white, purple and pink. In late spring the plants send up lovely spikes of flowers, about 8 inches tall. Usually they're an intense blue, but you can also find white, purple and red varieties. For some reason ajuga tends to appear, then disappear, in lawns according to a secret program all its own. A related species, *A. pyramidalis,* is attractive but doesn't have the spreading habit.

HOW TO GROW: Plant in sun or shade in any good garden soil, but make sure it is well drained. The plants spread by surface runners and can be easily divided in spring for propagation.

BEARBERRY
Arctostaphylos uva-ursi

DESCRIPTION: This native American plant, also called *kinnikinick,* can be seen scrambling over sand dunes in seaside areas. Though the stems can be many feet long, they are prostrate, and the plant is only about a foot tall. The stems root as they go and are good for holding the soil on steep banks. They also look terrific hanging over a wall. The attractive 1-inch leaves are evergreen, turning a bronze color in winter. Tiny, white, bell-like flowers appear in midspring, followed by red berries in late summer that stay on the plant a long time, to the delight of the birds. Hardy to Zone 2, the plant is widely grown on the west coast but will do well in many other areas. 'Point Reyes,' with good, dark green foliage, is a popular variety.

HOW TO GROW: Grow bearberry in full sun or part shade. It will do all right in good garden soil but is just as happy if the soil is dry, poor, rocky and sandy. It does not like to be transplanted and is best purchased and planted in sods, not bare-root. You can also grow it from cuttings or purchase small, nursery-grown plants and establish them while they're young.

EPIMEDIUM
Epimedium grandiflorum

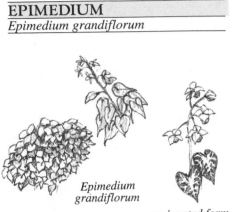

*Epimedium
grandiflorum*

variegated form

DESCRIPTION: Epimedium, also called "bishop's hat," is one of my favorite ground covers. It's one of those plants, like maidenhair fern, that looks dainty and delicate but is really as tough as they come—adaptable, easy to grow, and hardy to Zone 3. The small spurred flowers are supposed to resemble a bishop's miter, but they look to me like miniature columbines. The come in many different colors, depending on the variety—white, pink, red, yellow or lavender and appear in late spring. 'Rose Queen' is a good red, and 'Niveum' has large, showy white flowers. The heart-shaped leaves are pinkish when they first emerge in spring. They overlap in beautiful soft-looking mounds and last even into early winter, after turning a reddish bronze color.

Epimedium grows slowly when first planted, but like the tortoise that beat the hare it slowly and steadily establishes large, vigorous clumps. It will grow well even around the bases of trees, where it is a graceful addition.

HOW TO GROW: Epimedium prefers part shade but will grow in sun if you give it the moist, humusy soil in which it does best. Soil should be well drained and slightly acid. Since it is shallow rooted, try not to cultivate around it, but instead apply a light mulch to control weeds. Divide in spring, preferably while plants are dormant, cutting the tough roots with a knife.

HEATHER
Calluna vulgaris

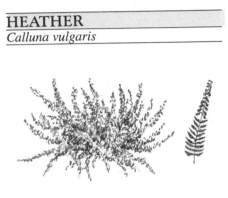

DESCRIPTION: Heather is one of my favorite plants because of its spiky shape, the subtle variations in its foliage colors and, best of all, its profuse, long-lasting summer bloom. Some varieties bloom for as long as three months, starting in summer and going into midfall. The plants vary in size but never exceed 2 feet. They bear their flowers along small spikes in shades of pink, red, purple, lavender or white. The tiny scalelike leaves are evergreen, often with startling colors such as yellow, red or gray, and it is fun to mix plants of different colors together. In fact, if you build a heather bed with different foliage colors, each of which has a different winter color as well and flowers of varied colors, you have quite a tapestry. While heather is outstanding in a bed all by itself, it also looks good as the foreground of a shrub planting. Some good standard varieties are 'J. H. Hamilton,' a pink; 'County Wicklow,' with double pink flowers and bright green foliage; and 'H. E. Beale,' a double pink that blooms very late. Most heathers are hardy to Zone 5.

HOW TO GROW: Plant heather in sun or part shade. It blooms best in sun, but part shade in winter will help it to withstand winter burn. In cold climates lay evergreen boughs over it in winter; these will protect it from sun, wind and cold, and will also trap the snow in an insulating blanket. In early spring you still may need to prune out winterkilled stems, but don't worry if the plants look beat-up at winter's end; as long as they are still alive, fresh new growth will appear after cutting. Give them acid, moist, well-drained soil, but don't make the soil too rich or the plants will be leggy. Heath (*Erica* species) is closely related and is also a fine plant; it is spring blooming, however, and has needlelike foliage.

LAMIUM
Lamium maculatum

Lamium
maculatum

Lamium
maculatum
'Beacon Silver'

Lamium
maculatum
'Album'

DESCRIPTION: Lamium is an excellent ground cover for shade. The common name is often given as "spotted dead nettle"—far too unattractive a title for this low-growing carpet of leaves with a stripe down the middle that can be white, yellow, red or silver. Lamium is evergreen from Zone 6 south. Even in Zone 5, where I live, they persist well into the winter. The erect flower clusters are long blooming, lasting from late spring to midsummer, and can be reddish purple, pink, or white depending

on the variety. 'Album' has white flowers and white-marked leaves; 'Beacon Silver' has pink flowers and silvery leaves.

If you set out a little nursery-grown pot of lamium in spring, you will have a lamium carpet by fall, and the following year you will probably be able to open your own lamium nursery with which to supply all your friends. It spreads rapidly by above-ground runners and is hardy to Zone 4.

HOW TO GROW: Grow lamium in part- or full shade if possible, but if the site is very sunny make sure the soil has plenty of moisture. Other than that lamium seems to have no special requirements and is easily propagated by division, cuttings or seed. If you do not want to open a lamium nursery, and it is crowding other plants, shear in midsummer to promote more compact growth.

LILY-OF-THE-VALLEY
Convallaria majalis

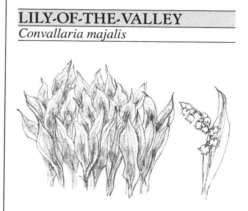

DESCRIPTION: Most people recognize the little white, bell-like flowers of this plant. Even the fragrance is unmistakable. The flowers are indeed beautiful and, naturalized in the right setting, lily-of-the-valley is a useful ground cover, but it can be a disappointment if it is in the wrong place. The leaves—two emerge to embrace each flower stalk—are not evergreen but start to turn brown in late summer and cannot be walked on at all. The roots are quite invasive, interfering with the growth of everything else in the plants' vicinity. Find a spot for it all its own. The plants produce orange berries after the flowers, but the berries are not profuse. The variety 'Rosea' is pink. Plants are hardy to at least Zone 3.

HOW TO GROW: Lily-of-the-valley does better in part- or full shade than it does in sun and will tolerate even dense shade. It likes a fertile, moist soil. Plants can be divided easily for propagation. If your bed is flowering poorly, divide and replant, or donate the excess to your favorite charity. Lily-of-the-valley is a good plant for a Mother's Day fundraiser.

LILYTURF
Liriope

DESCRIPTION: Lilyturf is valued for its evergreen, grasslike leaves and for the blue flower spikes, rather like those of grape hyacinth, that it sends up in late summer. These are followed by black berries. Big blue lilyturf (*Liriope muscari*) grows to 18 inches, with fairly broad, arching leaves; its flowers can also be lavender, purple or white de-

pending on the variety. It is clump-forming and an elegant ground cover in areas where it is hardy (to Zone 6). Creeping lilyturf (*L. spicata*) is a bit hardier (to Zone 5, generally), shorter (about 10 inches), with narrower leaves and a decidedly creeping growth habit. It spreads by underground rhizomes and bears pale lavender flowers in July and August.

HOW TO GROW: Lilyturf will grow in sun or shade and prefers fertile, moist soil enriched with plenty of organic matter. It dies to the ground in winter in the northern part of its range. If it looks bedraggled at winter's end, mow or cut it to the ground, and it will sprout fresh new growth.

PACHISTIMA
Pachistima canbyi

DESCRIPTION: Pachistima (also called "*paxistima*") is a woody shrub that grows along the ground, staying about a foot tall and rooting in the soil as it spreads. The narrow, dark green leaves, less than an inch long, are evergreen, turning bronze-colored in fall. Hardy to Zone 5, this is an excellent dense ground cover to use in shrub plantings, especially those with broad-leaved evergreens.

HOW TO GROW: Pachistima grows well in sun or shade but may need to be shielded from winter sun in cold areas. It likes a light, rich, acid soil and excellent drainage. The best way to propagate it is by layering, but it can also be grown from cuttings taken in midsummer, and by division.

PACHYSANDRA
Pachysandra terminalis

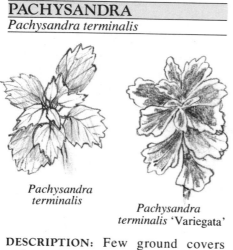

Pachysandra terminalis

Pachysandra terminalis 'Variegata'

DESCRIPTION: Few ground covers make such a thick, dense evergreen bed as pachysandra. It doesn't do its job overnight, but just wait, for, as the saying goes, the first year pachysandra sleeps, the second it creeps and the third it leaps. It is hardy to at least Zone 4, and is an excellent solution to the problem of what to plant right around tree trunks where sunlight is scarce and mowing is difficult. It grows up to a foot tall with attractive, dark green, tooth-edged leaves arranged in whorls. The white flower spikes in spring are neither numerous nor conspicuous; even less noticeable are the whitish berries that follow. The variety 'Variegata' has white-edged leaves and can effectively lighten up a dark, shaded area.

HOW TO GROW: Grow pachysandra in full or part shade, but avoid sunny sites. Not only will the leaves yellow in the sun, but grasses will come up amongst the pachysandra, and they are very difficult to eradicate. Any ordinary soil will do, but it should not be too dry and should be on the acid side. Plant pachysandra deeper than it was in the flat, so more roots will form along the stems. It roots very easily from cuttings. If you are planting some you have dug up at a friend's house, and are dismayed by all those long, tangled stems, separate them and tie each one in a knot, then plant them. I always mulch newly planted pachysandra, although once established it won't need mulch because it grows so thickly. If you have problems with leaf and stem blight, which begins with brown blotches on the leaves and spreads to the stems, don't use a heavy mulch, and rake fallen leaves and any diseased plants out of the bed. Euonymus scale is occasionally a problem with pachysandra; it is best dealt with by pruning out infested plants and spraying the others with dormant oil in early spring before growth starts.

PERIWINKLE
Vinca minor

DESCRIPTION: Also called "myrtle," this popular ground cover, about 6 inches tall, sends out runners over the soil surface that root where they touch ground. The handsome, dark green leaves are about an inch long, and the April-blooming flowers a cheerful blue. You can find varieties that are white or purple, but I like the old-fashioned "periwinkle blue" the best. There are also some varieties with variegated leaves. Periwinkle is probably the best all-purpose ground cover around and is hardy to at least Zone 5.

HOW TO GROW: Grow periwinkle in sun or shade, though some shade is preferable, especially in hot climates. Though it is not fussy about soils and will grow even in poor ones, it likes soil that is moist and slightly acid. I value it for its rather open growth habit, which allows me to interplant it with spring bulbs, but it can be sheared to promote denser growth.

PULMONARIA
Pulmonaria

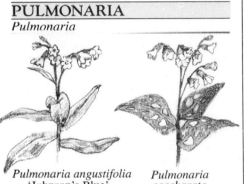

Pulmonaria angustifolia
'Johnson's Blue'

*Pulmonaria
saccharata*
'Mrs. Moon'

DESCRIPTION: This plant used to be called "lungwort" because its spotted leaves resembled diseased lungs and, in the homeopathic tradition of folk medicine, were thus supposed to be able to cure diseased lungs. Fortunately the plant has more demonstrable virtues. It spreads vigorously by creeping rhizomes, its broad leaves make it very attractive as a ground-cover planting and on top of that it bears beautiful clusters of tube-shaped flowers in spring, which generally open pink and turn to blue, resulting in both pink and blue flowers in the same cluster. *Pulmonaria angustifolia* is low growing (under 10 inches) and has leaves that are not spotted; pop-

ular varieties are 'Johnson's Blue' and the white 'Alba.' *P. saccharata,* called "Bethlehem sage," grows as tall as 15 inches. I like the variety 'Mrs. Moon,' whose blue flowers and spotted leaves are both large and very showy. If you find you get along well with pulmonarias, there are a number of other, less familiar species worth trying.

HOW TO GROW: Pulmonaria is a truly shade-loving plant and will wilt in sun. Even the morning sun that mine gets makes it wilt in hot weather. Soil need not be rich, but it should be full of organic matter to help it to hold moisture. Plants are easily divided in early spring but should be watered well after transplanting.

SWEET WOODRUFF
Asperula odorata (Galium odoratum)

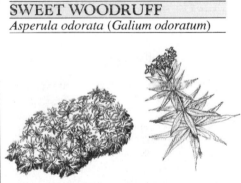

DESCRIPTION: Sweet woodruff carpets the ground with star-shaped whorls of bright green leaves, and blooms in frothy, fragrant white clusters in May and early June. It is the flavoring ingredient in May wine—something you can easily make yourself by steeping a handful of *Asperula odorata* in a good Moselle. It can be depended on as a ground cover under trees, even shallow-rooted ones.

HOW TO GROW: Grow sweet woodruff in part or full shade in fairly moist, well-drained, slightly acid soil. Divide it in early spring or early fall by simply picking up a clump and putting it somewhere else, then watering it well.

WILD GINGER
Asarum

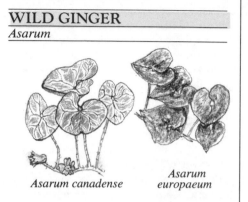

Asarum canadense   *Asarum europaeum*

DESCRIPTION: This is one of my favorite ground covers, the rounded leaves crowding together in a dense, tidy, elegant mat. (It bears flowers too, but these are completely hidden by the leaves.) Wild ginger gets its name from the pungent smell and taste of its leaves and roots. Our native species, *Asarum canadense,* is hardy to Zone 4 but is not evergreen. There are, however, two evergreen species you can grow (hardy to Zone 5): British Columbia wild ginger, *A. caudatum,* and European wild ginger, *A. europaeum.*

HOW TO GROW: Wild gingers like rich soil, but the essential ingredients are shade, moisture and a soil with plentiful organic matter. It will tolerate full shade, and the creeping rootstocks are easily divided and transplanted.

WINTERGREEN
Gaultheria procumbens

DESCRIPTION: This very low growing native plant has shiny evergreen leaves that turn purplish in fall and taste like peppermint. It bears little, nodding, white bell-shaped flowers in late spring, followed by bright red edible berries in fall, which last into winter. It is a delicate little plant, especially good in wooded areas, and is hardy to at least Zone 4.

HOW TO GROW: Wintergreen does best in part shade, in moist, acid, humus-rich soil. It spreads by creeping stems and is best transplanted from sods or nursery-grown clumps. Propagate it by division.

VINES

Vines are a little like willful children. They set forth with a great sense of purpose, determined to climb as fast as possible into the light-filled air above them, using anything they can to help themselves up and often taking up more space than you want to give them. But watch a vine when it finds no means of support: the growing shoot just hangs in midair, looking disappointed, and then falls to the ground, ready to try again. For all their ambition, most vines need attentive guidance from the gardener, who helps and directs them in their climb and restrains them at the same time.

Working with vines can be fun if you understand their habits and know some attractive ways to use them in the landscape. And yet the reasons that gardeners plant vines often sound rather negative. A building has a bare, ugly wall: let a vine cover it. The house next door is an obtrusive presence: build a fence covered with vines that will hide it. A terrace is too hot to sit on in summer: build an arbor so that a dense vine can shade it. But there are many positive reasons to grow vines too. Many have attractive leaves, flowers or fruits, and their twining, clinging or reaching growth habits make them a good visual contrast with the other plants around them. Some vines in the garden are "working vines," and some are displayed for their beauty alone. Most vines can be functional and ornamental at the same time.

Some vines are truly low-maintenance plants that will go their way with a minimum of nurturing and discipline; others you must fuss over. But all of them must be chosen carefully and placed carefully. Most troubles with vines come from using the wrong vine for a given spot.

Vines are not a distinct category of plant whose members have a lot in common. Some are annual, and some perennial. Some are herbaceous (soft stemmed), and some are woody. Some are hardy; some are tender. Some are vigorous and fast growing; some are more restrained. Vines also differ in the ways they climb. In fact the only thing that all vines have in common is that they have long but weak stems that must be supported, either by your efforts, theirs, or a combination of the two.

Types of Vines

Vines are generally divided into groups according to their primary method of climbing:

VINES THAT TWINE

Some vines grow by twining their stems around an object, preferably a vertical one. In the wild their support is most often a tree; in your garden it could be a tree, a pillar, a fence post, a downspout or anything small in diameter (a silo, for instance, would be too thick for a twining vine) yet sturdy enough to support the vine's weight. What support you provide will depend on the type of vine and the way it behaves in your climate. (See the individual descriptions in the List of Vines.) Wisteria is a typical twining vine.

A vine starts to twine when it touches an object. Sensitive tissues respond by producing cells faster on one side of the vine than the other, so that it bends as it grows and continues to bend round and round the object. Just as people are right- or lefthanded, so are twining vines, which you will hear described as twining "from right to left" and "from left to right." I find this terminolgy confusing, since the direction of twist is different depending on where you stand when you view the plant. I prefer "clockwise" and "counterclockwise" to describe vines' twists. These directions are easy to see when you look at a honeysuckle, which goes clockwise, and a bittersweet, which goes counterclockwise. Sometimes the direction varies even within a given species; some wisterias, for example, twine one way, and some twine the other. The only reason you'd ever need to know which way a vine twines is so you avoid trying to direct it the wrong way. As soon as it starts up its support you will be able to tell and thus cooperate with it.

VINES THAT CLING WITH TENDRILS

These vines sometimes twine, but their chief means of support is tendrils—little threads that grow out from the stem and wrap themselves around something. Sometimes tendrils are actually leaf stems. Examples are clematis and grape vines. When the vine touches an object it produces these tendrils very quickly, but the object must be thin enough for the tendrils to wind around. Wire mesh or lattice are both satisfactory supports for tendril vines, though here again the supports must be strong enough to hold them up. A clematis will do fine on a piece of chicken wire, but a grape vine needs a strong wooden or metal support. Vines that climb by tendrils in the wild use the branches of other vegetation.

VINES THAT CLING WITH HOLDFASTS

Some vines, when they touch an object, can quickly produce appendages that will adhere to it. The two chief kinds are aerial rootlets, which are short, hairlike projections from the sides of the stem, and adhesive disks, which are little round plates at the ends of thin tendrils.

The rootlets work by burrowing into even the tiniest fissures in the surface they are climbing, and the disks work by suction. Both devices enable vines to climb flat vertical surfaces, which would foil a twining vine or one with tendrils since they offer nothing for the vine or its tendrils to wrap around. In the wild, the support might be a tree trunk or a rock; in cultivation, a wall of brick, stone or any kind of masonry can provide a support. Ivy is an example of a vine with aerial rootlets. Virginia creeper has adhesive disks.

VINES WITHOUT SUPPORTS

Technically, perhaps, the plants in this category are not vines, but they are grown like vines. They have long, arching branches or canes that, in the wild, can reach through the stouter branches of other plants and thus be supported. Some, such as the climbing roses described in Chapter 11, have thorns that help them hook onto other plants; others just rely on the dense branching patterns of the plants that support them. The climbing jasmines are examples of this type. In the garden, vines without natural support might be given considerable assistance to keep them from falling down.

Landscaping with Vines

With these distinctions in mind, let's look at some of the vines that are available and the ways in which they can be used.

VINES ON FENCES

The most common request I hear for vines is from people with a fence they want to cover. Usually the fence is a necessary evil: the fence around the swimming pool that is required by law in some areas; the fence that keeps children or animals in—or out; the fence along the property boundary that hides the yard next door. Often there is quite a bit of fence, and the gardener is tempted to plant rather rampant vines that will cover it quickly. This is fine if the fence is a very sturdy one and can support a big, heavy vine, but many are not. I often advise people to plant ornamental vines that they enjoy looking at, which will merely soften the visual impact of the fence without covering it completely. Let's say you have a split-rail fence around your pool with wire mesh attached to it. If you plant clematis, climbing roses and morning glories along it they will not totally disguise the wire, but your eye will be drawn to them, not to the wire.

Similarly, a tall wooden barrier on your property line might be an eyesore, but if you plant the right vines it will seem as if the fence were there just to display them. Tendril vines like clematis can be grown if some green plastic-coated wire mesh is hung on the fence. Even a twining vine like wisteria will work if the fence is sturdy and if there are some wood or metal projections to which you can fasten the wisteria with wire. It is not, however, a good idea to grow vines that cling with rootlets or disks on wood fences; they injure the wood both by penetrating it and by keeping it too moist, causing it to rot. And you can't paint a fence with a clinging vine on it.

A chain-link fence is one that you might want to cover entirely with vegetation, and fortunately this is easy. Plant any big vines that you like on it and turn it into a hedge. Whatever the vines' own means of support, you can guide them through the openings in the mesh or secure them to it, even if they don't do it themselves.

VINES ON BUILDINGS

A vine and a building can have a good relationship or a bad one; it's a matter of choosing the right vine. If it's a good match, the vine will profit not only from the building's support but also from its warmth, which will cause the vine to grow rapidly and perhaps survive the winter in a zone in which it is only borderline hardy. In return the vine will not only lend beauty to the wall, but often cool it in summer and, if the vine is evergreen, warm it in winter.

If the vines and buildings are badly matched, however, the vines can do real damage. Vines that cling with disks or rootlets (and sometimes even vines with tendrils) are unsuitable for wooden buildings for the same reason they are unsuitable for wooden fences. They can also damage vinyl or aluminum siding, and even masonry if the mortar is loose or crumbly. Such vines are often grown on masonry structures, however, including brick, stone, concrete and stucco, and they will usually support themselves completely. Ivy on stone and brick buildings has become a veritable symbol of established tradition. But watch out for window frames, shutters and shingles, which these vines can damage. You may have to get up on a ladder from time to time and cut away parts of the vine that look like they mean mischief, and you'll have to provide wire supports if the surface is smooth or the vine very heavy.

If you have a wooden house but a large masonry chimney from the ground up, you can grow a clinging vine, but again, keep it off the wood. Similarly, a large expanse of ugly concrete foundation can be effectively hidden with a clinging evergreen vine such as *Euony-*

SOME WAYS TO SUPPORT VINES

Fig. 62

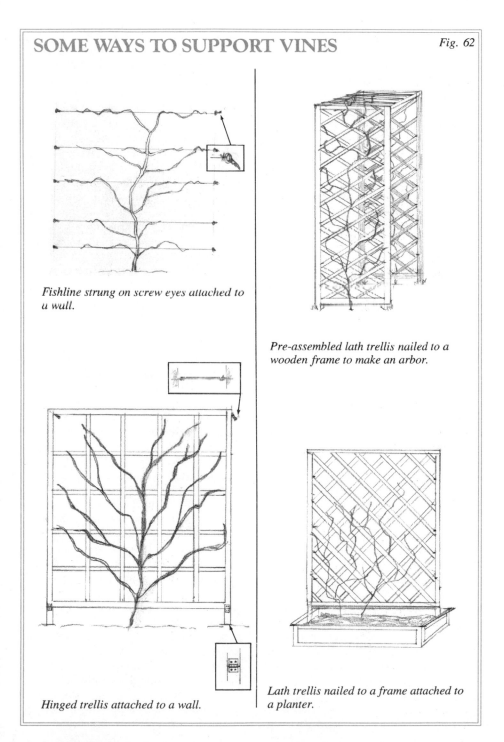

Fishline strung on screw eyes attached to a wall.

Pre-assembled lath trellis nailed to a wooden frame to make an arbor.

Hinged trellis attached to a wall.

Lath trellis nailed to a frame attached to a planter.

mus fortunei vegeta, as long as you clip it off as soon as it climbs high enough to reach wooden clapboards. With free-standing masonry walls that are not part of a building, this is not a problem; a vine like ivy or euonymus can ramble to its heart's content. Even a tumble-down stone wall is a fine place for a clinging vine. Let a climbing hydrangea cover it, for example.

You can grow vines that twine on both wood or masonry buildings, but you need to provide them with something to twine around. If the vine is a light one—a morning glory, for example, or a soft-stemmed clematis, you can tie horizontal lengths of transparent fishing line to screw eyes in the area you want the vine to climb. For heavier vines such as passion flower you can use copper wire, which will quickly weather to an unobtrusive green. For very heavy vines such as wisteria or honeysuckle you'll need a stout wooden trellis. If the building is wood you'll probably want to paint the trellis the same color as the building, position it so that there is a space for air to circulate between the vine and the building, and make your support removable. The hinged trellis shown in Figure 62 is one solution.

VINES ON TREES

Vines are usually thought to be bad for trees. Often this is indeed the case. Heavy, large-leaved vines such as grape can cut off the light from a tree and kill it, and even soft little vines like ground ivy—a common weed—can creep into a specimen shrub and, by depriving some branches of light, distort its shape. But properly chosen and properly pruned, vines can enhance the appearance of trees that support them.

For example a climbing hydrangea will cling to the trunk and gradually climb up into the tree without harming it. By clothing the trunk of a tall tree with a vine, you make use of a space that would normally have little interest. By growing a lightweight flowering vine such as a clematis or climbing rose on a small, nonflowering tree or shrub and letting it twine through the branches. This will only work if the branches are open enough to give the vine sufficient sunlight to grow and bloom.

Just use common sense in your choices. Don't introduce a vine onto a tree if the tree, or its trunk, is better appreciated without the vine. I wouldn't put a vine around the trunk of a white birch or let one climb throught the lacy foliage of a threadleaf Japanese maple. And don't use large heavy vines like bittersweet and honeysuckle unless you are prepared to prune the vines religiously, or unless the trees are dead or dying—dead trees can often support heavy vines for some years without your having to worry about what the vines are doing to them.

VINES GROWN ON SPECIAL STRUCTURES

While it may often be handy to use a freestanding support that is already there, like a fence, a house or a tree, very often the most sensible solution is to grow a vine on a support that you build for it and tailor to its particular needs. Various supports for light vines such as clematis are available in hardware stores and other places. You can also buy sections of lath trellis—thin wooden slats nailed together in a grid pattern—in the lumberyard and nail them to supports that you provide. The arbor shown in Figure 62 is one example. Again, you might sink freestanding pillars in the ground with crosspieces at the top where the vine can be displayed, or connect a series of posts with wires or chains for the vine to wind around.

In addition, there are pergolas and arbors that can be built, either freestanding or connected to a building, that are like open-walled, open-roofed rooms. Sometimes these are built with a series of connecting metal pipes; more commonly they are built of wood. It is important that they be solidly constructed and well sunk in the ground. I, for one, would not tackle the job of building an arbor or pergola but would hire a carpenter to do it.

Arbors and pergolas are a good way to support, display and enjoy large vines, especially fragrant flowering ones. Sitting on a terrace under an arbor and smelling wisteria, climbing roses, jasmine or honeysuckle is pleasant indeed. You might also try several different annual vines or use a different one each year. In addition to the morning glory and moonflower discussed in the List of Vines, there are many others you can try, such as climbing nasturtium, sweet pea, or black-eyed Susan vine (*Thunbergia alata*). You might even grow some of the vining food plants such as tomatoes, cucumbers, melons or scarlet runner beans on the sides of such a structure, planted either in containers or in the ground. If there is a special surface beneath the arbor, such as wood, flagstone or brick, you might want to be selective about what you grow above it, since falling fruits can stain these surfaces.

You can also grow vines on an arbor in order to create shade. A vine-covered arbor is a pleasant place to sit on a hot day, and if it is attached to a house wall, it will help to cool the house on that side. The best vines to use are ones with large leaves or dense foliage that will block the light, but which lose their leaves in winter when you want the sitting area or house wall to be warmed by the sun. Boston ivy (*Parthenocissus tricuspidata*) or grape would be good choices, as would silver fleece vine (*Polygonum aubertii*), and there are many other fine plants not mentioned in the List of Vines, such as Dutchman's pipe (*Aristolochia durior*), the lovely pink-flowered *Bougainvillea spectabilis* (in Zones 9 and 10) and hop vine (*Humulus lupulus*), which nurtures the "comma" or "hop merchant" butterfly.

VINES ON THE GROUND

Many vines will scramble over the ground just as readily as they will climb. English ivy, for example, is often used as a ground cover—on a steep, shady bank for example. Others that are suitable include *Euonymus fortunei*, Virginia creeper (if controlled) and *Rosa wichuraiana*.

VINES IN CONTAINERS

You might not think of vines as good plants to grow in containers because they do not naturally seem very—well—contained. But there are a surprising number of ways to do this effectively. Smaller vines such as morning glory and the other annual vines are nice in hanging baskets. Many of the ivies look well this way too, cascading out of, say, a hanging wire basket lined with sphagnum moss. You can also grow a vine in a large pot that is placed next to a support for it to climb. This is especially handy for plantings near the house where there are only paved surfaces and no earth. You can even erect a vine support that is part of the container itself, such as the wooden trellis attached to the wooden planter shown in Figure 62. If the planter is a masonry material you can stick the trellis into the soil, as long as the planter is deep enough for the soil to support it. Or set vine-filled planters on top of a wall and let the vines cascade down from there.

Or build a double wooden fence that has soil-filled boxes set into the top, and have vines spill out of those.

Growing Vines

How to plant, grow and maintain specific vines is discussed under the individual entries in the List of Vines. The important thing to understand in general is that you can have control over what the vine does.

CONTROL OVER GROWTH

Even though different vines grow at different rates, you can influence the growth rate of a vine to some degree. If you want it to grow in a hurry, dig a large hole into which you incorporate plenty of organic matter and fertilizer; then feed it regularly. If you want the vine to grow more slowly, go easy on the fertilizer and use peat to lighten the soil rather than a rich substance like manure. Then feed it only the amount it needs to stay healthy and grow at a rate that suits you.

You can also influence growth by the way you prune a vine. Though there is no single way to prune all the various vines, it is a general rule that pruning in late winter or early spring will stimulate more growth than summer or fall pruning will. If you have a rampant vine that you are trying to control, prune it late in the season, and make sure you thin out whole branches rather than just hacking away at the tips. Pruning large vines is a lot easier if you keep doing it each year instead of waiting until the thing is such a tangled mess that you want to cut it all down in disgust. This may be an option, however. Vines that are cut way back—in order to allow a building or porch to be painted, for example—often regenerate themselves beautifully.

TRAINING VINES

Though all of the true vines will go their own way, given the right support, you often need to direct them, either to make them go a certain direction, or because you are training them on a support that is not the one they would normally choose—for example, a twining vine grown on a flat wall. Training will almost always be necessary with vines that merely reach or arch upward without their own means of support. You will often need to tie vines to their supports, either permanently or until they use their own means to attach themselves. Even then you may sometimes have to anchor them if they become very heavy and look as if they might fall.

You can tie lightweight vines, or vines you are merely guiding temporarily, to their supports with soft twine, green plastic ribbon or pieces of paper-coated wire such as the ones that come with plastic garbage bags. A small vine stem can be anchored to a wooden support with a large metal staple, but don't hammer the staple in so far that you cannot pull it out as the vine grows. With large vines you will have to use pieces of heavy, plastic-coated wire. Again, never tie or staple a vine in a way that will constrict or girdle the stem as it becomes larger, because this can kill the stem. If a tie is a permanent one, make it large enough to accommodate the stem as it grows. Tie vines loosely in a figure eight, as with the tomato vine shown on page 302.

NO BAD VINES

The most important thing in growing vines is to be attentive, watch what the vine is doing, and be consistent in your attention to it. If you have picked the right vine, put it in the right place, given it the right support and kept it pruned and tied, it should do fine. Now, immediately I can hear some of you objecting: "What about kudzu?" (or whatever rampant vine you have had a traumatic experience with). It is true that some vines are uncontrollable in certain situations, and kudzu is a perfect example. Imported to this country from Japan as a way of controlling erosion on slopes, it escaped into the wild and now blankets a good part of the southeastern United States with its wide leaves. If you drive through Georgia you can see trees that rise up like prehistoric animals, totally covered with kudzu. My Louisiana grandfather used to tell me that when you sit on a porch covered with kudzu

you can actually *hear* it growing. It's true—you can.

The problem is that kudzu was introduced into a climate where it did too well. Admittedly kudzu is a bad vine in Georgia and Louisiana, but it might be a good vine in certain parts of Japan, or on a steep, eroding slope anywhere. If you are not sure whether a rampant vine will be a good or bad vine in your zone, it is probably best to choose a less vigorous one or plant it in a spot where rampant growth will not be a problem. Usually it is the vines that spread underground, such as kudzu, perennial pea (*Lathyrus latifolius*), Hall's honeysuckle and bittersweet (*Celastrus* species), that are hardest to eradicate. Use these with caution.

LIST OF VINES

The following list is a brief but representative sample of some of the more popular vines. It includes twining vines, all types of clinging vines, and those with arching branches. Most are perennial, a few are annual; most are hardy in the north, a few only in warm or tropical climates. Since vines vary so much in their growth habits, depending on where they are growing and in what type of soil, I have not, in most cases, given the growth rate or the ultimate height of the vines described. In some cases the height vines can attain almost appears to be infinite.

Seeds for annual vines can be obtained through local sources or from catalogs that sell seeds for annual flowers. Woody vines can be ordered from mail-order nurseries, but many are also available locally. For fruiting vines such as grapes, melons and raspberries see Chapter 9; for vegetable vines such as cucumbers see Chapter 7. For climbing roses see Chapter 11.

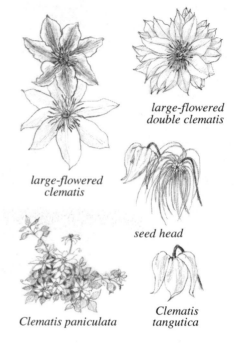

large-flowered double clematis

large-flowered clematis

seed head

Clematis paniculata

Clematis tangutica

CLEMATIS
Clematis

DESCRIPTION: This vine, pronounced *clem*-atis, is becoming increasingly popular because of its wonderful, long-blooming flowers and its manageable habit of growth. As if that were not enough, the flowers are followed by lovely plumed seeds that are decorative in themselves. The leaf stalks, used as tendrils, twine around everything they can, and very rapidly—if you set two or more potted clematis next to each other, watch out! They will soon look like one clematis. In most species the vines never become very heavy.

There are many different clematis species, and their hybrids, in cultivation. Most are hardy to Zones 4 or 5. They are generally divided into two categories, large-flowered and small-flowered. All can be grown on trellises, arbors, fences and other common vine supports, but supports for the larger woody ones must be strong.

Large-flowered clematis have flowers up to a foot across, but usually 5–8 inches. *Clematis* × *jackmanii* is an old favorite with purple flowers and hybrids of other colors ('Comtesse de Bouchard' is pink). Peak bloom is in July, with scattered blooms until fall. *C. lanuginosa* hybrids include the red 'Crimson King,' white 'Henryi' and 'Candida' and lavender-blue 'Ramona.' *C. patens* 'Nelly Moser' is mauve with pink stripes. These bloom from June on.

Many of the small-flowered clematis are large woody vines. *C. montana* has little white, starlike flowers in late spring or early summer; the variety *C. m. rubens* has purple flowers. *C. tangutica* bears little yellow, bell-like flowers in June and thereafter. *C. texensis,* an American native, has little red bells in June and thereafter. *C. paniculata* has small white, starlike flowers that are fragrant and appear in late summer and fall.

HOW TO GROW: Clematis likes sun but will tolerate partial shade and prefers it in warm zones. The soil should be a light, slightly alkaline loam with plenty of moisture but very good drainage. The plants like to have their roots cool. To ensure this, many gardeners put flagstones or pebbles on top of the soil around the plant. A mulch will also help, but if it is an acid one like shredded bark, add lime to the soil. In order to keep clematis roots cool you may allow them to crawl under tree roots as long as these are not the tree's feeder roots, which would compete with the vine for food and water. Remember, too, that the rest of the plant must be able to grow quickly into the light, not be shaded by the tree.

Clematis is transplanted in early spring in most climates (plants in containers can go in later if necessary). In mild climates fall planting is possible. Dig a hole at least 1 foot deep and 1½ feet wide and work in plenty of materials that will lighten and enrich the soil. A good combination would be a shovelful of rotted manure, a shovelful of peat, a shovelful of sand, and a few handfuls each of bone meal and lime. Plant with the crown 2 inches below the soil surface (it will form roots); water when you plant and when growth starts. Then have a little patience; the plants can be slow to establish and may not bloom for a few years. Some gardeners cut clematis back for a year or two to prevent bloom and

let the plant work on its root system. It is a good idea to feed young plants liquid fertilizer every six weeks or so while they are growing, and established plants can be given a handful of granular fertilizer in early spring and in fall. Some clematis die back to the ground in cool climates, so don't assume your plant has gone to clematis heaven just because you can't see it in spring; before long there will be fresh, little, light green shoots.

The rules for pruning clematis are confusing to gardeners, because they tell you to prune different species in different ways even though you cannot always tell which species a variety belongs to—often the seller does not know, and often your clematis is a hybrid of more than one species. The basic rule is: clematis that bloom on new wood (stems formed during the present growing season) are pruned in early spring before growth starts; those that bloom on old wood (the previous year's growth) are pruned just after flowering. (Usually it is the early-flowering ones that bloom on old wood.) Try to notice whether your clematis is blooming on new or old wood and prune accordingly: if on new, just cut back in early spring to promote fresh growth (unless of course the plant has died back to the ground); if on old, prune after bloom as needed to keep the plant the size you want it or to promote new growth.

The one troublesome thing about clematis is a fungus disease that can turn your beautiful vine into a string of blackened, dead foliage almost overnight. There is not much you can do about it. If you see rotted stems at ground level, it is too late to do anything, although wrapping a collar around the base of the plant while it is still healthy and spraying with a systemic fungicide like benomyl at least monthly are said to offer some protection. Sometimes one upper stem will die; if so you can try pruning it out below the blackened area, then spraying the rest of the plant with fungicide. If the plant succumbs, treat the soil with fungicide and it might regrow the following year. But just to be safe, don't grow another clematis in the same spot.

Buy two-year-old plants that have been grown on their own roots, not grafted. New ones are easily propagated from stem cuttings.

EUONYMUS (WINTERCREEPER)
Euonymus fortunei

DESCRIPTION: Many of the euonymus species are shrubs, and are considered in Chapter 14. This one is a vigorous vine, hardy to Zone 5, which clings to surfaces by means of rootlike holdfasts. It is a particularly useful vine because it is evergreen, with attractive, small, dark leaves. It will do well on a masonry wall or a chimney, hiding an ugly foundation, growing up a large tree and even as a ground cover—the stems root readily at points where they touch the ground. It has red berries in fall. There are a number of good varieties: *Euonymus fortunei vegeta* has oval leaves about 1½ inches long and orange berries; it also does well as a low shrub. *E. f. radicans* has slightly smaller leaves, pale pink berries, and can either climb or trail on the ground.

HOW TO GROW: Give euonymous moist, well-drained soil of average fer-

tility, and either sun or shade. When it is grown on a building in colder zones, some shade will keep the plant from becoming sunburned in winter. It can be propagated from rooting cuttings in moist sand or by layering. If euonymus scale is a problem, spray with dormant oil (page 73), and avoid planting on a south-facing wall, where scale insects will be more likely to breed.

HONEYSUCKLE
Lonicera

Lonicera japonica   Lonicera
                           sempervirens

DESCRIPTION: One of my childhood memories is sitting with my sisters under a huge honeysuckle vine in Pennsylvania, sucking the nectar out of the ends of the gold-and-white blossoms. It wasn't till long afterwards that I realized that not all honeysuckles were vines, that just as many of them were shrubs, and that among the vining ones not all of them grew as lushly as that childhood bower. Honeysuckles that are vines are twining ones; they bloom attractively and are quite varied in both their flowers and their berries.

Hall's honeysuckle (*Lonicera japonica* 'Halliana') is the one familiar to most people. It has white flowers that turn to gold in late spring and thereafter, followed by black berries. The foliage turns a nice bronze color in fall. A Japanese plant now naturalized in this country and hardy to Zone 5, it requires a strong support unless grown as a ground cover and can be very rampant if not controlled by pruning. If you want a more manageable vine, choose Henry honeysuckle (*L. henryi*), which is hardy to Zone 5 and has red flowers a bit later than those of Hall's, or try goldflame honeysuckle (*L. × heckrottii*), hardy to Zone 6 with long-blooming red flowers. Or try my favorite, trumpet honeysuckle (*L. sempervirens*), hardy to Zone 4, which bears red flowers and red berries. I like trumpet honeysuckle because of its restrained growth (in my northern climate) and late bloom—it helps to keep the hummingbirds around in July and August.

HOW TO GROW: Honeysuckle vines will grow in most soils, and in sun or shade, but they bloom best in full sun and in soil that is fairly moist. Don't feed the vigorous ones, and restrain them by pruning unless you are using them to control erosion and want rampant growth. Banish aphids as needed with a soap spray (page 73). Propagate by seed, softwood cuttings or by layering.

HYDRANGEA
Hydrangea anomala petiolaris

DESCRIPTION: Hydrangea is another plant most people think of as a shrub, not a vine, and most hydrangeas are indeed shrubs. But this climbing form of hydrangea is an excellent vine that ought to be more widely grown. Hardy to Zone 4, it clings by aerial rootlets, is excellent on a masonry wall and will even grow on a large tree without doing the tree harm. (It will harm the wall of a wooden building, however.) Large, heavy specimens may need additional support. The plant is quite slow growing and may not bloom for as much as five years after planting, but once established it is a large, woody vine with beautiful, large white flower clusters in

June, handsome, dark green foliage and peeling reddish bark that is attractive in winter. I like it on a fence, or spilling over a stone wall. If you have a pile of rocks you want to hide—rocks that are scarred from blasting, for example—climbing hydrangea is a beautiful way to cover them.

HOW TO GROW: Grow in full sun or part shade in rich, moist, well-drained soil that is a bit on the acid side. Feed and water until the vine is well established, and prune as needed, after flowering, to thin out abundant growth. Layering is the easiest way to propagate this hydrangea, but it can also be grown from seed.

IVY
Hedera

DESCRIPTION: Ivy clings by aerial rootlets but will also grow by rooting along the ground. So it is grown both on masonry walls and as a ground cover. Woven into a mesh fence it makes a good screen. It is prized for its handsome, dark evergreen leaves and for the fact that it does fine in shade (but beware the black berries, which are toxic). The common English ivy (*Hedera helix*) is hardy to Zone 6 and is the one to grow in cool areas, which it prefers; the variety 'Baltica' is hardier still. There are many varieties for those eager to explore unusual ivies, and some are variegated. In warmer areas grow the vigorous Algerian ivy (*H. canariensis*), hardy to

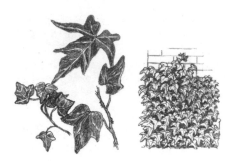

Zone 7. *H. c.* 'Canary Cream' is variegated. Or try the large-leaved Persian ivy (*H. colchica*), hardy to Zone 8. For Boston ivy see Virginia creeper.

HOW TO GROW: Shade or part shade is preferable, especially in the north where the winter sun can burn the leaves. Ivy is not a good vine for very dry climates. Give it rich, moist, well-drained soil, and prune in spring to control the vine's shape or produce bushy growth. Ivy is usually propagated by cuttings of young stems in sand or water.

JASMINE
Jasminum

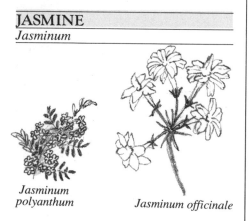

*Jasminum
polyanthum*   *Jasminum officinale*

DESCRIPTION: Some jasmines may twine to some extent, but as a group they are really in the category of shrubs. Some have long, arching stems, however, and are therefore grown as vines. They are very popular in warm climates, where they are usually evergreen and bear lovely flowers in spring or summer—sometimes even in winter;

many are extremely fragrant. Common jasmine (*Jasminum officinale*) is vigorous and hardy to Zone 7. It will grow to 30 feet; very fragrant white flowers appear in summer. Winter jasmine (*J. nudiflorum*) grows much less tall and is hardy to Zone 6. Yellow flowers, which are not fragrant, appear before the leaves in early spring in cooler climates, in winter in warm ones. Pink jasmine (*J. polyanthum*), whose flowers are more white than pink, has small, dainty leaves and starts blooming in winter in warm climates; it is hardy only to Zone 8 or 9 but can be grown successfully indoors and is very fragrant. Many jasmines, in fact, make good container plants, indoors or out. Some of the larger ones make good, dense, fragrant hedges. There are many other jasmines worth exploring, especially if you live in a warm climate.

The plant called "star jasmine" (*Trachelospermum jasminoides*) is actually not a jasmine. It is evergreen, bears fragrant white flowers in spring and summer and is a good screening plant in frost-free regions.

HOW TO GROW: Jasmines prefer sun, though some may do well in part shade. Any well-drained, light loam is suitable as long as there is some moisture. Most need pruning to keep them within bounds. With indoor plants especially it is important to cut them back hard after blooming to encourage branching and more bloom. The stems must be anchored to their supports. Propagate from cuttings or by layering.

MORNING GLORY AND MOONFLOWER
Ipomoea

DESCRIPTION: Morning glories are great vines to plant wherever you need some quick, temporary color—on a fence, lampost, mailbox or the post that

morning glory

moonflower

holds the clothesline. I grow them on the vegetable-garden fence, but I keep an eye on them lest they twine around my vegetables and thwart their growth. They can be supported by a very light trellis, and are also good vines to grow in containers. The common morning glory (*Ipomoea purpurea*) is a hardy annual; modern cultivars are derived from this and from other species which are tender perennials, including *I. tricolor* and *I. nil.* Most are bright blue, but some are pink, red, white, or one color striped or edged with another. All are twining vines with soft stems and heart-shaped leaves. The morning glory's name comes from the fact that it closes up its trumpet-shaped flowers against the afternoon sun, though it stays open on cloudy days.

Moonflowers, also called "moon vines," are closely related and look like large white morning glories. (Some botanists call them *Ipomoea alba* or *I. bona-nox,* others *Calonyction aculeatum.*) They are vigorous tender perennials that can be rather rampant in warm climates but are prized for their fragrant, night-blooming flowers, which are lovely in moon gardens (gardens planted to be admired at night) from midsummer to fall. Grow them as annuals north of Zone 8.

HOW TO GROW: Both morning glories and moonflowers need full sun and moist, well-drained soil; but too much water, as well as too much nitrogen-rich fertilizer, can lead to rampant stem and leaf growth but few flowers. Plant 8–12 inches apart, and ½ inch deep in a moistened furrow. In short-season climates give moonflowers a humusy soil, mulch it, and give it regular feedings with a balanced liquid fertilizer, all of which will speed growth. In long-season areas give it a strong support. The seeds of both vines germinate slowly; it helps to nick them with a file or soak them overnight before planting. I sow morning glories directly in the garden, but moon vines need a very long season to bloom and should be started indoors in peat pots about four weeks before you expect to plant them. Neither transplants easily unless peat pots are used.

PASSION FLOWER
Passiflora

DESCRIPTION: Passion flowers (also called "passion vines") are lovely vines, mostly tropical, with showy, long-blooming flowers, many of them fragrant. They are typically a broad, flat circle of pointed petals with a raised, fringed corolla in the center. Projecting from that are showy reproductive parts that later become oval, lemonlike fruits. Some of these fruits are edible. Colors vary widely. All cling by tendrils.

Blue passion flower (*Passiflora caerulea*) can actually be blue, pink, purple or white with a purple center. Its

Passiflora caerulea

passiflora hybrid

Passiflora manicata

Passiflora incarnata

hybrids produce showy flowers over 4 inches across that bloom most of the summer. There are many passion flowers to choose from; two of the red-flowered ones are *P. manicata* and *P. coccinea*. The hardiest passion flower is the native maypop (*P. incarnata*) which grows as far north as Zone 7 and has a 2-inch lavender or white flower with a purple corolla.

In warm climates passion flowers provide shade in an attractive way when grown on trellises, arbors or fences. In cool climates they are grown indoors.

HOW TO GROW: Give passion flowers full sun and light, moist but well-drained soil. They will tolerate heat well given sufficient water and are bothered by few pests. They sometimes die back in winter. To grow indoors, cut back hard in winter and keep dormant but slightly moist, with no fertilizer. Feed and water in late winter to produce fresh growth. Plants may be propagated by cuttings rooted in moist sand.

SILVER LACE VINE (FLEECE VINE)
Polygonum aubertii

DESCRIPTION: This vigorous twining vine is unusual because it blooms profusely in late summer, usually August.

The flowers are 6-inch clusters, usually greenish white, sometimes pinkish. It has many uses in the landscape because it not only provides a dense screen in a hurry (you can have a sizable vine within two years) but is attractive too. It is a good vine to shade an arbor because it is deciduous and will let the sun in when winter comes. It is a heavy vine that needs plenty of room and a strong support, but its vigor should not be a problem with regular pruning.

HOW TO GROW: Though the vine blooms best in full sun it will tolerate partial shade. It is not fussy about soil, though a moderately fertile sandy loam is best. It is drought-tolerant and has no serious pests. It may die back in winter in colder zones, and dead growth should be removed in spring. Where dieback does not occur the vine may be pruned back fairly hard in fall or winter and will then bloom profusely on new wood. Propagate by division, stem cuttings or from seed.

TRUMPET VINE
Campsis radicans

DESCRIPTION: Trumpet vine is a perfect example of a hummingbird plant. Its red-orange, 2- to 3-inch, trumpet-shaped flowers, which bloom in mid-July, have evolved along with the long, slender bill of the hummingbird, which

trumpet vine

'Madam Galen'

HOW TO GROW: Grow trumpet vine in full sun in moderately fertile, moist, well-drained soil. Prune it on top in winter or early spring as needed to lighten it and improve its appearance, especially if it is very heavy on top; you don't want the flowers—and the hummingbirds—to be too high for you to see and top-pruning will encourage new bottom growth. Propagate by layering, by removing and replanting suckers, from stem cuttings or from seed.

VIRGINIA CREEPER
Parthenocissus quinquefolia

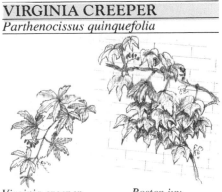

Virginia creeper   Boston ivy

pollinates them. Even the color, the hummingbird's favorite, is designed to attract this bird. The vine clings with aerial rootlets and is very large and heavy. Even if you have a massive masonry chimney for it to grow on, you might need to wire it for additional support, and make sure the roots do not cling to the house if it is made of wood. An easier place to grow it is on a free-standing masonry wall or over a rock pile. (If you do not have a suitable spot and want a good hummingbird vine, grow trumpet honeysuckle instead.) A hybrid, *Campsis radicans* × *tagliabuana* 'Madam Galen,' has even showier flowers. Both are hardy to Zone 4 or 5. Chinese trumpet vine (*C. grandiflora*) has large flowers but is hardy only to Zones 7–8. In warm climates trumpet vines can be invasive, but they are useful if you want to cover a lot of bare ground in a hurry.

DESCRIPTION: The Latin word *quinquefolia* means "five-leaved"—an important thing to know about Virginia creeper (what you see are actually five leaflets that make up one whole leaf). When I was a child the only way I could tell Virginia creeper from poison ivy, which it closely resembles, was to count these leaflets—if there were only three it was poison ivy. ("Leaflets three—let it be.") Virginia creeper, also called "woodbine," is relatively lightweight for a vine that can grow to 50 feet, and it is very attractive on a wall, fence or terrace. It would be one of my first choices if I wanted to see the wall behind a vine, since its growth is rather open. It also makes a good deciduous ground cover. The leaves turn bright red in fall, and the plant bears small blue-black berries. It clings with disk-tipped tendrils, is native to the eastern United States and is hardy to Zones 3–4.

There are a number of other *Parthenocissus* species that make a fine display. One is Boston ivy (*P. tricuspidata*). It is similar to Virginia creeper but has large, three-lobed leaves. The variety 'Veitchii' has smaller leaves that are purple, then green. Both are truly lovely ornamental vines that make a denser wall of leaves than Virginia creeper and are hardy to Zone 4. All cling well to stone or to trellises but, like most clinging vines, can harm wood clapboards and shingles.

HOW TO GROW: All will grow well in a loam of average fertility, lightened with humus (in the wild they choose woodland soil). They will tolerate either sun or light shade. Plant in spring or fall. They need pruning only to keep them within the space allotted them. Propagate from stem cuttings.

WISTERIA
Wisteria

DESCRIPTION: This is one of the most spectacular vines you can grow. It is heavy, twining, deciduous, long-lived and decorative in itself, but its chief virtue lies in the long clusters of pealike blossoms, which are borne in spring. These are followed by conspicuous seed pods, which last through the winter. The flowers are fragrant and usually blue-violet or white, sometimes pink or mauve. Wisteria looks best on an arbor or some other support where the flowers can hang down and be admired from below. They can also be grown in containers. Whatever support you give wisteria should be a strong one, and it should not be grown in trees, which it can harm.

Wisteria would probably be grown

more widely than it is, were it not for a few problems. The vines can be difficult to manage, especially in warm climates where they can be rampant. They can disrupt clapboards and shingles. And then, after you've put up with all that, they can refuse to bloom. Nonetheless, they are so fine when they work that many gardeners think they are worth a try, and manage to grow them well.

Several species are widely cultivated. Chinese wisteria (*Wisteria sinensis*) is the one most commonly grown in the western states and is hardy to at least Zone 6. The vines twine counterclockwise and bear blue-violet flower clusters up to a foot long. Japanese wisteria (*W. floribunda*) is similar, but its blue-purple flower clusters are longer and its leaflets somewhat smaller and more numerous. It is more commonly grown in the east, is a little hardier, and twines clockwise. The variety 'Alba' is white, 'Rosea' is pink and 'Macrobotrys' has very long, very fragrant violet flowers. *W. × formosa*, a hybrid of Japanese and Chinese wisteria, is hardy at least to Zone 5 and has a better fragrance than either of its parents. Its flowers, like those of Chinese wisteria, open all at once; those of Japanese wisteria open from the top down, and hence bloom longer. Wisterias often do not bloom until they are large, well-established plants.

HOW TO GROW: Grow wisterias in full sun, except in warm climates where they can take partial shade. Give them a strong support and a spot where air can circulate but keep them away from strong wind. Young plants should have a deeply dug soil lightened with humus, then be fed, watered and staked or tied against wind for a few years; but once established these deep-rooted plants do very well on their own. If the plants have been grafted, plant them with the graft union beneath the soil. Cut back to a few feet in late spring for the first few years. Then prune as needed to control shape, pruning after the vine has flowered (it blooms on the previous year's growth). Remove any suckers that grow up at the base of the plant.

Wisteria has no serious diseases or pests, but gardeners must often take rather drastic measures to force it into bloom, even after the plant is well established and has bloomed in previous years. Wisteria's reluctance can sometimes be due to the fact that the flower buds have been killed by cold. Try a more protected location, or grow a less tender vine. If a check in the fall reveals that flower buds have not formed, however, it may be that the plant is reproducing by adding to its mighty root system and by creating suckers, rather than by flowering and setting seed, and therefore has no interest in creating flowers. By root pruning the vine, slicing the roots with a sharp spade in a circle about 2 feet from the stem, you can often rob it of enough of its root system to make it produce flowers again. It is also a good idea to dig some high-phosphorus fertilizer deeply into the soil at this time, just beyond the point where you've severed the roots, because you do want the roots to start growing again. Sometimes pruning back long new growth part way in midsummer will help. If none of these tricks works, sit tight and see what happens. Wisteria, after all, hails from the inscrutable East, and it has a mind of its own.

SHRUBS

If you've ever been cheered by the sight of a forsythia in full bloom or been greeted by the fragrance of lilac or boxwood at the entrance to a house, you know what a few well-placed shrubs can do for a landscape. But you may not know how much they can do and how many different kinds of shrubs you, the gardener, have at your disposal.

No garden plants are grown as universally as shrubs except perhaps lawn grasses, and none are grown with so little imagination, not only in the choice of shrubs but in the way they are used. Shrubs are, unfortunately, something you are *supposed* to have—marching across the front of your house like Snow White's dwarves, clipped into the usual classic shapes: the Muffin, the Golf Ball, the Chicken Croquette. They are such unobtrusive clichés that often you only "see" them after someone cuts them down, just as with Muzak that you only "hear" when it is turned off. That's a pity, because shrubs are too versatile, and too beautiful, to be taken for granted.

A shrub is, generally speaking, a woody plant that is smaller than a tree—usually less than 15 feet tall—with more than one stem. Some shrubs can be grown as trees (that is, with one trunk), and some trees are shrublike (that is, grown with several trunks).

Shrubs vary not only in their size and habits of growth but in many other ways too. Some are deciduous, losing their leaves in winter or, in very warm climates, during the dry season, while others are evergreen. Of the evergreen shrubs, some have needles (these are often short versions of plants that normally grow as trees), and still more, like holly, have broad leaves. Many shrubs are grown for their flowers, some for their berries. Some shrubs have a particularly lovely shape, or their leaves have an interesting color or texture. Many have leaves that turn bright colors in fall in regions where cool nights bring bright fall leaf color. One of the pleasures of growing shrubs is finding ways to combine the different variations so that they complement one another.

Ways to Use Shrubs

The List of Shrubs beginning on page 500 describes some of the many shrubs appropriate for garden use and may give you ideas about which to grow. If the choice seems overwhelming, decide what you want from a shrub: what you want it to accomplish in its location, what time of the year you'd like it to be interesting, and any other requirements you have.

FOUNDATION PLANTINGS AND ENTRIES

You don't *have* to install a foundation planting just because every other house on the block has one. There are sometimes good reasons to plant one, however: the house foundation is made of an unattractive material or is very high, or perhaps the house simply needs some plants growing along the base to anchor it to the ground visually and give it solidity. But often the foundation planting is a cliché.

I find the idea of entry plantings more interesting. A group of plants that defines an entrance to a house (it could be a side or rear entrance as well as the front one) gives the house a welcoming appearance. The planting is a foretaste of hospitality to come and should be chosen as carefully as the carpet on the floor and the soup on the table. It should reflect your own taste, and it can be as interesting as you want it to be.

The plan shown in Figure 63 is just

one example. Two things make it different from entry plantings you usually see. First, the planting does not hug the foundation, but rather its main focus is farther out from the house. Second, instead of the usual needle evergreens, such as yews, junipers and sheared hemlocks, I've used broad-leaved evergreens and a few deciduous shrubs.

The house is entered by way of a winding path with plantings on either side. To the left is a clump of birch trees and a group of specimen rhododendrons —plants with special features that are meant to be looked at individually, not just as massed elements. The tallest is a small-leaved rhododendron called 'PJM' that will grow slowly to about 6 feet. The Yakusimanum rhododendron will form a 3-foot mound covered with pink-and-white blossoms. 'Purple Gem' is a small-leaved rhododendron that grows less than 2 feet tall. *Rhododendron impeditum* forms a low mat with bluish purple flowers. Closer to the door on the left are three slender deutzias (*Deutzia gracilis*), which are deciduous but have attractive, dark green leaves during the growing season and are covered with small white flowers in spring. A mountain laurel provides an accent to the left of the door—perhaps one of the new cultivars mentioned on page 516. To the left of the laurel, and at intervals along the house, are some inkberries (*Ilex glabra*) and dwarf evergreen azaleas, a hardy variety called 'Delaware Valley White.' The whole planting, on both sides of the walk, is unified by a carpet of periwinkle (*Vinca minor*), a broad-leaved evergreen ground cover (page 458).

The plants neither block the view from the windows nor obscure the view of the house from the street. The birch, though tall, does not have dense branches and does not hide the house; the PJM rhododendron is the only shrub in the planting that grows over 5 feet tall. A common mistake in planting near houses is to select shrubs that will ultimately grow both too tall and too wide, requiring constant shearing. This not only means a lot of unnecessary work, it means that you can never appreciate a shrub in its natural shape. In certain formal settings there is a place for closely sheared shrubs. But unless you are deliberately choosing this formal style, why not pick plants that will fit the spot to which they are assigned? In the List of Shrubs are many with low, compact growth habits that might also be appropriate to an entry planting. All the plants in this particular scheme are hardy to at least Zone 5; others on the list might be better suited to your own climate.

If you are not planting shrubs next to a building with windows, you are free to use some of the bigger ones. My feeling is that if a shrub like forsythia can't become the great weeping fountain that nature intended, there's no point in growing it. It won't flower very well if you keep chopping it back, anyway. One way to deal with a forsythia, or any large shrub, is to set it by itself, surrounded by lawn or next to a windowless wall where it can have your undivided attention. Another way is to plant a shrub border.

SHRUB BORDERS

A shrub border is a planting that displays a group of shrubs in a harmonious way. Often it borders a lawn or some other landscape feature, but it is meant to be beautiful in itself, just the way a flower garden is. Designing a shrub border is in some ways like designing the perennial flower gardens described in Chapter 6, because you are orchestrating heights, flower colors, foliage, plant shapes and blooming periods. But

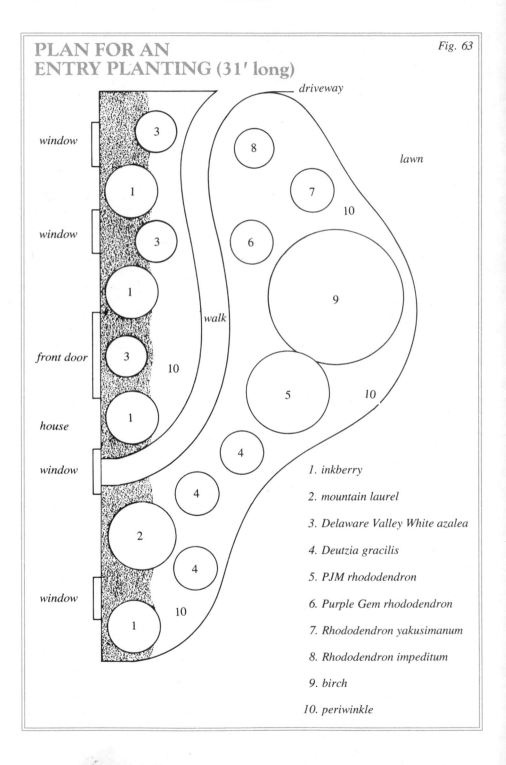

PLAN FOR AN
ENTRY PLANTING (31' long)

Fig. 63

driveway

lawn

window

window

walk

front door

house

window

window

1. *inkberry*

2. *mountain laurel*

3. *Delaware Valley White azalea*

4. *Deutzia gracilis*

5. *PJM rhododendron*

6. *Purple Gem rhododendron*

7. *Rhododendron yakusimanum*

8. *Rhododendron impeditum*

9. *birch*

10. *periwinkle*

now you are dealing with larger—and generally fewer—plants. As with perennials, you might strive for a border that is in its full glory during a particular season—usually spring, when most shrubs bloom. Or you might try to stretch the border's interest over the seasons by using late-blooming shrubs, those with colorful fall foliage, evergreens and even some shrubs with winter berries. If you do this you will never have the whole border in bloom at once, but since each shrub presents a large color mass that can stand alone visually, it won't matter. In fact, a fine shrub border can be built around shrubs with no conspicuous flowers at all, just effective foliage.

The plan shown on page 486 is for a shrub border that blooms from mid-April to August and ends with a fall foliage display. To plant it you'd need a space 50 feet long and 12 feet wide. It is important that the plants have room to spread out as well as up. To some extent they can mingle their branches with those of their neighbors and still look attractive, but you do need to give each one room for its branches and roots to grow without too much competition.

I've found that the best way to plan a border such as this one is to write the proposed shrubs' dimensions and blooming times right on the plan (with shrubs there is more room to write in the spaces than there is on a plan for smaller plants). Note in Figure 64 that the tallest plants—6 feet tall and over—are in the rear. In front of these are more compact shrubs under 6 feet tall. And in the foreground are some mixed heathers, which will in time spread together to form a mat that will unify the planting the same way the periwinkle did in the entry plan.

Bloom will start with the yellow of forsythia, followed by fothergilla with its white bottle-brush flowers, and a red

Japanese quince. Next come yellow broom and a yellow kerria, which also has beautiful variegated leaves. Potentilla, with its gray-green leaves, next puts on a show of yellow flowers that will continue intermittently throughout the summer; and the succession continues with a white-covered mound of Vanhoutte spirea, a vibrant Exbury azalea—perhaps a red-orange one like 'Balzac'—and the white mock orange 'Virginal' for exquisite fragrance. Summer blooms include reddish pink bumalda spirea, white oak-leaf hydrangea, and the heathers. The heathers will produce pink and white flowers from July to October if you mix a number of different varieties; they will eventually spread together to form a rich tapestry not only of flower tones but also of summer and winter foliage colors. Late-summer bloom is provided by orange-eye butterfly bush (*Buddleia davidii*) and rose of Sharon (*Hibiscus syriacus*); see their respective entries in the List of Shrubs for the available colors of each.

The 'Crimson Pygmy' barberries have been included in the shrub border for foliage interest. These compact plants have dark red leaves all summer that will look good next to the grayish leaves of the potentilla and the white-edged ones of the kerria. The barberry leaves will also lend their tones to the fall foliage display. The fothergilla will turn yellow-red, the Vanhoutte spirea a reddish orange, and the oak-leaf hydrangea will also have a reddish color.

Obviously there are many plants you might include in a border like this—there are no evergreens in the plan, for instance, no plants with berries and not a single lilac. I tried to choose plants of compact shape, even among the tall ones, so that none would monopolize the whole bed, and I tried to give each plant enough space to spread out. But even so they will have to be monitored

PLAN FOR A SHRUB BORDER (50' by 12')

Fig. 64

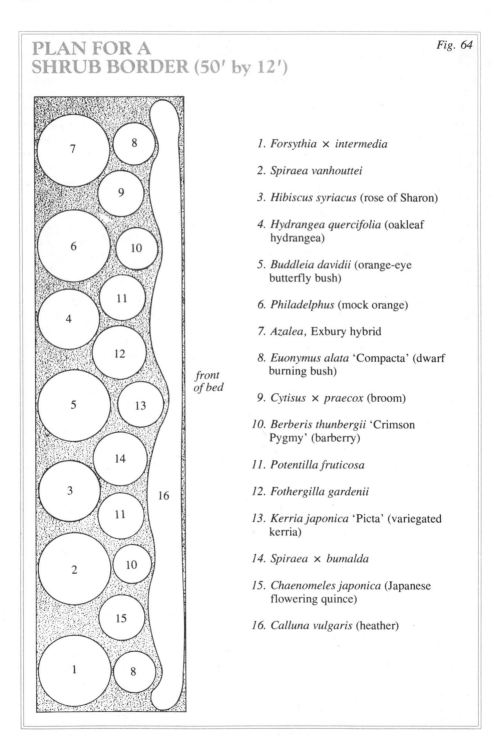

front of bed

1. *Forsythia × intermedia*

2. *Spiraea vanhouttei*

3. *Hibiscus syriacus* (rose of Sharon)

4. *Hydrangea quercifolia* (oakleaf hydrangea)

5. *Buddleia davidii* (orange-eye butterfly bush)

6. *Philadelphus* (mock orange)

7. *Azalea*, Exbury hybrid

8. *Euonymus alata* 'Compacta' (dwarf burning bush)

9. *Cytisus × praecox* (broom)

10. *Berberis thunbergii* 'Crimson Pygmy' (barberry)

11. *Potentilla fruticosa*

12. *Fothergilla gardenii*

13. *Kerria japonica* 'Picta' (variegated kerria)

14. *Spiraea × bumalda*

15. *Chaenomeles japonica* (Japanese flowering quince)

16. *Calluna vulgaris* (heather)

and pruned as needed to keep the bed from becoming a jungle.

SHRUBS IN ROCK GARDENS

Many shrubs, especially the smaller ones, are excellent rock-garden plants. The best are those like junipers and potentilla, which don't need a great deal of moisture or deep, rich soil. The dwarf conifers (evergreens with needles) are particularly appropriate, not only because of their small size, but because of the variety of their foliage colors and textures. Some of them are described in this chapter under false cypress and juniper, but there are also dwarf spruces, firs, arborvitae, hemlocks and pines. The important thing is to make sure the shrubs you get are really dwarf. Whoever sells you the plant should be able to tell you how tall it will ultimately grow and how quickly.

If you have a large rock garden, with either big boulders or extensive natural rock outcroppings, you can use larger specimen plants: a full-size azalea or Sargent's weeping hemlock for example. But in a garden of modest size with smaller rocks, look for spreading and creeping plants such as junipers, cotoneasters and some of the dwarf azaleas and rhododendrons. Plant them so that they will flow around the rocks or cascade over them from a spot above.

HEDGES

Hedges can serve a lot of purposes, often all at once. A hedge can give you privacy so that you won't have to look at the neighbors' yard, or they at yours. The same hedge can minimize noise and be a barrier against wind and even sun. A hedge can protect people and herbaceous plants in summer or broad-leaved evergreens in winter. A hedge can keep out roving pets and children, and even,

if thorny enough, be a deterrent to burglars. A hedge can also define a space in a number of ways. An impenetrable hedge might say, "This is my space—keep out," but a hedge with an enticing opening in it might say, "There is a private world in here—come in and take a peek." A hedge can be a frame or a backdrop for a garden, a seat or some other special feature, in which case it might say, "Now, may I present—the rose garden!"

Hedges can be formal or informal. Most of us know what a formal hedge looks like. It is closely sheared to a uniform width and height or even shaped to a specific geometric figure. Needled evergreens, and small-leaved shrubs like privet that put out dense twiggy growth when sheared, lend themselves best to this type of hedge. But don't use flowering shrubs such as forsythia, weigela or spirea in a formal hedge, for as you shear you will constantly be cutting off flower buds. Make these into informal hedges instead.

An informal hedge can be a row of a single type of plant, such as lilacs, or a mixture, rather like the shrub border in Figure 64. If you are making a mixed hedge, it is usually best to combine shrubs with similar growth habits.

If you really like informality, grow a hedgerow, which is simply a long thicket bordering a field or yard and containing a number of shrubby plants growing together. Traditionally hedgerows divided one field from another and kept wandering livestock out or in. If it sounds rather untidy, it is. That's the beauty of a hedgerow: it provides a touch of wilderness for small animals to hide in and birds to nest in, especially if berry plants are part of the mixture. And depending on your taste and where it is on your property, you may enjoy looking at the hedgerow as well.

Hedges can also be many sizes and

shapes. For the tallest ones, plant trees such as pine, spruce, hemlock or arborvitae. These make good windbreaks, too. For the smallest, try a hedge of low, clipped box if it's hardy in your area; if not, try 'Crimson Pygmy' barberry or *Viburnum opulus* 'Nanum.' In between are countless choices such as pyracantha, privet, burning bush, Japanese yew, bush honeysuckle, quince, rugosa rose and oleander. If you want a tall, skinny hedge, plant one of the columnar evergreens such as 'Skyrocket' or 'Gray Gleam' juniper; or try 'Tallhedge,' a columnar variety of the deciduous buckthorn (*Rhamnus frangula* 'Columnaris'). For a wide hedge, plant broad shrubs or two staggered rows of a narrower one.

OTHER WAYS TO USE SHRUBS

Perhaps you want a display of fall color; in this case plant a border composed of such shrubs as barberry, bridalwreath, and double-file viburnum. Perhaps you want to attract birds; then plant shrubs such as February daphne, arrowwood (*Viburnum dentatum*) and siebold viburnum (*V. sieboldii*). If your main interest is fragrance, plant shrubs like mock orange and the fragrant viburnums. If you have a deck, particularly one built high off the ground, shrubs will both hide the underpinnings and, if you choose fragrant ones, scent the air. Be sure to choose shrubs that are tall enough so that you can see and smell them from the deck. Many shrubs, especially butterfly bush, will lure butterflies to your home as well.

Another wonderful way to use shrubs is for winter interest. Most people do this by growing evergreens, and indeed it is lovely to look out on the mixed greens, blues, grays and purples of yews, spruces and junipers frosted with ice or snow. Some of them, such as Andorra junipers and heathers, have a special winter color. But I also look forward to seeing the branching patterns of deciduous shrubs in winter. And many have colored bark, such as the green-stemmed kerria or the red-stemmed dogwoods (page 541). Many shrubs, such as winterberry, keep their berries for a long time during the winter, too, and the berries add interest.

Another way to use shrubs is to plant them on a steep bank. Shrubs on a bank not only hold the soil but provide something decorative to look at that won't have to be mown. In fact if such a planting is well mulched it should not need any maintenance at all beyond pulling occasional weeds. The best shrubs for banks are low and spreading and will, within a few years, merge together to form a mat. Some that have worked well for me are shore junipers, which hold even the sliding dunes at the seashore, and cotoneasters. Other possibilities are bearberry (*Arctostaphylos uva-ursi*) and 'Arnold Dwarf' forsythia.

Choosing Shrubs That Will Thrive

When shrubs don't do well it is usually because they have not been chosen with an eye to climate and site. Here are some factors to take into account.

WINTER HARDINESS

It is important to find out the minimum winter temperature that particular woody plants can stand before you buy any, because they usually cost quite a bit more than herbaceous ones, and you want them to be around a long time. Sometimes it is worth taking a chance on a shrub's hardiness if you can give it a protected location. You might get lucky; then again, you might see it thrive for years only to have one severe winter finish it off. Use the hardiness ratings given in this chapter as a guide, but note the qualifying remarks on page 42. And see the comments on winter protection below.

If you live in a very cold climate, there are a number of shrubs you can grow with reasonable assurance that they will survive: potentilla, common lilac, burning bush, tatarian honeysuckle, sheep laurel and red-twigged dogwood for example. If you live in a warm climate, your choices are bounteous. The list in this chapter includes several shrubs for mild areas that do not fare well up north—box, camellia, ceanothus, some of the daphnes, nandina, oleander, and to some extent pyracantha. Others of interest to southern gardeners are pittosporum, vitex, Japanese aucuba, gardenia, skimmia, photinia, fatsia, jasmine and natal plum (*Carissa grandiflora*).

SHRUBS FOR DRY PLACES

If you live in a climate where it is very dry, there are shrubs you can pick that will feel right at home. These include broom, juniper, potentilla, privet, oleander, barberry, fountain butterfly bush, New Jersey tea (*Ceanothus americanus*), buckthorn, quince and vitex. If you live in a western area where dry conditions prevail but nights are cold, eliminate oleander and other tender shrubs from the list.

Many of these shrubs also do well by the seashore, where soil tends to be dry and sandy. Shrubs with grayish foliage such as potentilla are especially seaworthy; the tiny hairs on the leaves that give them their gray look protect them from wind, salt and dryness.

In a dry area you can still grow plants that need an average amount of moisture if you are prepared to irrigate them. But it might also pay for you to look further into the rather specialized field of drought-tolerant plants. California gardeners, for example, are particularly adept at landscaping with palms, cacti and other succulents that gardeners in cooler, moister regions would like to grow but can't.

SHRUBS FOR MOIST PLACES

If it rains a lot where you live, or if the spot where you want to grow shrubs is chronically moist from springs, streams or poor drainage, there are some shrubs you can plant that tolerate a great deal of moisture, such as clethra and blueberry, and others for which drainage can be less than perfect—red-twigged dogwoods, leucothoe, mountain laurel, winterberry and inkberry, and some of the viburnums such as American or European cranberry bush and arrowwood. Also, if you want to grow shrubs that don't like moist feet, consider some of the ways to improve drainage (page 40).

SHRUBS FOR SHADE

Many shrubs do well in a spot that gets sun for only part of the day, or in sunlight that is filtered through tree branches, or in the "bright shade" cast by trees with branches that are high off the ground. Some of these are camellia, holly, fothergilla, Japanese aucuba, coralberry, snowberry, mahonia, leucothoe, clethra, skimmia, pittosporum, barberry, nandina and privet. Some shrubs will do well in full shade, such as rhododendrons, azaleas, euonymus, mountain laurel and Japanese andromeda, although these may flower less heavily in shade. Consider this list not only for the usual "shady side of the house" situation, but for woodland areas and for areas under trees where it might seem as if little gardening would be possible. In some suburban areas all the yards are so shady that this is the only kind of gardening people do. Remember, though, that shallow-rooted trees such as maple, apple, beech, poplar, and elm will compete with shrub roots; deeper-rooted trees, such as oaks, pines and sweet gums, present less of a problem.

PREVENTING WINTER DAMAGE

A few shrubs, such as caryopteris and some hydrangeas, characteristically die back to the ground in winter, especially in cold climates. But for the most part shrubs' woody stems (and also leaves, if the shrubs are evergreen) are exposed to cold air, snow and ice. The amount and kind of winter damage a shrub will receive is sometimes hard to predict, because several factors are involved. Soil temperature is one. Each plant has a lower limit on the temperature its roots can stand—or can stand over a protracted period. Plant roots may also be affected by how constant the soil temperature remains; alternate freezing and thawing can damage the roots. Have you ever noticed how food can become mushy if you repeatedly thaw and refreeze it? Something similar can happen to plant roots, and freezing and thawing can break them and heave them out of the soil. Mulches (discussed in detail on page 63) can keep the soil temperature above a plant's danger zone and also work to keep frozen soil at a more constant temperature. This is why a good snow cover can be so beneficial to shrubs. The snow acts as a protecting mulch.

Soil moisture in winter is very important too, especially with evergreen shrubs. Evergreen leaves that remain on the plants transpire (that is, give off water) in winter, albeit at a slower rate than they exhibit in warm weather. If conditions have been dry prior to the time the ground freezes, the evergreen will not have stored enough water to get it through the winter. There is no way for the plant to replace the lost moisture until spring. Therefore, its leaves will inevitably dry out. If you live in a cold climate and are having a dry fall, it is a good idea to give your evergreen shrubs a thorough soaking once or twice a week as you head into winter.

Some evergreens are better adapted to winter than others. Needle-leaved shrubs transpire less than broad-leaved ones, and plants such as rhododendrons, whose leaves curl up when it is cold, also save moisture. But most broad-leaved evergreens are quite vulnerable to winter drying, and you often see their leaves turn yellow or brown in February or March, when the roots have run out of moisture in their effort to replace that lost by the leaves. Drying winds in winter can cause moisture loss, too, and the situation is further complicated by sunlight: the sun shining on the leaves causes them to lose water more quickly than they would in shade. On top of that, leaves can get a sunburn from the strong sunlight reflected off snow, or even off a light-colored building nearby. Certain shrubs like box and Japanese holly are particularly susceptible.

Thus, while mulching and fall watering can help to protect broad-leaved evergreens in winter, their location is equally important. It might seem to you that a warm, sunny, south- or west-facing spot would offer the most protection, but with broad-leaved evergreens the opposite is true. The ideal location is a north- or east-facing spot (since morning sun is less strong than afternoon), where the plants get bright shade and are protected from wind. If you can't give them a spot like this, some may have to be wrapped in a protective material such as burlap, which air and moisture can penetrate. (Support the fabric with wood or metal stakes.) Or use a covering of snow fence to create partial shade.

Planting Shrubs

G eneral advice for buying woody plants can be found on page 111, and for planting them on page 50. Following are a few more things to bear in mind about shrubs in particular.

WHEN TO PLANT

When you plant shrubs depends, in part, on where you live. In cold climates the best time to plant most shrubs is in early spring while they are still dormant. This gives them a long time to establish new roots before winter. In warm climates the greatest stress on a new plant is not winter cold and dryness but summer dryness and heat. In these areas fall planting, or even winter planting in frost-free regions, is preferable. The shrubs need to get well established before summer.

This does not mean that gardeners never plant shrubs in fall in the north. Nurserymen who wish their fall sales were as strong as their spring ones (and are trying to sell all their woody plants before winter) urge gardeners to plant then; landscapers eager to stretch their work out over the season plant then; and even busy home gardeners like to make use of those nice fall days, after the vegetable garden and other projects are over for the season. Fall planting can make a lot of sense, as long as you stick to plants that are easily moved and established. Most needle-leaved ever-

greens take fall planting well, as do a number of deciduous shrubs such as lilacs. Those at greater risk, such as most broad-leaved evergreens, are best planted in spring.

Shrubs that you do choose to plant in fall should be in the ground by late October at the latest, so that some new root growth is possible before the ground freezes. Make sure you water the plants very well during and after planting, and give them a 3- to 4-inch mulch.

In warm climates spring planting is possible too, especially for plants with needles, since needles transpire less than broad leaves do in hot weather. Be sure to water them well, mulch them, and soak them deeply during hot, dry weather.

When you plant also depends on whether the plant is bare-root, balled-and-burlapped or container grown. Most bare-root plants require spring planting, especially in cold areas, to give them time to re-establish their root systems before winter. You have greater flexibility with balled-and-burlapped plants that have been dug while dormant. Because there is soil around their roots, they have suffered less shock. These can be planted at any time except in very hot summer weather (especially in the south) or in very late fall (in the north). Container-grown plants carry the least risk of all, since their intact root systems have been growing inside the pot. But make sure shrubs you buy really are container grown and not "containerized" (that is, dug bare-root, stuck in a pot, and immediately put out for sale). If you're not sure, have the nurseryman pull the plant out of the pot partway; if you can see a tangle of roots, that's good—it means that the plant has been growing in the pot for a sufficient time.

SPACING SHRUBS

How far apart you place shrubs depends on how wide the plant will spread. I always like to give a plant enough room so that I can see its shape when it is mature and not have its growth impeded by other plants. Sometimes I don't know precisely how wide the shrub will get. My rule of thumb is to figure that it will spread about as wide as it will grow tall, unless (as is often the case) it is described as being "broad" or "spreading," or, on the other hand, "narrow," "fastigiate" or "columnar."

For hedges, the common advice is to plant shrubs 1–2 feet apart. I find that usually this is too close: most shrubs get wider than that very quickly and will be healthier if given more space. Planting 3 or even 4 feet apart will sometimes make a long hedge more affordable, too, if you are willing to wait a few years for the space between the plants to fill in. But of course it depends on the plant. I would space narrow shrubs like 'Tallhedge' buckthorn (*Rhamnus frangula* 'Columnaris') much more closely than I would a row of big, fat spireas or viburnums.

When planting low shrubs to hold a bank, I place them in staggered rows so that all the plants are equidistant from one another, usually about 3 feet apart each way. If the plants have been purchased in 1-gallon containers they will take a while to fill in and cover the bank, though in the meantime a mulch will keep the bank from eroding. Those in 5-gallon containers, planted 3 feet apart, will give a thick planting in as little as two years, depending on how fast they grow.

Pruning Shrubs

In Chapter 2 I stressed the importance of understanding how plants are structured and how they grow, so that you can identify their needs and give them what they want. But sometimes, as a gardener, you want to make a plant do what *you* want. Pruning is a case in point. For example a shrub may be naturally inclined to grow tall and leggy in order to compete with other plants for light, whether or not such competition is in fact at hand. So up it goes, not caring what it looks like—whether it has a nice, filled-out shape, or whether it has plenty of flowers or berries at eye level. But you care. So armed with pruners you take it in hand and give it some gentle guidance.

Plants do get pruned in the natural course of things—dead branches fall off, deer nibble twigs and cause them to branch—but it's a pretty haphazard pruning and one that you can improve on if you understand how pruning works. Shrubs are pruned for a number of different reasons: to give them a more attractive shape; to keep them from getting too tall or wide for the space they are in; to induce fresh new growth for more flowers, fruits or colored bark; to ease the shock of transplanting; to remove dead, diseased or damaged wood; to let light into a dense plant in order to improve its health; and to rejuvenate an old plant that no longer flowers well. Individual shrubs often have special pruning requirements, and these are mentioned in the List of Shrubs. But here are some general guidelines.

WHAT PRUNING DOES

It may seem at first that the chief reason to prune is to stop growth. Sometimes it is. If you remove an unwanted, mature branch from some kinds of woody plants the branch will not regrow. But just as often we prune to induce growth, paradoxical as this may seem. If you look at the twig in Figure 65 you'll see that there is a bud at the tip, called the "terminal bud," and also side buds along the twig's length. The terminal bud is responsible for the lengthening of that twig and actually produces hormones that keep the side buds from developing, which they are quite capable of doing if something should accidentally happen to the terminal bud and the secretion of the growth-inhibiting hormone should cease.

In pruning you cause this "accident" to happen by making a clean, slanted cut just above a side bud and getting rid of the terminal bud. The side bud will then start to send out a new shoot. Often the other buds on the stem will do likewise, and you may then choose whether to leave them all growing, perhaps cutting them all back to a side bud to make *them* branch or, kingmaker that you are, you may choose a single shoot that grows in a direction that suits you and eliminate the rest.

Usually you won't see any side buds low down on a branch, where the wood is old and thick. Severing the branch at this point may not produce any new growth. In some plants it may, however, because of the existence of invisible dormant buds beneath the bark, or because the plant is capable of producing brand-new ("adventitious") buds in a spot where a branch is cut.

Usually, when we prune a shrub, we are doing one of two things: thinning it by removing some branches altogether, or cutting back stems to side buds to induce branching and produce new, bushier growth. It is important to understand the difference between thinning and cutting back, because they produce different results and are used in different situations. Cutting back is sometimes referred to as "heading back" and can be done in varying degrees. If only the tips of the branches are cut, the process is called "shearing"; if a great deal of the branch is removed, it is called "cutting back hard." Cutting back produces new growth. Thinning by removing whole branches may produce new growth in some shrubs, even if done at soil level; but its main purpose is generally to curtail growth—to remove thick, overgrown sections of the plant and let in air and light.

PRUNING NEW SHRUBS

When shrubs are planted bare-root, they are cut back by from one-third to one-half their height. The main reason for this is to compensate for the loss of roots, especially feeder roots, that takes place during transplanting. The smaller the root system, the more the top of the plant is cut back. If you buy plants bareroot, especially if they come by mail, this will often have been done for you, and you will be able to see where recent cuts have been made. But if the plants come with long, wandlike stems you will have to cut them back yourself. Plants that are container grown or balled-and-burlapped do not need to be cut back, because their roots have suffered much less than those of bare-root plants. But if the stems are long and straggly, they will benefit by being cut back in order to cause branching and give the plant a better shape.

The most important pruning you do is this early pruning of newly acquired shrubs, because it determines whether or not the plant will grow into a pleasing shape. A plant like an azalea, for example, whose branching structure will always be very visible, will be much prettier if you control its branching from the start and don't let tall, awkward shoots

PRUNING SHRUBS

Fig. 65

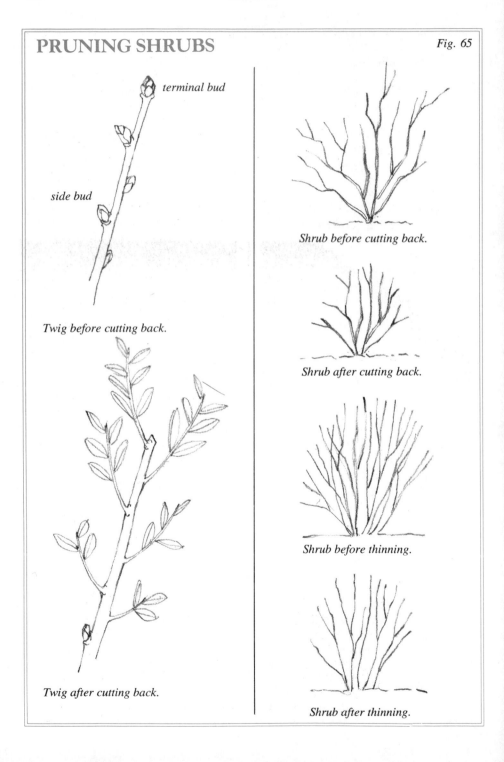

terminal bud

side bud

Twig before cutting back.

Twig after cutting back.

Shrub before cutting back.

Shrub after cutting back.

Shrub before thinning.

Shrub after thinning.

develop. And certain plants like junipers can never be brought back to a pleasing shape if you let them go too far without pruning.

It is especially important to cut back hedge plants while they are young, so that the bottom of the hedge will grow thick and bushy. The standard practice is to cut the newly planted shrubs back by at least a third, then each year cut back half of the plants' new growth until they reach their desired height. This may seem like excruciatingly slow growth if you want "instant hedge" for screening purposes, but if you don't do it you'll wind up with a hedge that is bare at the bottom. The only real short cut is to buy and plant a row of tall, bushy mature plants.

MAINTENANCE PRUNING

Once a shrub is established you may not have to prune it at all. If you have selected the right shrub for a given spot you won't have to worry about its getting too tall, and you can often let it simply achieve its natural shape. Unfortunately many gardeners regard shrubs the way they regard lawns—as something that must be cut regularly. So each year they go around giving them all crewcuts, not only ruining their grace but often preventing flowers and berries from forming.

How you prune is partly a matter of taste. Here is the way I go about it. For most shrubs I just watch the plant grow and remove any long, leggy shoots or branches that head out in an awkward direction. If a shrub is growing very thickly with lots of twiggy growth so that no light can reach the center, I might remove some of the twiggy ends or thin out some of the main stems at the base of the plant (Figure 65). I would cut back to a bud that faces outward (see page 434 for more discussion of this) so

that the shrub will open out like a bouquet. On the other hand, if it is too open and lax (a straggly-looking quince, for example) I might cut back to an inward-facing bud so that new branches will grow toward that gappy center and fill it in. Once you try this kind of sculpture pruning you'll realize how easy it is and will enjoy controlling shrub growth in a way that you consider beautiful.

One thing to keep in mind is that needled evergreens cannot be cut back as hard as broad-leaved evergreens or deciduous plants, because most of them do not regenerate from old wood that has been cut. Most of the long-needled ones such as pine and spruce don't even take shearing well. These should be pruned very selectively. Eliminate only branches that you don't want to regrow, or don't prune at all. Pines can be kept compact by pinching the "candles"— the little projections that shoot up from the tips of the branches.

Sometimes you want a plant to have a more geometrical, "shaped" look, however, whether for a formal garden or for a hedge that you want close-cropped and tidy. Frequent shearing with hedge trimmers will give you this smooth effect, but unless a plant or hedge is very large, I prefer to use hand pruners and give the plant a softer, less regular outline. I take a protruding twig and cut it several inches shorter than the ones around it so that the cut is hidden. I keep doing this until the size of the plant has been reduced a bit, but I leave it with roughly the same outline and with its surface more shaggy than smooth. I make sure that I prune hedges in such a way that the bottom is wider than the top; in this way the bottom receives enough sunlight to keep it green and growing, not bare.

I am also always on the lookout, in any shrub, for wood that is dead, diseased or dying, for this is neither healthy for the plant nor attractive. I cut bad wood back to a branch or bud, being careful not to leave a stub, which will only die and decay. If the plant is not in leaf and I am not sure whether a branch is dead or alive, I scratch it just a tiny bit with my thumbnail—if there is green under the bark, it's alive. I try to pick the right tool for the size branch I am cutting, and when I am dealing with diseased wood I disinfect the tool between cuts with a weak chlorine solution to avoid spreading the problem to healthy tissue.

REJUVENATING OLD SHRUBS

Old shrubs often become progressively less attractive because they have too many main stems, too much twiggy growth, and/or weakened branches that don't produce many leaves, flowers or fruits. They can also become either too leggy at the bottom, or they can produce a nest of suckers at the base that never flower. Some shrubs simply get too large. I spoke disparagingly a moment ago about the forsythia with a crewcut; at the opposite extreme is the forsythia that ate the yard—the one that is almost as large as your house and out of scale with the rest of the property.

If left alone, many of these shrubs would eventually weaken and die (except some, like lilacs, that can go on for several hundred years). But you can prune them in a way that will make them more attractive and also prolong their lives. In a few special cases, such as potentillas, honeysuckles and some hydrangeas, you cut old shrubs back hard to a few feet or even to the ground. But the basic and more usual technique of pruning old shrubs is to cut out some of the main stems at the base to let light in, sometimes cutting out some of the twiggy tip growth as well to promote

flowering and shorten a plant that has grown too tall. Often this is enough; but if the shrub is really a mess, or severely weakened, you can make pruning it a three-year program, cutting back a third of the old stems to the ground each year until all that is left is the new young growth that emerges from the base (this is less of a shock to the plant than doing it all at once). You can recognize old stems by their thickness and their shaggy, rough bark. New ones are thinner and smoother. With plants that already have a lot of suckers, as lilacs often do, you can prune out all but a few strong ones and let these replace the old stems that you cut.

WHEN TO PRUNE

Pruning at the wrong time of the year will rarely kill a plant, but doing it at the right time can make it more attractive and productive. Each plant has its own requirements, but here are some general principles.

Thinning a shrub to improve its looks or rejuvenate it is usually done in late winter or early spring while it is dormant. This is also the time to prune if you are trying to produce a lot of new wood; those buds will be primed to burst into action as the weather warms. (In hot, dry climates where there is no cold winter, you should prune at the end of the dry season when the plants' dormancy is about to end.) A hedge is usually pruned just after it has made its major spring growth, then as often as needed throughout the season to keep the hedge looking tidy.

If you are pruning to control the growth of a vigorous shrub, prune in summer or fall. Fall pruning is generally risky in cold climates, however, because new growth that results will not have time to harden off before winter and may be killed; in these areas, stop summer pruning soon enough to let any new growth harden.

The most common mistake people make is pruning flowering shrubs at the wrong time. These shrubs can be divided into two categories: those that bloom on new wood, produced during the same growing season as the flowers; and those that bloom on old wood, produced the season (or seasons) before. Those that bloom on new wood usually don't bloom until after June, because they're spending the first part of the season making new wood. They should be pruned in late winter or early spring before that growth starts. Plants that bloom on old wood usually bloom earlier in the season, and they should be pruned right after they bloom so that they can spend the latter part of the season making new growth unimpeded. So you see how great a mistake it would be to prune all your flowering shrubs at the same time. Unless they are all the same type, you would end up sacrificing some bloom. Shrubs grown for their fall foliage or berries are pruned after the show is over and the plants are dormant—usually late winter—or just thinned instead of cut back, so as to sacrifice as few berries as possible. Another trick with flowering plants such as lilacs is to deadhead them—remove the spent flowers after blooming. This not only puts more energy into plant growth but can also counteract the tendency of some plants to flower and fruit heavily only in alternate years.

ROOT PRUNING

Sometimes you want to prune a shrub's roots, for a variety of reasons. One is to restrict the shrub's growth if there is too much of it. Another is to prepare it for transplanting. Root pruning prospective transplants is done a whole season ahead and consists of severing the roots in a circle around the plant, at the point where you will dig a ball of earth when you come to move the plant. It causes the roots to branch and form a more extensive system of feeder roots, so the plant will suffer less root loss when moved. Root pruning is practiced frequently by nurserymen, less by the beginning gardener, who is usually better off not trying to move large, well-established shrubs and should hire a professional for such work. Still, root pruning is something you should know about. The other reason to root prune a shrub is to shock it into bloom. How this works, and how to do it, are explained on page 479 in the section on wisteria.

There are many other, more specialized forms of pruning, such as creating espaliers (training shrubs or small trees in a two-dimensional plane, either freestanding or against a wall), topiary (shearing to produce any specific shape, from a cube to an elephant), disbudding stems to produce huge blooms on one bud and selective pruning of pine candles to affect direction of growth. These involve techniques that you may research further once you are comfortable with the fundamentals of pruning.

As you prune your shrubs, keep the needs of your specific climate in mind. In general you can be more drastic with your pruning in areas that are mild and moist, and indeed you have to be, since plant growth there tends to be lush. In cold or dry areas, and especially in areas that are both cold and dry, you should be cautious about how much you prune and when you do it.

Other Maintenance Tasks

A part from pruning, most shrubs require very little care. If you have planted them with good soil amendments to start them off right, they usually do not need any additional feeding—unless they have suffered some stress, such as a severe pruning, or unless you want to produce rapid, vigorous growth for some reason (establishing a hedge quickly, for example). Usually fertilizing can be done just by top dressing with some well-rotted manure or liquid fertilizer just before growth begins in spring. The need of shrubs for nutrients also varies from one to another.

A mulch will help to promote root growth and keep the plant moist during dry weather as well as afford the winter protection described above. But some shrubs will still need a good soaking in severe drought, especially newly planted ones. Specific pests and diseases afflict specific shrubs; refer to the List of Shrubs and to the advice offered on page 68 and following.

Propagating Shrubs

Some propagating techniques, such as grafting, are beyond the scope of this book. The ambitious can grow shrubs from seed if the shrubs are not hybrids, or they can take cuttings—again a rather specialized skill. There are a few easier propagating techniques that you can practice, however.

TRANSPLANTING SUCKERS

To propagate shrubs, such as weigela, that send up rooted suckers near the base, expose the roots around a sucker and yank off the whole thing from the main stems of the plant. Replant it as you would any bare-root plant, making sure that the roots do not dry out. If a shrub has been grafted, don't replant suckers that grow from below the graft; these will be like the understock, not like the plant grafted onto it.

DIVIDING SHRUBS

Some shrubs can be increased simply by dividing their crowns, just as you would divide the crowns of herbaceous perennials. With some, all you need to do is slice the crown with a sharp spade or axe, using the motion pictured on page 56 and making sure there is a stem coming out of any section you replant. With others, it is a matter of clearing away the soil from the roots to expose them and severing sections of rooted stem with a pruning saw. How you tackle the job is pretty much a matter of common sense: you'll see what you need to do when you look at the plant and see how it is constructed. But it only works with plants that are very easy to transplant and so can be planted bare-root. Some of these are Japanese quince, lilac, azalea, clethra, glossy abelia, viburnum, winterberry and holly. Just to give you an idea of how easy dividing can be, I once dug up a Japanese flowering quince next to the front entrance of a restaurant and planted a rhododendron in its place. Since the quince was in bloom at the time, with beautiful flowers in a coral shade, we took all the little pieces we'd hacked up to my boss's nursery and planted them. They grew into fine plants in a row marked "coral quince." Ten years later I happened to stop at that restaurant for breakfast and noticed that the rhododendron was looking rather peaked, but that shoots of "coral quince" had sprouted up all around it. On the way out I said to the waitress, "You don't know me, but I planted that rhododendron, and I think you should take it out, because the quince loves the spot!" And I'm sure it's still there now.

LAYERING

To layer a plant, you simply bury part of a low-growing stem in the ground and wait for it to send down roots. Many plants grow roots this way without any help (ivy is a prime example), but you can initiate the process yourself if you want new plants from an established shrub. It works best for deciduous shrubs with long, flexible stems such as forsythia, quince, cotoneaster, daphne and some viburnums.

In early spring or fall, when the weather is cool, take a section of stem about 1 foot from the tip and bury it about 6 inches deep with the tip protruding (Figure 66). Set a flat rock over the soil to keep the stem down and the soil moist. With easy-to-layer shrubs this is all you need to do, but for extra insurance, and for shrubs that are more difficult to root, slice off a small section of the underside of the stem and dust the wound with a powdered rooting stimulant to make the stem root faster. Working organic matter and bone meal into the soil under the stem will help, too. Tying the new shoot to a stake will help it to grow upright.

After a year or so you can sever the plant from the old stem at ground level and transplant the newly rooted plant to a new location. Another method that makes transplanting easier is to layer directly into pots which you have buried up to their rims in the soil. While the plant is rooting you can feed it liquid fertilizer to hasten its development.

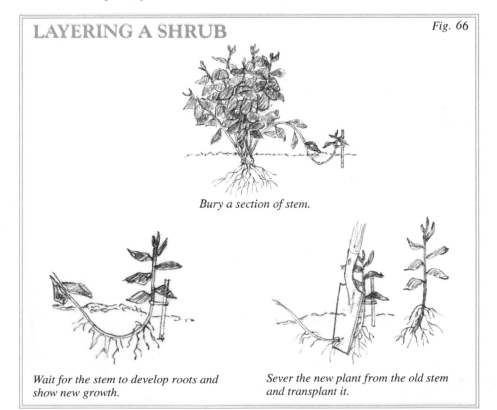

LAYERING A SHRUB   Fig. 66

Bury a section of stem.

Wait for the stem to develop roots and show new growth.

Sever the new plant from the old stem and transplant it.

LIST OF SHRUBS

The following list contains some easy-to-grow shrubs, chosen for their usefulness in the home landscape. Most, like forsythia, are old favorites; some, like fothergilla or clethra, might be new to you. Most can be grown throughout the country, though a few are listed with only warm-climate gardeners in mind. The preceding chapter suggests some additional species of shrubs, and other chapters in this book list a few shrubs masquerading in other guises. Roses, for example, are shrubs, though it is often said that the rose is a great flower but a poor shrub; its flowers are prized, not the rather sparse, lanky plants on which they grow. Some of the woody perennial herbs such as tarragon, sage, oregano and, where it is hardy, rosemary, can be used as small shrubs, as can the herbaceous perennials that make almost shrublike mounds in summer, like peonies or some of the artemisias. Refer also to euonymus and jasmine in the chapter on vines, and to some of the trees with shrublike varieties, as noted in Chapter 13: arborvitae, dogwood, fir, hemlock, spruce and willow (in addition to yew, holly, juniper and false cypress, which are considered here).

Most of your shrub purchases will probably be made at local nurseries where you can see the foliage and form of the plant, even if it is a small specimen. But you can often find more varied—and affordable—selections if you order shrubs by mail (see page 627 for some sources) and patiently wait for them to grow. They will usually come bare-root. Also note the advice given on page 527 for teaching yourself about trees; arboretums and botanical gardens often have fine shrub specimens as well.

You'll be able to see them in their mature form and so be better able to judge what the effect will be if you use them. Do you like their shapes? Is their scale right for the setting? Will they fit the spaces where you plan to use them? Your visit may inspire you to try something new and wonderful in your next shrub planting.

AZALEA
Rhododendron

DESCRIPTION: Azaleas are a group of plants that belong to the genus *Rhododendron*. The other members of the genus are simply called ''rhododendrons.'' While both can be either evergreen or deciduous, there are more deciduous azaleas than there are deciduous rhododendrons (almost all rhododendrons are evergreen). The main thing to remember is that all azaleas are rhododendrons, but all rhododendrons are not azaleas.

There are many azaleas to choose from. Some bloom in spring, with flowers appearing even before their leaves, others bloom as late as early July. The color range includes red, pink, lavender, salmon, orange, yellow and white. Heights also vary a great deal; some azaleas are nearly prostrate and some grow to over 12 feet. Your choice of azaleas will depend in large part on your climate. Some are cold-hardy, some not. Most azalea hybrids come from the orient, but there are also many beautiful native American azaleas, almost all of them to be found on the east coast from Florida to as far north as Maine. Here are some groups of azaleas that are widely grown:

Exbury and Knap Hill hybrids. These showy deciduous plants, hardy to at least Zone 5, can grow as tall as 12 feet. Colors include the whole azalea range. These are a good choice for northern gardens.

Kurume hybrids. These are evergreen, small leaved and small flowered, and grow 4–6 feet tall—shorter when trained as container plants. They can be sheared closely and still produce flowers in profusion in shades of pink, red, lavender, salmon and white. Most are hardy to Zone 7.

Indica hybrids. These tall, large-flowered evergreen azaleas are relatively sun-tolerant. They are popular in the south.

Torch azaleas (Rhododendron obtusum kaempferi). These are low-growing deciduous plants about 3 feet tall, with red, pink or salmon flowers in spring. They are hardy to Zone 5 or 6.

Mollis hybrids (R. × kosteranum). These grow 5 to 8 feet tall with yellow, red, orange, pink or white flowers in spring. They are deciduous and most are hardy to Zone 6.

Gable hybrids. These are evergreen, 3–4 feet tall, with pink, red or white flowers. They are generally hardy to Zone 6.

Native American azaleas. All of these are deciduous, and many have showy fall foliage as well as handsome flowers. They include swamp azalea (*R. viscosum*), which usually grows in wet places, has sticky white flowers in early summer and is hardy to Zone 3; sweet azalea (*R. arborescens*), which bears fragrant white or pink-tinged flowers in late spring on 9-foot plants and is hardy to Zone 5; pink-shell azalea (*R. vaseyi*), which is found in moist places, has pink flowers in spring and red foliage in fall, and is hardy to Zone 4; pinxterbloom (*R. nudiflorum*) (also known as "pink honeysuckle"), which grows 6 feet tall, bears pink flowers in spring before the leaves and is hardy to Zone 3; and flame azalea (*R. calendulaceum*), which bears stunning yellow, red or orange flowers on plants 9 feet or taller in late spring and is hardy to Zone 5 or 6.

Consult *Greer's Guide to Available Rhododendrons* for more guidelines in making your azalea selections. Experienced local nurserymen can also recommend ones that do best in your area.

Azaleas can be used in many ways—in shrub borders, as specimen plants, near terraces or entryways and in containers indoors or out. Their colors are so dazzling that an array of them can sometimes be too much of a good thing. I like them best in a woodland setting, mixed with plants like laurel and dogwood, where the intensity of the colors is softened.

HOW TO GROW: All the advice in the section on rhododendrons applies to azaleas. Remember that the native azalea species are indigenous either to sunny meadows or open woodlands with filtered light, so this is what they like best—too much sun can fade the blossoms of most natives; too little can result in less bloom. Plants transplanted from the wild should be cut back to compensate for the loss of roots and watered well.

Azaleas vary in their need for pruning. Many deciduous ones benefit from being cut back to encourage branching when they are young and then whenever they become leggy, especially the Exbury hybrids. Cutting back new shoots that emerge at the bottom of the plant to produce branching helps to fill in bare spaces near the ground. And all kinds of azalea will bloom more heavily if the tips of the stems are pinched. Both pruning and pinching are best done in early spring while the plants are still dormant—or just after flowering if you prefer not to sacrifice the flower display. Leggy stems can be removed from the bottom in summer as well.

BARBERRY
Berberis

high-growing

low-growing

DESCRIPTION: The barberry that grows wild in my neighborhood (*Berberis vulgaris*) is one of the first plants to leaf out in the woods and fields. In midspring tiny yellow flowers appear on its arching stems—they are only ¼ inch wide, but if you look closely they resemble miniature roses. In fall the plant turns a brilliant red-orange, and bright red berries appear; these last so long that they are sometimes still dangling there when it's time for the flowers. What more could you ask of an ornamental shrub? Apparently a lot; the plant is scorned because it is thorny and weedy. It's one of the first shrubs to take over neglected fields, along with such bad company as sumac, red cedar, multiflora rose and poison ivy. Barberry is even the host of a rust disease that afflicts wheat crops; in some areas it is illegal to plant it.

Nonetheless, some of the more civilized forms of barberry are popular garden specimens. Their berries and fall color make them attractive hedge plants, their thorns and dense habit make them practical ones. The most common cultivated form is Japanese barberry (*Berberis thunbergii*), which usually grows to about 6 feet and is hardy to Zone 4. More compact varieties include 'Aurea,' a 2-foot plant with yellow foliage, 'Kobold,' a compact 2- to 3-foot mound that is a hardy substitute for boxwood or Japanese holly, and the very popular 'Crimson Pygmy' ('Little Gem'), which usually stays about 2 feet tall and has purple-red leaves all summer, especially when grown in full sun.

Many other barberries are gardenworthy. Some are evergreen, such as warty barberry (*B. verruculosa*), which has black berries and quite showy yellow flowers and is hardy to Zone 6. Korean barberry (*B. koreana*), with dangling yellow flowers and red berries, and Mentor barberry (*B. mentorensis*), both hardy to at least Zone 5, are thorny shrubs that make good barriers.

HOW TO GROW: All the barberries are easy to grow in most soils and are drought-tolerant. They will grow in sun or shade, but foliage colors are more pronounced in sun. They transplant easily and respond well to shearing, either to create a hedge or, in the red-leaved varieties, to produce more colorful growth. They look best in their natural arching form, however. Old, overgrown plants can be thinned at the base. Shear or cut back in early spring, while the plants are dormant.

BOX
Buxus

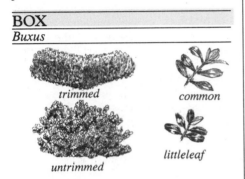

trimmed

common

untrimmed

littleleaf

DESCRIPTION: My climate, alas, is not kind to boxwood, which grows in lush evergreen mounds in the mid-Atlantic states on plants often several hundred years old. I can remember playing hide-and-seek as a child among the knurled trunks and fragrant billows of foliage while visiting my grandparents in Pennsylvania. Dwarf varieties such as 'Suffruticosa,'' or 'Green Pillow' are good choices if you want an edging box to outline a formal bed, though I still like the large ones best.

Common box (*Buxus sempervirens*), is slow growing but can sometimes grow as tall as a small tree; it is hardy to Zone 6. Littleleaf box (*B. microphylla*) is more compact. 'Wintergreen' is less apt to brown in winter than most; 'Vardar Valley' and 'Welleri' are compact, slow growing, and particularly hardy.

HOW TO GROW: The biggest problems with box are winter cold and winter dryness; they are prone to winter burn and should not be planted in exposed, sunny areas in cold climates. If you are a box lover, you may not mind wrapping your precious specimens in burlap for the winter or mulching their shallow roots to keep them cool and moist in summer and warm in winter.

Aside from this, box is not difficult to grow. It is not fussy about pH and needs feeding only while becoming established. Occasional ills such as root rot, leaf spot, stem canker and leaf miners are best dealt with by removing the affected parts and, if necessary, using fungicides or transplanting to a new location.

Box can be sheared as a hedge and also tolerates severe cutting back if damaged or overgrown. Generally all it needs is to have dead wood removed, however. Prune in early spring.

BROOM
Cytisus

DESCRIPTION: Broom makes a nice contrast to other flowering shrubs. The arching, wandlike stems are green all year long and are covered with yellow flowers, usually in spring. The leaves are relatively inconspicuous. Most brooms are fast-growing plants, 5 or 6 feet tall, and hardy to Zone 5 or 6. The vigorous Scotch broom, or common broom (*Cytisus scoparius*), is not quite as hardy as Warminster broom (*C.* × *praecox*). Most of the broom hybrids are derived from the former and are too tender for very cold climates, but they come in a variety of colors including red, apricot, pink, purple and white. Spike broom (*C. nigricans*) is low growing and blooms in midsummer. Ground broom (*C. decumbens*) is also late blooming and is even shorter, about 2½ feet; it is suitable for rock gardens.

HOW TO GROW: Brooms need full sun and prefer dry, sandy, well-drained, rather infertile soil. They seem oblivious to diseases and pests and tolerate the salty, drying winds of seaside gardens. They resent being transplanted or having their roots disturbed in any way. Plant container-grown plants in early spring and propagate by layering or softwood cuttings. Mulching in winter will help protect varieties that are not quite hardy for your region.

Brooms can be thinned out at the base if the plant is dense and overgrown, and the tips can be cut back to promote flowering. Prune spring-blooming brooms after flowering, summer-blooming ones before growth starts in spring.

BUTTERFLY BUSH
Buddleia

DESCRIPTION: Butterflies flock to these colorful, fragrant shrubs in throngs, to drink the nectar. Fountain butterfly bush (*Buddleia alternifolia*) forms a big

spreading mound as tall as 12 feet and as wide as 15, so give it plenty of room. Its flowers, in midspring, are long, slender, purple spikes. Foliage tends to be grayish, especially in the variety 'Argentea.' Orange-eye butterfly bush (*B. davidii*), so named because of the tiny orange centers in its flowers, is an upright, lanky plant. Available hybrids come in many colors—lavender, purple, blue, pink, red and white. Both *alternifolia* and *davidii* are hardy to Zone 5 with some protection such as mulch or a low mound of soil around the crown. Orange-eye butterfly bush dies back to the ground in winter in cold areas.

HOW TO GROW: Both species like full sun and well-drained soil enriched with some organic matter such as peat moss. Fountain butterfly bush should be allowed to grow like a fountain, but the tips of the branches can be cut back after bloom to encourage more flowers the following year. Orange-eye butterfly bush, which blooms on new wood, is often cut back very hard before growth begins in spring even in areas where it does not die back, to encourage fresh new growth. Dead or unproductive stems should be cut back at the base in either species.

CAMELLIA
Camellia

DESCRIPTION: Camellias were a wonder to me as a child because they bloomed in winter. My grandmother used to grow many of them in the Deep South, and one Christmas sent us a box of the beautiful flowers packed in dry ice. Camellias, alas, cannot take frost and are grown outdoors dependably only to Zone 8; but gardeners farther north often grow them in containers, keeping them indoors for all or part of the year.

The most common species is *Camellia japonica,* of which there are hundreds of hybrids. The plants, which are handsome, glossy-leaved evergreen shrubs, can get very tall when mature and are sometimes grown as small trees. From October to April they bear flowers that are usually 2–5 inches wide in several different forms—single, semidouble, double, peony form, anemone form and rose form—and in colors ranging from white to pink to dark red. *C. sasanqua* hybrids, which are smaller, more open-branched shrubs with smaller flowers, bloom from September to December. Camellias are equally effective as landscaping plants and in a natural woodland setting.

semi-double

double

HOW TO GROW: Camellias need to be protected from direct sun and drying winds. Give them moist, well-drained, slightly acid soil, and mulch the roots to keep them cool until the plants are well established. Keep the plants watered while they're young; even the leaves appreciate a sprinkling. Pruning young plants will help to achieve a compact shape; cut back after blooming to just above where the current year's growth begins. Old, overgrown plants can be thinned at the base in two stages, one year removing the lower branches to produce bottom growth and the following year cutting the tops back hard.

CEANOTHUS
Ceanothus × *delilianus*

DESCRIPTION: This evergreen shrub is sometimes called "wild lilac" because of the shape of its blossoms, but they are a true blue rather than lilac-colored. Ceanothus is very popular on the west coast where it tolerates dry, poor soil. Hybrids, which are varying shades of blue, are hardy to Zone 8. (Several deciduous species are hardy in the north but are white-flowered and not very showy.) Some grow as tall as 12 feet; others are prostrate creepers that are used as ground covers. The 3-foot New Jersey tea (*Ceanothus americanus*) is white-flowered and less showy, but it is a good shrub for dry, infertile soils and is hardy to Zone 5.

HOW TO GROW: Give ceanothus sun, a light, well-drained soil and not too much water. Keep foliage dry to avoid fungus diseases. The plants can be propagated by layering or cuttings. They don't need much pruning but can be pinched to encourage bushiness and thinned at the base if overgrown. Suckers at the base can also be removed, but cutting back severely will not induce branching.

CLETHRA (SUMMERSWEET)
Clethra alnifolia

DESCRIPTION: This native of the American northeast is a useful shrub for several reasons. It blooms at a time when

few other shrubs do—late summer—and it tolerates very wet soil. It also withstands the salty winds at the seaside. Flowers are very fragrant spikes about 5 inches long; there are also some pink varieties. The shrub can grow as tall as 9 feet, though it usually attains around 6. It is hardy to Zone 3 or 4.

HOW TO GROW: Give clethra moist, acid soil enriched with organic matter such as peat moss, and grow it in sun or light shade. The plant makes spreading clumps, and divisions of the roots can be made for propagation. It is best left to grow in its natural shape but can be thinned at the base or cut back at the tips if clumps get straggly; do this in early spring, since it blooms on wood of the current season.

COTONEASTER
Cotoneaster

DESCRIPTION: The name of this plant is pronounced "cah-*toe*-nee-*as*-ter" not, as you might think, "cotton-Easter."

Many species and varieties are used in gardens. Most are deciduous, have small, rounded leaves that turn red-orange in fall, tiny pink or white flowers in spring and red berries in fall that last most of the winter. The plants have long, graceful, arching stems with many side branches and are attractive for their shape alone. Spreading cotoneaster (*Cotoneaster divaricatus*) can grow to at least 6 or 7 feet tall and wide—a big mound of weeping branches. But many others are low growing, even prostrate, and are used as ground covers, on steep banks (where they grow quickly to hold the soil), or in the foreground of shrub plantings. Cranberry cotoneaster (*C. apiculatus*) and rockspray cotoneaster (*C. horizontalis*) stay under 3 feet tall (the latter is semievergreen in mild climates). Creeping cotoneaster (*C. adpressus*) is slow growing and only about a foot tall. All are tolerant of dry soil and the salty winds of seaside areas. Most are hardy to Zone 5.

HOW TO GROW: Give the plants full sun and well-drained soil. They do not transplant easily; it is best to buy container-grown plants and leave them in one place. They attract spider mites in some areas, which can be hosed off, and fire blight, which blackens the ends of the branches and should be pruned out. The plants should be grown in their natural shape, but long, awkward branches can be cut back to a side branch (early spring is the best time), and dense plants can be thinned at the base.

DAPHNE
Daphne

DESCRIPTION: Daphnes are small shrubs, mostly evergreen and mostly very fragrant; they should be planted in a spot where they can be easily seen and smelled. *Caution:* all parts of the plant

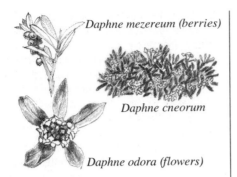

Daphne mezereum (berries)

Daphne cneorum

Daphne odora (flowers)

are poisonous, especially the berries; daphne should not be grown where children have access to the plant. Most bloom very early in spring. The deciduous February daphne (*Daphne mezereum*), hardy to Zone 5, has purple flowers in February or March (later in cold regions), followed by red berries, and grows about 3 feet tall. Lilac daphne (*D. genkwa*) is about the same size, has fragrant lilac-blue flowers and white berries and is hardy to Zone 6. Winter daphne (*D. odora*) is evergreen, as tall as 4 feet, bears fragrant purple flowers in early spring and is hardy to Zone 7. Rose daphne (*D. cneorum*) is a creeping evergreen mat less than a foot tall, with fragrant pink flowers in May, and is hardy to Zone 5.

HOW TO GROW: Give daphne full sun or light shade. It likes well-drained, humusy soil and a mulch to keep the roots cool in summer. Not easily transplanted, it should not be planted bare-root. It is propagated most easily by layering. Daphnes do not often need pruning, though they will tolerate severe cutting back. Awkward shoots are best dealt with by picking them for the house while they are blooming.

DEUTZIA
Deutzia

DESCRIPTION: For a few weeks in late spring, deutzia is covered with a froth of white flowers (in some varieties they are touched with pink, but I like the pure white ones best). I also like it because of its compact growth and use it in the front or middle of shrub plantings. It makes a good low deciduous hedge. In cool climates grow slender deutzia (*Deutzia gracilis*), which usually stays as low as 3 feet and is hardy to Zone 5. Lemoine deutzia (*D. × lemoinei*), hardy to Zone 4, can grow to 7 feet, though there are some compact varieties. Fuzzy deutzia (*D. scabra*), hardy to Zone 5 or 6, blooms in late June and can grow 8 feet tall.

HOW TO GROW: Deutzia is very easy to grow in most soils and will take either sun or part shade. In cold climates the low-growing varieties often die back considerably in winter. Prune out the dead growth carefully in early spring, being careful not to snip live shoots that are about to flower, since deutzias bloom on wood formed the previous season. After bloom you may cut back more severely, especially in the case of the taller deutzias, where you want to encourage lower branching. Old branches that no longer bloom can be cut out at the base, and branch tips can be sheared in order to promote more new flowering twigs the following season. Plants are easily propagated from stem cuttings.

ENKIANTHUS
Enkianthus campanulatus

DESCRIPTION: Sometimes called "red-

vein enkianthus,'' this handsome shrub has tiny, dangling yellow flowers tipped with red that appear just before the leaves in spring. As a bonus the leaves turn bright red in fall. There are also white- and red-flowered varieties. The plant usually grows to about 8 feet tall (sometimes as tall as 12). It is hardy to Zone 4 or 5.

HOW TO GROW: Enkianthus does well in full sun or part shade. It likes the same kind of soil that rhododendrons do: well drained, slightly acid and rich in organic matter. It doesn't transplant easily and is best propagated by layering. The upright-arching plants do not need pruning to look shapely, but can be cut back after flowering if more branching is desired, or thinned at the base if they are too dense.

EUONYMUS
Euonymus

DESCRIPTION: The deciduous and evergreen forms of euonymus are not at all alike. The most popular deciduous one is burning bush (*Euonymus alata*), also called ''winged euonymus'' or ''spindle tree.'' When it is very old it can become treelike, forming a wide, majestic umbrella of horizontal branches with corky ridges or ''wings'' along most of the branches and twigs. Growing it in the open, without competition, will result in a more beautifully shaped plant. In fall it turns pinkish red if growing in the woods, bright red if growing in sun-

shine. You can easily miss the red berries growing among that blaze of color, but the birds won't! A smaller variety, *E. alata* 'Compacta,' rarely grows higher than 6 feet and often less. Both kinds make good informal hedges and are hardy to Zone 3 or 4.

The chief evergreen euonymus is the *E. fortunei* described on page 472, hardy to Zone 5. Grown as a shrub without support, it will usually remain about 4 feet tall. There are many varieties with white or yellow variegation, and gardeners often choose them as specimen plants; these are more effective singly, I think, than in a mass. Another evergreen species, *E. japonica* (Japanese euonymus), is a large, glossy-leaved shrub that is hardy only to Zone 7 or 8; variegated forms of it also exist.

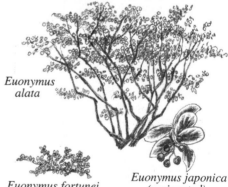

Euonymus alata

Euonymus fortunei

Euonymus japonica (variegated)

HOW TO GROW: Burning bush is very easy to grow, with few problems of any kind. Water it until it's well established; after that it will resist drought. The evergreen varieties are also vigorous and easy to grow, but in areas where euonymus scale is a problem, dormant oil should be routinely applied in spring. Propagation is most easily done by layering. Burning bush does not need much pruning—both as a single shrub and a hedge it is best in its natural form. To train it as a tree, remove lower branches and shoots from the ground in early spring. Dense shrubs can be thinned at the base. To curtail their growth, the evergreen types may need early-spring pruning, and even a second pruning later on in the growing season if particularly rampant. Don't prune after midsummer in cold climates. Remove long, awkward shoots or, in variegated varieties, those that lack the proper color.

FALSE CYPRESS
Chamaecyparis

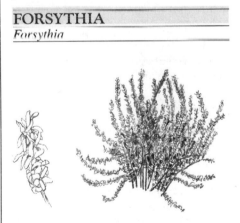

Chamaecyparis pisifera 'Compacta Nana'

Chamaecyparis pisifera 'Filifera Aurea'

DESCRIPTION: This evergreen tree usually goes under its Latin name, which is pronounced "Cam-i-*sip*-ar-is." It is a varied genus with many garden-worthy species, the most popular of which are native to Japan. Many are compact or dwarf and suitable for shrub borders, plantings near the house, and even rock gardens. The shapes and colors of the needles are often unusual and make the shrubs effective as specimen plantings and in rock gardens.

Hinoki false cypress (*Chamaecyparis obtusa*) is very tall if you get the original species. It has dark green needles like overlapping scales, arranged in a fan shape. The columnar varieties such as 'Erecta' are elegant alternatives to arborvitae either in a hedge or in a spot where you need a tall, narrow evergreen. The compact varieties grown as shrubs have the same lovely foliage.

'Gracilis' is broadly pyramidal and grows to 7 or 8 feet tall; 'Nana Gracilis' grows slowly to 4 feet. The *Chamaecyparis pisifera* varieties include many that are strikingly colored, such as 'Boulevard,' which is very blue and grows to 8 feet, and 'Filifera Aurea' ("gold-thread false cypress"), which is a pyramid of long, bright yellow, threadlike needles. While the latter can ultimately become a tall tree, it grows slowly and should be pruned to keep the form graceful. All of these mentioned are hardy to Zone 4.

HOW TO GROW: These plants do best in areas with some moisture in the air; they do not like hot, drying winds. They also appreciate a mulch as many of them are shallow rooted. Varieties with yellow foliage should grow in full sun to bring out the color. Branch tips may be pinched in spring or late summer to maintain a compact, bushy shape, but cutting back into old wood will not produce branching.

FORSYTHIA
Forsythia

DESCRIPTION: Nothing heralds spring quite as loudly as forsythia does; no wonder people love it. It does best in a spot where it can form a big mound and its long stems can arch and spill over without interfering with anything. I like it as a hedge when there is room for a very wide one, with the plants spaced 5 or 6 feet apart. Forsythia often affords a good way to block the view from the road, since even when it is bare of leaves you can't see through it. The most familiar forsythia is *Forsythia × intermedia*, of which there are many varieties ranging from pale to dark yellow. 'Spring Glory' is a popular variety because of its profuse bloom. Weeping forsythia (*F. suspensa*), and particularly the variety 'Sieboldii,' is excellent for slopes and banks, because the lax stems bend over and root along the ground. 'Arnold Dwarf' forsythia is 4 feet tall or less and a fast-spreading creeper that is also good for banks, though its flowers are nothing to brag about. All these are hardy to at least Zone 5, though cold winters may sometimes nip the flowers in the bud. *F. ovata* 'Northern Sun' is a hardier variety that will bloom well even in Zone 4.

HOW TO GROW: Forsythia will tolerate almost any growing conditions, though it prefers moist soils. It is not bothered by diseases or pests. Plants can be propagated easily from suckers or cuttings and by layering. Pruning forsythia is the trick. I sometimes think there should be a Forsythia Protection Society to make sure gardeners do it right. Shearing the plants into compact forms ruins the flower display, which is, to be honest, the only reason to grow most forsythias. If I have to tackle a plant that has become a monster (as some overgrown ones can), I have no choice but to crawl into the middle of it and remove the old stems (they look darker and rougher than the newer ones) to thin the plant out and let in light. As new growth develops at the base, more old stems can be cut out each year until there is a whole new compact plant, produced without loss of bloom. The whole plant can also be cut back to a foot or less, and it will eventually regrow. Pruning should be done after bloom, since flowers are made on the previous year's wood.

FOTHERGILLA
Fothergilla

DESCRIPTION: Also known as "witch alder," these shrubs offer so much to the gardener that it is surprising they are not more widely grown. In May they bear yellow-white flowers that look like bottle brushes (what you see are not petals but many prominent stamens) and have a spicy fragrance. In fall the leaves turn beautiful shades of yellow, orange and red. Large fothergilla (*Fothergilla major*) can grow as tall as 10 feet; the 2-inch flowers appear at the same time as the leaves. Dwarf fothergilla (*F. gardenii*) is usually about 3 feet tall, with slightly smaller flowers, and is a fine, compact choice for shrub plantings. Though native to the southeastern United States, both are hardy as far north as Zone 5.

HOW TO GROW: Fothergillas are easy to grow and are usually pest-free. Plant them in full sun or part shade (give them afternoon shade in hot climates). Soil should be moist but well drained and moderately acid. They rarely need pruning, but old wood can be thinned out at the base of the plant in late winter or just after bloom.

HOLLY
Ilex

Ilex meservae

Ilex verticillata

Ilex crenata

Ilex cornuta

DESCRIPTION: Some hollies are grown as trees, but a number of them, both deciduous and evergreen, make fine garden shrubs. Among the evergreen types the Meserve hybrids (*Ilex × meserveae*) are noteworthy because they are hardy as far north as Zone 5; they grow as tall as 12 feet and have names like 'Blue Angel' and 'Blue Prince' because of their lustrous, dark blue-green leaves. With most hollies it is necessary to have both a male and a female plant in order to ensure pollination of the female plant and the production of red berries. Japanese hollies (*I. crenata*) are an extremely useful evergreen group. Most have small, shiny leaves rather like those of boxwood. Their berries are black, but the more compact varieties, such as 'Hetzi,' 'Helleri' and 'Green Cushion,' form low mounds that are desirable in many landscaping situations. Most are hardy to Zone 5 or 6 but often need protection against winter burn. Inkberry (*I. glabra*) is an evergreen holly hardy to Zone 4. Its variety 'Compacta' usually grows 4–5 feet tall. Chinese holly (*I. cornuta*) is popular in the south and is hardy to Zone 7. 'Burfordii Nana' is a compact form.

A number of deciduous hollies native to the United States are fine garden plants. One is winterberry (*I. verticillata*), also called "black alder," which is hardy to Zone 3 or 4 and bears bright red berries that remain on the twigs a good part of the winter, for you to look at and for the birds to eat (as long as there is also a male plant). 'Nana' is a compact variety, 'Chrysocarpa' a yellow-berried one. Smooth winterberry (*I. laevigata*) doesn't need a male, is more compact, has bigger berries and turns a nice yellow color in fall.

HOW TO GROW: Most hollies need moist soil. Even those that are hardy in cold climates, such as Japanese holly, must be well watered before winter to prevent winter burn, and sometimes need screening with burlap. Inkberry and winterberry will both grow in very wet soil, though average soil suits them too. Most hollies benefit from a mulch year-round. There are no very serious pests or diseases, and plants rarely need pruning but can be cut back to lateral branches in late winter or early spring for more compact growth.

HONEYSUCKLE
Lonicera

DESCRIPTION: Vine honeysuckles are discussed on page 472, but a number of others are deciduous shrubs. They bear spring flowers, often fragrant, followed by showy berries—usually red but sometimes yellow. Most are hardy to at least Zone 4 and are upright-growing, problem-free plants. Among the best are the 9-foot tatarian honeysuckle (*Lonicera tatarica*), whose many cultivars have flowers that range from white to pink to dark red. Amur honeysuckle (*L. maackii*) is very tall with fragrant white flowers, and very hardy. Winter honeysuckle (*L. fragrantissima*) is more compact and evergreen in warm climates, with very fragrant white flowers. *L. xylosteum* 'Clavey's Dwarf' is low growing and is often used as a hedge plant.

HOW TO GROW: Honeysuckles will grow in part shade, but flowers and fruit are more abundant in sun. They are not fussy about anything, though most have a preference for moist soil. Prune them only to remove dead wood or thin overgrown plants. Most shrub honeysuckles bloom on new wood and can be pruned in early spring. One exception is winter honeysuckle, which blooms very early on old wood and should be pruned right after flowering.

HYDRANGEA
Hydrangea

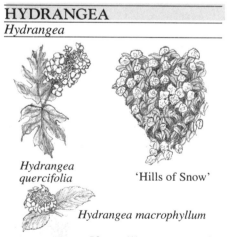

Hydrangea
quercifolia   'Hills of Snow'

Hydrangea macrophyllum

DESCRIPTION: If you like to grow a lot of large, showy flowers with a minimum of effort, hydrangeas are for you.

Peegee hydrangea (*Hydrangea paniculata grandiflora*) will grow to a large treelike plant with big balls of white flowers in July when few other shrubs are blooming, and the flowers will dry for winter bouquets right on the plant. It is hardy to Zone 4. *H. arborescens* 'Hills of Snow' is a small compact version only 3 to 4 feet tall that often dies back during the winter, though it is hardy to Zone 4. French hydrangeas (*H. macrophylla*) are often sold as houseplants and, hardy only to Zone 6 or 7, do best in warm climates. They usually stay well under 5 feet tall. Colors vary according to the many varieties, but most hydrangeas have the odd trait of turning pink in alkaline soils and blue in acid ones, just like litmus paper. (Add lime if you like pink hydrangea blossoms, aluminum sulfate or peat moss or other organic matter if you like blue.) I like the ones with flatter flower clusters, such as oak-leaf hydrangea (*H. quercifolia*), which blooms in early July but is, alas, not quite hardy in Zone 5 where I live. It forms short but wide-spreading clumps.

HOW TO GROW: Give hydrangeas fertile, humusy, moist but well-drained soil and they will take care of themselves unless it is very dry, in which case they'll need watering. Mulch helps. Either sun or part shade is suitable. Peegee and 'Hills of Snow' hydrangeas bloom on new wood, so can be cut back as needed in early spring. French and oakleaf hydrangeas should be pruned after flowering though winterkilled wood can be removed in early spring. Plants are easily propagated in spring from softwood cuttings.

JAPANESE ANDROMEDA
Pieris japonica

DESCRIPTION: Though very common

where I live, Japanese andromeda is held in great esteem as "the only shrub the deer do not eat." The plant also has other things to recommend it. The long evergreen leaves hang down in clusters, but new ones in spring are perky red-tinted rosettes. Flowers, in early spring, are dangling, creamy white bells. Andromeda grows fairly tall if not cut back and goes well with rhododendrons and laurel in the woods or near the house. It tolerates shade but flowers best in sun. I've noticed that hot afternoon sun can make it look wilted, but it soon revives.

HOW TO GROW: Plants do best in light, humusy, slightly acid soil. A mulch will help keep the soil sufficiently moist. Plant in early spring and prune after flowering to encourage branching, since plants bloom on old wood. Overgrown plants can be thinned gradually at the base or even cut to the ground; do either in early spring to give the plant a full season to make new growth.

JUNIPER
Juniperus

DESCRIPTION: Some junipers are trees (what we call "red cedar" is really a juniper). But many others are shrublike and as such are extremely useful in landscape plantings, especially since they will tolerate poor soil. They do well by the seashore as well as in hot, dry places, and they cover banks beautifully. There is great variety in their shapes, foliage textures and foliage colors; many make fine specimen plants, and the smaller ones look good in rock gardens, either as accents or trailing down over rocks. The low, spreading junipers make excellent ground covers.

Many varieties of Chinese juniper (*Juniperus chinensis*), such as the bluish 'Hetzii' and the flat-topped 'Pfitzerana,' may grow as tall as 10 feet and just as wide, sending out long, irregular horizontal branches. They are usually misused because people rarely understand how big they will grow; a compact juniper is more appropriate for most landscaping situations. But given the right space the big ones can be effective. The variety called "Sargent's juniper" forms a low, bluish mat. Varieties of common juniper (*J. communis*) include 'Depressa,' which grows under 4 feet tall, and 'Compressa,' a little gem of a plant that grows upright with a pointed top and never exceeds 2 feet. Tam juniper (*J. sabina* 'Tamariscifolia') is much used because it forms a low, wide, tidy mound of rich green. Varieties of creeping juniper (*J. horizontalis*) are the most prostrate of all: 'Wiltoni,' also called 'Blue Rug,' forms a blue mat just a few inches high that spreads widely and is excellent for the foreground of a shrub planting or in a rock garden. 'Bar Harbor' is gray-green and turns purplish in winter. Andorra juniper (*J. h. plumosa*) is taller than 'Bar Harbor' (under 2 feet) but also has a fine, purplish winter color.

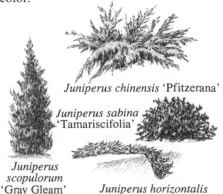

Juniperus chinensis 'Pfitzerana'

Juniperus sabina 'Tamariscifolia'

Juniperus scopulorum 'Gray Gleam'

Juniperus horizontalis

HOW TO GROW: Junipers like full sun and a soil that is rather dry, sandy, well drained and slightly acid. They rarely if ever need feeding. They should not need much pruning if you've chosen the right juniper for the spot, and they are usually appreciated for the irregularity of their branching patterns. But you can remove awkward shoots in spring or summer, trim recent growth in early spring if more bushiness is needed or cut all of the season's growth in summer to limit size. Cutting back hard to bare wood will not, however, produce branching.

KERRIA
Kerria japonica

DESCRIPTION: Kerria makes a showy display of yellow flowers in May. The original species has single ones and grows about 5 feet tall, but the more common 'Pleniflora' has flowers like little yellow balls and can grow as tall as 7 feet. The plants are vigorous almost to the point of being rampant, but in the right spot they can cheer you in two seasons, for the stems remain bright green year-round. Some have variegated leaves and make very pretty specimen plants; 'Picta' has white markings and 'Aureo-variegata' yellow ones.

HOW TO GROW: Kerrias like shaded sites but will grow in sun. Their favorite soil is rich in organic matter and well drained, but most soils will do. Plants can be propagated by dividing the roots or by layering. The major care involved is pruning tall shrubs yearly, removing stems at the base so new ones can replace them; stems can also be cut back part way, and they will branch. Prune after flowering.

LILAC
Syringa

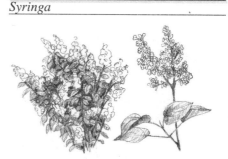

DESCRIPTION: Most lilacs are not very graceful; they get tall and leggy, and their leaves are a magnet for mildew in late summer. But their fragrant flowers redeem them, and they will always be a favorite with gardeners. The common lilac (*Syringa vulgaris*) is the one most often grown; it has spawned hybrids by the hundreds in shades of lavender, purple, rose and white. It is very hardy (to Zone 3), and I have seen it grow as tall as 20 feet.

The adventurous can experiment with other lilac species and their hybrids, for different flower shapes and growing habits and to stretch out "lilac time" to as much as six weeks. The early Korean lilac (*S. oblata dilatata*) is fairly tall and has large, fragrant lilac-pink flowers. Cut-leaf lilac (*S. laciniata*) is a short shrub (7 feet or less) with pale lilac flowers and finely cut leaves. Littleleaf lilac (*S. microphylla*) is also short but very wide; the variety 'Superba' has deep pink flowers. Persian lilac (*S. × persica*) is also very wide and spreading; the pale lilac flowers are small but very profuse.

Meyer lilac (*S. meyeri*) is short with deep purple flowers. For late bloom, try late lilac (*S. villosa*), which has long lilac or pinkish flowers, and Japanese tree lilac (*S. reticulata*, also called *S. amurenesis japonica*), which can grow as tall as 30 feet and bears long white flowers in mid-June. Most of these are hardy to at least Zone 5; early Korean lilac is hardy to Zone 4 and late lilac to Zone 3.

HOW TO GROW: Lilac likes a light, fertile, well-drained soil with a neutral pH. If yours is acid you might dig in some lime, bone meal and wood ashes. Lilacs are easy to transplant but should not be dug while the new leaves are emerging. The powdery mildew they get is unattractive but generally harmless; scale infestations should be controlled with dormant oil. The loss of branches can sometimes indicate borers in the lower stems—look for little holes with sawdust beneath them, and cut the stems and burn them.

Prune lilacs only after they have become well established. Remove the oldest stems and let a few new suckers grow up to take their place, but don't leave too many suckers that can rob the plant's energy and reduce the number of flowers. Carefully pinching off spent flowers just to the first leaves can result in more blooms the following year. Old plants can be cut as far back as 4 inches from the ground and still come back as bushy, rejuvenated plants, but this is best done over a period of three years, cutting back a third of the old stems each time. Severe pruning can be done in early spring before buds swell, lighter pruning just after bloom.

MOCK ORANGE
Philadelphus

DESCRIPTION: This lovely old-fashioned shrub bears clusters of fragrant white flowers 1 to 2 inches wide in June. Some are single, some double; the height and shape of the plants also vary, and the right size should be chosen to fit the spot. Often they have interesting peeling bark. (An old common name for this plant is "syringa," not to be confused with lilac.) Sweet mock orange (*Philadelphus coronarius*) grows as tall as 9 feet, with single flowers. *P.* × *virginalis* can be equally tall and rather leggy, but some varieties are more compact, and the flowers are usually double or semidouble. 'Albatre' is about 5 feet tall; 'Minnesota Snowflake' is tall but bushy and very hardy in cold climates. The Lemoine hybrids are among the choicest, growing 4 to 6 feet tall. 'Avalanche' and 'Belle Etoile' are compact singles; 'Boule d'Argent' a double; 'Mont Blanc' is an extra-hardy single. Most mock oranges are hardy to Zone 5.

HOW TO GROW: Mock oranges are very easy to grow, with no serious pests or diseases. Give them sun or part shade. They like moist, well-drained, humusy soil, but they aren't fussy. They can be propagated by layering or by removing and replanting suckers. Prune them lightly after bloom to keep them compact; old plants can be renewed by thinning at the base or cutting back the whole plant.

single

double

MOUNTAIN LAUREL
Kalmia latifolia

banded

freckled

DESCRIPTION: The best laurel species to grow is the American native mountain laurel, a broad-leaved evergreen that looks good as a specimen shrub, in group plantings or naturalized in a woodland setting. Most of those found in the wild have white to pale pink flowers, but new "banded laurel" hybrids are being developed with blotches, freckles or bands in vivid red, pink and purple shades. Other "red-budded" varieties have bright red buds that open gradually and give the whole flower cluster a rosy look, even in white-flowering varieties.

HOW TO GROW: Try to give mountain laurel a moist but well-drained, humusy soil just like the soil it would find in the woods. The plants will grow even in full shade, though they flower best in sun. But protect them from strong sun and drying winds in wintertime. Plant in early spring and mulch well. Mountain laurel is prone to leaf spot, which is usually just a cosmetic problem but can be treated with benomyl. Wash lacebugs off with a hose.

Mountain laurels often don't need pruning, but they can be cut back to forks or lateral branches—or even to the ground—to counteract a tendency to legginess. Those transplanted from the woods should be cut back in this manner. Drastic pruning should be done in early spring, but if you are pinching off recent growth to limit size or make plants bushy, do it after flowering, as plants bloom on old wood.

NANDINA
Nandina domestica

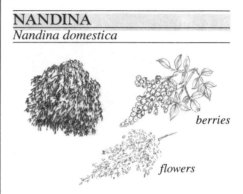

berries

flowers

DESCRIPTION: Popular in the south and on the west coast, this plant is sometimes called "heavenly bamboo" because of its bamboolike foliage. It bears large clusters of small white flowers in July, followed by even showier red berries. The foliage is evergreen, turning reddish and purple in fall and winter. Plants grow up to 8 feet tall, but there are a number of dwarf varieties such as 'Nana Purpurea,' and 'Compacta.' 'Alba' has white berries. If protected with a mulch it can grow in Zone 7 and even farther north, though the tops will be winterkilled.

HOW TO GROW: Nandina prefers sun, though it will take part shade. Though the plants will tolerate drought, a moist, light soil will produce more flowers and berries. Few pests or diseases bother it.

Large plants grow vigorously in warm climates and can become leggy. They are best pruned in early spring or after bloom, by removing some stems at the base each year and letting a supply of shorter new ones continually replace them. Old plants can be renewed by cutting half the stems to the ground one year and the rest the following year—or even by cutting all of them at once.

OLEANDER
Nerium oleander

DESCRIPTION: This southern plant actually blooms from spring to fall, with 3-inch flowers that are red, pink, yellow, purple or white, depending on variety. The leaves are evergreen and rather like those of bamboo. Oleander tolerates hot, dry conditions. Now for the bad news: Oleanders are very poisonous to people and animals. If you grow them you might warn your children against them the way my grandmother did, telling us the story of Leander's death upon eating the plant, and the exclamation of his lover, who discovered him: "Oh, Leander!" My grandmother kept the plant out of harm's way by training it as a tree (it can grow as tall as 20 feet).

HOW TO GROW: Oleander likes sun and well-drained soil. To contain its vigorous growth you may root prune it or cut the branches back to a fork in early spring. Deadheading the flowers will produce more bloom. Cutting the whole plant back to 6 inches will rejuvenate an old one. To grow as a tree, remove all stems but one and all suckers; keep removing lower branches as they start to sprout.

POTENTILLA
Potentilla fruticosa

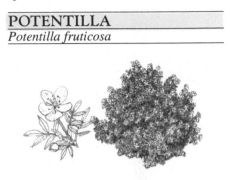

DESCRIPTION: Potentilla may not be as much of a household word as lilac or forsythia, but it is rapidly earning a place in the average gardener's repertoire. It is easy to grow, not at all fussy about soil, and compact; and though it blooms most heavily in early summer, you can count on it to come up with a few flowers all summer and into fall, especially if the weather is fairly cool. Flowers are about an inch wide and typically bright yellow, but varieties include pale yellows ('Katherine Dykes'), whites ('Mt. Everest'), and an occasional orange or peach ('Tangerine' and 'Daydawn'). Good bright yellow potentillas include 'Farreri' (also called 'Gold Drop') and 'Jackman's Variety.' Even without flowers the plants are attractive, with delicate gray-green foliage. Most form a tidy 4-foot-tall plant, though I find 'Mt. Everest' is almost prostrate. 'Klondyke' is another dwarf. I like to use potentilla near swimming pools for its summer color and because it can take the heat. It is also excellent in a foundation planting because it is both low and showy and because of the way its foliage contrasts with that of other plants.

HOW TO GROW: Potentillas like sandy,

slightly alkaline soils but will grow in most any soil. They like full sun but will be happy in part shade in very warm climates. They are pretty much pest-free. They can be propagated by layering, root division and softwood cuttings. They look fine without pruning, and it is best to plant them where they don't need to be contained, since they would need clipping often to contain them. Prune long or awkward shoots in spring, while the shrub is still dormant, and thin old shoots at the base if your plants seem overgrown.

PRIVET
Ligustrum

DESCRIPTION: Privet is an ideal hedge plant because it makes rapid, dense growth when sheared, because the leaves appear early in spring and remain for a long time in fall (some privets are even evergreen) and because the plants will withstand difficult conditions such as dry soil or the stresses of city life. They are sometimes used in other situations, though; the yellow-leaved kinds make good accent plants, for example. All bear small white flowers, in early-, mid- or late summer.

Hardy privets for the north include Amur privet (*Ligustrum amurense*), European privet (*L. vulgare*), border privet (*L. obtusifolium*) and the low-growing Regel's privet (*L. o. regelianum*)—all

hardy to Zone 4. Golden privet (*L. × vicaryi*), with yellow leaves, is hardy to Zone 5. Among the popular evergreen privets for warmer climates are Japanese privet (*L. japonicum*) and glossy privet (*L. lucidum*).

HOW TO GROW: Though privets thrive in most soils, they do need to have good drainage. Plant them in sun or part shade, about 1 or 2 feet apart for hedges. They are easy to transplant and will grow quickly. Shear privet hedges in early spring and early summer—and after that in areas where growth is very lush. Plants can be rejuvenated by cutting some old stems to the ground or by cutting the whole plant back to 6 inches.

PYRACANTHA
Pyracantha coccinea

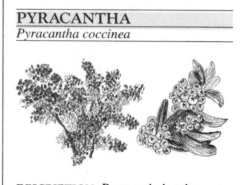

DESCRIPTION: Pyracantha's other common name is "firethorn"—appropriate because of its thorny branches and bright red or orange berries. The species listed here is the most popular, scarlet firethorn, and its most common variety is 'Lalandei,' which usually grows to about 6 feet. (Some pyracanthas grow very tall; others are low growing and used as ground covers.) Most varieties are hardy to Zone 6, but some only to Zone 7. Pyracantha is evergreen in warm climates. The most common way to use it is to let it climb up against a wall, but it also makes a good freestanding specimen plant; all kinds can be pruned into trees by removing the lower branches. It also makes a good hedge, especially if you want a thorny barrier.

HOW TO GROW: Give the plants full sun and well-drained soil. They are susceptible to fire blight, which can blacken the branches. Remove affected branches a foot below the blackened part, but never leave a stub, or it may rot. I think the plant looks best in its natural shape, but new growth can be pinched back to control the plant's size, and long or awkward branches can be cut back to a side branch after the fruits have fallen.

QUINCE
Chaenomeles

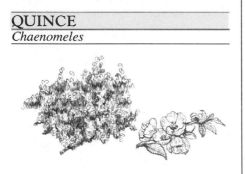

DESCRIPTION: I'd describe the growth habit of flowering quince as "picturesque"—in fact the irregularly shaped branches look much like something in a Chinese or Japanese painting. Flowering quinces are not to be confused with the large tree quinces grown for their pear-sized fruits. Flowering quinces are attractive landscape shrubs, useful either as specimen plants or as hedges. Shopping for them has been made very complicated by a number of changes in the genus's botanical names. The two most common species are Japanese quince (*Chaenomeles japonica*), which grows only 3 feet tall and has bright red-orange flowers, and common or flowering quince (*C. speciosa*), which can become a 10-foot plant, though low-growing hybrids have been developed. Both are hardy to Zone 5. You may, however, also find quinces sold as *Cydonia, Pyrus* or *Chaenomeles lagena-*

ria. But rather than engage your nurseryman in a fruitless discussion of the proper Latin name for quince, simply ask him how tall the shrub will grow, for this is the only distinction that need concern you. Hybrids come in a number of colors including white, reds, pinks and salmon or coral shades; flowers can be single, double and semidouble.

HOW TO GROW: Quinces are very easy to grow and will tolerate any reasonably good soil. Sun is best, but they will take some shade. Plants can be set in bare-root, though container-grown or balled-and-burlapped plants are best. Quinces are easily propagated by dividing the plant with a spade, especially if suckers have formed at a distance from the plant; they can also be layered. You may prune after the flowers have faded, to keep the plants compact and promote bloom. On compact plants this is rarely necessary, but some of the large ones can send out long, lanky stems that are best cut back to a side branch to make them more graceful. Old plants can be thinned at the base in winter.

RHODODENDRON
Rhododendron

DESCRIPTION: The large genus called *Rhododendron* includes many species and a huge number of varieties (including the azaleas, described on page 501).

The ones you select will depend in large part on which do well in your climate (again, see the section on azaleas). The plants are grown almost entirely for their spectacular flower clusters, which come in every color except true blue. The foliage, which is usually evergreen, is handsome during the growing season, but in cold weather the leaves droop and curl at the sides to conserve moisture— something I find rather depressing to behold on a day when I feel like drooping and curling myself.

Many gardeners find rhododendrons addictive, especially if they live in a climate that suits them, because there are always so many new ones to try. What climate suits them? One that is enough like the temperate woodland mountainsides where they grow wild (most are from the Orient, but some are native to the United States): the air is moist, but the soil drains well; leaf fall makes the soil acid; and summers are not too hot and winters not too cold.

Two American natives you might grow are rosebay rhododendron (*Rhododendron maximum*), a huge, treelike shrub hardy to Zone 4, and catawba rhododendron (*R. catawbiense*), hardy to Zone 5. The latter has produced a number of notable hybrids such as the hardy white 'Catawbiense Album' and the purple 'Roseum Elegans.' Other major groups include the Dexter hybrids, such as the lovely pink 'Scintillation,' hardy to Zone 5, and the Caucasian hybrids, including the very hardy and compact white 'Boule de Neige.' The Korean rhododendron (*R. mucronulatum*) is deciduous, hardy to Zone 5, and bears lavender flowers before the leaves. 'PJM' is a hybrid with fairly small leaves that have a nice purplish color in winter and rosy-purple flowers; it is hardy to Zone 4. Bloom times for rhododendrons can be as early as early May for Korean rhododendron, and as late as late June for rosebay rhododendron. Most fall in between.

Most rhododendrons should not be planted in front of windows or anything else you do not want obscured, for most grow at least 6 or 8 feet tall, many as tall as 15 feet and taller. They are all too often planted in spots where the owner must prune them drastically every year just to keep them in check. For sites like these choose a rhododendron like the exquisite *R. yakusimanum;* hardy to Zone 5, it slowly forms a 3-foot mound that is covered with big pink-white flower clusters in spring. Or plant some of the charming small-leaved rhododendrons such as *R. impeditum* or 'Purple Gem.'

HOW TO GROW: Give rhododendrons a light, moist soil with plenty of organic matter; moistened peat moss is the perfect thing to incorporate into the soil, because it is also acid. The plants are shallow rooted and don't need deep soil preparation, but a mulch such as shredded bark is an excellent idea to protect their roots and keep the soil moist. Plant them where they will not be exposed to drying winds or strong sunlight in winter, especially in very cold or very hot climates. A northern exposure in sunlight filtered through deciduous trees is excellent, though some varieties do not bloom quite as well in full shade.

Plant rhododendrons in early spring in cold climates, fall in warm ones. They cannot be planted bare-root. They generally do not need to be fed, though some liquid fertilizer or a top dressing of manure will help if growth is slow or if drastic pruning is anticipated. Well-grown plants do not often suffer diseases, and there are not many pests to worry about. Lacebugs will sometimes suck the undersides of the leaves, producing a stippled, yellowed look; these can be rubbed off with your fingers while active in late spring and early summer. Stems attacked by borers should be removed and burned.

Pruning is often not needed if the right site has been chosen, but sometimes plants are lanky and need some attention. The terminal buds (found in the center of a leaf rosette) can be pinched to cause side buds to develop and branches to form, or stems can be cut back to a leaf rosette (both are best done after flowering). Removing spent flowers at their base, just above the new buds, will produce heavier flowering the following year. For overgrown, leggy plants, cut back in early spring to produce lower growth. If possible, cut back to a leaf rosette, but if the stems are bare try to find the faint mark of a growth ring where dormant buds may be induced to grow. To rejuvenate gangly old plants you can cut a third of the stems back to a foot or so each spring; sometimes a whole plant cut back at once will regenerate, but this is risky.

ROSE OF SHARON
Hibiscus syriacus

DESCRIPTION: The chief value of this shrub, also known as "shrub althaea," lies in its late-summer bloom, usually coming in August. There are a number of varieties, in shades of pink, purple, blue, lavender, red and white. Flowers are usually 3 to 5 inches in diameter; extra-large ones can be produced by cutting stems back to two buds after blooming. They are tall, bushy plants growing as high as 15 feet and can be grown as trees by eliminating all but one stem and removing lower branches. They make good specimen shrubs, given enough space, and also can be used as informal hedges, though close shearing is detrimental both to bloom and to the shape of the plant.

HOW TO GROW: Plants should be set in while still young and protected with mulch until well established. Even so, until they are mature, they are susceptible to winterkill. They will grow in sun or part shade, and they like moist, humusy soil with good drainage. Pruning need only be done if you want a smaller, compact plant, or to produce larger flowers, as above. Cut back stems to laterals to control size and produce vigorous growth, and remove dead or damaged wood. Prune in winter in mild climates, early spring in cold ones.

SPIREA
Spiraea

DESCRIPTION: There are two very different groups of spireas. One consists of a number of fairly large spring-blooming shrubs with profuse white flowers. One of these is bridalwreath (*Spiraea prunifolia*), which grows as tall as 9 feet, has stems covered with buttonlike flowers in May and foliage that turns red or orange in fall. Thunberg spirea (*S. thunbergii*) grows to about 5 feet, bears clusters of flowers before the leaves, and has fuzzy foliage with some fall color. Vanhoutte spirea (*S. × vanhouttei*) grows up to 8 feet, has gracefully arching stems laden with small flower clusters in late May and some fall color. *S. nipponica* 'Snow-mound,' a more upright and compact

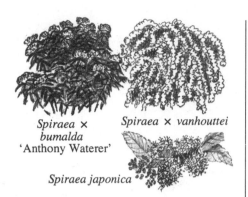

Spiraea ×
bumalda
'Anthony Waterer'

Spiraea × vanhouttei

Spiraea japonica

form than most, has flatter flower clusters. All are hardy to Zone 4, though twigs on some, particularly *S. thunbergii*, will often be winterkilled.

The other major group of spireas blooms in summer, with flat pink or red flower clusters, and includes bumalda spirea (*S. × bumalda*) and Japanese spirea (*S. japonica*). Some varieties are low and compact, others as tall as 6 feet. Ask your nurseryman how tall a plant will get before you choose a spot for it. These spireas are hardy to Zone 5.

HOW TO GROW: Spireas will be happy in almost any soil, though they do like it a bit moist if possible. They will grow well in part shade but bloom best in full sun. Give the big ones plenty of room to spill out in their lovely, arching shapes, because pruning them to a compact shape defeats their reason for being there. All the spring-blooming spireas bloom on old wood, so prune awkward shoots after flowering, unless you want to pick them for bouquets. Thinning at the base to remove old stems can be done in early spring; so can trimming to remove winterkilled twigs. The summer-blooming spireas can always be pruned in early spring since they bloom on new wood. They really do look better and flower better if old wood is thinned out regularly; this will also help to keep them low growing. Most spireas can be cut back almost to the ground.

VIBURNUM
Viburnum

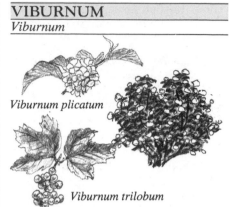

Viburnum plicatum

Viburnum trilobum

DESCRIPTION: Viburnums are a joy to grow because they are so trouble-free and because they offer so much. Most bear white flowers in mid- or late spring, some of them very fragrant; these are followed by berries, many of which are showy and either red, black or yellow. In addition many have colored foliage in fall, some of it quite striking. Sizes vary, so choose the right one for the site.

Among the best fragrant viburnums are Burkwood viburnum (*Viburnum burkwoodii*), whose flower clusters are 3-inch pinkish white balls; fragrant snowball (*V. carlcephalum*) is similar and grows to 9 feet; Korean spice viburnum (*V. carlesii*), the most fragrant of all, is only 5 feet tall, its variety 'Compacta' even smaller. All are hardy to Zone 5. Southerners favor sweet viburnum (*V. odoratissimum*), which grows to 10 feet and is hardy to Zone 8.

Other attractive viburnums include double-file viburnum (*V. plicatum tomentosum*), a tall and broadly spreading shrub with wide flower clusters atop the branches (in the variety 'Mariesi' they are especially showy). Linden viburnum (*V. dilatatum*) has very showy red berries as well as rust-red fall foliage and grows to 9 feet. Both are hardy to Zone 5. American cranberrybush (*V. trilo-*

bum) has flat flower clusters and red berries that are edible. It is hardy to Zone 3.

HOW TO GROW: Though not particular, viburnums appreciate a good, light, moist loam. They are shallow rooted and appreciate a mulch to keep roots moist and protected in winter. All will tolerate some shade, though full sun produces the best flowers and fruits. Viburnums can be propagated by layering. They rarely need pruning, though old plants can be thinned at the base. Spring-blooming species bloom on old wood, so prune the tops only after flowering, if needed.

WEIGELA
Weigela florida

DESCRIPTION: Formerly called *Diervilla,* this old-fashioned plant has only one trick, but a good one—producing small, bright flowers in May on long, arching stems. Typically red, they are little open-mouthed tubes designed just right for feeding the hummingbirds that suck their nectar. 'Vanicek' is a good red variety; there are also cultivars in shades of pink and white. (A related species, *Weigela middendorffiana,* is yellow.)

HOW TO GROW: Weigelas bloom more profusely in full sun, but they put on a

fairly respectable show even in shade. Most soils suit them fine, though they appreciate some moisture. They look best upruned, with the arching branches spilling out like a fountain, but some clipping must occasionally be done in spring in cold climates if tips have been winterkilled. Any pruning to shape is best done after flowering.

YEW
Taxus

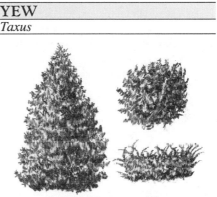

forms of Taxus cuspidata

DESCRIPTION: Most yew species are trees at maturity, not shrubs, but they are often used as shrubs, either by pruning them to keep them low, or by using compact varieties. No other evergreen responds quite so well to shearing, so yews make excellent evergreen hedges, possessing a fine, dark color that is the perfect backdrop for pale flower colors such as those of roses. Female plants have showy red berries, as long as there is a male plant around to pollinate them. Yews are trouble-free plants—in fact, their only drawback as far as I'm concerned is that they are absolutely the first food choice of our local deer. *Caution:* Yew berries are poisonous.

Most yews grown are derived from two species: English yew and Japanese yew. The English yew (*Taxus baccata*) is generally not hardy north of Zone 7, though some of its varieties, such as the low, flat-topped 'Repandens,' are hardier. Growth habits vary widely, from the tall, columnar Irish yew, 'Fastigiata,' to the 3-foot 'Nana.' Japanese yew (*T. cuspidata*) is hardy at least to Zone 5 and also comes in many forms. One of the best is 'Densa,' which grows no more than 4 feet high but can spread a lot wider than that, with very dark green needles.

HOW TO GROW: Yews will grow well in sun or shade. They appreciate moist but well-drained soil, and can be winter burned if they go into winter with dry roots and then are subjected to drying winds. A mulch will help to keep the soil moist. They may be sheared any time there is too much new growth, but more drastic pruning should be done before the season's growth starts. It is important to keep young plants shaped the way you want them as they grow, for heavy cutting back later will only result in plants that look like victims of a Pruning Shears Massacre and they may never develop a pleasing shape again.

TREES

People get attached to trees. They seem to feel more affection for them than they do for any other kind of plant. Perhaps this is because we once lived in trees, before we evolved from simian tree-swingers to human tree-planters. If you doubt the significance of that, look at children. As soon as they outgrow climbing all over their mothers, they're out there climbing into the trees if they're country children, or into "jungle gyms" and "monkey bars" if they're city kids. Having done both, I can say that trees are much more interesting. When I was a child my favorite climbing trees were old friends whose branches I'd hide in when I preferred not to be with people.

Even if all you do is look at your trees or pick up after them in fall, they take on individual personalities. Your rock-solid sugar maple cools your house in summer, eases you cheerfully into fall with the brightest and earliest color on the place and holds up your child's swing, all without asking anything in return. Your irresponsible weeping willow, on the other hand, sheds leaves all over the lawn, loses limbs in bad storms and is trying to get its roots into your septic system. But when it leafs out yellow in early spring like a long-haired blond, or does its dance of the seven veils in a summer storm, you're hooked again and let it stay another year.

Another reason we feel so strongly about trees is that they last so long. Usually they outlast us, if not in years, then by nature of the fact that we move from place to place and they remain. I have an old photo of me as a small girl, planting a 7-foot pine tree with my father. I am wielding a mattock over my shoulder, and he is holding a shovel. Before the house we lived in when the photo was made was sold, we both saw that tree tower over it—something that happens less and less as people move around more. When we do manage to live with a tree for a long time, it is sad indeed when it falls or must be cut down. It's like losing a companion. Even when a young tree doesn't work out and must be removed, its end is painful because it takes so long for a tree to grow that you feel you've wasted precious time. Mature trees give a sense of grandeur even to a modest homesite. They also add considerable value to a property. And there's no short cut—trees take a long time to attain their full size.

Growing trees is much trickier than growing smaller plants. Years may pass before you realize you've made a mistake in your choice of tree and where you've placed it, because the problems described below may not develop right away. Even when there are solutions to these problems, they get harder to implement as the tree gets bigger, encompassing a larger area to rid of insects and having higher branches to prune. And if the tree must be replaced—well, usually you can't replace it, except by waiting years for a new one to grow.

Choosing the Right Tree

Sometimes the untimely loss of a tree is unavoidable. A recent freak storm that devastated so many fine old trees in the south of England is a tragic example. Nonetheless there are things you can do as a gardener to prevent or minimize losses. Choosing the right tree in the first place is the most important one.

ORNAMENTAL FEATURES

Often the choice of a tree begins with a mental picture of a species you particularly like, either because of nostalgic associations or because it is attractive to you in some way. There are many different traits that make certain trees handsome "ornamentals" (garden trees), and these are not necessarily the same traits that make trees good for populating a forest or for producing lumber or firewood. A tree might be handsome because of its overall shape or because of its leaves—their color, shape or texture. Or it might bear showy flowers or fruits, or the bark might have an interesting color or texture. Most often a tree has a combination of several features that attract—for example, a copper beech is prized not only for its dark red leaves, but also for its massive, spreading form. A mimosa has fine-textured foliage that spreads out in a canopy, and it is also topped with fuzzy pink flowers all summer long. A paper birch has not only striking white bark, but also foliage that lets some light through (for "part-shade" gardens) and turns bright yellow in fall.

Which tree you choose will depend partly on how it looks in a specific place. The beech is an impressive sight when you drive up to a house, if placed on the front lawn. The mimosa is particularly effective if you look down on its flowers from a second-story deck or from a high embankment. The birch looks best in front of some dark evergreens that set off its white trunks.

It is also very important to give a tree plenty of room. It will neither grow well nor look good if crammed in among other trees, nor should its branches interfere with foot or vehicle traffic, and trees should never be planted under powerlines. For these and like reasons, you must make sure that when you select a tree you take into account its ultimate height and the ultimate spread of its branches. Keep scale in mind, too. So often a gardener plants a tree like a blue spruce that is a tidy

little cone when small but then grows into a 100-foot specimen that dwarfs the house and seems to bear no relation to it. Such a tree might complement a large structure, but would probably look better planted at a distance, as a background plant. Large deciduous trees often work well near to a house, however, because they shade it. But don't plant them any closer to the house than 25 feet. Their branches should not hang over the roof.

Especially if you have a small home, you may want to pick one of the smaller ornamental shade trees, such as European mountain ash, saucer magnolia, hawthorn, mimosa, the small maples such as Amur maple, paperbark maple and Japanese maple, or some of the ornamental fruit trees described in Chapter 9, such as crab apple, flowering cherry and Callery pear.

Trees vary enormously in their sizes and shapes. One might never get taller than 20 feet, another might go well over 100. Their heads (the leafy part) may be round, wide spreading, pendulous (weeping), broadly pyramidal, pointed like a church spire or even straight like a column. Try to visualize which shape will look best in the place where the tree will grow. It is unfortunate that gardeners do most of their thinking about trees when they are walking through a nursery, looking at infant trees. The best way to educate yourself about them is to visit a botanical garden or an arboretum, preferably one in the same climactic zone as yours, to see what various trees look like when they are full grown. You might even photograph some so they don't all blur together in your memory after you get home. This sounds like a lot of trouble to go to, but not when you consider how long you'll be living with those trees.

Try not to be taken too much with novelty. Sometimes new gardeners who are just discovering what a wealth of trees there are only plant their unusual discoveries. But just how many trees can you have with variegated leaves, weeping branches and peeling bark? These are accent trees that should be used judiciously. You may feel that having a yard with nothing but plain old ordinary green trees is like having a wardrobe with nothing but business suits. Maybe so. But build on the basics. As I said before, those trees will be there a long time.

Think about how your trees will look at different times of the year. Many are interesting during more than one season—with spring flowers and bright fall foliage, for example, in addition to summer greenery. And winter is just as important, especially in climates where deciduous trees are leafless for half the year or more. A number of trees, such as 'Bob White' crab apple or European mountain ash, have fruits that stay on the tree in late fall or winter. Others have bark—less visible in summer—that is a beautiful color or that peels to reveal patches of another color beneath: river birch, paperbark maple, kousa dogwood, Chinese elm, lacebark pine and Japanese stewartia to name a few. Evergreen trees can be all the more effective when the leaves are off the others, for different species have needles of varying textures, in shades of blue, gray or green. I also like to look at all the different bare shapes of deciduous trees in winter.

USEFUL TREES

Sometimes you plant a tree that will do a job. Shade trees are a prime example. For these you want a tree that will shade a house, lawn or terrace in hot weather but let in the sun when it is cold. Therefore, deciduous trees are usually chosen and planted southwest of the site to be shaded, to block the sun for as much of the hot part of the day as possible. To provide shade heavy enough for this purpose you need a tree with a dense head of leaves, like a maple or a beech. If you're not so much concerned with blocking the sun as you are with providing dappled shade for certain plants, choose trees such as birch, aspen and crab apple.

Trees make highly effective wind screens. They break the force of the wind by absorbing it rather than by rerouting it up over the barrier the way solid walls and fences can. Evergreens such as spruce, fir, cedar, arborvitae and pine are often used as wind screens, but some deciduous trees planted close together, such as beech, eucalyptus and the bushy Russian olive, can also be effective.

For visual screening, the best trees are those that have branches growing all the way to the ground. Often the most effective ones are the "fastigiate" or "columnar" trees such as 'Sentry Ginkgo,' Hinoki false cypress, columnar English oak, Irish yew and Armstrong red maple.

Plants that take hold quickly are used to hold banks and keep soil from eroding. While this can be done with ground covers or shrubs, trees such as pines also serve the purpose, especially when a screening effect is desired as well.

Generally when you are looking for a useful tree you want one that will be ornamental as well. But sometimes you just want to reforest an area that has been cleared or to plant a large number of trees to control soil erosion. In this case the trees you choose do not have to be the same kind you buy as landscaping specimens, and you do not have to buy them in large sizes. Your local Soil Conservation District or Forestry Service can advise you as to the best trees to choose for reforestation or erosion control in your climate and the specific site. They may even sell you tree seedlings at an affordable price.

If your land has woods on it, it is a very good idea to find out which trees are growing in them and learn how to manage them. Forests go through many changes in the course of time. Some trees crowd out others, and trees die and are replaced by new ones. You can control this process by eliminating less-desirable trees and by thinning the better ones to give more room to those that remain. Don't just go out in the woods with a chainsaw and start cutting, however, unless you have consulted with a forester or tree service first—they can mark trees to be eliminated or actually do the work itself for you. It takes a long time for a forest to grow and only a short time for a thoughtless person to undo nature's work. Also don't destroy all the understory plants (shrubs and small trees) in an effort to clean up your woods; these provide food and shelter for wildlife. You can make paths and remove some of the standing deadwood or fallen logs if you like (though I'd rather leave some—hollow trees and logs are homes to many creatures), but don't always feel you need to achieve the "parklike" grounds that realtors so often speak of in describing land. Find out what your woods have to offer before you take control of them.

CHOOSING TREES THAT WILL DO WELL

Finding a tree that will look good is useless if the tree will not survive. One important factor is winter-hardiness. Hardiness zone numbers are not always a good guide to how trees will fare in a given locale, for the reasons given on page 42, especially in areas where the climate varies because of changes in elevation or other conditions. For a major purchase like a tree, ask knowledgeable people in your own area to find out which ones do well. If the tree is an obscure one, buy it from a source that can advise you on its suitability. If you are taking a chance with a tree, even a slight chance, plant it where it will not be subjected to drying winds, especially in winter. Until it has weathered a few winters you might even wrap it in burlap. Very hot climates are also bad for some trees, such as larch and hemlock.

The amount of soil moisture can also be a factor in a tree's survival. Most will die if their roots sit in very wet soil. Unless your wet soil is easily corrected (page 40), choose moisture-loving trees such as swamp maple and any of the willows. For dry soils choose trees like paper birch, mimosa, red cedar and other juniper species, eucalyptus and honey locust.

If your lot is very shady, either from large trees of your own or your neighbor's, or from shade cast by a building, plant trees that naturally survive in forests, such as flowering dogwood, shadblow, and hemlock. If you are by the sea, Russian olive, Japanese black pine, Monterey pine (where hardy), blue spruce, arborvitae and hawthorn should do well.

Trees planted in cities must endure especially difficult conditions: soot and other air pollutants, dry soil, reflected heat from buildings and sidewalks. If they are street trees, add to this list such possibilities as damage from vandals or from vehicles striking the trunks, and poisoning from road salt and dog urine. Trees you can safely plant in city yards or lots include magnolia, mimosa, apple, Russian olive and Norway maple. Some good street trees are ginkgo, little-leaf linden, Washington hawthorn, red oak, Amur maple and Bradford pear.

Another thing to consider in choosing a tree is the risk of diseases or insect pests. Specific trees are susceptible to certain problems but often only in some parts of the country. I have mentioned some of these in the List of Trees, but consult your Extension Service or state university to find out which species are at risk in your area.

Finally, you should be aware that some trees are simply more long-lived than others. In general the faster a tree grows, the shorter its life will be and the more susceptible it will be to damage. Trees such as willows, poplars, birches and silver maples are short-lived and have brittle branches that break easily during storms. If you want large trees in a hurry, or if you simply like these trees very much, you can certainly plant them, especially if you have more long-lived trees as well. But you should be aware of their relative fragility and of the fact that their roots can be invasive, snaking their way into septic systems and drains in their quest for moisture. It is a good idea to keep any tree roots away from drains and leaching systems, but it is especially important with the species just mentioned.

Getting Started

G iving trees a good start in life is important. All of the advice on woody plants beginning on page 50 applies, but there are a few things to keep in mind about trees specifically.

BUYING TREES

For general information on buying woody plants see page 111. When purchasing trees, the gardener is faced with the decision of how large a tree to buy. Often it makes sense to buy very small specimens, especially if they are fast growing or you are buying a large num-

ber of them. Generally the younger the tree, the easier it is to establish. Some young trees can even be planted bareroot, which gives you the opportunity to order them through the mail and perhaps obtain varieties that are not available locally. Smaller trees are also much easier to plant than big ones—an important consideration if you are doing the work yourself. If you can patiently wait for them to grow you will have saved yourself both labor and money.

On the other hand, if you want one large specimen, or only a few, sometimes it makes sense to invest in larger stock. Perhaps you have a brand-new house on a lot devoid of trees or with no trees close by. The house looks stark and lonely sitting there by itself and may need the protection of shade trees in summer, or a line of trees to break the winter winds. In a situation like this I advise people to invest in a few large trees rather than spend money on many smaller ones. How large is large depends on your budget and also on the type of tree you're considering. (Those that are best transplanted while young are noted in the List of Trees.)

PROTECTING YOUNG TREES

After you've thought very carefully about where the tree should go, allowing for its ultimate size, plant it according to the directions beginning on page 50. Since most trees, unlike shrubs, only have one trunk, it is important to protect that trunk from damage. A tree trunk has a very thin layer of cells beneath the bark called the "cambium," which is necessary for the tree's survival. It cannot be replaced if lost, and thus if a tree is girdled—the bark cut in a complete circle around the tree—it will die (though an expert can sometimes save a girdled tree by a procedure called "bridge-grafting"). The chief threats to young tree trunks are animals such as rodents, rabbits and deer that nibble on the trunk, especially in winter, and can girdle it. A cylinder of hardware cloth, buried a few inches deep (or less, depending on what the tree's roots allow) to foil rodents and extending well above the anticipated snow level to foil rabbits and deer, will help considerably. But as trees grow, these collars should be removed so that they do not girdle the trunks themselves.

Another danger to the trunk in winter is sun scald—a burning of the trunk on its sunny side. A third is cracking of bark caused by sunny winter days followed by very cold nights. Both sun scald and cracking bark are less a problem in older trees with many branches, because even leafless branches provide some measure of shade for the trunk and because the bark of older trees is thick and tough. You can protect trunks from winter sun and wind by wrapping them in burlap or painting the trunks with white latex paint. Another form of protection is a commercial tree wrap, such as the white plastic guards that are wrapped in a spiral up the tree. These will help protect against animals, too, but should be removed during the growing season so that the trunk can get light and air.

Trees are often badly damaged by being struck with lawn mowers. The best solution to this problem is to mulch the area around the tree so that there is no need for the lawn mower to come close. If trees are planted near a parking area, driveway or road, you may need a barrier to keep vehicles from striking them. Sometimes just a row of railroad

STAKING TREES

Fig. 67

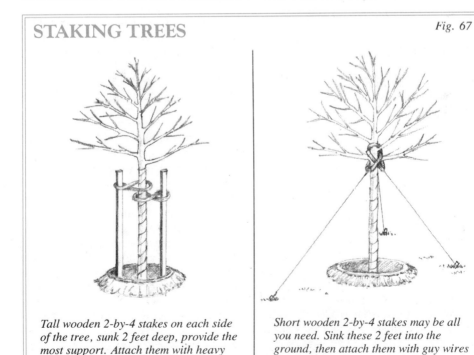

Tall wooden 2-by-4 stakes on each side of the tree, sunk 2 feet deep, provide the most support. Attach them with heavy wire threaded through sections of garden hose to protect the trunk.

Short wooden 2-by-4 stakes may be all you need. Sink these 2 feet into the ground, then attach them with guy wires looped around the lower branches and threaded through sections of hose.

ties that defines the driveway area will do the trick.

Staking new trees used to be a commonplace procedure, but the advisability of using tall stakes has recently come into question. Some studies have shown that the play of an unstaked tree in the wind helps it to develop a sturdy, tapered trunk that doesn't need support. Often a tree that is planted correctly, with a large enough root ball, won't need staking. If it is in a windy site, however, and it's a tall tree with a good, full head on it, stakes may be necessary, at least for the first year. If you are not sure whether a tree needs staking you might compromise by using the short stakes shown in Figure 67, which will allow some swaying but will prevent the tree from tipping or pulling out of the ground in strong winds.

Taking Care of Trees

M ost trees, once established, don't need much care. But while they are building new root systems and canopies of leaves to provide themselves with food, they usually need some help.

WATERING

It is important to keep young trees thoroughly watered. A deep soaking once a week in dry weather is much more valuable than a daily sprinkling that only wets the top inch or two of the soil and never gets down to root level. If you have built a dirt saucer around the tree when you planted it (page 52), you can simply put the end of a garden hose into the saucer, turn it on part way so a trickle runs out and leave it there for an hour or two. Or you can do the same with a soaker hose that you lay in a

circle around the tree. A 3- to 4-inch mulch of a material such as shredded bark, shredded leaves or wood chips will help the soil around the tree stay moist, as well as give the roots some winter protection (page 490). If mice are a problem, leave a few inches of unmulched ground close to the trunk or substitute a gravel mulch in that area.

FEEDING

Established trees don't usually need to be fed, but a young tree will benefit by a yearly feeding in late fall. Fall application will give the fertilizer time to work its way down to the roots by the following spring. You can use a pelletted commercial fertilizer (about 2 pounds of 10-10-10 for each inch of the tree's diameter), compost, a combination of rotted manure and bone meal, or whatever works best for you. Make sure you apply the fertilizer at the outermost circle of the tree's root system, where the feeder roots are. A mature tree's root spread is very large and reaches even farther out than the branches, whereas a tree that has only been in place a year will not have roots extending very much past the original root ball. In between it's a guessing game, but to be safe put some fertilizer out at least as far as the tree's branches reach (the "drip line"). With deep-rooted trees you can remove the mulch and scratch fertilizer into the soil; with shallow-rooted ones it is better just to scatter it or spread it on the ground. Some gardeners deep-feed tree roots by making holes with a crowbar or using an injection device, but I feel this is something you only need to do if a tree is badly stressed and needs fertilizing in a hurry. And even in cases like these I would be more apt to just spread a layer of manure or compost or give the tree periodic feedings with a liquid fertilizer and water it in well.

PESTS AND DISEASES

This subject is treated in general terms beginning on page 68. When you are dealing with trees, pest and disease control is more complicated than with smaller plants. You certainly can't hand-pick all the bugs off a tree, unless it's a very small one. One alternative is to spray. Spraying a tree is something best tackled by a professional. Consider, also, whether you need to spray at all: a great deal of spray is needed to treat a tree, and the spray must cover a vast area. The hazard to animal life from spraying trees can therefore be great. There are exceptions: if I had valuable trees that were prone to scale insects, for example, I might hire someone to spray them with dormant oil (page 73) before they leafed out, as protection, for insects that attack leaves may cause the trees to look unsightly and even defoliate them. If that doesn't happen every year, however (and many insect plagues come in cycles), the trees will probably recover from an insect attack. Furthermore, borers that attack trunks and branches can often be controlled without spraying by digging them out and destroying them.

All in all, the best way to deal with insect damage is to prevent it: avoid planting trees that commonly attract certain bugs in your area, and try to keep your trees as healthy and vigorous as possible by giving them good soil, water, food if they need it and the right amount of sun.

With diseases, control is similar: it is partly a matter of choosing trees that are not disease-prone where you live, and partly a matter of keeping trees healthy and vigorous. If possible, infected parts of the tree should be removed. Ends of twigs that are blackened by fire blight and stems infected with canker should be cut off, if you can reach them safely. Crown galls (knobby growths on the trunk and branches) can be cut out. If fungus diseases such as anthracnose or leaf spot appear on the leaves, rake up any that fall and destroy them, so that the disease will not overwinter in the soil.

It is difficult to diagnose tree diseases: the best approach is to put a sample of the diseased tissue in a plastic bag and bring it or mail it to your Extension Service for diagnosis. And don't give up on a tree too soon. It may surprise you and survive a plague that appears to be quite deadly. In a few cases where a serious disease threatens all trees of a certain type in your area, it is necessary to remove infected ones to prevent the spread, but these situations are rare.

WATCHING FOR SIGNS OF STRESS

Often when a tree is in poor condition no disease or insect is at fault. Many situations can cause trees simple physical stress. So before you start hunting for a bug or microbe, try asking yourself these questions about the tree.

Is the soil around it dry? If leaves look scorched or wilted it may be that the roots aren't getting enough water. The tree may also drop some of its leaves to prevent them from giving off too much water through transpiration. Soak the ground thoroughly and mulch the tree if possible.

Is the soil too wet? Leaves that turn brown and "dieback" (in which branches die at the top of the tree) are signs of general decline and may mean that a tree's roots are not getting enough oxygen because the soil is poorly drained (page 40). If the tree is small, consider moving it to a drier spot; if not, try to correct the drainage problem.

Is the soil compacted? If there is

general decline, determine whether the soil around the roots is receiving vehicle traffic or heavy foot traffic, or if it has been compacted by recent construction. Can the traffic be rerouted? If construction has caused problems, I try to dig some organic matter into the soil as deeply as possible without damaging the roots so that air, water and nutrients can circulate freely. Then I apply a heavy mulch—at least 4 inches. The spread of a tree's roots may seem like a very large area to mulch heavily, but mulch can often save a stressed tree, perhaps because it provides a cover so much like that of the forest floor.

Have the roots been damaged? If there has been construction near a tree—even outside the reach of the branches—the roots may be severely affected. Even digging a trench to lay a pipe can cause the death of a tree that is close by. If you suspect root damage, feed and mulch the tree as described above.

Trees can also suffer from construction that changes the grade of the soil around the tree—even by a few inches. Removing soil can bring the roots too close to the surface and even expose them; in these cases the soil should be replaced. Adding soil to a tree's site can rob the roots of food and air. If the soil level has been raised around the trunk of a tree, a tree well should be constructed. This involves digging down to the original soil level around the trunk, building a circular retaining wall to keep the excess soil away from the trunk and installing drainage tiles that will carry water and air out to the root tips. Ideally this should be done *before* the grade is changed; it is a job for professionals.

Are there enough nutrients? If the leaves are pale and small, flowers few or nonexistent and the tree spindly, the tree may need fertilizing.

Is the climate too cold or the site too unprotected? Even if a tree is hardy enough to survive your winters, leaf and flower buds may be killed in winter or by early-spring frosts that nip them after they start to open. The result may be poor leaf growth as well as lack of flowers and fruit. The best spot for a tender tree is one protected from winter winds and also from bright spring sunshine that will cause buds to open too soon. If the tree is well established and too big to move, you might try planting some sturdy, fast-growing evergreens such as white pines near it. They will shield it from wind or afternoon sun.

Have toxic materials affected the tree? If your trees are being poisoned by toxic elements in the environment, the cause of the trouble may be hard to diagnose, since different toxins produce different symptoms. But if deciduous leaves are scorched, glazed, or streaked, and if evergreen needles of recent growth are falling, air pollution may be the problem—one you can do little about. (An evergreen tree's dropping needles, however, is not *necessarily* a cause for concern. Even though they do not shed all of the present year's growth the way deciduous trees do, evergreens do shed some needles each year. Some species hold on to their needles longer than others. While three years is about average, pines shed needles the second fall after they appear, and junipers can hold them ten years or more.)

Trees that look as if they were suffering from drought may be contaminated by ground pollution; here you may be able to track the source and remove it. Injury to roots from herbicides used on weeds usually produces distorted new growth (twisted needles, puckered leaves). Use of the herbicide should be discontinued. Road salt is a very common culprit, causing branches and even whole trees to die. If the salt is from your own driveway or walkway, use mechanical means to remove ice and snow instead, or choose trees that are salt-resistant, such as oak, hawthorn, honey locust and the trees suggested above for seaside plantings. Avoid trees like pine and arborvitae, which are very susceptible to salt.

MAKING TREES FEEL AT HOME

In taking care of trees always remember where they naturally choose to grow: in the woods in the company of other trees. They do not choose to grow in the middle of lawns, surrounded by grass, a covering that affords the roots little shade or protection and competes with them for water and nutrients. Before planting a tree in the middle of your lawn, consider these alternatives:

Plant it at the edge instead. Often a tree on a house lawn sticks out like a sore thumb, especially a large tree that is not in scale with the house. Planted at the edge of the lawn, with other trees of varying heights, the same tree may fit in much better. A shade tree that must be fairly near the house can be visually tied in with a foundation or entryway shrub planting by using the same type of mulch or ground cover under it as you use for the shrubs.

Create a grove. Try planting several trees together as if they were a tiny woodland. Each tree must be given enough room to spread to its full width, but they may be grouped in a distinct area that is not treated as lawn but is rather mulched and underplanted with occasional groups of bulbs and ferns. Grass does not grow well under trees, anyway.

If you must plant a tree alone, at least mulch it. A thick layer of mulch will cool the soil and encourage feeder roots to come up to the topsoil where nutrients are most plentiful. Even raking the leaves from the lawn in fall and

piling them under the tree will help. In planting ground covers under trees I try to avoid those with thick, matted, hungry root systems, such as pachysandra. (See Chapter 12 for more information on ground covers.)

Pruning Trees

Many of the same principles explained in the section on pruning shrubs (page 492) also apply to trees. By cutting back twigs or branches you can induce branching and increase flower and fruit production. You can also thin trees by removing upper branches to let more light into the center of the tree, and you can stimulate growth of lower branches, though you would rarely thin at the base of the tree as you would with shrubs. A tree may even be thinned to lessen its wind resistance in very windy areas.

A tree will have a better shape when mature if you remove branches that grow in toward the center, or straight up, or straight down, and branches that crisscross one another either in a horizontal or vertical plane (Figure 68). Branches that simply look awkward or give the tree an asymmetrical appearance can also be removed. Eliminate branches with weak crotches—those that are tight and vertical as opposed to open and U-shaped. If a tree is of the type that should have a "leader," or central trunk, that continues up to the top of the tree but instead has two competing leaders, you should eliminate one of them early on. Multiple trunks can be thinned at the base to just one. If horizontal branches develop water sprouts (small branches that stick straight up) or suckers (branches that sprout from the bottom of the trunk), these too should be eliminated. If the tree's size must be restricted, upper branches can be cut back to an outward-facing side branch. Lower branches can be removed to expose an attractive trunk or allow you to walk under the canopy, though it is wise to await until at least several years after you plant the tree to do this, to keep the young trunk shaded against sun scald and to avoid reducing the number of leaves too much.

In general a tree will not look its best if you prune it in a way that interferes with its natural shape. If it is a round-headed tree, don't try to make it columnar. If it is a wide-spreading tree, let it spread, eliminating only branches that are too long or heavy and threaten to break.

It is important to do major shaping while the tree is young, for two reasons. First, early pruning for shape will start the tree off on the right road by giving it a pleasing form, something that cutting a large tree back will never really accomplish. Second, you will do the work while it can still be done safely. Small trees can be pruned with precision by using pruning shears, loppers and short-handled pruning saws while you stand on the ground. As they get larger you can still prune and stand on the ground by using a pruning saw on a pole, but this becomes more and more difficult to do well as time goes on. I will sometimes sit on a lower branch and lop off water sprouts or awkward branches, as shown on page 525, but believe me, in that picture I am not very far from the ground. Climbing high into trees is dangerous, and I would *never* climb up into a tree with a chainsaw. Pruning tall trees is, as far as I'm concerned, the work of a tree surgeon.

Sometimes there are pruning jobs that must be done on mature trees. Any deadwood should be removed. Branches that break should be cut back either to the trunk or to a healthy side branch. Prune large branches yourself only if you can do it with both feet on the ground. And cut the branch back gradually so that its weight will not tear the bark all the way to the trunk when the branch falls (Figure 68). In severing a branch, when you make your final cut, don't cut so close to the branch that you destroy the "branch collar"—the circular ridge that runs around the base of a branch. This collar will help the cut to close over and heal.

Wounds in a tree that are made by disease or physical blows should be cleaned out with a knife so there is no dead, rotting tissue. Then make an elliptical vertical cut (Figure 68) around the wound; this will heal better than an irregular or horizontal cut. Hollow cavities in trees do not need to be filled. There is much debate about whether cuts you make in tree branches should be covered with paint or a wound dressing or left bare. I'm not sure either treatment keeps out insects or disease organisms, so I cut as cleanly as possible and leave the wounds to heal themselves.

I think that when dealing with trees it is important to know your limitations. There is a lot to learn about trees, and each kind is a bit different from all others in the way it grows and the way it should be cared for. Unless you are quite expert you will not know when a tree needs to be cabled to prevent breakage, for example, let alone be able to do it safely and successfully. That's where the experts come in. Good tree surgeons, or "tree men," can be expensive, but I put them in the same category as doctors and vets—they are not something to skimp on when they are needed. Remember—you are not Paul Bunyan. You are not even Tarzan, even though you may once have loved to climb trees.

PRUNING TREES

Fig. 68

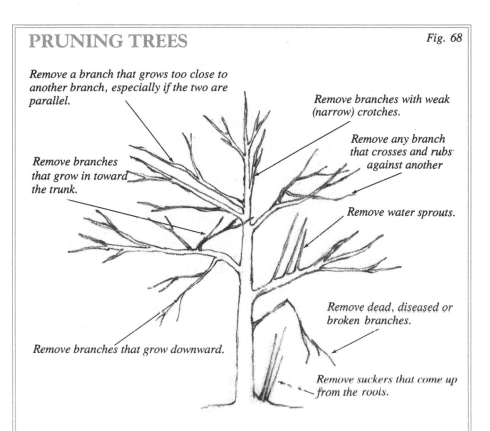

Remove a branch that grows too close to another branch, especially if the two are parallel.

Remove branches with weak (narrow) crotches.

Remove any branch that crosses and rubs against another

Remove branches that grow in toward the trunk.

Remove water sprouts.

Remove dead, diseased or broken branches.

Remove branches that grow downward.

Remove suckers that come up from the roots.

Pruning to make a well-spaced framework.

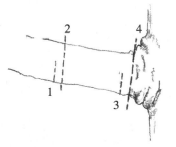

branch collar

Undercutting a branch to prevent the bark from tearing (numbers indicate the right order in which to make the cuts). The final cut should be flush with the branch collar but should not damage it.

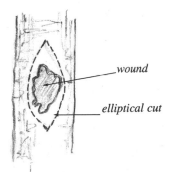

wound

elliptical cut

The right way to repair a wound in a tree.

LIST OF TREES

The trees included here are special because of their beauty and their general usefulness as landscape trees. While some are native American forest trees valuable for lumber or fuel, it is not their use for these purposes that has put them on this list. Nor were trees selected for their edible fruits, though many fruit-bearing trees are commonly grown as ornamentals. (Some are described in Chapter 9.)

Narrowing the list down to twenty trees was difficult. The result is merely a selection of popular trees that do well in at least 50 percent of the country. Do try some of the more unusual trees not on the list, such as smoke tree (*Cotinus americanus*), with its flowers like puffs of smoke, or franklinia (*Franklinia alatamaha*), which has white flowers and brilliant red-orange fall leaves and was named after Benjamin Franklin. And by all means use trees that are particularly effective in your part of the country, such as the blue gum trees (*Eucalyptus globulus*), which make such attractive wind screens in California, or the acacias (*Acacia decurrens, A. dealbata*), laden with fragrant yellow flowers in spring, which do so well in very warm climates. And consider growing some nut-bearing trees such as black walnut or pecan.

ARBORVITAE
Thuja

DESCRIPTION: Arborvitae is a good tree to use if you need a tall vertical evergreen either for an accent or for a hedge. A row of them planted 4–5 feet apart will grow into a dense barrier that will screen out sights, sounds and wind year-round. The trees are fairly slow growing and have flat, scalelike needles. The most popular species is American arborvitae (*Thuja occidentalis*), which grows as tall as 60 feet with a church-steeple shape, reaches about 15 feet across on the bottom if grown by itself and is hardy as far north as Zone 2. Unfortunately it tends to turn brown in winter. The many garden-worthy varieties, most of them much smaller than the original species, include the slender 'Fastigiata' and 'Columnaris,' and the dark green 'Techni,' or mission arborvitae, which grows to 15 feet. Dwarf varieties include 'Woodwardii,' or globe arborvitae. It is round and grows very slowly to 8 feet but can easily be kept as low as 3. There are also a number of gold-colored dwarf varieties.

Western arborvitae (*T. plicata*), also known as "giant arborvitae" or "western red cedar," stays green in winter, and while it can grow as tall as 200 feet, it can be kept smaller by pruning; it is hardy to Zone 5. Oriental arborvitae (*T. orientalis*, also called *Platycladus orientalis*), hardy to Zone 6 or 7, is popular in warmer climates.

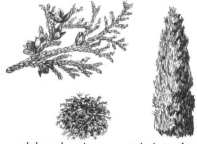

globe arborvitae   *mission arborvitae*

HOW TO GROW: Plant arborvitae balled-and-burlapped or container-grown, in full sun or part shade. In nature it chooses moist sites and should be given fertile soil with adequate moisture. Plants are susceptible to red spider mite and bagworm in some areas. Since the plant makes a rather tidy shape on its own it doesn't often need pruning, but it can be sheared in late winter to shape or contain it. Upright forms should be trained to one leader. Cutting back to bare wood will not produce branching.

ASH
Fraxinus

DESCRIPTION: Ash is a useful tree because many kinds of plants can be grown in the dappled shade that it casts. Varieties of several native American ashes are used as garden trees. White ash (*Fraxinus americana*) grows very quickly and can reach 120 feet; it is hardy to Zone 4. Fall foliage is yellow or purple, and in varieties such as 'Autumn Purple' and 'Rosehill' the fall color is especially showy. On the negative side the tree self-sows very aggressively. Green ash (*F. pennsylvanica lanceolata*) is a smaller tree, hardy to Zone 3. Male green ash trees do not produce seed, so are less of a nuisance in the garden; they are often sold as 'Marshall's' or 'Marshall's Seedless.'

Other ashes of interest to the gardener include velvet ash (*F. velutina*) which is popular in the south (to Zone 6) for its compact size and yellow fall color, and flowering ash (*F. ornus*),

which is also hardy to Zone 6 but dislikes intense heat. It bears profuse white flowers in late spring. For mountain ash (*Sorbus*), see page 549.

HOW TO GROW: Ash trees are easy to establish and can be planted bare-root. They like full sun and a deep, fertile, moist soil. They are sometimes bothered by scale insects and borers. As with all fast-growing trees, ash wood tends to be fragile, so it is important when pruning to eliminate branches with weak V-crotches and leave those that will grow strong. Ash trees should have one central leader. Prune in winter or early spring.

BEECH
Fagus

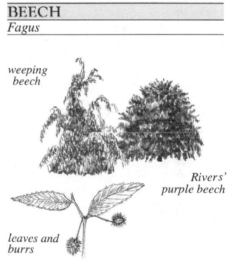

weeping beech

Rivers' purple beech

leaves and burrs

DESCRIPTION: Beeches are monumental trees that are long-lived and beautiful year-round. They form huge, round, spreading heads, whose branches often sweep the ground. The oval, toothed leaves turn dark gold in fall; the smooth gray bark is striking in winter. These trees need a large space all their own. The overhanging branches create an enclosed world of deep shade where nothing will grow, and the shallow roots emerge from the soil, forming great snakes along the ground.

The American beech (*Fagus grandifolia*) grows up to 90 feet tall and 60 feet wide, and is hardy to Zone 4. The European beech (*F. sylvatica*) is similar, and hardy to Zone 5. Most of the more unusual hybrids come from European beech: the weeping 'Pendula,' the fern-leaved 'Asplenifolia,' the upright 'Fastigiata,' the variegated ones such as pink-bordered 'Roseomarginata' and those that have deep red leaves year-round, such as the popular copper beech ('Cuprea'). All of these grow very large, and all but the upright ones get very wide.

HOW TO GROW: Give beeches a deep, well-drained, acid, fertile soil, well supplied with organic matter. They prefer full sun but will grow well in part shade. Plant them balled-and-burlapped, taking care not to plant too deeply or pile too much soil over the roots, which like to be near the surface. Prune in late winter. Young trees should be trained to a central leader, and branches with weak crotches should be removed since the wood is brittle and the branches grow long and heavy. Lower branches may be removed, if you like, so that you can walk under the tree and so that the handsome trunk will be visible.

BIRCH
Betula

DESCRIPTION: Birches are not long-lived trees, but they are graceful ones, and they are valued for their open branches that cast light shade, their yellow fall color, and their attractive bark, which varies from species to species. They are fast growing. Their flowers, born in spring, are fuzzy, dangling catkins. Birches look particularly fine with a background of evergreens, and are attractive planted in groves.

When most people think of birches they think of the paper birch, or canoe birch (*Betula papyrifera*), with its white bark marked with black bands and blotches. This native tree grows as tall as 90 feet, usually forming clumps. It is more long-lived when trained to one trunk, but the clumps are pretty, and it may be your choice to grow them that way. Paper birch is very hardy (to Zone 2) and resistant to borers, though like most birches its trunks and branches are easily broken by winter storms. Sweet birch (*B. lenta*) is another native, hardy to Zone 4, with attractive dark bark and good fall color. River birch, or red birch, (*B. nigra*), is valued for its beautiful reddish brown peeling bark. It is hardy to Zone 5 but needs a moist site.

Most of the fancier birch hybrids come from the tree called European white birch or silver birch (*B. pendula*, also known as *B. alba* and *B. verrucosa*). It grows up to 50 or 60 feet and has white bark that tends to darken with age. Silver birch is more or less weeping in habit, especially 'Youngii,' a popular variety. Others include 'Purpurea,' with purple leaves; 'Fastigiata,' which is narrow and upright, and cutleaf European birch ('Gracilis'), which is slightly weeping and has very fine foliage. The trouble with European white birch is that it is susceptible to both the bronze birch borer, which eats the wood underneath the bark, and the birch leaf miner, which can defoliate it (though trees are rarely killed). Paper birch, on the other hand, is resistant to both. A Japanese birch with white bark, *B. platyphylla japonica,* is resistant to birch borer.

HOW TO GROW: Birches are not easily moved and should be planted balled-and-burlapped. They like full sun and fairly moist but well-drained, moderately fertile soil. Birches are best pruned while young. Prune to form a single trunk and to remove awkward branches, branches with weak crotches, and branches growing low on the trunk that would obscure it. Try to restrict later pruning, as cuts do not heal easily. Prune before the sap starts to flow in late winter; otherwise pruning can be messy, since birches are bleeders, and cuts made after the sap begins to run will not heal well.

DOGWOOD
Cornus

Cornus kousa   Cornus florida

DESCRIPTION: The dogwoods comprise a varied group of trees and shrubs, useful for different purposes. The flowering dogwood (*Cornus florida*) is the most familiar—an extremely graceful tree with horizontal branches that tilt upward at the ends. Most are about 25 feet tall, though they can grow 30 feet and higher, and are hardy to Zone 5.

Little fat, pointed buds that perch on the branch tips bear showy white or pink flowers (which are actually leaflike structures called "bracts") in spring before the leaves appear, and are followed in fall by red berries. Fall foliage is a handsome dark red. 'Rubra' is the standard pink variety and 'Cherokee Chief' a red-flowering one. Kousa dogwood (*C. kousa*) has similar flowers, though they are always white and the bracts are pointed rather than notched. Their flowers appear several weeks later than those of *C. florida,* along with the leaves. Red raspberrylike fruits follow. The tree is less graceful in form and often has several trunks, though it can be trained to one; its chief advantage is that it is not affected by the disease problems that have devastated so many flowering dogwood trees in the northeast in recent years. Pacific dogwood (*C. nuttallii*) grows over 40 feet tall and is hardy to Zone 7; it has very large, showy white flowers in spring and sometimes reblooms in fall.

Cornelian cherry (*C. mas*) grows to about 25 feet with a spread of up to 15 feet and bears fluffy yellow flowers in early spring followed by edible red berries. Leaves are red in fall, and there are some variegated varieties. It is hardy to Zone 5 and resists drought, pests and diseases.

In addition there are two shrubby dogwood species grown for their bright red stems—especially striking in winter against the snow, and valuable for their extreme hardiness (to Zone 2). Tartarian dogwood (*C. alba*) usually grows to about 6 feet but can get as high as 10, with white flowers in spring followed by whitish berries in late summer. Variegated varieties included the yellow-edged 'Spaethii' and white-edged 'Elegantissima.' 'Sibirica' has stems that are a very bright coral red. Red osier dogwood (*C. stolonifera,* also called *C.*

sericea) can grow equally tall but is usually low and spreading. The variety 'Flaviramea' has bright yellow stems and can be planted with the red-stemmed varieties for a dramatic effect.

HOW TO GROW: Dogwoods like moist, well-drained soil, though red osier dogwood will grow in very wet soils as well. Soil should be slightly acid and fairly rich, and should contain plenty of organic matter. Plant dogwoods balled-and-burlapped in early spring while plants are young. Kousa dogwood does best in full sun but will take some shade. Flowering dogwood does well in sun or part shade, but the ideal site is at the edge of a wooded area, a site the tree would prefer in nature. It is much more vulnerable planted alone in a lawn where the shallow root system is not protected by leaf cover. Another problem with planting *C. florida* in a lawn is that it is especially susceptible to herbicide damage.

Flower buds, which are formed the year before blooming, can be killed during harsh winters. Borers can be dug out and cankers pruned out. Anthracnose, which causes the lower branches to die back, will eventually kill the whole tree and cannot be cured effectively.

Flowering dogwood should be pruned as little as possible; like birch it bleeds sap in spring, and its wounds heal slowly. Prune in late summer to remove injured or awkward branches as needed. Kousa dogwood and cornelian cherry can be pruned at the bottom to train them to one trunk, or left as tall shrubs. Tartarian and red osier dogwood should have old stems that have lost their red color cut out at the base regularly to promote bright red new growth. In addition suckers that come up from underground stolons must often be removed to control the plant's spread.

FIR
Abies

DESCRIPTION: Firs are imposing forest trees. Like any tall evergreen they are handsome in the right spot, where their size and form are in scale with their surroundings. They are all cold-climate trees. Concolor fir (*Abies concolor*), also known as "white fir," will eventually grow over 75 feet tall. It looks rather like a blue spruce but with longer needles (about 2 inches). It is hardy to Zone 4 and resists heat, drought and city conditions. Noble fir (*A. procera*) is a very tall fir that does well on the west coast and is hardy to Zone 6. Korean fir (*Abies koreana*) is small as firs go (to 50 feet), with fat, upright cones, and is hardy to Zone 6.

HOW TO GROW: Plant firs balled-and-burlapped or bare-root in moist, well-drained, slightly acid soil. They do not tolerate wind well, especially if it is hot and dry. Firs can be shaped while young by cutting back the tips in late winter or early spring, but cutting back hard will not induce branching. Trees should be trained to a central leader. If the leader is lost, a side branch can be pulled over and tied to the trunk to make it upright. The branch will become the new leader.

GINKGO
Ginkgo biloba

DESCRIPTION: The ginkgo is also called "maidenhair tree," because the fan-shaped, two-lobed leaves look something like fronds of maidenhair fern, to which the gingko is, oddly enough, related. Like ferns, gingkos are ancient—among the oldest plant species known. The gingko comes to us from China and is hardy to Zone 5. The tree will sometimes grow 100 feet tall or more in old age, but it grows quite slowly. Plenty of space should be allowed for it; its spread can be 40 feet wide. The ginkgo's greatest virtue is its ability to adapt successfully to city streets. The branches shoot out at odd, irregular angles, giving it an interesting appearance, then fill in as the tree grows older, to form a dense, round mass. Fall color is a glorious yellow. There are male and female trees, males being much preferred because the females produce foul-smelling fruit. (A reputable nursery will specify the sex of the tree it sells you.) There is a weeping variety, 'Pendula,' and an excellent columnar one, 'Sentry Ginkgo.'

HOW TO GROW: Plant ginkgos balled-and-burlapped in any reasonably fertile soil, but make sure the soil is well drained. They are easy to establish but should be thoroughly watered after planting. There are no serious pests or diseases. Usually ginkgos are not pruned but are left to go their eccentric way; nevertheless, pruning can be done in early spring if necessary.

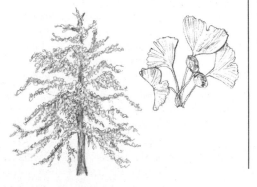

HAWTHORN
Crataegus

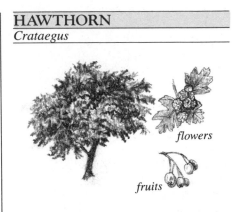

flowers

fruits

DESCRIPTION: Hawthorns are among the best ornamental trees, especially when a small tree is needed. They have thorns, as the name suggests, and fruit called "haws." The English hawthorn (*Crataegus oxyacantha*, also called *C. laevigata*) is the "may" tree about which there are so many folk traditions in the British Isles. Its clusters of small, white, spring flowers have such light-hearted associations as the "Queen of the May," but they have a dark side as well. An English friend of mine tells me his grandmother still considers it very bad luck to bring a branch of may indoors. Growing to about 15 feet, English hawthorn bears red berries in fall, but the fall foliage is not colorful. There are many varieties, including 'Paul's Scarlet,' with double red flowers, 'Rosea-plena,' a double pink, and 'Autumn Glory,' a white-flowering variety valued for its showy, long-lasting fruits.

Washington hawthorn (*C. phaenopyrum*) is rather upright but becomes more rounded as it ages, growing as tall as 30 feet. The white flowers generally bloom in June, the leaves turn red-orange in fall, and the red berries last till spring. Glossy hawthorn (*C. nitida*) is rather similar, with earlier flowers. Lavalle hawthorn (*C. × lavallei*) is May-blooming and about 20 feet tall, with red fall color and red-orange fruits.

All these mentioned are hardy to Zone 5. The cockspur thorn (*C. crus-galli*) is hardy to Zone 3. It grows well over 30 feet, but is multistemmed and often grown as a shrubby hedge.

HOW TO GROW: Hawthorns are best planted while they are small, because their long taproot makes them hard to move. Plant them balled-and-burlapped in early spring. They like full sun and will tolerate drought and rather poor soil, though a fine organic loam suits them best. They make good city trees. Leaf blight can spoil their appearance and even defoliate them, so sweep up and destroy all diseased leaves. Prune in winter or early spring, while the trees are dormant, thinning to let in light, to remove low branches, and to shape the tree, remembering that some irregularity and even shrubbiness is appropriate in a hawthorn. Suckers can be cut at any time.

HEMLOCK
Tsuga

DESCRIPTION: Hemlocks are tall, stately forest evergreens that adapt better than most trees to garden sites. One reason is the hemlock's graceful appearance: its slightly drooping branches and feathery needles seem to soften the tree's impact even when it is large, making it suitable as a specimen plant. Another is the ease with which hemlocks are sheared to a compact shape, allowing them to be used as hedges, either for screening or as a background for other plants. The most commonly used species for either purpose is Canadian hemlock (*Tsuga canadensis*) which grows as tall as 90 feet and is hardy to Zone 4. The unusual variety 'Pendula' (Sargent's weeping hemlock) forms mounds of drooping greenery in very picturesque shapes; it does not grow tall but spreads outward, cascading onto the ground, and is a much-prized specimen plant. Carolina hemlock (*T. caroliniana*) is a denser, shorter tree, hardy to Zone 5. Japanese hemlock (*T. diversifolia*), hardy to Zone 6, can get very tall but grows slowly and often remains shrublike, with multiple trunks.

HOW TO GROW: Hemlocks are best planted balled-and-burlapped, but since they are relatively easy to move, they can also be planted bare-root, which, being cheaper, may make more sense if hemlocks are to be used for hedges. They will be bushier, more filled-out plants if grown in full sun, but they will grow in part or full shade. Hemlocks need a deep, moist soil and dislike dry winds, drought and heat. They sometimes fall prey to hemlock scale, which is treated with a dormant oil spray. Hemlocks will put out new growth even when cut back hard. When used as hedges they should be sheared regularly from the time they are young. Shear each year in early spring before growth starts, and again in midsummer. Specimen trees are sheared by nurserymen to make them denser and bushier, but you may prefer the more open shape of the tree's natural growth. Normally hemlocks need little or no pruning, except that it is best to train to a single leader.

LARCH
Larix

DESCRIPTION: Larches look for all the world like evergreen trees. Their long, waving twigs have tufts of small nee-

branches can be removed for head room or if they are weak and straggly. The trees should have a central leader; if that is damaged, replace with another branch as described in the listing for fir.

LINDEN
Tilia

dles; they even have cones. But come fall those needles turn yellow and fall off, just like the leaves of any deciduous tree. And the wood is more like that of deciduous hardwood trees than the softer-wooded evergreens. Larches are beautiful in the wild; a stand of them will turn a hillside a bright pale green in early spring when the needles start to grow, and bright yellow in fall. But I have also lived with a larch on the lawn, as a specimen tree, and I found it a handsome, unusual accent. The native American larch (*Larix laricina*), also called "eastern larch" and "tamarack," grows as tall as 90 feet in an open pyramid. It is fast growing and one of the hardiest trees known. It will even live in Zone 1, regions of which are simply referred to as "the tamarack" because that's about all that grows there. European larch (*L. decidua*), hardy to Zone 2, is taller and is perhaps best known for the variety *L. d.* 'Pendula,' whose limbs have gracefully drooping side branches. Japanese larch (*L. leptolepsis* or *L. kaempferi*), hardy to Zone 4, is also pendulous, with peeling bark. It grows very fast and is more resistant to canker than other larches.

HOW TO GROW: Larches need a cool climate. They prefer a sunny location and deep, fertile, rather acid soil that is moist but well drained. They are easy to transplant but are best planted balled-and-burlapped in fall or early spring. Larches rarely need pruning. Lower

DESCRIPTION: Lindens are tall and fast growing, with an attractive, dense shape. They are used as shade trees and often as street trees. They bear dangling clusters of fragrant white flowers in early summer. Littleleaf linden (*Tilia cordata*), a European tree, is among the best. It grows up to 90 feet tall in a dense, compact pyramid and is hardy to Zone 4. Small, heart-shaped, dark green leaves turn yellow in fall in cool climates. 'Greenspire' is a particularly well-shaped, fast-growing variety. American linden, or basswood (*T. americana*), is a bit shorter and a bit hardier, but it lacks the good fall color. Silver linden (*T. tomentosa*, also known as *T. alba* and *T. argentea*) has leaves with whitish undersides that give the tree a silvery look when the wind blows; it is hardy to Zone 5.

HOW TO GROW: Grow lindens in deep, fertile, moist but well-drained soil in sun or part shade. Plant them balled-and-burlapped. Young trees should be pruned in late winter to develop a strong central leader, and lower branches can be removed to allow movement under them; but in general lindens develop a handsome, symmetrical shape on their own. Old trees can be thinned to remove deadwood and admit light.

MAGNOLIA
Magnolia

saucer magnolia

star magnolia

DESCRIPTION: Magnolias are handsome ornamental trees, with their showy flowers, their dark green leaves and their relatively small size. They are generally thought of as southern plants, but there are species that will do well in the north, even though they may not make you feel like Scarlett O'Hara. Saucer magnolia (*Magnolia × soulangiana*) grows about 25 feet tall, usually with several trunks, with smooth, dark gray bark. The large flowers, white streaked with pink and purple, sit upright at the tips of the branches before the leaves appear. Star magnolia is a considerably smaller tree; the flowers, which appear quite early in spring, are like large, fragile white stars. The foliage is much finer textured than that of saucer magnolia. Both are hardy to about Zone 5, but in cold climates are best grown in a partly shaded exposure to retard bloom—early flowers can be killed by

cold, and late snowstorms can turn star magnolia blossoms into tattered wrecks. Southern magnolia, also called "bull bay" (*M. grandiflora*), is a native evergreen, single-trunked tree that can grow as tall as 90 feet, though it is usually a good bit shorter. It is hardy to Zone 7, though it may survive farther north if grown in a sheltered location. It has huge, glossy, dark green leaves and fragrant white flowers that can be as large as a foot across. Its seed pods, which open in fall to reveal red seeds, are also ornamental.

HOW TO GROW: Magnolias generally like full sun, except in the situation described above, and except for southern magnolia, which is fairly shade-tolerant. All like fertile, loose, well-drained soil that is rich in organic matter, with a slightly acid pH. Magnolias do not transplant easily and should be planted balled-and-burlapped in spring. The roots are shallow, and care should be taken when cultivating around them. Keep the soil moist while the trees are becoming established, and mulch them. Magnolia scale can be treated with a dormant oil spray. Magnolias do not respond well to pruning because the wounds do not heal easily. But any dead or diseased wood should be removed. Remove water sprouts, suckers and any undesirable branches while they are small, if possible, pruning after flowering in early summer. Spent blossoms can be removed for better bloom the following year, but usually magnolias bloom prolifically on their own. The shorter kinds can be trained to one trunk or allowed to be shrublike.

MAPLE
Acer

DESCRIPTION: Everyone knows what a maple leaf looks like, right? It's the leaf on the Canadian flag, the one that lends its shape to maple sugar candies. Well, yes and no. While most maple leaves do have a three-lobed outline, they vary enormously in size and shape. With some the lobes are barely indented, with some they are so deeply cut they look like lace. Some even have three separate leaflets the way poison ivy does. Size of the tree also varies a great deal, and you can find a suitable maple whether you want a large shade tree or a small ornamental for a city yard. Most maples have especially fine fall color and seeds with wings on either side that you can spread apart and stick on the bridge of your nose if you are so inclined.

sugar maple

silver maple

Japanese maple

Of the large maples I especially like the sugar maple, also called "rock maple" (*Acer saccharum*), a fine shade tree that can grow well over 100 feet tall, with a big, round, dense head and leaves that turn shades of red, yellow and orange in fall. Collecting and boiling down the sweet sap to make maple syrup is a lot of work (it must be reduced to less than a thirtieth of its original volume) but it is a good way to get outdoors at the end of winter. 'October Glory' is a variety of sugar maple with especially good fall color; 'Newton Sentry' is a columnar form.

Red maple, also called "swamp maple" (*A. rubrum*), is nearly as popular as sugar maple, because its showy red flowers are such a welcome sight amid bare branches in early spring. Like sugar maple, it turns color early in fall, but in this case the leaves are blazing red. It is a bit less sturdy than sugar maple but will tolerate wet sites. Norway maple (*A. platanoides*), a big, round tree, casts a very dense shade and is rather shallow rooted, but it grows quickly as maples go. 'Erectum' is a columnar variety, and 'Crimson King' has red leaves all summer. All these are hardy to Zone 4. Silver maple (*A. saccharinum*) is often planted because of its very fast growth, its graceful, pendulous branches and its finely cut leaves with silvery undersides, which cast a dappled shade. It is also hardy to Zone 3. Silver maple has weak, breakable wood, however, and its roots can clog drains and septic systems if the tree is planted near them.

Of the smaller ornamental maples the choicest is Japanese maple (*A. palmatum*) and its hybrids. The original species, which can grow to 20 feet, has fine, deeply indented green leaves in summer that are reddish when they first emerge and turn red in fall. It is hardy to Zone 5 and self-sows freely. Varieties such as 'Atropurpureum' and 'Sanguineum' are dark red all season. The very slow growing cutleaf, or laceleaf Japanese maple (*A. p. dissectum*), can grow to 12 feet but is usually much smaller; an exquisite mound of cascading branches is supported by a twisted, picturesque trunk, with its lacy leaves often sweeping the ground. Varieties such as 'Atropurpureum' and 'Burgundy Lace' are red all season. In addition there are variegated varieties and some with leaves so fine they look like threads, such as 'Red Filigree.'

Among smaller maples those also worthy of note are Amur maple (*A. ginnala*), a tough little tree that grows up to 20 feet and has small, three-pointed leaves, fragrant white flowers in early spring, bright red fall foliage and showy red-winged fruits. It is even hardy to Zone 2. Often it has several trunks but can be trained to one if desired. Paperbark maple (*A. griseum*) grows about 25 feet tall, has leaves with three distinct leaflets and is valued most for its bark, which peels off in papery strips to expose a rust-colored layer beneath. It is hardy to Zone 6.

HOW TO GROW: Maples in general are easy to grow and have few pests or diseases. Most of them, especially red maples, need soil with adequate moisture. Most need plenty of sun, and if they are to develop a good fall color, they need a climate that is cool in winter. Cutleaf Japanese maple should be given a rich, moist, well-drained soil with plenty of organic matter and some light shade in hot climates. It should be staked until the trunk is well developed, and twiggy growth may be removed from the center as needed (though it is usually allowed to assume its own eccentric forms). Maples in general are pruned in late summer or fall when the sap is no longer running. Most need only occasional attention to remove dead, awkward or crossing limbs. But silver maples should be pruned to eliminate narrow, weak crotches and water sprouts. Paperbark maple should have lower branches removed to display the trunk.

MIMOSA
Albizia julibrissin

DESCRIPTION: Sometimes known as "silk trees," mimosas grow up to 35 or 40 feet tall, with very wide spreading branches and often several trunks. Fuzzy, pink-stamened flowers, which attract hummingbirds, bloom all summer—an unusually long period—and are followed by long, dangling seed pods. The leaves are finely textured, almost fernlike. The trees do not live a long time, possibly thirty years, but they have the advantage of blooming while very young. They are hardy to Zone 7 but will sometimes survive farther north in protected spots. Some varieties, such as 'Tryon,' are somewhat resistant to the wilt disease that lives in the soil and can plague mimosas in warm climates.

HOW TO GROW: Grow mimosa in full sun or part shade. It will tolerate dry, poor soil, but its soil must be well drained. Plant balled-and-burlapped in early spring while the plant is young, and stake until the roots are established. Mimosas can be pruned to a single trunk but are perfectly fine as multitrunked trees; lower branches are generally removed to enhance the shape of the canopy, as are any vertical ones that spoil the rather flat-topped effect. But prune as little as possible, never leaving a stub, because wounds on this tree can invite fungi and decay. Trees can be pruned while dormant in warm climates but not until after frost danger is past in cool ones.

MOUNTAIN ASH
Sorbus

DESCRIPTION: Though vulnerable to pests and diseases in some areas, mountain ashes are still popular ornamental or shade trees because of their size (most are under 50 feet), their rapid growth, their flat clusters of white flowers in spring, and in particular their showy, long-lasting red-orange berries, which the birds like as much as we do. Mountain ash even has showy red-orange foliage in fall. In short, it is worth trying,

though perhaps not a safe bet for mass plantings. There are a number of garden-worthy mountain ashes, some of them native to the U.S. European mountain ash, or rowan tree (*Sorbus aucuparia*), is the most widely grown, however. It is hardy to Zone 3 and grows as tall as 45 feet, with rather fernlike leaves. 'Fastigiata' is an upright variety, and 'Xanthocarpa' has yellow berries. Korean mountain ash (*S. alnifolia*), hardy to at least Zone 5, can sometimes grow as tall as 60 feet and has a rounded head that can extend all the way to the ground, though you might want to remove lower branches so as to view the smooth, gray bark of the trunk. Both the berries and the autumn leaves are extremely showy, though the foliage is not as finely cut as that of European mountain ash.

HOW TO GROW: Plant the trees balled-and-burlapped in full sun and a moist but well-drained soil. Newly planted trees benefit from staking. Fire blight may blacken the ends of branches, especially in the south. Affected branches should be pruned out. Young trunks may need to be protected from sun scald in the north. Borers may be found in the trunk near the ground in some regions in the east and can be destroyed by probing their burrows with a wire—laborious, but a labor of love if you have a fine tree. (Korean mountain ash is somewhat resistant to borers.) Older trees rarely need pruning, but young ones can be pruned in winter or early spring to produce one central leader and to remove crossed or vertical branches or ones with weak crotches. You may prune multi-trunked trees to a single trunk while they're young, if desired, and remove lower branches to allow headroom.

OAK
Quercus

white oak

red oak

DESCRIPTION: Oaks are very sturdy, deep-rooted, long-lived trees. Most are deciduous, but a few are evergreen. They tend to have round, spreading heads and cast a shade that is less dense than, for example, that cast by maples. The leaves are quite acid but make good compost or mulch because they don't mat. All oaks bear the familiar acorns and some hang onto their dead leaves in fall after the leaves of most other trees have fallen. White oak (*Quercus alba*), the classic "mighty oak," grows as tall as 100 feet with a large, round head and purplish red leaves in fall. It is low growing, taprooted and hard to move, so plant it young. White oak is hardy to Zone 5. Red oak (*Q. borealis* or *Q. rubra*) is somewhat shorter but grows faster and is easier to transplant. It also has bright red leaves in fall, resists pollution well and is hardy to Zone 4. Scarlet oak (*Q. coccinea*) has even brighter fall leaves but is a bit less hardy and is difficult to move. Pin oak (*Q. palustris*) has small, very indented leaves, a spire shape and dense, rather drooping branches that are attractive when planted with enough space to display them without interference. Leaves are red in fall, and the dead ones cling to the tree all winter. It is fast growing, easy to move and hardy to Zone 5.

English oak (*Q. robur*), hardy to Zone 5 or 6, lacks the colorful fall foliage of most oaks and is known mostly for its unusual ornamental varieties such as the columnar 'Fastigiata' and others that are purple-leaved or cut leaved. Willow oak (*Q. phellos*) has very fine, almost willowlike foliage that is yellow in fall. It is fast growing and hardy to Zone 6. Like pin oak, it tolerates wet soil. If you live on the west coast you can grow the splendid California oak, also called "coast live oak" (*Q. agrifolia*), a glossy-leaved evergreen that can grow quite tall but is more often 50 feet high or less, spreading widely on gnarled, twisted branches. Hardy only to Zone 9, it tolerates poor soil and drought. Southerners can grow the southern live oak (*Q. virginiana*), a large, wide-spreading tree that is evergreen in the Deep South, where it drips with Spanish moss. It grows quickly to as tall as 60 feet but can spread much wider than that, and is hardy to Zone 7.

HOW TO GROW: Oaks like full sun and average, slightly acid soil. Unfortunately they are rather like a big, strong man who constantly has a cold. They get various diseases, including a fungus that enters the trunk and creates gaping cavities. Borers and gypsy moths love oaks. The best defense is to give the trees a good site with sun and air circulation and good soil, and mulch them lovingly each year so as to help them resist these plagues. Oaks can be pruned while young to develop a strong central leader. They have a tendency to get twiggy. Side branches can be cut to induce longer branches to form, but they should be cut back to the main branch, since stubs left will produce more dense twigs. Mature oaks seldom need pruning. The strong wood resists breakage, but dead branches should be removed.

PINE
Pinus

DESCRIPTION: There are many pines suitable for use in the landscape, from small rock-garden specimens to towering forest trees; most are easy to grow. They have longer needles than most evergreens. Their branches generally have an open appearance, largely because most species shed their needles after the second season, so that only the ends of branches have foliage. A grove of pines with a carpet of fallen needles—even a small one with only three or four trees—is a lovely thing to have on your property.

Eastern white pine (*Pinus strobus*) has particularly long needles, and a rather bushy, pyramidal shape, growing as tall as 150 feet. It is hardy to Zone 3 and makes a fine specimen plant as well as a screen or hedge. There are columnar and weeping forms of white pine, as well as the excellent dwarf variety 'Nana,' which grows slowly and can reach 10 feet in height and as much as 10 feet in width, though it is usually much smaller. In shape, 'Nana' forms a tidy globe. Scotch pine (*P. sylvestris*) is

even hardier (to Zone 2), with bluish needles and reddish bark; because of its attractive dense shape it is often grown for Christmas trees. Japanese black pine (*P. thunbergii*) is a tall pine, hardy to Zone 5, that is very valuable in seaside plantings. Strong winds only seem to make it more interesting, and it displays trunks and branches at odd angles. It has long, dark green needles and dark brown bark. Mugo (or mugho) pine (*P. mugo mugo*) is a garden standby, because it behaves like a shrub, with long, thickly bunched needles. It grows slowly to 8 feet tall and at least as wide, and is hardy to Zone 2. But allow plenty of room for it to grow upward and spread outward, unless you buy one of the compact varieties (and in that case be sure it really *is* a compact one).

In the west, if you have the space, you can grow ponderosa pine (*P. ponderosa*), a stately, fast-growing tree that can attain a height of 150 feet and is hardy to Zone 6. Another fine western pine is Monterey pine (*P. radiata*), which can grow quickly to 60 feet and more and is hardy to Zone 7. As a seaside tree it has the same virtues that Japanese black pine has, and it is especially beautiful perched on the rocky headlands of the California coast.

Japanese white pine (*P. parviflora*) is another picturesque pine, especially the variety 'Glauca' (silver Japanese white pine), which has short, bluish needles growing in tufts. It is hardy to Zone 6, Zone 5 with protection. Perhaps the most choice pine of all is bristlecone pine (*P. aristata*), native to the American southwest. In the east it makes a very special rock-garden plant, with densely bunched needles, each plant having a shape all its own. Bristlecone pines look like gnarled old men, stunted by wind, drought and age. Plants in warm areas can grow to 45 feet, and these plants are often several thousand years old! In cool climates they grow very slowly and remain much smaller— a twenty-year-old plant might be 5 feet tall, and it can be kept even more diminutive by pinching it back. Bristlecones are hardy to Zone 5 or 6.

HOW TO GROW: Most pines seem to like a rather dry, sandy, well-drained soil on the acid side, though mugo pine will tolerate alkaline soil too. Pines like full sun. Most are easily transplanted and can be planted bare-root while young. White pine can be killed by a blister rust that is carried by gooseberries and currants; don't plant either if you or your neighbors grow white pine.

Pines are pruned by pinching their new shoots, or "candles," in half before the needles on them develop. This will both restrain growth and promote branching. You can treat the candles in two ways: pinch only the central candle in each bunch, or, for a more drastic effect, pinch each candle. Pines are trained to a central leader, and all dead branches should be removed where they join the trunk, including the lower branches, which tend to die as the tree ages. Cutting back to the part of the branch that has no needles will kill the branch.

RUSSIAN OLIVE
Elaeagnus angustifolia

DESCRIPTION: Russian olive is a fast-growing, round-headed tree that tends to be shrublike but can be trained to a single trunk. The trunks are wonderful gnarled, twisted things, with shedding, dark-colored bark. The tree can grow to 25 feet and spread equally as wide. It has long, willowlike leaves with silvery undersides. The leaves are Russian olive's chief ornamental feature. Fragrant flowers in early summer are greenish yellow, and the oval berries that follow are yellow with touches of silver. The trees are thorny and make good thick barriers, and they are also good wind screens. Like most gray-leaved plants they are excellent seaside specimens. You can even shear them like hedges. They are extremely hardy (to Zone 2) and long-lived. Don't expect them to produce anything resembling olives, though. The olives we eat come from another plant altogether (*Olea europaea*). I like to plant Russian olives in hot, exposed areas such as near swimming pools.

HOW TO GROW: These trees like a sandy loam best and will tolerate hot, dry, cold, salty and windy conditions. The only thing that really deters them is poor drainage. They can be planted bare-root and are pest-free, though a disease will sometimes kill the lower branches; prune these out, disinfecting your tools between cuts. You may leave healthy trees unpruned if you want a very dense plant, but you may also train them to a single trunk and remove lower branches so the trunks may be better seen. By the sea it is a good idea to shorten long branches that can break off in heavy winds, and to thin old trees. Russian olive responds very well to pruning; cutting them back hard promotes new growth.

SPRUCE
Picea

DESCRIPTION: Spruces are tall, fast-growing evergreen trees with symmetrical spire shapes. You can distinguish them from firs, which they resemble, in two ways: spruce needles can be rolled between the fingers, whereas the needles of fir (and hemlock) feel flat; and spruce cones hang from the branches rather than sit on top of them. Colorado spruce (*Picea pungens*) is a popular tree with a classic Christmas tree shape and smell. On healthy specimens, the branches extend all the way to the ground in dense, graceful layers. Blue spruce (*P. p.* 'Glauca') is very widely grown, though the caution expressed on page 527 should be noted. Needles of blue spruce have a bluish cast, but the degree of blueness varies from one tree to another. 'Koster' blue spruce (also called 'Argentea') is a more dependable true blue than most varieties. White spruce (*P. glauca*) likewise forms a tall, dense spire with a bluish cast. The variety 'Conica' (dwarf Alberta spruce) is a striking tree, growing slowly to 10 feet in a soft, fuzzy, pale green cone—an excellent accent plant. Norway spruce, whose botanical name, *Picea abies,* literally means "spruce fir," forms a broad, dense, dark green pyramid with distinctive upward-lifting branches and drooping side branches. It too is a massive tree that can be out of scale next to a home, but there are several small ornamental varieties of this spruce, such as 'Nidiformis' (bird's nest spruce), which grows to a mere 3 feet, with a flat top. All the spruces mentioned are hardy to Zone 2.

HOW TO GROW: To counteract their tendency to lose their lower branches, give spruces plenty of sun, and don't crowd them. They will tolerate heat or cold and most soils, including dry ones, but the soil should be well drained (Norway spruce likes a bit more fertility and moisture). Norway and Colorado spruce can be planted bare-root. Pests include spruce gall aphids, spider mites and scale; dormant oil sprays can be effective against all of them. It is difficult to prune large spruce trees without ruining their shape. They can be trained to one leader while young; awkward branches can be cut to a side branch if necessary. But for the most part pruning consists only of removing dead branches.

WILLOW
Salix

DESCRIPTION: Willows, whose vices and virtues are explained on page 526, are lovely trees in the right spot. Of all the species, the weeping willows are the most popular and are best planted by a pond or stream or where you want a pretty, fast-growing specimen tree but where the roots will not wreak havoc with your plumbing. Babylon weeping willow (*Salix babylonica*) is the best one where it is hardy (to Zone 6). It grows to about 40 feet, with long branches that sweep the ground and fine-textured leaves. In Zone 5 you can grow the Thurlow weeping willow (*S.* × *elegantissima*), which is similar, or one of the varieties of white willow (*S. alba*), which is hardy to Zone 2. It normally grows rather upright, but the one called 'Tristis' (golden weeping willow) is pendulous, with a fine fall color.

Pussy willows are a different story from willow trees. The native pussy willow, *S. discolor,* is a rather weedy, upright plant that produces the familiar gray, furry bumps along its stems just before the catkins leaf out in yellow bristles. It grows to 20 feet and is hardy to Zone 4. Goat willow, or white willow (*S. caprea*), is an import that grows a bit taller and has larger, showier "pussies" (which, by the way, are produced only on the male plant).

HOW TO GROW: Willows will grow in most average soils but prefer moist, even wet conditions. You may need to water them during dry spells until the root systems are developed. They grow best in full sun, though native pussy willows also thrive in the woods. They are among the easiest trees to establish and can be planted bare-root. They are easily propagated by cuttings or just by sticking a willow wand into moist soil. Weeping willows benefit from careful pruning, which encourages them to develop a strong central leader and strong upper branches—the idea is to get the branches to grow tall and arching so that they can support the long, weeping twigs. While the tree is young, prune to one central stem with a few good side branches, but keep removing the lower ones. Do this in late summer or fall, since willows bleed sap. Keep removing water sprouts from branches, and any suckers at the base of the plant. If you remove a branch, remove all of it; cutting back partway produces twiggy growth that will mar the overall effect. Trailing branches may be pruned at the ends, however, if they are in the way. Pussy willows are pruned like shrubs and should be cut back hard to produce fresh new stems. This will restrain the vertical growth and keep the twigs within reach for picking. You can cut out the old stems at the base, or even cut back all of them to force the whole plant to regrow.

CHAPTER 16

WILDFLOWERS

Throughout this book I've been telling you to look to nature for gardening advice: to see how nature fertilizes plants; to note how nature provides leaf mulches; to respect the balance of power that nature maintains among insects and plants; to take from nature ideas about grouping plants and designing gardens. With wildflower gardening this principle is especially important. It may seem obvious that wildflowers need to be grown the way nature grows them, but a surprising number of gardeners ignore this fact. As a result their wildflowers fail to thrive, and the gardeners become discouraged about growing them.

This is too bad, because if it's done right, growing wildflowers is one of the most satisfying forms of gardening there is. The bare spots in the lawn where shade once kept grass from growing can be a miniature woodland glade spotted with purple trilliums and Virginia bluebells in spring. The unmown grassy area out back could have patches of goldenrod, Queen Anne's lace and other meadow flowers, for color all summer. The boggy place where it seems nothing worthwhile could ever grow might nurture clumps of red cardinal flower and pink turtleheads in late summer. None of these lovely pictures can be counted on to happen by accident—but gardeners can create them. Certainly nature might put Queen Anne's lace in the meadow, but she might also decide that burdock and poison ivy would be more appropriate. As a gardener you can gently change her mind.

What Is Wildflower Gardening?

First, let me explain a few things that wildflower gardening is not.

It is not gardening with weeds. Both weeds and wildflowers grow wild, but a weed, by definition, is unwelcome. Interestingly enough, some of the worst weed pests are not native American plants, but plants introduced either intentionally or accidentally to our shores, their seeds mixed in with grain seed or hiding in the mud on visitors' boots. Without the ecological checks and balances nature maintained in their native lands, they have become rampant. Some of the weedy plants listed on page 58 do work well as wildflowers (tansy and jewelweed, for example) if given a spot where they can establish themselves and spread without interfering with anything. But the wildflower gardener also has many plants to choose from that are not invasive or "weedy." (See the List of Wildflowers for some especially good plants to start with.)

Sometimes the best wildflowers for gardening are imports—European wildflowers, or exquisite alpines, perhaps. But most of the ones that are best for the beginner's first attempt are native not only to the United States but to the specific area where the gardener lives. The less you have to adjust a site to give the plant a spot where it feels at home, the more rewarding your early attempts will be. With local species you can also go and see these plants growing in their native habitats and so better understand their needs.

Wildflower gardening is not digging up plants from the wild. If you go out walking in the woods or fields, see flowers you like, dig them up, bring them home and replant them, there is an excellent chance that they will die. For one thing, the time of year when wildflowers are showiest, prettiest and most recognizable is generally the worst time to transplant them. For another, even if you mark the spot where they grow and dig them later on when they are dormant, you may not be able to transplant them successfully. Just because a plant is growing happily in the woods without anyone's help does not mean that it is easy to grow at home or easy to transplant. Some wild plants are extremely particular about where they grow: how much sun or shade they get, how much moisture, what the soil texture or pH is, even what specific microorganisms inhabit the soil. Pink lady's slipper is a prime example of a plant that is very difficult to transplant from the wild (although its relative the yellow lady's slipper, *Cypripedium calceolus,* is a good plant for a beginner to grow). A certain fungus must be present in the soil for the pink lady's slipper to thrive, and it would be extremely difficult for anyone but a veteran wildflower gardener to provide just the right conditions for transplanting it.

The last and most important reason for not digging up wildflowers in the wild is that many are becoming endangered because of this very practice. Even species that seem quite plentiful are being depleted, often by nurseries that collect plants from the wild rather than propagate them.

The wisest—and most responsible —course for a beginning wildflower gardener is to start with a few species that are known as being easy to transplant and adaptable to the home setting. These should be live plants or seeds from a nursery or mail-order supplier that propagates its own stock. Your local nursery may sell some wildflowers potted up, but you will have a much wider choice if you order dormant plants from mail-order companies. Some reliable sources are listed beginning on page 614; but if you are buying from a place whose propagation policies are unknown to you, you should ask them to tell you what they are and avoid those that rely on collection.

If you really get involved in wildflower gardening you will probably want to learn how to grow wildflowers from seed. You can buy seed from mail-order companies that sell it, or you can collect seed yourself in the wild, taking only the few seeds you need. You can also join a society that, as part of its membership program, has a seed exchange. Both collecting and growing wildflower seeds can require considerable knowledge and skill—as well as patience. (The books listed on page 631 offer guidance.) With some species you must wait many years between the time you sow the seeds and the time they bloom. For these reasons a beginner is usually better off starting with dormant clumps of mature perennial plants. (These will sometimes arrive in the mail as "sods"—matted clumps with soil attached.) But if you enjoy this kind of gardening you might want to join a local native plant society, not only to learn more, but to meet other enthusiasts and to swap plant divisions and seeds with fellow gardeners (page 617).

Wildflower gardening is not maintenance-free. Often it is low-maintenance, but sometimes not. A colony of wildflowers will not maintain itself unless conditions are right. If you have successfully matched the plant with the right setting and planted it with care, it may look after itself, especially if it is a vigorous spreader. But many wildflowers, though easy to grow, will not withstand competition from other wild plants, including grasses. In addition, plants in nature often simply come and go. A wildflower you find in one spot may not be there the next year for a variety of reasons, and you'll probably want to help ensure the survival of those you plant by protecting them better than nature does—weeding, mulching and feeding them as needed.

In short, wildflower gardening is

much more like gardening with standard garden hybrids than you probably thought. It involves buying plants from nurseries, planting them in prepared soil, weeding them, mulching them, watering them and performing other tasks to help keep them alive and productive. If you undertand this, you'll save yourself a lot of disappointment.

Wild Plants Versus Hybrids

"Wildflower gardening" and "naturalizing" are closely related topics, but they are not precisely the same thing. "Naturalistic" or "naturalized" plantings are designed to look as if they were the work of nature, not man. They are most convincing when you use local wild species, but you can also achieve a natural, informal look by using species native to other parts of the country or the world, and even by using garden hybrids. The drifts of spring bulbs mentioned so frequently in Chapter 10 are a good example of this: all are hybrids of species native to other lands, but sprinkled here and there, even growing in grass, they look right at home. The same natural effect can be achieved with garden annuals and perennials that are planted where they can increase by self-sowing or by creeping rootstocks. Take bee balm, for example. You might choose to exclude it from your more formal garden because of its spreading habit but allow it to form large colorful clumps in a moist spot at the edge of the lawn. In doing so you might use either a hybrid bee balm or a wild species such as *Monarda fistulosa*—the effect would be much the same. My own feeling is that there is no reason to be a purist about wildflower gardening. If a hybrid is readily available and known to be a good garden plant, I would use it just as readily in a wild setting as I would the true native.

Wildflowers in Gardens

On other occasions you might want to take a wild species and use it in a conventional garden setting. A large number of the perennials that we use for sunny herbaceous borders are simply native meadow flowers, usually in a hybrid form but occasionally the wild species. Some of these are liatris, yarrow, New England or New York aster, butterfly weed, lupine and clustered bellflower. All are discussed in Chapter 6. Goldenrod and Queen Anne's lace, described in this chapter, are also suitable for a garden. Other wildflowers that you might use in a sunny perennial border are the tall, fuzzy-leaved mulleins (*Verbascum* species), pearly everlasting (*Anaphalis margaritacea*) with its white buttonlike flowers so useful in dried arrangements, bright blue chicory (*Cichorium intybus*) and the common white oxeye daisy (*Chrysanthemum leucanthemum*).

Native species that can be used in shaded perennial gardens include fringed bleeding heart, wild columbines, various monkshoods and wild blue phlox (all are discussed in Chapter 6). There are many more, including a number discussed in the List of Wildflowers, such as bottle gentians, Virginia bluebell, turtlehead and cardinal flower.

For the most part this chapter deals with native plants naturalized in a wild setting, or planted in well-supervised "wild gardens" that look natural but are collections of native plants carefully grouped together and conscientiously maintained. But keep in mind that with many plants you have the option of using wild ones in tame settings and hybrid ones in wild settings. In the List of Wildflowers, I have selected natives that are easy to grow. I hope that if you find these plants rewarding, you'll do some exploring on your own in this very large, fascinating and challenging field.

Matching the Plant to the Site

With wildflower gardening the choice of plant, soil preparation, planting and maintenance are all keyed to the site. Rather than creating a "lowest common denominator" soil that will support all the plants you decide will look good in the garden, as you would in a conventional flower bed, you are dealing with small microenvironments that are gardened in specific ways.

One of the smartest things you can do as a wildflower gardener is to explore the countryside in the area where you live and see which species thrive. Take along with you a good wildflower field guide, such as one of those listed in the back of this book, to help you identify them. Note which sites they choose in the wild and how they grow. Are particular wildflowers in small clumps or do they carpet the ground? Are they in full sun, part shade or full shade? Is the soil dry, average, damp or wet? What company do they keep? Often there are "companion plants," which appreciate the same conditions and might also look good in your plantings.

WOODLAND GARDENS

Woods are different everywhere you go, but in every kind of woods, there are certain plants that will do well. Each region has its own combinations of trees that predominate and its own "understory" plants—the shrubby plants that grow in the shade of these trees. Again, each woods has soil conditions that are much influenced by the depth of the tree roots and the materials that the trees' leaves add to the soil when they fall. Some woodland soils are very rich and moist, while others are rather dry and not as fertile. Some have extremely acid soil, others less so. These factors must all be kept in mind when you are choosing woodland plants to grow.

The light requirements of woodland plants also vary. Some woodland plants like to grow where a clearing in the woods admits some sunlight. Others are happy with just the sun they get in springtime before the deciduous trees leaf out and shade the forest floor. Some of these, called "spring ephemerals," actually go dormant in summer and disappear from view until the following spring; Virginia bluebell is an example. A few, such as bunchberry, will even tolerate the all-season shade and highly acidic soil of evergreen forests, but it is much easier to find plants for deciduous woods. Spruce trees, in particular, are virtually impossible to garden under; not only do they cast deep shade, but their needles are toxic to herbaceous plants.

You do not need woods to grow woodland plants, but if there are woods on your property you have the ideal situation. You can put plants in one specific spot in your woods where they can be admired together in an informal grouping. Or you can create a path that meanders through the woods, with wildflowers planted here and there, sited so that they can be admired from the path. Paths can be simply cleared periodically, by mowing, scything, and clipping individual woody plants with loppers. Or they can be mulched to deter unwanted growth permanently. One trick you might try is to lay down newspapers, say six sheets thick, then place about 4 inches of shredded bark on top of them. The newspapers will decompose after a year or two, but by then they will have permanently smothered much of the plant growth that might otherwise have poked up through the mulch.

To prepare the woods for planting you'll probably need to do some clearing to make them a bit tidier and to allow you to view your plantings better—but don't do too much. Remove unwanted trees or saplings (page 529) and standing dead trees to open up the woods and create the "open" or "dappled" shade that so many woodland plants like. You can also remove fallen trees and spindly underbrush. But leave some understory plants, especially if they are attractive ones. You may even want to plant some native shrubs such as azaleas and mountain laurel or small flowering trees such as shadblow or dogwood. And it is often helpful to remove some of the lower limbs from surrounding trees to let in a bit more light. But the woods should still look more like woods than a landscaped area.

In the spots where you are going to plant your wildflowers, look to see if there are existing plants—small woody shrubs, herbaceous flowering plants or foliage plants such as ferns—that you can incorporate into your scheme. You can leave clumps of bunch grasses (those that do not spread by rhizomes) and mosses, anything that looks woodsy and natural but won't compete with your new introductions. But you'll probably need to dig up a number of herbaceous and woody plants to make room for others. Dig them up by the roots so they won't reestablish themselves.

If the soil is lovely woodland soil,

enriched and lightened by years of leaf fall, you won't have to do anything to it—in fact, it should not even be tilled as you would an ordinary garden. Just dig holes large enough to accommodate your new plants, perhaps mixing a handful of bone meal into each hole to encourage root growth. Set the plants in the holes, spreading the roots out and then replacing the soil. Then water the plants well and either replace the ground litter of decaying leaves that you found there or add some additional light mulch of shredded leaves, salt hay, decaying straw, buckwheat hulls, grass clippings or shredded bark. (If the mulch looks too artificial you can scatter some leaves on top.) Moistened peat moss can be used as a mulch if another material such as leaves is spread on top to keep the surface from drying out and crusting. For plants that like very acid soil, a mulch of pine needles is beneficial as well as beautiful, and it's worth looking around for a source of needles if you don't have pine trees on your property. Apply any of these mulches carefully, making sure you don't cover the leaves and crowns of the plants, and don't forget that your mulch will be augmented by the leaves that fall from the trees. Many plants will rot if they are smothered with mulch.

How you arrange the plants in your woodland garden is important. You will want a less formal look than a perennial border might have, of course, but the same principles apply. Don't place tall plants where they will hide shorter ones. Try to achieve interesting foliage contrasts—combining the fernlike foliage of Dutchman's breeches with a broad-leaved plant like galax (*Galax urceolata*, also named *G. aphylla*), for example. And be mindful of what blooms when, so that you can visualize the various color combinations that will emerge as the plants flower. Try to think of what small pictures you can create in this or that corner of your woods, so that you will come upon them as you walk the paths. One of my favorite pictures is made with white foamflower, wild blue phlox and red-and-orange wild columbine (page 165), but the possible combinations are endless. Try a colony of Jack-in-the-pulpits emerging from a nest of maidenhair ferns; or plant trilliums with ferns. In other spots you might want to highlight just one kind of plant—for example, a clump of Solomon's seal—so that nothing else will distract from its very subtle beauty.

Many of the plants included in the List of Wildflowers make good woodland ground covers: bloodroot, Canada or wood anemone, bunchberry, May apple, Solomon's seal, foamflower and golden star. If you combine them with other plants, make sure that they can hold their own against the spreaders. Or else plant those that spread by roots in containers sunk in the ground so that their roots will be restrained. A bucket with the bottom removed works well for this. Plants that spread by self-sowing too abundantly can be controlled by snipping off the spent flowers before seed pods can form and scatter their seeds.

If you do not have woods on your property but are creating a woodland garden beneath or in the shade of ornamental trees, you may have to work harder at preparing your site. If there is lawn grass you must remove it (page 57) as well as any other competing plants. It's unlikely that the spot already has good woodland soil, so you should dig in plenty of moistened peat moss, compost or other soil amendments, trying for soil that is dark colored, light textured and rich. If your soil is heavy clay, it might be better to start from scratch by replacing the clay with soil that you mix yourself to imitate rich woodland

soil. Build raised beds to contain it and edge them informally with stones or old logs. Raised beds will also help if the soil is too wet for the plants you want to grow. The garden can then be designed and planted in the same manner as the shaded perennial garden described on page 149, except that you will probably aim for a more informal look, with creeping plants like foamflower drifting across some areas and accent plants like bottle gentians or turtleheads highlighting others.

The plants described as woodland species in the List of Wildflowers will do fine in the shade of most deciduous trees. Some others you can try are herb-Robert and other wild geraniums; the bright red-orange wood lily (*Lilium philadelphicum*); the *Erythronium* species, which are variously called trout lily, fawn lily and dogtooth violet, and which have small, dangling, lilylike flowers; various species of wild violets; partridgeberry (*Mitchella repens*), a creeper with beautiful white-veined leaves and bright red berries in fall; wintergreen (*Gaultheria procumbens*), a woodland ground cover with evergreen leaves and red fall berries; Oconee bells (*Shortia galacifolia*), with its dainty white, bell-like spring flowers; shooting star (*Dodecatheon meadia*), with flowers like little rosy cyclamens; pink-flowered spring beauty (*Claytonia virginica*); and wild ginger (*Asarum canadense*), which carpets the forest floor with its shiny round leaves. For woods that are very deeply shaded, try miterwort (*Mitella diphylla*), also called "bishop's cap," with dainty white flowers borne high above the spreading foliage, or plant bluebead (*Clintonia borealis*), noted more for its fat, bright blue berries than its dainty yellow flowers. Most woodland flowers bloom in spring, although you might spot your woods with some summer and fall color by planting wood lily, turtlehead, cardinal flower and snakeroot (*Cimicifuga* species).

MEADOW FLOWERS

Woodland gardening is the easiest type of wildflower gardening for the beginning gardener because so many of our native plants are woodland species. Before our country was settled, most of it was woods, with only occasional sunny clearings. Thus a large proportion of our native plants are woodland dwellers. There are a few parts of the country, however, where natural meadows are prevalent, for example the high meadows of the Rocky Mountains and the Midwestern prairies. In the mountain meadows, wildflowers do well because competing grass is rather sparse, giving them a chance. On the prairies certain flowering plants have naturally adapted to coexist with prairie grasses. But the acres and acres of fields cleared for crops or pastureland are a recent development, and so are many of the wildflowers that populate them; often they represent species brought in by settlers and now naturalized. They are fields that have been plowed and fertilized and support many tall, vigorous grasses with creeping roots that can quickly crowd out broad-leaved flowering plants.

For this reason the recent popularity of growing "wildflower meadows" has resulted in a lot of very discouraged gardeners. While grassy fields sustaining a number of flowering species are sometimes seen in nature, they are not easy to duplicate, depite the great number of wildflower-seed mixtures on the market. If you scatter these seeds in a grassy meadow, few if any will grow because they cannot compete with the established plants that are already there. If you start from scratch with bare ground you will have more success, but it will be short-lived. Mixes with annual wildflower seeds may give you something like an instant meadow the first year, but there is no guarantee that any will self-sow in subsequent seasons. Mixes that contain seeds of perennial flowers often contain many plants that are unsuitable to your particular climate and terrain, and the perennials that do bloom are likely to be crowded out over time by one or two of the stronger, more rampant wildflowers, by grasses, or by other undesirable, competitive plants that self-sow from the wild.

I see these seed mixes as interim solutions. Let's say you have had some construction done that has left a lot of unattractive bare ground that will soon erode if you don't cover it quickly. If you intend the spot to be a wild area rather than lawn, broadcasting a seed mix that combines grasses and some annual and/or perennial wildflower seeds can be a pretty means of dealing with the problem, even though its full effect is short-lived. Or, if you are starting a meadow garden on bare ground, a wildflower-seed mix can be useful, even though you will have to follow it up with more permanent plantings.

The only way to establish a truly permanent wildflower meadow is to plant clumps of perennial plants and then maintain them, as if they were part of a garden. In fact, the more you think of your meadow as a garden and not as a self-sufficient environment, the more successful your attempt will be.

I think the best way to embark on meadow gardening is to try a mini-meadow in some spot on your property that is readily accessible and that you can keep an eye on in the course of your regular activities. A perfect spot would be a corner or strip of the back lawn—a place that is wild already or one that is currently growing lawn grass that you simply let go unmowed. Select several perennial wildflowers that will naturalize, such as goldenrod, New England aster, butterfly weed, liatris, bee balm, yarrow, pearly everlasting (*Anaphalis margaritacea*), tansy, chicory and ox-eye daisy. Not only does this collection include a number of different colors, it spans the season from early summer to fall. If the meadow is a bit moist you might also try turtlehead, cardinal flower, jewelweed (page 60), gentians and the *Eupatorium* species such as Joe-Pye weed (*E. maculatum*) and boneset (*E. perfoliatum*). Remove the grass and prepare little beds for these plants. Put just one species in each bed, but plant at least three clumps or divisions of that one species. They can all be set out in early spring, or you can start the early-blooming ones the previous fall. Water them well, mulch them with a material like straw or shredded bark, and then keep checking them—weeding out grass and other competing plants around them until they become fully established. Even after that, they may need some protection against competition.

If your meadow is not a mini-meadow, but rather a whole field, you can use the same approach, but you will have to be all the more vigilant about your little planting beds, watching to see that they don't get swallowed up by the growth of the other vegetation. The best way to handle the meadow is to keep some paths mowed through it leading to the planted areas, so that you can not only take care of the plants but also admire them. You might even put mulch on the paths if you like to walk them often, using the same method described for woodland paths.

As your clumps become established and spread they may need much less care, especially the most vigorous ones and those best suited to the soil and climatic conditions of your particular meadow. But there will always be a few tasks to perform. As your meadow grows, keep removing any plants that you don't want there—obvious ones like poison ivy, or ones that you might like in another situation but choose not to have in the meadow, such as burdock, wild raspberry brambles and thistles. Mow the entire meadow once a year after the last species has finished blooming and dropped its seeds. This will keep woody plants (shrubs and trees) from growing up. You might, of course, want to have some woody plants in your meadow, either ones you have planted or ones that occur there naturally, such as sumac, blueberries, sweet fern or bayberry; if so, just mow around them. You might even want to encourage a few tree seedlings. Those that are considered too "weedy" to be ornamental specimens, such as wild cherry, locust or field junipers, might be just right in your meadow.

Watch and see what nature contributes to your meadow: wild purple clover, milkweed and buttercups, perhaps. And keep thinking of new things that you can add as well. The meadow will always be in flux and will never be quite the same from one year to the next. And of course it will vary according to what part of the country you live in. Out west your meadow might include penstemon, Indian paintbrush, blue mountain beard-tongue or one of the columbines such as western red columbine or the yellow *Aquilegia chrysantha*. In Maine it might include wild lupine (*Lupinus perennis*); in Texas another lupine, the annual bluebonnet (*L. subcarnosus*). If you live in the Midwest you'd grow one of the liatris species native to the Great Plains—*Liatris punctata* and *L. pycnostachya;* in the south you'd grow the southern species *L. elegans;* in the northeast *L. scariosa* or *L. spicata*. If you live in the Midwest you'd want to explore the various prairie grasses and flowers, many of which are supplied by specialty nurseries. Wherever you live, consult a local wildflower society for more ideas.

WILDFLOWERS FOR WET AREAS

The woodland stream I played in as a child was a perfectly landscaped water garden. In early spring skunk cabbages poked up their purplish flowers all along it—odd bulbous things that came to a point and smelled like skunks if you bruised them; later their leaves opened into wide green cabbagelike rosettes. Bright yellow marsh marigolds appeared right down next to the water, and ferns unrolled their fronds, forming a lush carpet in summer.

Many attractive wild plants grow like this in wet spots all by themselves, whether these are stream beds, marshes, bogs, the banks of ponds, woods and fields where the soil is soggy, or just roadside ditches where the water sits when it rains. If there is a wet spot on your property you may have had some unkind thoughts about it. You can't walk through it or drive through it. You couldn't build anything on it without great difficulty, even if the local wetlands commission would let you. You suspect it's full of snakes and mosquitoes, and you're considering having it drained at great expense.

But wait! Your wet spot is a valuable resource that many gardeners would envy. Chances are it's full of wildlife, including frogs that eat those mosquitoes, nesting waterfowl and perhaps even fish. If you look closely you may find that it has already been "landscaped," just as my old stream was, with native plants. What's more, there are many new ones that you can introduce and grow there.

Even though you've decided to keep the place wet, you may want to change its configuration. I happen to like marshes, swamps and boggy places. For one thing they are beautiful to look at; for another it's important to have some parts of the landscape that people can't walk in easily, so wildlife can be protected there. In preference to a marsh, however, you may want to create something that is more of a body of water, like a small pond, by having some grading and damming done. Streams can be diverted if their current course is causing problems. Your local Soil Conservation Service office can give you advice on how to go about projects like these. If you want a more modest homemade pond, order some of the catalogs listed on page 629 and discover what aids are available—from preformed fiberglass pools to heavy plastic liners that you simply spread out over a dug pond bottom and fill with water. You can also buy aquatic plants, fish, snails and other creatures that help keep a pond ecology in balance.

Finding plants for your wet spot is not at all difficult. You go about it just as you would for any of the environments I've been talking about. See what is there already that you'd like to encourage. Find other species that are either native to your area or will do well there. Plant them carefully in designated areas. And maintain them, both while they are becoming established and thereafter. Inform yourself about the needs of the plants you use. While some moisture-loving species like blue flag can grow right in the water with their roots submerged, others like Canada anemone cannot, and merely prefer damp soils to dry ones.

Some other plants you might consider for wet sites are the dainty meadow rues (*Thalictrum*); yellow flag (*Iris pseudacorus*); sweet flag (*Acorus calamus*), which has leaves like those of an iris but flowers like a yellow cattail; monkshood; tall, frothy white goatsbeard (*Aruncus dioicus*); tall, spiky *Ligularia;* Japanese primrose (page 177); and foliage plants such as cattails (*Typha latifolia*) and sedge (*Carex* species). And don't forget all the wonderful native ferns, such as the dainty maidenhair (*Adiantum* species), the wood ferns (*Dryopteris* species), the magnificent ostrich fern (*Matteuccia pensylvanica*), the tiny spleenworts (*Asplenium* species), and the evergreen Christmas fern (*Polystichum acrostichoides*).

Trees to frame your water garden might include swamp maple, willow, river birch and sycamore. Some shrubs that like wet feet are clethra (page 505), blueberry, spicebush and witch hazel.

When you are working in wet soil, remember to take care that it does not become compacted. Don't till it or cultivate it, just do what is necessary to keep it free of too-vigorous weeds or grasses, and try to avoid walking on the areas you have planted.

ROCKY AREAS

Rocks are almost always an asset in wildflower planting. Rocks that occur in woodland plantings blend beautifully with the plants, especially if they are covered with lichens and mosses. And they can help you to highlight plants. Place specimens behind rocks so that they stick up above them when they flower, or flow over the rocks. Or put a special plant in front of a rock so that the rock forms a background for it. If you are creating a woodland garden or small shade garden where no rocks exist, you might even consider bringing some in. If you do, place them carefully so that they look natural, burying the bottom third of the rock in the soil so that it looks as if it "grew" there. Also, use types of rocks that occur in your area for a more natural look: granite rocks if those are typical; limestone rocks if those predominate. In open areas rocks can be an asset too, whether they are large boulders or outcroppings of ledge. Here again you can place rocks in the landscape artifically, but make them look as natural as possible. And if you have rocks already, by all means make the most of them.

An old friend of mine named Bluie Piel, then in her seventies, once led me out the front door of her house to admire her half-shaded lawn, where grass was fighting it out with slabs of New England granite that broke the soil surface like the backs of half-submerged whales. It was spring, and drifts of self-sown blue scilla were all over the grass, blending exquisitely with the clumps of red-and-yellow wild columbine that had also self-sown there, taking hold even in tiny soil pockets in the rocks. It looked like a miniature alpine meadow, Connecticut-style. "Now, dearie," Bluie said, "God didn't do that. *I* did that." And so, I might add, can you. That's what wildflower gardening is all about.

LIST OF WILDFLOWERS

This list is a sampling of common, herbaceous flowering plants of woods, marshes and fields. Most of them are native to North America. Start with these easy-to-grow favorites, then experiment further, exploring wild shrubs and trees, ferns and other foliage plants as well. Most states have native plant societies (many of them noted in the List of Plant Societies in the back of this book). These can steer you toward species that can be grown successfully in your area.

BLACK-EYED SUSAN
Rudbeckia hirta

DESCRIPTION: Even most nongardeners recognize this bright wildflower with its yellow, daisylike petals and raised, dark brown center. It generally grows 2–3 feet tall, usually in sunny meadows or by the sides of roads. It blooms a long time—from June to September—and I find it a good cut flower for summer bouquets. Sometimes it is called "brown-eyed Susan," the name usually associated with *Rudbeckia triloba,* a southern version that grows a bit taller—though frankly in my view it doesn't matter which name you give to either. Black-eyed Susans are perennials and may persist for a few years if cut back

after bloom, but more often than not they bloom once from seeds dropped in late summer.

HOW TO GROW: Black-eyed Susans are prairie flowers that will compete fairly well with other meadow flowers and even with grasses if the latter are sparse and without long, vigorous roots. Black-eyed Susans like a sunny spot best but will tolerate part shade. Soil need not be moist or fertile; in fact in the rich soil of a garden the plants will rapidly become too much of a good thing. Grow them in a meadow or in a spot all their own. They are difficult to divide; best to grow them from seed sown in late summer or early fall, then let them self-sow over the years.

BLOODROOT
Sanguinaria canadensis

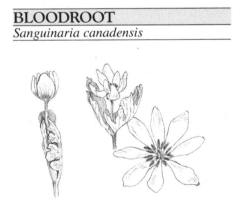

DESCRIPTION: Bloodroot's white, star-like flowers emerge from the forest floor or next to streams in early spring, opening like little cups, then flat saucers, to reveal yellow centers. The flowers last only a few days, but the attractive light green leaves, which wrap around the stems, then unfold, last all summer and make a good ground cover for shady areas. (Bloodroot may go dormant in late summer if it is very dry.)

The plants are also attractive in smaller groups in a shade garden. Bloodroot rarely grows more than 8 inches tall and is hardy to Zone 3. A very showy double variety is also available.

HOW TO GROW: Bloodroot needs soil with adequate moisture, but its soil must be well drained. The ideal is a fertile woodland soil with plenty of humus. Level of pH is not especially important, but if the soil is poor in nutrients a top dressing of compost or even a liquid fertilizer is beneficial. The plants need some filtered sunlight to bloom in spring but should not have hot sun in summer. The roots are rhizomes that bleed red when cut. Plant in fall or in spring if the plants are dormant, with the rhizomes lying horizontally just below soil level; they will send up new shoots. Plants can be divided for propagation, but dense clumps can also be left alone. They will spread by self-sowing as well as from the root system.

BLUE FLAG
Iris versicolor

DESCRIPTION: These small, elegant iris have flowers that are blue marked with gold and that appear from late spring to midsummer. The plants grow 2–3 feet tall. The flowers look something like a Siberian iris, but the leaves are sword shaped, like those of bearded iris. Blue flag grows wild in wet meadows and like places and can even grow with its roots submerged, beside ponds and streams and in marshes. Crested iris (*I. cristata*) is another good wild iris to grow; it grows from bulbs and forms a low carpet in moist areas, with small blue flowers.

HOW TO GROW: Blue flags prefer full sun but will tolerate part shade. They are grown very easily in any fertile soil, including that of a perennial border, as long as it is kept reasonably moist by watering or mulching. They are not fussy about soil pH. Plant them either in early spring or in late summer or fall. Some people's skin is sensitive to iris roots; if yours is, wear gloves. Dividing every few years after bloom will promote flowering. To do this cut the plants back to about 6 inches and divide the rhizomes into clumps with leaves attached. Replant the rhizome horizontally just below soil level with the crown at soil level. The plants will spread themselves by means of the creeping rhizomes and also by seed.

BOTTLE GENTIAN
Gentiana andrewsii (*G. clausa*)

DESCRIPTION: These late-summer bloomers are also called "closed gentians" because the petals of the blue flowers appear to be tightly closed. They aren't, though—bees do get inside to pollinate them. Bottle gentians grow

1–2 feet high, with a cluster of flowers on top of the stems and a whorl of leaves just below them; often there is another flower cluster and leaf whorl farther down the stem. One plant can form a large clump, sending out thick roots from the crown. Usually bottle gentians are found in moist meadows or next to streams, sometimes in bogs; in warmer climates they grow in the mountains in open woods. Hardy to Zone 3, bottle gentians are the easiest of the many gentian species that wildflower gardeners grow. They are the one to start with, therefore, but you can explore others, including the beautiful, elusive fringed gentian (*Gentianopsis crinita*). It is a biennial that must be grown from seed, and you never know where it will turn up in the wild from one year to the next.

HOW TO GROW: Bottle gentians can either be naturalized in a wild garden or grown in a more formal garden. Give them full or filtered sun. They cannot take strong competition from other perennial plants, and it is best to weed around the clumps from time to time and mulch them. Although they like moist soil, a soil that is only moderately moist will usually do, especially with a mulch. A rich, sandy loam is best, with plenty of organic matter and a neutral or slightly acid pH. Plant them in early spring or fall, while they're dormant. Plants do not need to be divided to stay vigorous, but can be divided to propagate them—as long as you keep plenty of soil around the roots when you replant them. Crowns should be at about soil level.

BUNCHBERRY
Cornus canadensis

DESCRIPTION: These little woodland plants grow 8 inches tall or less, yet are closely related to dogwood trees. The white flowers, in fact, look very much

like those of flowering dogwood, though they are much smaller, blooming in late spring, and are followed by clusters of red fruits. The leaves are a handsome glossy green. The plants grow in open woods with deciduous trees, the roots extending along the soil surface just under the leaves littering the forest floor. They will thus do well as a ground cover in a partly shaded area, but only if summers are fairly cool. They grow naturally in cool climates and are hardy to Zone 2.

HOW TO GROW: There is not much to growing bunchberries—just make sure the plants are shaded and the moisture around the roots is fairly constant. Beyond that they like a rather acid soil, organic matter and a light mulch to cover the spreading roots. The woody roots are hard to establish bare-root, and it is best to purchase sods, planting them in spring or fall with the eyes (buds) just below the soil surface. Divide in early spring or late fall, making sure each piece of rhizome has an eye.

CANADA ANEMONE
Anemone canadensis

DESCRIPTION: Also called "meadow anemone," this plant spreads rapidly to make masses of 1¾-inch white flowers in damp meadows or next to bodies of water. It also makes a good ground cover for shady areas. The flowers, which usually appear in June, are single with raised gold centers; they are borne atop stems 1–2 feet high. The plants

increase quickly by means of thin rhizomes, holding their own even against grass, and are best given a spot of their own to naturalize in. If you are growing Canada anemone right next to other herbaceous plants, you should contain the roots. Planting in a bottomless bucket will do the trick. A close relative, wood anemone (*Anemone quinquefolia*), is similar but shorter, the flowers touched with pink in the center; it too forms a carpet.

HOW TO GROW: The ideal site is partly shaded with moderately fertile, slightly acid, moist but well-drained soil. Plant while dormant in spring or fall with the eyes at soil level, and mulch lightly. Divide in spring or fall to propagate or increase flowering.

CARDINAL FLOWER
Lobelia cardinalis

DESCRIPTION: Cardinal flowers are about the most intense red of any flower I know. As perennials they tend to be rather short-lived, but I can remember my great-aunt's pride in the fact that

they came up every year, without fail, next to her brook. The ideal situation is a sunny, damp spot that never dries out completely, even in summer. But you can also grow cardinal flowers in the herbaceous garden, as long as you keep the plants watered. The flowers are in spikes, as tall as 5 feet, with little tube-like petals that hummingbirds love to drink nectar from and that bloom for a month or more in late summer. They are lovely grown with another wild lobelia species, great blue lobelia (*Lobelia siphilitica*), which blooms at the same time.

HOW TO GROW: Cardinal flower likes light, humusy soil of average fertility and a slightly acid pH. Grow it in sun or part shade, but in sun make sure the soil is quite moist. Plant in spring in cold climates, spring or fall in mild ones, with the crowns at soil level. Clumps can be divided and the individual rosettes replanted in spring. They also self-sow.

DUTCHMAN'S BREECHES
Dicentra cucullaria

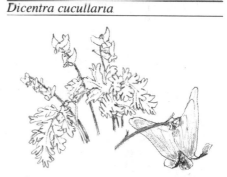

DESCRIPTION: These plants are closely related to bleeding hearts. They have the same deeply cut, fernlike foliage and long, arching stems. But instead of flowers like little hearts dangling in a row from these stems, they have flowers like a Dutchman's pantaloons hanging upside down. Flowers are generally white or pinkish. They grow in large spreading colonies, but don't work as an all-summer ground cover, because the leaves go dormant not long after the early-spring flowers have faded. They are most effective naturalized in the woods where they can spread freely or mingle with ferns and other vigorous plants.

HOW TO GROW: Dutchman's breeches are best grown among deciduous trees, where the sun shines through the bare branches in early spring. A light, humusy, slightly acid soil suits them best—moist but well drained. A fertile soil will promote flowering, and a light organic mulch such as shredded leaves will best duplicate natural forest conditions. (Salt hay is also good.) Plant or divide the small white tubers in summer after the plant's natural period of dormancy sets in, and up until late fall. Don't be discouraged if new plants fail to bloom; they will when they are well established.

FOAMFLOWER
Tiarella cordifolia

DESCRIPTION: This is one of my favorite shady ground covers; its maplelike leaves spread on runners that just seem to touch the soil, root and move on. Frothy white flowers appear in spring. Despite the apparent fragility of the runners, there are sturdy underground roots

beneath the crowns, once the plants are established. En masse, foamflowers are spectacular, looking just like foamy waves flowing through the woods, around rocks and trees. In warm climates the plants are evergreen. Their natural habitat is fertile, moist woodland.

HOW TO GROW: Foamflowers prefer part shade in cool climates but can take full shade in warm ones. They are not fussy about pH but like moderately rich soil and mustn't dry out at any point. A soil rich in organic matter, and a light mulch, will help keep them happy in warm weather. Plant or divide in spring or fall; new plants, formed where the runners touch down, can be transplanted by cutting the runners and replanting the new crowns at soil level.

GOLDENROD
Solidago

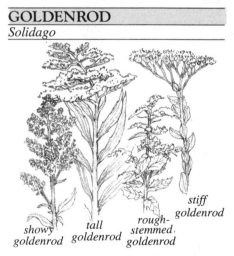

showy goldenrod   *tall goldenrod*   *rough-stemmed goldenrod*   *stiff goldenrod*

DESCRIPTION: Most people are familiar with goldenrod, with its bright yellow plumes in late summer and early fall. For years it has been blamed for the hay fever that so many people get at that time of year, perhaps because the fuzzy goldenrod flowers *look* so pollen-laden. In fact it is the sly, less-conspicuous flowers of ragweed that cause most of the trouble.

People also don't realize that there are many different species of goldenrod. Hybrid forms are even sold. (In Europe goldenrod is more treasured as a garden plant than it is here.) The best goldenrods to grow are probably the ones native to your area, though goldenrods are very adaptable. Most are typically found in rather infertile meadows. (In fact farmers where I live know the soil of an abandoned field needs work if they see goldenrod growing there. Canada goldenrod (*Solidago canadensis*) is a common species that likes meadows slightly moist in spring and dry in summer, and grows up to 4 feet. Wrinkled, or rough-stemmed goldenrod (*S. rugosa*) is similar, though sometimes taller. Both are hardy to Zone 3. Showy or noble goldenrod (*S. speciosa*) can grow quite tall and has particularly fine gold flowers, hardy to Zone 5 or 6. Seaside goldenrod (*S. sempervirens*), hardy to Zone 5, blooms a long time, even into late fall, and the leaves are evergreen. It is the best species to grow in seaside locations.

HOW TO GROW: Goldenrods prefer full sun. They can be very invasive, spreading by creeping rootstocks and self-sowing, especially in moist, fertile soil. They may need to be controlled in a garden setting but are good flowers for a meadow garden. To propagate, divide in late winter or early spring.

GOLDEN STAR
Chrysogonum virginianum

DESCRIPTION: This plant's other name is "green-and-gold," probably because the flowers are bright gold with green centers. The leaves are an attractive, rather dark green, the plants less than a foot tall. I often wish golden star were more easily available, for few plants are longer blooming. It usually starts flow-

ering in April, with great profusion, then throws out sporadic blooms all summer and into fall—and even through the winter in warm climates! The leaves are also evergreen in warm areas. Alas, it is not reliably hardy past Zone 6 or 7, though with winter protection you can often grow it in Zone 5. In areas where it does very well it makes a fine ground cover, but also try it in flower gardens or in a rock garden.

HOW TO GROW: The plants seem to do well either in sun or shade, though filtered shade is probably best; too much shade will restrict flowering. They like a fertile, well-drained soil, rich in organic matter. It is better to give them too little moisture than too much; a mulch may keep them too moist and also impede self-sowing, which they generally do prolifically. (For winter protection, mulch with salt hay, then remove it promptly in early spring.) Plants can be divided in late winter, early spring or late fall by cutting the rhizomes with a knife, making sure each one has a crown with a rosette of leaves visible. Replant and water thoroughly.

HEPATICA
Hepatica americana

DESCRIPTION: Generally called "round-lobed hepatica," this plant sends up clumps of little flowers in very

early spring, before the leaves appear. The flowers are usually white, sometimes pale blue and sometimes (in alkaline soil) pink. They only flower on sunny days and close at night. The leaves stay on the plants all summer and winter too, though then they turn a brownish green color and are replaced by fresh leaves after the plants flower. Native to open woodlands, they are fine used as ground-cover plants for partly shaded areas, as specimens in the woodland garden, and in rock gardens. They are hardy to Zone 3. Sharp-lobed hepatica (*Hepatica acutiloba*) is very similar, but the leaves have pointed lobes rather than rounded ones, and the plant prefers soil with a neutral pH.

HOW TO GROW: Give round-lobed hepaticas humus-rich, slightly moist acid soil. Plant with the crowns at soil level and mulch lightly. Clumps will enlarge by themselves and will often self-sow, but they may be propagated by dividing them in fall. Don't remove the leaves, though, since they should remain during the winter.

JACK-IN-THE-PULPIT
Arisaema triphyllum

DESCRIPTION: I used to love to find these plants in the woods when I was a child. In mid- to late spring they send up a stalk about 2 feet tall with a strange flower that flops over like a canopy over an enclosed "pulpit." Inside the pulpit is a small protuberance called a "spa-

dix" (that's Jack). The pulpit, or "spathe," is usually green-and-brown striped. In late summer a cluster of red-orange berries forms where Jack once stood. The root is a corm once valued by the Indians as a cooked food—hence the plant'§ other name, "Indian turnip." The corm is poisonous if eaten raw. It grows in rich, moist woodlands, or places like seasonal stream beds that flow only in spring and dry out in summer.

HOW TO GROW: Giving Jack-in-the-pulpits a humus-rich soil is more important than finding them a moist spot. They like full or part shade but not full sun. Soil should be rather light and acid. Plant little corms about 3 inches deep; larger ones can go deeper—as deep as twice their diameter. Corms can be divided, but handle them with care; some people get a rash from touching them. Once established, the plants can take care of themselves very well, often forming large colonies.

MAY APPLE
Podophyllum peltatum

DESCRIPTION: This is a charming plant if used in the right way. In late spring each plant sends up what look like two little, folded-up beach umbrellas; these unfold as two broad, umbrellalike leaves

from June to August in most areas, which means you have them throughout the summer to lighten and soften bouquets of brighter, less delicate flowers. I even like the way the flowers look when they are fading and start to close up like little cups. They are the same species as our common garden carrot, and in fact if you pull one up you'll see a carrot-shaped, carrot-smelling taproot, though it's stringy and white instead of fat and orange. The plants are hardy to Zone 3.

under which you have to peek to see the small white or pinkish flowers. But I like them just for the foliage; an established clump forms a large mat that is a sea of umbrellas all summer long. In May a small, yellow fruit (the "apple") forms where the flowers were. You can eat the fruit, but don't ever eat the roots or leaves—both are poisonous, and even touching the roots can cause a rash. The other name for the plant is "wild mandrake."

HOW TO GROW: Naturally growing in open, damp, deciduous woods, May apple likes a rich, moist soil and a fairly acid pH. It makes an excellent ground cover for shaded or semishaded sites. Plant or divide the rhizomes in fall, leaving at least one bud on each division and spreading out the rhizomes 1 inch below soil level.

QUEEN ANNE'S LACE
Daucus carota

DESCRIPTION: This flower is so common that you might assume it to be an American native, but it's really from Afghanistan and was introduced to the New World from Europe in colonial times. Meadows, roadsides and overgrown fields are full of its lacy, flat umbels made up of many tiny white flowers and a solitary purple one right in the center. They bloom a long time,

HOW TO GROW: Queen Anne's lace will grow in cultivated gardens, though if the soil is very fertile the stems may become leggy. It will tolerate dry, infertile soil quite well but needs at least a half-day of full sun. Despite the fact that it chooses to live in meadows, it cannot compete with vigorous-rooted perennials and grasses. It is best simply to naturalize a clump of it somewhere and keep the soil weeded and cultivated so that the plant will self-sow abundantly. Like many members of the *Umbelliferae* (page 184), Queen Anne's lace does this well anywhere, but in cultivated ground it will do so best. On the other hand, if you don't want it to self-sow, deadhead the plants—or just pick them. (There's always a place for another bouquet of Queen Anne's lace.) Like other tap-rooted plants, they can't be divided, but seeds can be collected when dry and sown outdoors in late spring.

SOLOMON'S SEAL
Polygonatum biflorum

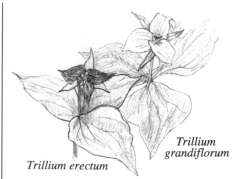

Trillium
grandiflorum

Trillium erectum

DESCRIPTION: Another favorite woodland plant, Solomon's seal has arching stems about 2 feet high with two rows of lance-shaped, drooping leaves; from their axils (where the leaves join the stem) hang yellow-green flowers, usually in pairs, in late spring. In summer blue-black berries appear and are eagerly consumed by small mammals and birds. Solomon's seal makes a good shade-loving ground cover, forming big clumps eventually. A close relative, great Solomon's seal (*Polygonatum commutatum*) grows to 5 feet and more and is very showy but also very vigorous; make sure you have adequate space to accommodate it. Both species are hardy to Zone 3.

HOW TO GROW: Ideal conditions are shady, with moist, acid soil, but the plants will tolerate sun, neutral soil, and even some dryness. It is wise to mulch them, though, as it is for most woodland plants, to keep soil moisture relatively constant. Divide the rhizomes in spring (fall in warm climates), with at least one bud per division, and lay them horizontally 1 inch below the soil surface.

TRILLIUM
Trillium

DESCRIPTION: The trillium I grew up with was *Trillium erectum,* variously called "purple trillium," "wake robin" and "stinking Benjamin." (Its flowers smell putrid, but that's not a problem if you keep your nose out of them.) The name "trillium" refers to the fact that there are three leaflets in each leaf cluster, but there are also three purple petals, alternated with three green sepals. These May-blooming flowers are followed by large, dark red berries, which birds and small mammals eat. Plants are a little over a foot tall and very hardy (to Zone 2). They grow in wet, cool, fertile woodlands. Actually there are many species of trillium for the wildflower gardener to grow, and if you like this one I urge you to try others, such as the white or snow trillium (*T. grandiflorum*), which has lovely white flowers several inches across. Like purple trillium it is easy to grow; it is hardy to Zone 5.

HOW TO GROW: Trilliums have bulblike rhizomes with stringy roots attached that extend deep into the soil. They like sun in early spring, then part shade as the trees leaf out. Give them a rich, moist, acid, organic soil and a mulch; top dress with compost if your soil is poor. They are planted in fall, with the rhizomes about 2 inches below the soil surface.

TURTLEHEAD
Chelone lyonii

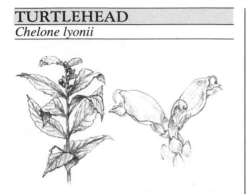

VIRGINIA BLUEBELL
Mertensia virginica

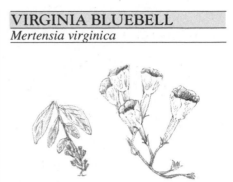

DESCRIPTION: This rather showy pink-to-purple flower is native to the south but has naturalized throughout the east. It grows about 3 feet tall and is one of the few good wildflowers for late summer, blooming anywhere from July to September. The flowers, atop a spiky stem, look like, well, the heads of turtles. It is found in boggy places. A related species called "snakehead" (*Chelone glabra*) has white flowers and similar growing habits; it is a larval food for the black-and-orange Baltimore butterfly. Both species are hardy to Zone 3.

HOW TO GROW: Plant in full sun if the soil is moist all summer; otherwise light shade is best. Plant in rich, light, humusy, acid soil and mulch to keep soil moisture constant. You can divide the fibrous roots in early spring for propagation, but they usually spread well without your help.

DESCRIPTION: This plant is a typical "spring ephemeral," sending up broad, apple-green leaves in early spring and pretty, clustered, bell-like flowers that are shades of pink, lavender and blue, all on the same flower. After blooming, the flowers, big leaves and stems simply disappear. It may be helpful to mark the spot where they grow while they are blooming so you won't disturb the roots later on when the plant is dormant. They choose to live in moist, semishaded places.

HOW TO GROW: Give Virginia bluebells rich, fairly acid soil that is moist but well drained. Though hardy to Zone 3, they benefit from a light winter mulch. The tuberous roots do not need to be divided, but for purposes of propagation you can do it carefully after the plants go dormant, replanting them 2 inches deep. Keep new plants watered well.

HOUSEPLANTS

It usually starts with one plant. You are a nongardener until your Valentine gives you an azalea. Or your mother brings over a philodendron when you move into your new apartment. Or you go to the hospital with pneumonia and come back with a streptocarpus. Much to your astonishment the new plant doesn't die. In fact, after you follow a friend's advice about its care, it thrives, blooms, and puts out new growth. Encouraged, you buy another plant to keep it company, then another, and another. Pretty soon your apartment looks like the set of a Tarzan movie. You're hooked.

There are a lot of reasons why people get started with houseplants. Plants make the indoors look like the outdoors, softening the lines of the furniture and architecture and making any place look more hospitable. With their flowers and foliage they bring spring and summer into our rooms in the dead of winter. They also make us healthier: plants give off moisture that's a good antidote for a dry, central-heated atmosphere, and they emit oxygen that enriches the air we breathe. And part of the appeal of houseplants comes from a basic need to have other living things around us; even something as uncommunicative as a plant can help to fill that need.

Often indoor gardening is the only way a person can satisfy the gardening urge. If you live in an apartment or a house with a yard that is too small or too shaded, or just generally unsuitable for plants, or if you like to garden year-round but live in a cool climate, growing houseplants is the answer. While houseplants can be fussy about specific things and are less self-sufficient than outdoor plants growing in the ground, they are also less time-consuming to grow as a rule (no weeds!). You can turn indoor plants into a hobby if you like, experimenting with new ones and propagating

them, or you can just let them be decorative. It's your choice.

Best of all, houseplants open up a whole world of variety. While there are many species to explore in any kind of gardening, houseplants offer more choices than do other forms of gardening. It is especially exciting to be able to grow the beautiful, often weird specimens of the tropical rain forests or the desert—environments so different from your own that the plants that grow there seem like exquisite works of art. Setting a bromeliad on your table, its jewel-like flower emerging from a circle of spiny leaves, is like setting a priceless vase there, except that the bromeliad is affordable. Hanging a staghorn fern on the wall is even better than hanging a painting, because its shape changes as its "antlers" grow.

As your interest in houseplants develops, you may want to acquire a structure like a greenhouse that will let in more light, allow you to grow plants in a more carefully controlled environment and give you a place to perform messy tasks like potting. Small models are available that can be added onto a house easily; there are even miniature greenhouses you can attach on the outside of a window so plants can be grown with maximum light. For the purposes of this chapter, however, I'll assume that you are working with whatever resources your living space already provides.

Ways to Use Houseplants

Any plant can be displayed singly like the ones just mentioned. The more interesting the plant, the more it lends itself to this treatment. But sometimes plants work better in groups. For one thing each will benefit the others by giving off moisture, thus making the air a bit more humid around the plants than it is in the rest of the room. For another, you can create lovely decorative effects, massing plants to resemble an outdoor scene, be it a cool-climate woodland "planted" with ferns, trailing ivy and Norfolk Island pine, a tropical rain forest with spider plants, Christmas cacti and bromeliads, or a desert of cacti and tall succulents. And you needn't be a purist about grouping plants according to their origins. Simply combining a diverse group of plants with foliage of different shades, shapes and textures is always effective. When you do this you may plan your grouping by using a few complementary foliage types or flower colors. Or you might make a composition of one plant type alone, but with species and varieties that vary slightly— such as a windowsill of cacti with different shapes, a mini-forest of different dracaena species, or a tray of rex begonias with different foliage patterns.

Let's face it, though: with indoor gardening more than with any other kind, there is the temptation to be a collector. If you have succumbed you probably violate the rule of design that insists on using masses of a few plant types rather than "one of this, one of that." So be it. There is, after all, limited room in which to put plants without having asparagus fern dripping into your tea or hoya vines crawling into your bed. So collect as many different ones as you have the space and interest to try.

Finding the Right Location

While you are being creative with your plants, you must always remember that while they may be artworks they are also alive, and they have specific individual needs. Where you put a plant is not just a matter of deciding where it looks good; also crucial is picking a spot where it will get the amount of light it needs to do best, where it will have the right temperature and the right degree of humidity. Sometimes this is a matter of choosing the spot to fit the plant, but sometimes it means choosing a plant to fit the spot, especially if your surroundings do not offer an unlimited choice of conditions. Fortunately there are plants that do well even in the most unlikely spots. The List of Houseplants includes a description of the specific needs of each of the plants covered. When you are trying others you usually can obtain information on culture from the nursery that sells them to you.

One thing to keep in mind when placing plants in your home is that some are toxic to humans and/or pets. I would avoid having children or pets nibble on *any* plant that is not a known, safe food plant. But with some common houseplants special care must be taken that they are displayed out of harm's way. These include philodendron, spider plant, dieffenbachia, oleander (*Nerium oleander*), croton (*Codiaeum*), mistletoe (*Phoradendron serotinum*), poinsettia (*Euphorbia pulcherrima*), and Jerusalem cherry (*Solanum pseudocapsicum*).

After you find the right spot for a plant, you must care for it in just the right way. It must be in the right pot, have the right soil and be given the right amounts of water and fertilizer. Various maintenance needs such as washing and pruning must be met, and any insect or disease problems must be taken care of. Unfortunately a number of different houseplant problems have very similar manifestations. Rather than give you a confusing list of symptoms and their possible causes, I suggest the following approach: whenever a plant is not doing its best, run down the list of factors in plant growth discussed below and make sure you are giving the plant the recommended treatment in all these areas. Note the ways in which the factors are interrelated—the kind of pot and the potting medium affect how much water the plant needs; the amount of light affects the amount of fertilizer it needs; the time of year affects many needs too. Always look at the total picture.

LIGHT

Few homes are lit as well or as uniformly as the great outdoors. Our plants tend to cluster on windowsills, sunning on one side at a time like beach goers on a row of lounge chairs. To be sure, modern homes have more light than traditional ones, where windows are small. Nowadays many houses have picture windows or entire glass walls, or skylights and bubbles that let light in from above. Homes are lit with more artificial light as well. Instead of lamps perched on end tables there's now track lighting, spot lighting and more convenient and attractive versions of the fluorescent lights that plants dearly love. You can even buy fixtures specially designed to light plants.

But it's very important to give a plant exactly the right kind of light. Some will tolerate very low light, others need a good four hours of sun each day, and yet others, the great majority in fact, prefer bright light that is not direct sun. Bright light might be sunlight that fills a room with a glow so that even plants set back from the window are lit. It might be light reflected off white walls. It might be sunlight filtered by a gauze curtain or a fiberglass screen. Or it might be the morning sun from an east window or late-afternoon sun from a west one, neither of which are as strong

as direct midday sun from a south window. An excellent site for some plants is a north window where there is no direct sun at all; but in that case there should be no trees or other obstructions to keep the outside light from flooding in.

Plants often do well in offices that are brightly lit throughout with fluorescent lighting. As long as the plants get 14–16 hours of light each day, they need not be very close to the lights themselves. If you have fluorescent lights in the bathroom or kitchen and can keep them turned on all day, these can be good spots for plants too. But if you want to grow flowering houseplants you may have to put together the kind of fluorescent-lighting apparatus shown on page 45 to suit their greater need for light. Try setting the lights about 18 inches above the plants; then watch to see how they react and adjust the distance accordingly. Even if you don't find such a setup an attractive way to display plants, you can bring them into flower under lights and then remove individual plants at their peak to grace a table. This is a good solution to the problem of having no bright light at all—often the case in city apartments. Incandescent light is not as good as fluorescent light for plants, chiefly because it gives off more heat. To get the leaves close enough for them to benefit from the light, you risk scorching them.

Foliage plants in general are tolerant of low light conditions, while flowering ones tend to need brighter light (though often not direct sun). If a plant is not getting enough light, the leaves will be thinner than normal—the result of the plant's having used the sugars and starches stored there in order to grow. (With enough light to carry on photosynthesis actively it can replenish the supply.) The leaves of light-deprived plants may also be smaller, and the stems will have long stretches between the nodes where leaves form, resulting in a gangly, leggy appearance. The plants may also be bending toward a light source in order to get more light and may drop leaves. Light-starved plants will usually not bloom. On the other hand, if a plant gets too much light the leaves turn yellow, then brown between the veins or on the edges.

TEMPERATURE

While some houseplants can tolerate a wide temperature range and probably prefer about the same degree of warmth that you do, others are rather fussy and may not thrive in your environment. Many apartment buildings are kept very warm in winter, even at night. If you live in warm rooms, and the temperature is out of your control, you may have trouble with "cool-room" plants such as cyclamens and camellias and with plants that need a period of winter dormancy (during which they are kept cool) in order to bloom, like clivia and Christmas cactus. On the other hand, if you can control your environment and are one of the many homeowners who once considered 72 degrees "room temperature" but now, in an energy-conscious, economy-conscious age, put it closer to 65 (and even lower at night), you had best bypass "warm-room" plants such as African violets and moth orchids, although you can, of course, treat them to a space heater if needed. In many houses some rooms are cooler than others. Even parts of a room can vary drastically in temperature, so if you are really interested in indoor gardening, a minimum–maximum thermometer is a wise investment. It will let you find out exactly how cold the living room gets, or how hot your plants will be if you set them near a heat register, or how much a spot is affected by drafts. Plants that are too cold will grow very slowly, if at all.

Those that are warmer than they like to be will wilt or their leaves will look scorched or dried out (though many plants will tolerate high temperatures if you keep the air moist).

HUMIDITY

Apartment buildings and houses with central heating often have very low humidity—as low as 5 to 10 percent, especially in winter when the heat is turned up—causing dry skin for you and your plants. If they are cacti they'll shrug it off, but if they're ferns they'll turn brown and perhaps even die. Most plants prefer a humidity of 50–60 percent. (Some like it even higher, but these are best grown under greenhouse conditions.) Humidity is measured by a device called a "hygrometer"—not an essential tool for the average gardener, but if you are curious, you might borrow one just to see what the humidity in your living space is on an average day.

If the air is too dry for a plant, its young leaves may be small and yellowed or may not even form. Old leaves may dry out, brown and drop off. If the air is too humid, plants can get mold or mildew; the leaves may have soggy spots or rot altogether. Buds may form, then rot.

If the humidity is low there are several things you can do to help your plants fare better. You can group them together, for the reason explained above. You can mist them, using an inexpensive plastic bottle as shown on page 577, or an empty window-cleaner bottle filled with warm water. The trick is not to wet the leaves but to envelop them in a cloud of mist by spraying around them. Try to mist at least once a day. Ferns especially love misting, but don't mist fuzzy-leaved plants such as African violets. Another good trick is to set plants on a "humidity tray." To set one up, just get a tray of some waterproof material such as plastic or metal at least 2 inches deep, and fill it with pebbles in the bottom. If you use attractive pebbles the tray can be a decorative asset; I love the black Mexican beach pebbles that you can buy in bags, for example. Set your potted plants on the pebbles and fill the tray with water that almost covers the pebbles but does not quite come up to the level of the pots. To create even more humidity throughout the room you can set a tray of water on the radiator, heat register or woodstove and let it evaporate into the air. You may find that there is a room in your house that is more humid than the others—the bathroom because people shower there, perhaps, or the kitchen because people cook there. You can also create some "jungle air" in one room by means of a humidifier, and put all your humidity-loving plants in there.

Sometimes there is too much humidity in a house—in summer perhaps, or in rooms that are below ground. This can be remedied with a dehumidifier and sometimes with just a fan to increase air circulation. If this fails try another spot for the plants or grow plants that love high humidity such as bromeliads and ferns.

Buying Houseplants

See Chapter 4 for a general discussion of how to buy plants. When you are buying houseplants you should be especially careful to examine plants for signs of insect infestation or disease, because both spread more readily indoors than out and can infect your healthy specimens. Look for compact plants with good foliage color. To make sure they have not been weakened by being grown in the same pot for too long, turn the pot upside down and see if there are roots coming out.

There are new houseplants appearing on the market all the time, and even if you are familiar with the field, many may be new to you. Try to find a salesperson who can tell you what growing conditions each plant needs. Often plants come with labels that give you directions for their proper care.

Houseplants can also be ordered by mail. You may find this is the best way to acquire an interesting collection, since a wide range of varieties will be available from catalogs. Generally they will arrive bare-root (see page 112 for information about buying plants through the mail).

Potting Your Plants

After you've bought your plant, check out the pot it's in. It may look fine to you or it may need to be replaced, either because the pot doesn't have the look you want, or because it is a temporary container made out of pressed peat or some other short-lived material, or because it is too small and the plant is outgrowing it. It is important to get the plant off to the right start with the right kind of pot and the right kind of soil, and also to pot it up correctly.

PLANT CONTAINERS

The right plant container is one that will keep just the amount of soil around the plant that it needs. In a too-small pot there will be little soil, and the plant will be "potbound" or "rootbound"—its roots will fill the pot so that there is not enough room for soil or nutrients. In a too-large pot with too much soil, excess water will be held around the plant's roots, depriving them of air and killing them. A good rule of thumb is to give the plant a pot that is an inch wider than its root ball.

Make sure the pot provides for drainage. If water is to drain away, obviously the pot needs to have at least one hole in the bottom, and the pot must be set on a saucer or some sort of tray to receive the excess when you water the plant. The humidity tray described above serves this purpose as well.

When you bring home a new houseplant chances are it will either be in a plastic pot or a standard, reddish brown clay one. Each has its advantages. A plastic pot is light and holds moisture better, so that the plant does not have to be watered so often. This can be a drawback, however, because if you overwater a plant in a plastic pot the water will take longer to drain away. Clay pots, on the other hand, are of a porous material that releases excess water over the pot's entire surface, not just at the bottom, and also lets air in and out. The soil in them dries out faster, so they need to be watered more often, but there is less danger of overwatering. Clay pots are heavier than plastic—a problem with a large pot full of heavy soil, but a plus if a pot contains a top-heavy plant in a light soil mix, which might tip over in a light pot. Clay pots often have white deposits on their outsides after they have been used a while. These are salts from fertilizers that have leached through the pot's porous sides. The stains can be unattractive but are useful as a way of monitoring the amount of fertilizer you give a plant; if a lot of white appears soon after you clean off the pot and flush out the soil (see below), you have overfertilized.

Both kinds of pots have their uses. Clay pots are, to my mind, the more attractive. I especially like to group a collection of them in different shapes and sizes. But if you prefer to use plastic pots, you can always hide them inside something more decorative.

There are many other containers that plants look good in: glazed ceramic, wooden, straw, metal, and so forth. You can experiment to suit your own taste. By monitoring my watering very carefully, I have grown certain plants successfully in pots that were not designed for holding plants and hence had no drainage holes, but I don't advise this unless you know exactly what you are doing. Nevertheless, if you want to try because your beautiful plant container has no holes and you cannot drill holes without damaging the pot, put an inch or two of stones on the bottom and set the plant in a plastic or clay pot on top of them. Excess water will drain safely into the stones, but don't let so much collect that it reenters the pot.

There are also decorative planters you can buy called *cache-pots* (French for "hide the pot"), which are made specifically to hide a utilitarian container. If the decorative planter is a basket, put a water-catching saucer inside so the basket doesn't rot.

Plant containers should be kept clean, not only for appearance' sake but to get rid of disease organisms. When reusing a pot, *always* wash it out first with soap and water and a mild chlorine-bleach solution (about 9 to 1), scouring it to remove all dead leaves, algae and fertilizer deposits. If the pot is made of clay, soak it in water for a while so it will not draw water out of the soil when you pot the plant.

There are various containers available for hanging plants, often with holes in the rim so that cords or wires can be attached. If there are no holes you have to sling something around the bottom of the pot that will support it, such as those macramé supports that have been used so much—overused, you may feel. (I think the simpler ones, without a lot of dripping tassels, look all right.) If there are holes in the rim and the pot is not too heavy, try this trick: use heavy transparcnt fishing line to support the pot. It will be almost invisible, so that the plant will appear to float in midair. (Using a soil-less mix inside the pot will make it lighter.) Another option is to get a wire basket and line it with moistened sphagnum moss (not peat moss, which would fall through the holes), then fill this with your soil mix. Wire baskets are too messy to use indoors but they are pretty and natural looking and plants drain well when growing in them.

Make sure that there is something to catch the excess when you water a hanging plant. Many pots come with a saucer attached, but you still must water carefully so that the saucer doesn't overflow onto the floor. A hanging planter without holes in the bottom works fine if you put an inch or two of pebbles in the bottom, then set a conventional pot on top of them. It is helpful if the plant hangs within easy reach for watering. If not you can water it by setting ice cubes on the soil surface and letting them melt into the soil—although the best way is to just take down the pot and give the plant a good soaking in the sink.

SOIL

The kind of soil that goes into your pot is very important. A plant in a pot needs soil that is lighter in texture than soil for an outdoor plant, because drainage is so important. Ordinary garden soil may work fine for some potted plants, but it holds too much moisture for many of them. It is best to use a mixture of soil and soil lighteners. There are many different formulas for soil mixes. A typical "standard potting mix" might be one part soil, one part peat and one part sand. For the soil I usually dig some up in fall before frost so that I can have it handy during the winter. It is a good idea to sterilize garden soil in a 180- to 190-degree oven for at least an hour to kill disease organisms and weed seeds. If you don't have access to garden soil, or if nongardeners in the house balk at your cooking dirt in the oven, you can buy bags of potting soil. But try to get "real" soil if you can; I find the bagged kind has a pulverized, uniform texture that does not drain as well as what I dig up, which has particles of more varied size, including little stones. For peat, use a medium-textured type if you can find it, not the fine, powdery kind. For sand, use sharp builders' sand, never beach sand, which is rounded and has salt in it. Beware of sand provided for use on icy roads, which may also contain salt.

There are other nonsoil ingredients that might go into your mix. Vermiculite, which is made from mica deposits, is a light, very absorbent material. If you want your mix to hold water a bit longer you might substitute this for the sand, which drains very fast and makes for a rather heavy pot when combined with soil. Perlite, a natural mineral product that looks, nonetheless, like little pieces of white styrofoam, seems almost weightless and is good for lightening and aerating a mix. Composted bark is another good organic soil lightener. Charcoal is sometimes added to soil mixes as well because it absorbs toxic agents.

With many plants you may decide that you don't want any soil at all, just a soilless mix—say, equal parts of perlite, vermiculite and peat. Such mixes can be bought in bags and usually contain some lime to counteract the acidity of organic materials like peat and bark. Soilless mixes usually contain some fertilizer as well. One advantage of them is that they are sterile. I find a soilless mix extremely handy and always keep a large bag of it around. I use it for adding to garden soil, or I use it by itself for starting seeds and for plants that like a very light, well-drained potting medium. Remember, though, that if used straight a soilless mix may make the pot so light that a top-heavy plant will tip over. For hanging baskets, however, it is often ideal. Always moisten a soilless medium thoroughly before you use it so it will not draw moisture away from the plant's roots. You may also have to fertilize the plant more often if you use a soilless mix.

Each plant has its own requirements as to growing medium. Cacti and succulents, for example, need particularly good drainage and prefer either a soilless mix or one to which a large amount of sand has been added. Ferns like a more moisture-retentive mix such as one containing soil, vermiculite and peat.

Any growing medium you use should be replaced from time to time if possible, for several reasons. For one thing it can become compacted. For another, the organic matter in both soil and soilless mixes breaks down eventually. Also fertilizer salts can accumulate in any medium. If a plant has been diseased, it is wise to unpot it, shake the soil out of its roots and put the plant in fresh soil that does not harbor the disease organisms. Start with fresh soil whenever you pot up a plant, whether for the first time or when moving it from one pot to another. If a plant needs to remain in the pot for years with its roots undisturbed, you can still do it a favor by removing and replacing the top inch or so of soil every so often, because this is where the greatest concentration of salts, debris or algae will be.

POTTING UP

When you're all set with the right pot and the right growing medium, you're ready to pot up the plant. Do your potting on any hard surface where you can make a mess. If you have a table you can use, that's great. I pot outdoors if weather permits, or on a brick floor indoors on the side porch. While you are getting a pot ready, make sure the roots of the plant do not dry out. If the plant has arrived in the mail bare-root, leave it in its packing material till the last minute. If it is in a pot, leave it there till you're ready for it. Take a fresh, clean pot and put a piece of broken clay pot over the hole in the bottom (several if there is more than one hole), laying its concave side down; this will keep soil from falling out the hole. You can also use a piece of fine plastic mesh like the bags onions are sold in. Then put some of your soil or mix in the bottom, suspend the plant over it with the roots where you want them and carefully start to add soil at the sides, poking it gently with your fingers to firm it as you go. Every now and then whack the pot down firmly on your floor or table to settle the soil. It is important not to have air pockets in the soil as they will cause the roots to dry out. Fill to within an inch or two of the top (the bigger the pot, the more space you should leave), whacking and poking as you go. With most plants the crown should be just at the soil surface so that the foilage is not covered with soil but the roots are. When you're all done, water the plant until water runs out the bottom hole.

Sooner or later, as the top grows and the root system gets too big for the pot, you will need to repot the plant. When a plant is potbound you may see roots on the soil surface, or they may literally crawl out of the top of the pot or through the hole in the bottom. Water may have trouble sinking into the soil—or may drain out very quickly because organic matter in the soil mix has broken down and been replaced with roots. The pot may also feel abnormally light. If you're not sure what's going on in there, lift the plant out and see if there are many roots visible along the outside of the soil.

Here's how to remove a plant from a pot: hold it upside down and rap the rim on a hard surface as shown on page 50. Support the plant with the stem between your fingers so that you can catch it when it slides out.

When you have the plant out of the pot, look carefully at the roots. If any look rotted or mushy remove them; in fact if the roots look badly damaged and other signs have also led you to suspect a disease that might spread to other plants, it is probably best to throw the plant away. If the plant is very potbound and the roots are matted or circling the pot, break them up with a sharp knife. By forcing them to repair themselves you are ensuring that they will strike out into their nice new soil; otherwise they might stay in a matted lump.

When repotting plants, take their individual needs into account. Some plants such as clivia like to be potbound. Some grow quickly and need frequent repotting. Others grow very slowly but even these like to have their soil replaced periodically.

Taking Care of Your Plants

M aintenance is the part of houseplant care that confuses most people, but it's really a pretty simple business. There are some dos and don'ts, which I'll describe below, but one thing to remember about houseplant care is that although you are giving plants a very consistent environment in which factors such as temperature fluctuate much less than they would if the plant were outdoors, the plant is still conscious of the seasons. Unless its environment is totally controlled by artificial lighting and a carefully monitored temperature, it will respond when fall comes and the days are shorter, the light weaker, the humidity less, and the drafts cooler. Many plants will do best subjected to natural seasons, because they are biologically designed to go through a resting period in winter. Some plants even go completely dormant, and all their above-ground growth dies back; these should be left alone almost completely, usually with nothing more than a tiny amount of water. Others simply grow more slowly, or not at all in winter, and just need to have less water and less fertilizer. If you feed and water them to produce active growth when there is too little light, the growth will be weak and leggy. Plants' individual needs are discussed in the List of Houseplants.

If you can bring your plants outdoors in summer it will benefit them greatly, even if you only set them on a balcony. You will need a spot that gives the plants the degree of light they like (sun, part sun, bright filtered light, low light, etc). And you will need to water them when they are dry, since they'll dry out much faster after a rain than plants in the ground will. Also, after a lot of rain I always go around and empty their saucers so the roots don't rot. Another great trick is to bury the pots up to their rims in the soil. This usually takes care of the plants' watering needs, and you can even go off for a month or two and leave them. But don't forget to dig them up again in fall! And bring any frost-tender plants inside as soon as a frost threatens.

WATERING

Everyone knows that houseplants need to be watered, but it's a classic case of a little knowledge being a dangerous thing. More houseplants are killed by faulty watering than by any other cause. And it's almost always overwatering, not underwatering, that does it. If a plant is underwatered it shows its dissatisfaction very quickly by wilting or, in the case of succulents, by wrinkling—obvious signals that most people respond to immediately, and unless the plant stays wilted a long time it will usually recover as soon as it is watered.

It's much harder to tell when a plant has been overwatered. People try to be too kind to their plants and end up drowning them—the roots can't get enough oxygen in overwatered soil, and so they start to die. If roots are drowning, they can't absorb nutrients, and this failure eventually makes itself visible in poor growth of the plant, though usually not until the roots are damaged beyond repair. As this point the plant will also wilt, since the dead roots cannot absorb water, and so the hapless gardener rushes up with *more* water, thereby finishing the plant off altogether. Watching for earlier, easier to recognize signs of overwatering, such as failure to produce new leaves, darkened, mushy leaves and stems, and leaves that curl, yellow or brown at the edges is one way out of the dilemma, but frankly the best course is to be attuned to each plant's individual needs for water. When in doubt, or when you are learning the ways of a new plant, underwater, just to be on the safe side.

The best way to water is to really soak the plant with tepid or room-temperature water until it runs out the bottom of the pot. You need to get water to the roots at the bottom of the pot, not just those near the surface. If a plant has become very dry it is a good idea to immerse the entire pot in water until it stops bubbling, this way you are letting it drink up as much as it can hold, especially in a porous pot, which could otherwise drain moisture from the soil if

the pot itself has dried out. But never let the plant sit indefinitely, either in the sink or in a saucer full of water. If the water has not been absorbed after half an hour or so, pour it off. Then leave the plant alone until it needs water again. This will usually be when the soil on top has been dry for a day or two. Plants that need soil that is "evenly moist" prefer to be watered just as the surface is starting to dry out, but even most of these will take a day of dryness, and if in doubt it is best to give them one.

The best way to tell if the soil is moist is to feel it with your finger. To see how far down the dryness goes, stick your finger down into the soil. This is especially important to do with nonporous pots, in which the surface can be dry but the rest of the soil quite wet. (Porous clay pots dry out more uniformly.)

There are certain factors you should be aware of that will help you to anticipate a plant's water needs. A plant will need to be watered more often if the room is warm, if the air is dry, if it is in a small pot, if it is in a clay pot, if the pot contains light soil or a soilless mix, if the plant is a large or fast-growing or lush-leaved specimen, or if the plant is at a stage when it is actively growing, flowering or fruiting.

When you water a potted plant, try not to get the leaves wet since this can foster diseases. A watering can with a long, thin spout that you can poke under the leaves is ideal. Bottom watering (submerging the bottom of the pot in water and letting the plant absorb it) spares the leaves and is efficient, but it can easily lead to overwatering. Bottom watering is sometimes recommended for fuzzy-leaved plants such as gloxinias, whose leaves do not like to get wet, but it must be closely monitored. Don't let the plant sit in water for more than half an hour. Also, any plant should be top watered every now and then to flush out fertilizer salts.

If you have to leave your plants, don't make other people responsible for watering them unless they are gardeners or have been fully instructed about your plants' needs. If it is mild weather and you have an outdoor area, bury the pots up to their rims in the ground in a shaded spot. Another trick, indoors or out, is to soak the whole pot, then encase the entire plant in a transparent plastic bag—a food-storage bag for the small ones, a dry-cleaner's bag for the large ones or for a group of plants. The air inside will be very humid and will recycle lost moisture back to the plant's leaves. This will get most of your plants through a week or two of neglect. But always keep bagged plants out of the sun. They will bake inside the bag, and the soil will dry out faster. There are also wick watering devices you can purchase that will water your plants for you when you are away.

FERTILIZING

It's a natural impulse to overfeed a growing plant. "Have another helping," you say, adding a tad more than it says on the label, figuring that the little bit extra will give your plant just that much more encouragement, especially if it isn't looking good.

This is not the right approach to fertilizing houseplants. For one thing plant food, unlike chicken soup, does not cure everything. Feeding will not make a plant flower—light will. Feeding will not necessarily make a sluggish plant grow if what it needs is more or less water or more or less light. Even a nutrient-starved plant won't respond to fertilizer if there is not enough light for photosynthesis to take place, or if it does respond, it will produce growth that is weak and spindly.

A potted plant can use some fertilizer at certain times but probably less than you'd think. It needs it at the time it is actively growing, because nutrients are required for leaf, stem and root production. If a plant has gone through a period of winter dormancy it will benefit from feeding during the growth spurt with which it emerges from dormancy and produces a lot of new leaves, lengthens its stems and enlarges its root system. But don't feed it right away; in most cases it's best to let a plant break dormancy on its own by showing new growth, then give it light and water to encourage it, and *then* feed it.

It is easiest to feed your plants a formulation specially designed for houseplants, feeding not more, and preferably less than the amount specified on the label. Plants grown chiefly for their foliage need fertilizer relatively high in nitrogen. (Fish emulsion has given me good results.) Those grown for their flowers usually prefer a formula lower in nitrogen but higher in phosphorus. Pay attention to the needs of individual plants described in the List of Houseplants or by the greenhouse or store where you bought them.

Moisten the soil thoroughly before you feed, if you are applying a dry fertilizer. Roots cannot absorb fertilizer unless they are thoroughly moistened. Don't feed a plant if it is diseased or has been severely damaged by an insect invasion. The roots may not be able to absorb the fertilizer, and it will only collect in the soil, leaving excess salts. Don't feed plants heavily if they are growing in low light. Don't feed plants that have gone into dormancy or are resting. And don't feed newly purchased potted plants for, say, six months; they have probably been given a good shot of slow-release fertilizer in the nursery. Plants you have repotted yourself should also be given a rest from feeding. Just let light, warmth and water do their work until there is enough of a new root system to absorb extra nutrients.

If a houseplant is starved of nutrients you will see the leaves turn pale or yellow; usually these are old leaves that are suffering at the expense of new growth, which is getting whatever resources the plant has. Overfed plants may show vigorous growth initially, with large, crisp, dark green leaves. But eventually the leaves will brown as salts accumulated from overfertilizing diminish root growth. You may see white salt deposits and green algae on the pot and on the soil surface. If you think that you have overfed a plant the best thing to do is flush it with water. This means watering until the water runs out of the pot, waiting till it stops and doing it again. Do this about four times.

INSECT PESTS

Dealing with insects on indoor plants can be aggravating. You can't depend on other creatures in the environment to help you out, because except for a few spiders, they aren't there. You can't bring bug-eating birds and toads into the house. To be sure, gardeners with greenhouses and even some windowsill gardeners have had excellent results with bringing in natural predators—for one thing they are a captive crew and won't disperse into the countryside the way they do in your vegetable garden. But someone in your household may object to your releasing swarms of ladybugs, lacewings and ichneumon flies in the house—probably the same person who leaves for the day when you sterilize soil in the oven.

It is also more difficult to ignore a few insect pests indoors, since a few can rapidly become an infestation and spread to other plants. Furthermore, you should be even more reluctant to use toxic sprays and dusts or other toxic materials inside than you are outside, since contact by breathing or touching is even harder to avoid. But fortunately there are some simple, safe means of controlling insects on houseplants. And the fact that the plants are relatively small makes control easier than it is on large outdoor specimens.

Start by keeping your plants as vigorous as possible by giving them proper care, as described above. Good health won't make them less appealing to bugs, but it will make them better able to withstand any insect damage they receive. Keeping the area free of dead leaves and other debris where insects can hide or lay eggs may help some too. Washing plants with soap as part of your regular maintenance program can be very beneficial.

One of the most important things to understand here is that few houseplant pests originate in the house; they have to come in on a plant, either one you have bought or have been given or one that has summered outside. Therefore any new arrival should be isolated from other plants for a week or two while you examine it for possible problems. Putting it in a separate room is often sufficient, but you may even want to tie a plastic bag over it to be really sure new bugs don't leave the plant and roam at large. Examine the whole plant daily, especially the undersides of the leaves and the places where leaves and branches join the stem.

If you do see injured plant parts or a lack of vigor that suggests insect damage, be sure to identify the pest correctly. Don't just reach for a pesticide spray. The problem may be due to a disease or some other form of stress. Even if it is an insect that's causing the trouble, you'll need to apply the controls that work best against it. Some insccts, such as whiteflies, are visible and obvious; some, such as scale, may be best identified with a magnifying glass (a handy tool for any gardener to have); others, like mites, may be too small to see at all, and you'll need other clues (see below).

Always try to use the safest possible means of control. If you must use a toxic spray, even a relatively safe one like rotenone or pyrethrum, spray outdoors if at all possible; and observe the safety precautions described on page 74. Prune out badly infested parts of the plant and get them out of the house right away. If the plant is badly afflicted it is sometimes easier just to discard the whole thing. But not on the compost pile—you don't want insect pests there, either.

Here are some of the visitors you might expect to receive:

Aphids. These are visible as clusters of tiny dots, usually green but sometimes red or brown. They are most often found on new growth, at the tips or forks of branches, and in buds or flowers. Look for new growth that is stunted or distorted, and for yellowed leaves. Aphids do harm not only by sucking plant juices, but also by spreading viruses. And they secrete a sweet, sticky substance called "honeydew," which in turn attracts the black sooty mold fungus, which is both unattractive and harmful. Wash aphids off by spraying with insecticidal soap, which will also remove honeydew. Dabbing with a cotton swab soaked in alcohol will also help. As a last resort use rotenone.

Mealybugs. These strange little bugs look like tiny spots of white cotton and are usually found in the forks where two stems meet. Leaves may look yellow, or plants stunted. If you watch mealybugs long enough you'll see that they move—but not much, and very slowly. Mostly they just sit there suck-

ing plant juices, secreting honeydew and toxins that harm the plant. I have been able to control them by dabbing with alcohol but find that you have to repeat the treatment several times till the bugs are gone. Insecticidal soap also helps. Use pyrethrum if all else fails.

Scale. A number of scale insects afflict houseplants. Crusty-looking patches along the stems prove under the magnifying glass to be tiny oval objects, usually whitish, tan or brown. They too suck sap, causing discolored leaves and stunted plants, and they secrete honeydew—in fact the most noticeable symptom may be stickiness. Best treatment is to spray with insecticidal soap and rub them off with a soft cloth. Alcohol is also effective.

Spider mites. If your plants' leaves have pale-colored, almost transparent spots, and there are fine webs on the undersides, they have spider mites, which sprape away the leaf tissue and then suck up the sap that accumulates. The mites will probably be too tiny to see, even with a magnifying glass. Since they like hot, dry air, you may be able to prevent infestations by misting or raising the humidity in the room and at the same time giving the plants plenty of fresh, free-circulating air. A soap spray, or just a forceful spraying with water may eradicate them, but be sure to spray the undersides of the leaves. If spider mites are on wide-leaved plants, wiping them off with a soft cloth can also help to control them.

Thrips. These are very small, narrow insects with feathery wings. They can be yellow, brown or black. They attack plant parts in the same way that spider mites do, and the damage looks similar. They like buds, especially those of white flowers. Best treatment is to remove infested buds and use insecticidal soap on the whole plant. Use pyrethrum or rotenone only if necessary.

Whiteflies. These tiny flying insects are annoying to deal with because they do not sit still. As soon as you put your hands near the plant they fly up in a cloud. You can try spraying the remaining ones with insecticidal soap, rotenone or pyrethrum, or you can wave strips of flypaper around the plant, then spray with soap. Or hang a yellow sticky trap nearby (page 73).

Cyclamen mites. These are invisible, but their damage appears as a pronounced twisting and deforming of new plant growth. They afflict cyclamens and a number of other plants, including African violets. You may be able to prune out affected parts, but the surest control is to immerse the entire plant—pot, leaves and all—in water that is at exactly 110 degrees for 30 minutes. If this is difficult for you to do, it is best to discard the plant before others are infested.

HOUSEPLANT DISEASES

Houseplant diseases are hard for the average gardener to identify and even harder to treat. The best course is prevention. Houseplants will usually ward off diseases by themselves if you give them proper care to keep them vigorous. Giving them fresh air is also important, either by opening a window from time to time, or by simply making sure that air circulates in the house. Use a fan if necessary or just put the plants in an airier spot rather than in a corner or a room whose door is seldom opened. While misting usually benefits plants, don't mist a plant that is fighting a disease, and when watering, try very hard to keep its leaves dry. Changing a sick plant's soil may also help, or at least changing the top inch or so.

Giving new plants a quarantine period and close scrutiny during that time is as important for detecting diseases as it is for bugs. You must also isolate a plant with a disease so the problem won't spread. Diseased parts of the plant should be pruned out and destroyed, and you should be prepared to throw out the whole plant if necessary. Don't let a dead or dying plant sit around until you can get around to removing it.

Most houseplant diseases are caused by fungi. Leaf-spot diseases, which cause brown, black or tan spots to appear on the leaves, are among the most common. Affected leaves later drop off. Leaf spot and like diseases are best fought by reducing humidity, improving air circulation, and pruning out affected leaves or stems. Bacterial leaf-spot diseases (in fact, most bacterial diseases) cause watery-looking patches to appear and are dealt with in the same way.

Powdery mildew makes leaves whitish; just remove affected leaves and improve the air circulation. Virus diseases such as mosaic are much harder to control. Plants with mosaic are stunted, with mottled, deformed leaves. If aphids have transmitted the disease, destroy the aphids and remove infected parts; the plant may recover. But generally a plant with a virus is best destroyed before it affects others.

If you're not sure what's wrong with the plant, first check for bugs, then see if you're giving it the location it likes. Perhaps you should try it in another spot. Make sure it's getting the proper care. If you still suspect a disease, take a sample of the affected parts to your Extension Service to have it diagnosed, then try the control methods detailed above.

OTHER MAINTENANCE TASKS

You can forget about talking to your

houseplants. Whatever people tell you, a plant is no more ready to hear what you have to say than is a puppy who would rather sniff. But hovering over plants does seem to make them grow better; one theory is that in standing over them a lot you breathe enough carbon dioxide on them to improve their general vigor. Perhaps. But in any case, the more ways you find to fuss over your plants, the more apt you are to notice bugs or other small signs of trouble and deal with them before they become big trouble. In addition to hovering, here are some other good things to do:

Pinching and pruning. Pinching indoor plants is the same process as pinching outdoor ones, as described on page 156. In some cases it is done to make the plant bushier, with a more graceful, compact shape; in others it is done to keep the plant a manageable size. Often the biggest problem with a thriving houseplant is keeping it from outgrowing its confined quarters and turning into a monster. Unfortunately, pinching doesn't work on single-stemmed plants like palms and dracaenas, but on other large ones such as schefflera, citrus fruits and *Ficus benjamina* it works fine. Pinch the ends of stems that have several sets of leaves on them just above a node.

If a plant has already gotten out of hand a more drastic pruning may be in order. Prune as illustrated in Figure 65, cutting back to a node and being careful not to leave a stub. Some plants can even be root pruned by removing the plant from the pot and cutting off the tips of the roots (leaving at least two-thirds of the root system intact), then repotting in the same size pot, with soil added where the old roots were. The plant should have a third of its top growth removed at the same time. The best time to do both types of pruning is

spring, when plants are actively growing and can recover well.

Washing. It may seem odd to give plants a bath, but they love it. Plant leaves get dirty, and even if you dust them, they can still accumulate grime that will keep them from producing food efficiently. Wash them outdoors if you can, or in a sink or bathtub, using a teaspoonful of mild liquid soap (not a detergent) in a quart of water—or use one of the insecticidal soaps designed for plants. Either kind will also help to keep the plants pest-free. Rinse with a stream of water. Indoors a hand-held shower nozzle at the end of a hose is ideal. Or just let the shower rinse them. Outdoors use a hose, adjusting the nozzle so that the spray is forceful enough to do the job, but not forceful enough to break the stems or wash the soil out of the pot.

Turning the pot. Just giving your pots a quarter turn each week will do wonders for them if the light they receive is strongest on one side (as from a window). Turning will ensure that all the leaves get the full benefit of the light and grow better, and it will keep the plant from growing more on one side than another, making it lopsided. You needn't turn plants grown directly beneath artificial lights, but even then you may need to change their position to give them uniform light. The center of a fluorescent light tube gives more light than the ends.

Tidying up. Be sure to remove any dead leaves or stems from the plants promptly, and any plant matter that falls into the pots, saucers, trays, table surfaces or onto the floor. Such trash not only looks a mess, but it can harbor insects and disease organisms.

It may be a good idea to set a particular day aside for these small maintenance tasks each week. But don't let such an efficiency move cause you to feed and water improperly. Many plants need to be watered more or less often than once a week, and feeding schedules also vary from plant to plant. If your plants are surrounded by many gardeners, whether in a home or in an office, make sure that only one person is in charge of feeding and watering. Otherwise the plants will be either fed and watered too little or too much—usually the latter. In every office where I have worked I have heard this conversation:

"The plant is dead."
"But I've been watering it!"
"So have I."
"So have I."
"So have I."

Plant care, like so many other things in life, is better done by one than by a committee.

Propagating Houseplants

E veryone who becomes enthusiastic about growing houseplants winds up propagating them. It's so easy to do! If you like a plant, you can propagate it and have several or give some to friends, swapping them for plants that *they* have propagated. If a beloved plant has overgrown its spot or just gotten too big to be beautiful, propagate it, and by the time you have a nice, compact new plant you can chuck the old one with equanimity. The only thing you shouldn't do is propagate a diseased or otherwise unhealthy plant. The propagation may not even work if the mother plant (the plant from which the new plants are made) has been weakened, and if it is diseased or buggy it can just pass on the problem to its offspring.

There are several ways to propagate houseplants. Sometimes one method works better than the others for a partic-ular species, sometimes you have a choice of several methods.

DIVISION

Dividing houseplants is no different from dividing herbaceous perennials that you grow outdoors, as described on page 151. Houseplants that can be divided are those with multiple crowns. With these you can pull or cut the plants apart to produce smaller plants, each with its own root system and at least one stem or an "eye" where a stem will form. Plants that divide well are streptocarpus, bromeliads, aloe, snakeplant, ferns, clivia and some begonias.

Many plants that grow from bulbs can also be divided. A plant like amaryllis can be divided after its rest period by breaking off a bulblet that forms at the side of the main bulb and replanting it.

ROOTING PLANTLETS

Some houseplants have a charming habit of making "babies" by themselves, often without the benefit of soil. Spider plant is the perfect example: the tufts of leaves that grow at the end of the long stems are little plants that need only a bit of soil and moisture to induce them to root. If you set the mother plant on a table surrounded by small pots you can root the plantlets without even removing them from the stem, then cut the stem when new growth on the subsidiary plants indicates that they have rooted. But I've had equally good luck just taking off a plantlet and sticking it in a moist planting mix.

STEM CUTTINGS

This is the most common way to propagate houseplants (Figure 69). You simply cut a section of stem and root it in a medium such as sand, perlite, vermiculite, peat moss or a combination of these. It is easiest to use a commercially prepared soilless mix. Usually the growing end of the stem is cut, in which case it is called a "tip cutting." Middle sections of stems can also be used, though. It is best to take your cuttings while the plant is actively growing, because a fresh young shoot will root best, but don't try rooting a shoot so immature that it is very limp and tender.

The night before you take the cutting, water the plant so the stems and leaves will have plenty of moisture in them. Have your potting mix all ready before you take the cuttings. Sterilize it, if it is not a material sold already sterilized, and put it in a container such as a shallow clay pot or a small plastic flat (the kind annual seedlings are sold in). It doesn't much matter what you use, but the container must be thoroughly cleaned and have drainage holes in the bottom.

Using a clean, sharp knife or razor blade, cut a stem 4 to 6 inches long, one that has several sets of leaves on it. Make the cut at a slant and cut just below a node (the point where a leaf joins the stem). Remove the leaves from that node; you can remove the next set too, but there should be at least one set of leaves left on the cutting. You will give the rooting process an extra boost if you then dip the end of the cutting in a rooting compound—a white powder

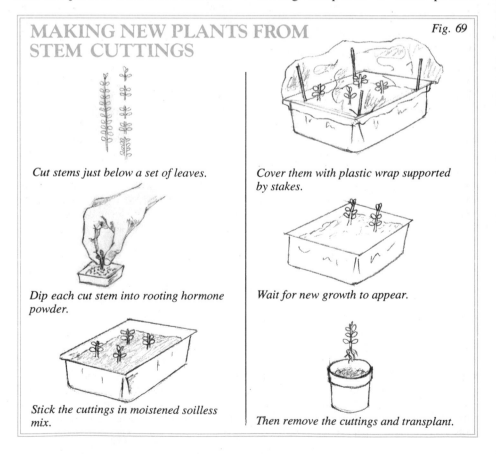

MAKING NEW PLANTS FROM STEM CUTTINGS

Fig. 69

Cut stems just below a set of leaves.

Dip each cut stem into rooting hormone powder.

Stick the cuttings in moistened soilless mix.

Cover them with plastic wrap supported by stakes.

Wait for new growth to appear.

Then remove the cuttings and transplant.

containing rooting hormones, available at stores that sell plant supplies. Don't dip the cutting into the container of compound; take out whatever you'll need, and if there is any compound left after you've treated the cutting, discard it. Then make a hole in the potting mix with a pencil. It should be an inch or two deep, depending on the length of the cutting. Stick the cutting in so that the end is at the bottom of the hole. Firm the mix lightly around the cutting and water it gently but thoroughly.

Now all you have to do is cover your container with plastic film to keep the air inside humid, and wait for the cuttings to root. You can either put the container in a plastic bag or spread plastic wrap over it, supporting the wrap with wire hoops or sticks inserted into the mix so the plastic doesn't touch the plant. Or just put your flats and pots in a large transparent plastic box. While they are rooting the cuttings should have plenty of light but not direct sun, and should be kept at a temperature of 65–75 degrees. Watch to make sure that the potting mix and the air around it do not dry out. The plastic should look moist or foggy. Water as needed or let air in if it looks too sodden in there or if you see mold. Cuttings of fuzzy-leaved plants like the air to be drier. These should have the soil moist but not the leaves.

Your cuttings should root in two to five weeks. Usually you can tell they have rooted by the fact that they stand up in a perky way with good color and even fresh new growth, but if you're not sure, tug on the cutting ever so slightly. If it resists it has rooted. Dig up the rooted cuttings very gently using a spoon or fork, and plant them individually in small pots using a similar potting mix or one with a larger percentage of soil. Don't fertilize the cuttings at all until about a month after they root; the roots aren't ready for it yet.

LEAF CUTTINGS

For fleshy-stemmed plants such as gloxinia, African violets, streptocarpus, rex and Rieger begonias, peperomia, jade plant and sedum, leaf cuttings are an excellent way of propagation. It may take a bit longer to get full-sized plants with this method than with stem cuttings, but since each leaf makes several plants you'll have more of them. In spring or summer (or any time if you are growing under artificial light), cut a healthy young leaf (a clean, sharp razor blade works best) with 1½ to 2 inches of stem attached, making a slanted cut. Rooting compound is not always used with leaf cuttings, although I always figure it can't hurt. Insert the stem ½ inch into the soil and lightly firm the medium around the stem. With some plants, such as rex begonias, the stem or the underside of the leaf vein is split lengthwise; plantlets grow from this wound. With large-leaved plants such as these you can also cut the leaf into a wedge-shaped section that includes the central vein, and plant that. Some plants, such as jade, geraniums and Christmas cactus, are so easy to root from leaves that all you need to do is stick the bottom end of the leaf rather unceremoniously into the ground. Succulents also like to be left for a day or two to callus the cut a bit; leaves of nonsucculents must be set in the medium right away, however, so they don't dry out.

One advantage of propagating with leaf cuttings is that you can watch the result above ground—little plantlets form around the leaves. Keep the soil and air moist, as above, and remove plantlets from the mother leaf when they are large enough to have adequate root systems. (You'll learn easily by experience.) Then plant each one in a small pot (a peat pot is fine).

OTHER METHODS OF PROPAGATION

Some of you are probably asking, "When is she going to talk about the glass of water?" To many people plant propagation is a jelly glass on the windowsill with a cutting inside it growing roots that you can *see*. Yes, you can see them, but relatively few plants can sit with their roots in water without rotting. It is always fun to try, however, and in the case of some plants such as philodendron, coleus, impatiens and the tall, cane-type begonias, rooting in water works excellently. But if you try it, be sure to pot the cuttings soon after they develop roots and before they turn to mush.

At the opposite extreme of complexity is a sophisticated technique of propagation invented by the Chinese called "air layering," in which a plant stem is cut partway through, then enclosed in a material like damp sphagnum moss with plastic film wrapped around that. The moss should be kept moist. In a few weeks roots will grow, making a new plant, which is then removed and replanted. Air layering is useful if you have a plant that has grown too tall. Simply air layer it at the desired height. If it then branches in an attractive way you will have two plants.

I have been describing methods of propagation that don't require plants to flower and produce seed. Many houseplants can be grown from seed as well. Some of the choicest new varieties of African violets, gloxinias and cyclamens, for example, are available as seeds.

MAKING NEW PLANTS FROM LEAF CUTTINGS

Fig. 70

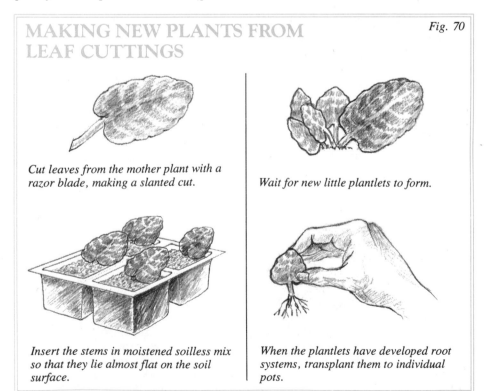

Cut leaves from the mother plant with a razor blade, making a slanted cut.

Wait for new little plantlets to form.

Insert the stems in moistened soilless mix so that they lie almost flat on the soil surface.

When the plantlets have developed root systems, transplant them to individual pots.

LIST OF HOUSEPLANTS

Almost any plant can be a houseplant if you want it to be—even a tree if it's grown as a bonsai. Other chapters have covered some plants that can be grown indoors, such as the herbs in Chapter 8, some annuals in Chapter 5, vines like passion flower in Chapter 13, perennials like sedum in Chapter 6, bulbs that can be forced indoors for winter bloom (page 399) and even vegetables like patio tomatoes or indoor lettuce crops. If you've ever watched a sweet-potato plant grow in a glass of water or carefully nourished an avocado pit even though you knew it would never produce avocados, you know the fun of growing things when it is not gardening season.

In growing houseplants the limitations are the space and light available; but the plant choices are almost infinite. The following list includes many old favorites, some plants that are becoming old favorites, and a few exotic-but-easy plants you might not have heard of. But please explore further! I have ignored many succulents, such as *Echeveria, Euphorbia, Kalanchoe,* aloe and agave. And many fine hanging plants, such as grape ivy *(Cissus incisa),* Swedish ivy *(Plectranthus australis),* wax plant *(Hoya carnosa)* and wandering Jew *(Zebrina pendula).* And foliage plants such as *Fatsia japonica, Aspidistra, Monstera* and *Sansevieria* (snake plant). And those that flower! What about the ghostly white *Spathiphyllum,* the festive *Euphorbia pulcherrima* (poinsettia), the papery *Abutilon* (flowering maple), the flamboyant *Strelitzia reginae* (bird of paradise) and the incredible orchids, many not hard to grow. Use the catalogs in the List of Mail-Order Sources to experiment further.

AFRICAN VIOLET
Saintpaulia

DESCRIPTION: If you only have patience for one little houseplant, this might be the perfect one. It blooms almost all the time, even in winter. It's tidy and compact, with pretty, oval, fuzzy leaves surrounding the flowers, which grow up in the center, making the plant look like a bouquet. (Sometimes the leaves are bronzed or variegated.) Hybridizers have produced thousands of varieties whose flower colors range from a wonderful intense blue, to purple, magenta, lavender, pink, coral and white (but no real red as yet). The flowers are usually about an inch wide, some are ruffled or fringed and some bicolored. All have bright yellow stamens in the center. Standard-sized plants grow up to a foot tall, and semiminiatures are 6–8 inches, as are the true miniatures, which have tiny flowers, too. There are also trailing varieties.

The Optimara, Ballet and Rhapsodie series all contain excellent varieties. If your interest is sparked you may want to investigate the wider world of African violets. If you do not have much light and your rooms are on the cool side, you won't have good luck with them unless you grow some of the newer varieties bred for low light and cooler temperatures. Consult the African Violet Society (see the List of Plant Societies) for more information.

HOW TO GROW: Most African violets do best in a warm room where it is at least 70 degrees during the day and no colder than 60 degrees at night. Light should be bright but not direct sun; fluorescent lights and growing lights designed for plants seem custom-made for African violets, and many enthusiasts use these alone. The plants prefer quite humid air (especially the trailing ones) and soil that is kept evenly moist, though it is all right for the soil to dry out for a day if the plants are not actively growing. They respond very poorly to overwatering and poor drainage. Use water that is at room temperature and try to keep the leaves dry to avoid leaf-spot diseases.

The easiest way to give African violets the soil they like is to buy a bag of commercial "African violet soil." Or, you can make your own mix using one part peat or leaf mold for organic matter and one part sand or perlite for good drainage. Feed about once a month with "African violet food" or a standard houseplant fertilizer (one that is not too high in nitrogen, or you'll get lots of beautiful fuzzy leaves and no flowers). Overfeeding is also a grave error, caus-

ing the leaves to turn gray and the leaf stems to rot. Flush out excess fertilizer salts regularly.

Use fairly small, shallow pots, keeping the plants a bit rootbound, and turn the potted plants from time to time if most light comes from one side— otherwise your flower display will be lopsided. Crowns can be divided, but leaf cuttings are the best way to propagate African violets. Use a medium-sized leaf and dip the stem in rooting powder. African violets don't last forever; after they become woody they often decline—that's the time to take leaf cuttings.

BEGONIA
Begonia

Rieger begonia

rex begonia

DESCRIPTION: There are many kinds of begonias you can grow indoors, all of them very different from one another in the way they look and grow, and all with their own special virtues. The fibrous-rooted wax begonias, which are grown most often as outdoor annuals, make fine ever-blooming houseplants (page 136). Tuberous begonias (page 403) also can be grown as houseplants, though they'll only bloom in summer. Angel-wing begonias (*Begonia coccinea*) are fibrous rooted, cane-type begonias that grow up to 4 feet and more and bear dangling clusters of small red flowers almost year-round. Iron-cross begonias (*B. masoniana*) are foliage plants, growing 1½ feet tall from rhizomes; they are valued for their crinkly, apple-green leaves, which are marked in the center with a dark green cross.

Probably the most spectacular and popular begonias grown as houseplants are rex and Rieger begonias. Rex begonias (*B. rex-cultorum*) grow from rhizomes and have small pink or white flowers in spring, but they are most prized for their large, magnificent leaves, which are an intricate brocade of green, red, bronze, pink or silver. They make a lavish mound a foot tall or a bit more; miniature varieties are 6 to 8 inches. Rieger begonias (*B.* × *hiemalis*) often have colored leaves but are grown for their profuse, showy flowers at least 2 inches across, in shades of red, pink, orange and yellow, which provide months of color in winter. They are fibrous rooted.

HOW TO GROW: Begonias, in general, like plenty of light, and flowering types should have several hours of sun each day for best winter bloom. Daytime temperature should be in the 65- to 75-degree range (a bit cooler for Rieger begonias) and not below 50 degrees at night. All, especially rex begonias, like humid air, but it must circulate well to avoid mildew, especially with the large-leaved types. Soil should be a nice, light, organic mix, like that sold for African violets, and should be kept evenly moist, or just slightly dry between waterings. But drainage *must* be excellent, and you should avoid wetting the leaves. Fertilize lightly with a balanced fertilizer about every two weeks while plants are in active growth, or, in the case of Rieger begonias, all year. Fibrous-rooted kinds should be repotted in spring as needed; those with rhizomes go in shallow pots and should remain rootbound until you can see rhizomes all over the soil surface.

Rieger begonias that stop blooming can be cut back to several inches to produce fresh, flowering growth. Stems of rex begonias should be cut back to the base if they start to get leggy. Wax begonias also benefit from being cut back, and stems of angel-wing begonias without leaves should be cut back in early spring to make new growth. All begonias can be propagated easily by stem cuttings. With rex and Rieger begonias leaf cuttings are also a good method.

BROMELIAD
Many genera

Guzmania lingulata

Aechmea fasciata

DESCRIPTION: These fascinating plants are among the most exotic houseplants a gardener can grow—and also among the easiest! Not a genus in themselves, but a large group of genera, they include *Aechmea, Billbergia, Cryptanthus, Dyckia, Guzmania, Neoregelia, Nidularium, Tillandsia* and a number of others. Bromeliads come from the jungles of South America. Some are terrestrial, but many are air plants (epiphytes), living high up in the trees without any soil and taking nourishment only from whatever organic matter washes their way. (They are not parasitic and do not draw nourishment from the trees themselves.) Tree-growing bromeliads catch rainwater in cuplike urns of leaves.

Bromeliads are grown mainly for their spectacular flowers, but the leaves are often particularly handsome too. A typical bromeliad has a rosette of leaves, sometimes soft and green, sometimes stiff and spiky with variegated markings. A flower stalk usually emerges from the center of the rosette. The showiness of these flowers really lies in the brilliantly colored bracts that surround them, though the tinier flowers are also beautiful. A plant blooms only once, but the flower is often extraordinarily long lasting, and bromeliad plants readily produce offshoots. You may remove these from the mother plant and repot them or cut out the spent mother plant and let the cluster of new ones bloom together.

If you're looking for a bromeliad to start with, try *Aechmea fasciata.* You might find it marketed under various names such as "urn plant" or "silver vase," but you'll recognize it by its vase of stiff, tooth-edged green leaves, marked horizontally with silver bands. The flower spike has toothed bracts of a bright pink color; little blue-purple flowers nestle among the pink spikes. Best of all, this colorful spectacle lasts about six months. The plant grows 1–2 feet tall. Another gorgeous, long-blooming bromeliad is *Guzmania lingulata,* which is about the same size, with long green, straplike leaves (sometimes striped with purple), and a red-orange cluster of bracts enclosing white flowers from late winter to summer.

HOW TO GROW: Bromeliads with stiff, variegated leaves like good, bright light and often will take some direct sun (but don't expose them to strong midday sun in summer); those with softer, green leaves are fairly shade-tolerant. They do well under artificial lights. They are happiest in warm rooms (65–75 degrees) which can be as low as 50–60 degrees at night (even lower for *Aechmea fasciata*). Give them humid air and a very light, porous organic soil or soilless mix—remember that many bromeliads are air plants, and their roots don't normally grow in soil. Some gardeners grow the ephiphytic types on pieces of tree branch wrapped in moistened sphagnum moss, but a shallow clay pot will do fine. You can allow the top inch or so of the pot to dry out between waterings (overwatering can lead to fungus diseases), but always keep the cup inside the leaves filled with water. Feed lightly—a balanced liquid fertilizer at half the suggested strength added to the soil and cup once a month in spring and summer is about right. Propagate by dividing offsets with a knife and repotting them.

CACTUS
Many genera

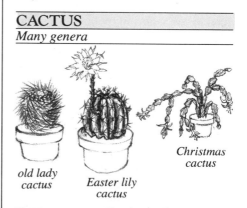

old lady cactus

Easter lily cactus

Christmas cactus

DESCRIPTION: Cacti are fun to grow because of their eccentric, even comical shapes. They're also beautiful, especially when they bloom. If your air is dry and you have trouble growing plants that like high humidity, put away your mister and pebble-filled trays and try cacti instead. They also need less attention than other houseplants. They are part of the large group of desert plants called "succulents," which store water in their fleshy leaves to get them through the long dry spells their native climates are known for. Cacti don't have conventional leaves, just stems, which are often jointed. They also have "areoles"—small holes from which tufts emerge. Sometimes the tufts are soft, like hairs; sometimes they are sharp and spiny. (The tufts shelter them from the sun and, if sharp, against creatures who might bite them to get at the water inside). The flowers, which appear in spring and summer, also emerge from the areoles.

Cacti are a large family, with many genera that make good houseplants. Here are some good ones to start with. *Mammillaria* cacti are sometimes called "pincushion" or "nipple" cacti. Most look like small round globes covered with nipples and bear clusters of small, pretty flowers in a crown around the top. Some good ones to try are old lady cactus (*Mammillaria hahniana*), which is covered with long white hairs, produces red flowers and generally grows well under 10 inches; the tiny golden star cactus (*M. elongata*), which is composed of a cluster of long projections with yellow spines and white flowers; *M. zeilmanniana*, which forms a little round ball and produces pinkish red flowers even at a young age.

Easter lily cactus (*Echinopsis multiplex*) is a little round cactus with vertical ribs and large, pink flowers borne on tall stems; these open in the evening and have a lovely fragrance. Hybrids, which are crossed with species of *Lobivia* cactus, come in other colors such as red and orange, and may be day-blooming. Among the many other good flowering cacti to try are species of *Opuntia* (prickly pear), *Aporocactus* (rattail), *Echinocereus* (hedgehog), *Ferocactus*

(barrel) and *Rebutia* (crown).

One of the most popular cacti is the Christmas cactus (*Schlumbergera truncata* or *Zygocactus truncatus*), a jungle epiphyte that sends out long, arching, jointed stems. Lovely red or white tube-shaped flowers dangle from the tips around Christmas time. The variety known as "Thanksgiving cactus" blooms a few weeks earlier and can be distinguished by the fact that the last joint on a stem has two prominent teeth. A similar plant, Easter cactus (*Rhipsalidopsis gaertneri*), is spring blooming. Plants are long-lived and can grow as tall as 3 feet and at least as wide.

HOW TO GROW: Most cacti prefer full sun, so give them as much of it as you can. Some will do all right in bright light or under fluorescent lights. They like warm temperatures during the day but can tolerate 40–45 degrees at night (don't let them freeze, though) and may even bloom better if you turn down your thermostat at night. They like dry air but will take average humidity. In spring and summer when growth is active they should be watered thoroughly. During the winter they go dormant for a time, a period they need in order to bloom. They probably won't need water at all during this time, unless they wrinkle. If your water is softened, water them with bottled water, since they cannot tolerate salt.

Plant cacti in small, shallow clay pots, with a light, sandy soil (except Christmas cacti—see below). Repot in spring if you see roots in the drainage hole. Don't feed new plants for a year, then feed about once a month during the growing season with a weak concentration of low-nitrogen liquid fertilizer; don't feed cacti at all while they're dormant. They love to be summered outdoors, in fact the cooler days and shorter nights at the end of summer can help to trigger bloom, but bring them indoors when temperatures start to get down into the 40s. Propagate them by transplanting offsets that have developed their own roots.

Christmas and Thanksgiving cacti need more water and fertilizer than other cacti, and they need a more organic soil. Feed them twice a month in spring and summer, and let the soil dry out a bit between waterings. But starting eight weeks before the time you want them to bloom, give them a rest. Keep them in a cool place that gets no light at night (50–60 degrees), give them no fertilizer and just enough water to keep them from wrinkling, and don't repot them during this time (do it in spring). Gradually introduce them to warmer temperatures. Water while blooming, then keep the cacti on the dry side until spring. They are propagated easily by stem cuttings.

CITRUS
Citrus

Meyer lemon   Calamondin orange

DESCRIPTION: You may not think of citrus fruits as houseplants, but some of them make excellent ones! If you've ever dropped an orange or lemon seed into a pot you know that they grow easily, but chances are you got a plant that didn't do anything except look green. If you choose the right kinds of citrus, however, you can produce fragrant white flowers, followed by fine

fruits, even when very young. Citrus are broad-leaved, evergreen plants that will put up with a lot, I find. Even if they drop all their leaves they can pull themselves together and regroup. The hardiest lemon is the Meyer lemon (*Citrus limon* 'Meyer'), which bears 3-inch fruits. This is a good one to start with, but also try the ponderosa lemon (*C. l.* 'Ponderosa'); just one of its 5-inch fruits yields enough juice and rind for two large pies. Both can be kept to 4 feet or less with a little pruning. For a good indoor orange, try Calamondin orange (× *Citrofortunella mitis*), which bears little tart fruits about 1 inch wide, often at the same time that it is bearing flowers. It too can be kept very compact. When buying indoor citrus plants, look for those specified as dwarf varieties.

HOW TO GROW: Citrus plants are sun loving and should get at least four hours of direct sun a day. In summertime set them outdoors. They do best with fairly warm temperatures by day—around 70 degrees—but prefer about 55 at night, especially in winter. Give them fairly humid air. Citrus plants are best potted or repotted in early spring just when new growth is starting. Grow them in a well-drained, all-purpose potting mix a bit on the acid side. Keep plants potbound. Let the soil get almost dry, then water thoroughly. Feed every two weeks from early spring to late summer with a houseplant fertilizer, then feed about once a month, skipping December and January altogether. Pinch the tips whenever you want to control growth and make the plants bushy, and propagate from stem or tip cuttings any time from midsummer to late fall.

CLIVIA
Clivia miniata

DESCRIPTION: Clivia, also called

"Kaffir lily," grows from a thick-rooted bulb. It looks something like the more familiar amaryllis, to which it is related, but I think it is prettier and its clusters of orange, red or gold flowers more subtle than the huge amaryllis flowers. Flowers can appear any time from December to April (most often in March), rising on 18-inch stalks from the tidy, dark green, straplike leaves and opening over a period of several weeks. Most plants get about 2 feet tall, but there are more compact varieties.

HOW TO GROW: Clivias are very easy plants to grow once you understand them. They will take morning or late-afternoon sun, but too much midday sun will scorch the leaves. Bright indirect light all day is best. Give them average room temperature and humidity by day, but cool temperatures at night if possible. During the dormant period before bloom, a temperature of 50–55, day and night, will help to induce bloom. Clivias like an organic soil like that used for African violets and need to be potbound in order to flower. Repot only when the roots are crawling out of the top of the pot. A heavy pot is often necessary to keep them from tipping over.

In spring and summer keep the plants evenly moist, fertilizing every two weeks. A summer outdoors in filtered sun will do your clivias good.

Bring them in before frost, and stop feeding them. Starting around Thanksgiving, give them little or no water, and if possible keep them in a cool room that gets no light in the evening. When a flower stalk emerges, bring the plant into a warm, light place and start feeding and watering it again. Plants may be propagated by removing and replanting side bulbs in spring when new growth starts.

DIEFFENBACHIA
Dieffenbachia

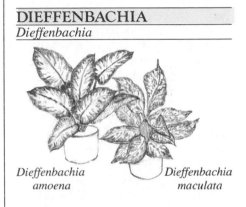

Dieffenbachia amoena   *Dieffenbachia maculata*

DESCRIPTION: This plant's common name is "dumb cane," because the sap irritates your tongue and causes it to swell so that you can't talk. It is a large plant from the American tropics, grown for its wide leaves, and there are many species and cultivars to choose from, many with attractive markings in shades like chartreuse or cream. Usually they are single stemmed. The most common species is *Dieffenbachia maculata*, which often has striking yellow or white variegations. *D. amoena* has large, dark green leaves with white blotches. Both can eventually reach the ceiling. Their leaf variegations make them good plants for brightening up a corner, though they will grow best if the corner is not a very dark one.

HOW TO GROW: Among the most easy-to-please of houseplants, dieffenbachias like bright, indirect light but will toler-

ate much lower light conditions. *D.
amoena* especially prefers shade. All
dieffenbachias grow best in fairly humid
rooms that are warm during the day and
no colder than 50 degrees at night. Plant
them in a light, organic potting mix that
drains easily, and keep them fairly potbound to control their size. Repotting, if
needed, can be done at any time. Water
thoroughly, then let the soil dry out
before watering again. (Don't ever overwater, or both roots and stems will rot.)
Feed once or twice a month in warm
weather but not in winter.

Leggy plants can be cut back to
within 4–6 inches of the soil and will
sprout new growth (this is best done in
spring). Propagate by tip or stem cuttings. It is best to wear gloves when you
are working with the plants so that the
sap cannot get in your eyes or mouth.
Keep children away from dieffenbachias
for the same reason.

DRACAENA
Dracaena

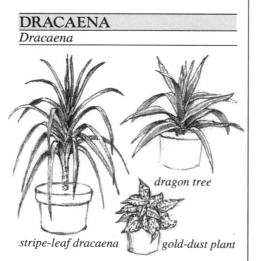

dragon tree

stripe-leaf dracaena   gold-dust plant

DESCRIPTION: Among the tallest of
houseplants, the treelike dracaenas are
perfect when you need a strong accent.
They have swordlike leaves, often with
attractive variegations. Although they
are single stemmed, several plants of
different heights can be grown together

in the same pot for a bushier look. They
are easy-to-grow plants, very tolerant of
indoor environments.

Dracaena fragrans 'Massangeana,'
sometimes called "corn plant," has
leaves that resemble those of corn, with
a yellow stripe down the middle. *D.
marginata* (dragon tree) has a cluster of
red-edged leaves atop a tall stem that
twists in picturesque ways. In the variety 'Tricolor' the leaves are green, red
and yellow. *D. deremensis* 'Warneckii'
has rather stiff leaves, striped with
white. All these can grow to the ceiling
eventually. If you want a more compact
dracaena, grow *D. surculosa* (*D. god-
seffiana*), called "gold-dust plant,"
which only grows a few feet tall. The
flat oval leaves are dark green with
cream-colored spots; in the variety
'Florida Beauty' the leaves are so spotted they are almost all white.

HOW TO GROW: Dracaenas will tolerate
quite low light, though brighter light
will bring out foliage variegations better. They will also tolerate low humidity
to some degree, but they do prefer warm
rooms. Plant them in an average potting
mix, repotting any time they look
crowded. Water freely from spring to
fall, keeping the soil evenly moist but
never letting them become waterlogged.
In winter let the soil dry out between
waterings. Feed every two weeks or so
during the growing season. Plants can
be cut back to 4 to 6 inches, and new
growth will sprout. New plants can be
propagated by removing and replanting
suckers that form at the base or by
cutting sections of the canes that have at
least one node and laying them on moist
sand.

FERNS
Many genera

DESCRIPTION: Ferns give a better softening effect to an indoor environment

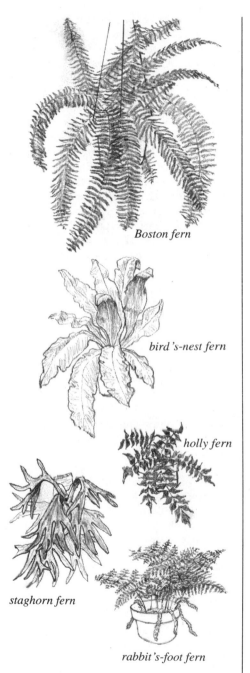

Boston fern

bird's-nest fern

holly fern

staghorn fern

rabbit's-foot fern

that make good houseplants. Many people are familiar with that old favorite, the Boston fern (*Nephrolepsis exaltata* 'Bostoniensis'), a very easy indoor plant with rich green, arching fronds; in the variety 'Fluffy Ruffles' they are rather upright and have frilled edges. Even more foolproof is its relative, the Dallas fern (*N. e.* 'Dallasii'), which grows less than a foot tall. Bird's-nest fern (*Asplenium nidus*), a type of spleenwort, has wide, shiny, wavy-edged fronds that look more like leaves and can grow 2–3 feet tall. Holly fern (*Cyrtomium falcatum*) also has leaflike fronds (a bit like large holly leaves) and is extremely adaptable as an indoor plant.

If you want something a bit unusual that's very easy to grow try rabbit's-foot fern (*Davallia fejeensis*), a beautiful feathery fern from the South Pacific. Its long rhizomes look like brown, furry paws and can be seen crawling out of the pot and hanging from its rim. When supplying an office with plants I once set one of these on a woman's desk, and the fern made her so nervous that she couldn't sit next to it. But most people find *D. fejeensis* charming, myself included. Another exotic that is not terribly hard to grow is the staghorn fern (*Platycerium bifurcatum*), whose gray-green fronds look like antlers (I'd say more like those of a moose than those of a stag). It is an epiphyte, generally grown on a piece of wood or bark, with its roots wrapped in moistened sphagnum moss.

HOW TO GROW: Few ferns can tolerate much, if any, sun, and most grown indoors don't like deep shade either. Give them bright indirect or filtered sun and an average room temperature. The one thing they are really fussy about is humidity. Generally, the more feathery its fronds, the more moisture in the air a fern needs. Ferns with leaflike fronds

than any other type of plant. They are easy to grow if you have a fairly humid environment, and there are many kinds are more drought-tolerant. Misting or using a humidity tray may make the difference for you.

Ferns are shallow rooted and should be grown in shallow pots in a light, organic soil mix. Keep the soil evenly moist but not soggy (the phrase "like a squeezed-out sponge" is often used to describe the right degree of wetness). The surface can be permitted to dry out between waterings in winter, however. Water the base of a staghorn fern when it feels dry. Indoor ferns do not need a period of dormancy, though they may go dormant if the temperature is below 50 degrees; and they can be fed lightly about once a month all year. You can move them outdoors in summer but not into direct sun. Ferns spread by runners, which can be severed and replanted for propagation. To propagate rabbit's-foot fern, pin the tip of a "foot" to the surface of moist sand with a hairpin.

FICUS
Ficus

weeping fig   *rubber plant*

DESCRIPTION: One of the most popular houseplants these days is the weeping fig (*Ficus benjamina*), usually just called "ficus." Though related to the edible fig, it does not bear fruit, but it makes a beautiful display as an indoor plant. A bushy tree that might grow to 50 feet in its native Malaya, it can easily be kept to 6 feet or so or allowed to grow

to ceiling height, which it will do within a few years. Its 3-inch, shiny, pointed leaves tolerate low humidity well—one reason why ficus is such a popular plant. Another oft-grown ficus is that old standby the rubber plant (*F. elastica*). It looks almost like an artificial plant, with its large, dark green, oval, shiny leaves, and it can grow to the ceiling if you don't pinch its tip. Though now out of fashion because of overuse, *F. elastica* is still a good plant to grow if you need something big and green in a spot with little light. (It will grow in bright light too). The variety 'Decora' has very broad leaves, and there are variegated varieties as well, though these need more light in order to show their colors.

HOW TO GROW: Ficus plants like fairly warm rooms but will tolerate low humidity because their leaves are rather leathery. *F. benjamina* needs more light than *F. elastica*—filtered sun or bright, indirect light is best. Soil for both can dry out a bit between waterings, but don't overwater: *F. elastica* will get leggy, and *F. benjamina* will drop its leaves. Sudden changes in the environment, such as being moved or exposed to drafts, can also cause leaf drop in the latter, making it seem like a delicate, fussy plant. But it will usually recover promptly with new growth. Feed both regularly except in fall or winter and wash the leaves with warm water. They like to be rather potbound, and their size can be controlled by root-pruning them and putting them back into the same pot. Stems can also be cut back to the desired height and will produce new, compact growth.

GLOXINIA
Sinningia speciosa

DESCRIPTION: This is a very beautiful plant when in bloom, and this is when you are apt to receive it as a gift—a

cluster of large, bell-shaped flowers rising out of a circle of large, dark green
fuzzy leaves. After blooming a gloxinia
goes into a dormant state during which
the leaves and stems die and there is
nothing left but a little, flattish tuber. At
this point most people throw the thing
away, not realizing that they can keep
growing it and reflowering it for decades. Gloxinias come in many vibrant
colors—chiefly red, purple, pink and
white; some are spotted or edged with a
contrasting color.

HOW TO GROW: You can purchase a
gloxinia at any point in its life. If it's in
bloom you can see what the flowers
look like, of course, but often it is easier
and less expensive to purchase a tuber in
midwinter, planting it about ½ inch
deep in a soilless mix. Water it sparingly while it is starting to root, then
keep soil evenly moist but not soggy
while the leaves appear. Try not to get
the leaves wet. Gloxinias will do well in
a room whose temperature is normal or
cool, but the air should be fairly humid,
and the plant should have bright light
but not direct sun. Like other members
of the gesneriad group, which includes
African violets and streptocarpus, gloxinias do well under fluorescent lights
(give them fourteen to sixteen hours per
day). Feed with a balanced or high-
phosphorus fertilizer once a month
while plants are growing.

After bloom stop feeding and gradually stop watering. When the leaves turn
yellow and the plant goes dormant you
can either leave the tuber in the pot or
repot it in a slightly larger one, then
store it in a dark, cool place (about 50
degrees), keeping the soil almost dry
until a few months later when new
growth starts. Or you can dig up the
tuber and store it in peat moss for at
least forty-five days, then place it in
barely moistened peat or a soilless mix
when you want it to start growing, just
as you do when you buy a new tuber.
New plants can be propagated by dividing the tubers just when they show eyes,
making sure there is an eye for each
division, or by taking leaf cuttings.

JADE PLANT
Crassula argentea

DESCRIPTION: This almost indestructible South African plant has fat, oval,
usually dark green leaves. It is a succulent, so the leaves hold water, helping it
to survive droughts in its native land and
forgetful waterers in others. It also tolerates low humidity and low light. It is
very long-lived, and will grow into a
thick-trunked, 4-foot, treelike shape,
though you can very easily keep it
smaller and bushier by pinching the
stem tips. Though plants rarely bloom
while young, an old one will suddenly

cover itself with fragrant, starlike white flowers if it is potbound.

HOW TO GROW: Give a jade plant the average-to-cool temperatures it prefers, even though it will tolerate a very wide temperature range. Sun or bright light is best but not necessary, and it will also take direct sun. Let plants dry out slightly between waterings in spring and summer, then water less and less as winter comes, giving them only enough in winter to keep the leaves from shriveling. Feed every two weeks or so during spring and summer. Jade plants will do fine if rootbound, though it is best to repot them every two years or so using an average soil mix. If the plant looks graceless and overburdened, remove pendulous growth as needed. Use the cut stems or single leaves for propagation. (Both are easily rooted.)

PALMS
Many genera

parlor palm

lady palm

sentry palm

DESCRIPTION: Palms make great indoor plants because of their graceful shapes and because they tolerate a multitude of ills—dry air, overheating, cold drafts and low light. Fronds are divided into leaflets; some plants grow on a single stem, while others have many stems coming up from the base. There is a palm for every situation—here are some to try. The parlor palm (*Chathe bella*) is a feathery, fairly slow growing palm that makes clumps up to 4 feet, sometimes taller. It prefers a warm, humid room and does best when potbound. The lady palm (*Rhapis excelsa*) is also slow growing but can reach the ceiling eventually, with dark green, fan-shaped fronds on hairy, bamboolike canes. There are variegated forms with yellow stripes. This is a very tolerant palm that will even take fairly cool temperatures. The kentia palm *(Howea)* is another graceful, feathery palm that grows slowly and adapts to either low or bright light, though it needs a warm room. Species include *Howea forsterana,* also called "paradise palm," which grows fairly quickly, its long fronds arching out in a vase shape, and the sentry palm (*H. belmoreana*), which is more compact. Both are single-stemmed and can be potted in clumps of several.

HOW TO GROW: Picture the filtered light of a tropical jungle, then see if you can find a spot like that for your palm. Try to give it a warm spot with fairly high humidity, even though it will tolerate dry air to some extent. (Humidity also helps it to avoid red spider mites.) Use a standard potting mix, not soilless but with some loam. Keep the soil consistently moist (again, like a jungle) but let the top inch dry out between waterings in wintertime; overwatering a palm in winter can cause the roots to rot. There is no dormant period, but growth does slow in winter, and palms should not be fed then, though a monthly feeding in spring and summer with a balanced fertilizer will benefit them.

PEPEROMIA
Peperomia

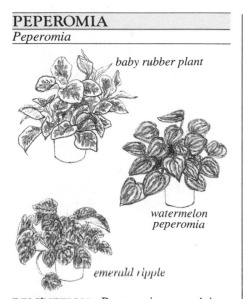

baby rubber plant

watermelon peperomia

emerald ripple

DESCRIPTION: Peperomias are dainty little plants, rarely more than a foot tall, well suited for terrariums, dish gardens or wherever a small plant looks good. Though they produce little spiky flowers, they are grown for their thick heart-shaped leaves. These can be smooth or wrinkled and range in color from very dark green to almost silver. There are many peperomias you can try. One popular one is *P. caperata,* emerald ripple, which has dark green, crinkled leaves and is very easy to grow. Another is *P. argyreia* (*P. sandersii*), often called "Watermelon peperomia" because its leaves, held on red stems, are striped like a watermelon. Another is *P. obtusifolia,* sometimes called "baby rubber plant" because the shape and texture of its leaves are a bit like those of a rubber plant. Its leaves often have white variegations. But this is only a small selection of these delightful plants, some of which have are trailing and grow well in baskets.

HOW TO GROW: Peperomias are not fussy about temperature, though they do appreciate a humid atmosphere. They like bright light but not direct sun. Many are epiphytes (air plants) and so prefer a light, very well drained soil or soilless mix. It is most important not to overwater peperomias, especially in winter; let the soil dry out on the surface between waterings. They can be fed monthly with a balanced liquid fertilizer during spring and summer, but not in fall or winter, and overfeeding should always be avoided. Peperomias do not need frequent repotting, since they are so small and compact, but you can repot them in early spring. This is also the time to propagate them by division, if they make offsets, or by tip, stem or leaf cuttings.

PHILODENDRON
Philodendron

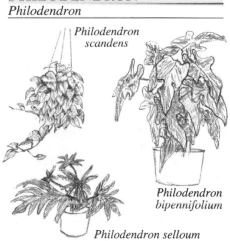

Philodendron scandens

Philodendron bipennifolium

Philodendron selloum

DESCRIPTION: The name "philodendron" means "tree-loving"—inspired by the tree-climbing habit of many of these South and Central American jungle plants. Some species are not so vining in their habit, however, forming new growth at the base, branching and creeping along the ground; these are known as the "self-heading" types. Philodendrons may seem like rather mundane plants simply because they are so common—common because they are so easy to grow. *Anyone* can grow a philodendron. But they can be used in interesting ways—cascading from indoor balconies, for instance. And there are many species and cultivars you've probably never heard of but might like to grow once you start to explore them.

The most familiar philodendron, a vining plant with smooth, heart-shaped leaves, is sometimes called "heart leaf" and is known by three Latin names: *Philodendron scandens, P. oxycardium* and *P. cordatum.* You also might try the vining *P. bipennifolium,* or fiddle-leaved philodendron, which has large, violin-shaped leaves when full grown. Like many vining plants it is often grown on a bark-covered support (usually a piece of wood). *P. selloum,* saddle-leaved philodendron, has deeply lobed leaves and is a self-heading type, as is *P. wendlandii,* which looks something like a bird's nest fern. There are also philodendron varieties with brightly colored or variegated leaves.

HOW TO GROW: Give philodendrons bright light if possible; they will tolerate low light but don't like strong, direct sun. Average warmth and humidity are fine, though they prefer quite humid air, and the variegated ones like it pretty warm. Keep the soil evenly moist but not too wet, and feed about once a month with a liquid houseplant fertilizer. Feed less in winter, a bit more in spring and summer. They like an average potting soil with organic matter and should be repotted only when very rootbound. Pinch straggly, vining specimens if you want them bushier. They are propagated very easily from stem cuttings (tip cuttings for vining types).

SCHEFFLERA
Schefflera actinophylla

DESCRIPTION: This plant is sometimes called "umbrella tree," because of the

umbrellalike shade it casts in the wild. Its leaves grow in hand-shaped leaf clusters. (The Latin name is sometimes given as *Schefflera macrostachya* and *Brassaia actinophylla.*) Schefflera is the classic, easy-to-grow indoor tree, branching nicely and adapting to a variety of light conditions. It grows fairly slowly and can be easily kept to a manageable size, though in its native Australia it grows to 20 feet.

HOW TO GROW: Grow schefflera in a room of average temperature but with a humid atmosphere if possible, misting as needed. It likes bright light but can also tolerate low light and some direct sun. Pot it in a standard potting mixture, and repot any time it seems potbound, unless you are trying to keep the plant small. You can let the top inch or so dry out between waterings, especially in fall and winter when growth is slower. Feed about once a month in spring and summer, but don't overfeed. I find that washing the leaves regularly is one of the most important things you can do to keep a schefflera healthy.

SPIDER PLANT
Chlorophytum comosum (C. elatum)

DESCRIPTION: Ah, the spider plant. Creeping into the health-food restaurants, then into all the other restaurants, then into the car dealerships, the travel agencies, the government agencies, and probably heaven, hell and purgatory. But cliché or not, the spider plant will always be with us because it is attractive and outrageously easy to grow. Narrow, grassy green leaves with a central white (sometimes yellow) stripe erupt in rosettes at the tips of hanging stems that can get 5 feet long, looking much like a spider's legs. It is most often grown as a hanging plant.

HOW TO GROW: Spider plant likes an average room temperature and humid air but will survive in fairly dry air too. It likes bright light, but will tolerate medium light and weak sunshine. Rotate the pot from time to time, or you'll have a lopsided spider. Give it an all-purpose potting soil, and repot it any time you think it looks crowded. Water the plant thoroughly, then let it dry out on the surface or even a bit deeper; it will tolerate dry soil much better than wet. Feed your spider plant every two weeks in spring and summer if you want to encourage growth. Plants can be di-vided, but the simplest way to propagate is to remove a leaf cluster from the end of a stem and root it in a small pot. You can put many clusters in one pot if you're impatient to get a big, lush plant.

STREPTOCARPUS
Streptocarpus

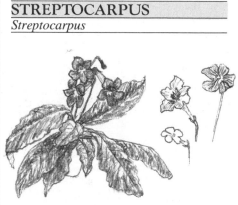

DESCRIPTION: The common name for this plant is "Cape primrose" (because it comes from the Cape of Good Hope in South Africa), but most people these days call it by its Latin name. "Streptocarpus" may sound like a disease, but actually it's the best new plant to appear on the scene in quite a while: it's compact, easy to grow, and blooms most of the year, even in winter. The 2- to 5-inch flowers are most typically blue-violet but can also be red, pink, purple, lavender and white. Some have frilly edges or throats of contrasting colors. The flowers' shape is much like that of an azalea bloom, but they are borne on wiry stems above a large rosette of stemless, crinkled, primroselike leaves. *Streptocarpus saxorum* is a trailing type. The Nymph hybrids are especially long-blooming; 'Constant Nymph' is lavender-blue with a yellow throat and blooms most of the year. The John Innes hybrids are similar but with even more variety of colors. The Weismoor hybrids have especially large blossoms on plants as tall as 2 feet. 'Good Hope' is a good, sun-tolerant, light blue variety. Often the best new hybrids are only available as seed.

HOW TO GROW: Streptocarpus are in some ways similar to African violets, but they will take cooler temperatures (usually down to 50 degrees—below that they may go dormant). They need good, bright light, although they don't like direct sun, and they do well under fluorescent lighting. Plant them in shallow clay pots in a light soil mix like that used for African violets, and keep the soil moist. If the plant stops blooming, however, let it rest for at least a month or two, giving it just enough water so that the leaves do not wilt. Feed once or twice a month in spring and summer, with a balanced or high-phosphorus liquid fertilizer, but don't overfeed, and never feed while the plant is resting. Wait till new growth appears, repot if necessary and then start feeding and watering again. To propagate streptocarpus, divide mature plants while they are dormant.

APPENDIX

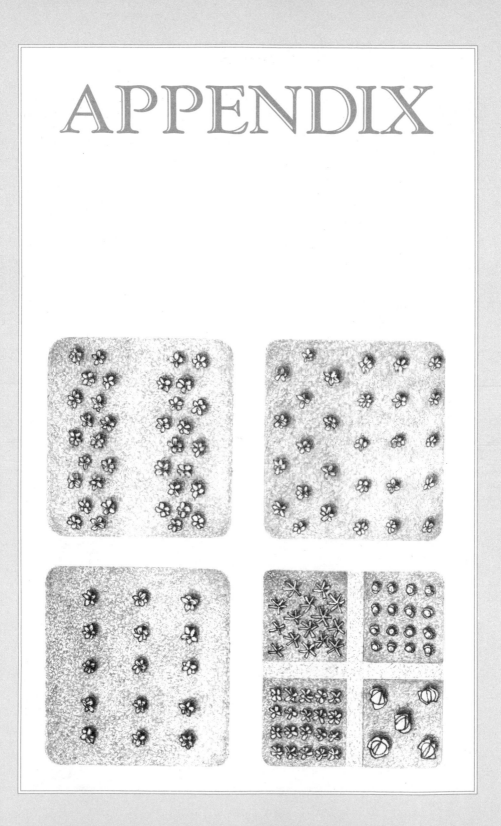

PLANT HARDINESS ZONE MAP

Prepared by the U.S. National Arboretum, Agricultural Research Service, U.S. Department of Agriculture in cooperation with

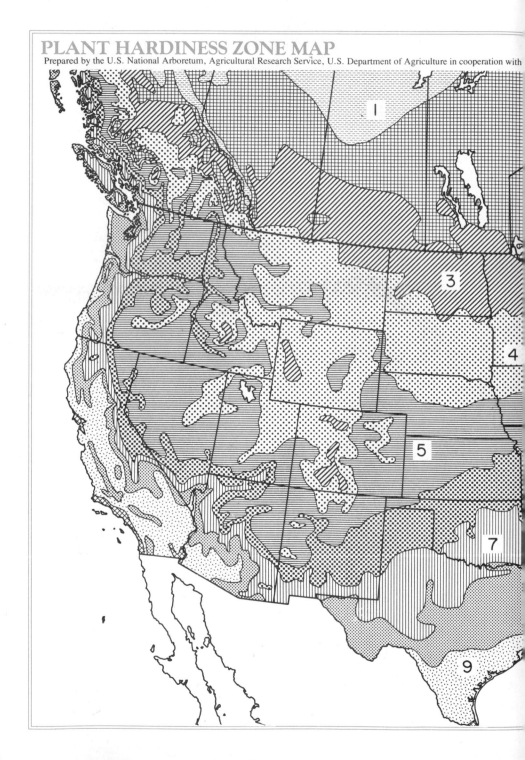

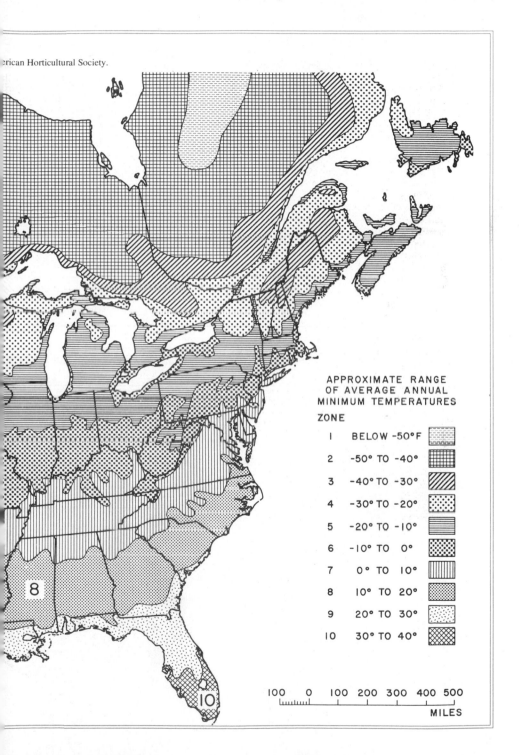

erican Horticultural Society.

APPROXIMATE RANGE
OF AVERAGE ANNUAL
MINIMUM TEMPERATURES

ZONE

1	BELOW -50°F
2	-50° TO -40°
3	-40° TO -30°
4	-30° TO -20°
5	-20° TO -10°
6	-10° TO 0°
7	0° TO 10°
8	10° TO 20°
9	20° TO 30°
10	30° TO 40°

100   0   100   200   300   400   500
MILES

Plant Societies

African Violet Society of
America, Inc.
P.O. Box 3609
Beaumont, TX 77704

American Begonia Society
P.O. Box 1129
Encinitas, CA 92024

American Camellia Society
c/o Ann Blair Brown
P.O. Box 1217
Fort Valley, GA 31030-1217

American Conifer Society
c/o Maxine Schwarz
Box 242
Severna Park, MD 21146

American Daffodil Society, Inc.
c/o Mrs. Leslie Anderson
Rt. 3, 2302 Byhalia Rd.
Hernando, MS 38632

American Dahlia Society
c/o Michael L. Martinolich
159 Pine St.
New Hyde Park, NY 11040

American Fern Society
c/o Dr. David S. Barrington
Botany Department
University of Vermont
Burlington, VT 05405

American Gloxinia & Gesneriad
Society, Inc.
5320 Labadie
St. Louis, MO 63120

American Hemerocallis Society
c/o Sandy Goembel
Rt. 5, Box 6874
Palatka, FL 32077-9578

American Horticultural Society
7931 E. Boulevard Dr.
Alexandria, VA 22308

American Hosta Society
c/o Jack A. Freedman
3103 Heatherhill Dr. SE
Huntsville, AL 35802

American Iris Society
c/o Mrs. Jeane Stayen
7414 E. 60th St.
Tulsa, OK 74145

American Peony Society
c/o Greta Kessenich
250 Interlachen Rd.
Hopkins, MN 55343

American Pomological Society
c/o Dr. L.D. Tukey
103 Tyson Building
University Park, PA 16802

American Primrose Society
c/o Larry Bailey
1370 9th Avenue West
Edmonds, WA 98020

American Rhododendron Society
c/o Mrs. Paula L. Cash
14885 S.W. Sunrise Ln.
Tigard, OR 97224

American Rock Garden Society
c/o Buffy Parker
15 Fairmead Rd.
Darien, CT 06820

American Rose Society
P.O. Box 30,000
Shreveport, LA 71130-0030

Azalea Society of America
P.O. Box 6244
Silver Spring, MD 20906

BIRC (Bio-Integral Resource
Center)
P.O. Box 7414
Berkeley, CA 94707

Bromeliad Society, Inc.
2488 E. 49th
Tulsa, OK 74105

Cactus & Succulent Society of
America
c/o Ms. Virginia Martin
2631 Fairgreen Ave.
Arcadia, CA 91006

Canadian Chrysanthemum &
Dahlia Society
c/o G.H. Lawrence
83 Aramaman Dr.
Agincourt, Ontario, Canada
M1T 2PM

Canadian Rose Society
c/o D. Lask
686 Pharmacy Ave.
Scarborough, Ontario, Canada
M1L 3H8

Canadian Wildflower Society
c/o James A. French
35 Bauer Cres.
Unionville, Ontario, Canada
L3R 4H3

Friends of the Trees
P.O. Box 1466
Chelan, WA 98816

Herb Society of America
300 Massachusetts Ave.
Boston, MA 02115

Heritage Roses Group
c/o Lily Shohan
RFD 1
Clinton Corners, NY 12514

Home Orchard Society
c/o Marian Dunlap
2511 S.W. Miles St.
Portland, OR 97219

Horticultural Society of New
York
128 West 58th St.
New York, NY 10019

Indoor Citrus & Rare Fruit
Society
c/o Randy Peterson/Annette
Fabri
176 Coronado Ave.
Los Altos, CA 94022

Indoor Gardening Society of
America
c/o Horticultural Society of New
York
128 West 58th St.
New York, NY 10019

International Geranium Society
c/o B. Tufekian
4610 Druid St.
Los Angeles, CA 90032

International Lilac Society
c/o Walter W. Oakes
P.O. Box 315
Rumford, ME 04276

Massachusetts Horticultural
Association
300 Massachusetts Ave.
Boston, MA 02115

National Chrysanthemum
Society, Inc.
c/o Galen L. Goss
5012 Kingston Dr.
Annandale, VA 22003

National Gardening Association
c/o Betsy Bradbury
180 Flynn Ave.
Burlington, VT 05401

New England Wild Flower
Society
c/o Bea Entwisle
Garden in the Woods
Hemenway Rd.
Framingham, MA 01701

North American Lily Society
c/o Mrs. Dorothy Schaefer
P.O. Box 476
Waukee, IA 50263

Pennsylvania Horticultural
  Society
c/o Betsy Gullan
325 Walnut St.
Philadelphia, PA 19106

Rhododendron Society of
  Canada
c/o Dr. H.G. Hedges
R.R. 2
St. George, Ontario, Canada
  N0E 1N0

The Scatterseed Project
(unusual or endangered seed
  varieties)
Box 1167
Farmington, ME 04938

Seed Savers Exchange
RFD 3, Box 239
Decatur, IA 52101

Mail-Order Sources of Plants, Seeds and Supplies

To the best of my knowledge at
the time of publication, the
catalogs listed here are free
except as noted. There may be an
additional charge in the case of
suppliers that have added a
catalog fee or raised the price
from that noted here. In selecting
sources of seeds and plants it is
best to order from suppliers
closest to your own growing
area, except in the case of indoor
plants. Nearby suppliers are most
apt to carry plants that will do
well in your region.

BULBS

Antonelli Brothers
2545 Capitola Rd.
Santa Cruz, CA 95062
408-475-8828
$1.00
Specializing in tuberous

begonias; calla lilies and
gloxinias also available.

Breck's
U.S. Reservation Center
6523 N. Galena Rd.
Peoria, IL 61632
309-691-4616
$2.00
Spring and summer bulbs.

Dutch Gardens, Inc.
P.O. Box 200
Adelphia, NJ 07710
201-780-2713
or
Vennestraat
2160 AA Lisse-Holland
02521-1 46 48
A large variety of spring and
summer bulbs, many hybridized
on the company's own growing
fields in Holland and shipped
directly at close-to-wholesale
prices. The catalog includes
amaryllis, lilies, peonies,
bearded iris, day lilies and
allium.

Flad's Glads
2109 Cliff Ct.
Madison, WI 53713
608-255-5274
Specializing in gladiolus
hybrids.

John D. Lyon Co.
143 Alewife Brook Pkwy.
Cambridge, MA 02140
617-876-3705
Large and unusual selection of
species bulbs, spring-, summer-
and fall-blooming.

McClure & Zimmerman
1422 W. Thorndale
Chicago, IL 60660
312-989-0557
Large and unusual collection of
spring, summer and fall bulbs,
including many species bulbs,
"for the dedicated bulb
enthusiast."

Oregon Bulb Farms
14071 N.E. Arndt Rd., Dept.
  MO
Aurora, OR 97002
503-226-7425
$2.00
Specializing in lilies: Oriental,
Asiatic and Aurelian hybrids.

Quality Dutch Bulbs, Inc.
50 Lake Dr.
P.O. Box 225
Hillsdale, NJ 07642
201-391-6586
$2.00
Spring bulbs shipped directly
from Holland.

Rex Bulb Farms
P.O. Box 774
Port Townsend, WA 98368
206-385-4280
$1.00
Large selection of lily bulbs,
freesias and dahlias.

John Scheepers, Inc.
Phillipsburg Rd., R.D. 2
Middletown, NY 10940
914-342-1135
914-342-3727
$3.00
Complete selection of spring
bulbs; also bulbs for indoor
culture and outdoor planting in
southern regions. Some lily
bulbs, day lilies, peonies.

Swan Island Dahlias
P.O. Box 800
Canby, OR 97013
503-266-7711
$2.00
Large selection of dahlia
hybrids, including a few new
introductions.

TyTy Plantation Bulb Co.
Box 159
Ty Ty, GA 31795
912-382-0404
Specializing in American-grown
bulbs, particularly canna lilies,
of which many are their own
introductions; also a number of
other summer bulbs and some
perennials.

Van Bourgondien Bros.
P.O. Box A
245 Farmingdale Rd., Rt. 109
Babylon, NY 11702
516-669-3500
Wide variety of spring and
summer bulbs, as well as some
perennials, houseplants and
others.

Van Engelen Inc.
Stillbrook Farm
307 Maple St.
Litchfield, CT 06759
203-567-8734
203-567-5662
*Wide selection of spring bulbs
from Holland in large quantities
at wholesale prices.*

Vandenberg
Black Meadow Rd.
Chester, NY 10918
914-469-2633
$2.00
*Spring and summer bulbs; also
perennials.*

The Waushara Gardens
Plainfield, WI 54966
715-335-4462
$1.00
*Specializing in gladiolus,
including their own hybrids, and
a number of other summer bulbs.*

Wyatt–Quarles Seed Co.
P.O. Box 739
Garner, NC 27529
919-832-0551
*Assortment of spring bulbs, as
well as some summer bulbs and
amaryllis.*

Also see under Miscellaneous:
International Growers'
Exchange, Inter-State; see under
Perennials: Holbrook.

FRUITS

Allen Co.
P.O. Box 1577
Salisbury, MD 21801
301-742-7122
*Specializing in strawberry
plants; also asparagus roots,
raspberries, blackberries and
blueberries.*

Applesource
Tom Vorbeck
Route 1
Chaplin, IL 62628
*Antique and specialty apples for
examining and tasting.*

Bear Creek Nursery
P.O. Box 411
Bear Creek Rd.
Northport, WA 99157
Specializing in a very large

*selection of antique apple
varieties. Also some antique
pears, Asian pears, berries, a
large nut-tree selection, other
unusual fruits, trees and shrubs.*

Boston Mountain Nurseries
Rt. 2, Box 405-A
Mountainburg, AR 72946
*Strawberries, bramble fruits,
grapes and blueberries for the
commercial or home grower.*

Brittingham Plant Farms
P.O. Box 2538
Salisbury, MD 21801
*Specializing in strawberry
plants; also asparagus roots,
grape vines, blackberries,
raspberries and blueberries.*

Buntings' Nurseries Inc.
Box 306
Selbyville, DE 19975
302-436-8231
Strawberry plants only.

California Nursery Co.
Niles District, Box 2278
Fremont, CA 94536
415-797-3311
*Standard and dwarf fruit trees,
table and wine grapes, citrus
fruits, and other choices for
warm climates.*

Country Heritage Nurseries
P.O. Box 536
Hartford, MI 49057
616-621-2491
*Especially wide selection of
berry fruits; also tree fruits,
bush fruits, asparagus, rhubarb,
onion sets, seed potatoes.*

Cumberland Valley Nurseries,
  Inc.
P.O. Box 471
McMinnville, TN 37110
800-492-0022
615-668-4153
*Specializing in peaches, plums
and nectarines; also apples,
pears, cherries and pecans.*

Emlong Nurseries Inc.
P.O. Box 236
Stevensville, MI 49127-0236
616-429-3431
616-429-3612
*Large catalog emphasizes tree
fruits and small fruits; also trees,
shrubs, perennials, vines, roses.*

Johnson Nursery
Rt. 5
Ellijay, GA 30540
404-273-3187
$1.00
*Selection of tree fruits and some
small fruits includes unusual
varieties.*

Lawson's Nursery
Rt. 1, Box 294
Ball Ground, GA 30107
404-893-2141
*Very large selection of Georgia-
grown apple trees; also pears,
peaches, plums, cherries and
southern blueberries.*

Henry Leuthardt Nurseries, Inc.
Montauk Hwy., Box 666
East Moriches, NY 11940
516-878-1387
*Dwarf and semidwarf apples,
pears, plums, peaches,
nectarines and apricots;
semidwarf cherries; rare and
choice old apple varieties;
espaliered apples and pears;
some grapes and small fruits.*

Miller Nurseries
West Lake Rd.
Canandaigua, NY 14424
800-828-9630
800-462-9601 (in New York
  State)
*Wide selection of tree fruits and
small fruits; also roses,
landscaping trees and other
items.*

New York State Fruit Testing
  Cooperative Assoc., Inc.
Geneva, NY 14456
315-787-2205
$5.00 membership fee
*Wide selection of tree fruits and
small fruits tested for quality,
winter hardiness, disease
resistance and productivity; new
introductions as well as old
standards and heirloom
varieties. Very informative
catalog.*

Nourse Farms, Inc.
Box 485, RFD
South Deerfield, MA 01373
413-665-2658
Specializing in strawberry

plants; also raspberries, asparagus, rhubarb, horseradish and evergreens.

Makielski Berry Farms and
   Nursery
7130 Platt Rd.
Ypsilanti, MI 48197
313-434-3673
313-572-0060
Specializing in raspberries; also blackberries, currants, gooseberries, strawberries, blueberries, grapes and some tree fruits.

Rayner Bros., Inc.
P.O. Box 1617
Salisbury, MD 21801
301-742-1594
Wide selection of strawberry plants; also asparagus, rhubarb, grapes, bramble fruits, blueberries, some tree fruits and evergreen trees.

Southmeadow Fruit Gardens
Lakeside, MI 49116
616-469-2865
"Choice and unusual fruit varieties for the connoisseur and home gardener"; many heirloom varieties. Includes apples, plums, cherries, quince, medlar, currants, gooseberries, grapes, crab apples and others.

Stark Brothers' Nurseries
Louisiana, MO 63353-0010
800-843-5091
Very large selection of tree fruits and small fruits; varieties for the south included. Also nut and shade trees, ornamental flowering trees, roses, gardening aids.

SunSweet Fruit and Bulb
   Nursery
Box Z
Sumner, GA 31789
912-386-8400
Tree fruits, small fruits, summer bulbs and perennials selected for Zones 8, 9 and 10.

Van Well Nursery
P.O. Box 1339
Wenatchee, WA 98801
509-663-8189
800-572-1553 (in Washington)
Large selection of standard and

dwarf fruit trees; some small fruits.

Waynesboro Nurseries
Waynesboro, VA 22980
703-942-4141
Large selection of fruit trees, nut trees, ornamental trees and shrubs.

Also see under Miscellaneous:
Kelly Bros., Henry Field's, J.W.
Jung, Krider, Savage Farms,
Vernon Barnes.

GARDEN GEAR

Brookstone
127 Vose Farm Rd.
Peterborough, NH 03458
603-924-9541 (24 hours a day)
603-924-9511
Unique and hard-to-find gadgets for indoor and outdoor gardening.

Clapper's
1125 Washington St.
West Newton, MA 02165
617-244-7909
Top-of-the-line tools, furniture and ornaments.

Gardener's Eden
A Garden Catalog from
   Williams–Sonoma
P.O. Box 7307
San Francisco, CA 94120-7307
415-421-4242
Primarily garden accessories, furniture and ornaments; some tools and equipment.

Gardener's Supply
128 Intervale Rd.
Burlington, VT 05401
802-863-1700
Large selection of tools, equipment and supplies, with an emphasis on organic methods and aids for cool-climate gardeners.

Indoor Gardening Supplies
P.O. Box 40567
Detroit, MI 48240
313-427-6160
A full range of supplies for the indoor garden.

A.M. Leonard, Inc.
6665 Spiker Rd.
Piqua, OH 45356
800-543-8955
513-773-2694
An encyclopedic horticultural tool and supply catalog for home gardeners, nurserymen, florists, foresters, landscapers and arborists.

Natural Gardening Research
   Center
Hwy. 48, P.O. Box 149
Sunman, IN 47041
812-623-3800
Informative catalog offers safe pest-, disease- and weed-control products and other organic-gardening supplies.

Necessary Trading Co.
New Castle, VA 24127
703-864-5103
Pest-control products, fertilizers, books and equipment for organic gardeners.

Walter F. Nicke
Box 667G
Hudson, NY 12535
518-828-3415
50 cents
Garden tools and equipment; many unusual items.

The Plow & Hearth
560 Main St.
Madison, VA 22727
800-527-5247
703-948-6821
Garden accessories, furniture, tools and gadgets.

Ringer
9959 Valley View Rd.
Eden Prairie, MN 55344-3585
800-654-1047
Lawn and garden tools, gadgets, fertilizers, pest-control products and composting aids for organic gardeners.

Smith and Hawken
25 Corte Madera
Mill Valley, CA 94941
415-383-4050
Top-of-the-line tools, equipment, garden furniture and ornaments.

Also see under Miscellaneous:
Mellinger's.

HERBS

Caprilands Herb Farm
Silver St.
Coventry, CT 06238
203-742-7244
Herb plants and seeds, in addition to books on herbs, craft items and other herb-related products.

Casa Yerba Gardens
3459 Days Creek Rd.
Days Creek, OR 97429
Organically grown herb plants and seeds, many of them rare and unusual. Catalog costs $1.00 when they have it. Otherwise, to get their list, send a stamped, self-addressed envelope.

Fox Hill Farm
444 W. Michigan Ave., Box 9
Parma, MI 49269-0009
517-531-3179
$1.00
Large selection of container-grown herb plants, including everlastings and scented geraniums.

The Herb Greenhouse
Box 22061
Louisville, KY 40222
502-893-5198
Large selection of herbs available as plants, seeds and bulbs.

Hemlock Hill Herb Farm
Hemlock Hill Rd.
Litchfield, CT 06759-0415
203-567-5031
50 cents
Perennial and biennial herb plants.

Lost Prairie Herb Farm
805 Kienas Rd.
Kalispell, MT 59901
406-756-7742
Large selection of herb plants, including some that repel fleas.

Merry Gardens
P.O. Box 595
Camden, ME 04843
207-236-9064
$1.00
Large selection of container-grown herbs and other plants, including ivies and fuchsias; many miniature, dwarf and scented-leaved geraniums. Additional catalog of flowering plants, vines, ferns, mosses, foliage plants, oxalis, gesneriads, cacti and other succulents available for $2.00

Misty Meadow Gardens
301 E. South St.
Hillsboro, OH 45133
513-393-9606
Specializing in herbs and some ornamental plants, sold inexpensively as "speedling plugs."

Richter's
Box 26
GoodWood, Ontario, Canada
L0C 1A0
416-640-6677
$2.50
Very large selection of herb seeds, many of them rare, and some wildflower and gourmet vegetable seeds. Some herb plants as well.

The Rosemary House
120 S. Market St.
Mechanicsburg, PA 17055
717-697-5111
717-766-6581
$2.00
Herb plants and seeds in addition to books and other herb-related products.

The Sandy Mush Herb Nursery
Rt. 2, Surrett Cove Rd.
Leicester, NC 28748
704-683-2014
$2.00
Very large selection of herb plants, including many unusual ones, and many thymes, sages, and scented-leaved geraniums. Herb seeds also available. Informative handbook.

Sunnybrook Farms
9448 Mayfield Rd.
P.O. Box 6
Chesterland, OH 44026
216-729-7232
$1.00
Large selection of herb plants, including ivies and scented geraniums; herb seeds from Comstock Ferre and Co.

Taylor's Herb Gardens, Inc.
1535 Lone Oak Rd.
Vista, CA 92084
619-727-3485
Field-grown herb plants include annuals, perennials and biennials. Herb seeds also available.

Also see under Seeds: Herb Gathering.

HOUSEPLANTS

Altman Specialty Plants
553 Buena Creek Rd.
San Marcos, CA 92069
619-744-8191
$1.00
Well-illustrated catalog offers a wide variety of unusual succulents.

California Epi Center
P.O. Box 1431
Vista, CA 92083
619-758-4290
$2.00
Flowering jungle cacti and other succulents; color photographs throughout.

Cape Cod Violetry
28 Minot St.
Falmouth, MA 02540
617-548-2798
$1.00 (credited toward purchase)
Very extensive list of African violet varieties.

Davidson–Wilson Greenhouses
RFD 2
Crawfordsville, IN 47933
317-364-0556
Selection includes geraniums, African violets and other gesneriads, begonias, impatiens and other houseplants, both familiar and unusual.

Fairyland Begonia Garden
1100 Griffith Rd.
McKinleyville, CA 95521
707-839-3034
50 cents
Specializing in begonias (rex, tuberous, fibrous and hybrid) and lily bulbs.

Fischer Greenhouses
Oak Ave.
Linwood, NJ 08221
609-927-3399
25 cents
African violets, companion plants, supplies; catalog photographed in color.

Grigsby Cactus Gardens
2354 Bella Vista Dr.
Vista, CA 92084
619-727-1323
$2.00
Large selection of cacti and other succulents.

K & L Cactus Nursery
12712 Stockton Blvd.
Galt, CA 95632
209-745-4756
$2.00
Well-photographed catalog with an extensive offering of cacti and other succulents; books and planters also available.

Kartuz Greenhouses
1408 Sunset Dr.
Vista, CA 92083
619-941-3613
$2.00
Extensive selection includes begonias, gesneriads, miniature and terrarium plants and many rare flowering plants.

Lauray of Salisbury
Undermountain Rd., Rt. 41
Salisbury, CT 06068
203-435-2263
$1.75
Very large selection includes cacti and other succulents, begonias, orchids, gesneriads and many others.

Logee's Greenhouses
55 North St.
Danielson, CT 06239
203-774-8038
$3.00 (credited toward $25.00 purchase)
Huge selection of houseplants with a specialty in begonias; also includes herbs, geraniums, citrus plants, ferns and mosses, hoyas, jasmines and many others.

Lyndon Lyon Greenhouses, Inc.
14 Mutchler St.
Dolgeville, NY 13329-0249
315-429-8291
$1.00
African violets and companion plants including streptocarpus and gloxinias; color photographs.

Orchids by Hausermann, Inc.
2N 134 Addison Rd.
Villa Park, IL 60181
312-543-6855
$1.25
Informative catalog with color photographs lists a large selection of orchids.

Rainbow Gardens
P.O. Box 721
La Habra, CA 90633
213-697-1488
$1.00
Tropical cactus and other exotic plants; specializing in orchid cactus.

Ray's African Violets
Rt. 1, Box 244
College Station, TX 77840
409-690-1407
Specializing in miniature African violets.

Shady Hill Gardens
821 Walnut
Batavia, IL 60510
$1.00 (credited toward purchase)
Specializing in geraniums; long list includes many unusual types such as cactus-flowered, fancy-leaf, zonal, painted lady, regal, scented, cascade, ivy-leaf, dwarf, miniature and species geraniums.

Suni's Violets
South Kent Rd., P.O. Box 32
South Kent, CT 06785
203-927-4486
Send S.A.S.E.
African violets; standard and miniature varieties.

Tinari Greenhouses
2325 Valley Rd.
Huntingdon Valley, PA 19006
215-947-0144
35 cents
African violets and supplies; color photographs.

PERENNIALS

American Daylily & Perennials
P.O. Box 7008
The Woodlands, TX 77387
713-351-1466
$3.00
Large selection of day lilies for both the collector and the home gardener; also cannas, Louisiana iris and lilyturf.

Bluestone Perennials
7211 Middle Ridge Rd.
Madison, OH 44057
216-428-7535
800-852-5243
Large selection of perennials; small, container-grown plants at affordable prices; also shrubs.

Borbeleta Gardens, Inc.
15974 Canby Ave.
Faribault, MN 55021
507-334-2807
$3.00
Day lilies, Siberian iris, dwarf bearded iris and bulb lilies (Asiatic, Oriental and trumpet hybrids).

Lee Bristol Nursery
Box 5
Gaylordsville, CT 06755-0005
203-254-6951
Large selection of day lilies; prices geared to the average gardener.

Caprice Farm Nursery
15425 S.W. Pleasant Hill Rd.
Sherwood, OR 97140
503-625-7241
$1.00
Peonies, day lilies, hostas and Japanese and Siberian iris.

Carroll Gardens
444 E. Main St.
P.O. Box 310
Westminster, MD 21157
800-638-6334
301-848-5422
301-876-7336
$2.00
Wide selection of perennials, including wildflowers, ferns, ground covers, lily bulbs and rock-garden plants; also summer bulbs, scented geraniums, herbs, vines, roses, shrubs and trees.

Clifford's Perennial & Vine
Rt. 2, Box 320
East Troy, WI 53120
414-642-7156 (after 5 P.M.
  EST)
*Selection of flowering perennials
and vines, particularly clematis;
also some shrubs.*

Cooley's Gardens
P.O. Box 126
Silverton, OR 97381
503-873-5463
$2.00
*Very large selection of tall
bearded irises including new
introductions.*

The Country Garden
Rt. 2, Box 455A
Crivitz, WI 54114
715-757-2045
*Large and unusual selection of
annuals, perennials and bulbs
with an emphasis on those that
make good cut flowers. Includes
plants for drying. Annual and
perennial seeds, potted
perennials, and bulbs available.*

The Crownsville Nursery
P.O. Box 797
Crownsville, MD 21032
301-923-2212
$2.00
*A variety of perennials, azaleas,
wildflowers, ferns, herbs and
ornamental grasses, with a
specialty in day lilies.*

Dooley Mum Gardens
Rt. 1
Hutchinson, MN 55350
612-587-3050
*Chrysanthemums for the home
gardener.*

Englerth Gardens
2461 22nd St.
Hopkins, MI 49328
616-793-7196
*Specializing in Japanese and
Siberian iris; day lilies including
tetraploids; hostas.*

Garden Place
6780 Heisley Rd.
P.O. Box 388
Mentor, OH 44061-0388
216-255-3705
*General selection of herbaceous
perennials.*

Russell Graham
4030 Eagle Crest Rd. N.W.
Salem, OR 97304
503-362-1135
$2.00
*Interesting selection of unusual
perennials and bulbs, including
hardy cyclamen, ferns,
ornamental grasses, lily bulbs,
novelty daffodils and dwarf
narcissi; many native species
including iris and violets.*

Holbrook Farm & Nursery
Rt. 2, Box 233B
Fletcher, NC 28732
704-891-7790
$2.00
*Basic selection of herbaceous
perennials; some woody plants
and bulbs.*

Huff's Gardens
P.O. Box 187
Burlington, KS 66839
316-364-2933
*Large selection of
chrysanthemums.*

Illini Iris
RFD 3, Box 5
Monticello, IL 61856
217-762-3446
$1.00
*Specializing in Siberian and
bearded iris.*

King's Mums
P.O. Box 368
Clements, CA 95227
209-759-3571
$1.00
*Extensive list of chrysanthemums
for the exhibitor or gardener;
includes blooming times.*

Klehm Nursery
Rt. 5, Box 197
South Barrington, IL 60010
312-551-3715
$2.00
*Specializing in herbaceous and
tree peonies; also a number of
day lilies, hostas and bearded
iris.*

Lamb Nurseries
E. 101 Sharp Ave.
Spokane, WA 99202
509-328-7956
509-328-1505
$1.00

*Specializing in hardy perennials,
alpines and rock-garden plants.*

Lenington-Long Gardens
7007 Manchester Ave.
Kansas City, MO 64133
816-454-9163 (early morning or
  late evening)
Send 2 first-class stamps.
*Large selection of day lilies
including tetraploids and new
introductions.*

Mid-American Iris Garden
P.O. Box 12982
Oklahoma City, OK 73157
405-946-5743
$1.00
*Specializing in tall bearded iris
including new introductions; also
border, miniature-tall,
intermediate and standard-dwarf
varieties.*

Milaeger's Gardens
4838 Douglas Ave.
Racine, WI 53402-2498
414-639-2371
$1.00
*Complete selection of flowering
perennials; also perennial herbs,
prairie plants and grasses,
woodland plants, hardy roses
and books.*

The Primrose Path
RFD 2, Box 110
Scottdale, PA 15683
412-887-6756
$1.00
*A variety of garden perennials
including some native species.*

Powell's Gardens
Rt. 3, Box 21, Hwy. 70
Princeton, NC 27569
919-936-4421
$1.50
*Specializing in iris, day lilies,
dwarf evergreens, perennials
and rock-garden plants.*

Reath's Nursery
P.O. Box 521
100 Central Blvd.
Vulcan, MI 49892
$1.00
*Specializing in hybrid peonies,
including both herbaceous and
tree peonies.*

Rice Creek Gardens
1315 66th Ave. N.E.
Minneapolis, MN 55432
612-574-1197
$1.00
*Unusual rock-garden plants,
alpines, wildflowers, ground
covers, dwarf ferns, ornamental
grasses, vines, waterside plants,
dwarf evergreens and unusual
flowering shrubs.*

Rocknoll Nursery
9210 U.S. 50
Hillsboro, OH 45133-8546
513-393-1278
Send 2 first-class stamps.
*Unusual perennials including
rock plants, wildflowers, hostas,
day lilies, succulents, shade
plants, Japanese and Siberian
iris; also dwarf evergreens and
flowering shrubs.*

Savory's Greenhouses and
    Gardens
5300 Whiting Ave.
Edina, MN 55435
612-941-8755
$1.00
Large selection of hostas.

Saxton Gardens
1 First St.
Saratoga Springs, NY 12866
518-584-4697
25 cents
*Day lilies for the collector or
average gardener; specializing
in cold-hardy varieties.*

Schreiner's Gardens
3625 Quinaby Rd. N.E.
Salem, OR 97303
$2.00
*Large selection of bearded iris,
including new introductions,
dwarf and intermediate varieties.*

Shady Oaks Nursery
700 19th Ave. N.E.
Waseca, MN 56093
$1.00
*Perennials, wildflowers, ferns
and shrubs for shady places.*

Smirnow's Son
11 Oakwood Dr. W., Rt. 1
Huntington, NY 11743
516-421-0836
$2.00
Hybridizer of Japanese, lutea

*and European tree peonies. A
good selection of herbaceous
peonies also available.*

Sunnyslope Gardens
8638 Huntington Dr.
San Gabriel, CA 91775
818-287-4071
*Large selection of
chrysanthemums for the
exhibitor or the average
gardener.*

Thon's Garden Mums
4811 Oak St.
Crystal Lake, IL 60012
815-459-1030
*Selection of chrysanthemums for
the average gardener includes
the hardy Cheyenne series;
blooming times indicated.*

Andre Viette Farm & Nursery
Rt. 1, Box 16
Fishersville, VA 22939
703-943-2315
$2.00
*Extensive list of herbaceous
perennials, some unusual.
Includes large selection of day
lilies, ornamental grasses,
peonies and bearded, Siberian
and Japanese iris.*

Wayside Gardens
Hodges, SC 29695-0001
800-845-1124
$1.00 (credit toward order)
*Very large variety of perennials,
shrubs, roses, trees, vines and
ground covers; also summer
bulbs, gourmet fruits and herbs.*

White Flower Farm
Litchfield, CT 06759-0050
203-496-9600
203-496-1661
$5.00 per year for two catalogs
    and supplements, credited
    toward orders over $25.00.
*Very informative catalog offers
extensive collection of
perennials, as well as flowering
shrubs, spring and summer
bulbs, books and supplies.*

Gilbert H. Wild and Son, Inc.
Sarcoxie, MO 64862
417-548-3514
$2.00
*Very large selection of day lilies;
also herbaceous peonies.*

Also see under Wildflowers:
Forest Farm.

ROSES

The Antique Rose Emporium
Rt. 5, Box 143
Brenham, TX 77833
409-836-9051
*Very extensive selection of
antique roses; also companion
perennials.*

Armstrong Roses
P.O. Box 2666
Chatsworth, CA 91313
800-338-7428
*Selection of modern roses
grouped in special collections.
Some companion perennials.*

High Country Rosarium
1717 Downing at Park Ave.
Denver, CO 80218
303-832-4026
*Antique and modern roses grown
on their own roots and chosen
for hardiness on mountains and
high plains. Includes
drought-tolerant roses.*

Jackson and Perkins Co.
1 Rose La.
Medford, OR 97501
*Modern rose selection, new
introductions.*

MB Farm Miniature Roses, Inc.
Jamison Hill Rd.
Clinton Corners, NY 12514
914-266-3138
Selection of miniature roses.

Nor'East Miniature Roses, Inc.
58 Hammond St.
Rowley, MA 01969
617-948-7964
P.O. Box 473
Ontario, CA 91762
714-984-2223
*Selected miniature roses
including miniature tree roses.*

Roses by Fred Edmunds, Inc.
6235 S.W. Kahle Rd.
Wilsonville, OR 97070
503-638-4671
Selection of modern roses.

Roses of Yesterday and Today
802 Brown's Valley Rd.
Watsonville, CA 95076-0398
408-724-3537
$2.00
*Very large selection of old, rare
and unusual roses; also selected
modern roses.*

Also see under Perennials:
Milaeger's; see under
Miscellaneous: Krider, Inter-State.

SEEDS

Abundant Life Seed Foundation
P.O. Box 772
Port Townsend, WA 98368
206-385-7192
$1.00
*Nonprofit foundation
specializing in heirloom
vegetable seeds, seeds of herbs,
annual and perennial flowers,
wildflowers, trees and shrubs;
many seeds in bulk. Books also
available.*

Allen, Sterling & Lothrop
191 U.S. Rt. 1
Falmouth, ME 04105
207-781-4142
*Vegetable seeds, annual and
perennial flower seeds, lawn
mixtures.*

Bountiful Gardens
c/o John Jeavons
5798 Ridgewood Rd.
Willits, CA 95490
707-459-0150
*Organically grown, open-
pollinated (nonhybrid) vegetable
seeds; also herb and flower
seeds, books, supplies.*

W. Atlee Burpee and Co.
Warminster, PA 18974
215-674-4915
*Extensive collection of vegetable
and flower seeds; also fruits,
trees and shrubs, garden
equipment, pest-control supplies.*

D.V. Burrell Seed Growers Co.
Rocky Ford, Co. 81067
303-254-3318
*Complete basic selection of
vegetable seeds available in both
small quantities and bulk. Also
herb and flower seeds.*

Comstock, Ferre & Co.
Box 125
Wethersfield, CT 06109
203-529-6255
800-346-6110
*Vegetable, flower and herb
seeds.*

The Cook's Garden
P.O. Box 65
Londonderry, VT 05148
802-824-3400
$1.00
*Vegetable and herb seeds
including many unusual
varieties, especially lettuces and
other salad greens.*

William Dam Seeds Ltd.
P.O. Box 8400
Dundas, Ontario, Canada
   L9H 6 M1
416-628-6641
*Wide selection of vegetable seed,
includes many varieties for
northern gardens. Seeds of cover
crops, trees, grasses, herbs,
wildflowers, annual flowers,
houseplants, perennials,
everlastings. Also summer bulbs,
books, supplies. All seeds
untreated.*

DeGiorgi Seed Co., Inc.
P.O. Box 413
Council Bluffs, IA 51502
712-323-2372
*Extensive catalog of vegetable
seeds, annual and perennial
flower seeds. Many unusual
varieties.*

Farmer Seed & Nursery
818 N.W. 4th St.
Faribault, MN 55021
507-334-1623
*Long-established seed company
with an emphasis on varieties for
northern zones. Also lawn seed,
cover crops, fruits, shrubs and
trees, perennials, summer bulbs,
supplies.*

The Fragrant Path
P.O. Box 328
Fort Calhoun, NE 68023
$1.00
*"Seeds for fragrant, rare and
old-fashioned plants." Includes
annuals, perennials, herbs,
vines, trees and shrubs.*

Gleckler's Seedmen
Metamora, OH 43540
*Very unusual vegetable seeds,
especially tomatoes.*

Good Seed
P.O. Box 702
Tonasket, WA 98855
$1.00
*"Modern and heirloom seeds for
northern and mountain
gardeners." Vegetables, herbs,
flowers.*

Harris Seeds
Moreton Farm
3670 Buffalo Rd.
Rochester, NY 14624
*Complete selection of vegetable
and flower seeds; also gladiolus
bulbs, lawn seed, gardening
supplies.*

Heirloom Garden Seeds
P.O. Box 138
Guerneville, CA 95446
707-869-0967
*Rare and unusual seeds, chiefly
herbs and wildflowers; some
vegetables, salad greens.*

Herb Gathering, Inc.
5742 Kenwood
Kansas City, MO 64110
816-523-2653
$2.00
*Gourmet French vegetable seeds
and an assortment of culinary
herbs.*

J. L. Hudson
P.O. Box 1058
Redwood City, CA 94064
$1.00
*An encyclopedic collection of
rare and unusual seeds—
vegetables, herbs, flowers,
fruits, shrubs, trees, ferns,
grasses—many from the far
corners of the globe.*

Johnny's Selected Seeds
Foss Hill Rd.
Albion, ME 04910
207-437-4301
207-437-9294
*Large selection of both
traditional and new varieties,
many of them unusual and many
geared to cold-climate
gardeners. Includes seeds for
Oriental vegetables, herbs,*

flowers; also books and gardening supplies.

Kilgore Seed Company
1400 W. First St.
Sanford, FL 32771
$1.00
Vegetables and flower seeds geared to Florida gardeners.

Kitazawa Seed Company
1748 Laine Ave.
Santa Clara, CA 95051-3012
Oriental vegetable seeds.

Le Jardin du Gourmet
West Danville, VT 05873
Gourmet vegetable seeds, many from France. Also herb plants and seeds, flower seeds, leeks and shallots. Small 22-cent seed packets available.

Le Marché Seeds International
P.O. Box 190
Dixon, CA 95620
916-678-9244
$2.00
Informative catalog of gourmet vegetable seeds.

Orol Ledden & Sons
P.O. Box 7
Sewell, NJ 08080-0007
609-468-1000
Vegetable seeds, annual and perennial flower seeds, grasses and cover crops, gardening supplies.

Liberty Seed Co.
P.O. Box 806
New Philadelphia, OH 44663
216-364-1611
Complete selection of vegetable seeds; also herbs, flowers, garden equipment.

Nichols Garden Nursery
1190 N. Pacific Hwy.
Albany, OR 97321
503-928-9280
Gourmet herb and vegetable seeds; flower seeds including everlastings and pansies; "beer-and wine-making supplies."

Park Seed Co.
Cokesbury Rd.
Greenwood, SC 29647-0001
803-223-7333
Very large selection of annual and perennial flower and

vegetable seeds. Also herb and wildflower seeds, bulbs, perennial plants, small fruits, garden supplies.

Pinetree Garden Seeds
RFD #1, Box 397
New Gloucester, ME 04260
207-926-3400
Large selection of vegetable seeds includes new hybrids, heirloom varieties, Italian, Oriental, French and Latin-American vegetables and herbs. Also lists books and supplies.

Plants of the Southwest
1812 Second St.
Santa Fe, NM 87501
505-983-1548
$1.00
Unusual seed catalog features grasses, wildflowers, trees and shrubs, modern and ancient American vegetables, herbs and books.

Porter and Son, Seedsmen
1510 E. Washington St.
P.O. Box 104
Stephenville, TX 76401-0104
Large selection of vegetable seeds, particularly tomatoes, melons and peppers; onion plants, flower seeds, supplies.

The Redwood City Seed Company
P.O. Box 361
Redwood City, CA 94064
415-325-7333
$1.00
Open-pollinated (nonhybrid) vegetables, herbs and flowers; books also available.

Seeds Blüm
Idaho City Stage
Boise, ID 83706
$2.00
Large selection of heirloom vegetable seeds and unusual varieties. Also herbs, flowers, garlic and onions, and a specialty in unusual varieties of seed potatoes. Active seed-saver program.

Seedway, Inc.
Hall, NY 14463-0250
716-526-6391
Vegetable, flower and lawn seeds

for home and commercial growers.

Shepherd's Garden Seeds
7389 W. Zayante Rd.
Felton, CA 95018
408-335-5311
30 Irene St.
Torrington, CT 06790
203-482-3638
$1.00
Unusual selection of vegetable, herb and flower seeds; emphasis on foreign vegetable varieties, particularly European.

R.H. Shumway's
P.O. Box 1
Graniteville, SC 29829
803-663-6276
Wide selection of both old-fashioned and up-to-date vegetable seeds and plants, as well as flower seeds, lawn and pasture grass, cover crops. Many available in bulk at wholesale prices. Also fruit trees, small fruits, roses.

Siberia Seeds
Box 2026
Sweetgrass, MT 59484
Canadian home address:
Box 3000
Olds, Alberta, Canada T0M 1 P0
50 cents and SASE
Seeds for tomato varieties that do well in cold climates.

Stokes Seeds, Inc.
Box 548
Buffalo, NY 14240
716-672-8844
Canadian address:
39 James St., Box 10
St. Catharines, Ontario
Canada L2R 6R6
Very large, basic selection of vegetable and flower seeds.

Thompson and Morgan
P.O. Box 1308
Jackson, NJ 08527
201-363-2225
Very large selection of seeds for vegetables, annual and perennial flowers, ornamental grasses, houseplants, trees, shrubs and herbs.

Tomato Growers Supply Co.
P.O. Box 2237
Fort Myers, FL 33902
Huge selection of tomato varieties; sweet and hot peppers; books and supplies.

Tsang & Ma
P.O. Box 294
Belmont, CA 94002
415-595-2270
Large selection of Oriental vegetable seeds; also cooking equipment and supplies.

Twilley Seeds
P.O. Box F65
Trevose, PA 19047
800-622-7333
215-639-8800
$1.25
Up-to-date selection of vegetable seeds, including Oriental varieties; also annual flowers.

Vermont Bean Seed Co. (Seeds for the World)
Garden Lane
Fair Haven, VT 05743
802-265-4212
802-265-3387
Primarily vegetable seeds, many unusual varieties, some herb and flower seeds. All seeds are untreated.

Vesey's Seed Ltd.
P.O. Box 9000
Houlton, ME 04730-0829
207-892-1048
Vegetable and flower seeds, with an emphasis on seeds for areas with a short growing season.

Willhite Seed Co.
P.O. Box 23
Poolville, TX 76076
817-599-8656
Vegetable seeds; a very large selection of melons, many of them the nursery's introductions. Also Texas wildflower seeds.

Woodruff and Royce Seed Co.
RFD 2, Box 145
Whitehall, NY 12887
518-499-0628
New and old vegetable seeds, herbs, annual and perennial flowers, supplies.

Also see under Miscellaneous: Mellinger's, Henry Field's, Gurney's, Earl May, J. W. Jung; see under Perennials: Country Garden.

SHRUBS AND TREES

Bosley Nurseries
9579 Mentor Ave.
Mentor, OH 44060
216-352-3308
Azaleas and rhododendrons.

Bovees Nursery
1737 S.W. Coronado
Portland, OR 97219
503-244-9341
503-244-9381
$2.00
Unusual rhododendrons and azaleas; other trees and shrubs available.

Carlson's Gardens
Box 305
South Salem, NY 10590
914-763-5958
Large selection of azaleas and rhododendrons.

Cascade Forestry Service, Inc.
Rt. 1, Cascade, IA 52033
319-852-3042
Northern hardwood trees, evergreens, native-American nut trees, ornamental and shade trees, evergreen and deciduous shrubs.

The Cummins Garden
22 Robertsville Rd.
Marlboro, NJ 07746
201-536-2591
$1.00
Azaleas, rhododendrons, dwarf evergreens, deciduous and broad-leaf evergreen shrubs.

Ferris Nursery
811 Fourth St. N.E.
Hampton, IA 50441
515-456-2563
Ornamental and shade trees, evergreens, windbreaks, flowering shrubs; also roses, fruits, perennials.

Girard Nurseries
P.O. Box 428
Geneva, OH 44041
216-466-2881
Specializing in azaleas and rhododendrons; also flowering trees, flowering shrubs, bonsai plants, ground covers, broad-leaf evergreens, conifers, ornamental and shade trees, fruits and nuts, tree and shrub seeds.

Gossler Farms Nursery
1200 Weaver Rd.
Springfield, OR 97478-9663
503-746-3992
503-747-0749
$1.00
Specializing in magnolias and unusual shrubs and trees.

Greer Gardens
1280 Goodpasture Island Rd.
Eugene, OR 97401-1794
503-686-8266
Huge selection of hybrid and species rhododendrons, deciduous and evergreen azaleas, camellias, mountain laurel, Japanese maples and many unusual shrubs and trees, both evergreen and deciduous.

Musser Forests
P.O. Box 340-S88M
Indiana, PA 15701-0340
412-465-5685
Ornamental and shade trees, evergreens, flowering shrubs, hedge plants, ground-cover shrubs.

Pacific Tree Farms
4301 Lynwood Dr.
Chula Vista, CA 92010
$1.50
Fruit and nut trees for tropical and subtropical climates.

Roslyn Nursery
211 Burrs La.
Dix Hills, NY 11746
516-643-9347
Large selection of rhododendrons, azaleas, hollies, deciduous and broad-leaf evergreen shrubs, dwarf conifers; also deciduous trees, ferns, perennials.

Washington Evergreen Nursery
P.O. Box 388
Brooks Branch Rd.
Leicester, NC 28748
704-683-4518 (April through
  October)
803-747-1641 (November
  through March)
$2.00
*Specializing in dwarf evergreens;
some broad-leaf evergreens.*

Also see under Miscellaneous:
Mellinger's, Kelly Bros.; see
under Wildflowers: Yerba
Buena, Woodlanders, Las
Pilitas.

WILDFLOWERS

Applewood Seed Co.
P.O. Box 10761, Edgemont
  Station
Golden, CO 80401
303-431-6283
*Informative catalog offers
wildflower seeds, many native.
Regional mixes available.*

Clyde Robin Seed Co., Inc.
Box 2855
Castro Valley, CA 94546
415-581-3467
*Seeds of wildflowers, shrubs and
trees, mostly native species;
mixtures available.*

Environmental Seed Producers,
  Inc.
P.O. Box 5904
El Monte, CA 91734
818-442-3330 (in California)
213-442-3330
*Large selection of wildflower
seeds including regional mixes.*

Forest Farm
990 Tetherow Rd.
Williams, OR 97544-9599
503-846-6963
$2.00
*Very large selection of wild trees
and shrubs and many herbaceous
perennial species; most native to
the northwestern U.S.*

Las Pilitas Nursery
Star Rt. Box 23 X
Santa Margarita, CA 93453
805-438-5992
$4.00

*California native plants;
primarily shrubs and trees but
also perennials and some bulbs
and seeds.*

Little Valley Farm
RFD 1, Box 287
Richland Center, WI 53581
608-538-3180
*Nursery-grown perennial
wildflowers; also trees, shrubs,
vines, books, wildflower seeds.*

Prairie Nursery
Rt. 1, Box 365
Westfield, WI 53964-0116
608-296-2607
*Native Midwestern prairie plants
and seeds; wildflowers, grasses,
wetland species.*

Siskiyou Rare Plant Nursery
2825 Cummings Rd.
Medford, OR 97501
503-772-6846
$1.50
*Rare plants including alpines,
rock-garden plants, ferns, dwarf
shrubs and woodland perennials.*

The Vermont Wildflower Farm
P.O. Box 5, Rt. 7
Charlotte, VT 05445-0005
802-425-3831
Wildflower mixes.

We–Du Nurseries
Rt. 5, Box 724
Marion, NC 28752
704-738-8300
*Extensive selection of wild
perennials, many native to the
southeastern U.S.; includes
rock-garden and woodland
plants, Oriental species, shrubs.*

Windrift Prairie Shop
RFD 2
Oregon, IL 61061
815-732-6890
*Seeds of prairie grasses and
perennials; publications.*

Woodlanders, Inc.
1128 Colleton Ave.
Aiken, SC 29801
803-648-7522
$2.00
*Extensive selection of wild
shrubs and trees; also many wild
herbaceous perennials.*

Yerba Buena Nursery
19500 Skyline Blvd.
Woodside, CA 94062
415-851-1668
*California native plants;
primarily trees and shrubs, also
many perennials and ferns.*

Also see under Perennials:
Crownsville, Garden Place,
Primrose Path; see under Seeds:
J. L. Hudson, Redwood City,
Plants of the Southwest.

MISCELLANEOUS

Vernon Barnes & Son Nursery
P.O. Box 250 L S 1 2 3
McMinnville, TN 37110
*Shrubs, trees, fruits, vines,
bulbs, perennials and
wildflowers.*

Henry Field's Seed and Nursery
  Company
Shenandoah, IA 51602
712-246-2011
*Large selection of vegetable
seeds and fruits; also roses,
shrubs, summer bulbs,
perennials and nut, shade and
ornamental trees.*

Fred's Plant Farm
Rt. 1, Box 707
Dresden, TN 38225-0707
901-364-5419
Sweet potato plants.

Gurney's Seed and Nursery Co.
Yankton, SD 57079
605-665-1671
605-665-1930
*Large selection of vegetable
seeds and plants, with potatoes a
specialty; flower seeds,
houseplants, fruits, nuts,
ornamental shrubs, trees and
vines, perennials, summer-
blooming bulbs, roses and
supplies.*

International Growers'
  Exchange, Inc.
P.O. Box 52248
Livonia, MI 48152-0248
313-422-0747
Catalog subscription $5.00 for 3
  years, includes 2 catalogs per
  year; subscription deductible
  from first order.

*Large selection of perennials,
wildflowers, houseplants, herbs
and bulbs for spring, summer
and fall. Most items offered only
in quantity, at quantity rates.*

Inter-State Nurseries
P.O. Box 208
Hamburg, IA 51640-0208
800-843-5091
314-754-4525
$1.50
*Large rose selection; also
perennials, fruits and other
plants. Separate catalog with
spring bulb selection.*

J.W. Jung Seed Co.
335 S. High St.
Randolph, WI 53957-0001
414-326-3121
*Large selection of vegetable
seeds; also fruits, roses, shrubs,
trees, perennials, other plants,
supplies.*

Kalmia Farm
P.O. Box 3881
Charlottesville, VA 22903
*Onion sets, including potato
onions, multiplier onions,
Egyptian top onions, shallots
and garlic; also ornamental
alliums, kiwi trees, narcissus,
crocus and saffron crocus.*

Kelly Bros. Nurseries, Inc.
Dansville, NY 14437
800-828-697
800-462-6836 (in New York
State)
*Large selection of fruits; also nut
trees, vines, ornamental shrubs
and trees, perennials, roses.*

Krider Nurseries, Inc.
Box 29
Middlebury, IN 46540
219-825-5714
*Large rose selection; also fruits,
trees, shrubs and perennials.*

Lilypons Water Gardens
6800 Lilypons Rd.,
P.O. Box 10
Lilypons, MD 21717-0010
201-874-5133
301-874-5133 (Washington D.C.)
Brookshire, TX 77423-0188
713-934-8525
713-391-0076 (Houston)
$4.00

*Large selection of hardy and
tropical water lilies, hardy and
tropical bog plants and
water-gardening supplies.*

Earl May Seed & Nursery L. P.
208 N. Elm St.
Shenandoah, IA 51603-0099
800-831-4193
*Vegetable and flower seeds,
fruits, perennials, nut trees,
vegetable plants, ornamental
trees and shrubs, roses.*

Mellinger's
2310 W. South Range Rd.
North Lima, Oh 44452-9731
800-321-7444
216-549-9861 (in Ohio)
*Very large selection of tools,
equipment and supplies; large
tree and shrub selection; also
seeds, fruits, bulbs, wildflowers,
ground covers and perennials.*

Piedmont Plant Co.
P.O. Box 424
Albany, GA 31703
912-883-7029
*Vegetable plants including
tomatoes, peppers, eggplant,
sweet potatoes, Chinese
cabbage, lettuce, cole crops,
beets, onions and leeks; garlic
and shallot bulbs.*

Savage Farms Nurseries
P.O. Box 125 SF 123
McMinnville, TN 37110
*Fruits and nuts; ornamental
shrubs, trees and vines.*

Steele Plant Co.
Gleason, TN 38229
901-648-5476
Two first-class postage stamps
*Vegetable plants, including
onions, cabbages, Brussels
sprouts, broccoli, cauliflower
and sweet potatoes.*

William Tricker, Inc.
P.O. Box 31267
7125 Tanglewood Dr.
Independence, OH 44131
216-524-3491 or 3492
*Large selection of hardy and
tropical water lilies, hardy and
tropical bog plants and
water-gardening supplies.*

For Further Reading

BOOKS

You will surely wish to consult
some books that treat in greater
detail specific plants and
gardening practices that interest
you. Here are some that I
consider to be helpful.

General Reference

American Horticultural Society
Staff. *North American
Horticulture: A Reference
Guide.* New York: Charles
Scribner's Sons, 1982.

Bailey, Liberty Hyde, and
Bailey, Ethel Zoe; revised by
the staff of L. H. Bailey
Hortorium. *Hortus Third: A
Concise Dictionary of Plants
Cultivated in the United States
and Canada.* New York:
Macmillan Publishing Co.,
Inc., 1976.

Bush-Brown, James, and
Bush-Brown, Louise.
America's Garden Book, rev.
ed. New York: Charles
Scribner's Sons, 1980.

*Organic Gardening and Farming
Magazine*, ed. *The
Encyclopedia of Organic
Gardening.* Emmaus, PA:
Rodale Press, Inc., 1978.

Raven, Peter H., et al., *The
Biology of Plants*, 4th ed. New
York: Worth Publishers, 1986.

Wyman, Donald. *Wyman's
Gardening Encyclopedia,*
updated edition. New York:
Macmillan Publishing
Company, Inc., 1987.

Vegetables, Fruits and Herbs

Creasy, Rosalind. *The Complete Book of Edible Landscaping: Home Landscaping With Food-Bearing Plants and Resource-Saving Techniques.* San Francisco: Sierra Club Books, 1982.

Foster, Gertrude B., and Louden, Rosemary F. *Park's Success With Herbs.* Greenwood, SC: George W. Park Seed Co., 1980.

Hill, Lewis. *Fruits and Berries for the Home Garden.* Pownal, VT: Garden Way Publishing, 1977.

Jabs, Carolyn. *The Heirloom Gardener.* San Francisco: Sierra Club Books, 1984.

Kline, Roger A., et al. *The Heirloom Vegetable Garden,* rev. ed. Ithaca, NY: Cornell Cooperative Extension, 1986.

Kourik, Robert, *Designing and Maintaining Your Edible Landscape Naturally.* Santa Rose, CA: Metamorphic Press, 1986.

National Gardening Association. *Gardening: The Complete Guide to Growing America's Favorite Fruits and Vegetables.* Reading, MA: Addison-Wesley Publishing Co., Inc., 1986.

Owen, Millie. *A Cook's Guide to Growing Herbs, Greens, and Aromatics.* New York: Alfred A. Knopf Inc., 1978.

Seymour, John. *The Self-Sufficient Gardener: A Complete Guide to Growing and Preserving All Your Own Food.* New York: Doubleday & Co., 1979.

Taylor, Norman. *Taylor's Guide to Vegetables and Herbs,* edited and revised by Gordon P. DeWolf, Jr. Boston: Houghton Mifflin Co., 1987.

Simmons, Adelma G. *Herb Gardening in Five Seasons.* New York: E.P. Dutton, 1977.

Tolley, Emelie and Mead, Chris. *Herbs: Gardens, Decorations and Recipes.* New York: Clarkson N. Potter Inc., 1985.

Annuals and Perennials

Bloom, Alan. *Perennials for Your Garden.* Portland, OR: International Specialized Book Services, 1981.

Fell, Derek. *Annuals: How to Select, Grow and Enjoy.* Tucson, AZ: HP Books, 1983.

Harper, Pamela, and McGourty, Frederick. *Perennials: How to Select, Grow and Enjoy.* Tucson, AZ: HP Books, 1985.

Randall, Harry, and Wren, Alan. *Growing Chrysanthemums.* Portland, OR: Timber Press, 1983.

Taylor, Norman. *Taylor's Guide to Annuals,* edited and revised by Gordon P. DeWolf, Jr. Boston: Houghton Mifflin Co., 1986.

———. *Taylor's Guide to Groundcovers, Vines and Grasses,* edited and revised by Gordon P. DeWolf, Jr. Boston: Houghton Mifflin Co., 1987.

———. *Taylor's Guide to Perennials,* edited and revised by Gordon P. DeWolf, Jr. Boston: Houghton Mifflin Co., 1986.

Shrubs and Trees

Bartels, Andreas. *Gardening with Dwarf Trees and Shrubs.* Portland, OR: Timber Press, 1987.

Brooklyn Botanic Garden. *The Hundred Finest Trees and Shrubs for Temperate Climates.* Brooklyn: Brooklyn Botanic Garden, 1957.

Davis, Brian. *The Gardener's Illustrated Encyclopedia of Trees and Shrubs.* Emmaus, PA: Rodale Press, Inc., 1987.

DeGraaf, Richard M., and Witman, Gretchin. *Trees, Shrubs and Vines for Attracting Birds: A Manual for the Northeast.* Amherst, MA: University of Massachusetts Press, 1981.

Dirr, Michael A. *Manual of Woody Landscape Plants,* 3rd ed. Champaign, IL: Stipes Publishing Co., 1983.

Fell, Derek. *Trees and Shrubs.* Tucson, AZ: HP Books, 1986.

Flint, Harrison L. *The Country Journal Book of Hardy Trees and Shrubs.* Harrisburg, PA: Historical Times, Inc., 1983.

Galle, Fred. *Azaleas.* Portland, OR: Timber Press, 1985.

Greer, Harold E. *Greer's Guidebook to Available Rhododendrons,* rev. ed. Eugene, OR: Offshoot Publications, 1987.

Horticultural Committee of the Garden Club of America. *Plants That Merit Attention, vol. 1: Trees.* Portland, OR: Timber Press, 1984.

Hudak, Joseph. *Shrubs in the Landscape.* New York: McGraw-Hill, 1984.

———. *Trees for Every Purpose.* New York: McGraw Hill, 1980.

Symonds, George W. *The Shrub Identification Book.* New York: William Morrow and Co., Inc., 1963.

———. *The Tree Identification Book.* New York: William Morrow and Co., Inc., 1973.

Taylor, Norman. *Taylor's Guide to Shrubs,* edited and revised by Gordon P. DeWolf, Jr. Boston: Houghton Mifflin Co., 1987.

———. *Taylor's Guide to Trees,* edited and revised by Gordon P. DeWolf, Jr. Boston: Houghton Mifflin Co., 1988.

Trelease, William. *Winter Botany: An Identification Guide to Native and Cultivated Trees and Shrubs.* Mineola, NY: Dover Publications, 1967.

Wyman, Donald. *Shrubs and Vines for American Gardens,* rev. ed. New York: Macmillan Publishing Co., Inc., 1969.

———. *Trees for American Gardens,* rev. ed. New York: Macmillan Publishing Co., Inc., 1965.

Bulbs

Lawrence, Elizabeth. *The Little Bulbs.* Durham, NC: Duke University Press, 1986.

Rix, Martyn, and Phillips, Roger. *The Bulb Book: A Photographic Guide to Over Eight Hundred Hardy Bulbs.* Eureka, CA: Mad River Press, 1981.

Scott, George H. *Bulbs: How to Select, Grow and Enjoy.* Tucson, AZ: HP Books, 1982.

Taylor, Norman. *Taylor's Guide to Bulbs,* edited and revised by Gordon P. DeWolf, Jr. Boston: Houghton Mifflin Co., 1986.

Roses

Brooklyn Botanic Garden. *Handbook on Roses.* Brooklyn: Brooklyn Botanic Garden, 1980.

Jekyll, Gertrude, and Mawley, Edward. *Roses,* revised by Graham Stuart Thomas. Salem, NH: The Ayer Company, 1983.

Taylor, Norman. *Taylor's Guide to Roses,* edited and revised by Gordon P. DeWolf, Jr. Boston: Houghton Mifflin Co., 1986.

Thomas, Graham Stuart. *The Old Shrub Roses,* rev. ed. London: J. M. Dent, 1979.

Wildflowers

Art, Henry W. *The Wildflower Gardener's Guide: Northeast, Mid-Atlantic, Great Lakes, and Eastern Canada Edition.* Pownal, VT: Garden Way Publishing, 1987.

Birdseye, Clarence, and Birdseye, Eleanor G. *Growing Woodland Plants.* New York: Dover Publications, 1972.

Craighead, John J., et al. *A Field Guide to Rocky Mountain Wildflowers.* Boston: Houghton Mifflin Co., 1974

Dennis, John V. *The Wildlife Gardener.* New York: Alfred A. Knopf Inc., 1985.

Foster, F. Gordon. *Ferns to Know and Grow,* rev. ed. Portland, OR: Timber Press, 1984.

Newcomb, Laurence. *Newcomb's Wildflower Guide.* Boston: Little, Brown and Co., 1977.

New England Wild Flower Society. *Garden in the Woods Cultivation Guide.* Framingham, MA: New England Wild Flower Society, 1986.

Niehaus, Theodore F., and Ripper, Charles L. *A Field Guide to Pacific States Wildflowers.* Boston: Houghton Mifflin Co., 1976.

———. *A Field Guide to Southwestern and Texas Wildflowers.* Boston: Houghton Mifflin Co., 1984.

Niering, William, and Olmstead, Nancy. *The Audubon Society Field Guide to North American Wildflowers: Eastern Region.* New York: Alfred A. Knopf Inc., 1979.

———. *The Audubon Society Field Guide to North American Wildflowers: Western Region.* New York: Alfred A. Knopf Inc., 1979.

Peterson, Roger Tory, and McKenny, Margaret. *A Field Guide to the Wildflowers of Northeastern and North-Central North America.* Boston: Houghton Mifflin Co., 1974.

Phillips, Harry R. *Growing and Propagating Wild Flowers.* Chapel Hill: The University of North Carolina Press, 1985.

Smyser, Carol A. *Nature's Design: A Practical Guide to Natural Landscaping.* Emmaus, PA: Rodale Press, Inc., 1982.

Sperka, Marie. *Growing Wildflowers: A Cultivator's Guide.* New York: Charles Scribner's Sons, 1984.

Steffek, Edwin F. *New Wild Flowers and How to Grow Them,* rev. ed. Portland, OR: Timber Press, 1983.

Stevenson, Violet. *The Wild Garden.* New York: Penguin Books, 1985.

Sullivan, Gene A., and Daley, Richard H. *Directory to Resources on Wildflower Propagation.* St. Louis, MO: National Council of State Garden Clubs, 1981.

Houseplants

Crockett, James U., and the Editors of Time-Life Books. *The Time-Life Book of Flowering Houseplants.* New York: Henry Holt and Co., 1986.

———. *The Time-Life Book of Foliage Houseplants.* New York: Henry Holt and Co., 1986.

Rowley, Gordon D. *The Illustrated Encyclopedia of Succulents.* New York: Crown Publishers, Inc., 1978.

Taylor, Norman. *Taylor's Guide to Houseplants,* edited and revised by Gordon P. DeWolf, Jr. Boston: Houghton Mifflin Co., 1987.

Miscellaneous Techniques

Beckett, Kenneth, and Stevens, David. *The Contained Garden: A Complete Illustrated Guide to Growing Plants, Flowers, Fruits and Vegetables Outdoors in Pots.* New York: Viking Press, 1983.

Brooklyn Botanic Garden. *Propagation for the Home Gardener.* Brooklyn: Brooklyn Botanic Garden, 1984.

Browse, Phillip M. *Plant Propagation.* New York: Simon and Schuster, 1988.

Bubel, Nancy. *The Seed Starter's Handbook.* Emmaus, PA: Rodale Press, Inc., 1978.

Chamberlin, Susan. *Hedges, Screens and Espaliers: How to Select, Grow and Enjoy.* Tucson, AZ: HP Books, 1982.

Foster, H. Lincoln. *Rock Gardening: A Guide to Growing Alpines and Other Wildflowers in the American Garden.* Portland, OR: Timber Press, 1982.

Gallup, Barbara, and Reich, Deborah. *The Complete Book of Topiary.* New York: Workman Publishing, 1987.

Hill, Lewis. *Pruning Simplified,* updated ed. Pownal, VT: Garden Way Publishing, 1986.

———. *Secrets of Plant Propagation: Starting Your Own Flowers, Vegetables, Fruits, Berries, Shrubs, Trees, and Houseplants.* Pownal, VT: Garden Way Publishing, 1985.

Kramer, Jack. *Drip System Watering for Bigger and Better Plants.* New York: W. W. Norton and Co., 1980.

Morse, Harriet K. *Gardening in the Shade.* Portland, OR: Timber Press, 1982.

Perkins, Harold O. *Espaliers and Vines for the Home Gardener,* repr. of 1964 ed. Ames, IA: Iowa State University Press, 1979.

Taylor, Norman. *Taylor's Guide to Garden Design,* edited and revised by Gordon P. DeWolf, Jr. Boston: Houghton Mifflin Co., 1988.

Williams, T. Jeff. *Garden Construction,* rev. ed. San Francisco: Ortho Books, 1985.

Pests and Diseases

Carr, Anna. *Rodale's Color Handbook of Garden Insects.* Emmaus, PA: Rodale Press, Inc., 1983.

Metcalf, Clell L., et al. *Destructive and Useful Insects,* 4th ed. New York: McGraw-Hill, 1962.

Philbrick, Helen, and Philbrick, John. *The Bug Book: Harmless Insect Controls.* Pownal, VT: Garden Way Publishing, 1974.

Pirone, Pascal P. *Diseases and Pests of Ornamental Plants,* 5th ed. New York: John Wiley and Sons, Inc., 1978.

Yepsen, Roger B., Jr., ed. *The Encyclopedia of Natural Insect and Disease Control.* Emmaus, PA: Rodale Press, Inc., 1984.

Regional Advice

Batson, Wade T. *Landscape Plants for the Southeast.* Columbia, SC: University of South Carolina Press, 1984.

Duffield, Mary R., and Jones, Warren D. *Plants for Dry Climates: How to Select, Grow and Enjoy.* Tucson, AZ: HP Books, 1981.

Editors of Sunset Books and *Sunset Magazine. New Western Garden Book,* 4th ed. Menlo Park, CA: Lane Publishing Co., 1979.

Gardening Staff of *Southern Living* and Floyd, John A., Jr. *Southern Living Gardening Guide.* Birmingham, AL: Oxmoor House, 1981.

McNeilan, Ray A., and Ronningen, Micheline. *Pacific Northwest Guide to Home Gardening.* Portland, OR: Timber Press, 1983.

For Inspiration

Damrosch, Barbara. *Theme Gardens.* New York: Workman Publishing, 1982.

Henderson, Marge, and Wilkinson, Libby, eds. *The House of Boughs.* New York: Viking Penguin, Inc., 1985.

Hobhouse, Penelope. *Color in Your Garden.* Boston: Little, Brown and Co., 1985.

Jekyll, Gertrude. *Wood and Garden,* rev. ed. Salem, NH: Ayer Publishers, 1984.

King, Ronald. *The Quest for Paradise: The History of the World's Gardens.* New York: W. H. Smith Publishers, 1979.

Lloyd, Christopher. *The Well Chosen Garden.* New York: Harper and Row Publishers, 1984.

Mitchell, Henry. *The Essential Earthman.* New York: Farrar, Straus and Giroux, 1983.

Morse, Harriet K. *Gardening in the Shade.* Portland, OR: Timber Press, 1982.

Page, Russell. *The Education of a Gardener.* New York: Random House, 1985.

Perenyi, Eleanor. *Green Thoughts: A Writer in the Garden.* New York: Random House, Inc., 1983.

Schenck, George. *The Complete Shade Gardener.* Boston: Houghton Mifflin Co., 1984.

Schinz, Marina, and Littlefield, Susan. *Visions of Paradise: Themes and Variations on the Garden.* New York: Stewart, Tabori and Chang, 1985.

Thomas, Graham Stuart. *Colour in the Winter Garden,* 3rd rev. ed. London: J. M. Dent, 1984.

Verey, Rosemary, and Samuels, Ellen, eds. *The American Woman's Garden.* Boston: New York Graphic Society/ Little, Brown and Co., 1984.

Wilder, Louise Beebe. *The Fragrant Garden: A Book About Sweet Scented Flowers and Leaves,* rev. ed. New York: Dover Publications, 1974.

PERIODICALS

In addition to these gardening publications, many of the plant societies listed on page 617 put out informative periodicals.

The Avant Gardener. Horticultural Data Processors, P. O. Box 489, New York, NY 10028. Monthly.

B.U.G.S. Flyer. P. O. Box 76, Citrus Heights, CA 95611-0076. Quarterly newsletter about ecologically sound horticultural techniques.

Flower and Garden. 4251 Pennsylvania Ave., Kansas City, MO 64111. Bimonthly.

Garden. The Garden Society, New York Botanical Garden, Bronx, NY 10458. Bimonthly.

Garden Design Magazine. American Society of Landscape Architects. 1733 Connecticut Ave. N.W., Washington, DC 20009. Quarterly.

Harrowsmith. The Creamery, Charlotte, VT 05445. Bimonthly.

The Herb Quarterly. Box 275, Newfane, VT 05345. Quarterly.

Horticulture. Subscription Dept., P. O. Box 2595, Boulder, CO 80323. Monthly.

Plants and Gardens. Brooklyn Botanic Garden, 1000 Washington Ave., Brooklyn, NY 11225. Issues published quarterly, each on a specific topic, with over 50 available.

Rodale's Organic Gardening. 33 E. Minor St., Emmaus, PA 18049. Monthly.

Sunset Magazine. Lane Publishing Co., Willow and Middlefield Rds., Menlo Park, CA 94025. Monthly magazine for western gardeners.

OTHER SOURCES

Capability's Books. Box 114, Highway 46, Deer Park, WI 54007. Books for gardeners.

Combined Rose List. Beverly R. Dobson, 215 Harriman Rd., Irvington, NY 10533. Sources of roses.

The Cooperative Extension Service. Located in every county of every state. Phone may be listed under "Extension," "Cooperative" or under the name of the county.

Directory of Seeds and Nursery Catalogs. National Gardening Association, 180 Flynn Ave., Burlington, VT 05410. Published annually.

The Herb Gardener's Resource Guide. Paula Oliver. Northwind Farm. Route 2, Box 246, Shevlin, MN 56676.

Hortulus. 101 Scollard St., Toronto, Ontario, Canada M5R 1G4. Horticultural books.

The Garden Seed Inventory, edited by Kent Whealy. Seed Saver Publications, P. O. Box 70, Decorah, IA 52101. Sources of heirloom and open-pollinated fruit and vegetable seeds.

Gardening by Mail. Barbara Barton, 1986. Tusker Press, P. O. Box 597004, San Francisco, CA 94159.

Gardening by Mail—Where to Buy It. The Mail-Order Association of Nurserymen. Dept. MB, 210 Cartwright Blvd., Massapequa Park, NY 11762.

The Gardener's Book of Sources by William Bryant Logan. Published by Viking, 1988.

Nursery Source Manual. Brooklyn Botanic Garden. Published November 1982.

Nursery Sources: Native Plants and Wildflowers. New England Wild Flower Society, Inc. Garden in the Woods, Hemenway Rd., Framingham, MA 01701.

Sources of Native Seeds and Plants. Soil Conservation Society of America, 1979. 7515 Northeast Ankeny Rd., Ankeny, IA 50021.

Source List of Plants and Seeds. Anderson Horticultural Library, Minnesota Landscape Arboretum, 3675 Arboretum Drive, Box 39, Chanhassen, MN 55317.

Elizabeth Woodburn. Booknoll Farm, Box 398, Hopewell, NJ 08525. Bookseller.

Index

(Page numbers in **boldface** refer to main references and definitions of terms. Page numbers in *italics* refer to illustrations. Plants are listed both by common name, in roman type, and by botanical name, in *italic* type.)

M